FIELDING'S WORLDWIDE CRUISES 1998

Fielding Titles

FIELDING'S WORLDWIDE CRUISES 1998

Shirley Slater
and
Harry Basch

Fielding Worldwide, Inc.
308 South Catalina Avenue
Redondo Beach, California 90277 U.S.A.

Fielding's Worldwide Cruises 1998

Published by Fielding Worldwide, Inc.

Text Copyright ©1997 FWI

Icons & Illustrations Copyright ©1997 FWI

Photo Copyrights ©1997 to Individual Photographers

FIELDING WORLDWIDE INC.

PUBLISHER AND CEO	**Robert Young Pelton**
GENERAL MANAGER	**John Guillebeaux**
OPERATIONS DIRECTOR	**George Posanke**
ELECTRONIC PUBLISHING DIRECTOR	**Larry E. Hart**
PUBLIC RELATIONS DIRECTOR	**Beverly Riess**
ACCOUNT SERVICES MANAGER	**Christy Harp**
PROJECT MANAGER	**Chris Snyder**
MANAGING EDITOR	**Amanda K. Knoles**

PRODUCTION

Martin Mancha	**Reed Parsell**
Ramses Reynoso	**Craig South**

COVER DESIGNED BY	**Digital Artists, Inc.**
COVER PHOTOGRAPHERS—Front cover	**Princess Cruises**
Back cover	**Windstar Cruises**
INSIDE PHOTOS	**Harry Basch, Shirley Slater and various cruise lines**
AUTHORS' PHOTO	**Patricia Viamontes**

Inquiries should be addressed to: Fielding Worldwide, Inc., 308 South Catalina Ave., Redondo Beach, California 90277 U.S.A., Telephone *(310) 372-4474*, Facsimile *(310) 376-8064*, 8:30 a.m.–5:30 p.m. Pacific Standard Time.
Web site: http:/www.fieldingtravel.com
e-mail: fielding@fieldingtravel.com

ISBN 1-56952-156-5

Printed in the United States of America

Letter from the Publisher

Fifty years ago Temple Fielding began the first of what would be a remarkable new series of well-written, highly personalized guidebooks for independent travelers. Eighteen years ago Fielding invented the first guide to the cruise industry. Today, Fielding Worldwide is known for seeking out new destinations and is quickly becoming the leading expert in emerging travel trends.

Today it would be wrong to assume that cruising is just catching on. Cruise travel is big and getting bigger. Only seven percent of Americans have taken cruises but the growth rate, both in terms of total passengers and the new super ships, is increasing at a phenomenal rate. The new *Carnival Destiny* will carry 3400 people (plus another 1000 crew members) and have a gross tonnage of over 100,000 tons. The seas haven't seen ocean liners of this magnitude since the *QE2* hit the water at 83,000 tons back in 1938. The *Destiny* is so big it cannot even fit through the Panama Canal. This year alone there are 31 new ships under construction, some of them costing up to half a billion dollars each.

In the last few months there have been major changes in the cruise industry so it's no surprise that *Fielding's Worldwide Cruises* is not an update but an entirely new book every year. Harry Basch and Shirley Slater have personally been aboard all 184 ships reviewed in *Fielding's Worldwide Cruises* and have taken more than 200 cruises during the past 15 years. Their in-depth reviews give you the information you need to choose not only the right ship, but compare the various levels of luxury (or adventure) each cruise line offers.

Enjoy your cruise adventures with Harry, Shirley and Fielding.

R Y P

Robert Young Pelton
Publisher and CEO
Fielding Worldwide, Inc.

DEDICATION

To the late Edwin Self, founder of *San Diego Magazine*, a gentleman and a scholar, who published our first cruise story in 1979.

And Jerry Hulse, former travel editor of the *Los Angeles Times*, who, when he ordered our column "Cruise Views" in 1983, said, "Do you think you guys can find enough to write about for a year?"

ABOUT THE
AUTHORS

Shirley Slater and Harry Basch

Called by the *Chicago Sun-Times* "America's premier cruise specialists," Shirley Slater and Harry Basch are an award-winning husband-and-wife travel writing and photography team whose work has been published internationally since 1976. For more than a decade, they have been the world's most widely read cruise experts.

They are authors of *Fielding's Alaska Cruises, Fielding's European Cruises* and editors of *Fielding's Cruise Insider,* an online news-and-reviews journal about the cruise industry that can be accessed from the Fielding Website at www.fieldingtravel.com, as well as authors of *Fielding's Freewheelin' USA* and the monthly newsletter *Shirley and Harry's RV Adventures.*

As contributing editors for the trade magazine *Cruise & Vacation Views,* their monthly ship reviews are read throughout the travel agent community. They have also written ship reviews for trade publications *Travel Weekly, TravelAge* and *ASTA Agency Management* magazine.

Their syndicated column "Cruise Views" has appeared regularly in the *Los Angeles Times* and other major newspapers for 15 years. They have also contributed to magazines such as *Bon Appétit, Vogue, Modern Maturity, Travel & Leisure, Islands* and *Travel Holiday,* as well as various auto club and inflight publications.

For the million subscribers to Prodigy Computer Services, they have created six editions of an annual North American Ski Guide, two Cruise Guides and a Caribbean Ports of Call Guide. Slater is also the author of *The Passport Guide to Switzerland.*

At the 60th World Travel Congress in Hamburg, Germany, in 1990 the couple was awarded the prestigious Melva C. Pederson Award from the American Society of Travel Agents for "extraordinary journalistic achievement in the field of travel," the third time the award was given and the first time it was awarded to freelance writers.

They also received the 1995 award for distinguished RV writing for their *Fielding's Freewheelin' USA.*

FOREWORD

When we were very young (if that were ever possible), we lived in Europe for several years, traveling on the cheap but always willing to splurge whenever we could afford it on the best of something. Our guidebook and bible, text and verse, was Temple Fielding's *Europe* guide, because it was the only guidebook that made us laugh, gave us a sense of fun and was absolutely honest—we literally couldn't afford to make any wrong choices.

In this cruise guide, we go back to the basics, to Temple Fielding and his philosophy of always telling the reader honestly but with style, verve and an occasional grumpy touch, about the best and worst of travel.

If we also occasionally sound a little curmudgeonly, it's only because we've been "being there and doing that" for the past 20 years all over the world as full-time professional travel writers and photographers, tallying up along the way 175 countries and more than 200 cruises aboard virtually everything that floats.

This is the book we've always wanted to write. We hope you like it.

—Shirley Slater and Harry Basch

TABLE OF CONTENTS

EVERYTHING YOU WANT TO KNOW ABOUT CRUISES AND MORE...

THE RATINGS

* Asterisks after the ship's name represent ships that are in transition from one company to another, which the authors have been aboard in the vessel's earlier life, or new vessels that are sister ships to existing, already inspected vessels due to come on line in 1998.

EVERYTHING YOU WANT TO KNOW ABOUT CRUISES AND MORE...

INTRODUCTION:
LOOK WHO'S
AFLOAT

This romantic couple could be mistaken for companions of Noel Coward.

> "Why do the wrong people travel, travel, travel
> And the right people stay at home?"

Noel Coward song lyrics

Even the late Noel Coward, the most urbane and unflappable cruise passenger one can imagine, probably would have been rendered speechless at who and what's afloat these days.

On the decks he frequented, there were no earphone-wearing joggers or aerobics classes, just stately promenaders (the kind who nod only after being properly introduced) or dozing readers wrapped in steamer rugs. Certainly nobody ever requested a no-smoking table or a low-calorie lunch.

Coward definitely would have raised an eyebrow at cruise-ship dress codes allowing gentlemen to appear at dinner not only without black tie but without any tie or jacket at all. And he hardly could have imagined couples stealing away after dinner to screen a video in their cabin instead of dancing cheek to cheek to the ship's orchestra.

Suddenly 4 million Americans a year were going down to the sea in ships. They weren't all wealthy retirees, and they weren't all looking for love and attention. They were all ages, from all economic groups, singles, honeymoon couples, working couples on a budget, families with small children, grandparents with grandchildren.

We've been on cruises with—

- Amanda at 2 and Amy at 86
- High rollers and bingo buffs
- A fitness nut who found out she could cruise on a spa ship cheaper than going to a famous spa for a week
- Surfers, divers and joggers who run their daily mileage on deck from Bora Bora to Bequia
- A septuagenarian learning to operate a computer
- A purple-haired teen-aged punk rocker who spent more time on the deck than in the disco
- Bird-watchers, whale-watchers and girl-watchers
- Women competing to see who could stuff the most ping pong balls into their bikinis
- A tycoon who has a long stretch limousine waiting to take him sightseeing in every port
- An accountant who celebrated his 50th birthday by cruising to both the Arctic and Antarctic within the same year
- Best-selling novelists and supermarket checkers, retired teachers and circus owners, movie stars and mechanics—and none of them have ever been boring—or bored.

To Cruise or Not To Cruise

A girl never really looks as well as she does on board a steamship, or even a yacht.

Anita Loos, *Gentlemen Prefer Blondes,* **1925**

Life aboard cruise ships used to be thought of as a sedentary vacation for the very old and very rich, who reclined on wooden deck chairs reading books and sipping bouillon when they weren't wearing tuxedos and eating caviar.

Then along came the slick TV version, based on the premise that all a lovelorn individual had to do was get on board the "Love Boat" and the captain and his meddlesome staff would make everything smooth sailing. All problems would be settled, true love would triumph and, since the ship never seemed to move anyhow, no one's hairdo would even get mussed.

The real world of cruising today is volatile, ephemeral, constantly changing as lines are acquired, new ships come into service and old ships are retired or sold down the river into ignominious retirement as hotels or casinos.

Cruise lines are selling you a dream. And anyone old enough to remember the days of radio knows that the images the aural programs created in the mind were stronger, more dramatic and more compelling than the pallid stuff that came along later on TV. The power of your dream, your imagination, creates a challenge that the cruise industry is trying to meet. Sometimes they do, sometimes they don't.

Getting Real

TV commercials and brochures about cruises all promise the glamour life.

TV commercials and glossy color brochures about cruises all promise the same thing—an unexcelled excursion into the glamour life, with romantic evenings, a perfect tan, six or eight gourmet meals a day, and intermittent forays into picturesque and exotic ports of call where the sun always shines, the shopping is splendid and the natives friendly and photogenic.

Oddly enough, more often than not, it works out that way.

But based on some of the complaints we've had from readers over the years, several of them signed up for a cruise that should have been advertised more like this:

"You'll have fun aboard the friendly, 30-year-old *SS Rustbottom*, which failed her last five sanitation inspections in spite of heavily spiking the drinking water with chlorine.... Our bottom-of-the-line cabins are so small you have to take turns getting dressed inside, and our menus are created by a Miami-based computer programmed to give you the maximum number of calories for the lowest possible cost.... Our inexperienced and incompetent staff could not care less about your comfort or pleasure, and the residents of our popular ports of call make their livelihoods by harassing you in the streets to purchase their overpriced souvenirs."

What are some of the things that make passengers angry?

First and foremost seem to be promises the passenger felt were implied in the brochure or claimed were actually made by the travel agent prior to the trip. Ambiguous terms such as "first class," "deluxe," "elegance"—and, of course, the ever-popular "five-star-plus," the monster created by this very guide—typical hyperbole churned out by ad agency copywriters who may never have been aboard the ship—are echoed bitterly by disappointed letter-writers who expected something grander than they received.

Some expectations appear unrealistic to more experienced cruisers—24-hour room service does not necessarily mean hot four-course meals are served in the cabin at 3 a.m., for instance, and no cruise-savvy travel agent would promise clients they could spend the entire disembarkation and turn-around day aboard the ship in their cabin until time to catch their evening flight home.

One of our favorite reader complaint letters was from a female attorney celebrating her 40th birthday on her first cruise. The ship was one of the former Royal Viking Line vessels, always top of the line in food and service, but the attorney was suing to have the price of her cruise refunded because at breakfast every morning the waiters persisted in offering her a silver tray of pastries despite the fact that she had told them she was on a diet.

Hey lady, get a life!

Take a Vacation from Vacations

The real pleasure of a cruise is not having to do anything you don't want to do.

At some point in every traveler's life, there comes a moment, bittersweet as the end of a love affair, when the vacation is over, the workaday world is looming and there's nothing you need worse than a vacation to recover from your vacation.

Next time, maybe you should take a cruise.

Cruise lines spend a lot of time and money telling us about the unending procession of meals and the nonstop fun and games, when the real pleasure of a cruise is not having to do anything you don't want to do—except attend the obligatory lifeboat drill at the beginning of the cruise.

No packing and unpacking to move from one hotel to another, no cars to rent or trains to catch, no lunchtime arguments about which restaurant or picnic spot looks more appealing, no bungled hotel reservations on a weary midnight arrival in Budapest because a convention of Bulgarians came to town.

Coming back to your ship after a day ashore is like coming home. Your waiter knows how you like your breakfast eggs, your steward knows what time you go to dinner so he can turn your bed down and put a chocolate on your pillow.

A travel agency that specializes in cruises can help you select the ship and itinerary that's best for you, as long as you make your wishes and your budget considerations clear to them. Don't just ask for a Caribbean cruise and take whichever one is mentioned first. Ships and ports of call vary tremendously, and everybody loses if you don't enjoy yourself.

Take the right cruise, and you'll come home rested and happy. Of course, you will be expecting to be served breakfast in bed the first few days home, and you'll miss finding that good-night chocolate on your pillow.

DID YOU KNOW?

"I rather wished that I had gone first class," Evelyn Waugh wrote about sailing from Port Said aboard P&O's Ranchi in 1929. "It's not that my fellow passengers were not every bit as nice as the Port Said residents had told me they would be, but that there were so many of them."

Future Trends

Passengers on today's cruise ships are far from sedentary, with deck games, gyms, spas and aerobics classes always available.

If we can believe present trends, passengers of the future are going to be healthy, wealthy and wise.

Healthy, because virtually every ship menu afloat is offering low-calorie, low-fat and vegetarian options; because more and more cruise lines are banning smoking in their dining rooms and show lounges; and because well-equipped fitness centers and aerobics classes are as common as casinos. We're also seeing more stringent inspections of water and air-conditioning systems and tougher restrictions on food handlers.

Wealthy (well, at least less poor), because money-saving early booking discounts that let you cut costs from the published brochure rate are in effect closer and closer to sailing time; no matter how late you book, have your travel agent check to see if you qualify. Frequent cruisers can qualify for free cruises with accrued cruise days from Cunard, and Seabourn passengers in the line's WorldFare program may purchase blocks of 45 to 120 cruise days at a reduced price and use them on any cruises over a period of three years.

Wise in the ways of the world, because there is more of it to see by ship than at any time in recent history.

Fear of Cruising

Paddlewheel cruises on the Mississippi River as on the **American Queen** *from Delta Queen Steamboat always keep you within sight of land.*

A lot of people who think nothing of buying a package coach tour to a foreign country, driving the car across the continent or booking a week at a resort hotel on the recommendation of a casual friend over lunch, shy away from the idea of taking a cruise. Why?

Here's what they tell the pollsters:

Six Common Excuses

1. "Stuck in the middle of an ocean somewhere? I might get bored or feel trapped."

2. "I'm scared I'd get seasick."

3. "I can't plan my vacations that far in advance."

4. "I'd feel uncomfortable—I wouldn't know what to wear or how much to tip or which cabins were good."

5. "I'm afraid of gaining weight with all that food around."

6. "What if I don't like the ship? Then I've wasted my whole vacation."

Six Quick Answers

1. Forget about the ocean if you don't want to go out on one. Alaska cruises that depart from Vancouver travel the Inside Passage through some of the most spectacular scenery on earth and never out of sight of land. The same is true aboard paddlewheelers on the Mississippi River, yachtlike luxury ships in the Intracoastal Waterway or friendly, low-key vessels on the St. Lawrence, along the Columbia or in the San Juan Islands. As for boredom, most first-time cruisers claim they need a vacation when they get home from a cruise because they're exhausted from the non-stop activity.

2. If your previous seagoing experience is limited to sailboats, fishing boats or a hitch in the Navy, modern cruise ships equipped with stabilizers that eliminate much of the rolling motion may surprise you. Less than five percent of the passengers on any cruise complain of motion sickness; medications are readily available on board if you're bothered by *mal de mer*. (See Scoping Out Seasickness and Sidestepping Seasickness, page 113.)

3. If there's one thing there's plenty of, baby, it's cruise ship cabins in 1998. A good travel agent can book you on almost any ship for any destination on short notice— sometimes with a deep discount.

4. If you're bugged by the unfamiliar, a cruise is the least complicated vacation you'll ever have to deal with; it all comes in one neat prepaid package. You don't need a special wardrobe for cruises; chances are, everything you need is already in your closet. (See Eleven Tips to Lighten Your Luggage, page 105.) Tipping suggestions are spelled out on board toward the end of the sailing (also, see Tipping, page 117.) and there's a checklist on what to look for in a cabin (see Choosing A Cabin on page 44.)

5. Every ship offers a variety of seafoods, salads, fruits and vegetables, along with low-calorie, low-fat dishes. Some offer full spa menus. Even on small ships you'll find exercise classes and a full array of gym facilities. You could come back home in better shape than when you left. As for temptation, repeat after us—"Just because I paid for it doesn't mean I have to eat it all." (See How to Avoid Pigging Out at Sea, page 49.)

6. Selecting the right ship is the biggest single decision you'll have to make. Don't let anyone tell you all cruises are alike—they're not—or that Brand X Cruise Line is "the best" because there's not one single "best." The best cruise for you is the one you'll enjoy the most. See Choosing A Cruise, page 43 and How To Read A Brochure, page 23, below.

DID YOU KNOW?

Nearly 15 years ago when we first began writing our cruise column, a brusque California businessman planning his first cruise called us. He said he'd asked three travel agents which was the best cruise line–the first said Princess, the second said Carnival, the third said Sitmar (now defunct). So he called us to find out which of those three was the best. When we tried to counter by finding out something about him and what kind of cruise experience he was seeking, he screamed angrily into the phone, "I knew it! You don't know any more about it than those travel agents!" And he hung up.

The New Cruisers

More and more young singles and couples are discovering cruises as a fun and affordable mini-vacation.

A funny thing happened to ocean liners on the way to the 21st century—they got democratized.

The great and famous ships that carried royalty, heads of state, the Astors and the Glorias (Swanson and Vanderbilt) in first-class luxury, relegating to second and third class all other passengers from potato-famine Irish immigrants to '50s college students, have turned into one-class cruise ships where everyone on board is equal, more or less.

Meanwhile, the transatlantic jumbo jets that hastened the demise of ocean liners have become almost a parody of the old class system themselves, fawning over first-class passengers with sofa-sized seats and leg rests, personal video monitors and champagne and caviar, and cramming everyone else into steerage, where bodies are jackknifed into tortuous positions, babies cry all night and unidentifiable foods in plastic compartments are slapped down at intervals on wobbly trays.

Even a decade ago, the change was apparent, as cruise lines began to notice the huge numbers of first-timer cruisers aboard. Carnival's president, Bob Dickinson, then vice president of sales and marketing, pointed out in 1985 that 70 to 75 percent of all his line's passengers were first-time cruisers. "We don't think we're in the cruise business; we're in the vacation business." He went on to predict—correctly—that Carnival would have a 10-ship fleet by 1995. And it's still growing!

The mini-cruise market, offering short, affordable getaways, was booming with Eastern Cruise Line's *Emerald Seas* (now in the Mediterranean as the *Sapphire Seas*) sailing from Miami to the Bahamas and Western Cruise Line's *Azure Seas* (now Dolphin's *OceanBreeze*) cruising down to Ensenada from Los Angeles.

A lucrative and previously untapped new market was discovered— couples and singles from the world of young, upwardly-mobile professionals; baby boomers with income and leisure time for longer vacations; blue-collar and clerical workers who appreciated one up-front, all-inclusive ticket price for a vacation as luxurious as any they could find at a land-based resort and often less expensive.

In contrast to the retired and/or wealthy passengers who make up the rosters on around-the-world cruises, the new cruise passengers are looking for mini-vacations at sea, comparing a weekend cruise to a weekend spent in Nassau, Palm Springs, Las Vegas or Atlantic City.

You'll get the picture the minute you step aboard a cruise ship these days. Hardly a ship leaves dock without announcing a party for singles within a day or two of sailing, and guest hosts are on board many vessels expressly to dance, play bridge and socialize with unattached women.

If you're one of the new cruise passengers, you can count on more and more variety in the world of cruises. The day is not far off when you'll be able to cruise anywhere you wish for the length of time you prefer at a price you can afford, not once in a lifetime but once or twice a year.

Short Sails, Big Sales

The burgeoning mini-cruise market is the fastest-growing segment of cruising today as more and more first-timers decide to try the waters. They like the idea of sampling the experience for a few days before booking a longer sailing.

Short cruises seem to fit today's lifestyles, too, with people opting for several small vacations throughout the year rather than one big one. The newest wrinkle is family reunion cruises aboard mini-cruises where nobody has to host, cook or clean—and you can get a group discount as well. For every 15 or so people, there's usually a free or discounted escort or organizer's ticket.

The major mini-cruise home ports are Miami, Port Canaveral, Fort Lauderdale, Los Angeles and San Juan.

DID YOU KNOW?

David Gevanthor, former president of now-defunct SeaQuest Cruises, once said about first-time cruisers starting out on modest ships or sailings, "That's like saying you start off buying a Ford and gradually work up to a Mercedes, and that ignores a guy that buys a Mercedes for his first car. Price is not a determiner; it's the lifestyle and desires of the client that determine what kind of cruise they take."

Anatomy of a Cruise Ship: A Curmudgeon's Guide

The funnel or stack is where the cruise line displays its logo and sends out its combustion gases; never sit downwind of the funnel without checking for soot.

The Basics

- **FUNNELS** or **STACKS** are where the cruise line displays its logo, such as Princess Cruises' sea witch with flowing hair or Costa Cruises' blue-and-yellow C or Celebrity's big white X, Greek for Chi or C. The stack also carries away the ship's combustion gases and occasional bursts of black smoke. When wearing white pants, never sit in a deck chair downwind of the funnel without checking first for soot.

- **GANGWAYS** are the external stairways or ramps leading to the ship from the shore. It is also the place where the ship's photographers take pictures of passengers embarking or disembarking in every port, thereby creating a traffic jam in both directions.

- **LIFEBOATS** are the orange and white vessels that hang outside your cabin window blocking your view if your travel agent doesn't know how to read a deck plan. Some lines such as Crystal and Princess point out in their brochures where a cabin view is partly or entirely obstructed and reduce the price accordingly. Some lines, however, sketch the boats in on the deck plan but fail to point out or reduce the price on partially obstructed views. And still other lines fail to indicate the lifeboats at all, leading to *Titanic*-tinged visions.

Deck Areas

- **SWIMMING POOLS** on some ships may be mistaken for a footbath or an ornamental fountain. Fancy pool areas with swim-up bars, waterfalls and other pool novelties tend to get clogged up with passengers under 16.

- **JOGGING TRACKS** can be found on many of the newer ships on a sports deck high atop the ship. Some of these are so short that it takes 13 (on *Radisson Diamond*) or 14 (on *Seabourn*) laps to make a mile. Never, under any circumstances, book a cabin under the jogging track.

- **CHILDREN'S WADING POOLS** can be found on some ships and can be identified by its singular lack of children; most prefer to spend their time belly-whopping into the adult pool.

Shuffleboard can reach fever pitch on classic cruiseships.

- **SHUFFLEBOARD** is a popular deck game that can reach fever pitch on classic liners. On some ships, new cruisers mistake it for hopscotch.

- **PROMENADE** is the deck that goes all the way around the ship, giving passengers a chance for a brisk, breezy walk. Six or seven times around usually equals a mile. Do not attempt to exchange pleasantries with a grim-faced walker counting laps.

Lounges and Public Rooms

- **SHOW LOUNGES** in the daytime are the setting for line dancing lessons, bingo games and port information lectures, but in the evening become Broadway and Las Vegas with musical extravaganzas or, all too often, the last refuge of magicians, jugglers, puppeteers and ventriloquists last seen on the "Ed Sullivan Show."

- **CINEMAS** are where recent movies are screened; on some ships they are also considered an ideal spots to nap after lunch. Passengers under 12 vie with each other for the record number of times they can come and go opening the entry doors wide enough to wipe out the image on the screen.

The disco is the place to meet junior officers in white uniforms late at night. Never book a cabin over, under or beside the disco.

Fielding

CRUISE SHIPS

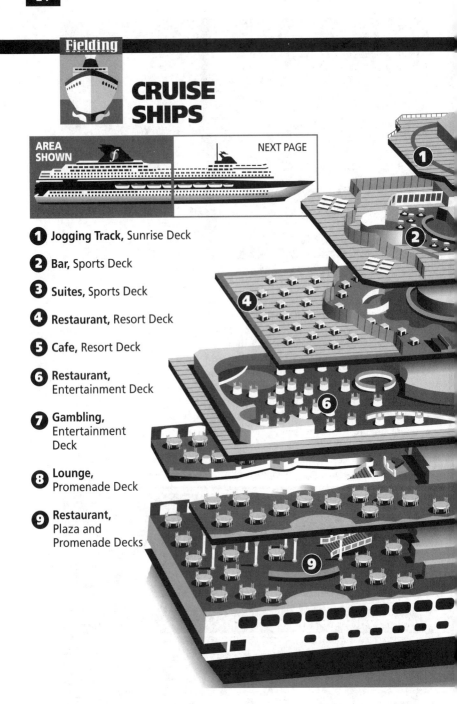

AREA SHOWN

NEXT PAGE

1. **Jogging Track,** Sunrise Deck

2. **Bar,** Sports Deck

3. **Suites,** Sports Deck

4. **Restaurant,** Resort Deck

5. **Cafe,** Resort Deck

6. **Restaurant,** Entertainment Deck

7. **Gambling,** Entertainment Deck

8. **Lounge,** Promenade Deck

9. **Restaurant,** Plaza and Promenade Decks

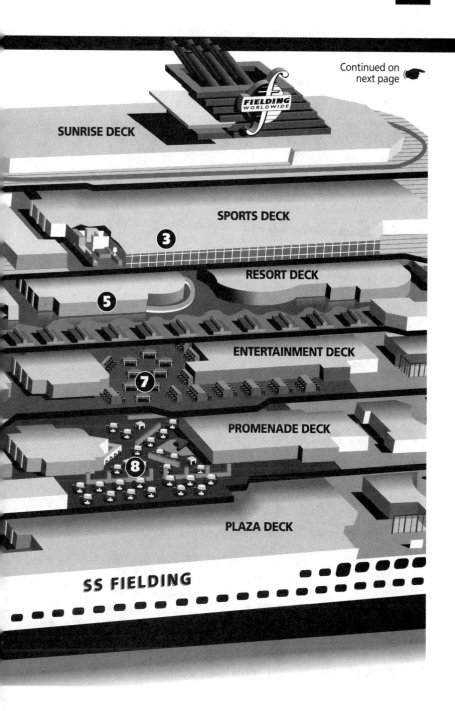

Continued on next page

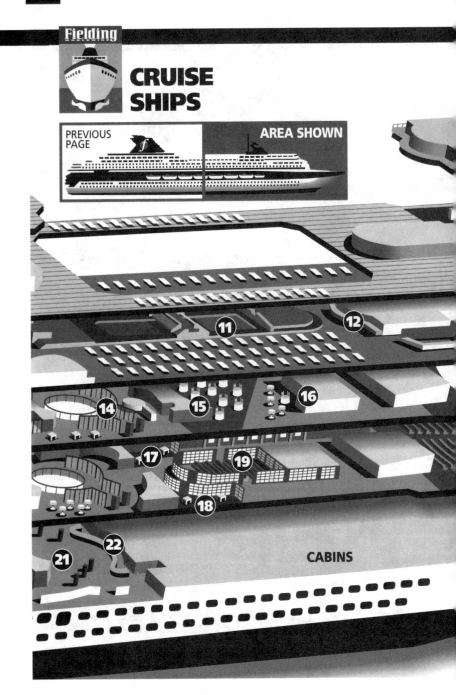

Fielding
WORLDWIDE

CRUISE SHIPS

PREVIOUS PAGE

AREA SHOWN

CABINS

10 **Lounge**, Sports Deck

11 **Swimming Pools**, Resort Deck

12 **Bar**, Resort Deck

13 **Spa**, Resort Deck

14 **Lounge**, Entertainment and Promenade Decks

15 **Cafe**, Entertainment Deck

16 **Lounge**, Entertainment Deck

17 **Card Room**, Promenade Deck

18 **Library**, Promenade Deck

19 **The Cinema and Conference Center**, Promenade Deck

20 **Theatre**, Entertainment and Promenade Decks

21 **The Grand Foyer**, Plaza Deck

22 **Guest Relations and Lobby**, Plaza Deck

SS FIELDING

- **DISCOS** are the place to meet junior officers in white uniforms late at night. On older ships such as the *Dolphin IV*, *OceanBreeze* and *SeaBreeze*, they are located deep in the bowels of the vessel and in the daytime look like a place where Dracula would sleep. On Carnival ships they flash with neon and rock videos and throb with amplified sound. Never book a cabin over, under or beside the disco.

- **PHOTO GALLERIES** are where the ship's photographers mount the pictures of passengers they've snapped at odd moments throughout the cruise. They are always crowded with people buying photos they want to keep and others buying photos they don't want anyone else to see.

- **TEEN CENTER** is a euphemism for a video games arcade that is frequently filled with males far past their teens. A modern refinement introduced by Carnival's *Holiday* lets the kids use their own ship ID card to access the games in lieu of dogging Dad for more quarters; the charge goes right into the billing computers along with Dad's bar bills and Mom's shipboard shopping.

- **DUTY-FREE SHOPS** are the places to buy Lladro porcelain, Rolex watches, sequinned garments and other useless items. Essentials such as toothpaste, aspirin and sunblock are harder to find since the profit margin is considerably smaller.

- **CASINOS** are a philosophical proving ground where optimists arrive and pessimists depart. A real gambler heads for the roulette table, taking a chance on whether the sea motion is in his favor or against it.

- **LIBRARIES** on most ships are the place to find books to read. They are also populated by competitive trivia quiz aficionados looking up answers in order to win still another bookmark or key chain. You can tell how much your cruise line trusts you by noting whether the glass cases are locked or unlocked.

- **CARD ROOMS** are the refuge of avid bridge players whose conversation beyond bids is limited to port of call observations such as, "It's only Hong Kong, shut up and deal." Only a masochist should let himself be roped into being a fourth for bridge after lunch.

Elevators come in all shapes and sizes, including this neon-lit glass elevator on Carnival's **Fantasy**.

- **ELEVATORS** on ships should be avoided at all costs, since the exercise of going up and down stairs is a major defense against weight gain. Elevators should only be used in an emergency except, of course, they do not operate during emergencies.

- **BEAUTY SALONS** are where all the women on board gather between 5 and 7 p.m. on formal nights. Naughty hairdressers direct them back to their cabins via the deck, where the wind destroys the comb-out and everything has to be done all over again.

All About Cabins

- **CABINS** come in all shapes and sizes, mostly small. As a rule, the higher the deck location, the higher the price, but the smoothest ride is amidships (in the middle) on a lower deck.

- **OUTSIDE CABIN** with a window has a square or rectangular panel of glass with light coming through. If the glass is round, it is a **PORTHOLE**. If you fling the curtains open and find yourself facing a blank wall, you have an **INSIDE CABIN**.

- **OUTSIDE CABINS ON PROMENADE DECK** (premium priced) are always admired by passers-by who look into the windows as they stroll by. On some ships the glass is covered with a special tinted film so outsiders see their own reflections during the daytime. But after dark, the situation is reversed, with the cabin occupants starring in their own X-rated TV shows for the passersby outside. Windows and portholes cannot be opened, except on very ancient vessels such as the *Mayflower*.

- **VACUUM MARINE TOILET**, which flushes with a loud "whooooosh," along with a tub or shower and wash basin are found in each cabin's private bathroom. The best toilets have the flushing device situated where it cannot be activated until the toilet lid is closed, an essential safety feature for absent-minded passengers.

- **ELECTRICAL APPLIANCE**—Before plugging a hair dryer or other appliance into a wall socket, check whether the ship's electrical system is 110 volts and AC (alternating current) or 220 volts and DC (direct current). Plugging one of the former into one of the latter may blow more than the hairdo. Many ships carry voltage converters that will solve the problem; check with the purser's desk.

- **TEMPERATURE CONTROL KNOBS** can be found in each cabin. When your choices are limited from cold to colder or hot to hotter, call Housekeeping to send up a repairman.

- **CABIN WALLS** on all but the newest ships can be very thin, and an entertaining alternative to a TV set or radio. The disembodied voice that gives greetings or commands from the cabin walls is usually the cruise director on the public address system, unless he's droning on about sea temperatures and windspeeds and nautical miles, in which case it's the captain. A panel of knobs located near the bed can tune in shipboard music programmed by overworked staffers at the reception desk who play "The Sound of Music" for three days in a row.

- **CLOSETS** are designed to remind passengers that they should have left behind half the clothes they brought.

- **LIFE JACKETS**, somewhere within the closet or under the bed, appear humorous at first glance but are extremely important should there be a problem at sea. Always attend the lifeboat drill and never leave without learning to don the jacket properly, check for the whistle and light, and find which lifeboat is yours.

- **PAPERS** that arrive under the cabin door are not junk mail. Each has some message to impart, whether it is the full schedule of activities for the next day with the suggested dress code for the evening or a 20 percent discount on perfume or gold chains in the gift shop. Read all papers shoved under the door, no matter how boring they appear. One might be an invitation to dine at the captain's table.

Service Areas

- **PURSER'S DESK**—usually located in the lobby. It's the desk with the long line of people waiting to register a complaint, break a $100 bill into singles or buy postage stamps.

- **SHORE EXCURSIONS DESK**—where you go to buy overpriced bus tours of minor Mexican cities which always stop at the cathedral, the cliff-divers and then an hour-long shopping opportunity at the gift shop of the guide's cousin.

- **RADIO ROOM**—where you arrange to pay $15 a minute to send a fax to your office or make a call home to your answering machine and find out bad news that ruins your vacation.

The dining room — this one is aboard RCI's Viking Serenade *— is a favorite shipboard gathering spot.*

The Dining Room

- **TABLES** rarely come with only two chairs but most often in fours, sixes, eights or even tens. Couples who worry about being bored (or boring) are safer at tables of six or more. After dining together throughout the cruise, passengers always wind up sending Christmas cards to each other.

- **MEAL SEATINGS** are the arbitrary times the cruise line has decided its passengers will eat. **MAIN** or **FIRST SEATING** offers lunch at noon and dinner at 6 or 6:30 a.m., but breakfast is at 7 a.m. **SECOND** or **LATE SEATING** passengers dine fashionably at 8 or 8:30 a.m., breakfast at a comfortable 8:30 or 9 a.m. in the morning, but can't have lunch until 1:30 p.m. This is why three-hour deck buffet breakfasts and lunches were invented.

- **SECOND SEATING** is preferred by really dedicated gourmands, who can fit in early riser's coffee and a few samples from the buffet breakfast before reporting for the regular dining room breakfast. Then morning bouillon at 11 settles any remaining hunger pangs until time for a hot dog or hamburger from the deck grill as an appetizer for the buffet lunch. Lingering over the 1:30 p.m. lunch fills the empty moments until teatime, with cocktail hour, dinner and midnight buffet left to round out the day—and the figure.

- **SPECIAL DIET MENUS**—low in fats, calories or salt—demanded by passengers at the beginning of a seven-day cruise are usually thrown to the winds about Wednesday, after which they wonder why their shipboard diet plan didn't work.

- **MIDNIGHT BUFFETS** served at 10:30 p.m. rank high on the senior circuit. Swinging singles should seek vessels like Carnival's with 24-hour pizzeria service.

The Only Ten Nautical Terms You Ever Need to Know

1. **Port**: the left side of the ship when you're facing the pointy end.
2. **Starboard**: the right side of the ship when you're facing the pointy end.
3. **Forward**: toward the front, or pointy end.
4. **Aft**: toward the back, or blunt end.
5. **Bow**: the pointy end.
6. **Stern**: the blunt end.
7. **Tender**: a boat carried aboard the ship that can ferry you ashore if the ship is not tied up at the dock; to use the boat to ferry passengers ashore.
8. **Gangway**: the detachable outside stairway from the ship's deck down to the dock or tender.
9. **Embark**: to get on a ship.
10. **Disembark**: to get off a ship.

Ten Questions to Ask Yourself Before Calling a Travel Agent

Before you sail away into the sunset, you need to know what you want and be able to communicate that information to a travel agent, since virtually all cruise lines prefer or require bookings to be made through agents. Read these questions and know the answers to them before you call the travel agent. It will make her job much easier and ensure that you'll get the right cruise for you.

1. What are you looking for—sunny island beaches, duty-free shopping, a stress-free, do-nothing getaway, a razzle-dazzle good time with plenty of entertainment?

You can get them all on a cruise, but not necessarily on the same ship. Try to be specific as to what you want. A working couple with young children might opt for a family cruise combined with a Disney World package, giving them quality time with the kids and still the chance to be alone together while the youngsters join in special shipboard youth programs. On the other hand, a grade-school teacher seeking a break from workaday reality would probably want to set sail in exactly the opposite direction from ships that carry hundreds of romping children.

2. How long can you be away?

Cruises can be three-day weekend sailings, seven-day cruises, 14-day sailings, even 100-plus day world cruises. First-timers usually opt for three to seven days, frequent cruisers for a longer period of time.

3. Where do you want to go?

Weekend or mini-cruises usually set out from Florida for the Bahamas or from Los Angeles to Catalina Island and Baja California. Seven-day cruises with air/sea packages let you sail around the Hawaiian Islands, the Caribbean, Mexican Riviera, Alaska, the South Pacific or Europe. It usually takes 10 days for a Panama Canal cruise with a full transit, although several ships offer a cruise into part of the canal during a seven-day itinerary.

4. Are you traveling as a single, one of a pair, or part of a group of family and friends?

Others may have different needs or desires, so confer with them before making any decisions. A ship good for singles may not work so well with family groups.

5. What do you want in the way of shipboard lifestyle?

Decide what you think are the most important elements of a good vacation, jot them down and have them handy when you make your initial call to a travel agent. While many stressed-out travelers picture a cruise ship as a place to lounge quietly by the pool with a good book, they may be ready after a couple of days for livelier activities. Virtually all cruise ships today offer gym equipment, aerobics, lectures, shoreside golf and tennis, dancing, bridge or crafts classes and even shopping.

6. Do you want a large, medium-sized or small ship?

Big ships have more entertainment, bigger casinos and spas and longer lines; medium-sized ships have scaled-down versions of the same. Small ships are more apt to be free of regimentation and rigid dress codes, but you may be on your own for entertainment. Small to mid-sized vessels usually provide a more relaxed ambiance, while glittering megaliners throb with music and bright lights most of the night. But there's not a vessel afloat that doesn't have a sunny, secluded corner for reading or a lively spot around the bar for socializing.

7. Do you want a classic (read older) or contemporary (read newer) ship?

Most new ships will remind you of a chain resort hotel like Hyatt or Marriott, complete with atrium, glass elevators and identical modular cabins, while ships built 20 or more years ago have ocean liner looks, odd-sized cabins and nostalgic promenade decks.

8. Do you want frequent opportunities to wear your nicest party clothes, or would you prefer to stay casual day and night?

Super-deluxe small ships are quite dressy, expedition and sailing ships casual, and big ships usually have two dress-up evenings a week. Sometimes people who work in an office that requires business attire every day welcome the indulgence of casual sailing or adventure cruising where the only dress code may request "no bathing suits or bare feet at dinner."

9. Do you want to go island-hopping on a ship that stops at a lot of ports or spend your time relaxing aboard ship?

If relaxing is more important, look for itineraries that designate one or two days at sea during a seven-day cruise. You'll still have ports to visit but can get some rest in between.

10. What do you want to learn about the places you'll visit?

If the history, culture, flora and fauna is important, look to expedition ships that emphasize natural history lectures and birdwatching boatrides. Adventure and expedition cruises always seem to attract a lot of doctors, lawyers, teachers and other professionals who diligently attend all the lectures, then happily splash ashore in rubber landing craft to go on nature hikes. If you prefer to know where to pick up brand names like Rolex, Lladro or Colombian emeralds, any big mainstream cruise ship will fill the bill with its "guaranteed shopping" programs subsidized by the very merchants being recommended.

INSIDER TIP

Don't let price be the major factor when you choose your first cruise, especially if you assume all ships and cruises are alike. They're not, and the difference of $20 a day could mean a huge improvement in the quality of your shipboard experience. Once you've taken a couple of cruises, then you can afford to experiment, but a first-time cruise experience that doesn't meet your expectations could turn you away from cruising for good. A smart travel agent will try to steer you toward the most positive cruise experience for you and your family; that means future repeat business for the agent.

How to Read a Brochure

Whenever a new flock of brightly plumaged cruise brochures arrive, we find ourselves leafing through them and visualizing, not the romantic days at sea they portray, but an overworked copywriter in a tiny cubicle high atop a metropolitan office building.

Our fantasy copywriter, thesaurus at the ready, stares through a dirt-streaked window at a rainy sky between bouts of turning out hyperbolic sentences about "hibiscus-scented nights" and "elegant lounges where the decor is luxurious and plush."

Sometimes we wish cruise lines would spend a little less on the four-color pages and take the poor copywriter out on a cruise someday. It would certainly help clear up the vague and overblown prose.

In the meantime, however, the safest path for a potential cruise passenger is to skim the prose lightly and **CONCENTRATE ON THE PICTURES AND CHARTS**—you'd be surprised how much information you can glean from them—and then turn immediately to **READ THE "FINE PRINT"** on the inside back pages for the real nitty-gritty.

First, take a careful look at all the color photos. Don't get lost in reverie, imagining yourself standing on the deck with that Technicolor tropical drink in your hand—that's the intention of most successful advertising photography.

Instead, first **STUDY THE MODELS**, those beaming, bronzed beauties in each shot, then notice the slightly out-of-focus "real people" in some, but not all, of the backgrounds. The models represent the line's idealized version of their perfect prototype passengers, while the people in the background are real passengers on board during the photo shoot. If the ship seems suspiciously empty, the real passengers were all chased away so they could photograph the models alone. If the background people and the foreground people look as if they would be invited to the same party, you have a cruise line that is marketing realistically.

Next, flip quickly through the entire brochure to **GET AN OVERVIEW**. Where is the emphasis? If you see lots of nightlife and casino shots, the company is trying to tell you it is proud of the ship's after-dark entertainment. Where you see smiling waiters and cabin attendants, the line is telling you you'll get special treatment from its staff. If you see smiling children and their happy parents, the line is tipping you off that they welcome families on board. And if you see lots of food pictures, they're telling you, Miss Scarlett, you'll never be hungry again!

The **ITINERARY TABLES** are also valuable sources of information. If the copywriter extols a particular Caribbean island where you'll get a breathtaking view from atop a volcanic mountain in the island's center, and the itinerary says you dock at 9 a.m. and sail at noon, there's no way you'll see that view. And if your Greek Islands cruise arrives in Hydra at 9 p.m. and departs at 10:30 that same evening, you won't have many slides to show the folks back home.

Watch out for the little **ASTERISKS THAT DENOTE "CRUISE BY"** for some ports or islands. While you may get a look at them through binoculars or telephoto lenses, you won't set foot ashore.

If the itinerary has two cities shown, one of them in parentheses —say, Civitavecchia (for Rome) or Livorno (for Florence)—you can expect a long bus ride from the port town to the destination city. A 9-to-5 stop in Civitavecchia would allow you only a couple of hours in Rome by the time the ship clears immigration and the bus makes its way through heavy traffic.

Be sure, too, to note the **DAY OF THE WEEK** you're scheduled to arrive in each port. If there's a special museum you want to visit, check to be sure it's open on the day you're there. If you're counting on some serious shopping in St. Thomas, remember that stores are closed on Sundays, except for a few that open for a quick couple of hours in the morning when a ship is in port.

DECK PLANS are helpful in spotting extra niceties on board that aren't always promoted—the library, card room, sauna and spa, beauty and barber shop, hospital, covered decks and enclosed galleries.

DINING ROOM DIAGRAMS can tip you off as to how close together the tables are and if there are many tables for two available. Note that on older ships the dining room is usually on a lower deck, where your only view is of closed draperies backlit with fluorescent tubing to give the illusion of daylight.

What **ABOUT THE FOOD** on board? A discerning gourmet can usually tell from the photographs. Don't waste too much time studying the overwrought, gelatin-encased gala buffet; it's as standard on mass-market seven-day Caribbean ships as the deck chairs and about as tasty.

In today's more health-conscious world, salmon has supplanted beef as the food photo of choice in cruise brochures, and more space is given to appetizers and small plate dishes than main courses or gala buffets, suggesting to the nervous first-timer that he won't necessarily gain weight on this ship.

You can usually tell from the pictures whether the cruise line will go out of its way to offer an interesting excursion ashore or simply **sell you a three-hour bus tour**.

CABIN SIZE is better determined from deck plans than photographs. In the latter, the photographer is usually shooting with a wide-angle lens while braced in the doorway or crouching in the shower. These lenses can distort a standard-sized berth into a bed fit for Magic Johnson.

And watch out for the brochure that shows **ONLY PICTURES OF DESTINATIONS AND CLOSE-UPS OF ATTRACTIVE MODELS DRINKING CHAMPAGNE.** Unless the ship was still under construction or undergoing extensive refitting when the photos were made, you suspect, maybe rightly, that they're trying to hide something from you.

After practicing a while with the pictures and diagrams, you should be in fine shape to tackle the prose and read between the lines. For additional assistance, check out **The Brochure Says** and **Translation** segments for each ship in the ship review section.

EAVESDROPPING

"I expected something Noel Cowardish on my first cruise, but instead there were all these people in polyester acting like every night was New Year's Eve, the deck chairs were all jammed up together and the man next to me was listening to Mexican rock-and-roll on his radio. Later I learned ways of finding quiet, remote hiding places for reading, and some of the people turned out to be very nice." A female passenger who chose the wrong cruise line for her first cruise.

Working on a Cruise Ship

We frequently get letters from readers wanting to know how to get a job on a cruise ship. If you think it's all exotic ports, partying with the passengers and glamorous high pay, think again. Most of the waiters and cabin stewards depend on tips as the primary source of their wages. They do get room and board, but they have to share cabins, have little privacy and often work seven days a week for a month at a time. A large cruise ship employs more than 1000 crew members, however, and there is frequent turnover as people move on, settle down, or decide to pursue other opportunities on land. Job opportunities range from ship photographer to shop clerk, cruise director, engineer, ship doctor and entertainer to hairdresser, casino dealer, exercise instructor, nurse or electrician. Contact the cruise lines that interest you in this book and find out who to contact at their employment recruitment office. You may also want to check out Web Sites for cruise employment opportunities. (Be careful of agencies charging exorbitant recruitment fees.) Other useful addresses include:

Global Ship Services, Inc.

141 NE Avenue, Ste 203, Miami, FL 33132 (305)374-8649.
Positions ranging from pursers to secretarial staff, housekeepers, cabin stewards, bar staff and restaurant personnel.

Onboard Promotions Group

777 Arthur Godfrey Boulevard, Ste. 320, Miami Beach, FL (305)673-0400.
Port Lecturers.

Ship Services International

370 W. Camino Gardens Boulevard, Boca Raton, FL 33432 (407)391-5500.
Entertainers and general cruise staff.

Greater Atlantic Casinos

990 Northwest 166 Street, Miami, FL 33169 (954) 359-0001.
Casino workers.

Cruise Ship Picture Company

1177 South America Way, Ste. 200, Miami, FL 33132 (305)539-1903.
Ship Photographers.

For more information on ship employment opportunities, you may want to read *Working On Cruise Ships* by Sandra Bow, published in 1996 by Vacation Work, Oxford, UK.

WHO GOES WHERE

WORLD CRUISING

These ships move continuously throughout the world during the year. Those marked **World** do a long cruise in the winter/spring.

Crystal Cruises	World	Crystal Symphony	page 353
Cunard Line	World	QE2	page 366
	World	Royal Viking Sun	page 372
Delphin Seereisen	World	Delphin	page 388
Holland America Line	World	Rotterdam VI	page 512
P & O (Princess Tours)	World	Arcadia	page 610
	World	Oriana	page 615
Princess Cruises	World	Island Princess	page 653
Saga International Holidays	World	Saga Rose	page 783

ALASKA

Alaska Sightseeing/Cruise West	*Spirit of Alaska*	*page 191*
	Spirit of Columbia	*page 191*
	Spirit of Discovery	*page 196*
	Spirit of Endeavour	*page 200*
	Spirit of Glacier Bay	*page 204*
	Spirit of '98	*page 207*
Carnival Cruise Line	*Jubilee*	*page 258*
Celebrity Cruises	*Galaxy*	*page 283*
	Mercury	*page 283*
Clipper Cruise Line	*Yorktown Clipper*	*page 298*
Crystal Cruises	*Crystal Harmony*	*page 353*
Glacier Bay Tours & Cruises	*Executive Explorer*	*page 475*
	Wilderness Adventurer	*page 479*
	Wilderness Explorer	*page 483*
Holland America Line	*Nieuw Amsterdam*	*page 506*
	Noordam	*page 506*
	Ryndam	*page 500*
	Statendam	*page 500*
	Veendam	*page 500*
Norwegian Cruise Line	*Norwegian Dynasty*	*page 563*
	Norwegian Wind	*page 558*
Princess Cruises	*Crown Princess*	*page 640*
	Dawn Princess	*page 646*
	Regal Princess	*page 640*
	Sky Princess	*page 663*
	Sun Princess	*page 646*
Radisson Seven Seas	*Hanseatic*	*page 673*
Royal Caribbean International	*Legend of the Seas*	*page 716*
	Rhapsody of the Seas	*page 716*
Special Expeditions	*Sea Bird*	*page 851*
	Sea Lion	*page 851*
World Explorer Cruises	*Universe Explorer*	*page 923*

BAHAMAS

Carnival Cruise Line	*Ecstasy*	*page 264*
	Fantasy	*page 264*
Canaveral Cruise Line	*Dolphin IV*	*page 244*
Norwegian Cruise Line	*Leeward*	*page 582*
Premier Cruise Lines	*Star/Ship Oceanic*	*page 628*
Regal Cruises	*Regal Empress*	*page 694*
Royal Caribbean International	*Nordic Empress*	*page 730*
	Sovereign of the Seas	*page 739*

BERMUDA

Celebrity Cruises	*Horizon*	*page 289*
	Zenith	*page 289*
Cunard Line	*QE2*	*page 366*
	Royal Viking Sun	*page 372*
Norwegian Cruise Line	*Norwegian Crown*	*page 554*
	Norwegian Majesty	*page 567*
Regal Cruises	*Regal Empress*	*page 694*
Royal Caribbean International	*Song of America*	*page 735*

CANADA/NEW ENGLAND

American Canadian Caribbean Line	*Grande Caribe*	*page 216*
	Mayan Prince	*page 216*
	Niagara Prince	*page 216*
Clipper Cruise Line	*Clipper Adventurer*	*page 303*
	Nantucket Clipper	*page 298*
Cunard Line	*QE2*	*page 366*
Holland America Line	*Westerdam*	*page 515*
Norwegian Cruise Line	*Norwegian Crown*	*page 554*
Princess Cruises	*Royal Princess*	*page 657*
Regal Cruises	*Regal Empress*	*page 694*
Royal Caribbean International	*Vision of the Seas*	*page 716*
Seabourn Cruise Line	*Seabourn Pride*	*page 800*
Silversea Cruises	*Silver Cloud*	*page 823*
St. Lawrence Cruise Line	*Canadian Empress*	*page 791*

CARIBBEAN

American Canadian Caribbean Line	*Grande Caribe*	*page 216*
	Grande Mariner	*page 216*
	Mayan Prince	*page 216*
	Niagara Prince	*page 216*

CARIBBEAN

Carnival Cruise Line	*Carnival Destiny*	*page 253*
	Carnival Triumph	*page 253*
	Celebration	*page 258*
	Ecstasy	*page 264*
	Fascination	*page 264*
	Imagination	*page 264*
	Inspiration	*page 264*
	Sensation	*page 264*
Celebrity Cruises	*Century*	*page 283*
	Galaxy	*page 283*
	Horizon	*page 289*
	Mercury	*page 283*
	Zenith	*page 289*
Clipper Cruise Line	*Nantucket Clipper*	*page 298*
	Yorktown Clipper	*page 298*
Club Med Cruises	*Club Med 1*	*page 308*
Commodore Cruise Line	*Enchanted Isle*	*page 316*
Costa Cruises	*CostaClassica*	*page 332*
	CostaRomantica	*page 332*
	CostaVictoria	*page 342*
Crystal Cruises	*Crystal Harmony*	*page 353*
	Crystal Symphony	*page 353*
Cunard Line	*QE2*	*page 366*
	Royal Viking Sun	*page 372*
	Sea Goddess I	*page 377*
	Vistafjord	*page 381*
Dolphin Cruise Line	*IslandBreeze*	*page 423*
	OceanBreeze	*page 427*
	SeaBreeze	*page 432*
EuroCruises	*Black Prince*	*page 454*
Holland America Line	*Nieuw Amsterdam*	*page 506*
	Noordam	*page 506*
	Rotterdam VI	*page 512*
	Ryndam	*page 500*
	Statendam	*page 500*
	Veendam	*page 500*
	Westerdam	*page 515*
Mediterranean Shipping Cruises	*Melody*	*page 530*
Norwegian Cruise Line	*Leeward*	*page 582*
	Norway	*page 548*
	Norwegian Crown	*page 554*
	Norwegian Dream	*page 558*
	Norwegian Sea	*page 572*
	Norwegian Star	*page 577*
	Norwegian Wind	*page 558*
P & O	*Oriana*	*page 615*
	Victoria	*page 619*

CARIBBEAN

Princess Cruises	*Grand Princess*	*page 651*
	Crown Princess	*page 640*
	Dawn Princess	*page 646*
	Sun Princess	*page 646*
Radisson Seven Seas Cruises	*Radisson Diamond*	*page 680*
Regal Cruises	*Regal Empress*	*page 694*
Royal Caribbean International	*Enchantment of the Seas*	*page 716*
	Grandeur of the Seas	*page 716*
	Majesty of the Seas	*page 724*
	Monarch of the Seas	*page 724*
	Nordic Empress	*page 730*
	Rhapsody of the Seas	*page 716*
	Splendour of the Seas	*page 716*
Royal Olympic Cruises	*Stella Solaris (Sun Line)*	*page 777*
Seabourn Cruise Line	*Seabourn Pride*	*page 800*
Sea Cloud Cruises	*Sea Cloud*	*page 805*
Seawind Cruise Line	*Seawind Crown*	*page 814*
Silversea Cruises	*Silver Cloud*	*page 823*
Star Clippers	*Star Clipper*	*page 862*
	Star Flyer	*page 862*
Tall Ship Adventures	*Sir Francis Drake*	*page 891*
Windjammer Cruises	*Amazing Grace*	*page 898*
	Fantome	*page 900*
	Flying Cloud	*page 900*
	Legacy	*page 900*
	Mandalay	*page 900*
	Polynesia	*page 900*
	Yankee Clipper	*page 900*
Windstar Cruises	*Wind Spirit*	*page 912*
	Wind Star	*page 912*
World Explorer Cruises	*Universe Explorer*	*page 923*

WEST AFRICA AND CANARY ISLANDS

Clipper Cruise Line	*Clipper Adventurer*	*page 303*
Cunard Line	*QE2*	*page 366*
	Sea Goddess I	*page 377*
Costa Cruises	*CostaRiviera*	*page 338*
EuroCruises	*Black Prince*	*page 454*
	Black Watch	*page 458*
OdessAmerica	*Adriana*	*page 587*
P & O Cruises	*Oriana*	*page 615*
Seabourn Cruise Line	*Seabourn Pride*	*page 800*

EAST AND SOUTH AFRICA

Mediterranean Shipping Cruises	*Symphony*	*page 539*
OdessAmerica	*Royal Star*	*page 594*
Orient Lines	*Marco Polo*	*page 601*
Princess Cruises	*Pacific Princess*	*page 653*
Renaissance Cruises	*Renaissance ship*	*page 705*
Silversea Cruises	*Silver Cloud*	*page 823*

GREEK ISLANDS AND TURKEY

Costa Cruises	*CostaClassica*	*page 332*
	CostaRiviera	*page 338*
	CostaVictoria	*page 342*
Crystal Cruises	*Crystal Symphony*	*page 353*
Cunard Line	*Royal Viking Sun*	*page 372*
	Sea Goddess II	*page 377*
	Vistafjord	*page 381*
EuroCruises	*Azur*	*page 450*
OdessAmerica	*Adriana*	*page 587*
P & O Cruises	*Oriana*	*page 615*
	Victoria	*page 619*
Princess Cruises	*Pacific Princess*	*page 653*
Radisson Seven Seas Cruises	*Radisson Diamond*	*page 680*
	Song of Flower	*page 685*
Renaissance Cruises	*Aegean I*	*page 702*
	Renaissance ships	*page 705*
Royal Olympic Cruises	*Odysseus (Sun Line)*	*page 769*
	Olympic (Epirotiki)	*page 754*
	Orpheus (Epirotiki)	*page 758*
	Stella Oceanis (Sun Line)	*page 773*
	Stella Solaris (Sun Line)	*page 777*
	Triton (Epirotiki)	*page 762*
Silversea Cruises	*Silver Wind*	*page 823*
Star Clippers	*Star Flyer*	*page 862*
Swan Hellenic Cruises	*Minerva*	*page 886*
Windstar Cruises	*Wind Spirit*	*page 912*
	Wind Star	*page 912*
	Wind Surf	*page 917*

HAWAII/TAHITI

American Hawaii Cruises	*Independence*	page 228
Carnival Cruise Line	*Jubilee*	page 258
Club Med Cruises	*Club Med 2*	page 308
Crystal Cruises	*Crystal Harmony*	page 353
Cunard Line	*Vistafjord*	page 381
Princess Cruises	*Sky Princess*	page 663
Radisson Seven Seas Cruises	*Paul Gaugin*	page 677
Royal Caribbean International	*Legend of the Seas*	page 716
Seabourn Cruise Line	*Seabourn Legend*	page 800

MEDITERRANEAN

Clipper Cruise Line	*Clipper Adventurer*	page 303
Costa Cruises	*CostaAllegra*	page 326
	CostaMarina	page 326
	CostaRiviera	page 338
	CostaRomantica	page 332
Crystal Cruises	*Crystal Symphony*	page 353
Cunard Line	*QE2*	page 366
	Royal Viking Sun	page 372
	Sea Goddess I	page 377
	Sea Goddess II	page 377
	Vistafjord	page 381
Delphin Seereisen	*Delphin*	page 388

MEDITERRANEAN

EuroCruises	*Ausonia*	*page 446*
	Black Watch	*page 458*
Holland America Line	*Maasdam*	*page 500*
	Rotterdam VI	*page 512*
Norwegian Cruise Line	*Norway*	*page 548*
	Norwegian Dream	*page 558*
Orient Lines	*Marco Polo*	*page 601*
P & O Cruises	*Arcadia*	*page 610*
	Oriana	*page 615*
	Victoria	*page 619*
Princess Cruises	*Grand Princess*	*page 651*
	Island Princess	*page 653*
	Royal Princess	*page 657*
Radisson Seven Seas Cruises	*Radisson Diamond*	*page 680*
	Song of Flower	*page 685*
Renaissance Cruises	*Renaissance ship*	*page 705*
Royal Caribbean International	*Splendour of the Seas*	*page 716*
	Vision of the Seas	*page 716*
Saga International Holidays	*Saga Rose*	*page 783*
Seabourn Cruise Line	*Seabourn Legend*	*page 800*
	Seabourn Spirit	*page 800*
Sea Cloud Cruises	*Sea Cloud*	*page 805*
Silversea Cruises	*Silver Cloud*	*page 823*
	Silver Wind	*page 823*
Special Expeditions	*Caledonian Star*	*page 842*
Star Clippers	*Star Flyer*	*page 862*
Swan Hellenic	*Minerva*	*page 886*
Windstar Cruise	*Wind Song*	*page 912*

MEXICO WEST COAST

Carnival Cruise Line	*Elation*	*page 264*
	Holiday	*page 258*
	Jubilee	*page 258*

MEXICO WEST COAST

Clipper Cruise Line	*Yorktown Clipper*	*page 298*
Crystal Cruises	*Crystal Harmony*	*page 353*
	Crystal Symphony	*page 353*
Royal Caribbean International	*Song of America*	*page 735*
	Viking Serenade	*page 747*
Silversea Cruises	*Silver Cloud*	*page 823*
Special Expeditions	*Sea Bird*	*page 851*
	Sea Lion	*page 851*

ORIENT/ASIA

Carnival Cruise Line	*Tropicale*	*page 272*
Crystal Cruises	*Crystal Harmony*	*page 353*
Cunard Line	*Sea Goddess II*	*page 377*
Delphin Seereisen	*Delphin*	*page 388*
Esplanade Tours	*Bali Sea Dancer*	*page 438*
	Oceanic Odyssey	*page 442*
EuroCruises	*Black Watch*	*page 458*
Holland America	*Nieuw Amsterdam*	*page 506*
Orient Lines	*Marco Polo*	*page 601*
Princess Cruises	*Sky Princess*	*page 663*
Radisson Seven Seas Cruises	*Song of Flower*	*page 685*
Royal Caribbean International	*Sun Viking*	*page 743*
Seabourn Cruise Line	*Seabourn Legend*	*page 800*
	Seabourn Spirit	*page 800*
Silversea Cruises	*Silver Wind*	*page 823*
Star Cruises	*MegaStar Aries*	*page 870*
	MegaStar Taurus	*page 870*
	Star Aquarius	*page 874*
	Star Pisces	*page 874*
	SuperStar Capricorn	*page 877*
	SuperStar Gemini	*page 880*
Swan Hellenic	*Minerva*	*page 886*

PANAMA CANAL

SCANDINAVIA, BALTIC and BRITISH ISLES

SCANDINAVIA, BALTIC and BRITISH ISLES

Costa Cruises	*CostaAllegra*	*page 326*
	CostaMarina	*page 326*
Crystal Cruises	*Crystal Symphony*	*page 353*
Cunard Line	*QE2*	*page 366*
	Royal Viking Sun	*page 372*
	Vistafjord	*page 381*
Delphin Seereisen	*Delphin*	*page 388*
EuroCruises	*Black Watch*	*page 458*
	Funchal	*page 465*
	Kristina Regina	*page 468*
Holland America Line	*Maasdam*	*page 500*
Norwegian Cruise Line	*Norway*	*page 548*
P & O Cruises	*Arcadia*	*page 610*
	Oriana	*page 615*
	Victoria	*page 619*
Princess Cruises	*Pacific Princess*	*page 653*
	Royal Princess	*page 657*
Radisson Seven Seas Cruises	*Radisson Diamond*	*page 680*
	Song of Flower	*page 685*
Renaissance Cruises	*Renaissance ship*	*page 705*
Royal Caribbean International	*Splendour of the Seas*	*page 716*
	Vision of the Seas	*page 716*
Seabourn Cruise Line	*Seabourn Pride*	*page 800*
Silversea Cruises	*Silver Cloud*	*page 823*
Special Expeditions	*Caledonian Star*	*page 842*
	Swedish Islander	*page 856*
Swan Hellenic	*Minerva*	*page 886*

SOUTH AMERICA

Clipper Cruise Line	*Clipper Adventurer*	*page 303*
Cunard Line	*Royal Viking Sun*	*page 372*
	Vistafjord	*page 381*

SOUTH AMERICA

Crystal Cruises	*Crystal Harmony*	*page 353*
EuroCruises	*Black Prince*	*page 454*
Holland America	*Nieuw Amsterdam*	*page 506*
Ivaran Lines	*Americana*	*page 524*
Norwegian Cruise Line	*Norwegian Crown*	*page 554*
OdessAmerica	*Ambasador I*	*page 590*
	Skorpios	*page 587*
	Terra Australis	*page 587*
Princess Cruises	*Royal Princess*	*page 657*
Regal Cruises	*Regal Empress*	*page 694*
Royal Olympic Cruises	*Odysseus (Sun Line)*	*page 769*
	Stella Solaris (Sun Line)	*page 777*
Seabourn Cruises	*Seabourn Pride*	*page 800*
Silversea Cruises	*Silver Cloud*	*page 823*

SOUTH PACIFIC

Club Med Cruises	*Club Med 2*	*page 308*
Cunard Line	*Sea Goddess II*	*page 377*
Esplanade Tours	*Bali Sea Dancer*	*page 438*
	Oceanic Odyssey	*page 442*
Orient Lines	*Marco Polo*	*page 601*
Princess Cruises	*Sky Princess*	*page 663*
Renaissance Cruises	*Renaissance ship*	*page 705*
Seabourn Cruise Line	*Seabourn Legend*	*page 800*
Silversea Cruises	*Silver Wind*	*page 823*

NORTH AMERICAN COASTAL AND RIVERS

American Canadian Caribbean Line	*Grande Caribe*	*page 216*
	Grande Mariner	*page 216*
	Mayan Prince	*page 216*
	Niagara Prince	*page 216*
American West Steamboat Company	*Queen of the West*	*page 238*
Alaska Sightseeing/Cruise West	*Spirit of Alaska*	*page 191*
	Spirit of Columbia	*page 191*
	Spirit of Discovery	*page 196*
	Spirit of Endeavour	*page 200*
	Spirit of Glacier Bay	*page 204*
	Spirit of '98	*page 207*
Clipper Cruise Line	*Clipper Adventurer*	*page 303*
	Nantucket Clipper	*page 298*
	Yorktown Clipper	*page 298*
Delta Queen Steamboat Company	*American Queen*	*page 398*
	Delta Queen	*page 403*
	Mississippi Queen	*page 407*
Glacier Bay Tours and Cruises	*Executive Explorer*	*page 475*
	Wilderness Adventurer	*page 479*
	Wilderness Explorer	*page 483*
Special Expeditions	*Sea Bird*	*page 851*
	Sea Lion	*page 851*
St. Lawrence Cruise Lines	*Canadian Empress*	*page 791*

EXPEDITIONING

AF = Africa; ANT = Antarctica; ARC = Arctic; WW = Worldwide

Abercrombie & Kent	ANT, WW	*Explorer*	*page 168*
Clipper Cruise Line	ANT, ARC, WW	*Clipper Adventurer*	*page 303*
Hapag-Lloyd	ANT	*Bremen*	*page 488*
Marine Expeditions	ANT, ARC	*Fleet*	*page 928*
Orient Lines	ANT	*Marco Polo*	*page 601*
Quark Expeditions	ANT	*Akademik Golitsyn*	*page 929*
	ARC	*Kapitan Dranitsyn*	*page 929*
	ANT, ARC	*Kapitan Khlebnikov*	*page 929*
	ANT, WW	*Professor Molchanov*	*page 929*
	ARC	*Sovetski Soyuz*	*page 929*
Radisson Seven Seas Cruises	ANT, ARC, AF, WW	*Hanseatic*	*page 673*
Society Expeditions	ANT, WW	*World Discoverer*	*page 833*
Special Expeditions	WW	*Caledonian Star*	*page 842*

CHOOSING A CRUISE

Sometimes equating a ship with a hotel can help a first-time cruiser visualize it better; this soaring atrium lobby from Royal Caribbean's **Nordic Empress** *may remind you of your favorite Marriott or Hyatt.*

Pick a Ship, Any Ship

OK, you say, a cruise sounds great. Where do I sign up?

That's like saying a hotel is a hotel, book me a room. If you're a Ritz-Carlton regular, you might not be happy at the Motel 6. We feel a lot of otherwise experienced travelers might be more comfortable with cruising if they could equate a cruise line with a hotel company, so we've taken a bit of poetic license to give you a chance to relate your favorite type of land accommodations to the possibilities at sea. Bear in mind, however, that although ships are looking more and more like land hotels, the cruise ship experience is often superior, especially in service and entertainment, to its shoreside equivalent.

Bed-and-breakfasts	Alaska Sightseeing	*page 185*
	American Canadian Caribbean Line	*page 213*
	American Hawaii Cruises	*page 223*
	Clipper Cruises	*page 295*
	Delta Queen Steamboat Company	*page 393*
	Glacier Bay Tours and Cruises	*page 471*
	St. Lawrence Cruise Lines	*page 789*
Club Med	Club Med Cruises	*page 305*
	Star Clippers	*page 859*
	Windjammer Barefoot Cruises	*page 895*
Four Seasons	Silversea Cruises	*page 819*
Holiday Inn	Sun Line	*page 766*
Howard Johnson	Commodore	*page 313*
	Dolphin	*page 421*
	Regal Cruises	*page 691*
Hyatt Regency	Costa Cruises	*page 321*
	Princess Cruises	*page 633*
Inter-Continental	Celebrity Cruises	*page 277*
Marriott	Norwegian Cruise Line	*page 543*
	Royal Caribbean International	*page 711*
MGM Grand	Carnival Cruise Lines	*page 247*
Relais & Chateaux	Sea Goddess	*page 377*
	Radisson Seven Seas Cruises	*page 669*
	Windstar Cruises	*page 909*
Ritz-Carlton	Crystal Cruises	*page 349*
	Cunard Royal Viking Sun	*page 372*
	Seabourn	*page 795*
	Vistafjord	*page 381*
Small Luxury Hotels	Renaissance Cruises' Small Ships	*page 699*
Westin	Holland America Line	*page 493*
Summer camp	World Explorer Cruises	*page 921*

Choosing a Cabin

Prices for the cruise are determined by the cabin category, which in turn is based on deck location, amenities, whether the cabin is outside (with a porthole or windows) or inside (with no daylight), and sometimes, but not always, on cabin size.

Don't expect to snap up the bottom-priced loss leader (the one advertised in big print in the ads) because some cruise ships may have only four or six of these, long since allotted or sometimes assigned to cruise staff or entertainers.

Standard cabin amenities always include a bed or berth for each passenger, closet and storage space, some sort of table or dresser, private bathroom fa-

WE DON'T *claim* TO BE THE *best.*

SHIPS' REGISTRY: NETHERLANDS, BAHAMAS

OUR GUESTS *consistently* CLAIM IT FOR US.

For the past 7 years Holland America Line has been the highest-rated major cruise line† in *Condé Nast Traveler's* "Reader's Choice Awards." It's an honor that makes us especially proud, because it comes not from our industry, but from the people we welcome on board week after week. Call 1-800-426-6593 today for a free brochure, and begin planning the cruise that will spoil you for others.   †Fleet of 5 ships or more

Holland America Line
A TRADITION OF EXCELLENCE®

Alaska · Canada · Caribbean · Europe · Hawaii · Mexico · Panama Canal · South America · Grand Voyages

Grand foyer, Celebrity Cruises' *Galaxy*

cilities (except on some sailing ships) with toilet, sink, tub or shower. Most have individual temperature controls, telephone and radio and/or TV.

Grand suites such as the Royal Suite aboard RCI's Majesty of the Seas have many pleasurable extras, including separate living and sleeping areas and entertainment centers.

Pleasurable extras in upper price categories may include private verandas, suites with separate living room and bedroom, mini-refrigerators, sitting areas and picture windows.

Families with children or several people traveling together will save money by booking cabins with third and fourth upper berths, pull-down bunks that go for much less money (sometimes free) than the first two beds in a cabin.

Disabled travelers will find most vessels have one or more cabins that are specially configured to take care of wheelchairs with wider doors, turning space, low or flat sills and grab rails in the bathroom.

Dining Room Know-How

Your cruise ship dining room will operate in one of three ways:

1. **Totally open seatings**, usually on small or ultra-luxury vessels, in which the passenger arrives within a given time frame and sits where and with whom he pleases.

2. **Single meal seatings**, in which the passenger arrives within a given time frame and occupies an assigned table for the duration of the cruise.

3. **Two meal seatings**, in which passengers are assigned to dine at a particular table at a specified time, usually 6 or 8:30 p.m. for dinner, with breakfast and lunch comparably early or late as well.

The two-seating arrangement is the most common. You'll probably be asked at the time of booking which you prefer, but there's no guarantee you'll get it. If you don't get a card with a specified dining time and table number in advance or find it in your cabin when you arrive on board, go immediately to the maitre d'hotel in the dining room or another designated area and arrange your seating.

Some ships offer in addition to the regular dining room an alternative restaurant available at no extra charge but by reservation only, such as An Evening at Don Vito's aboard Radisson Seven Seas' Radisson Diamond.

Second seating times are the most in demand on Caribbean and Mediterranean cruises, first seating times in Alaska. Don't be upset if you don't get your first choice on a cruise, particularly if the ship is full, but if it means a lot, chat quietly with the maitre d'hotel, expressing your desire while tactfully holding a $20 bill and you may be able to negotiate a change.

You can request first or second seating, a smoking (on those ships that still allow smoking in the dining room) or nonsmoking table and the table size you wish. Most first-time cruisers request tables for two, which are relatively rare, but find they enjoy being seated at a larger table for six or eight. The most potentially problematic table size is for four. If you can't stand your tablemates and want to move, be decisive—make your move at the end of the very first dinner. Don't wait a couple of days to see if they get more charming. They won't.

Some ships offer alternative restaurant dining by reservation; there is no charge except sometimes a request to tip at point of service. This enables passengers seated at a large table in the regular dining room to have a private dinner for two or an opportunity to dine with new acquaintances.

Cruise Line Cuisine

It seems to us that TV's "The Love Boat" was on the wrong track. Episode after episode, the passengers seemed to spend an inordinate amount of time falling in and out of love. You hardly ever saw anybody agonizing about what to order for dinner.

But if you took a poll of real-life cruise passengers, you'd find more of them looking forward to encountering a lobster thermidor than a shipboard romance, and to lighting into a dish of cherries jubilee instead of starting a flame in someone's heart.

Italian buffet night brings a taste-tempting dessert display.

Cruise ship brochures entice us with full-color photographs of voluptuous midnight buffets, centerfolds of sensuous bananas flambé, lush melons and wicked croissants on a bedside tray. Is it any wonder we bound up the gangway anticipating a tryst with a tournedos of tenderloin Rossini?

But all too often our hopes are cruelly dashed, like the heartsick swain on a recent trans-Pacific cruise who spent six fruitless days and nights searching for the grand buffet of his dreams. "It was right there on page 8 in the brochure," he sighed, "but I couldn't find it anywhere on the ship."

In the fantasy world of cruise-ship advertising, every meal is a gourmet feast fit for a king, or even a restaurant critic. But in the real world on board, that's not always the case.

Think for a minute about your favorite little gourmet restaurant, the place you go once or twice a year to celebrate a special occasion. Does it serve two full dinner seatings an evening to between 500 and 3000 people, plus offering breakfast and lunch?

Does it operate a cafeteria on the side, along with a tearoom, half-a-dozen bars with snacks and hot hors d'oeuvres, a specialty pizzeria or ice cream parlor, and a catering service that produces beach picnics, deck barbecues and delivers meals to your door?

Is it atop a remote mountain peak or on an island in the middle of the ocean, hundreds of miles from a reliable source of food supplies?

No? Then don't try to compare most cruise ship cooking to a three-star *Michelin Guide* restaurant. Of course, there are a few exceptions (see Best Floating Dining Rooms, page 157).

Small ships, on the other hand, may turn out tastier food because they don't have to deal with as much volume, but on the down side, their menus are usually more restrictive.

Five Food Fanatic Tips About Ships

1. Most large ships serve high-quality hotel banquet food, most often capably prepared and attractively served. You'll encounter a few truly memorable dishes, some mediocre ones and, at least once during your cruise will be served something unidentifiable that you're sure you didn't order until the waiter affirms that it is indeed the chef's version of gazpacho or pecan pie.

2. Before you sign on the dotted line with your friendly neighborhood travel agent, ask to see some menus from the ship you're considering—not prototype menus like some publish in their brochures, but actual menus that have the date printed on them from a recent cruise, preferably one the agent picked up during her cruise. (You fussy eaters are not going to accept an agent's recommendation unless she's been aboard that ship, at least for lunch, are you?)

3. Most mass-market, mini-cruise and seven-day Caribbean lines have rotation menu plans that are not repeated during a single cruise but rather follow each other every seven or 14 or 21 days. Theme evenings are popular—French night with onion soup, *escargots* and *coq au vin*, Italian nights with antipasto, pasta and veal scaloppine, American nights with shrimp cocktail, corn on the cob and roast turkey with cranberry sauce. In this book, such cuisine is referred to as Themed.

4. Once on board, shop around early in the cruise for the location of the breakfasts, lunches and snacks that really sing out to you, and once you've found a winner, stick with it. Menus are usually posted ahead of time, so you can do your window-shopping in advance.

5. Talk to your waiter, and if he's good, learn to trust him. He's there to make you happy; his tip depends on it. Let him know what you like and dislike early in the cruise, and he'll always lead you through the menu. We treasure a memory of one of our first cruises, a Sitmar waiter named Tony who delivered the luncheon dish we'd ordered but materialized a few minutes later with another dish we hadn't ordered, murmuring, "I thought you might like to taste this one, too." Our choice was wrong; his was right.

DID YOU KNOW?

Cruise line food has improved tremendously in the 15 years we've been covering the scene. We remember a Dutch chef on the Rotterdam world cruise in 1985 who was going to retire at the end of that 100-day journey, and went to bizarre extremes not to repeat a single dish during the entire cruise. By the time we got on for the last leg, he was down to truly terrible combinations.

Five Tips on Reading a Shipboard Menu

1. See if it gives you a variety of lunch options from brunch-type dishes if you missed breakfast (omelets, for instance) to lighter fare (sandwiches and main-dish salads) to something hearty if you're hungry.

2. Check the light or low-calorie recommendation. We saw a ship once listing the day's diet special as Cobb Salad, that high-fat, high-calorie concoction of chopped bacon, blue cheese, avocado, and eggs with a gloppy-thick dressing. You'd never lose weight on that diet.

3. See how much fresh food versus canned or pre-prepared dishes they offer. Fresh catch of the day may be pre-frozen, but that's to be expected unless you're cruising in Alaska. Watch out for that long list of seven appetizers, most of them tinned juices.

4. See if they're pulling out all their stops on the dessert menu. A lot of lines cut food costs by stuffing passengers with sugary sweets and stodgy starches—you'll note the macaroni salads and Jello on the buffets—spending about $1.98 a day per passenger on raw materials.

5. Eye the dish descriptions carefully to make sure the line isn't blending out all the dishes with cream-based sauces instead of fresh herbs, garlic or imaginative seasoning.

INSIDER TIP

Check the nationality of the ship's officers, chef or dining room staff. Princess ships have British and Italian officers but an Italian dining room and galley staff, so you can expect continental cuisine with a definite Italian accent. Greek ships are going to serve continental dishes plus Greek salads and appetizers and at least one Greek menu a cruise. The Norwegians like to put out lavish seafood smorgasbords somewhere along the way.

How to Avoid Pigging Out at Sea

Take advantage of the exercise classes and spa aboard the ship; you've paid for them just as you have all that food you feel compelled to eat. Here, wanna-be Antarctic explorers work out aboard the **World Discoverer.**

1. Shop around, reading posted menus in advance and checking out the entire buffet display before plowing in.

2. Don't stuff yourself. Help save the whales by not being one; let the fishes finish your food.

3. Unless your metabolism is fantastic, skip a meal every now and then, substituting teatime for lunch or scheduling an hour in the disco before judiciously checking out the late buffet.

4. Beware of Greeks (or Italians or Jamaicans or Austrians) bearing dishes; a soulful-eyed waiter usually has his tip rather than your figure in mind when he coaxes you into ordering an appetizer, soup, salad, fish, meat and two desserts.

5. Steer clear of piña coladas and any other drink you can't see through or that has an umbrella in it. Opt instead for mineral water or diet soda, a glass of wine or light beer.

6. Take advantage of the exercise classes and spa; you've paid for them just as much as you have all that food you feel compelled to eat.

7. You'll find vegetarian and low-fat or low-calorie dishes on practically every menu these days, as well as a wider range of fish and poultry and less red meat.

8. If we want a vegetarian dinner, we sometimes order a plate of all the side vegetable dishes on the menu rather than the same old boring steamed cauliflower, broccoli and carrots.

9. Try ordering dishes without the sauce. Contrary to the famous Jack Nicholson "whole wheat toast" scene from *Five Easy Pieces*, most waiters will be happy to bring you sauce on the side or lemon wedges instead of salad dressing.

10. When you lunch on deck, plan to wear your bathing suit or shorts, and check out the row of slender young sylphs and Adonises by the pool (or for that matter, the not-so-slender ones) for positive reinforcement before you fill your plate.

Ship Sanitation Inspections

The way food is handled from its very arrival aboard the ship to its storage, as here in the food storage lockers on Cunard's **Vistafjord,** *and its final holding and preparation can affect the ship sanitation score.*

A great deal of attention is being paid these days to the "green sheet" ship sanitation inspection scores from U.S. Public Health's Center for Disease Control that are issued every two weeks.

It's laudable that the Center for Disease Control is carrying out the program because it keeps the cruise lines on their toes, making them train and carefully observe the galley employees, who may speak a dozen different languages.

But by the time the score has been published, it's history, and the infraction has been corrected long ago. As a rule, ships are inspected every six months, but may go a year or even longer without a reinspection unless the cruise line requests one. Many cruise lines employ a trained sanitation expert to establish and monitor their own sanitation practices.

The only real value of the scores for a potential passenger is as a longtime study of a specific ship over a couple of years. If the vessel is a consistent failure, then chances are its galley and sanitation practices are sloppy.

A single 30-point infraction causes the ship to fail automatically, since 86 out of a possible 100 is the passing grade. Improper methods of handling food are responsible for most major point losses, with temperature violations in food holding, preparation and serving areas the most critical.

Unannounced inspections are carried out at regular intervals on foreign-flag ships that call even occasionally in U.S. ports. When a ship fails, it can (and almost always does) request a reinspection as soon as possible to show the problem has been cleared up.

We went through all the "green sheets" for a one-year period and found an interesting pattern. Some of the cleanest and most highly-regarded ships were occasionally among the failures. The super-deluxe *Seabourn Pride*, which scored a 74 on February 19, 1995, but was retested March 21 and scored a 94; the spic-and-span *Rotterdam*, which scored a 78 on April 18, 1995, but bounced back with a 93 on May 24; and the stately *Sagafjord*, (now the *Saga Rose* for Saga Holidays), which failed with an 81 on April 23, 1995, but rescored a 96 on June 12. On the other hand, some vintage budget ships—notably the *Regal Empress* from Regal Cruises—held a score of a 95 during most of the time period, dropped to an 86, still passing, during a later period, and scored a 97 on the June 24, 1995, inspection. This despite the fact that before its first scheduled sailing from New York, officials went down to the dock and handed out flyers pointing out sanitation levels so low passengers might not wish to sail with her. In the first quarter of 1996, the *Crystal Symphony* and Celebrity's *Century* both scored a rare 100. And Celebrity's *Galaxy* achieved the same score in January of 1997.

Ships most commonly fail on the last inspection before they're sold or transferred, probably because the crew is less motivated. New ships or cruise lines (the latter the case with Regal Cruises) are usually given a couple of preliminary inspections with notes before getting a published score. "It's not unusual for a new ship to fail, because generally you have a lot of new people with new equipment," one of the inspectors told us.

The CDC inspectors have improved the quality of ship sanitation tremendously over the years, as well as carrying on an education program for kitchen workers who may come from a culture with different sanitation standards. Very few land-based restaurants could score an 86 or better under the CDC standards, according to former program head Tom Hunt, who had previously been a restaurant inspector. Unless a ship consistently fails over a period of time, there's no real way of determining whether a passenger might suffer a gastrointestinal illness aboard.

In fact, we were inadvertently once the cause of a ship sanitation rating failure when photographing the dining room for a food magazine. The chef had stuck a bouquet of fresh flowers in the walk-in refrigerator to keep them fresh until the shoot, and the CDC inspectors on the surprise inspection seized them as a major infraction—nonfood items stored with food items.

Six Questions About Ship Sanitation Scores

1. Does anyone ever score a perfect score?
    Yes, the first ship to make 100 on the numerical listings, which were initiated in 1989, was Carnival's *Fantasy* on April 30, 1990, followed by Windstar's *Wind Spirit* which scored 100 on August 27, 1990. More recently, *Crown Dynasty*, now *Norwegian Dynasty*, scored 100 on February 8, 1994, and the *Crystal Symphony* and Celebrity's *Century* made it in early 1996. Celebrity's *Galaxy* scored a perfect 100 on her first inspection in January 1997.

2. What's the lowest score ever recorded?
    The lowest one we've found was a 23 for Epirotiki's *Oceanos* back in 1989; that ship sank off the coast of South Africa in 1991.

3. Can the CDC keep a ship from sailing because of poor sanitation?
    Cooperation is voluntary on the part of the ship being inspected. The vessel sanitation program cannot forbid a ship with extreme sanitation problems to sail until its problems are corrected; it can only recommend that it not sail.

4. Who pays for these inspections?
    The cruise lines themselves.

5. Are all cruise ships inspected?
    The CDC's jurisdiction covers all ships carrying 13 or more passengers that sail in international waters. It does not include U.S.-flag vessels sailing in U.S. waters such as those of American Hawaii, Delta Queen Steamboat, Alaska Sightseeing/Cruise West or American West. Those ships are the responsibility of the Food and Drug Administration and the state health departments within their cruising areas.

6. How can I get a copy of the latest scores?
    Via Internet, ftp.cdc.gov//pub/ship_inspections/shipscore.txt, or by calling ☎ *(404) 332-4565* and requesting Document No. 510051.

Safety of Life at Sea

Commonly called SOLAS, Safety of Life at Sea regulations govern cruise ships that call at U.S. ports. Whenever a new ship comes into service, or enters a U.S. port for its first call, it must undergo a rigorous set of inspections by the U.S. Coast Guard covering fire safety drills, use of emergency equipment, crew drills and detailed examinations of the condition and safety of the vessel's hull and its machinery. After the initial series of inspections, the ships are reinspected quarterly. Unlike the CDC inspectors described above, the Coast Guard has the power to detain a ship from sailing if it is deemed unsafe for its passengers.

The Coast Guard's Traveling Inspectors team boards ships with emergencies to investigate causes, such as ships running aground, engine room fires, main engines down and sweltering passengers aboard ships with no electricity, air conditioning or hot food.

Stringent new SOLAS regulations implemented in 1997 have seriously affected the cruise industry, because they required detailed (and costly) amendments and additions to older vessels, from sprinkler systems to freon-free air-conditioning systems and low-level lighting systems. As a result, many cruise lines sold off or repositioned their vintage vessels.

INSIDER TIP

Many of the older ships are being sold to operators abroad to sail exclusively from non-U.S. ports, and so do not come under U.S. Coast Guard inspections and SOLAS regulations. Be cautious about buying a bargain cruise on a ship that sails only from Mediterranean or Asian ports if you're concerned about ship safety.

Where in the World Do You Want to Go?

The Caribbean, Alaska, Mexican Riviera, New England and Canada, Panama Canal, the Mediterranean, Northern Europe, South Pacific and Asia are all familiar, at least in concept, and easily accessible.

But with the magic of overland excursions, riverboats and canal barges, you can also consider as ports of call the Taj Mahal, Kenya's game parks, the city of St. Louis, the Burgundy wine country or the Pyramids.

No poll, rating system or expert travel agent can tell all potential cruise passengers that any one experience is "best." A well-worn truism says neophyte cruisers care most about ports of call, veteran cruisers about which ship. In either case, you'll want to concern yourself about more than where you're going and how much it's going to cost.

Five Hints for a Hassle-Free Cruise

1. The shorter the cruise, the younger and more casual the group on board is likely to be. For most first-time cruisers, the introduction to cruising is aboard a three- or four-day mini-cruise from Florida or California. See Short Sails, Big Sales, page 11.

2. If you want a smooth, trouble-free sailing, avoid any shakedown, inaugural, maiden voyage or first sailing on the heels of major renovations. Although some ships have sailed through these with flying colors, this is when the vessel is most vulnerable to plumbing, heating, air conditioning and water pressure problems.

3. If you are considering booking a ship that never sails from a U.S. port and your travel agent has no firsthand knowledge of it, take some time to check it out before putting down a deposit no matter how tempting the price. Some lesser-known vessels or very low-priced sailings may feature discounted cabins left over from a group or charter, or a cruise marketed primarily in another country, and you could find yourself odd man out. Also, these vessels are no longer inspected regularly by the U.S. Coast Guard and could represent a safety hazard.

4. When dealing with waiters and stewards to whom English is a second or third language, speak slowly and distinctly and be ready with an alternative word when they don't understand your initial request. That way you'll be spared the problem one infuriated passenger had with her Scandinavian stewardess who did not know what a "cantaloupe" was; if the passenger had switched to the word "melon," she would have gotten a serving of breakfast fruit instead of the envelope that was delivered by the bewildered Norwegian.

With waiters and stewards to whom English is a second language, such as this Greek bartender, speak slowly and distinctly when ordering something.

5. Read the fine print at the end of the company brochure and on the back of your ticket/contract, and you'll find the line is not responsible for missed ports of call, changed itineraries or liabilities in connection with independent contractors such as airlines and ground tour operators.

Seven Ways to Protect Yourself from Travel Scams

1. Be skeptical. If an offer seems too good to be true, it probably is. Unsolicited "prizes" you get through the mail or over the phone promising a free cruise usually involve your calling in and giving someone your credit card number or paying a "service fee" for a trip that never materializes.

2. Follow up. If you book through a discount agency's 800 number, don't send them checks or money orders. Use a credit card, but only after ascertaining that the cruise line rather than the agency will process the charge. Verify the reservation by demanding the vendor's confirmation number.

3. Never give out your credit card number on the phone to someone who called you.

4. Don't buy a cruise from a toll-free 800 telephone number if you haven't checked them out; it's better to visit the office in person and talk face-to-face with a travel agent. Several major cruise travel agencies with 800 numbers, some of them in business for years and regarded as reliable, went bankrupt suddenly in the last year or two, leaving clients high and dry and cruise-less.

5. Check any agency you're dealing with to see if they're members of professional travel organizations such as ASTA (American Society of Travel Agents), ARTA (Association of Retail Travel Agents), CLIA (Cruise Line International Association) or NACOA (North American Cruise-Only Agencies).

6. Double-check with the cruise line itself to confirm bookings and all payments.

7. When in doubt, call the National Consumer's League Hotline, ☎ *(800) 876-7060.*

SPECIAL CASES

Many ships sail with a number of gentlemen hosts aboard to dance with unattached ladies; here a dance class is in progress.

Singles

Anyone browsing through a cruise brochure notices sooner or later that ubiquitous term "per person, double occupancy" in conjunction with prices.

But what happens to passengers, as many as 25 percent of all potential travelers, who travel alone?

Generally, when one person occupies a double cabin, a surcharge that runs from 125 to 200 percent of the per person double occupancy rate is charged.

There are only two surefire ways to avoid the singles surcharge:

Opt for a **"guaranteed share"** from lines that offer it, which means the line will attempt to find another passenger of the same sex, general age range and smoking preference to match up with you or let you have the double cabin to yourself at the per-person double occupancy rate.

Find a ship, usually an older vessel, that has **designated single cabins** and pay the listed fare, which often works out to be nearly as much as a double cabin surcharge. Single cabins are available aboard Cunard's *Vistafjord* and *QE2*, American Hawaii, World Explorer, Norwegian Cruise Line's *Norway* and Ivaran's *Americana*, which often prices single cabins at the same or lower price as the per person double occupancy rates.

For 20- to-40 year-olds, Windjammer Barefoot Cruises offers a half-dozen "singles cruises" throughout the year on designated dates, with half the passengers male and half female, they promise. (They cite five marriages from previous singles sailings.)

Over-50 travelers might want to opt for something a little less casual. Single women with social dancing and bridge-playing on their minds will find ships that carry social hosts (see below) have a definite appeal.

Everything You Ever Wanted to Know About Social Hosts

1. Which lines carry them?

Cunard Line, Silversea Cruises, Delta Queen Steamboat Company, Crystal Cruises, Holland America (on longer cruises), American Hawaii (on selected Big Band sailings).

2. Who are they?

Usually retired businessmen or military men, single, divorced or widowed, and upwards of 50 years old.

3. Can I count on romance?

No, just socializing, dancing, bridge playing and companionship at mealtimes and on shore excursions. Anything else, including spending too much time with one passenger, is forbidden. However, some social hosts have met ladies aboard and continued to see them on land without having to follow the cruise line's rules. Several marriages are said to have come out of meetings between social hosts and passengers.

4. How many hosts are usually on board?

Anywhere from two to 10 or more, depending on the size of the ship and how many single female passengers are booked for that sailing.

5. How can someone get a job as a social host?

The leading (and perhaps only) agent for social hosts is Lauretta Blake of **The Working Vacation**, *4277 Lake Santa Clara Drive, Santa Clara, CA 95054,* ☎ *(408) 727-9665.* She screens and books hosts for several cruise lines for $150 fee per week at sea, paid by the host.

The cruise lines themselves do not charge a fee for placing hosts; you could send a letter, picture and resume directly to the cruise line's personnel department or director of entertainment. Most hold regular "auditions."

The hosts usually receive no payment beyond the free cruise, economy class airfare to and from the ship, and a modest allowance for onboard expenditures such as wine and bar bills. Cruise lines usually require their hosts take two or three cruises back to back, and sleep two to a cabin.

Five Tips for Cruising with Kids

Shipboard playrooms provide innovative outlets for energetic kids.

1. Book a ship that is likely to have other young children aboard. Whether a kid is 6 or 16, he's happy if he can find someone near his own age. Otherwise he can get bored and fidgety. (See "Best Ships for Families with Kids," page 149.)

2. Don't expect free 24-hour baby-sitting. The youth counselors are there to enrich your child's vacation, not take him off your hands. A few lines offer baby-sitting in the evenings in the youth center, usually with a surcharge.

3. Don't take the kids on a cruise line that doesn't offer a children's program, discounts on their fare and counselors on staff—that's a tip-off the ship and its regular passengers would be happier without children on board.

4. Check with the cruise line if your child is under two; many lines have minimum age limits.

5. Look for the'toons—The Big Red Boat of Premier has a contract with Warner Brothers' Looney Tunes, which means Bugs Bunny and Tweety Bird on deck; Dolphin sails with Hanna Barbera's Fred Flintstone and Yogi Bear aboard.

INSIDER TIP

In case you're wondering who's inside the furry suit animating Yogi Bear or Andy Panda, it's usually a member of the ship's crew–perhaps a dishwasher or night cleaning person–who's paid extra to portray the cartoon character. Look at it this way–he's in show biz.

Ten Cruise Tips for Seniors

Pick and choose among the many meals and snacks offered every day, perhaps enjoying teatime treats, such as passengers aboard Cunard's **Royal Viking Sun.**

1. A ship's size and itinerary have a direct relationship with how quickly sophisticated medical care can be obtained in an emergency; large ships have more medical staff and facilities on board, and more importantly, some have a landing pad for a helicopter to land and evacuate a seriously ill passenger.

2. Have your doctor write the details of any ongoing medical condition, as well as any prescription drugs or serious allergies, on an index card and give it to the ship's doctor when you board.

3. Study the deck plan of the vessel you're considering for elevators if you use a wheelchair or tire easily climbing stairs.

4. Check to make sure the cabin category you're booking provides two lower beds rather than an upper and a lower, which can make getting in and out of bed more difficult.

5. Check itineraries to determine where the ship will dock as opposed to where it anchors and tenders; going down a gangway on the side of the ship and transferring to a bobbing launch calls for steady footing.

6. Exercise care and moderation in food and drink; avoid any major changes in your normal eating pattern.

7. Pick and choose; sample the six or eight meals a day a few at a time, skipping lunch, perhaps, in favor of a big breakfast and afternoon tea, or have a light dinner to save room for the midnight buffet.

8. Don't overtax yourself in every port of call; take a half-day tour instead of a full-day tour, or take an early morning stroll around the port town, come back to the ship for a midday break and then go back in late afternoon for a second look if you wish.

9. Remember that comfort is more important than fashion in tropical areas; wear broken-in walking shoes and loose-fitting clothing.

10. Mix and mingle; don't seclude yourself or limit your choice of companions to others your own age.

Getting Married Aboard

While the popularity of honeymoons at sea has been increasing steadily for the past five years, some cruise lines now offer the additional option of getting married aboard ship. Then the bride and groom can sail away on their honeymoon cruise with—or without—other members of the wedding party.

Couples on a budget like the convenience and romance of a shipboard wedding, where they can have a smaller ceremony with only a few guests. By marrying on a ship instead of celebrating a big wedding ashore, they might even save enough to pay for the honeymoon cruise.

Contrary to popular belief, a ship's captain is not empowered to conduct a wedding ceremony, "at least not one that will last longer than the cruise," one captain jokes.

But couples booked on the sailing may get married in port, using either an officiate provided by the cruise line, or a minister, rabbi or priest they bring themselves.

Packages vary from basic (under $300 for a notary and witnesses, cake and champagne for the newlyweds) to elaborate (a two-hour reception with open bar, hot and cold buffet and champagne toasts for around $75 a person). Many are coordinated for the cruise line by private wedding consultant companies.

Most common ports where weddings can be arranged include Miami and Los Angeles, several Hawaii ports including Honolulu, Hilo and Kona, St. Thomas in the U.S. Virgin Islands, Tortola in the British Virgin Islands, Vancouver, B.C., and Juneau, Alaska.

Cruise lines that offer wedding packages include American Hawaii, Carnival, Celebrity, Dolphin, Holland America, Norwegian Cruise Line, Princess, Royal Caribbean and Windjammer Barefoot Cruises.

EAVESDROPPING

"Twenty-five years ago if you took a honeymoon cruise, your name was Rockefeller. Now it's Smith or Jones," says Bob Dickinson, president of Carnival Cruise Lines.

Five Tips for Honeymooners at Sea

1. Check when booking if you want a double or king-sized bed; some vintage vessels have twin beds that cannot be pushed together.

2. Tables for two are not always guaranteed; some cruise lines put couples at tables of six or eight. Your travel agent can request a table for two or arrange for you to be seated with other honeymooners at a large table.

3. If you want to be singled out for congratulations, special onboard parties for newlyweds and the like, let your agent know. But if you want anonymity, say so in advance or you may be serenaded by the waiters in the dining room when you'd rather be left alone.

4. Check to see which lines offer complimentary champagne, souvenir photos or special receptions with other honeymooners. Others can provide extra goodies with add-on packages adoring friends or relatives might like to donate.

5. Since most cruise lines limit the number of onboard weddings per sailing, it's a good idea to make plans and reservations as far in advance as possible.

Cruising for the Physically Challenged

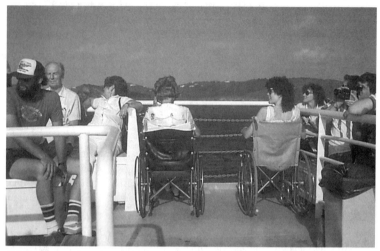

While going ashore by tender is normally difficult or impossible for wheelchair travelers, the large tender from NCL's **Norway** *handles them with ease.*

More and more of the estimated 36 million physically challenged Americans are booking cruise vacations, either with groups or as independent travelers. Most experience the same pleasurable holiday other cruise passengers do, but a few report everything from minor inconveniences to major problems.

The problem for some independent physically-challenged is the requirement or request from virtually every cruise line that they be accompanied by an "able-bodied" companion. One way around this would be to book a special group tour that would have its own escorts and personnel aboard to take the extra responsibility away from the ship's staff for alerting deaf or sightless travelers in case of an emergency.

Cruising is one of the very best vacations for wheelchair travelers so long as the ship has elevators, wide corridors, and cabins specially configured to take care of wheelchairs with wider doors, turning space, an absence of high sills, and grab rails and a pulldown shower seat in the bathroom. Often, but not always, these cabins may also have a lower hanging rack and storage shelves placed conveniently low. But sometimes cabins are designated accessible and their bathrooms don't comply. Even if there is no sill to negotiate and the door is 25 inches rather than the standard 22 inches wide—both adequate for wheelchairs—should the door open in and to the right, for instance, and the toilet is behind it, there's no way a wheelchair occupant can use it.

While some wheelchair travelers will improvise with portable toilet and basin facilities in order to be able to sail on an otherwise inaccessible ship, others are rightly indignant if a line promises accessibility and they don't get it. Unfortunately, many cruise line employees don't have access to the specific cabin measurements for all their ships. You're better off booking through a travel agency that specializes in trips for the disabled.

Going ashore by tender in some cases is difficult or impossible for wheelchair passengers. An exception is the broad-decked Little Norway from NCL's *Norway*, which can be loaded level with the gangway doors, allowing wheelchairs to be rolled on and off the tender. Other cruise lines such as American Hawaii can offload mobility-impaired passengers through the lower deck crew gangway, which is level with the dock, rather than the passenger gangway, which can be steep in many island ports.

Under the cruise lines and ship reviews beginning on page 131, we have tried to point out ships that have accessible cabins we have personally inspected.

AGENCIES SPECIALIZING IN TOURS AND CRUISES FOR THE DISABLED

Flying Wheels Travel
PO Box 382
143 West Bridge Street
Owatonna, MN 55060
☎ (800) 535-6790

Mada Edmonds
Cobb Travel Agency
905 Montgomery Highway
Birmingham, AL 35216
☎ (205) 822-5137

Joe Regan
Able to Travel
247 N. Main Street, Suite 308
Randolph, MA 02368
☎ (800) 557-2047

Joan Diamond & Jill Bellows
Nautilus Tours & Cruises Ltd.
17277 Ventura Boulevard, Suite 207
Encino, CA 91316; ☎ (818) 788-60004
Outside CA (800) 797 6004

Marilyn Ryback
Dahl's Good Neighbor Travel
7383 Pyramid Place
Los Angeles, CA 90046
☎ (213) 969-0660

Murray Vidocklor
SATH Handicapped Travel
347 Fifth Avenue, Suite 610
New York, NY 10016
☎ (212) 447-2784

Judi Smaldino
Tri Venture Travel
1280 Court Street
Redding, CA 96001
☎ (916) 243-3101

Five Tips for Physically Challenged Travelers

1. Be honest with yourself about what you can and cannot do and pass that information on to the travel agent.

2. Be sure your doctor says your condition will allow you to travel.

3. Take it easy; don't try to do everything that's offered just to prove you can.

4. Take along an aide or companion. Some agents have a list of retired nurses who'll accompany disabled travelers and share a cabin in exchange for the trip.

5.   Seeing-eye dogs are accepted on some ships, but each case has to be individually arranged with the cruise line.

Nude Cruises

Nude cruising is the latest wrinkle, according to Roslyn Scheer, executive director of the American Association for Nude Recreation, who says 92 percent of her organization's members are over 35, and half of them earn more than $50,000 a year.

Several nude cruises a year are offered by **Bare Necessities Tour & Travel** of Austin, Texas, who boast a database of 20,000 names. The company charters small to mid-sized vessels ranging from the sailing ships of Star Clipper to mainstream cruise ships. **Travel Au Naturel** in Land O'Lakes, Florida, charters sailings with costume parties, dancing and a special celebrations. "Some nude shore excursions are also scheduled on certain sailings," says the agency's Christie Musick.

For more information, contact the **American Association for Nude Recreation**, *1703 N. Main Street, Suite E, Kissimmee, FL 34744-3396,* ☎ *(800) TRY-NUDE* or *(407) 933-2064.*

Cruises for Gays

Cruises for gays and lesbians is one of the most rapidly growing speciality segments of the cruise industry, with more and more agencies organizing both charters of small ships or group bookings on large ships. Some of them include the following.

RSVP Cruises, *2800 University Avenue Southeast, Minneapolis, MN 55414,* ☎ *(800) 328-7787 or (612) 379-4697.*

Our Family Abroad, *40 W. 57th Street, Suite 430, New York, NY 10019,* ☎ *(800) 999-5500.*

Advance Damron Vacations, *Houston, TX.* ☎ *(800) 695-0880.*

Pied Piper Travel, *New York, NY.* ☎ *(800) TRIP-312 or (212) 239-2412.*

Cruises for Women Only

Olivia Cruises, *4400 Market Street, Oakland, CA 94608,* charters small cruise ships with sailings exclusively for women. In the past, Greek Islands and Mediterranean cruises have been a particular specialty. Call them at ☎ *(510) 655-0364.*

Cruises with College Classes

Semester At Sea sailings conducted by the Institute for Seaboard Education and the University of Pittsburgh gives a student academic credit for some 50 courses from Global Ecology to Caribbean Literature. Classes meet daily when the ship is at sea, and go on field trips when the ship is in port.

Some 500 students sail on each Semester at Sea program, which also operates a cruise ship in Alaska during the summer. The ship serves as the student dormitory, with sailing students sharing two- and three-berth cabins. All meals are provided on board.

Adults who also would like to participate in a "voyage of discovery" may enroll either for academic credit or may audit classes or sit in on lectures that interest them. A 100-day around-the-world voyage is offered twice a year for $14,880 per person, double occupancy, or $17,880 for singles. For details call **World Explorer Cruises** at ☎ *(800) 854-3835.*

Christian/Church-Oriented Cruises

Vacations-in-the-Son, *PO Box 91591, Longwood, FL 32791*, markets religion-oriented cruises for groups and charters with born-again Christians. Contact them at ☎ *(407) 862-6568.*

Alcohol-Free Cruises

Serenity Trips, a company that specializes in alcohol-free vacations, schedules family cruises. For details, call ☎ *(800) 615-4665.*

Friends of Bill W meetings are scheduled frequently on many cruise ships.

Theme Cruises

More cruise lines than ever before are offering theme cruises to appeal to passengers with special interests, or to attract people who might not consider a cruise otherwise. Celebrities, sports stars, best-selling authors, and specialists in every field imaginable sail on selected cruises, hobnobbing with passengers and sharing tidbits from their area of expertise. You might find Martha Stewart sharing gardening tips on a cruise to Bermuda, Wolfgang Puck giving instructions on cooking gourmet dishes on a Mediterranean cruise, or Troy Aikman and Tiger Woods sailing on sports cruises to Alaska. Themes range from art and architecture to golf, history, wine tasting, or music and entertainment. Special events such as solar eclipses, regional festivals and New Year's sell out quickly.

Fielding's CruiseFinder™

Theme cruises change so frequently it's impractical to list them all here, but do check out Fielding's CruiseFinder™ on the Worldwide Web for up-to-date schedules. (www.fieldingtravel.com)

ALTERNATIVE CRUISES

In Burgundy, barging and ballooning often go hand-in-hand.

The captain of the *QE2* is not likely to give you a turn at the wheel, and you won't be wading ashore at some tiny Caribbean island from the *Splendour of the Seas*. Big cruise ships are like seagoing deluxe hotels, lavishly appointed, self-contained cities.

But just as travelers seek out little country inns and bed-and-breakfast establishments in off-the-beaten-track locations, cruise passengers seek alternative cruises, smaller vessels that sail to out-of-the-way corners of the globe.

You'll probably never see these ships in TV commercials. They don't have glittering casinos and Las Vegas-style shows, glamorous passengers dolled up in sequins and satins, miles of midnight buffet and cruise directors organizing fun and games.

Not all of them sail the ocean blue, and few of them boast sleek, streamlined curves and acres of teak decks. Some of them, in fact, are downright funny-looking—squat, sturdy barge-hotels that meander along the canals of Europe at five or six miles an hour, beetle-browed Russian icebreakers capable of moving through pack ice, ferries and freighters, mail boats and coastal steamers from Alaska's glaciers to the fjords of Norway.

Canal Barges

Barging Along the Burgundy Canal

Lazing along the canal at six or eight miles an hour is a wonderful way to see the French countryside.

A perfect antidote for an exhausting if-it's-Tuesday itinerary is a leisurely, luxurious cruise aboard a hotel barge along France's scenic and historic Burgundy Canal. Instead of eight countries in seven days, you'll get a close-up acquaintance with a handful of French towns, a couple of vineyards where you sample vintages with the winemaker himself, several chateaux where you may have tea with the titled owners, and perhaps a lunch or dinner in a *Michelin Guide* three-star restaurant, along with breakfast croissants and brioche bicycled back, still warm, from a village bakery.

Lolling lazily on the deck sipping a glass of champagne, you see Burgundy at eye level, waving at farmers in dazzling canary-yellow fields of rapeseed or fishermen in blue work smocks dozing along the banks of the canal as you glide past, almost close enough to touch the scarlet poppies and wild iris, purple lupine and feathery white Queen Anne's lace that bloom there. Life on a barge is as lighthearted as a floating house party with a dozen congenial friends.

The historic 600 miles of canals in Burgundy, like the rest of France's 3000 miles of manmade waterways, were begun in 1604 by Henry IV as a commercial artery. Today, trucks and trains have taken over the shipping, and Burgundy's canals are used for recreational sailing.

There are usually bicycles on board, one for each guest, so when you feel curious or energetic, you can disembark at one of the locks and ride along the towpaths, or explore nearby villages and countryside.

Days are easy and effortless, perfect for people who want to let city-jangled nerves slow down to a gentle, contented purr. While almost everyone promises get-away-from-it-all vacations, barge companies really deliver them, because once you're afloat, you won't hear the headlines or be paged for a long-distance call—there are no telephones, radios or TV sets on board. In fact, we spent most of a day driving in a van on barge towpaths along the Burgundy Canal with a barge company president who couldn't find his boat for hours. On the other hand, if you want to reach out and touch someone, it's easy to hop off and make a phone call from one of the towns along the way, or pick up a copy of the *International Herald Tribune* if you must.

Ballooning

Soaring in a hot-air balloon is an easy option from a barge cruise.

The most magical addition to a barge cruise is a balloon excursion over the vineyards and villages of Burgundy. Everything about ballooning is hypnotic, from the moment the brightly colored balloons are unloaded from the gondola baskets, through the inflation procedure with the gas burner forcing hot air inside, to the easy liftoff as you soar above castles or meadows. There's no sense of air rushing past; you drift in smooth silence broken only by occasional blasts from the burner. It's so quiet you can carry on conversations with people in the vineyards below or friends in another balloon. And when you finally do set down, sometimes in the last rays of the setting sun, you find a friendly crowd of Burgundians waiting—children rushing out of houses calling and waving, motorcyclists and bicyclists zipping along dirt roads, eyes fixed on the balloon as they bounce and jounce through the ruts trying to get where you're landing. By the time the bottles of champagne are uncorked, everyone is chatting eagerly away in French and English.

Balloon excursions are optional add-ons for barge cruises at a cost of about $245 per person, per flight in Burgundy. Flights average around two hours, plus the time spent inflating and deflating the balloon. Passengers are encouraged to help. Spots should be reserved in advance, according to Abercrombie & Kent, which arranges balloon excursions on all its barges except the *Rembrandt*, and can be paid by check or credit card to the operator on the day of the flight.

Hotel Barges in Burgundy

The Horizon II *cruises the canals of Burgundy.*

NOTE: In parentheses after each barge's name are the initials of the company or companies that book it, which you can match with the full names, addresses and phone numbers of the barge marketing firms below (page 74).

Our very first barge cruise was more than 20 years ago on *L'Escargot* (F&L), a 24-passenger vessel sailing the Burgundy Canal, and it was love at first sight, despite the compact cabins with upper and lower berths. Extensively refurbished in 1994, *L'Escargot* is back, cruising between Dijon and Vandenesse-en-Auxois. Excursions to Clos de Vougueot, Cote de Nuits, Beaune and Chateauneuf are sure to please wine fanciers.

A similar route is followed by *La Reine Pedauque* (F&L), which carries 12 passengers and has facilities for the handicapped. Cruises are three or six nights, and accommodations include twin or double bed cabins and two suites.

The 12-passenger *Nenuphar* (FCW) sails central Burgundy between Sens and Ancy-le-Franc, stopping in Chablis for wine-tasting, in Sens for the Monday morning farmers' market, in Joigny for a spectacular dinner at the *Michelin* three-star restaurant La Côte Saint Jacques.

In western Burgundy, the *Liberte* (FCW) carries eight passengers along the Canal du Nivernais, and excursions include a visit to Auxerre, wine-tasting in Chablis, a *foie gras* sampling at a 17th-century farm, and dinner ashore in Vezelay at the *Michelin* three-star L'Esperance, where chef Marc Meneau makes a marvelous appetizer from local fresh *foie gras*.

For charter only, the little *Niagara* (F&L) takes six passengers through central Burgundy between Dijon and Vandenesse-en-Auxois, while the luxurious new *Saint Louis* (F&L, SLI) takes the same number of charter passengers between Dijon and Pont Royal, which includes an excursion to Vezelay and its magnificent hilltop basilica, as well as optional customized wine and gourmet cruises. *Le Papillon* (F&L), also a six-passenger charter barge, offers three different itineraries in central Burgundy, on the Canal du Nivernais or Burgundy and Franche-Comte.

One unforgettable summer we sailed aboard the *Horizon II* (FCW) with a hot-air balloon trip over the vineyards of Burgundy, a fantastic experience. The 12-passenger luxury barge sails between Tonnerre and Venarey-les-Laumes, with a special dinner one night at the famed *Michelin* three-star La Côte d'Or in Saulieu.

Another of our longtime favorites, *La Litote* (A&K), takes 20 passengers around the heart of Burgundy, visiting a Cistercian abbey at Fontenay, the chateau at Tanley and the winemakers of Chablis for a scenic six-night holiday.

Wine enthusiasts might consider one of the 22-passenger barges in lower Burgundy, the *Lafayette* (A&K, F&L), which makes several special wine cruises with estate tours and wine tastings aboard and in the vineyards around Beaune and Chagny, or the *L'Abercrombie* (A&K) which visits vineyards in Santenay and Mersault.

Esprit (FCW) sails the Burgundy Canal between Santenay and Dijon, with dinner at the *Michelin* three-star restaurant Lameloise in Chagny, an excursion to the 12th-century Castle of Rochepot and a visit to the historic Clos de Vougeot.

The *Luciole* (F&L), a 14-passenger hotel barge, offers some sailings on the Canal du Nivernais, others on the Burgundy Canal, with various excursions tailored to the tastes of the guests.

La Belle Epoque (EW) sails the Burgundy canal, stopping for wine tastings in a cellar in the medieval town of Chateauneuf and a visit to Dijon's Ducal Palace. It's also the first hotel barge with spa and health club facilities aboard.

Exclusively for charter, the sumptuous seven-passenger *Fleur de Lys* (A&K, AIF, F&L) has suites with four-poster beds and bathtubs, grand piano, TV set, and even a small swimming pool. A six-night sailing through upper Burgundy would make a splendid splurge for three couples for about $11,500 a couple.

Sister barges *Alouette* (A&K, AIF) and *Hirondelle* (A&K, AIF, F&L) sail through Burgundy and the Franche Comte with an accent on vineyards, wine-tastings, ancient abbeys and châteaux. *Alouette* carries six, *Hirondelle* eight, and both can be chartered for a group of 14 (A&K).

Anacoluthe (A&K) sails the Seine and Yonne Rivers from Paris, highlighted by an evening cruise through the city to see the illuminated buildings. Excursions include a visit to Monet's home and gardens at Giverny, the artists' village of Barbizon and a wine-tasting in Chablis.

Even in these days of automation, some locks still have live locktenders.

Other Barge Journeys In France

While Burgundy is hands-down the most popular canal for both luxury hotel barges and drive-your-own vessels, France has 23,300 miles of navigable rivers and canals.

Cruising in Champagne in summer on three- and six-night itineraries, the six-passenger *Saroche* (KPS), converted to a luxury hotel barge from a Dutch cargo barge in 1994, boasts some unique features, including a wood-burning fireplace, a fish pond with waterfall and goldfish, and split-level lounge and dining room. The same barge relocates to Provence and the Camargue in autumn.

The newly built *Libellule* (A&K) cruises the Champagne and along the Marne, with optional add-on tours of Paris.

The new 12-passenger *L'Impressionniste* (EW) cruises the Champagne region and Alsace-Lorraine, with excursions to Moet & Chandon for a Champagne tasting and a visit to Chateau Conde en Brie, built for Louis de Bourbon.

The charming *Napoleon* (A&K, AIF, F&L), decorated in Rhône French provincial fabrics and furniture, takes 12 passengers along the Rhone in Provence with visits to outdoor markets, the clifftop village of Les Baux, the Roman theater at Orange and the vineyards of Chateauneuf-du-Pape. Sailings are six nights, and the vessel is available for individual or charter bookings.

In Alsace-Lorraine, the doughty Dutch-built *Stella Maris* (EW) usually takes passengers to a crystal factory, to see the Marc Chagall stained-glass window in the Chapelle des Cordeliers in Sarrebourg and through the Plan Incline de Louis-Arzvillier, an engineering marvel that lowers boats some 135 feet in a sort of vertical lock.

The new eight-passenger *Princess* (FCW) offers huge suites on her cruises of the Loire, Champagne, Moselle and Alsace-Lorraine.

In the Upper Loire Valley, the 24-passenger *Chanterelle* (A&K) sails between Nevers and Rogny, pausing for wine-tastings in Sancerre and Pouilly Fume, visits to *faience* and ceramic factories. Certain summer sailings are set aside as family departures, meaning children under 15 will be permitted aboard.

Also in Loire, *La Joie de Vivre* (F&L) carries 10 passengers between Montargis and Chatillon-sur-Loire on six-night sailings that visit the Palace of Fontainebleau, wineries in Sancerre and Chateau La Bussiere.

Cruising on the Canal du Midi in the south of France accesses some sensational sightseeing, including the walled city of Carcassone, where the six-passenger hotel barge *La Tortue* (F&L) sets out from on its cruises to Beziers. Here, unlike further north in France, the cheapest fares are during the hot months of July and August, with spring and fall the high season. Also in the Midi is the *Anjodi* (EW), carrying 10 passengers.

Gascony, famous for its food and wine, draws gourmets and wannabe chefs aboard the modest little *Julia Hoyt* (JHCC) where skipper/chef Kate Ratliffe prepares *pâtés* from the local *foie gras* and has the option of cooking classes for interested passengers.

The six-passenger charter barge *Lanikai* (LCC) sails in Champagne, along the Marne Canal, the Canal du Rhone au Rhin, Burgundy Canal and the Nivernais Canal, with special off-season discounts for seniors or for four or more passengers traveling together.

Hotel Barges in the British Isles

The 12-passenger *Actief* (A&K, F&L) cruises the Upper Thames, a popular region for hotel barges, sailing past country homes and riverside inns between Windsor and Oxford.

Cruising through Cambridgeshire between Brampton and St. Ives is the 10-passenger *Barkis and Peggotty* (A&K, F&L). We should really say "are" because *Barkis* and *Peggotty* are two barges that travel in tandem. The *Peggotty* has five small, thin-walled, twin-bedded cabins, each with its own private bathroom facilities, and the *Barkis* carries the dining room, salon, bar and galley. They cruise independently during the day and are lashed together at night so passengers can cross from one to the other at will. During the day, crossovers from one barge to the other can be made at the locks, but passengers should plan ahead.

Golfers can cruise the Caledonian Canal in the Scottish Highlands and get in five rounds of golf during the week aboard the eight-passenger, Dutch-built *Vertrouwen* (FST). Its special golf package includes a night at Gleneagles Hotel.

In Ireland, the family-owned *Shannon Princess* (CCG) cruises the Shannon River, framing Irish country scenes, visiting off-the-beaten track archeological sites, Roman ruins and Irish pubs.

Canal Cruising in Holland and Belgium

The all-suites *Meanderer* (F&L) makes six-night roundtrip sailings out of Amsterdam in tulip season into the bulb fields, to the Aalsmeer flower market and Keukenhof Gardens, as well as summer sailings between Paris and Amsterdam that cruise through the Belgian and Dutch countryside.

Also out of Amsterdam, the 20-passenger *Rembrandt* (A&K) sails on spring tulip cruises, as well as summer voyages through Holland and Belgium that stop at the Zaansche Schans "living history" windmill area, the Frans Hals Museum in Haarlem, Delft's porcelain factory, Ghent's Church of the Holy Blood and Bruges' network of canals. In March and again in October and November, special bicycling departures are scheduled for organized biking jaunts through Belgium.

The new 30-passenger *Vincent Van Gogh* (A&K) offers sailings in Holland and Belgium. Cabins and suites contain remote-control TV sets with VCR, among other luxuries formerly unknown in the world of barge cruises.

INSIDER TIP

While hotel barges are famous for their largesse with open bar, a few exceptions still charge for cocktails—L'Escargot, the Rembrandt on some discounted sailings, the Anacoluthe and Barkis & Peggotty. Wine is always included with meals.

Bicycles and mopeds are carried aboard barges for both crew and passenger use.

Ten Most-Asked Questions About Canal Barge Cruises

1.   Can you take children aboard?
Some barge companies have a minimum age for child passengers, usually not permitting anyone under 15 except on charter sailings. If yours does not specify, consider this: If the children are babies or toddlers, we'd definitely advise against taking them on a luxury hotel barge.

There are no play areas or places they can get away from the other passengers, and barge galley crews are usually too busy to prepare separate, less-sophisticated meals for kids. We've sailed with well-behaved older children (from Australia), however, who did not create problems for the other passengers. If you have small children and want to cruise the canals, consider renting and handling your own boat or booking a small charter barge with two or three other families with children.

2. Won't I feel confined on one of these small boats?

No, on the contrary. Passengers spend most of their time aboard on deck or in the main lounge rather than in the cabins, and every barge we know carries bicycles along for side jaunts. You can also disembark in any of the many locks and get back on later down the line if you want to go jogging or walking, as well as bicycling.

3. The prices seem fairly high compared to some Mediterranean cruise ships. What extras are included in the fare that might not be on regular cruises?

The average per diem for barge cruises is $335–$400 per person, double occupancy, cruise only. Most barges include all beverages, including cocktails and wines, and emphasize wines and cheeses of the region. Transfers to and from the barge are usually included, as well as all shore excursions, except hot-air ballooning. Bicycles are aboard for passenger use at any time, and some barge cruises include a special gourmet meal ashore at a top-rated restaurant. Gratuities for the barge crew are usually extra.

4. What about seasickness?

There's no need to worry about getting seasick on a barge. You're moving on very smooth waters at a low rate of speed with no sense of motion at all.

5. Do I need to be able to speak French?

Not unless you want to have conversations in the villages or with the locktenders along the route. Your barge captain and crew are not only fluent in English—in many cases, they are English.

6. Do I need any special wardrobe?

No, life aboard a barge is casual. Your daytime clothing can be jogging suits, jeans or shorts, whatever is comfortable. In the evenings, you may want to slip into something a bit dressier, but it's not essential. Do carry good sneakers or walking shoes for the deck and the towpaths alongside. If you plan to go ballooning, layer your clothing for early morning flights, since the weather warms up as the sun gets higher in the sky. If your itinerary includes a meal at one of the *Michelin*-starred restaurants, take along a dress-up outfit.

7. I plan to tour Europe extensively, and take a barge cruise for only a small part of the time. How much luggage can I take aboard?

If you have more than two suitcases, you may want to consider storing some of your luggage on shore, perhaps at one of the hotels you'll be using.

8. Can I expect the same kind of amenities I'd find in a hotel or on a large cruise ship?

Generally, you'll find electrical connections but they will usually be 220 volt with 110 connections limited to electric razors. Some companies provide hair dryers in the cabins as well. Barge operators may request conservation of fresh water, which means shorter showers.

9.   Are all barges pretty much alike?

Not at all. In the beginning, the novelty of the experience managed to supersede the sometimes basic accommodations—upper and lower bunk beds with the bath down the hall—and dowdy decor. Now you'll find new all-suite barges, barges with saunas, fitness rooms or swimming pools, fully air-conditioned cabins with adjoining private bath, even a few bathtubs. You'll want to carefully examine the deck plans for the barge you're considering to gauge the relative size of the cabin and read the fine print. It's a favorable sign if the brochure offers a photograph of the cabins. They are usually located on a lower deck just above the waterline, so your window will give you closeup views of canal banks.

10.   What kind of evening entertainment can I expect?

Barge passengers usually linger over drinks and dinner through most of the evening, but since the barges tie up overnight, you may want to walk into the village to a disco or cafe. Conversation is a major pastime aboard most barges. At least one barge, the *Lanikai* (LCC), offers a half-board cruise option, serving welcome aboard dinner in arrival and all the remaining breakfasts and lunches, with evenings free to dine at local restaurants.

The best local wines and cheeses are served aboard French luxury barges.

The following are some of the companies that provide barge cruises in Europe. If you think there seem to be an inordinate number of barges plying the canals, be aware that many of the barge owners may use several companies to sell their sailings. Most of the following are American travel wholesalers or barge marketing firms.

Abercrombie & Kent

1520 Kensington Road, Oak Brook, IL 60521, ☎ *(800) 323-7308.*

Twelve barges in France, Holland, Belgium, England, Germany and Austria; features antiques, golf theme barge cruises in Britain.

Afloat in France

Box 6616, FDR Station, New York, NY 10150, ☎ *(416) 364-0903, (800) 313-2702.*
Four barges in France, two in Burgundy and two in Provence.

Cruise Company of Greenwich

31 Brookside Drive, Greenwich, CT 06830, ☎ *(800) 825-0826.*
Provides barge tours of Ireland aboard the little *Shannon Princess.*

European Waterways

Suite 4C, 140 E. 56th Street, New York, NY 10022, ☎ *(212) 688-9489, (800) 296-4554.*
Sixteen barges in France, England, Holland and Belgium, including the new *Belle Époque,* the first hotel barge with a spa pool, fitness room and sauna, and the barge *L'Impressionniste* for 12 passengers.

Fenwick & Lang

100 W. Harrison, South Tower, Suite 350, Seattle, WA 98119, ☎ *(800) 243-6244.*
Fourteen barges in France, England and Holland; optional hot air ballooning is also available with your barge cruise.

Five Star Touring

60 E. 42nd Street, Suite 612, New York, NY 10165, ☎ *(212) 818-9140, (800) 792-7827.*
The *Vertrouwen* takes eight passengers on the Caledonian Canal in the Scottish Highlands.

French Country Waterways

PO Box 2195, Duxbury, MA 02331, ☎ *(800) 222-1236.*
Four barges in France, special early and late season discounts.

Julia Hoyt Canal Cruises

5 Ledgewood Way, No. 6, Peabody, MA 09160, ☎ *(800) 852-2625, (508) 535-5738.*
The *Julia Hoyt* makes foodie sailings in France.

Kemwel's Premier Selection

106 Calvert Street, Harrison, NY 10528, ☎ *(800) 234-4000.*
Twenty-five barges for charter and scheduled sailings in France, England and Holland.

Lanikai Charter Cruises

98-985 Kaonohi Street, Aiea, Hawaii 96701, ☎ *(808) 487-6630.*
A six-passenger crewed barge available for seven-day charters in France between April and October.

The Barge Lady

225 North Michigan Avenue, Suite 324, Chicago, IL 60601, ☎ *(800) 252-9400.*
The new *Saint Louis,* specialized French food and wine cruises (and an on-board cellular telephone—*quel dommage!*)

Self-Drive Barges

If you're resourceful enough to make your own minor repairs, want to plan your own itineraries and prepare your own meals, by all means consider the less-expensive option of renting a barge.

No experience is necessary, say the rental agencies, and you don't need a license. Instead, you get a guide and manual, and are checked out on the boat with a demonstration run before you take over.

Crown Blue Line, for instance, has 26 boat models that take care of two to 12 passengers, and all are fully equipped, with bedclothes and towels, cooking utensils, cutlery and glassware. You'll find a refrigerator, sink, cooker with oven grill, bathroom with shower and toilet, hot and cold running water and heating system.

Figure on a price of around $1700 a week for a basic boat for two, up to $4400 for a luxury vessel for eight. The fare includes taxes, tolls, fuel and damage waiver. Rentals are available from 17 different locations in France and one in Holland. You can even arrange for your boat to be stocked with a starter kit of groceries.

Rive de France has rental bases in Aquitaine, Burgundy, Franche-Comte and Alsace-Lorraine. Five boat models that sleep from four adults and two children to eight adults and one child are available.

The British Tourist Authority can send you a brochure called Inland Waterways that lists companies that book motor cruisers and narrow boats for British canals.

Barge Rentals:

Crown Blue Line

c/o Fenwick & Lang, 100 W. Harrison, Suite 350, Seattle, WA 98119, ☎ (206) 216-2903, (800) 243-6244

Rive de France

172 Boulevard Berthier, F-75017 Paris, ☎ 00-33-1-46-22-10-86.

British Tourist Authority

551 Fifth Avenue, New York NY 10176, ☎ (212) 986-2266.

River Cruises

*The **Dresden** is one of the modern riverboats in Europe.*

The rivers of Europe invite travelers to sail along the Rhine, the Danube, the Volga, the Elbe, the Thames, even Shakespeare's beloved Avon, stopping along the way for wine tastings in Austria or folk dancing in Hungary, to see the circus in St. Petersburg or the pottery makers of Delft.

Unlike group land-tours which tend to be made up of Americans only, the river boats attract a number of Europeans, so you're socializing with a cosmopolitan crowd. While some riverboats we've cruised aboard during the years are more lavish than others, all have offered a unique close-up look at a lovely part of Europe, delicious meals, regional wines and a silk-smooth ride.

The famous coasts of Europe, too, from the glamorous Cote d'Azur of France to the lush and lovely Turquoise Coast of Turkey, are best seen from the water.

While the vessels described below are special riverboats that cruise in Europe, some of the smaller cruise ships in the preceding section may also offer European river cruises as a part of their itineraries. We took such a cruise aboard the *Seabourn Pride* from Seabourn Cruise Line in late spring, with an itinerary that included sailing along some of the great rivers of France, a two-day overland tour through the chateaux country of the Loire, a visit to Mont St.-Michel, a day in Paris, stops in Hamburg and Amsterdam and a spectacular finale—sailing the Thames under the Tower Bridge into the center of London.

About Riverboats

For veterans of America's traditional river vessels, such as the paddlewheelers from Delta Queen and American Queen Steamboat Companies, European riverboats may appear squat and undistinguished without that rakish red sternwheel and tall black funnels we're accustomed to seeing.

But they offer the same shallow draft and smooth ride, the same sociable open decks where passengers spend much of the day watching the scenery along the riverbanks, and the same care and attention to meals and service. Menus will not be as expansive, in some cases, or offer as many choices as traditional sea cruises, but all meals are usually included on riverboats, unlike many of the European ferries. Often, a single fixed menu with perhaps two main dish choices is provided.

Don't expect much entertainment aboard beyond shore excursion lectures, port videos and a little teatime or after-dinner dance music. In some cities, local bands or concert artists may come aboard to perform, or an optional evening excursion to the opera, theater or ballet may be offered.

Cabins are generally on the small side, usually with two lower beds, bathroom with shower, a lounge, restaurant and sundeck. A few of them, notably KD's *Deutschland* (KD), *Britannia* (KD), *Danube Princess* (EAC), *Blue Danube* (EC), *DeltaStar* (EC&T) and *Rousse* (EC&T), even boast small swimming pools on deck. EuropAmerica's *Mozart* and *Heinrich Heine* (KD) have indoor swimming pools and the former offers a fitness center as well. *Prussian Princess* (EAC) and *Princesse de Provence* (EAC) offer full-length French doors in their deluxe-category cabins that open to the scenery and fresh air.

While most river cruises marketed in the United States begin and end at a specified port, the vessels from KD River Cruises of Europe allow embarkation and disembarkation at a variety of ports along the way, making an add-on cruise particularly flexible on a longer itinerary. Few if any young children are aboard most of Europe's river boats, with the exception of KD River Cruises, which offers discounts for children 4 to 14 and lets children under 4 sail free.

The Rivers of Europe

NOTE: In parentheses after each boat's name are the initials of the company or companies that book it, which you can match with the full names, addresses and phone numbers of the river boat companies and marketing firms below (page 86).

Cruising the Elbe

An impromptu party on deck as the **Prussian Princess** *cruises along the Elbe.*

It is so quiet as we move along the river, we can hear the birds singing in the nearby trees when our cabin's French doors are open. There's no deck or balcony outside, just waist-high metal bars, but the open doors provide fresh air and a closer rapport with the scenery.

From our mooring in the Czech Republic village of Decin, we can see a fairy-tale castle atop the hill. A brass oompah band in bright costume greeted us on our return from a day in Prague with some loud and lively tunes. Along the river we have seen ducks, swans, geese, a few storks, even a blue heron, and once we glimpsed deer standing stock-still in a misty green meadow.

This vessel, the *Prussian Princess* (EAC), is the most luxurious of the European river vessels we've sailed aboard, with its antique-style furnishings, oil paintings, Tiffany stained-glass and big vases of fresh flowers. Passengers sit at sociably small tables set with crisp white linen. Service is swift and sophisticated and the cuisine is continental, with elaborate evening menus that often include a sorbet between the fish course and the meat course. Desserts from the Viennese chefs, not surprisingly, are delectable.

Recently, the *Prussian Princess* has been repositioned to sail the Rhine (see below) and sister boat *Dresden* (EAC), equally elegant, cruises the Elbe through the former East Germany into the Czech Republic, part of the former Czechoslovakia.

An Elbe cruise usually begins in Hamburg and calls in the medieval Hanseatic town of Tangermunde; magnificent Magdeburg, with the oldest Gothic church in Germany; Wittenberg, where Martin Luther lived and taught; Meissen and Dresden and their eponymous porcelain factories; Pillnitz and its impressive palace; Bad Schandau, jumping-off point for an all-day visit to Prague; Decin and Saxony's "Little Switzerland;" Worlitz and its canals.

Overland pre- or post-cruise visits to Berlin, Dresden, Prague or Hamburg are options as well. Figure from $225 to $300 per person, double occupancy, for a two-night land package add-on.

In addition to the *Dresden*, the 124-passenger *Clara Schumann* (KD) also cruises the Elbe between Dresden and Wittenberg (for Berlin) or Hamburg, and between Wittenberg and Prague. Cabins have color TV, and there's an observation lounge with bar, sun deck and sauna aboard.

Cruising the Danube

Shore excursions offer the option of colorful cafes such as this one in Budapest.

The beautiful blue Danube varies from steel blue to dark gray to, on occasion, muddy brown—"It's always blue when you're in love," one Viennese lady told us—but it waltzes past lush green hillsides and castle ruins that date from the Crusades, through the vineyards of Austria, along the borders of the Czech Republic, Slovakia and Hungary to Budapest. Expect lots of music and wine, romantic ruined castles and majestic abbeys.

One of our favorite stops along the Danube is Durnstein in the Wachau wine region, with the ruins of Kuenringer Castle where Richard the Lion-hearted was said to have been held prisoner, colorful wine taverns along narrow, cobblestoned streets and the 17th century Hotel Schloss Durnstein looming like something out of a Grimm fairy tale. (The rumor is that it was an inspiration for some of the stories.)

The cruise itineraries include seven-day roundtrip sailings from Passau, Germany; roundtrip cruises from Vienna; and seven-day cruises between Vienna and Nuremberg, Budapest and Nuremberg, between Budapest and Berching, Germany, or between Frankfurt and Vienna.

The 207-passenger *Mozart* (EAC) and the 200-passenger *Danube Princess* (EAC) both cruise the Danube on weeklong roundtrips from Passau. Major ports of call along Europe's second-longest river are Melk with its Baroque abbey; Grein and its 12th-century monastery; Bratislava, Slovakia, at the foot of the Carpathian mountains; Esztergom, Hungary, and its cathedral that is a replica of St. Peter's in Rome; the twin cities Buda and Pest, divided by the Danube; and Durnstein.

An 11-day itinerary along the Danube between Regensburg and Budapest is scheduled in summer aboard the *Rembrandt van Rijn* (SHC) with special music programs aboard and concerts on shore in abbeys and classic theaters.

The eight-passenger *Marjorie* (A&K) is probably the smallest vessel making the Passau roundtrip six-night itinerary between late May and late October, and it is available for charter as well as individual bookings. An all-inclusive, barge-type package conveniently includes shore excursions and all beverages and wines, unusual on riverboats. A six-night charter for eight costs around $25,000.

Newest luxury boat on the Danube is the *River Cloud* (ET&C) which carries 96 passengers in a richly decorated boat filled with marble and rosewood, teak and brass. There is more public space indoors and out than is usual on a riverboat. Cabins are spacious and attractive, with TV sets, telephones and private baths with showers. Six of the accommodations are suites with panoramic windows and sitting areas. It cruises between Budapest and Nuremberg, and calls at Visagrad, Esztergom, Bratislava, Vienna, Durnstein, Passau, Regensburg and Kelheim, visiting a total of four countries. You can also book a package with the *River Cloud* that includes an overnight journey aboard the Venice Simplon-Orient Express between Venice and London.

The *DeltaStar* (ET&C) carries 160 passengers on its roundtrip six-night sailings from Vienna, and offers special seasonal classical music cruises plus options in Budapest of attending an evening at the opera or theater, a city tour or a Csardas party at a Hungarian farm with gypsy music, riding displays and local food and wine.

The new *Amadeus* (ROE) offers 11-day cruises of the Danube between Bucharest and Passau, as well as some seven-day sailings between Budapest and Nuremberg and seven-day roundtrips from Passau. Children under 12 are permitted aboard.

The Berching-to-Budapest seven-night itinerary operated by *Blue Danube* (EC) sails through Kelheim, Regensberg, Passau, Linz, Melk and Durnstein on its way to Vienna, Bratislava and Budapest.

The 106-passenger *Wilhelm Tell* (KD) makes six-night sailings between Nuremberg and Vienna, with overnight calls in Regensburg, Germany, with its 12th-century stone bridge spanning the Danube; Passau; Linz; and Durnstein at fares from $1130 per person, double occupancy. KD's *Heinrich Heine* carries 104 passengers on a similar itinerary at slightly higher prices.

OdessAmerica also books a number of Danube River sailings.

Cruising The Rhine/Main/Moselle

The **Theodor Fontane** *sails the Rhine, Main and Moselle.*

River cruising on the Rhine dates back more than 170 years, and that majestic river, 820 miles long, in combination with its tributaries the Moselle and the Main, offers travelers a splendid look at the heart of Europe.

Ports of call along the route include Volendam, Enkhuizen, Kampen and Arnhem in Holland; Cologne, Koblenz, Rudesheim and Speyer in Germany; and beautiful Strasbourg in France with its half-timbered buildings and superb cuisine (look especially for *choucroute Alsacienne,* a hearty meal of wine-simmered sauerkraut, ham and sausages, a specialty of the little restaurants around the cathedral, or, for a magnificent splurge, book a lunch at Le Crocodile, a three-star *Guide Michelin* restaurant also in the old town.)

The recently refurbished *Rhine Princess* (EC, EC&T), a sister boat to the *Blue Danube* (above), carries 120 passengers on seven-night sailings between Basel and Amsterdam at fares that begin around $1100 per person, double occupancy. The vessel contains a whirlpool spa, sauna, sun deck, swimming pool and single meal seatings, along with menus themed to the country being sailed through. Half the cabins aboard have bathtubs, the other half showers, so you should request your preference when booking.

The 184-passenger *Deutschland* (KD) makes two- to four-night cruises along the Rhine between Amsterdam and Basel, Amsterdam and Strasbourg; Strasbourg and Cologne; or Cologne and Basel; visiting, depending on the cruise, Heidelberg, Mannheim, Rudesheim, Speyer, Mainz and Dusseldorf.

Three- and four-night cruises on the 184-passenger *Britannia* (KD), sister boat to the *Deutschland,* and the very similar 184-passenger *Austria,* offer comparable itineraries out of Rotterdam. Approximate fares for the sailings range from $320 to $1800, depending on season and accommodation.

The 184-passenger *Italia* (KD), sister boat to the *Austria,* and the 124-passenger *Theodor Fontane* sail three-river "Magic Triangle" itineraries of the Rhine, Moselle and Main with two-, three and seven-night programs between Trier and Wurzburg, Frankfurt and Trier, Frankfurt and Cologne or

Trier and Cologne that emphasize optional guided walking tours in the villages and towns along the way.

Our old favorite, the 142-passenger *Prussian Princess* (EAC), covers Switzerland, France, Germany, Belgium and Holland in her perambulations along the Rhine. April and May are the months for tulip season, with some interesting northern ports, including Amsterdam, Maastricht, Nijmegen, Rotterdam, Delft, Antwerp, Brussels and Ghent, along with some grand cathedrals, canals, art museums, diamond cutters and limestone caves.

The *Rembrandt van Rijn* (SHC) carries 90 passengers along the Rhine on 10- and 11-day sailings in summer that also include excursions along the Moselle. In spring, the same boat visits Holland and the bulb fields, cruising the North Sea Canal, the Amsterdam/Rhine Canal and the River Lek.

Finally, if you have trouble deciding whether you want to cruise the Rhine or the Danube, why not do both? The sleek new Dutch-built *Erasmus* (AHI) offers a "Face of Europe" program that makes a 17-day sailing between Amsterdam and Budapest, utilizing the new Main/Danube Canal to sail from the Rhine to the Main, then along the engineering marvel that is the new canal to the Danube. Ports of call include Cologne with its twin-spired Gothic cathedral; Boppard and the Rhine Gorge, where the legendary Lorelei lured sailors to their deaths; Rudesheim and its famous wines; Wurzburg and its Marienberg Fortress on the Main; Bamberg and Nuremberg; Heidelberg on the Neckar River; Regensberg; Passau, Melk, Durnstein and Vienna in Austria; and Bratislava, Slovakia. Fares begin at under $5000 per person, double occupancy, including roundtrip airfare from New York. And the *Rembrandt van Rijn* (SHC) offers a similar itinerary in a 15-day program between Frankfurt and Budapest that combines the Rhine with the Main/Danube Canal from $3020 per person, double occupancy, including airfare from London.

Cruising The Seine

Passengers aboard KD's **Normandie** *take a scenic sailing along the Seine.*

The picturesque charm that attracted artists more than a century ago remains in the coastal village of Honfleur. Colorful fishing boats still cast their reflections in the harbor; narrow old buildings cling to the hillsides; fishwives sell seafood fresh from the boats; and every Sunday morning, as it has for centuries, the market gathers around the wooden Saint Catherine's Church.

When you travel along the Seine from the sea to Paris, you follow the river's broad, lazy loops and scribbles through the rich, green countryside, watching the soft colors and shapes give way to the stark angularity of 12th-century stone at the ruins of Richard the Lionhearted's Gaillard fortress, and pausing in the village of Giverny to visit Monet's home and gardens, where you can stand on his wisteria-covered Japanese bridge and watch the changing light and color in the slow-moving water below.

Riverboat cruisers in France can make this stunningly beautiful sailing between Paris and Normandy's Honfleur aboard the *Normandie* (KD) and have the option of visiting Giverny ($31). The seven-night cruise also calls at Rouen, its marketplace still surrounded by some of the black-and-white timbered houses that stood when Joan of Arc was burned at the stake in 1431, and at Jumieges, an 11th-century monastery near the pretty little town of Caudebec-en-Caux.

Cruising The Rhone and The Saone

Cabins aboard the **Princess de Provence** *have large French doors that open for fresh air and grand river views.*

The elegant *Princesse de Provence* (EAC), decorated in Provençal style with full-length French doors that open to the scenery and fresh air in the deluxe cabins, carries 148 passengers along the Rhone and Saone on round trips from Lyon, the food capital of France. Ports of call include Arles with its Greco-Roman ruins; Avignon and its noted bridge; Tournon with an optional excursion into the gorgeous Ardeche region; Macon and its wineries; Chalon-sur-Saone in the heart of Burgundy; Tournus and Vienne. Add on a pre- or post-cruise hotel package in Nice, Paris or Lyon. Basic cruise fares range from $980 to $2950 per person, double occupancy, with two-day hotel package add-ons from $235 to $300 per person double.

The 106-passenger *Arlene* (KD) cruises between Avignon and Losne (for Geneva) along the Rhone and Saone, past vineyards and Roman ruins, the *pont* at Avignon, the Pont du Gard at Arles, the marshy Camargue with its wild ponies; Les St. Maries-de-la-Mer, traditional gathering spot for the Gypsies; and Macon's wine country. Hotel stays can be added on for Geneva before or after the cruise.

Cruising The Duoro

On Portugal's Duoro River in Porto, the port wine boats called barcos *rabelos traditionally carried the wine along the river until replaced by a railway in the late 19th century.*

The 160-passenger *Lady Ivy May* (EC) sails along Portugal's Duoro River on seven-day roundtrip itineraries from Porto, the famous port wine city. The winding river meanders through the northwestern part of the country, crossing over Europe's highest dam, the Carrapatelo Barrage. Passengers dine one evening at a local winery; visit the Monastery of Alpendora; take motorcoach jaunts into the ancient town of Lamego and the frontier towns at the Spanish border; and enjoy a narrow-gauge train trip in the Duoro River Valley. Besides port tastings, wine enthusiasts will find the opportunity to sample Portugal's crisp and fruity *vinho verde*. Shoppers will want to snap up some of the handpainted pottery, traditional tiles and weavings.

Cruising The Volga

If all you know about the Volga River is that the boatmen used to sing, "Yo heave ho" as they trudged along the banks pulling the boats by rope, you have some surprises coming on this popular river boat itinerary.

The German-built *Sergei Kirov* (BE, CMI, EC, FW, SLT) carries 250 passengers and 50 Swiss-trained crew members between Moscow and St. Petersburg on a Golden Ring itinerary that cruises the Volga from Moscow north to the Volga-Baltic Canal, then along Lake Ladoga, the Svir River and Lake Onega into St. Petersburg. A three-day city stay at either end of the journey includes the boat as your hotel. Fares begin at around $2000 per person, double occupancy, including roundtrip airfare from New York.

The Summer Palace at Pavlovsk is a tour option on the Golden Ring itinerary.

The German-built *Pakhomou* (AHI), run by a Swiss-trained hotel staff, cruises between Moscow and St. Petersburg with both food products and chef from western Europe. Rates range from around $3695 to $4395 per person, double occupancy, including airfare from New York for 14 days.

There's also a riverboat, the Austrian-built, 184-passenger *Anton Tchekhov* (OA, EC) that cruises along the Yenisey through the heart of Siberia between Dudinka and Krasnoyarsk. Perhaps the most exotic of all the river cruises, the 12- or 13-day land/sea package (the cruise/tour length depends on which direction you're headed, with the southbound itinerary one day shorter) is bracketed with a brief stopover in both Moscow and St. Petersburg. Most passengers aboard are German-speaking Europeans, but guides are also conversant in English. Fares range from around $3033 to $3846 per person, double occupancy, including airfare from New York.

A 12-day itinerary between Moscow and St. Petersburg aboard the 90-passenger *Sergei Yesenin* (SHC) includes overland sightseeing at both ends of the cruise. The Austrian-built boat was recently refurbished. Fares range around $3000 per person, double occupancy, including airfare from London with a choice between main or boat deck twins, single occupancy of double cabins or suites.

Cruising Sweden's Gota Canal

The historic Gota Canal cuts across the heart of Sweden between its two most populous cities, Stockholm and Gothenberg. Vintage 60-passenger steamers called *Juno, Wilhelm Than* and *Diana* (EC) negotiate 65 locks along the way, providing passengers with some low-key, close-up views of rural Sweden. The food aboard is tasty and typically Swedish, with gravlax, reindeer, dilled potato salad, flatbreads and cloudberries among the smorgasbord treats. All cabins are outsides with portholes or windows, but they're small and basic, with upper and lower berths, wash basins en suite, toilets down the hall and showers on Main and Bridge decks. Think train compartment rather than cruise ship cabin and you'll be acclimated by the time you arrive. Fares range from a low of $775 per person, double occupancy, for a four-day sailing to a high of $1590 for a top-category cabin with fruit basket and robes provided. Shore excursions are included. No children under 7 are permitted.

Stockholm is a starting point for Gota Canal cruises through Sweden.

Quiz: Up Which Lazy River?

See if you can match the scenery or activity, listed on the left, with the correct European river on the right. The answers appear on page 88.

1. A Heurige evening with schrammelmusik.	*a. The Rhine*
2. Any old port-tasting in a storm.	*b. The Volga*
3. Famous fireworks displays "burn" this river every summer.	*c. The Rhone*
4. No "yo heave ho" these days on modern river boats.	*d. The Elbe*
5. Shop for world-famous porcelain at the factories.	*e. The Duoro*
6. A Year in Provence.	*f. The Danube*

The following are some of the companies offering river cruises in Europe:

Abercrombie & Kent

1520 Kensington Road, Oak Brook, IL 60521, ☎ *(800) 323-7308.*
Three river cruisers in France, Holland, Germany and Austria, including the *Anacoluthe*, which emphasizes art-oriented cruises in France.

AHI International

701 Lee Street, Des Plaines, IL 60016, ☎ *(800) 680-4244.*
River cruises in Europe on the Rhine, Main, Danube and Moselle and along Russia's Volga and China's Yangtze.

ATS Tours

2381 Rosecrans Avenue, Suite 325, El Segundo, CA 90245, ☎ *(800) 423-2880.*
Handles catamaran cruises aboard the new *Reef Escape, Coral Princess* and *Kangaroo Explorer* along Australia's Barrier Reef.

Berrier Enterprises, Ltd.

1 Sutter Street, Suite 308, San Francisco, CA 94104, ☎ *(415) 398-7947.*
Various waterways journeys in Russia and other European areas.

Blue Lagoon Cruises

c/o Fiji Visitors' Bureau, 5777 West Century Boulevard, Suite 220, Los Angeles, CA 90045, ☎ *(800) YEA-FIJI.*
Six small vessels that sail on short, casual cruises to Fiji's Yasawa Islands from Lautoka near Nadi Airport.

Cruise Company of Greenwich

31 Brookside Drive, Greenwich, CT 06830, ☎ *(800) 825-0826.*
Provides cruises to the national parks of Costa Rica and Belize aboard the 62-passenger *Temptress.*

Cruise Marketing International

1601 Industrial Way, Suite A, Belmont, CA 94002, ☎ *(415) 592-1397, (800) 5 RUS-SIA.*
Russian river sailings.

Elegant Cruises & Tours, Inc.

31 Central Drive, Port Washington, NY 11050, ☎ *(516) 767-9302, (800) 683-6767.*
Various European itineraries and vessels.

Esplanade Tours

581 Boylston Street, Boston, MA 02116, ☎ *(800) 426-5492.*
For 20-passenger sailings aboard the *Myat Thanda* along the Irrawaddy in Myanmar.

EuropAmerica River Cruises

1800 Diagonal Road, Alexandria, VA 22314, ☎ *(703) 549-1741 or (800) 348-8287.*
Five luxurious river vessels that sail the Danube, the Rhine, the Elbe and the Rhone, including the *Prussian Princess,* described above, the *Mozart, Danube Princess, Dresden* and *Princesse de Provence.*

EuropAmerica Cruises

1800 Diagonal Road, Alexandria, VA 22314, ☎ *(703) 549-1741, (800) 348-8287.*
Five luxurious river vessels that sail the Danube, the Rhine, the Elbe and the Rhone, including the *Prussian Princess,* described above, the *Mozart, Danube Princess, Dresden* and *Princesse de Provence.*

EuroCruises, Inc.

303 West 13th Street, New York, NY 10014, ☎ *(212) 691-2099, (800) 688-3876, (800) 661-1119 (brochures).*
For Europe Cruise Lines' new *Rhine Princess* and *Blue Danube* on the Rhine, Moselle and Danube, Gota Canal sailings, the *Lady Ivy May* on Portugal's River Douro and the *Anton Tchekhov* on the Yenisey River in Siberia.

FinnWay, Inc.

228 E. 45th Street, New York, NY 10017, ☎ *(212) 818-1198, (800) 526-4927.*
Russian Golden Ring itineraries aboard the *Kirov, Litvinov, Andropov* and *Lenin*

Hebridean Island Cruises

c/o British Tourist Authority, 551 Fifth Avenue, New York, NY 10176-0799, ☎ *(800) GO 2 BRITAIN.*
Scottish coastal cruises aboard the 48-passenger *Hebridean Princess.*

KD River Cruises of Europe

2500 Westchester Avenue, Purchase, NY 10577, ☎ *(800) 346 6525 from the eastern U.S., or Suite 619, 323 Geary Street, San Francisco, CA 94102,* ☎ *(800) 858-8587 from the western U.S.*

Now 170 years old, the oldest and largest river cruise line in Europe, with 13 vessels sailing the Rhine, Danube, Elbe, Moselle, Main, Seine, Rhone and Volga. KD's river vessels are *Deutschland, Britannia, Austria, Europa, Italia, France, Wilhelm Tell, Clara Schumann, Theodor Fontane, Heinrich Heine, Normandie, Arlene* and *Kirov*.

Nabila Cruises/Naggar Tours

605 Market Street, Suite 1310, San Francisco, CA 94105, ☎ *(800) 443-NILE.*
For (what else?) cruises along the Nile, as well as yacht cruises along the Turquoise Coast of Turkey.

OdessAmerica

170 Old Country Road, Suite 608, Mineola, NY 11501, (516) 747-8880, (800) 221-3254.
Book river cruises in eastern Europe, including the Danube, Volga and Elbe.

Regal China Cruises

57 West 38 Street, New York, NY 10018, ☎ *(800) 808-3388.*
Three new luxury river vessels, *Princess Sheena, Princess Jeannie* and *Princess Elaine*, that cruise the Yangtze, plus a Shanghai harbor overnight cruise on *Spirit of Shanghai*.

Roylen Endeavour Cruises

c/o Queensland Tourist and Travel Corporation, 516 Fifth Avenue, New York, NY 10036, (212) 221-4505, or 2828 Donald Douglas Loop North, Santa Monica, CA 90405, (310) 452-1225.
Offers two-, three- and five-night cruises in the Whitsunday Islands, off eastern Australia, on vessels carrying up to 50 persons each.

Rivers of Europe

5250 W. Century Boulevard, Los Angeles, CA 90045, ☎ *(310) 641-8001, (800) 999-0226.*
Represents the new *Amadeus* for Danube Cruises.

Sunny Land Tours

166 Main Street, Hackensack, NJ 07601, ☎ *(800) 783-7839.*
Offers tours of Siberia and the Ukraine aboard the *Russ*, the *Leonid Krasin* and the *Kirov*.

Swan Hellenic Cruises

77 New Oxford Street, London, WC1A 1PP, ☎ *011-44-171-800-2200, (800) PRINCESS.*
This P & O-owned company is noted for its excellent lecture programs.

Uniworld

16000 Ventura Boulevard, Encino, CA 91436, ☎ *(800) 733-7820.*
Offers cruises on the Amur River in the Russian Far East, Russia's Volga, Svir and Moscow Canal, and the Rhine, Moselle, Main and Danube in Western Europe.

Answers to Lazy River Quiz: 1, f; 2, e; 3, a; 4, b; 5, d; 6, c.

Adventure and Eco-tourism Sailings

The little pier is lined with people, a hundred or more, curious for the sight of us. They have been waiting since 8 a.m., and it is now 3 p.m. We have arrived on a expedition ship commanded by Captain Heinz Aye, and we are the first group of white tourists ever to appear on Jamdena Island in the Tanimbars. As we come down the gangway, a dozen hands reach to touch our bare arms...

Penguins are sighted frequently on Antarctic cruises.

In one house, preparation is under way for a wedding feast, with a pig tethered ready to kill and roast and hundreds of coconuts piled up in heaps. An old woman, her mouth stained with betel nut, approaches, holding out a small and intricately woven basket. We are not sure whether she is showing it to us or trying to sell it, so we smile politely and nod. Later, after we're back on the ship, one of the other passengers flaunts it. "Look what I got for only $5!"

The next day we are ferried by Zodiac to a seemingly deserted island opposite the town of Tual. By the time the first Zodiac-load has waded into the soft, sandy beach, two small boats have arrived from town to have a look at us, and other islanders materialize from the bushes with white paste smeared on their faces against the relentless sun. They stare gravely and silently as these peculiar pale visitors don snorkeling gear and splash into the water. The film star and her sister have stretched out on towels in the sand, and are soon surrounded by young men staring with open curiosity. The sand is clean and golden and dappled with tiny, elegant shells. Evelyn has unfurled a silk Chinese umbrella for shade as she strolls along collecting shells. Seth has put up the windsurfer, to the great delight of the little boys watching, and they touch the vivid, silky sail with tentative strokes.

Expedition ships go to extremes, to the icebergs of Antarctica, the steamy jungles of the Amazon, through the Northwest Passage or to some of the remote islands of Indonesia (as in the Tanimbars, above).

Average per diem: Around $400 PPPD for cruise only aboard the major expedition ships, much less from the small family operations.

The following are some companies who offer expedition and eco-tourism cruises:

Canadian River Expeditions Ltd.

3524 W 16th Avenue, Suite 1A, Vancouver, BC, Canada V6R 3C1, ☎ *(604) 738-4449.*
A family operation making river expeditions into the Queen Charlotte Islands, the
Yukon and coastal British Columbia.

Captain Al Parce

X-Ta-Sea, PO Box 240250, Douglas, AK 99824, ☎ *(907) 364-2275.*
Takes four people at a time out in his 49-foot vessel into Tracy Arm, Frederick
Sound and Admiralty Island on various itineraries from one to six nights.

Cruceros Australis

The Chilean Desk, 10250 SW 56th Street, Suite A-201, Miami, FL 33165, ☎ *(800)*
541-8938.
The *Terra Australis*, previously one of the U.S.-built coastal cruisers of now-defunct
American Cruise Lines, sails in Tierra del Fuego from Punta Arenas. Although there
are hints that she also ventures into the Antarctic, she should not, since there's no
ice-hardened hull on this vessel.

Eco-Expeditions

1414 Dexter Avenue N., #327, Seattle, WA 98109, ☎ *(800) 628-8747.*
Operates out of the same office as Zegrahm Expeditions (below), with a series of
Galapagos sailings and a cruise around Britain on the *Caledonian Star.*

The Explorers Club

46 East 70th Street, New York, NY 10021, ☎ *(800) 856-8951.*
Makes adventure expeditions, including occasional Antarctic sailings on the Russian
icebreaker *Kapitan Khlebnikov.*

Glacier Bay Adventures

PO Box 68, Gustavus, AK 99826, ☎ *(907) 697-2442.*
Makes eco-tour explorations of Alaska's Glacier Bay Country aboard the *Stellar*, a
research vessel built for the Alaska Department of Fish and Game.

InnerAsia Expeditions

2627 Lombard Street, San Francisco, CA 94123, ☎ *(800) 777-8183.*
Once again offering Alaska coastline cruises on its little 12-passenger *Discovery* after
several years of inactivity while the vessel was under charter during the Exxon oil
spill cleanup.

Lifelong Learning, Inc.

101 Columbia, #150, Aliso Viejo, CA 92656, ☎ *(800) 854-4080.*
Programs in the Antarctic, Costa Rica, the Amazon, North Africa, Asia Minor, the
Yucatan, Japan, Europe, Canada and the U.S.

Metropolitan Touring/Adventure Associates

13150 Coit Road, Suite 110, Dallas, TX 75240, ☎ *(800) 527-2500.*
Markets the *Santa Cruz, Isabella II* and hotel/yacht *Delfin* in the Galapagos.

NWT Marine Group

17 England Crescent, Yellowknife, N.W.T., Canada, X1A 3N5, ☎ *(403) 873-2489.*
A family-run company that cruises Canada's Arctic along the Great Slave Lake and
MacKenzie River aboard the 20-passenger *Norweta.*

Special Expeditions

720 Fifth Avenue, Department 235, New York, NY 10019, ☎ *(800) 762-0003.*
Cruises the Galapagos Islands aboard the *Polaris* and the Amazon aboard the *Flotel
Orellana.*

TCS Expeditions

2025 First Avenue, Suite 830, Seattle, WA 98121, ☎ *(800) 727-7477.*

Veteran expeditioner T.C. Swartz, former head of Society Expeditions, provides adventure cruises to Iceland, Greenland, the Canadian Arctic and the North Pole.

Zegrahm Expeditions

1414 Dexter Avenue N., #327, Seattle, WA 98109, ☎ *(800) 628-8747.*
Longtime expedition leader Werner Zehnder and his team of experts explore the Arctic and Antarctic, and offer dive excursions to Galapagos, cruises of the Seychelles aboard the *Caledonian Star* and catamaran explorations of Australia's Kimberley Coast.

In addition, see under Cruise Lines, above, Abercrombie & Kent, Bergen Line, Odessa America Cruise Company, Quark Expeditions, Radisson Seven Seas Cruises, Society Expeditions and Special Expeditions.

Sailing Ships

We drive through endless back roads of Maine trying to link up with the motorless sailing ship *Victory Chimes* we are to board for a *Bon Appétit* story. Finally the variable winds wind down and she slips easily into the harbor at Stonington on Deer Isle. Maine Windjammers don't follow a precise itinerary but sail with the wind.

The three-masted "ram" schooner, so called for her prominent thrust-bow profile, was built in Bethel, Delaware, in 1900 and christened *Edwin & Maud.* As no-nonsense as her name, she hauled lumber up and down the Chesapeake Bay.

Like the ship, our 30 or so fellow passengers are doughty, no-nonsense types with their birding binoculars, stout deck shoes and windbreakers with Elderhostel patches sewn on them.

We stow our small carry-on bag of casual clothing atop one of the two bunk beds in the compact cabin, noting an adjacent wash basin while realizing that both toilet and shower are elsewhere on the vessel. Since there's no need to change for dinner, we return up on deck in our rumpled traveling clothes. Nobody cares or even notices, because Monday night is the highly anticipated lobster night, and most of our fellow passengers, veterans of more than one cruise aboard, stand around chatting and sipping their BYOB cocktails with one ear cocked for the dinner bell.

As soon as it sounds, everyone hurries down to the dinner tables, where platters heaped with the huge, steaming crustaceans are plopped without ceremony into the center of each table, enough lobsters for everyone to have two apiece. Accompanying them, corn on the cob, potato salad, and later, for dessert on deck, a crumbly double-crusted fresh strawberry and rhubarb pie topped with a huge dollop of hand-whipped cream.

Everything aboard is cleaned, polished and shined with a palpable pride by the crew of nine, so that the *Victory Chimes* gleams like burnished gold in the setting sun. As the ship's colors are lowered in the lingering dusk, the passengers spontaneously applaud.

"She's the only one left of the three-masted schooners," Captain Kip Files says softly, "she's the only one to survive."

Average per diem: Around $125 PPPD.

The following are some of the companies that offer sailing ship cruises:

Absolute Asia

155 West 68th Street, Suite 525, New York, NY 10023, ☎ *(800) 736-8187.*
Indonesian culture and wildlife cruises aboard SongLines Cruises' new luxury sailboat *Maruta Wind.*

Captains Ken & Ellen Barnes

70 Elm Street, Camden, ME 04843, ☎ *(800) 999-7352.*
Operate the schooner *Stephen Taber* along the coast of Maine in summers, as well as the 1948 motoryacht *Pauline.*

Cruise Company of Greenwich

31 Brookside Drive, Greenwich, CT 06830, ☎ *(800) 825-0826.*
Offers sailing cruises aboard the new 50-passenger sail cruiser *Lili Marleen,* starting in the Azores in April, the Med in May, the Baltic in midsummer and the Atlantic coast of Europe and the Canary Islands in autumn.

Maine Windjammer Association

PO Box 137, Rockport, ME 04856, ☎ *(800) MAINE-80.*
Operates a fleet of ten individually owned, historic, two- and three-masted vessels, including the 132-foot *Victory Chimes* (see above), that sail along the coast of Maine in summer.

Metropolitan Touring/Adventure Associates

13150 Coit Road, Suite 110, Dallas, TX 75240, ☎ *(800) 527-2500.*
Offers sailings in the Galapagos aboard two historic sailing vessels, the 12-passenger brigantine *Diamant* and the eight-passenger ketch *Rachel III.*

Worldwide Travel & Cruise Associates, Inc.

400 SE 12th Street, Suite E, Fort Lauderdale, FL 33316, ☎ *(800) 881-8484.*
Book several notable sailing yachts, including the *Savarona, Sea Cloud* and *Le Ponant.*

Yankee Schooner Cruises

PO Box 696FL, Camden, ME 04843, ☎ *(800) 255-4449.*
Sails the historic, two-masted 137-foot schooner *Roseway* off the coast of Maine in summer and in the Virgin Islands in winter.

Zeus Tours & Yacht Cruises, Inc.

566 Seventh Avenue, New York, NY 10018, ☎ *(800) 447-5667.*
Markets the 24-passenger sailing cruiser *Pan Orama* in the Caribbean as well as small ships in Greece and Turkey, including the yachts *Zeus I, II and III.* In the Seychelles, under the Galileo Cruises label, the line also books the 18-cabin sailing cruiser *Galileo Sun.*

In addition, see under Cruise Lines, above, Club Med Cruises, Special Expeditions, Star Clippers, Tall Ship Adventures, Windjammer Barefoot Cruises and Windstar Cruises.

Freighters

It's a rare person who hasn't daydreamed about getting away from everyday routine by hopping a freighter to some distant port to stand gazing across the rail, pretending to be Somerset Maugham or Jack London—or even Alex Haley, the late author of *Roots,* who wrote many of his books while on long freighter cruises.

A few years ago it looked like freighter travel was fading into the sunset as more and more familiar companies such as San Francisco-based Delta Lines began closing down their cargo carriers to passengers. ("Cargo doesn't eat and doesn't complain," said one.)

Freighters take passengers to many colorful ports where cargo is loaded.

Now, in the wake of the fast-growing cruise industry, freighters are seeing a resurgence of passenger travel as well.

The biggest misconception about freighter travel, according to Freighter World Travel executives, is that people expect the accommodations to look like something out of an old Humphrey Bogart movie, whereas actually, some lines are adding new ships and upgrading public areas for passengers.

But before you dash out and book passage on a slow boat to China, there are some things you need to know, both about yourself and about freighter travel. Here's a quick quiz.

Freighter Fitness: A Quiz

1. Are you fussy about food and service?
   Very, add 5. Sort of, add 4. Occasionally, add 3. Rarely, add 2. Never, add 1.

2. How flexible are you?
   Very, add 1. Sort of, add 2. Occasionally, add 3. Rarely, add 4. Never, add 5.

3. Are you self-reliant and can easily amuse yourself?
   Very, add 1. Sort of, add 2. Occasionally, add 3. Rarely, add 4. Never, add 5.

4. Do you get along easily in close quarters with strangers?
   Always, add 1. Sort of, add 2. Occasionally, add 3. Rarely, add 4. Never, add 5.

5. Are you worried about getting bored aboard a ship?
   Very, add 5. Sort of, add 4. Occasionally, add 3. Rarely, add 2. Never, add 1.

Here are some helpful hints to guide you through the quiz.

1. On 12-passenger freighter cruises, your meals will be the same served to the officers, which means on a foreign-flag vessel, say, Greek or German, you should be prepared to enjoy the cuisine of that country, because that's what the galley usually cooks for the crew. You'll also usually be sharing the officers' cabin steward, so don't expect breakfast in bed or lots of pampering.

2. If the itinerary lists a port you've always wanted to visit, but the ship cancels that call at the last minute; if you're expecting to spend three days in Rio but end up getting only eight hours; if you plan to be home on the 58th day but actually don't get back until the 67th day—can you handle it?

3. On a freighter, you won't have a cruise director to cajole you into fun and games, nor a shore excursions manager selling guided bus tours to Yokohama, nor an orchestra playing for after-dinner dancing. You may have to take your own reading materials and games (although most freighters have small libraries and a few cards and games on hand), or even, in the case of Lykes Lines, your own dinner wine and liquor.

4. Remember that you'll be sharing a dinner table with the same 10 or so other passengers for a lot of days, and what seems only vaguely irritating at the beginning can be infuriating after a week or two. We remember a woman on the *Americana* named Janet who constantly made pronouncements at the dinner table, like "This is not a real freighter; I know, because I've taken 35 freighter cruises," or "I'm the poor relation on board, because I'm the only one in an inside cabin."

5. Amiable loners and couples whose world is complete within themselves make good freighter passengers, as do creative people with portable projects they need to work on free of interference or telephone calls. It's a laid-back atmosphere where you make your own entertainment.

SCORES:

If you scored higher than 20, book a cruise ship, not a freighter.

If you scored 15, the only cargo-carrier you'll be happy aboard is Ivaran's *Americana* (page 524).

If you scored under 10, you should be able to manage a freighter cruise.

Freighter cabins like this one aboard Columbus Lines are spacious.

Five Things You Need to Know Before You Go

1. There's no doctor aboard; if a vessel carries fewer than 12 passengers, he's not required.

2. There may be an age limit. Because of the medical rule above, many cargo companies have stringent upper age or medical condition rules. You can expect to asked for a medical certificate.

3. No special dietary requests can be handled.

4. Most freighter companies refuse to carry children or pregnant women.

5. The per diem cost of a freighter trip is slightly lower than most cruise ships, but don't book just because it's cheaper. You'll pay a flat rate, and if it lasts longer, you won't have to pay any more, but if it ends early, you don't get a refund.

The following companies can help you book passage on a freighter:

Compagnie Polynesienne de Transports Maritime
595 Market Street, #2880, San Francisco, CA 94105, (415) 541-0677.
The 64-passenger *Aranui* carries mail, cargo, deck passengers and tourists around the islands of French Polynesia.

Freighter World Cruises, Inc.
180 South Lake Avenue #335, Pasadena, CA 91101, (818) 449-3106.
Represents virtually every freighter company that takes passengers, notably CAST, Columbus Line, Bank Line ATW, Mineral Shipping, Reederei Bernhard Schulte, NSB, Ivaran, Egon Oldendorff and the new *Cielo di Los Angeles* that cruises from the west coast of Canada and the U.S. to the Mediterranean.

TravLtips Cruise and Freighter Travel Association
Box 188, Flushing, NY 11358, (800) 872-8584.
This group handles bookings for the cargo liner and Royal Mail Ship *RMS St. Helena*, which cruises to the remote South Atlantic island of St. Helena, where Napoleon spent his last years in exile. It also books Blue Star Line's *Columbia Star* and *California Star* from the West Coast to Australia, New Zealand and Fiji.

In addition, see under Cruise Lines, above, Ivaran Cruise Line.

European Coastal Cruises

Scandinavian ferries offer roundtrip mini-cruises out of several cities.

European Coastal Cruises, Ferries and Yachts

NOTE: In parentheses after each vessel's name are the initials of the company or companies that book it, which you can match with the full names, addresses and phone numbers of the companies and marketing firms below (page 98).

While the most famous series of coastal cruises in Europe is probably the Bergen Line's Norwegian Coastal Voyages (see page 241), there are also a number of ferries, sailing ships and other small vessels offering holiday sailings, including yacht rentals in the Aegean.

Like **a floating Scottish country hotel**, the exquisite little 50-passenger *Hebridean Princess* (HIC) cruises the coastlines of Scotland, Ireland and Norway with a crew of 35 and a local guide on every sailing. Instead of a casino and jugglers, your entertainment may be fishing trips, clay pigeon shoots, bicycling or exercising in the trim little gym aboard. Instead of theme night and two-seating dinners, passengers enjoy superb Scottish cuisine at single seating meals. Take tea in a lounge with chintz-covered furniture and half-timbered brick fireplace, and settle into a lavish cabin or suite, perhaps one with a private balcony. Figure an average of around $300–$400 a day per person, double occupancy, depending on the season and cabin selection.

Fjord Holidays (EC) offers cruise tour packages that let you **cruise by day through the Norwegian fjords**, take the Flaam scenic railway and spend the night in country hotels. The four- or five-day programs begin in either Bergen or Oslo and include a stopover at Balestrand. Daily departures between mid-May and mid-September cost from $500–$750 per person, double occupancy, including the fjord cruises, rail excursion, hotel stay and daily breakfasts.

"Impressions of A Swedish Summer" is the name Sven-Olof Lindblad gives to his Special Expeditions sailings aboard the little *Swedish Islander* (see page 856) The 49-passenger boat sails around the islands of the Stockholm Archipelago, cruising by day and stopping for overnights in quiet country inns along the way. You'll meet the Swedish people, go bicycling, fishing and swimming, and celebrate summer in the part of the world that welcomes it most warmly.

Far to the south in the sunny Aegean, the 36-passenger sail-cruiser *Galileo Sun* (ZT&C), built in 1994, sets out on seven-night Greek Islands itineraries that include **plenty of watersports** and fishing opportunities, with water-skiing, windsurfing, and snorkeling equipment aboard. The season runs throughout the summer and into mid-October, and fares are around $1800 to $2000 for the week, including American buffet breakfasts daily and either lunch or dinner daily, depending on shipboard activities.

The 45-passenger sailing/motor yacht *Pan Orama* (CC&T, ZT&C), built in 1994, offers cruises around the Greek Islands or along the coast of Turkey from Kusadasi, near the ancient city of Ephesus, to Antalya on the gorgeous Turquoise Coast. You can **go swimming off the stern** of the boat. All cabins are outsides with a choice of double or twin beds and private bath facilities.

And the 50-passenger *Lady Catarina* (ZT&C), a sleek new yacht built in 1995, provides TV sets in each of its outside cabins, single unassigned seatings for mealtimes and a swimming platform on the ship's stern.

Even **more intimate** are the 20-passenger yachts from Zeus Tours & Cruises, also cruising on seven-day Greek Islands itineraries from late May through late October. Fares range from around $1025 to $1275 per person, double occupancy; lower prices are for cabins with upper and lower berths, toilet and shower. Again, daily American breakfasts and either lunch or dinner are included, along with a beach barbecue, a captain's dinner and a Greek Night.

Caiques are **traditional wooden Greek sailing vessels** that can carry from 20 to 30 passengers in double cabins with private facilities (NC/NT). Figure from $1000 to $1500 per person, double occupancy, for a week, with American breakfast and either lunch or dinner daily, a captain's tour, English-speaking tour leader and lots of watersports opportunities.

For some, the ultimate getaway might be taking **your own private yacht through the Greek Islands**. Zeus Tours operates a fleet of 120 sailing yachts, motor yachts and motorsailers that can be chartered with or without captain and crew, and Nabila Tours offers a choice of 500 motor yachts, sailing yachts, motor sailers and bareboat sailing yachts. Yachts from 20 to 60 feet, handling from two to 10 people, go for a daily rate of around $160 to $950; two passengers should be qualified sailors, one of them a qualified skipper. Motor sailers from 46 to 150 feet range from $800 to $8800 a day, while motor yachts without sails, accommodating six to 80 passengers, cost from $1700 to $7600 a day.

Among the Scandinavian ferries, Viking Line's *Isabella, Mariella, Cinderella, Rosella* and *Amorella* (EC) offer overnight sea transportation on a 2000-plus passenger vessel that is equivalent to a giant cruise ship, with nightclubs, discos, entertainment, swimming pools, saunas and shops on board. Prices range from around $85 to $600 per person, double occupancy, one way, depending on the route and type of cabin. The cheapest are four-berth insides with two upper and two lower berths with shower and toilet. Viking Line's ferry sailings include **overnight trips between Stockholm and Helsinki or Turku, Finland**. Fares include one buffet breakfast and one buffet dinner, but there are a variety of à la carte restaurants in various price ranges. You can carry along your car for an additional $19 in low season, $51 in high season.

A three-day, two-night roundtrip sailing from either Stockholm or Helsinki, staying in port all day in the other city, costs from around $225 per person, double occupancy, including two breakfasts and two buffet dinners.

Estline's 856-passenger *Mare Balticum* (EC) offers a two-night roundtrip **mini-cruise year-round from Stockholm to Tallinn, Estonia**, which includes two breakfasts and a city sightseeing tour with lunch. Prices range from around $110 to $625, depending on date and cabin accommodations. The cheapest are inside economy cabins with upper and lower berths and shared bathroom facilities. If you book a one-way passage between Stockholm and Tallinn ($105 to $473 per person double occupancy), meals are not included. Unlike cruise ships, ferries do not usually include meals in the basic fare.

Scandinavian Seaways (EC) operates **overnight ferries between Oslo and Copenhagen**, as well as two-night mini-cruises as a roundtrip voyage out of either city with a full day spent in the other city. On the mini-cruise package, rates range from around $205 to $521 per person, double occupancy, including two breakfast and two dinner buffets and a city tour.

The following are some of the companies that offer coastal cruises, sailing ship cruises, yacht charters and ferry cruises in Europe:

Classical Cruises & Tours

132 E. 70th Street, New York, NY 10021, ☎ *(800) 252-7745.*
Mediterranean and Aegean sailings with an emphasis on history and culture.

Cruise Company of Greenwich

31 Brookside Drive, Greenwich, CT 06830, ☎ *(800) 825-0826.*
Offers sailing cruises aboard the 50-passenger sail cruiser *Lili Marleen*, starting in the Azores in April, the Med in May, the Baltic in midsummer and the Atlantic coast of Europe and the Canary Islands in autumn.

Elegant Cruises & Tours, Inc.

31 Central Drive, Port Washington, NY 11050, ☎ *(516) 767-9302, (800) 683-6767.*
Books sailings in Europe on the *Sea Cloud*.

EuroCruises

303 West 13th Street, New York, NY 10014, ☎ *(212) 691-2098, (800) 688-3876, (800) 661-1119 (brochures).*
Books ferries, river boats and coastal cruises as well as larger European cruise ships.

Hebridean Island Cruises

Acorn Park, Skipton, North Yorkshire, England BD23 2VE, ☎ *011-44-1756-701338.*
Scottish coastal cruises aboard the *Hebridean Princess*.

Nabila Cruises

Naggar Tours, 605 Market Street, San Francisco, CA 94105, ☎ *(800) 443-NILE.*
Yacht cruises along the Greek and Turkish coasts.

Worldwide Travel & Cruise Associates, Inc.

400 SE 12th Street, Suite E, Fort Lauderdale, FL 33316, ☎ *(800) 881-8484.*
Books several notable sailing yachts, including the *Savarona, Sea Cloud* and *Le Ponant*.

Zeus Tours & Cruises, Inc.

566 Seventh Avenue, New York, NY 10018, ☎ *(212) 221-0006, (800) 447-5667.*
Markets the 24-passenger sailing cruiser *Pan Orama* in the Caribbean as well as small ships in Greece and Turkey, including the yachts *Zeus I, II and III*. The line also books the 18-cabin sailing cruiser *Galileo Sun*.

In addition, see under Cruise Lines, above, Club Med Cruises, Special Expeditions, Star Clippers, and Windstar Cruises.

CRUISE LINE CONTACTS

Most cruise lines do not book cruises directly but will send brochures and information free of charge. More and more lines are putting up web sites that feature itineraries, photos and contacts. There are a number of travel agents who operate web sites complete with links. We recommend using Fielding's CruiseFinder, a searchable database from which this book is created. We also provide an extensive links page for cruise and other travel sites.

Company	Phones	Web Site
Abercrombie & Kent	(630) 954-2944 (800) 323-7308	www.abercrombiekent.com
Airtours (U.K.)	(01144) 1706-260-000	www.airtours.com/airtours/ news.html
Alaska Sightseeing/ Cruise West	(206) 441-8687 (800) 426-7702	www.smallship.com
American Canadian Caribbean Line	(401) 247-0955 (800) 556-7450	www.accl-smallships.com
American Hawaii Cruises	(800) 765-7000	www.cruisehawaii.com
American West Steamboat Company	(206) 292-9606 (800) 434-1232	
Bergen Line	(212) 319-1300 (800) 323-7436 (reservations) (800) 666-2374 (brochures)	www.bergenline.com
Canaveral Cruise Line Inc.	(904) 427-6892	
Carnival Cruise Line	(305) 599-2600 (800) CARNIVAL	www.carnival.com
Celebrity Cruises	(305) 262-6677 (800) 242-6374	www.celebrity-cruises.com
Clipper Cruise Line	(314) 727-2929 (800) 325-0010	www.ecotravel.com/clipper
Club Med Cruises	(212) 977-2100 (800) 453-7447	www.clubmed.com

Company	Phones	Web Site
Commodore Cruise Line	(954) 967-2100 (800) 237-5361	www.commodorecruise.com
Costa Cruises	(305) 358-7325 (800) 462-6782	www.costacruise.com
Crystal Cruises	(310) 785-9300 (800) 446-6620	
Cunard Line	(212) 880-7500 (800) 5-CUNARD	www.cunardline.com
Delphin Seereisen	(01149) 699-840-3811	
Delta Queen Steamboat Company	(504) 586-0631 (800) 543-7637	www.deltaqueen.com
Disney Cruise Line	(407) 939-3500 (offices) (407) 566-7000 (information)	www.disney.com/ DisneyCruise/
Dolphin Cruise Line	(305) 358-5122 (800) 222-1003	www.dolphincruise.com
Epirotiki Cruise Line	(212) 397-6400 (800) 872-6400	www.epirotiki.com
Esplanade Tours	(617) 266-7465 (800) 426-5492	
EuroCruises	(212) 691-2099 (800) 688-EURO	
Galapagos Cruise Line	(800) 221-3254	
Glacier Bay Tours and Cruises	(206) 623-7110 (800) 451-5952	www.glacierbaytours.com
Golden Sun Cruises	[30] (1) 452-1260 (800) 473-3239 (Aegean TravelVisions), in North America	
Hapag-Lloyd	(01149) 421-350-0333 (800) 551-1000 (for Bremen) (800) 334-2724 (for Europa)	
Holland America Line	(206) 283-2687 (800) 426-0327	www.hollandamerica.com
Ivaran Cruise Line	(201) 798-5656 (800) 451-1639	
Jardrolinjia Cruises	(212) 695-8229	
Marine Expeditions	(416) 964-9069 (800) 263-9147	
Mediterranean Shipping Cruises	(212) 764-4800 (800) 666-9333	
Norwegian Cruise Line	(305) 436-4000 (800) 327-7030	www.ncl.com/ncl

Company	Phones	Web Site
OdessAmerica Cruise Co.	*(516) 747-8880* *(800) 221-3254*	
Orient Lines	*(954) 527-6660* *(800) 333-7300*	
P & O Cruises	*(310) 553-1770* *(800) PRINCESS*	www.p-and-o.com
Premier Cruise Lines	*(407) 783-5061* *(800) 327-7113*	www.bigredboat.com
Princess Cruises	*(310) 553-1770* *(800) PRINCESS*	www.princesscruises.com
Quark Expeditions	*(203) 656-0499* *(800) 356-5699*	www.quark-expeditions.com
Radisson Seven Seas Cruises	*(305) 776-6123* *(800) 333-3333*	www.cruising.org/radisson
Regal Cruises	*(813) 867-1300* *(800) 270-SAIL*	www.regalcruiscs.com
Renaissance Cruises	*(954) 463-0982* *(800) 525-5350*	
Royal Caribbean International	*(305) 539-6000* *(800) 327-6700*	www.royalcaribbean.com/ main.html
Royal Olympic Cruises	*(212) 397-6400* *(800) 872-6400*	www.epirotiki.com
Saga International Holidays	*(617) 262-2262* *(800) 952-9590*	
St. Lawrence Cruise Lines	*(613) 549-8091* *(800) 267-7868*	
Seabourn Cruise Line	*(415) 391-8518* *(800) 929-4747*	
Sea Cloud	*(516) 767-9302* *(800) 683-6767*	
Seawind Cruise Line	*(305) 573-3222* *(800) 854-8787*	
Silversea Cruises	*(305) 522-4477* *(800) 722-9055*	
Society Expeditions	*(206) 728-9400* *(800) 548-8669*	
Special Expeditions	*(908) 654-0048* *(800) 348-2358*	
Star Clippers	*(305) 442-0550* *(800) 442-0551*	
Star Cruises	*(Singapore) (011) 65-733-9766* *FAX: (011) 65-733-8622*	
Sun Line Cruises	*(212) 397-6400* *(800) 872-6400*	

Company	Phones	Web Site
Swan Hellenic Cruises	*(01144) 171-800-2200 (in U.K.) (888) MINERVA (in U.S.) (800) PRINCESS*	www.swan-hellenic.co.uk
Tall Ship Adventures	*(303) 755-7983 (800) 662-0090*	www.tallshipadventures.com
Windjammer Barefoot Cruises, Ltd.	*(305) 672-6453 (800) 327-2601*	www.windjammer.com
Windstar Cruises	*(206) 298-3057 (800) 258-7245*	www.windstarcruises.com
World Explorer Cruises	*(415) 393-1565 (800) 854-3835*	www.wecruise.com
Zeagrahm Expeditions	*(206) 285-4000 (800) 628-8747*	
Zeus Tours and Cruises	*(212) 221-0006 (800) 447-5667*	

Web sites are coming online as we speak so check for new sites by using www.excite.com and searching for cruise lines.

Can I send e-mail to passengers onboard a ship?

Fielding is frequently asked which ships allow passengers to receive e-mail. Remember that ships do not have access to phone lines but must use expensive satellite and radio communications. So, forget the concept of free e-mail. Phone calls from ship to shore can cost $25 a minute or more, so that means faxes and e-mail are expensive as well. Although the official policy of most cruise lines is not to accept e-mail for passengers on ships, unofficially the cruise lines with Websites listed above may make an effort to pass on your message, but they can't guarantee it will be received. Before you leave on your cruise give a copy of the satellite communications number for the ship to whomever should contact you in the event of an emergency. (This will be included with your ticket package.) If you have an emergency onboard and need to contact someone onshore, the purser's desk will make arrangements for you with the radio officer.

Note: Fielding publishes cruise information only. We do not book cruises and we cannot forward e-mail to passengers on cruises. For last minute updates on cruises and for information on ships no longer in service or in transition, check out Fielding's Cruise Insider online at www.fieldingtravel.com.

GETTING READY TO GO

If you have a special occasion to celebrate, let the line know ahead of time and it'll bake you a cake, as Cunard did for this couple.

Timetable

Two Months or More Ahead of Time:

—Get a passport (see Nuts and Bolts, page 121) or get your old one renewed if it's within six months of expiring.

—Apply for any visas you may need for ports of call. Some countries let you travel on a group visa so long as you stay with group excursions when ashore. If you want to strike out on your own, check to see if you need an individual visa. Then get it either through a visa service (usually quite costly and time-consuming) or, if you're in a city where there is a consulate or embassy from the country you're planning to visit, go down in person and apply. It takes only a few days, as a rule.

When Your Tickets Arrive:

—Sit down and examine carefully everything in the package, because there may be forms you need to fill out and mail or fax back to the line. At the very least, there are forms that you should fill out at home before leaving rather than at the check-in counter at embarkation, when you may be holding up a long line. And there will be valuable information dealing with life aboard the ship, wardrobe and how to communicate with you on the ship for those at home.

—Give a copy of the satellite communications telephone number for the ship to whomever should contact you in an emergency, and threaten violence if they call when there is no emergency. (There's nothing scarier than to be relaxing aboard a ship miles from land and have the radio officer ring your cabin with a call from home.)

—If you're traveling independently to the ship, take with you the name and telephone number of the port agent for the city of embarkation, because sometimes a ship isn't where it's supposed to be when you arrive.

The Day or Night Before:

—Pack your bags, being sure to affix to each one the baggage tags the cruise line has sent, with your name and cabin number clearly written on each.

The Day of Your Flight or Transfer to the Ship:

—Get to the airport (or the ship) comfortably early in case there's a traffic delay. Pay careful attention to boarding time and sailing time instructions. If you're too early, you'll sit around on a folding chair in a large terminal waiting until you can board.

Carry casual clothes to wear on deck in the daytime, like this couple aboard the **Star Clipper;** *bathing suit coverups are always useful.*

Eleven Tips To Lighten Your Luggage

1. **Lightweight Bags:** We carry soft-sided but durable bags in small to medium sizes, tucking in an empty folding bag to bring dirty laundry or souvenirs back home. Try never to carry more than you can handle yourself, since you may arrive in some primitive place where there are no baggage carts, as in the Miami airport. While a ship doesn't care how much baggage you bring on board, the airline that gets you there can be sticky about overweight luggage. Also, cabin closet and drawer space may be limited on smaller ships or in lower category accommodations.

2. **List:** Work out a wardrobe list in advance to avoid those just-in-case clothes that get thrown in at the last minute and never worn. Remember that separates multiply, you can wear an outfit more than once, and sticking to basic color combinations means fewer shoes and accessories to coordinate.

3. **Laundry:** Virtually every cruise ship has a laundry, either self-service or send-out. Daytime clothes are casual and if they're washable as well, you don't need to take many. Dry-cleaning is available on most of the newer ships, and you'll often find irons and ironing boards in self-service laundries or from the housekeeping department for last-minute touch-ups.

4. **Layering:** Bulky garments add weight and take up space; instead, layer lightweight garments for air-conditioned areas and cool mornings on deck. You'll have more wardrobe variety as well. Wear your bulkiest clothing and shoes to the ship to save having to pack them.

5. **Lightweight fabrics:** Carry more light natural fibers such as cottons and linens to tropical climates; avoid synthetics, which tend to cling and don't breathe. Silks are nice for dressy evenings but wrinkle in the humidity on shore.

6. **Location purchasing:** Since you're going to be tempted by clothing in ports of call—T-shirts, caftans, pareus—you might as well plan for it. Take fewer casual items and shop with a clear conscience.

7. **Little sizes:** No, we don't mean clothing but toiletries; save those samples that come in the mail or buy the smallest possible tubes and containers before leaving. All but a few ships have complimentary toiletries in the cabins; we've tried to point out those that don't. (See Five Things You Won't Find Aboard under the cruise ship you're sailing aboard.)

8. **Less is more:** We've long ago limited gifts and souvenirs for friends back home to small, unbreakable, easily packed items such as scarves, flat placemats, leather goods including wallets or belts, rather than outsized, fragile items that have to be hand-carried.

9. **Libraries:** Don't carry a collection of hardbound best-sellers to read aboard; every ship has a library of some sort, from the *QE2's* magnificent collection to a small group of dog-eared paperbacks on an ACCL expedition vessel. Tuck a paperback or two into your luggage and then trade with someone else when you've finished.

10. **Logic:** Carry essentials including passport, tickets, traveler's checks, cash, extra glasses, cameras and prescription medications in hand baggage you always keep with you; never put them in a suitcase that may be checked.

11. **Leave it out when in doubt:** We've never yet come back from a cruise without at least one garment we carried and never wore. Other passengers usually don't notice if you're wearing the same thing several times; it's the pleasure of your company, not your wardrobe, that counts.

For many people, dressing up for formal night is a special part of the cruise.

Wardrobe Tips: Sequins Don't Wrinkle

Chances are, everything you need to pack for your cruise is already in your closet—(we know this doesn't make a good argument for someone using the cruise as an excuse to buy some smashing new clothes)—because people on ships wear the same clothes as people on land, regardless of what some department store fashion buyers seem to think.

In the daytime, casual shorts and T-shirts or jogging suits pass muster all over the ship, and in the evening, dress-up clothes of the sort you'd wear to a dinner party or nice restaurant will do just fine.

On the most classic and elegant ships, the dreaded words "formal night" do mean a tuxedo, dinner jacket or dark suit for a man, and a cocktail outfit or evening dress for women, but a blazer or sports jacket and tie for men, a dress or pantsuit for women, will be acceptable on most big Caribbean mass-market lines such as Carnival, RCI or NCL.

A few lines such as Star Clipper and Windstar ask only for "casual elegance" in the evenings and never require a jacket or tie. And Windjammer Barefoot Cruises in their clever little "Windjammer Survival Booklet" (☎ 800-327-2601 to get a copy) says "With us dressing for dinner means putting on a clean T-shirt."

Five Essentials to Pack in Your Hand Baggage

1. Prescription medications in their original containers.

2. Sunblock and a hat.

3. An extra pair of prescription eyeglasses or contact lenses.

4. A sweater to combat overzealous air conditioning on board.

5. Proof of citizenship—passport, copy of birth certificate or voter registration card; a driver's license is not acceptable.

Nice to Take Along

1. Camera and film (if you're a novice, practice at home with a roll or two before you leave).

2. Lightweight binoculars.

3. Small, packable guidebooks for the area.

INSIDER TIP

It's a good idea not to pack anything firm whether valuable or not in your checked baggage. In several major airports that handle a lot of cruise traffic (including New York's JFK) cameras and jewelry have a way of disappearing between the time the bag comes off the plane and when it gets into the baggage area.

Air/Sea Packages

If you've bought an air/sea package, the travel agent or cruise line has forwarded your air tickets to you a distressingly short time before departure. Take a moment and double-check the departure times and other details to be sure they coincide with the date and departure time of the cruise. If you're traveling with a spouse, you may or may not be seated together on the plane, since the block of tickets is run through a computer that couldn't care less about your marital bliss. If this happens to you, see if another member of your group will change seats with one of you if you're all clumped together.

Your route between home and the port may also be circuitous because of the airline hub system. If there's a long way to get there, you can count on that being your route. Should you have plenty of frequent flyer miles, you could book the cruise at the cheaper cruise-only price and use your mileage to get to and from the port. The only downside there is if your cruise is cancelled at the last minute, the cruise line would probably not refund the value of your lost mileage.

Arriving at the Airport of Your Port City

With an air/sea package, you will find somewhere in the arrival airport a uniformed meet-and-greet holding a sign with the name of your ship or cruise line on it. She may be at the gate or in the baggage area. She will tell you to claim your luggage and then mill about with the rest of your group until everyone has his or her bags, or until the couple whose bag was lost go to the baggage window and fill out the lost luggage forms.

Then you'll all be led as a group to your vehicles, and the meet-and-greets will supervise loading you and your baggage into the same or different vehicles. It's not a bad idea for a couple traveling together for one to get into the bus and get a seat for the two of you and the other watch the baggage until it is actually put into a vehicle.

Arriving at the Pier

The main difference between the port of Miami and the port of Los Angeles is that you'll be surrounded by porters to help you with your luggage at the former, and you'll be surrounded by passengers trying to find a porter at the latter. The porter will ferry your baggage from the taxi to the baggage-loading area for the ship, or, if you've arrived by transfer on an air/sea package, the meet-and-greets will see to its transfer. Again, it's a good idea to keep an eye on your bags as they're transferred.

You'll be ushered into a large hall where a lot of people are milling about or standing in line. There will be from one to 10 counters with letters of the alphabet above them. Queue up under the letter for your surname; if you are a couple with different surnames, as we are, select the shorter of the two lines. You will turn in your cruise tickets, passports, and (please, please, please) your already-filled-out forms, give them a credit card to imprint for onboard charges, and they in turn will give you a boarding card, perhaps a cabin key and part of your ticket. You will then be directed to the security point where you'll put everything through the machines again, just as you did at the airport. (If you're carrying 1000 ASA film for your cameras, this second X-ray dose could damage the film.)

> ### INSIDER TIP
>
> *You'll be expected to turn in your passport to the purser's staff when checking in aboard a ship and should not expect to see it again until the morning you disembark, except in certain Baltic and Black Sea ports where you pick it up from the purser and immediately turn it in to the port security officers at the bottom of the gangway. They return it to you when you come back to the ship and you turn it back into the purser's office.*

Security

Cruise passengers have gotten accustomed to the same security drills as airline passengers, running baggage through the X-ray devices and showing a

Here's where we go. Here's how we get there.

CENTURY • GALAXY • HORIZON • MERCURY • ZENITH

It's a long way from Hamilton, Bermuda, to Alaska's Hubbard Glacier. Or from Cabo San Lucas, on the tip of Baja California, to the twin Pitons on St. Lucia in the Lesser Antilles. But each destination, and dozens more, shares one thing in common – the presence of a most uncommon cruise line. Celebrity. Five Celebrity ships comprise one of the world's newest, most modern fleets. And each sails the seas in a style that is singularly Celebrity. Nothing compares to the acclaimed cuisine of Master Chef Michel Roux or our museum-worthy paintings and sculpture. Nothing compares to our Five Star service, expansive staterooms, or to AquaSpa,^{SM} the most luxurious spas afloat. Celebrity is uniquely qualified to present you with the best of Bermuda, Alaska, the Caribbean, the Panama Canal and beyond. Call your Travel Agent or 1-800-CELEBRITY, ext. 633, for a free brochure.

Celebrity Cruises
Exceeding expectations.™

Norwegian Cruise Line's *Windward* in Alaska

Orion restaurant, Celebrity *Galaxy*

America West Steamboat's *Queen of the West* on the Columbia River

boarding pass to reboard the vessel. The newest precautionary safety measure introduced on some lines recently is the requirement of a photo ID to
back up the usual boarding card for passengers boarding and reboarding the
ship. This is particularly enforced in the Bahamas, where illegal immigrants
have been caught boarding ships with legitimate passengers by using another
traveler's boarding card.

Visitors who have not made previous arrangements are not permitted to
board most ships in port. If you want to invite a friend on board for lunch or
a drink, be sure to ask well ahead of time at the purser's desk if it can be arranged.

Boarding

You will follow a long line of people carrying their hand baggage along an
interminable gangway, perhaps up some stairs or an escalator, perhaps along
a covered walkway, to the point where a strip of tape has been stuck across
the floor and a man with a camera will order you to stop by a life ring and
smile. Try to look as cheerful as you can, because this photograph will be put
on display the next day for everyone on the ship to see.

When you cross over the threshold from the gangway into the ship, you
will be simultaneously greeted with a smile, handed some sheets of paper
that you don't have anywhere to put, told to watch your step and watch your
head, and have a white-gloved steward try to wrestle your hand baggage off
your shoulder while asking you your cabin number. He'll lead you to your
cabin, where you may or may not be greeted by your cabin steward or stewardess, who introduces himself or herself politely and explains how to turn
on the TV and flush the toilet.

*Check to see that your dining table assignment card is waiting in your cabin; if
not, go immediately to the maitre d'hotel and arrange it. The dining room here
shows the variety of table sizes available.*

The First Five Things to Do After Boarding

1.   Check the shipboard program to see when the lifeboat drill is held and what time the welcome-aboard buffet lunch service shuts down.

2.   Be sure your dining table assignment is set. If not, hie yourself to the maitre d's table and get one.

3.   Go to the spa or beauty salon in person to book all upcoming appointments for hair, nails, massage and facials.

4.   Hurry to the library to check out that new best-seller or videotape you want to see; if the library is not staffed and things are locked up, make a mental note of what you want and check the shipboard program for the first opening time.

5.   Unpack.

On Board

—Establish credit for your shipboard account.

On check-in or after boarding, you'll be asked to leave a credit card imprint to establish your shipboard charge account. Most ships make it impossible to spend cash until check-out time. (On a few small vessels without a completely computerized billing system, you may find that sales revert to cash at midnight the night before disembarkation to facilitate billing.) The purser's office slips a bill under your cabin door the last night of the cruise, usually long after bedtime, and you don't need to stop by the desk at all unless you have a question about it.

Almost every ship sailing today has some sort of gym and fitness center, as well as indoor and outdoor pools where water exercises are held; this is the lap pool on Princess Cruises' **Royal Princess.**

Spas

Almost every ship today sails with some sort of gym or fitness center; a jogging or walking track, either a specially surfaced ring around an upper deck or the passenger promenade deck; a daily exercise program that includes aerobics and other energetic activities; and a menu that includes designated low-fat, low-salt, low-calorie dishes. In addition, most have a full range of beauty, hair, nail and spa services, including manicures, pedicures, massage, steam baths, hydrotherapy, facials, herbal wraps and even mud/steam baths. The bigger the ship, the more the facilities.

Like most casinos, shops and photographic services, spas and beauty shops at sea are operated by concessionaires. Steiner of London, which dates back to 1903 when the company got its first royal warrant for hairdressing, has the lion's share of ship contracts, around a hundred vessels at last count.

Passengers are urged to book massage and beauty services as quickly as possible after boarding, since the best times go quickly. Busiest days are when the captain's formal welcome aboard and farewell parties are held.

Five Ways to Get Invited to the Captain's Table

1. Occupy the most expensive cabins aboard.
2. Be a many-time repeat passenger.
3. Be rich and/or famous, a travel agent or a member of the media.
4. Be an extremely attractive blonde, preferably Norwegian.
5. Have your travel agent make the request, describing you as a rich, famous, beautiful, Scandinavian, blonde travel writer.

The Lifeboat Drill

A mandatory lifeboat drill for all the ship's passengers and crew will be called within 24 hours after sailing from the port of embarkation. You will be told to go to your cabin and get your life jacket, then report to your lifeboat station as designated on a sign affixed to your cabin wall or door. Sometimes you report to a public lounge on the ship, sometimes directly to your boat station on deck. Crew members will be posted in each stairwell and hallway to direct you to your station. It is requested that you not use the elevators since in a real emergency, they might be disabled. The signal to gather for the lifeboat drill is seven short and one long blast on the ship's whistle. You stay at your station until released by the crew member in charge. Don't worry about struggling into your life jacket in the cabin; a crew member will help you at the boat station if you need assistance. Smoking and drinking during the lifeboat drill is prohibited.

Five Money-Saving Tips On Board

1. Take along your own soft drinks, wine or liquor (or buy them along the way in port) for pre-dinner libations in your cabin (but don't take your own drinks into the ship's public areas—that's a no-no). A few lines state that bringing your own liquor to your cabin is not allowable, but we've yet to see it enforced.
2. Ask the shore excursion staff about ways of doing your own sightseeing program ashore instead of buying a costly shore excursion; a group of four can sometimes negotiate a Caribbean island tour with a local cab driver for less than the cost of four excursions, and a couple can walk around a town in Alaska on their own and catch the highlights, using the shore excursion booklet as a guide.
3. If you have kids along, persuade them to participate in the youth programs and activities rather than hang out in the video arcades, where quarters have a way of melting away quickly.

*Steer clear of the ship's casino, such as this one aboard RCI's **Majesty of the Seas**, as well as the bingo games, if you're on a tight budget.*

4.   Steer clear of the casino and bingo games on board if you're on a tight budget, or set aside the amount of money you can afford to lose and don't dip any deeper.

5.   If your shopping resistance is low, concentrate on sightseeing instead; otherwise you'll end up with bulky shopping bags full of things that are not as irresistible as you thought when you get them home.

INSIDER TIP

To get better service than the other passengers doesn't cost a thing; just read a crew member's name tag, look him in the eye, call him by name, smile and say thank you and show an interest in him as an individual. And remember the name next time without having to look at the name tag.

KEELHAUL

Many cruise lines now offer "port lecturers" who hand out maps to what they call "recommended" shops where the merchandise is "guaranteed." All this means is that the shops listed on the maps have paid to be listed and give commissions to both the "lecturer" and the cruise line. Most promise a 30-day opportunity to return or exchange defective merchandise, but any legitimate shopkeeper should promise the same. Too many passengers read these maps without realizing they are commercial ventures, and become fearful of going into a "non-guaranteed" shop and getting ripped off.

Shore Excursions

A few cruise lines, primarily expedition vessels, include shore excursions in the base price, but aboard most ships, you'll be offered a variety of optional group port tours that may range from an inexpensive walking tour of Key West to a costly helicopter flight over a glacier or volcano.

Early in the sailing, the shore excursions director will hold one or more sessions to describe the tours as well as shopping pointers and ways to tour on your own. You're usually given a printed form with the excursions and prices on them, which you fill out and turn in to the shore excursions office. The excursions are then charged against your shipboard account, and the tickets or vouchers delivered to your cabin. Take care of your tickets and remember to have them along with you, "ripped and ready" as one shore excursions manager used to say, when you go ashore to take the tour. No ticket, no tour.

If you're on a budget, you'll want to weigh carefully which excursions to take and which to skip. Consider taking your own walking tour in a small port rather than getting on a bus or in a van with the others. The shore excursions manager can usually give you some advice.

Remember too that certain excursions have limited participation, so if there's something you can't live without, get to the shore excursions office as soon as possible after that tour is open for booking. Some cruise lines will let your travel agent book a tour for you ahead of time so you're guaranteed a spot.

Scoping Out Seasickness

The removal of the Transderm Scop seasickness "patch" from the market was a better-late-than-never move for this often-dangerous drug perceived as innocuous by its users because it resembled the harmless and familiar Band-Aid. Over the years we've encountered numerous serious medical incidents because of the patch, whose main medical ingredient was scopolamine. The former prescription-only medication carried a lengthy cautionary sheet in fine print inside each package which we are confident few if any of its users ever read. Adverse reactions ran from dryness in the mouth (two-thirds of its users) to disorientation and loss of memory, particularly in older users.

There are much safer and equally effective treatments for seasickness, as well as some unusual remedies, included in the following roster:

1. Sea Band or Travel Garde bracelet-like knit bands worn around the wrist at acupressure points to relieve symptoms of nausea.

2. Ginger root capsules, available in health food stores or Asian pharmacies, taken before meals.

3. Nonprescription antihistamine remedies such as Dramamine, Antivert or Bonine can be taken one or two hours before sailing but may cause drowsiness.

4. Some shipboard doctors recommend a Dramamine injection, which works more quickly than an ingested tablet for a sudden or severe onset of seasickness.

Sidestepping Seasickness

But we have a more revolutionary cure for seasickness—a malady we must confess we've never suffered, but we do have sympathy for its victims. Here are three things to do if you're worried about a little mal de mer.

1. Select the right ship.

2. Sail the smoothest waters.

3. Sleep in the steadiest beds.

Pick a ship with little rolling and no pitching motion, such as the unique twin hulled *Radisson Diamond*, which moves smoothly (if rather slowly) through the water with little discernible side to side motion and no back to front motion. Fixed inboard stabilizers counteract both roll and pitch, and pitch and heave are reduced because the water is funneled between the two pontoons of the catamaran-like ship.

Sail-cruise vessels such as the Windstar ships have computer-trimmed and operated sails that keep the ships at an even keel when they proceed under sail, with heeling kept well under 6 percent.

Ships with a deeper draft (the measurement of the ship's waterline to the lowest point of its keel) usually perform better in rough seas than ships with shallow drafts. For instance, Norwegian Cruise Line's *Norway*, built as the transatlantic liner *France*, has a 35-foot draft that forces her to anchor rather than come alongside in her Caribbean ports but sure does make getting there smoother.

Destinations and itineraries can make a big difference for passengers concerned about ship motion. Plan to sail in sheltered waters such as Alaska's Inside Passage or along one of the great rivers of the world, where land is in sight and waters are calm. Conversely, in areas where two seas meet—Cabo San Lucas, Mexico, where the Sea of Cortez meets the Pacific, for instance, or South Africa's Cape of Good Hope or South America's Cape Horn—are notorious waters. Areas with powerful currents that have a speed greater than 0.8 knots an hour—the Falklands, South Indian Ocean, Bay of Bengal, Bay of Biscay, Solomon Sea, Java Sea, Bering Strait, Spitsbergen and the Angulhas Current along the southern tip of Africa—can really stir up the water.

Other rough sea reliables include the North Atlantic, the South China Sea, the Aegean in summer, the Shetlands and west coast of Scotland. In our experiences over the years, areas that stand out dramatically are an April crossing on the North Atlantic, Cape Horn and the Drake Passage on a January Antarctic sailing, a November sailing along the coast of West Africa off Namibia, and the seas around Nome, Alaska, anytime.

The smoothest ride on most ships is on a lower deck in an amidships cabin. The higher-priced sun and boat deck cabins give more bounce and roll. But book a cabin too close to the bow or stem, and you may feel every swell. Taking an outside cabin near the waterline bothers some cruisers, because the seas slosh across the little round window like a washing machine in the laundromat.

Ten Tips for First-Time Photographers

1. Take your camera manual with you on the cruise so if you have problems, a more experienced photographer on board can help you figure it out.

2. Always take a set of spare batteries and have them along with you when you go ashore.

3. When photographing people on deck or ashore against bright backgrounds, use your flash to fill in extra light on their faces.

4. Don't rest your elbows or camera against the ship's rail to steady it; the ship's vibrations will make your photo blur.

Take your camera manual and spare batteries with you on your cruise, especially if you're going into severe weather areas such as the Antarctic to photograph icebergs from the deck of the **World Discoverer.**

5. If you want to shoot pictures through the window of a tour bus, put your camera as close as possible to the glass without touching it; be aware tinted windows can cut down on your light and alter the colors of the subject. And using the flash will give you a beautiful picture of a white light in the bus window.

6. On deck, in small boats and Zodiacs, carry a plastic bag to slip over your camera to keep the salt spray from splashing it.

7. If you're traveling with a borrowed camera, get it far enough in advance so you can shoot a practice roll and develop it before leaving home.

8. When photographing lounge shows or lecturers indoors on a cruise ship, be aware how far the light from your flash will carry; it may be necessary to move forward into a better position to get your shot, but do it quietly and don't block anyone else's view. Some ships do not allow flash pictures during a show and almost all ban the use of video cameras.

9. If you hold your camera firmly in both hands, push your elbows against your rib cage, begin mentally counting backwards from 10 to 1 and midway squeeze the camera button, strange as it may sound, you can get a steadier shot in a low light situation.

10. Think in terms of telling a story with your cruise photographs—photograph the life ring with the ship's name on it, your cabin, your waiters and stewards, even yourself in the mirror dressed for the captain's dinner.

Where to Complain

Cruises score higher on passenger satisfaction surveys than any other form of leisure travel. But if things go wrong, the worst thing you can do is seethe silently and complain to your travel agent after you get back home, or mutter about it to fellow passengers. That only aggravates the annoyance.

The purser's or hotel manager's desk, usually in the main lobby, as here aboard a Renaissance ship, is the place to take your complaints in most cases.

Instead, when you have a specific problem during your cruise, take it immediately to the person responsible for that area of service, speak calmly and explain the situation in a reasonable tone of voice.

—Cabin or cabin service complaints should go to the housekeeper; if it doesn't work out, go to the hotel manager.

—Dining room complaints should be taken up with the maitre d'hotel or the dining room captain responsible for your table area; if you don't get satisfaction, go to the hotel manager or chief purser.

—Ship charges or procedures should be discussed with the purser's desk or information desk.

—Always point out any problems or complaints on the questionnaire you're given at the end of the cruise. Everyone up to and including the chairman of the board and the ship owner read these whenever there is a serious complaint. And don't be coerced by an anxious waiter or steward to give an excellent rating when not warranted just because he says he may lose his job as a result.

KEELHAUL

We give a punishing Keelhaul Award to those litigious passengers who threaten to sue cruise lines because there happened to be a hurricane or storm at sea that spoiled their vacation. When was the last time they sued Holiday Inn or Marriott under similar circumstances?

THE END OF THE CRUISE

Despite the highly polished service, the cadre of dining room stewards aboard the **Seabourn Spirit** *does not accept gratuities.*

Tipping

It used to be that any article on shipboard tipping—"shipboard gratuities," as the cruise line brochures like to call it—dealt simply with whom, how much and when. At some point in his disembarkation lecture, the cruise director would say, "So many passengers have asked us about whom and how much to tip…" and launch into an easy-to-compute per-person-per-day figure for the waiters and the cabin stewards.

Then you would go back to your cabin and figure out how much to tip each, get some change and slip that amount into the little envelopes that had a way of appearing in your cabin just when needed. You might put a little extra cash in for someone who was extra solicitous, knock off a little from someone else who had done less than you expected.

That was the way it used to be.

In the late 1970s, Holland America Line, which trains its own employees at special hotel schools in Indonesia and the Philippines, implemented a "no tipping required" policy. "We don't say tipping is not permitted," a line spokesman explained, "simply that it is not required. A passenger is free to tip any of our serving personnel if he wishes, but those personnel are not permitted to solicit tips in any fashion."

Then in 1984, Sea Goddess Cruises came along with an even more explicit rule—"If you are concerned about tipping, the Sea Goddess concept is quite simple: gratuities are discouraged."

Seabourn went them one further in 1990; the company "strictly prohibits all staff for any solicitation or acceptance of gratuities."

Even more astonishing is that we were getting excellent service on all three lines, erasing that notion that the word "tip" was an acronym "to insure promptness."

Well, if that isn't the case, what is a gratuity? Is it a voluntary reward for extra-special service, or is it, as in most European hotels and restaurants, a percentage charged for service and as routine a part of the bill as taxes? And if that's so, why couldn't it be added into the base cruise fare?

An automatic up-front payment would eliminate the problem crew members face called "stiffing"—a passenger leaving no tip whatsoever on a cruise where tipping is expected.

Aboard some ships, tips are automatically calculated and added to the passenger's shipboard account. And on most ships, bar service charges of 15 percent are automatically added to the drink tab.

On Crystal's ships, you can even charge your tips on your shipboard account and receive in exchange small printed cards to sign and present to your waiters and cabin steward, who later turn them in for cash. This relieves you of adding and multiplying chores and the necessity of going down to the purser to get change.

Some of the confusion about tipping comes from ships with open-seating policies. Since you may have a different waiter each time, how do you know whom to tip?

The Greek stewards' union requests each passenger set aside a prescribed amount that is pooled and divided among the crew under a prescribed formula. The usual argument that a crew member will work harder if he's hoping for a tip doesn't apply here, since everyone's going to get the same. (Insiders say peer pressure shapes up any lazy stewards on a Greek ship.)

Some of the smaller American ships and expedition vessels also use the pool system for tips.

Anytime we mention tipping in our newspaper columns, the mail is fast and furious, very little if any of it defending the practice of tipping. The most audible complaints come not from first-timers but veteran cruisers.

Here are some of the questions raised—Should the person who eats breakfast and lunch from the self-service buffet and goes ashore for dinner when the ship is in port be expected to leave the same amount as the passenger who shows up in the dining room for all three meals every day? And should the couple in the small inside cabin on the lower decks give the same steward's tip as the couple in the big boat deck suite?

These are questions for which there are no easy answers. In the meantime, to find out the recommended tip amounts for each ship, check that ship's listing in the guide.

The Last Day: Don't You Love Me Anymore?

Everyone at your table has hugged goodbyes the night before, after each has discreetly handed out the tips in their proper little envelopes and expressed a heartfelt thanks to the dining room stewards. The evening is always long and loud after a short cruise, with everyone getting in their last few hours of drinking and gambling and dancing, and quiet and downbeat after a long cruise, when the difficult transition to going home has to be made.

Bags go into the hall at midnight or sometime before 6 a.m. They'll be gathered up and ferried to a central area on the ship and transferred ashore after the ship has been secured the next morning.

No passengers are permitted to disembark until all the luggage has been unloaded and put ashore.

> **INSIDER TIP**
>
> *Obvious as this may seem, you must be scrupulously careful setting aside the clothing you need to travel in the next day, all the items including shoes and underwear, before putting your bags outside your door for collection. You won't see them again until you're back on shore. Pajamas are not proper debarkation attire.*

Breakfast service is more limited on disembarkation day, with the added aggravation in U.S. ports that the tea is terrible because there's so much chlorine in the water in case the kitchen has a surprise public health inspection, and there are no poached eggs because for some mysterious reason, the kitchen cannot poach eggs if the public health inspectors are aboard.

If your waiters are friendly but a little withdrawn, it's because, on many ships, they're the same busy beavers that spent the night lugging luggage down the halls and so have had maybe two hours of sleep maximum. Your tablemates, your best friends for life during the past week or so, may seem inordinately concerned with airport and getting home details, but you all exchange addresses and phone numbers.

You say goodbye a dozen times to everyone while you're milling about waiting for the ship to be cleared by customs and immigration and for your group's turn to depart.

Getting Off

You have been given color-coded baggage tags depending on aircraft departure times or ongoing arrangements, and your baggage will be waiting in the customs hall in the color-coded group. Do not panic; it is probably there somewhere. Gather it up, getting a porter if you need one or lugging it out by yourself if you don't.

You will have been given a U.S. customs form to fill out, which you will turn in at the gate as you leave. Most cruise ships arriving in U.S. ports have customs and immigration officials on board who have precleared your passport and customs forms before you disembark the ship.

INSIDER TIP

It's a good idea to take a close look at your bag before setting it out in the hall. When you get on the dock, you'll see a dozen just like it. The idea is to pick up the one belonging to you. We have seen passengers wandering around with no idea of what their bags actually look like.

Going Home

If you're on the air/sea package, your return to the airport and home will be very similar to your arrival, with the meet-and-greets on hand with their signs and advice. If you're in the port of Miami or Fort Lauderdale and flying with a major airline, after you claim your baggage and clear customs at the port, you can trundle it right over to the airline's baggage truck at the pier and check it in there, trusting it will arrive in your home airport when you do. It usually does.

THE NUTS AND BOLTS

How to get a passport:

Apply in person at one of the 3500 clerks of court or post offices which accept applications, or at one of the 13 passport agencies in the United States.

Present two passport photographs (go to a photographer who specializes in these), a photo ID with your signature such as an active driver's license, and proof of citizenship or nationality—a certified copy of a birth certificate, a Certificate of Naturalization or an expired U.S. passport.

Pay $65 if you're over 18, $40 if you're under 18, and turn in or mail in the completed printed form you were given to fill out. You can expediate the process (allow three working days) by paying an additional #30. If you're renewing your passport, pay $55.

How to select a travel agent:

Take as much time and care with your choice as when choosing a mate, looking for intelligence, warmth, patience, friendliness and diligence. A knowledge of basic geography is helpful too.

Look for professional associations; the agent should be a member of ASTA (American Society of Travel Agents), ARTA (Association of Retail Travel Agents), CLIA (Cruise Lines International Association) and/or NACOA (National Association of Cruise Only Agents). The latter specialize in cruises, but it does not mean they are more qualified on the subject than "full service" agents, only that they are specialists.

Whenever you book a cruise ticket through an agent, the agent receives a commission from the cruise line, not from you. There may be surcharges on other agency services, however, with the recent airline caps restricting the commission an agent can make from booking an air ticket.

How to go through immigration:

Have your passport ready and in your hand.

Be sure you're in the correct line; signs often indicate certain lines are restricted to airline crews, nationals of that country or members of European Community nations only.

When you near the immigration officer, be sure to remain behind the taped or painted line on the floor until the person ahead of you has finished and left.

Answer any questions asked, but don't volunteer comments, and don't fidget while he's examining your passport.

How to go through customs:

Have ready any receipts for large purchases you may have made on the trip.

Fill out the requisite form honestly.

Be prepared to open any bags or suitcases if requested, but never hesitate or ask the officer if he wants it opened, even when the man in front of you has had to open his.

Trip cancellation insurance:

This covers you if you have to cancel your cruise at the last minute, after the full fare has been paid and the cancellation penalties kick in, because of illness, death in the family or business emergencies.

Travel agents usually recommend a client take this insurance; some of the more cautious even ask a client who refuses it to sign a form indicating they were offered the insurance. Cruise lines, while not wanting to appear heartless, point out that while an emergency of this sort may happen once in your lifetime, it happens to them every sailing.

Vaccinations and medications:

If you are going to exotic areas of the world, check with your doctor or public health authorities about any medications or vaccinations recommended for travelers to that region. Remember that if you eat and sleep only aboard the cruise ship you will not be taking the same risks as someone on a trek or a safari.

Port Taxes:

Those friendly tropical islands who love tourists also love slapping on huge port taxes, also sometimes called "head taxes," for visitors. The highest one we've encountered in North American waters is Bermuda's $60 a passenger.

Some sharp-eyed cruisers may note that the cruise line's port fees may actually exceed the total of the individual ports' actual taxes. The usual explanation for this is administrative costs, whatever that means.

In 1997, the state of Florida brought a civil suit against certain cruise lines for adding on these fees to the advertised cruise price. As a result, some companies have factored in those add-on fees into advertised cruise prices. Check the small print for your cruise line.

Pre- and post-cruise packages:

Most cruise line brochures have add-on pre- or post-cruise packages for the cities of embarkation and disembarkation. If you're interested in such a package, discuss it with your travel agent to be sure the hotel being used is one you would like and that the price is less than you could get on your own. The upside of these packages is that they usually include transfers, which could save a lot of money in some cities.

WHERE ARE THEY NOW?

A Work in Progress

We all wonder whatever became of our favorite ships when they seem to have dropped off the planet or at least out of the travel agencies. Too many times cruise lines either never mention them again or say they "retired" them. That doesn't necessarily mean the ships are sent out to pasture, mothballed or sent to the breakers; it may mean they've been sold or leased to another cruise company. So we set out in chase of recently familiar ships, the vintage vessels that are changing hands rapidly these days because of the 1997 SOLAS (Safety of Life at Sea) and IMO (International Maritime Organization) safety requirements that are difficult and expensive to implement. Here's where they were and what they were doing in mid-1997. To Be Continued...

Achille Lauro

This ship was little-known in the United States until the dramatic events on board in October 1985, when terrorists took control of the vessel as it was sailing between Suez and Alexandria, while most of the passengers were on an overland excursion, and killed an American passenger. The bad-luck ship was built as the *Willem Rhys* in Holland, with its keel laid in 1939 but the vessel not launched until 1946 and delivered in 1947, for service between Rotterdam and Indonesia. She sailed around the world with two-class service for Rotterdamsche Lloyd until she was sold to Flotta Lauro, renamed the *Achille Lauro*, and rebuilt in Palermo in 1965. The work was delayed by an explosion and fire. She made her first voyage under the new name in 1966, then suffered another fire in 1972 during a refit in Genoa. In 1975, she collided with the livestock carrier *Youssef* in the Dardenelles, which sank with the loss of one life (plus some of the livestock, presumably). In 1982 she was impounded in Tenerife because of unpaid repairs, and then laid up the following year. In 1984 she returned to Mediterranean service. Despite being engulfed in world-wide publicity after the terrorist attack, the ill-fated ship continued cruising for Lauro; by then the line was renamed *StarLauro*. We passed her in the Bosphorus Straits in the summer of 1990, rusty, weary, and listing heavily to port. A disastrous fire aboard when she was off the Horn of Africa in 1994 totally destroyed the ship. She sank as rescuing tugs came in sight of her.

American Adventurer

The kids' cruise line ship spent only a year in extra-heavy duty with high-density family cruises before returning to Genoa to revert to its previous identity as *CostaRiviera*.

Atlantic

The sturdy veteran of many kids cruises as one of Premier's Big Red Boats was sold to Mediterranean Shipping Cruises and now sails as the *Melody*.

Aurora I, Aurora II

Sold to Singapore-based Star Cruises to become the *MegaStar Taurus* and the *MegaStar Aries*.

Boheme

Once a popular budget cruise ship sailing the Caribbean. Since 1985, it's the *Freewinds*, owned by the Church of Scientology. According to insiders, members get a free cruise if they make a donation of $5000 to the church.

Britanis

At this writing, the beloved old American-built *Britanis* is no longer under U.S. government charter as offices and housing in Guantanamo Bay, Cuba. Instead, the ship is laid up.

Caribbean Prince

Now sailing as the *Wilderness Explorer* for Glacier Bay Tours and Cruises.

Carnivale/FiestaMarina

Carnival's short-lived *FiestaMarina* version of its longtime "fun ship" *Carnivale* directed at the Latin American market fizzled, despite the high-quality product, and with running mate *Mardi Gras* was sold to Epirotiki during another short-lived marketing agreement that ended with the Greek company, in effect, buying the two ships from Carnival. The ship now sails as the *Olympic*.

Constitution

The *Constitution* has been retired by American Hawaii, who said it would be too expensive to renovate the ship and bring it up to new SOLAS standards.

Crown Monarch

Now sailing in Asia as the *Nautica* for Singapore-based Cruise Lines International.

Cunard Countess

Sold to Awani Cruise Line of Indonesia for $23 million.

Cunard Crown Jewel

Sold to Singapore-based Star Cruises to become the *SuperStar Gemini*.

Cunard Dynasty

Sailed briefly as Majesty Cruise Lines' *Crown Majesty* before being leased to Norwegian Cruise Line as the *Norwegian Dynasty*.

Cunard Princess

Now sails as the *Rhapsody* for Mediterranean Shipping Cruises.

Danae

After being burned and scuttled in Venice harbor, the ship was resurrected as the *Baltica* for Sunshine Cruises (aka Greek-based Festival Shipping) and subsequently renamed *Danae Princess* by new operators Italia Cruise Lines.

Daphne

Sold to Swiss-run Leisure Cruises, a new company, for $11 million.

Dawn Princess

The former *Fairwind* for now-defunct Sitmar, the *Dawn Princess* reverted to Vlasov's V.Ships in Monaco, its former owners, and was leased to a German travel company, which renamed her *Albatros*, with one 's.'

Dolphin

Sold to a central Florida shipping company named Kosmas, a.k.a. Canaveral Cruise Line Inc., in July 1995, the vessel makes two-night cruises out of Port Canaveral.

Emerald Seas

Last seen sailing in the Mediterranean as the *Sapphire Seas*.

Enchanted Seas

Now sailing as the *Universe Explorer* for World Explorer Cruises.

EnricoCosta

Now sailing as the *Symphony* for Mediterranean Shipping Cruises.

EugenioCosta

Sold to Bremer Vulkan Shipyard for a 1997 delivery.

Fair Princess

After a potential sale to now-defunct Regency Cruises fell through, Princess towed the *Fair Princess*, the former *Fairsea*, to Mazatlan. The ship repositions to Australia to replace the *Fairstar*.

Festivale

The former Carnival ship is now sailing as Dolphin's *IslandBreeze*.

Kazakhstan II

Sold to Lady Lou/Sea Delphin Shipping Ltd. Malta. Renamed *Delphin* and registered in Malta.

Majestic

Leased by Premier Cruises to London-based CTC Cruises for a four-year period. Now sailing as the *Southern Cross*.

Mardi Gras

After being leased out for a year as *Pride of Galveston*, the ship was renamed *Apollo* by owner Epirotiki.

Mermoz

The ships remaining from the trio of cruise lines owned at the end of 1994 by the French-based Accor Group went to Costa but *Mermoz* was expected to be sold after the Carnival/Airtours takeover of Costa.

Monterey

It's been nearly five years now that the U.S.-built *Monterey* has been sailing as flagship of the former StarLauro Cruises, now Mediterranean Shipping Cruises. It was picked up at bank auction for a song by a Panamanian company called Cia Naviera Panocean SA in Honolulu after parent company Aloha Pacific filed for bankruptcy in 1989.

Nordic Prince

Sold by Royal Caribbean Cruises Ltd. in early 1995 to Airtours, a British travel company, who renamed it *Carousel*.

Ocean Islander

This trim, mid-sized vessel that sailed for Ocean Cruise Lines in Europe, the Caribbean and South America, is now the *Royal Star* for Star Line Cruises in Mombasa.

Ocean Princess

Ran aground and was badly damaged in South America in 1993; we had gone aboard her only a couple of days before in Rio. Two decks were partly flooded and she was declared a total loss. Ellice Navigation in Piraeus bought her and towed her to Greece, where she was reconstructed as the *Sea Prince*. A subsequent sale to Louis Cruise Line of Cyprus has netted still another new name—*Princesa Oceanica*.

Odessa

The recently refurbished vessel from Black Sea Shipping was impounded in Italy a year ago, joining a number of other Black Sea vessels being detained by creditors in various ports of the world.

Pearl, Pearl of Scandinavia, Ocean Pearl

Poor pitiful *Pearl* had a lot of names during her illustrious career. Most recently she was the *CostaPlaya*, marketing cruises to Cuba from the Dominican Republic, sold only to Europeans and Latin Americans by parent company Costa Crociere in Genoa to circumvent U.S. trading-with-the-enemy restrictions. But with the Carnival/Airtours takeover of Costa she's slated to be sold.

Royal Odyssey

The ship built as the *Royal Viking Sea* has been turned into the *Norwegian Star* sailing year-round from the port of Houston for Norwegian Cruise Line.

Royal Majesty

The flagship of Majesty Cruise Line was sold to Norwegian Cruise Line to become the *Norwegian Majesty*.

Sagafjord

Cunard decided to retire this prestigious and beloved ship after an engine room fire off the Philippines interrupted her 1996 world cruise. She had previously been scheduled to leave the fleet at the end of her 1996 Alaska season. Now she sails as the *Saga Rose* for Saga Holidays.

Sea Princess

The *Sea Princess* was renamed *Victoria* in mid-1995, in order to free the name for a new Princess ship due in 1998.

Song of Norway

Sold to Britains's Airtours, who previously bought its former RCCL running mate *Nordic Prince*. Now sails as the *Sundream*.

Southward

The longtime Norwegian Cruise Line vessel was sold to Airtours to become the *Seawing* for the British-based travel company. See Airtours.

Star Princess

Transferred to P & O to become the *Arcadia*, replacing the *Canberra* in late 1997.

Starward

The last of the Norwegian Cruise Line "white ships" to leave the fleet, the *Starward* has been turned into the *Bolero* for Greek-based Festival Shipping's Azur-Bolero Cruises.

The Victoria

Now at Louis Cruise Line in Cyprus as the *Princesa Victoria*.

Universe

The doughty old *Universe*, which served for years as the Semester-at-Sea ship and made summer Alaska sailings for World Explorer Cruises, was sent to the breakers. She has been replaced by the *Universe Explorer*, the former *Enchanted Seas*.

Vasco De Gama

The schizophrenic, dual-named vessel—its other monicker and present legal name is *Seawind Crown*—was finally officially renamed and able to sail under only one name. Today it's part of the Cruise Holdings family of vintage vessels.

World Renaissance

Sold in August 1995, by Epirotiki (it was the line's flagship) to an Indonesian travel company.

THE RATINGS

A GUIDE TO THE GUIDE

The main body of this book is a thorough compilation of cruise lines, ships and alternative cruises around the world, with 184 ships reviewed, plus details on dozens of other smaller and alternative vessels.

The cruise companies—most are cruise lines but a few are marketing companies who represent various foreign cruise lines—are described first, in alphabetical order, and following each company's description the ships are then described individually or, in the case of identical sister vessels, in a group, but rated individually.

You may note in the book and even within certain segments of it information repeated several times, because we feel many readers will dip into the book at random rather than read it in sequence.

Eight Cruise Terms You May Meet for the First Time

1. **Repositioning**—When a vessel moves seasonally from one cruising area of the world to another, it makes a "positioning" or "repositioning" cruise; because the ship has to make the journey whether passengers are aboard or not, the cruises may be discounted, offer an eclectic and unusual itinerary or a lot of leisurely days at sea.

2. **Refit**—The redecoration or remodeling of a vessel, which can be in drydock (the ship above the waterlevel so hulls can be repainted) or wetdock (the ship in the water). "Soft furnishings" are all the upholstery, draperies, sheets, towels, tablecloths and so on. "Cosmetic" refits are sort of like face-lifts—they don't make the ship's life longer, just help her look a little fresher.

3. **The Jones Act**—The term commonly applied to the 1886 Passenger Service Act, an obscure turn-of-the-century passenger cabotage act designed to protect American shipping by not permitting any foreign-flag vessel to transport people between two points in the United States without calling at one or two foreign ports in between. Since there is very little American passenger shipping left, movement has been under way to strike out the antiquated law, but cargo shipping interests zealously protect it because they feel if it were struck down it would threaten their cargo shipping as well.

4. **U.S.-flag ship**—For a ship to qualify as a U.S.-flag vessel, it must have been built and registered in the United States, be staffed by a primarily or totally American

crew and never have been re-flagged to another country. The only exception to this rule was made in 1979 by Congress for American Hawaii's *Independence*, which lost its U.S. flag when it was sold to a Hong Kong shipping company. See American Hawaii Cruises, page 223.

5.   **Flags of convenience**—A euphemism for ship registrations made in Panama, Liberia, the Bahamas, Cyprus and other nations with low ship taxes and non-hindering union requirements by ship owners who want to save money.

6.   **Cruise-only**—The fare quoted is for the cruise itself and does not provide an air transfer from your home town to the port where you board the ship. You're responsible for getting yourself to the port on time, and getting yourself back home afterwards.

7.   **Air add-ons**—Usually extra fees added on top of a cruise fare that may (or sometimes may not) already include some airfares. The usual routine is to book an air/ sea package through the cruise line whenever it's available since the airfare will usually be lower than you could negotiate on your own. But some travelers want to use frequent flyer awards or fly a specific airline or upgrade to business or first class. While upscale lines may offer this option in their air add-ons, the normal cruise line is going to fly you in the cheapest seats on the most inconvenient schedule that can be blocked out. They don't like it; you don't like it. They're at the mercy of the air carriers, and that's why you don't get your air tickets until a few days before you leave on your cruise.

8.   **Meet-and-greets**—These are land-based employees of the cruise line who do all the gathering up and shuttling of passengers between the airport and the ship. They are usually in a uniform of some sort and always carry a sign or clipboard with the name of your cruise line or ship on it. When you see them, check to make sure they have your name on their clipboard list or you may not get a seat on the bus that will take you to the ship.

Eight Things to Remember

1.   **Report Card**—the ratings for ship cabins, food and entertainment based on the way your high school English teacher used to grade your book reports.

2.   **Average Price PPPD**—the average per person per day price, based on double occupancy, for the cruise ship cabin under review.

3.   **The Bottom Line**—Personal observations and ruminations about the vessel or cruise line under review.

4.   **GRT**—Gross Registered Tonnage, not a ship's weight, but rather a measurement of a ship's enclosed cubic space which tallies all revenue-producing areas aboard for the purpose of harbor dues.

5.   **Passengers—Cabins Full**—the maximum number of passengers aboard if all the beds, including upper berths, are filled.

6.   **Passengers—2/Cabin**—The normal complement of passengers with two passengers to each cabin.

7.   **PSR**—Passenger Space Ratio, a figure reached by dividing the number of passengers carried into the Gross Registered Tonnage, which gives a general idea of how much total enclosed space is available for each passenger; a sort of seagoing comfort index.

8.   **Seating**—The number of meal seatings per evening; most ships have two seatings, a first, early or main seating, and a second or late seating. When there is a single seating, passengers often have some latitude in arrival time, unlike two seatings, which require on-time arrival.

SHIPS BY ALPHABETICAL LISTING
The Ratings

Fielding invented the star ratings system for cruise ships in 1981. Today our ratings are key indicators to a ship's quality of experience and value. Our ratings should not be confused with the ratings created by Fodor's, Frommer's, Berlitz or other guides who attempt to emulate this book. Also beware of self-appointed star ratings by a cruise line or out-of-date listings posted by other publications.

We have been aboard all the rated ships without asterisks in the following pages, and the ratings reflect our personal opinion of the ship and the cruise experience it offers.

Asterisks after the ship's name represent ships that are in transition from one company to another, which we have been aboard in the vessel's earlier life, or new vessels that are sister ships to existing, already inspected vessels due to come on line in 1998.

Anchor ratings reflect a cruise experience that was enriching and rewarding aboard an adventure, expedition, river or coastal vessel where the pleasure of the journey far exceeds the physical quality of the cruise vessel. A few ocean-going ships that offer expedition and educational sailings will carry both star and anchor ratings.

Unrated ships are those the authors have not been aboard in the ship's present incarnation, most of them new ships not yet on line.

★★★★★★   The ultimate cruise experience

★★★★★   A very special cruise experience

★★★★   A high quality cruise experience

★★★   An average cruise experience

★★   If you're on a budget and not fussy

★   A sinking ship

Ship	Rating	Page
Adriana	**Unrated**	587
Aegean I	**Unrated**	702
Amazing Grace	**Unrated**	898
Ambasador I	★★, ⚓⚓⚓⚓	590
American Queen	⚓⚓⚓⚓	398
Americana	★★★	524
Arcadia	★★★★	610
Ausonia	★★★	446
Azur	★★★	450
Bali Sea Dancer	★★★, ⚓⚓⚓	438
Black Prince	★★★	454
Black Watch*	★★★★	458
Bolero	★★★	462
Bremen	★★★★★, ⚓⚓⚓⚓⚓	488
Caledonian Star	★★★, ⚓⚓⚓⚓⚓	842
Canadian Empress	⚓⚓⚓⚓	791
Carnival Destiny	★★★★★	253
Carnival Triumph*	★★★★★	253
Carousel*	★★★	175
Celebration	★★★	258
Century	★★★★★	283
Clipper Adventurer	**Unrated**	303
Club Med 1	★★★	308
Club Med 2	★★★	308
CostaAllegra	★★★★	326
CostaClassica	★★★★★	332
CostaMarina	★★★★	326
CostaRiviera	★★	338
CostaRomantica	★★★★★	332
CostaVictoria	★★★★★	342
Crown Princess	★★★★★	640
Crystal Harmony	★★★★★★	353
Crystal Symphony	★★★★★★	353
Dawn Princess	★★★★★	646
Delphin	★★★★	388
Delta Queen	⚓⚓⚓⚓	403
Disney Magic	**Unrated**	415
Disney Wonder	**Unrated**	415

Ship	Rating	Page
Dolphin IV	★★	244
Ecstasy	★★★★★	264
Elation*	★★★★★	264
Enchanted Isle	★★	316
Enchantment of the Seas*	★★★★★	716
Europa	**Unrated**	492
Executive Explorer	⚓⚓⚓	475
Explorer	★★, ⚓⚓⚓⚓	168
Fantasy	★★★★★	264
Fantome	⚓⚓⚓	900
Fascination	★★★★★	264
Flying Cloud	⚓⚓⚓	900
Funchal	★★	465
Galaxy	★★★★★	283
Grand Princess	**Unrated**	651
Grande Caribe	⚓⚓⚓	216
Grande Mariner	⚓⚓⚓	216
Grandeur of the Seas	★★★★★	716
Hanseatic	★★★★★, ⚓⚓⚓⚓	673
Holiday	★★★	258
Horizon	★★★★★	289
Imagination	★★★★★	264
Independence	★★★	228
Inspiration	★★★★★	264
IslandBreeze	★★	423
Island Princess	★★★	653
Jubilee	★★★	258
Kristina Regina	**Unrated**	468
Leeward	★★★★	582
Legacy	⚓⚓⚓	900
Legend of the Seas	★★★★★	716
Maasdam	★★★★★	500
Majesty of the Seas	★★★★	724
Mandalay	⚓⚓⚓	900
Marco Polo	★★★★	601
Mayan Prince	⚓⚓⚓	216
MegaStar Aries	★★★★	870
MegaStar Taurus	★★★★	870

Ship	Rating	Page
Melody*	★★★	530
Mercury*	★★★★★	283
Minerva	⚓⚓⚓⚓	886
Mississippi Queen	⚓⚓⚓⚓	407
Monarch of the Seas	★★★★	724
Monterey*	★★★	533
Nantucket Clipper	⚓⚓⚓⚓	298
Niagara Prince	⚓⚓⚓	216
Nieuw Amsterdam	★★★★	506
Noordam	★★★★	506
Nordic Empress	★★★★	730
Norway	★★★★	548
Norwegian Crown	★★★★	554
Norwegian Dream (Dreamward)	★★★★★	558
Norwegian Dynasty	★★★★	563
Norwegian Majesty	★★★★	567
Norwegian Sea	★★★	572
Norwegian Star	★★★★	577
Norwegian Wind (Windward)	★★★★★	558
OceanBreeze	★★★	427
Oceanic Odyssey	★★★★	442
Odysseus	★★★	769
Olympic	★★	754
Oriana	★★★★★	615
Orpheus	★★	758
Pacific Princess	★★★	653
Paradise*	★★★★★	264
Paul Gauguin	**Unrated**	677
Polaris	★★★, ⚓⚓⚓⚓	847
Polynesia	⚓⚓⚓	900
Queen Elizabeth 2	★★★★★	366
Queen of the West	⚓⚓⚓	238
Radisson Diamond	★★★★★★	680
Regal Empress	★★	694
Regal Princess	★★★★★	640
Renaissance V–VIII	★★★★	705
Rhapsody of the Seas	★★★★★	716
Rhapsody*	★★★	536

Ship	Rating	Page
Rotterdam VI	**Unrated**	512
Royal Princess	★★★★★	657
Royal Star	★★★	594
Royal Viking Sun	★★★★★★	372
Ryndam	★★★★★	500
Saga Rose	★★★★	783
Sea Bird	★★, ⚓⚓⚓⚓	851
Seabourn Legend	★★★★★★	800
Seabourn Pride	★★★★★★	800
Seabourn Spirit	★★★★★★	800
SeaBreeze	★★★	432
Sea Cloud	★★★★, ⚓⚓⚓⚓⚓	805
Sea Goddess I	★★★★★★	377
Sea Goddess II	★★★★★★	377
Sea Lion	★★, ⚓⚓⚓⚓	851
Sea Princess*	★★★★★	646
Seawind Crown	★★★★	814
Seawing*	★★★	178
Sensation	★★★★★	264
Silver Cloud	★★★★★★	823
Silver Wind	★★★★★★	823
Sir Francis Drake	⚓⚓⚓⚓	891
Sky Princess	★★★★	663
Song of America	★★★	735
Song of Flower	★★★★★★	685
Sovereign of the Seas	★★★★	739
Spirit of '98	⚓⚓⚓⚓⚓	207
Spirit of Alaska	⚓⚓⚓⚓	191
Spirit of Columbia	⚓⚓⚓⚓	191
Spirit of Discovery	⚓⚓⚓⚓	196
Spirit of Endeavour	⚓⚓⚓⚓⚓	200
Spirit of Glacier Bay	⚓⚓⚓	204
Splendour of the Seas	★★★★★	716
Star Aquarius	★★★	874
Star Clipper	★★★★	862
Star Flyer	★★★★	862
Star Pisces	★★★	874
Star/Ship Oceanic	★★★	628

Ship	Rating	Page
Statendam	★★★★★	500
Stella Oceanis	★★★	773
Stella Solaris	★★★	777
Sun Princess	★★★★★	646
Sun Viking	★★	743
Sundream*	★★★	181
SuperStar Capricorn	★★★	877
SuperStar Gemini	★★★★	880
Swedish Islander	⚓⚓⚓	856
Symphony*	★★★	539
Triton	★★	762
Tropicale	★★★	272
Universe Explorer	★★, ⚓⚓⚓	923
Veendam	★★★★★	500
Victoria	★★★★	619
Viking Serenade	★★★★	747
Vision of the Seas*	★★★★★	716
Vistafjord	★★★★★	381
Westerdam	★★★★	515
Wilderness Adventurer	⚓⚓⚓	479
Wilderness Explorer	⚓⚓⚓	483
Wind Song	★★★★★	912
Wind Spirit	★★★★★	912
Wind Star	★★★★★	912
Wind Surf	★★★★★	917
World Discoverer	★★★, ⚓⚓⚓⚓⚓	833
Yankee Clipper	⚓⚓⚓	900
Yorktown Clipper	⚓⚓⚓⚓	298
Zenith	★★★★★	289

SHIPS BY RATING

Rating	Ship	Page
★★★★★★	Crystal Harmony	353
★★★★★★	Crystal Symphony	353
★★★★★★	Radisson Diamond	680
★★★★★★	Royal Viking Sun	372
★★★★★★	Sea Goddess I	377
★★★★★★	Sea Goddess II	377
★★★★★★	Seabourn Legend	800
★★★★★★	Seabourn Pride	800
★★★★★★	Seabourn Spirit	800
★★★★★★	Silver Cloud	823
★★★★★★	Silver Wind	823
★★★★★★	Song of Flower	685
★★★★★, ⚓⚓⚓⚓⚓	Bremen	488
★★★★★	Carnival Destiny	253
★★★★★	Carnival Triumph*	253
★★★★★	Century	283
★★★★★	CostaClassica	332
★★★★★	CostaRomantica	332
★★★★★	CostaVictoria	342
★★★★★	Crown Princess	640
★★★★★	Dawn Princess	646
★★★★★	Ecstasy	264
★★★★★	Elation*	264
★★★★★	Enchantment of the Seas*	716
★★★★★	Fantasy	264
★★★★★	Fascination	264
★★★★★	Galaxy	283

Rating	Ship	Page
★★★★★	Grandeur of the Seas	716
★★★★★, ⚓⚓⚓⚓⚓	Hanseatic	673
★★★★★	Horizon	289
★★★★★	Imagination	264
★★★★★	Inspiration	264
★★★★★	Legend of the Seas	716
★★★★★	Maasdam	500
★★★★★	Mercury*	283
★★★★★	Norwegian Dream (Dreamward)	558
★★★★★	Norwegian Wind (Windward)	558
★★★★★	Oriana	615
★★★★★	Paradise*	264
★★★★★	Queen Elizabeth 2	366
★★★★★	Regal Princess	640
★★★★★	Rhapsody of the Seas	716
★★★★★	Royal Princess	657
★★★★★	Ryndam	500
★★★★★	Sea Princess*	646
★★★★★	Sensation	264
★★★★★	Splendour of the Seas	716
★★★★★	Statendam	500
★★★★★	Sun Princess	646
★★★★★	Veendam	500
★★★★★	Vision of the Seas*	716
★★★★★	Vistafjord	381
★★★★★	Wind Song	912
★★★★★	Wind Spirit	912
★★★★★	Wind Star	912
★★★★★	Wind Surf	917
★★★★★	Zenith	289
★★★★	Arcadia	610
★★★★	Black Watch*	458
★★★★	CostaAllegra	326
★★★★	CostaMarina	326
★★★★	Delphin	388
★★★★	Leeward	582
★★★★	Majesty of the Seas	724
★★★★	Marco Polo	601

Rating	Ship	Page
★★★★	*MegaStar Aries*	870
★★★★	*MegaStar Taurus*	870
★★★★	*Monarch of the Seas*	724
★★★★	*Nieuw Amsterdam*	506
★★★★	*Noordam*	506
★★★★	*Nordic Empress*	730
★★★★	*Norway*	548
★★★★	*Norwegian Crown*	554
★★★★	*Norwegian Dynasty*	563
★★★★	*Norwegian Majesty*	567
★★★★	*Norwegian Star*	577
★★★★	*Oceanic Odyssey*	442
★★★★	*Renaissance V–VIII*	705
★★★★	*Saga Rose*	783
★★★★, ⚓⚓⚓⚓	*Sea Cloud*	805
★★★★	*Seawind Crown*	814
★★★★	*Sky Princess*	663
★★★★	*Sovereign of the Seas*	739
★★★★	*Star Clipper*	862
★★★★	*Star Flyer*	862
★★★★	*SuperStar Gemini*	880
★★★★	*Victoria*	619
★★★★	*Viking Serenade*	747
★★★★	*Westerdam*	515
★★★	*Americana*	524
★★★	*Ausonia*	446
★★★	*Azur*	450
★★★, ⚓⚓⚓	Bali Sea Dancer	438
★★★	*Black Prince*	454
★★★	*Bolero*	462
★★★, ⚓⚓⚓⚓	Caledonian Star	842
★★★	*Carousel**	175
★★★	*Celebration*	258
★★★	*Club Med 1*	308
★★★	*Club Med 2*	308
★★★	*Holiday*	258
★★★	*Independence*	228
★★★	*Island Princess*	653

Rating	Ship	Page
★★★	Jubilee	258
★★★	Melody*	530
★★★	Monterey*	533
★★★	Norwegian Sea	572
★★★	OceanBreeze	427
★★★	Odysseus	769
★★★	Pacific Princess	653
★★★, ⚓⚓⚓⚓	Polaris	847
★★★	Rhapsody*	536
★★★	Royal Star	594
★★★	SeaBreeze	432
★★★	Seawing*	178
★★★	Song of America	735
★★★	Star Aquarius	874
★★★	Star Pisces	874
★★★	Star/Ship Oceanic	628
★★★	Stella Oceanis	773
★★★	Stella Solaris	777
★★★	Sundream*	181
★★★	SuperStar Capricorn	877
★★★	Symphony*	539
★★★	Tropicale	272
★★★, ⚓⚓⚓⚓⚓	World Discoverer	833
★★, ⚓⚓⚓⚓	Ambasador I	590
★★	CostaRiviera	338
★★	Dolphin IV	244
★★	Enchanted Isle	316
★★, ⚓⚓⚓⚓⚓	Explorer	168
★★	Funchal	465
★★	IslandBreeze	423
★★	Olympic	754
★★	Orpheus	758
★★	Regal Empress	694
★★, ⚓⚓⚓⚓	Sea Bird	851
★★, ⚓⚓⚓⚓	Sea Lion	851
★★	Sun Viking	743
★★	Triton	762
★★, ⚓⚓⚓	Universe Explorer	923

Rating	Ship	Page
Specialty Ships		
⚓⚓⚓⚓	American Queen	398
⚓⚓⚓⚓⚓, ★★★★★	Bremen	488
⚓⚓⚓⚓⚓, ★★★	Caledonian Star	842
⚓⚓⚓⚓⚓	Delta Queen	403
⚓⚓⚓⚓⚓, ★★	Explorer	168
⚓⚓⚓⚓⚓, ★★★★★	Hanseatic	673
⚓⚓⚓⚓⚓	Minerva	886
⚓⚓⚓⚓⚓	Mississippi Queen	407
⚓⚓⚓⚓⚓	Nantucket Clipper	298
⚓⚓⚓⚓⚓, ★★★	Polaris	847
⚓⚓⚓⚓⚓, ★★★★	Sea Cloud	805
⚓⚓⚓⚓⚓	Spirit of '98	207
⚓⚓⚓⚓⚓	Spirit of Endeavour	200
⚓⚓⚓⚓⚓, ★★★	World Discoverer	833
⚓⚓⚓⚓⚓	Yorktown Clipper	298
⚓⚓⚓⚓, ★★	Ambasador I	590
⚓⚓⚓⚓, ★★★	Bali Sea Dancer	438
⚓⚓⚓⚓	Canadian Empress	791
⚓⚓⚓⚓	Executive Explorer	475
⚓⚓⚓⚓	Fantome	900
⚓⚓⚓⚓	Flying Cloud	900
⚓⚓⚓⚓	Grande Caribe	216
⚓⚓⚓⚓	Grande Mariner	216
⚓⚓⚓⚓	Legacy	900
⚓⚓⚓⚓	Mandalay	900
⚓⚓⚓⚓	Mayan Prince	216
⚓⚓⚓⚓	Niagara Prince	216
⚓⚓⚓⚓	Polynesia	900
⚓⚓⚓⚓	Queen of the West	238
⚓⚓⚓⚓, ★★	Sea Bird	851
⚓⚓⚓⚓, ★★	Sea Lion	851
⚓⚓⚓⚓	Sir Francis Drake	891
⚓⚓⚓⚓	Spirit of Alaska	191
⚓⚓⚓⚓	Spirit of Columbia	191
⚓⚓⚓⚓	Spirit of Discovery	196
⚓⚓⚓⚓	Swedish Islander	856
⚓⚓⚓⚓	Yankee Clipper	900

Rating	Ship	Page
⚓⚓⚓	*Spirit of Glacier Bay*	*204*
⚓⚓⚓, ★★	*Universe Explorer*	*923*
⚓⚓⚓	*Wilderness Adventurer*	*479*
⚓⚓⚓	*Wilderness Explorer*	*483*
	Unrated Ships	
Unrated	*Adriana*	*587*
Unrated	*Aegean I*	*702*
Unrated	*Amazing Grace*	*898*
Unrated	*Clipper Adventurer*	*303*
Unrated	*Disney Magic*	*415*
Unrated	*Disney Wonder*	*415*
Unrated	*Europa*	*492*
Unrated	*Grand Princess*	*651*
Unrated	*Kristina Regina*	*468*
Unrated	*Paul Gauguin*	*677*
Unrated	*Rotterdam VI*	*512*

THE BEST OF 1998

★★★★★★
The Six-Star Ships

Fantasy suites like the Crystal Penthouse aboard the **Crystal Symphony** *exemplify the six-star cruising experience.*

The Dazzling Dozen, the Top Cruise Experiences for 1998

Ultra-deluxe vessels with sophisticated cuisine, excellent service, far-reaching and imaginative itineraries, and a highly satisfying overall cruise experience.

Crystal Harmony	**Crystal Cruises**	*page 353*
Crystal Symphony	**Crystal Cruises**	*page 353*
Radisson Diamond	**Radisson Seven Seas Cruises**	*page 680*
Royal Viking Sun	**Cunard Line**	*page 372*
Seabourn Legend	**Seabourn Cruises**	*page 800*
Seabourn Pride	**Seabourn Cruises**	*page 800*
Seabourn Spirit	**Seabourn Cruises**	*page 800*

Sea Goddess I	**Cunard Line**	*page 377*
Sea Goddess II	**Cunard Line**	*page 377*
Silver Cloud	**Silversea Cruises**	*page 823*
Silver Wind	**Silversea Cruises**	*page 823*
Song of Flower	**Radisson Seven Seas Cruises**	*page 685*

The Five-Star Ships

Carnival's newer ships, such as the Carnival Destiny *above, are an example of how cruise lines are consistently turning out a quality product.*

Stylish, comfortable ships, each vessel or class with its own distinct personality catering to a variety of different audiences with a high overall quality in its price range.

Carnival Destiny	**Carnival Cruise Lines**	*page 253*
Carnival Triumph	**Carnival Cruise Lines**	*page 253*
Century	**Celebrity Cruises**	*page 283*
CostaClassica	**Costa Cruises**	*page 332*
CostaRomantica	**Costa Cruises**	*page 332*
CostaVictoria	**Costa Cruises**	*page 342*
Crown Princess	**Princess Cruises**	*page 640*
Dawn Princess	**Princess Cruises**	*page 646*
Ecstasy	**Carnival Cruise Lines**	*page 264*
Elation	**Carnival Cruise Lines**	*page 264*
Enchantment of the Seas	**Royal Caribbean International**	*page 716*

Fantasy	**Carnival Cruise Lines**	*page 264*
Fascination	**Carnival Cruise Lines**	*page 264*
Galaxy	**Celebrity Cruises**	*page 283*
Grandeur of the Seas	**Royal Caribbean International**	*page 716*
Hanseatic	**Radisson Seven Seas Cruises**	*page 673*
Horizon	**Celebrity Cruises**	*page 289*
Imagination	**Carnival Cruise Lines**	*page 264*
Inspiration	**Carnival Cruise Lines**	*page 264*
Legend of the Seas	**Royal Caribbean International**	*page 716*
Maasdam	**Holland America Line**	*page 500*
Mercury	**Celebrity Cruises**	*page 283*
Norwegian Dream	**Norwegian Cruise Line**	*page 558*
Norwegian Wind	**Norwegian Cruise Line**	*page 558*
Oriana	**P & O Cruises**	*page 615*
Paradise	**Carnival Cruise Lines**	*page 264*
Queen Elizabeth 2	**Cunard Line**	*page 366*
Rhapsody of the Seas	**Royal Caribbean International**	*page 716*
Regal Princess	**Princess Cruises**	*page 640*
Royal Princess	**Princess Cruises**	*page 657*
Ryndam	**Holland America Line**	*page 500*
Sensation	**Carnival Cruise Lines**	*page 264*
Splendour of the Seas	**Royal Caribbean International**	*page 716*
Statendam	**Holland America Line**	*page 500*
Sun Princess	**Princess Cruises**	*page 646*
Veendam	**Holland America Line**	*page 500*
Vision of the Seas	**Royal Caribbean International**	*page 716*
Vistafjord	**Cunard Line**	*page 381*
Wind Song	**Windstar Cruises**	*page 912*
Wind Spirit	**Windstar Cruises**	*page 912*
Wind Star	**Windstar Cruises**	*page 912*
Wind Surf	**Windstar Cruises**	*page 917*
Zenith	**Celebrity Cruises**	*page 289*

Ten Best Buys at Sea

The Sun Terrace dining rooms aboard the Norwegian Dream *and* Norwegian Wind *are airy and multilevel.*

Delta Queen Steamboat Company	*American Queen*	A warm and richly rewarding experience in Americana in **a floating Victorian bed-and-breakfast**.
Carnival	*Fleet*	Providing a big, splashy **Las Vegas/theme park experience for the whole family** at affordable prices.
Celebrity	*Fleet*	Offering the finest cruise ship food and service in handsome, tasteful surroundings at an excellent value, **the best large-ship buy afloat**.
Norwegian Cruise Line	*Norwegian Dream* *Norwegian Wind*	Well-designed ships with a feeling of **intimate spaces in sophisticated surroundings** for young to middle-aged couples and singles.
Holland America Line	*Fleet*	**The most beautiful traditional cruise ships at sea**, a solid value for the money with tasty, imaginatively served food and warm friendly service, classy and classic.
Orient Lines	*Marco Polo*	A vintage vessel with **great itineraries, excellent food**, a chic, art deco style—and the price is right.

Royal Caribbean International	*Nordic Empress*	An **outstanding short-cruise experience** for first-time cruisers because of a tactful and caring staff that make you feel at ease.
Silverseas	*Fleet*	Looks expensive until you **see what you get for your money**, with airfare, all beverages and tips included.
Radisson Seven Seas Cruises	*Song of Flower*	Everybody's favorite little luxury ship with everything included in a base fare, **the best small-ship buy afloat.**
Alaska Sightseeing/ Cruise West	*Spirit of '98*	A replica turn-of-the-century coastal steamer with **an all-American staff and home-cooked cuisine**, giving a great close-up look at Alaska and the Northwest.

Best Ships for Families with Kids

Play areas such as those aboard the **Disney Magic** *make the new Disney Cruise Line more appealing to families.*

Disney Cruise Line	*Disney Magic*	The biggest name in family fun debuts March 12, 1998.
Premier Cruise Lines	*Oceanic*	Premier goes on sailing with a new owner and one Big Red Boat.
Royal Caribbean	*Grandeur of the Seas*	Teens have their own disco and younger kids their own Club Ocean playroom.

Carnival Cruise Lines	*Holiday*	A $1 million "virtual reality" room, great for teens and preteens.
Princess Cruises	*Sun Princess* *Dawn Princess*	The Fun Zone for kids and Cyberspace for teens is super.
P&O Cruises	*Oriana*	The biggest and most complete kids area at sea.

Going to Extremes: Top Adventure Vessels

Passengers aboard the **World Discoverer** *go birdwatching in a Zodiac.*

Marine Expeditions	*Fleet*	To the ends of the earth with the basic comforts but not many frills.
Esplanade Tours Spice Islands Cruises	*Bali Sea Dancer*	Familiar to expeditioners as the *Illiria*, a small comfortable vessel sailing from Bali to Komodo these days.
Hapag-Lloyd	*Bremen*	The former *Frontier Spirit*, a purpose-built expedition ship that goes from the Arctic to the Antarctic and points in between.
Special Expeditions	*Caledonian Star*	A comfortable, homey ship that sails from Bodrum to the British Isles and Spitsbergen.
Abercrombie & Kent	*Explorer*	The original expedition cruise ship that pioneered China and the Antarctic and made the first passenger transit of the Northwest Passage.

Radisson Seven Seas Cruises	*Hanseatic*	Newest and most elegant of the expeditioners with music at teatime and the probable speed record for the Northwest Passage transit.
Quark Expeditions	*Kapitans Dranitsyn, Khlebnikov et al*	Russian icebreakers that crunch their way around the Antarctic or up to the North Pole.
Special Expeditions	*Polaris*	A sturdy, comfortable, unpretentious vessel is based year-round in the Galapagos Islands.
Society Expeditions	*World Discoverer*	Another expedition champion that has garnered a lot of records on its worldwide wandering.

The Most Romantic Ships at Sea

Sea Goddess I offers elegant touches with its afternoon tea service.

Cunard	*Sea Goddess I* *Sea Goddess II*	Unfettered, laissez-faire cruise with a few like-minded romantics looking to **rekindle romance or launch a love affair**. Take your lover along with you, however, since the ships rarely carry single passengers; recommended for couples only.

Silversea	*Silver Cloud* *Silver Wind*	Larger than Sea Goddess, so there's more anonymity if you really want to hide out. They also offer **those lovely private balconies** the Sea Goddess ships don't have. Couples are best, but there have been a few unattached males and females on both sailings we've made.
Windstar Cruises	*Wind Star* *Wind Song* *Wind Spirit* *Wind Surf*	Attract a lot of handsome couples of all ages, but the **romance here comes from the sails**, from sitting alone together on the big gray-and-yellow cushions on the stern deck in the dark in the balmy tropical breezes.
Norwegian Cruise Line	*Norway*	The former *France* from the great French Line of the 1960s still reverts to her ocean liner romance when she makes her summer sailings in France. **Young couples could get caught up in the lushly romantic art deco atmosphere. Great for honeymooners who splurge on a top cabin.**
Sea Cloud Cruises	*Sea Cloud*	Romantic in every sense of the word, particularly if you've booked one of the two owner's suites, where cereal heiress Marjorie Merriweather Post and her husband E.F. Hutton sequestered themselves (separately) in lavish 1930s splendor. If you're stuck in one of the newer, cheaper, smaller cabins, spend your free time **cuddled together on the big, blue-cushioned "blue lagoon" on the fantail**.
Costa Cruises	*CostaRomantica*	The name doesn't hurt but the spare and elegant suites with private verandas that are named after operas are among the most romantic digs at sea. Burled brierwood furniture and cabinetry, gauzy white bedroom, **an electronically operated floor-to-ceiling window shade for total privacy, plus a large whirlpool tub, discreet butler service,** terry-cloth robes and reclining deck chairs on the veranda. Yes!

Outer Space: The Sweetest Suites at Sea

The new duplex penthouses aboard the Vistafjord *include a private veranda with outdoor whirlpool.*

Cunard	*Vistafjord*	Offers a pair of dazzling, duplex penthouses complete with private sauna, outdoor hot tub on private veranda, two marble bathrooms with Jacuzzi tubs, wet bar and treadmill for a morning workout.
Crystal	*Crystal Symphony*	Two Crystal Penthouses, separate living rooms, dining area, large private veranda, big walk-in closets, extra guest half-bath, wet bar, Jacuzzi tub, lovely cabinetry.
Royal Caribbean International	*Legend of the Seas and her five sisters*	The Royal Suite has a huge white piano dominating one corner of a spacious living room, green marble compartmented bathroom, wet bar, long private veranda, full entertainment center—drop-dead gorgeous.
Holland America	*Maasdam Ryndam Statendam Veendam*	A single huge owner's suite on each ship has a wide private veranda, separate living room, dining room and bedroom, huge walk-in closet, compartmented bath, butler pantry to have meals prepared in suite.

)

Princess Cruises	Royal Princess	The Royal and the Princess Suites have big elegant marble bathrooms, wide veranda, light, bright and airy, handsomely furnished.
Princess Cruises	Dawn Princess Sun Princess	Spacious suites with private balcony, bedroom, living room, dining area and huge divided bath with stall shower and Jacuzzi tub.

Splashy Ships for Watersports

The platforms aboard the Club Med ships show their emphasis on watersports.

American Canadian Caribbean Line	Fleet	These ships have bow-landing capacity that lets swimmers and snorkelers disembark on a tropical island anywhere by walking down the steps.
Fred. Olson Line	Black Prince	Its Marina Park extends from the stern of the ship at anchor with teak decks, enclosed swimming pool and watersports galore.
Club Med	Club Med 1 and 2	Has a similar watersports platform sans pool.
Norwegian Cruise Line	Fleet	Offers a super Dive-In Program.
Seabourn Cruises	Fleet	Watersports platform with pool.
Sea Goddess Cruises	I & II	Watersports platform sans pool.
Windstar Cruises	Fleet	Watersports platform.

Best Ships for Singles

The pool deck on Royal Caribbean's Sovereign of the Seas *is a popular place for people to meet.*

Under 30	Windjammer Barefoot Cruises	Try the special Singles Sailings that promise equality between the sexes.
Females Under 30	Carnival Cruise Lines	These ships attract a lot of single guys under 30.
30-50	Royal Caribbean International	A good mainstream place to meet.
Females 30-40	Norwegian Cruise Line	Lots of great-looking guys in the sports bars watching The Game; just don't stand between them and the screen.
Women 50-up	Crystal Cruises Cunard Line	Dancing hosts, dress-up evenings and live music almost around the clock.
Men 50-up	Crystal Cruises Cunard Line	Try being a dancing host. See Everything You Ever Wanted to Know About Social Hosts, page 56.
Over 70	Ivaran's *Americana*	Inexpensive single cabins and no upper age limits.

Three Most Off-the-Wall Onboard Events

Toga Night on Costa Cruises solves the what to wear dilemma.

Costa Cruises	Toga Night	Virtually everyone on board dons a custom-made toga (with or without street clothes under them) and makes like Messalina and Claudius.
Tall Ship Adventures' *Sir Francis Drake*	BLT night	Everyone dons buccaneer, lingerie or toga, including the captain.
Carnival	Men's Knobby Knees Contests	Men model their best knee-revealing outfits, or roll up their pants legs.

Three Best Theme Buffets at Sea

Crystal	Both Ships	Italian deck buffet
Cunard's	*Royal Viking Sun*	Norwegian seafood buffet
Cunard's	*Vistafjord*	The Bavarian Brunch

The Best Cruise Lines For Buffets

The breakfast buffet aboard Holland America's Maasdam *is an example of the consistently high service they provide.*

Holland America Line	Consistently the best day-in, day-out Lido food service.
Celebrity Cruises	The prettiest arrangements and most convenient layouts, plus wine by the glass on a rolling cart.
Crystal Cruises	Outstanding special theme buffets and great deck grills.
Cunard's *Sea Goddess*	Imaginative deck food.
American Hawaii Cruises	Its deli counter and food court options are crowd-pleasers.

Best Floating Dining Rooms

Besides serving the finest food at sea, each of the following ship dining rooms has additional special qualities.

Radisson Seven Seas	*Radisson Diamond*	The prettiest: The Grand Dining Room
Radisson Seven Seas	*Song of Flower*	Best service
Cunard	*Sea Goddess I, Sea Goddess II*	Most convivial: The Dining Salon

Seabourn	Seabourn Legend, Seabourn Pride, Seabourn Spirit	The most-formal service
Cunard	Royal Viking Sun	Most-spacious dining room
Celebrity	Century	Grandest entrance

Best Alternative Restaurants

A sampling of the fare aboard the Vistafjord.

An alternative restaurant is an option to dine occasionally somewhere other than the ship's regular dining rooms, where you usually have assigned seating.

Radisson Seven Seas Cruises	Radisson Diamond	**An Evening at Don Vito's** where they serve up a delicious (and fun) all-Italian evening in a casual atmosphere.
	Song of Flower	**Angelino's** offers classic Northern Italian dishes for up to 30 guests.
Crystal Cruises	Crystal Symphony	**Prego Restaurant**, also Italian and very elegant.
Cunard	Vistafjord	**Tivoli Restaurant**, an intimate and romantic little Italian restaurant with candlelight.
	Royal Viking Sun	**Venezia** is a glamorous Italian addition to the mealtime options on the Sun.
Crystal Cruises	Crystal Harmony	**Kyoto Restaurant**, austere and Oriental, with spare decor and clean but simple dishes.

Best Spas at Sea

The Nautica spas aboard Carnival ships feature large whirlpools,well-equipped gyms and lots of glass.

Celebrity	*Century Galaxy Mercury*	The most innovative health, beauty and fitness centers afloat.
Carnival	*Carnival Destiny and Fantasy-class ships*	**Nautica Spa** offers 15,000 square feet of space, with a huge glass-walled gym and full-time instructors, aerobics room, beauty services, spas with skylights overhead.
NCL	*Norway*	**The Roman Spa and health and fitness centers** with lavish indoor pools like a Roman bath.
Cunard	*QE2*	The **Spa and Health and Fitness Center**, two decks of complete beauty and spa treatments, including a full thalassotherepy center.
Royal Caribbean International	*Legend of the Seas and her sisters*	**The Solariums**, with a glass canopy-covered pool, water jets, Roman marble everywhere.

Best Cruise Entertainment at Sea

Crystal Cruises	*Crystal Harmony* *Crystal Symphony*	**"Some Enchanted Evening,"** a magnificent performance staged on both ships, is the first authorized Rogers and Hammerstein production at sea.
Carnival	*Carnival Destiny*	**The new "Palladium,"** a spectacular three-deck show lounge, presents two dazzling new shows, **"Formidable" and "Nightclub Express,"** with flying scenery, fog and laser lights.
Princess Cruises	*Megaships*	**"Mystique,"** a sensational production set under the sea with 23 performers, including nine acrobats, has scenery that "grows" in front of your eyes. It's a knockout.
Norwegian Cruise Line	*Fleet*	Offers well-performed Broadway shows like "Crazy For You," "42nd Street," "George M" and "Pirates of Penzance" on the stages of its ships; the classic *Norway* has a particularly fine theater with balcony and orchestra seating.

Good Ships for First-Timers and Why

Budget

Dolphin Cruise Line	*OceanBreeze, IslandBreeze and SeaBreeze*	Clean, comfortable, affordable vintage vessels

Moderate

Seawind Cruise Line	*Seawind Crown*	Offers a good Southern Caribbean itinerary on a classic and comfortable ship that also carries some free land stays to extend your vacation.
Royal Caribbean International	*Nordic Empress*	Offers top-drawer surroundings, excellent entertainment and good food and service with tactful attention to first-timers.

Norwegian Cruise Line   *Fleet*   Dive-in and onboard sports programs, themed dinners and costume evenings on all ships add energy and direction to the overall experience.

The teak and tile pool deck of the Seawind Crown are a couple of the nice touches on this classic cruise ship.

Splurge

Radisson Seven Seas   *Radisson Diamond*   This twin-hulled ship is funny-looking to traditionalists, but it's great for first-time cruisers who want a top-drawer luxury sailing with space and stability.

Special Experiences at Sea

Passengers aboard American Hawaii Cruises learn the hula.

American Hawaii Cruises	Tells you everything you ever wanted to know about Hawaiian culture, tradition and legends—and teaches you to hula, make leis and play the ukulele besides.
Royal Olympic Cruises	Takes you around the Mediterranean on Greek Culture and Mythology 101 cruises that will have you reeling from the tragedies of the House of Atreus before you make a dent in your sunblock.
Swan Hellenic	Carries some of the most erudite and entertaining lecturers in the world. You can hobnob with them at mealtimes and cocktails.
World Explorer Cruises	Tells you more about Alaska than you could ever have imagined, with videos, films, lecturers, shore excursions and lots of ports of call in the 14-day cruise, plus a scholarly library that serves on the winter Semesters at Sea for college credit as well.

Maximizing Mini-Cruises

A jazz band from New Orleans performs aboard the Delta Queen.

For the Kids

Disney Cruise Line	*Disney Magic*	Port Canaveral to the Bahamas.
Premier	*Oceanic*	Port Canaveral to the Bahamas.
Carnival	*Holiday*	Los Angeles to Ensenada.
Carnival	*Fantasy*	Port Canaveral to the Bahamas.

For Singles

Carnival	*Ecstasy*	Miami to the Bahamas.
NCL	*Leeward*	Miami to the Bahamas and to Mexico's Caribbean.
Regal Cruises	*Regal Empress*	Sailing from New York on party cruises in summer, from St. Petersburg on four-, five- and six-day sailings in winter.

For Couples

RCI	*Viking Serenade*	From Los Angeles to Ensenada.
RCI	*Nordic Empress*	From San Juan to the Caribbean.
Radisson Seven Seas	*Radisson Diamond*	Some special short sailings in the Caribbean aboard a super-luxury ship.

For Seniors

Delta Queen Steamboat	*Fleet*	Various short sailings from New Orleans on the Mississippi.
Regal Cruises	*Regal Empress*	Short sailings from New York in summer, from Port Manatee on four-, five- and six-day sailings in winter.

Inaccessible Vessels for Wheelchair Passengers

Abercrombie & Kent	*Explorer*
ACCL	*Caribbean Prince, Mayan Prince, Niagara Prince, Grand Caribe*
Alaska Sightseeing/Cruise West	*All ships*
Clipper Cruises	*Nantucket and Yorktown Clipper*
Club Med Cruises	*Club Med 1 & 2*
Esplanade Tours	*Bali Sea Dancer*
EuroCruises	*Ausonia, Funchal*
Ivaran Lines	*Americana*
Marine Expeditions Fleet	*All ships*
Quark Expeditions Fleet	*All ships*
Regal Cruises	*Regal Empress*
St. Lawrence Cruise	*Canadian Empress*
Sea Cloud Cruises	*Sea Cloud*
Special Expeditions	*Polaris, Sea Bird, Sea Lion, Caledonian Star*
Star Clippers	*Star Clipper and Star Flyer*
Tall Ship Adventures	*Sir Francis Drake*
Windjammer Fleet	All sailing ships

ABERCROMBIE & KENT

1520 Kensington Road, Oak Brook, IL 60521
☎ *(630) 954-2944, (800) 323-7308*
www.abercrombiekent.com

History..

Abercrombie & Kent started as a safari operator 35 years ago, founded by the father of present CEO Geoffrey Kent, who made up the mythical Abercrombie as his partner because he liked the way it sounded. One of the most respected of all luxury tour operators, A&K had booked a number of groups and charters on ships over the years, but got into the cruise business firsthand when it went into a marketing agreement with Seattle-based Society Expeditions in 1990, and ended up buying the company's 96-passenger expedition ship *Society Explorer* (the former *Lindblad Explorer*) in 1992 when Society Expeditions went into Chapter 11 bankruptcy reorganization. (The Seattle company is back in business again, operating its other expedition vessel *World Discoverer*. See Society Expeditions, page 833.) The *Explorer*, as it was renamed, was refurbished in 1992 at a cost of $1 million.

—The first passenger ship to cruise to Antarctica (*Lindblad Explorer*, 1969).

—First passenger ship to successfully negotiate the Northwest Passage (*Lindblad Explorer*, 1984).

Concept ....

Expedition and adventure cruising as we know it today began with the late Lars-Eric Lindblad and his *Lindblad Explorer* in 1969, and has been going to the penguins ever since. Lindblad introduced a basic travel pattern that is still followed today—to bring along experts in geology, flora and fauna on every sailing, to use inflatable rubber landing craft called Zodiacs to leave the mother vessel to explore ashore or to get closer to icebergs or rocky cliffs where seabirds are nesting, and to rehash the day's events before dinner nightly in a recap, usually with the experts interpreting what the expeditioners had seen. Expeditioners would receive volumes of material and recommended reading lists before, during and after the sailing. Shore excursions would be included in the fare.

Signatures. . . . .

Red expedition parkas issued to each Antarctic cruiser; Zodiac explorations ashore; follow-up trip logs prepared by lecture staff and issued to all passengers after they've returned home from the trip.

Gimmicks . . . .

The red hull of the *Explorer* stands out dramatically against the snow and ice in photographs. To this day, some of those early expeditioners think every expedition ship's hull has to be red.

Who's the Competition. . . . .

There's plenty of competition these days for A&K, especially in the Arctic and Antarctic regions, although most of the organizers and operators came out of either Lindblad Travel or Society Expeditions in the late 1970s and early 1980s. Quark Expeditions and Zeghram Expeditions use Russian icebreakers to crunch through the ice to the North Pole and to make a full circumnavigation of Antarctica. Society Expeditions' *World Discoverer*, Radisson Seven Seas Cruises' *Hanseatic*, Hapag-Lloyd's *Bremen* (the former *Frontier Spirit*) and Orient Cruise Line's *Marco Polo* are the major competitors in the Antarctic, while Special Expeditions (founded by Lindblad's son Sven-Olof Lindblad) uses its *Polaris* in the Galapagos and the *Caledonian Star* for some expeditions around the world.

Who's Aboard. . . . .

Older couples and singles who have the time and money to go adventuring; members of the Century Club; members of the Explorers Club; veterans of earlier expeditions. They're mostly North Americans and Europeans, particularly German and Swiss, although we often find Brazilians and Japanese on Arctic and Antarctic expeditions. It can be very clubby.

Who Should Go . . . .

Anyone interested in learning more about the world around us.

Who Should Not Go. . . . .

Small children; people with impaired mobility (there are no elevators on the ship and exploring involves climbing down steep gangways into Zodiacs bobbing in icy water); and anyone who wants to know how many formal nights are scheduled.

The Lifestyle. . . . .

Instead of oiling up to soak in the sun or sipping piña coladas on deck, expedition passengers stand at the ship's rail in the polar breeze watching for whales or icebergs, penguins or polar bears, tufted puffins or royal albatross. Shipboard life is casual; there is no need to dress up. Dining is at open seating, and everyone usually arrives right on time. If whales are spotted, everyone jumps up from the table and runs out on deck. If you've signed up to be called when the Northern Lights are out, you may be awakened at 3 a.m. to struggle out onto an open deck shivering.

Wardrobe . . . .

Because there is little closet space in the *Explorer's* cabins and no fashion police on board, take along practical and rugged outdoor clothing that can be layered so items can be donned or removed as the weather changes. In the Arctic and Antarctic, we find lightweight long silk underwear very practical, because it gives warmth without weight and dries quickly when you get wet wading ashore. In the evenings, expeditioners may or may not change into something clean, depending on their mood and how long the afternoon's excursion lasted. Some passengers bring jacket and tie for the captain's dinners, usually two per sailing. The important items to pack on most expedition cruises are headgear and footwear—rubber boots, some sort of raingear, hiking shoes or boots, rain hats, sun hats with strings that tie them down, and, if you must, safari hats.

Bill of Fare . . . . B

The food aboard is well prepared by European chefs who have introduced new menus recently. Breakfasts and lunches are usually built around buffet self-service items, while dinners are served course by course. Cocktails and wines are available.

Showtime . . . .

The nightly "recap" from the naturalists and expedition leaders tells you what you saw today and what you'll do tomorrow. On days at sea, lectures and films are scheduled frequently except for a two-hour window after lunch when most of the rugged expeditioners take their naps.

Discounts . . . .

Early booking discounts of $500 per person are available on Antarctic expedition sailings of the *Explorer.* Make consecutive bookings of two back-to-back sailings and get 20 percent off the lower priced cruise.

The Bottom Line

The intrepid little *Explorer* can tackle just about any part of the globe, and in her 28 years of wandering probably has. The cabins are small but comfortable, the food is good and your fellow passengers congenial, as a rule. Expeditioners are just cruisers who go to extremes.

★★ ⚓⚓⚓⚓⚓

EXPLORER

As the days went by, the ice of the Antarctic began to seem like confectionery instead of glaciology—some of it cracked meringues, shiny and crunchy-looking; others the sculpted cold sheen of ice-blue marble where an iceberg had split. There was the window-display, fake-snow glitter of an ice floe in the sunshine with a dozen penguins perched on it out for a ride, and glossy marshmallow mountains, divinity peaks and sugar-dusted chocolate rocks.

The *Explorer* was built with polar cruising in mind, and has a double ice-hardened hull, shallow draft, extensive navigational equipment and bow thrusters to help her maneuver among the icebergs and floes of Arctic and Antarctic oceans. All cabins are outsides and have private baths with showers; there is a lounge, bar, library, lecture hall, dining room, gift shop, laundry service, beauty shop, English-speaking doctor and single seating meal service.

Between The Lines

The Brochure Says

"After a day of adventure, return to the ship to enjoy all the amenities of a traditional cruising vessel: like-minded company, excellent Continental cuisine and comfortable, air-conditioned cabins."

Translation

You can see the world without hardly leaving the comforts of home.

INSIDER TIP

All shore excursions and on-board tips are included on the Antarctic and Amazon sailings.

Cabins & Costs

Fantasy Suites: C

Average Price Per Person, Double Occupancy, Per Day: $536 in the Amazon, $928 in the Antarctic, both plus air add-ons and port charges.

There are two suites aboard the *Explorer*, not really on the fantasy level but more comfortable and spacious than the other quarters, each with a queen-sized bed, separate sitting area with sofa and chairs, a coffee table, mini-refrigerator and bath with shower.

Small Splurges: C

Average Price PPPD: $388 in the Amazon, $668 in the Antarctic, plus air add-ons.

Since there's no elevator, one of the two upper cabin decks is more convenient, say one of the 10 standard cabins on the boat deck, with a window, two lower berths, a small desk/dresser with stool and five drawers, and a tiny bathroom with shower.

Suitable Standards: C

Average Price PPPD: $370 in the Amazon, $579 in the Antarctic, plus air add-ons.

Go for one of the Yacht Deck amidships cabins for the best ride in rough waters. These standard outside doubles have portholes instead of windows and the same furnishings (see "Small Splurges," above) in a smaller space.

Bottom Bunks: .... C-

Average Price PPPD: $274 in the Amazon, $434 in the Antarctic, plus air add-ons.

Portholes in the bottommost deck cabins get what we call the laundromat treatment—either you're watching the seas sloshing over them or they're covered against severe weather and you're in the equivalent of an inside cabin. They contain the same basic furniture as the other standards (see "Small Splurges," above) but are even narrower.

The Routes

The *Explorer* spends the winter months in the Antarctic, cruising along the peninsula and sometimes visiting nearby island groups such as the Falklands, South Georgias or South Orkneys.

In the spring and fall a series of Amazon River cruises is offered, some traveling between Iquitos and Manaus, and some between Iquitos and Belém, the entire 2000-mile length of the river.

For the remainder of the season, various companies charter the *Explorer*.

The Scoop

Nine of the bottom-category cabins designated as doubles are primarily sold as single cabins with a 50 percent single supplement added on. These cabins are located forward on Explorer and Yacht Decks. They're also the smallest cabins with the potential of offering the bumpiest ride in rough seas, plus the washing-machine porthole view of the oceans of the world. But the overall experience outweighs the small drawbacks of this vessel, as you can see from the two-star, five-anchor rating.

Insider Tips

Five Essential Places

1. The lecture hall, where passengers gather for slide lectures and learned discussions (and sometimes a quick nap).

2. The sun deck with its small pool can be a shelter from the wind or a good place to read.

3. Explorer Lounge is where the expeditioners gather at the end of the day to compare notes, buy a drink and nibble on chips and pretzels.

4. The dining room is big enough to seat all the passengers in one seating, but can get noisy if everyone decides to talk at once.

5. The library, a great place to go to catch up on research between shore excursions; published material about the regions being cruised is all there.

Five Good Reasons to Book This Ship

1. To cruise the Antarctic Peninsula on the first passenger ship that ever sailed there.

2. To get the equivalent of a college course about geology, marine mammals, cacti, icebergs, parrots of the Amazon—whatever your interest.

3. To meet people you'll probably stay in touch with—perhaps even take other expedition cruises with—for years.

4. To go bird-watching in a Zodiac.

5. To take and bring back incredible photographs of icebergs, and a lot of mysterious shots of where the whale was.

Five Things You Won't Find On Board

1. A dance orchestra.

2. An elevator.

3. A Jacuzzi.

4. A casino.

5. A cabin designated wheelchair-accessible; this vessel is not appropriate for mobility-impaired travelers.

EXPLORER   ★★, ⚓⚓⚓⚓

Registry	**Liberia**
Officers	**European**
Crew	**International**
Complement	**61**
GRT	**2,398**
Length (ft.)	**239**
Beam (ft.)	**46**
Draft (ft.)	**14.7**
Passengers-Cabins Full	**114**
Passengers-2/Cabin	**100**
Passenger Space Ratio	**22.83**
Stability Rating	**NA**
Seatings	**1**
Cuisine	**Continental**
Dress Code	**Casual**
Room Service	**Yes**
Tip	**Included**

Ship Amenities

Outdoor Pool	**1**
Indoor Pool	**0**
Jacuzzi	**0**
Fitness Center	**Yes**
Spa	**No**
Beauty Shop	**Yes**
Showroom	**No**
Bars/Lounges	**1**
Casino	**No**
Shops	**1**
Library	**Yes**
Child Program	**No**
Self-Service Laundry	**No**
Elevators	**0**

Cabin Statistics

Suites	**2**
Outside Doubles	**55**
Inside Doubles	**0**
Wheelchair Cabins	**0**
Singles	**9**
Single Surcharge	**150-200%**
Verandas	**0**
110 Volt	**No**

Airtours

Wavell House, Holcombe Road, Helmsmore, Lancashire BB4 4NB, Great Britain
☎ *(01144) 1706-260-000*
www.airtours.com/airtours/news.html

History . . . .

The second-largest tour operator in the United Kingdom will soon become a more familiar name to North Americans, because Carnival Cruise Lines in early 1996 invested $310 million to purchase 29.54 percent of the company. The company also owns Scandinavian Leisure Group AB, formerly a travel property of SAS airlines, and Sunquest Vacations of Canada.

The two companies complement each other in marketing air/sea/land packages throughout Europe and North America.

For several years, Airtours has operated two ships familiar to North Americans under their previous names—the former *Nordic Prince* of Royal Caribbean Cruise Ltd. is Airtours' *Carousel*, and the former *Southward* of Norwegian Cruise Line has become the *Seawing*. They operate in the Sun Cruises division of Airtours. The former *Song of Norway* has joined the fleet recently as the *Sundream*.

Gimmicks . . . .

Passengers can pre-order duty-free items for delivery on either their outbound or homebound flights.

Passengers can pre-book guaranteed seating in order to be able to sit together, make a later check-in at the airport and pre-order special meals to be served during the flight.

Who's The Competition . . . .

Besides the obvious British giants Cunard and P & O, Airtours also competes in Europe with active North American marketers there such as Royal Caribbean International, Princess, Costa and Royal Olympic.

Who's Aboard . . . .

Holiday-makers from the United Kingdom looking for an affordable and convenient package for vacations in the sun. Many are young to middle-aged couples looking for the same active lifestyle as North America's new cruisers.

Wardrobe.

Casual and comfortable garb is in order for daytime, both ashore and on deck, while a gesture toward dressing for evening—"a sport jacket and trousers for men and elegant separates for ladies"—rather than full formal wear is recommended in the brochure.

Bill Of Fare

Big English breakfasts, "elevenses" mid-morning snacks, luncheon in the dining room or on deck, afternoon tea, a four-course dinner and a midnight supper are on the menu daily. While designed to please British palates, many of the dishes on board will strike Americans as rich or over-elaborate.

Showtime.

While typical cruise ship production shows are presented on some evenings, British passengers are less inclined to sit back and be entertained than Americans. Instead, they enjoy participating, so you'll find many more passenger talent shows, singalongs, karaoke nights, costume parades, trivia quizzes and name-that-tune contests, as well as slow dancing to the ship's orchestra.

Discounts

Airtours promises passengers the lowest available price on their holiday bookings, and guarantees that if they find a lower price within 28 days of booking, they will match that fare or allow cancellation free of charge.

The Bottom Line

As with most North American cruise lines aiming at young and first-time cruisers, the emphasis is on destinations and pre- and post-cruise hotel stay-overs rather than shipboard life. Cabins may be booked by category but not by cabin number, which is assigned when passengers board the ship.

★ ★ ★
CAROUSEL*

As the Nordic Prince, *one of the ship's most popular bars was the Viking Crown Lounge high atop the ship with fantastic views to the sea. But you won't find it on the* Carousel. *As a trademarked signature of Royal Caribbean Cruise Ltd., the lounge had to be removed when the ship was sold.*

The ship has an easy layout for first-time cruisers, with most of the passenger cabins on the three lower passenger decks, except for the two top categories, which are located on the Promenade Deck. The topmost deck has a sunwalk and space for sun loungers, while the Sun Deck one deck down contains an amidships pool, a cafe and gymnasium and spa. The Midsummer's Night Lounge (Airtours has retained the musical theater titles RCI gave the ship) aft on Promenade Deck doubles as the disco, with children's clubs adjacent. The Showboat Lounge serves as a second or cabaret room aft on Restaurant Deck, while the main show lounge is forward on the same deck. Amidships is the Camelot Dining Room and a small casino. The beauty salon, gift shop and purser's desk are located amidships on Main Deck.

· Between The Lines ·

The Brochure Says

"It's often said that sea air makes you hungry and that may well be true. . . but you will never know, for the ships' chefs and their team make sure no one on board would ever test the theory."

Translation

With six meals a day, like Scarlett O'Hara, you'll never be hungry again.

Cabins & Costs

NOTE: All prices are approximate, translated into U.S. dollars from British pounds, and are the prices per day per person double occupancy, plus airfare.

Fantasy Suites . . . . **N/A**
N/A

Small Splurges. . . . .
Average Price Per Person, Double Occupancy, Per Day: $241 plus airfare.
The cabins categorized as Deluxe are the top-ranked aboard, but don't expect a gala suite. A location on Promenade Deck, nightstands and chairs to supplement the pair of twin beds which can be joined as a double, and a full-sized closet are the amenities.

Suitable Standards. . . . .
Average Price PPPD: $158 plus airfare.
There are two categories between the Deluxe (above) and these standard outsides, which have twin beds or double beds (make your choice when booking), portholes and a desk/dresser, plus some with additional pulldown berths for families traveling with children.

Bottom Bunks . . . .
Average Price PPPD: $141
The basic standard inside cabins match the Suitable Standards above, except they have no porthole. Decide whether the relatively minimum savings is worth not having daylight.

The Routes

In summer, the *Carousel* cruises the western Mediterranean coasts from Barcelona to Rome with an emphasis on French and Italian Riviera ports, as well as southern Mediterranean that include Malta, Sicily, Tunis and the Balearic Islands. In winter, the ship repositions from Tenerife in the Canary Islands to the Caribbean, offering longer cruises for the Europeans who have flown the distance to join the ship.

CAROUSEL* ★★★

Registry	**Britain**
Officers	**British**
Crew	**International**
Complement	**400**
GRT	**23,200**
Length (ft.)	**637'**
Beam (ft.)	**80'**
Draft (ft.)	**22'**
Passengers Full	**1160**
Passengers 2/Cabin	**1062**
Passenger Space Ratio	**21.8**
Stability Rating	**Good**
Seatings	**2**
Cuisine	**British/Continental**
Dress code	**Casual**
Room service	**Yes**
Tip	**$7 PPPD**

Ship Amenities

Outdoor Pool	**1**
Indoor Pool	**0**
Jacuzzi	**0**
Fitness Center	**Yes**
Spa	**No**
Beauty Shop	**Yes**
Showroom	**Yes**
Bars/Lounges	**3**
Casino	**Yes**
Shops	**Yes**
Library	**No**
Child Program	**Yes**
Self-Service Laundry	**No**
Elevators	**4**

Cabin Statistics

Suites	**0**
Outside Doubles	**343**
Inside Doubles	**188**
Wheelchair Cabins	**0**
Singles	**0**
Single Surcharge	**Yes**
Verandas	**0**
110 Volt	**Yes**

AIRTOURS

★ ★ ★
SEAWING*

As the Starward, this was our favorite of the Norwegian Cruise Line "white ships," so called for the white hulls in contrast to the line's flagship Norway with its dark blue hull. All the "white ships" are gone from NCL now, sold to other companies, but still popular in the European markets for their sun-and-fun deck designs.

Except for a dozen deluxe cabins sharing space on the Boat Deck with the dining room, all passenger accommodations are on the three lower decks on the *Seawing*. Above the Boat Deck is the Mayflower Deck, with the Clipper Lounge, a venue for shows and dancing, forward, and the card room, beauty salon, children's clubs, gym, sauna, piano bar and tiny casino aft. Above is the Beach Deck, an appropriate name for the sunbathing area, which also includes a small amidships pool and an aft sports deck plus the Riviera Bar forward. Topmost is the Tropicana Deck, with the higher Panorama Deck area reached by stairs, plus the large Crows Nest nightclub with dance floor and bar.

The Brochure Says

"...the Crows Nest...holds a late night disco with a difference. While regular music features up-to-date dance floor hits, special theme nights include '40s sounds and '50s and '60s rock and roll, guaranteed to bring back memories, or country and western classics for a complete change of mood."

Translation

Pack all your glad rags, Myrtle.

Cabins & Costs

NOTE: All prices are approximate, translated into U.S. dollars from British pounds, and are the prices per day per person double occupancy, plus air.

Fantasy Suites . . . .**N/A**
N/A

Small Splurges . . . .
Average Price Per Person, Double Occupancy, Per Day: $241 plus airfare.
Deluxe cabins are somewhat larger than on *Carousel*, with sitting area, picture windows and bedside tables, plus a bath/shower combination in the bathroom. Some have rollaway beds for children that slide under the double bed for storage.

Suitable Standards . . . .
Average Price PPPD: $158 plus airfare.
Standard cabins have two lower beds, privacy curtain in sleeping area and desk/dresser combination, portholes and optional upper berths for children. Space is adequate but not generous for two adults.

Bottom Bunks . . . .
Average Price PPPD: $141
The inside double cabins at the lowest price offer similar furnishings to the standards (above) except instead of the porthole, there is a blank wall covered with a curtain.

The Routes

The *Seawing* cruises in Europe and North Africa year-round, offering 12-night holidays along the coast of Spain, seven- and 14-night sailings around the western Mediterranean, southern Mediterranean sailings to the Balearics, Sicily, Malta, Naples and Tunis, and, in winter, sailings to Madeira, the Canaries and North Africa, plus the eastern Mediterranean, Egypt and Israel.

SEAWING* ★★★

Registry	Britain
Officers	British
Crew	International
Complement	300
GRT	16,607
Length (ft.)	536
Beam (ft.)	75
Draft (ft.)	22
Passengers Full	916
Passengers 2/Cabin	798
Passenger Space Ratio	20.81
Stability Rating	Good
Seatings	2
Cuisine	British/Continental
Dress code	Casual
Room service	Yes
Tip	$7 pppd

Ship Amenities

Outdoor Pool	1
Indoor Pool	0
Jacuzzi	0
Fitness Center	Yes
Spa	Yes
Beauty Shop	Yes
Showroom	Yes
Bars/Lounges	4/3
Casino	Yes
Shops	Yes
Library	Yes
Child Program	Yes
Self-Service Laundry	No
Elevators	4

Cabin Statistics

Suites	10
Outside Doubles	266
Inside Doubles	120
Wheelchair Cabins	0
Singles	0
Single Surcharge	Yes
Verandas	0
110 Volt	Yes

★ ★ ★
SUNDREAM*

RCI was certainly music-minded when it launched its first ship with rooms named after musicals—South Pacific Lounge, The King and I Dining Room, My Fair Lady Lounge—but the first time we went aboard this ship in the early 1980s, we were struck more by the Kool-Aid colors everywhere—raspberry, tangerine, lemon-lime and strawberry.

Now the former Song of Norway (shown above) has relinquished its Viking Crown Lounge aft on the stack and become the Sundream for Airtours.

When the *Song of Norway* debuted back in 1970, she had a capacity for 740 passengers, probably considered quite enough in those days, but the demand was soon such that the line decided to lengthen the vessel in 1978 in the first-ever "stretching" operation and the ship now carries 1004 passengers. As the *Sundream*, she manages to retain some intimacy but is big enough to give passengers a sense of choice when they're out and about, with three big lounges and a good expanse of deck space, plus a full round-the-ship promenade.

We wish we could say passengers get a sense of personal space as well, but most of the cabins are quite small—around 120 square feet—with the exception of three modest suites.

Between The Lines

The Brochure Says

"Like the beautiful and cultured countries she visits, the ship is known for her understated elegance...No wonder she visits such irresistible places—otherwise, you might never go ashore."

Translation

She's not very glitzy or glamorous, but you'll find her comfortable enough as a floating hotel to take you to some places you want to go without packing and unpacking all the time.

Cabins & Costs

Fantasy Suites: C

Average Price Per Person, Double Occupancy, Per Day: not available.

The Owner's Suite, while a little short on fantasy, is the biggest accommodation on board (266 square feet) with sitting area, mini-refrigerator and bar, larger-than-usual wardrobe area, bathroom with tub and shower and two lower beds that cannot be pulled together for a queen-sized bed.

Small Splurges: C

Average Price PPPD: not available.

The category C deluxe staterooms are up around the Owner's Suite but a bit smaller. Still, they're adequate, with two lower beds and bathroom with tub. Strollers along the Promenade Deck outside the window provide additional diversions.

Suitable Standards: .... C-

Average Price PPPD: not available.

Lots of "outside staterooms" and "larger inside staterooms" (read "smallish cabins") are in the mid-range categories on the A and B decks. Expect a double or two lower beds, sometimes configured in an L-shape in the larger ones, or parallel in the smaller ones.

Bottom Bunks: .... D-

Average Price PPPD: not available.

Q category bottom-of-the-line inside cabins have a single double bed suitable for petite romantics who don't want any sunlight coming in to wake them up. Bathrooms have showers only. There are only four of these.

INSIDER TIP

Young singles shouldn't plan on crowding four into a cheap inside cabin, no matter how appealing the prices are, without taking into consideration how little dressing, showering and storage space is available. If you travel really light, however, you might be able to manage it.

The Routes

The *Sundream* cruises sunny seas in Europe and elsewhere for Airtours.

The Scoop

Standard accommodations still feature what we call the "interlocking knees" double cabin, from a long-ago brochure photograph that showed an attractive pair of models ensconced in that small, chairless cabin, gamely smiling, one sitting on each bed facing each other with, yes, their knees interlocked.

AIRTOURS

And this high-density vessel has a low passenger-space ratio, meaning when the ship is full, which it frequently is, conditions can get crowded.

Overall, this ship is best for competitive types, who can vie in the fitness/sports program; couples, who can rekindle romance in the very cozy cabins; and kids, who fit into the upper Pullman-style berths easier than adults.

Insider Tips

Five Special Spots

1. The pool on Sun Deck, a convivial gathering spot just steps away from the Pool Bar and the Pool Cafe; a dedicated sun worshipper could spend most of the day here without missing a thing.

2. The Sun Walk, a balcony which looks down on the pool but offers a peaceful getaway from the pool activity.

3. The My Fair Lady Show Lounge, redecorated in subtler, deeper shades instead of its formerly flashy orange, raspberry and green.

4. The King and I Dining Room, trim and shipshape and with windows big enough to see out from, as well as nightly themed dinner menus to take you around the world.

5. Stroll the Sun Walk to check out the sunbathers below.

SUNDREAM* ★★★

Registry	**Britain**
Officers	**British**
Crew	**International**
Complement	**423**
GRT	**22,945**
Length (ft.)	**637**
Beam (ft.)	**80**
Draft (ft.)	**22**
Passengers-Cabins Full	**1138**
Passengers-2/Cabin	**1004**
Passenger Space Ratio	**22.85**
Stability Rating	**Fair**
Seatings	**2**
Cuisine	**British/Continental**
Dress Code	**Traditional**
Room Service	**Yes**
Tip	**$7 PPPD**

Ship Amenities

Outdoor Pool	**1**
Indoor Pool	**0**
Jacuzzi	**0**
Fitness Center	**Yes**
Spa	**No**
Beauty Shop	**No**
Showroom	**Yes**
Bars/Lounges	**4**
Casino	**Yes**
Shops	**3**
Library	**Yes**
Child Program	**No**
Self-Service Laundry	**No**
Elevators	**4**

Cabin Statistics

Suites	**3**
Outside Doubles	**325**
Inside Doubles	**177**
Wheelchair Cabins	**0**
Singles	**0**
Single Surcharge	**Yes**
Verandas	**0**
110 Volt	**Yes**

Alaska Sightseeing CruiseWest

Fourth and Battery Bldg., Suite 700, Seattle, WA 98121
☎ *(206) 441-8687, (800) 426-7702*
www.smallship.com

These homey, unpretentious vessels are ideal for people who want to see Alaska close-up and personal.

History...

The near-legendary World War II pilot Charles B. "Chuck" West came back from the China-Burma-India theater to start an Alaska bush pilot service in 1946, which he turned into world-famous Westours Inc. After selling Westours to Holland America Line in 1973, he went on to found Alaska Sightseeing/Cruise West, at first offering day cruises on Prince William Sound and along the Inside Passage, and in 1990, adding overnight cruises in Alaska on the 58-passenger *Spirit of Glacier Bay.*

In May, 1991, West, by now also known as "Mr. Alaska," reintroduced U.S.-flag sailings between Seattle and Alaska for the first time since Alaska Steamship Company suspended its passenger operations in 1954. He used one 82-passenger ship the first year, adding a second 84-passenger vessel in 1992, then a 101-passenger ship in 1993.

Today, with West's son Richard as president and CEO, the family-owned company's vessels cruise in Alaska, British Columbia, Puget Sound, the Columbia and Snake Rivers and the San Francisco Bay/Sacramento Delta.

—AS/CW is the biggest little-ship cruise company in North America, with six overnight vessels and two day-cruise vessels, each carrying fewer than 101 passengers.

—All the line's vessels are under 100 tons, which allows the company full access to Glacier Bay without having to qualify for the limited number of permits issued annually for entrance.

—The company runs a longer sailing season in Alaska than its rivals, beginning in early April and continuing until October.

—Captain Leigh Reinecke and Captain Becky Crosby, two of the very few female captains at sea, command AS/CW vessels.

Concept . . . .

This Alaska-savvy company feels that putting passengers in small vessels is the best way to get a close look at and a feel for the true Alaska experience. Eco-tourism and the environment are primary concerns at AS/CW, and schedules are deliberately styled to be flexible so the captain can take a different course to show passengers a mother bear and her cubs feeding in a rich patch of grass, or spend an hour watching a chorus line of 15 orcas lined up across British Columbia's narrow Grenville Channel, so close to the ship that one frustrated passenger complained she couldn't get them all in one shot with her 50-millimeter lens.

Signatures . . . .

A unique bow-landing capability on four of the line's vessels allows passengers to troop down a front gangway and right onto shore without using a tender or inflatable landing craft. This device was originally designed and built by Luther Blount of American Canadian Caribbean Line, whose company also promotes its own bow-landing vessels. Blount's Warren, Rhode Island, shipyard constructed the former *New Shoreham I* and *New Shoreham II*, which now sail as the *Spirit of Glacier Bay* and the *Spirit of Columbia*.

An open bridge policy gives passengers daytime access to the navigation bridge except in severe weather, letting wanna-be skippers chat with the captain, stare at the radar or study the charts. It's also a good place to watch for wildlife without getting wet when it's raining.

There is an emphasis on the foods, wines and boutique beers of the Pacific Northwest. Several regional wines are usually available by the glass as well as by the bottle.

A new repeat passenger club called Quyana ("thank you" in Yupik Eskimo dialect) has been introduced with its own newsletter.

Seamless Service is the line's new trademarked program, providing "a high degree of personalized service, and linking that service from ship to shore."

CHAMPAGNE TOAST

Bartenders aboard these small vessels will let passengers who want a glass of wine at cocktail time in the bar, then another with dinner in the dining room, save money by buying a full bottle at the bottle price and keeping it in the bar refrigerator with the cabin number written on the label.

Gimmicks . . . .

"Our Bear...Their Bear" ad campaign has a closeup photo of bears on a rocky shore taken by an amateur photographer from the deck of the *Spirit of Alaska*. Beside it is a long view photo of an Alaska shoreline with a circle pointing out a distant speck on the shore..."Their Bear."

DID YOU KNOW?

In addition to its overnight cruise ships, AS/CW also operates two highly successful day-cruise vessels which are not rated in this guide–the Glacier Seas, *which makes daily eight-hour crossings of the Prince William Sound, and the* Sheltered Seas, *which takes passengers on five- or six-day cruises of the Inside Passage with overnights spent at land hotels.*

Who's the Competition. . . . .

AS/CW competes head-on with Glacier Bay Tours & Cruises, as well as New York-based Special Expeditions which offers a somewhat more rugged version of Alaska and Pacific Northwest cruises with excursions in inflatable rubber landing craft and a permanent rather than transitory company of naturalists. Clipper Cruises *Yorktown Clipper* carries 140 passengers on similar sailings into hidden fjords and glaciers from Juneau and Ketchikan.

The AS/CW flagship *Spirit of '98*, a replica riverboat built in 1984, has a new competitor in the *Queen of the West*, a replica paddlewheeler built by Seattle-based Bob Giersdorf, who operated now-defunct Exploration Cruise Lines with some of the vessels now in AS/CW's fleet, and who is a longtime rival of the West family in Alaska tourism services.

Who's Aboard . . . .

American and Canadian couples and a few singles, most past retirement age, with a sprinkling of younger (read late 40s–early 50s) people and some parents with adult offspring. On each sailing there's usually a handful of foreigners—British, Germans, Australians and New Zealanders—who have come to experience Alaska for themselves after hearing about it from friends or relatives back home. For many aboard, it is their first cruise and they have deliberately chosen what they anticipate is an untraditional, non-fancy cruise experience.

Who Should Go . . . .

These vessels are ideal for people who want to see Alaska up close and personal with a friendly and energetic staff of young Americans (most of whom are here because they love Alaska). While most of the passengers on the cruises we've taken are seniors, we feel younger couples interested in the environment and wildlife would also enjoy the bed-and-breakfast ambience of the vessels for a casual, low-key holiday. There are plenty of options for active rather than passive shore excursions, including kayaking, river rafting, salmon fishing or bicycling down a mountain. As the company's brochure says, it's "for people who'd rather cruise in the wilderness than shop-till-you-drop."

Who Should Not Go

Families with young children, because there's nowhere on these small vessels for children to play or run about.

Night owls who like a lot of slick entertainment, casinos and discos.

People who want to dress up and show off their jewelry.

Anyone who decided to take a cruise after watching a Carnival commercial.

NO NOs

Smoking is not permitted anywhere indoors on this line's ships; passengers are requested to smoke only on the open decks.

The Lifestyle

Casual, very nature-oriented, friendly and unpretentious. Passengers dine at one seating, arriving soon after the meal call is broadcast and sitting where they please at tables for six. Most choose to wear their handwritten name tags that give first name and home state or country, to make casual conversation that much easier with fellow passengers.

All the ships have deck areas for brisk walking, as well as a couple of exercise machines tucked away in a corner somewhere, which is as close as they come to a fitness center.

Entertainment is provided by energetic young crew members who perform improvisational comedy and re-enact corny melodrama scenes so badly they break themselves up as passengers look on with paternal pride. Lectures are ad hoc, provided perhaps by a pair of wilderness rangers paddling in by kayak to show off their territory from an inside point of view (as in, "Right over there last week we found a mountain goat that had slipped and fallen a couple of thousand feet and drowned.") Daytime activity at sea consists of watching the scenery from indoors or out, chatting with each other, reading, playing cards and writing postcards. It's very relaxed and family-like, and passengers share many interests and common backgrounds.

Wardrobe.

There is no dress code and no dressing up for dinner. You may show up in whatever you happen to be wearing, so long as it's decent. Casual clothing prevails, with sweaters and slacks or jeans with jogging shoes the Alaska uniform. An in-cabin booklet says it best: "Dress is always casual...(you can) save on dry-cleaning bills once you have returned home...(and) there is no time wasted changing clothes."

Bill of Fare. B

Young chefs prepare American-style food that is quite tasty compared with the sometimes bland banquet cuisine aboard the big ships, even veering giddily close to the cutting edge for some passengers. One day when the breakfast special was described as lox and bagels, a woman at our table from California's Central Valley asked in sweet confusion, "And what exactly is that?"

Meals are served family-style; you sit where and with whom you please.

There is a set menu for each meal with one or two or, sometimes at dinner, three choices, perhaps fresh Alaska salmon, Cornish game hen or a vegetarian eggplant or lentil dish, but a limited range of alternatives can be ordered ahead of time by people who want something different. At the end of dinner each evening, the chef appears and describes what he's preparing for the next day. Passengers turn in their orders on a slip of paper, somewhat as one does in a railway dining car.

Hot hors d'oeuvres are served in the lounge before dinner, perhaps baked brie in a pastry crust with a garnish of grapes, a pâté, pizza or hot sausages with mustard.

The first course is often already on the table when passengers arrive, so that "yes" or "no" is more appropriate than "this" or "that." Desserts are usually familiar and tempting (a rich pecan tart and a Klondike pound cake were memorable).

Breakfast may be a choice of almond seven-grain pancakes or eggs, bacon and hash brown potatoes, enhanced by a self-service buffet at the room entrance with oatmeal, fresh fruit, juices and muffins. In addition, there's a self-service early riser breakfast of coffee, tea, juice and breakfast pastries.

At lunch, there's usually a substantial salad and/or sandwich, along with a hot soup, or you can request a hamburger or hot dog on special order.

Special dietary requirements—i.e., vegetarian, low-salt, low-fat or Kosher—can be requested at time of booking.

There is no cabin food service (except in the Owners Suite on the *Spirit of '98*), but if you're feeling under the weather, one of the cheerful and caring Passenger Service Representatives (a euphemism for cabin and dining room stewardesses) would probably bring you something anyhow.

A modest selection of wines, most of them from California and the Pacific Northwest, are available by the glass or bottle at reasonable prices.

Discounts . . . .

No special fares or discounts are offered, but low-cost air add-ons from 75 gateway cities are available. Early booking is essential on these ships, which frequently sell out by spring for the entire season.

The Bottom Line

This is a particularly beguiling cruise experience for novices and veterans alike. Quintessentially American in style and cuisine, it should be a must for non-North Americans who want to get a sense of typical American hospitality, humor and food. The staff is young, dedicated and genuinely enthusiastic about what they're showing you, and there's never a discouraging word on board. This is due in equal measure to the passengers, who are the kind of people who travel cheerfully without a litigious attitude or complaint-driven monologue. While not pretending to claim they're perfect for everyone, AS/CW has a way of winning over even a dyed-in-the-wool curmudgeon, should one ever clomp aboard.

Interestingly, the company, like Carnival, has apparently chosen to compete with land-based vacations rather than other cruise products, and it structures its brochures and marketing efforts toward audiences who might book a Tauck Tour or Grand Circle Travel trip, spelling out the itinerary in coach tour terms. "Breakfast, lunch, dinner" is listed as included on each day's itinerary aboard ship, as if other cruise lines did not also provide them gratis. Photos of destination highlights far outnumber depictions of life on board in the land-oriented brochures.

On the down side, there is nowhere to get away from your fellow passengers except in the cabin or ashore. Most of the ships have a single lounge that doubles as bar, lecture room, card room, reading room and gift shop.

⚓⚓⚓⚓
SPIRIT OF ALASKA
SPIRIT OF COLUMBIA

Our first cruise aboard the Spirit of Alaska *was sailing through Washington's San Juan Islands, something like bopping along a scenic maritime road, watching the scenery and looking for wildlife, then pulling into sleepy little port towns. We found a whaling museum staffed by volunteers dedicated to the three pods of 89 or so orcas who inhabit the San Juans, a hotel where Teddy Roosevelt once slept (he'd still recognize it today) and evening concerts on an Aeolian pipe organ in a turn-of-the-century mansion turned resort hotel.*

A forward seat in the lounge offers a good vantage point for seeing glaciers.

Seeing the gradual transformation on these two vessels from basic boats to attractive cruise options has been inspiring. The *Spirit of Columbia*, which we first sailed when it was ACCL's *New Shoreham II*, is dramatically changed after being stripped down to the bare bones and rebuilt in a somewhat more luxurious mode. The *Spirit of Alaska*, built in 1980 as the former *Pacific Northwest Explorer* from Exploration Cruise Lines, has also been considerably spiffed up recently.

These sister ships are clean and comfortable without a lot of big-cruise-ship extras such as beauty parlor, casino or buffet restaurant. But then there's little need to have your hair groomed, since a few minutes in the fresh breeze (or fog and rain) can make it a mess again; gambling is not of interest to most of the passengers aboard; and having an alternative place in which to eat is superfluous when you have a menu of very tasty food at every meal and all-day self-service coffee and tea available. A bow-landing ramp on the front of the vessels allows passengers to disembark quickly and easily at remote island beaches.

Between The Lines

The Brochure Says

"The sleek *Spirit of Alaska* is equipped for bow landings, with ample outside viewing areas and an open wheelhouse."

Translation

You can sometimes get off the ship by queueing up behind the rest of the passengers and trooping down a steep, narrow gangway onto land. There's a lot of open deck with railings and various items of nautical hardware underfoot where you can lounge about if you don't mind sharing space with the handful of smokers that are usually aboard, and you can drop by the bridge any time to share your navigational observations with the patient captain.

Cabins & Costs

Fantasy Suites: . . . . **B**

Average Per Person, Double Occupancy, Per Day: $485 plus airfare.
The brand-new Owner's Suite added to the *Spirit of Columbia* forward on the Upper Deck, with its queen-sized bed, view windows, TV/VCR, mini-refrigerator, bathtub with shower and stocked bar, has generous storage space in both drawers and hanging closets.

Small Splurges: . . . . **C-**

Average Price PPPD: $456–$532 plus air add-ons.
While not strictly suites since the sitting area and the sleeping area are awfully close together, these accommodations will meet the requirements of most non-fussy passengers who don't like big cruise ships. What you get is a window or two, a sink that's in the cabin rather than in the bathroom and a shower.

Suitable Standards: . . . . **D**

Average Price PPPD: $395 plus air add-ons.

You get two lower beds, a nightstand, closet, in-cabin lavatory and bathroom with toilet and shower in an area that measures roughly nine feet by 11 feet.

Bottom Bunks: .... **D-**
Average Price PPPD: $228–$289 plus air add-ons.
Take the same facilities as above, push them into a somewhat smaller space, and eliminate the window in favor of a portlight, a hole high up on the cabin wall that you can't see through but that lets a little daylight in, and you have the bottom category C cabin. The good news is, there's only one of these on each ship.

The Routes

The *Spirit of Alaska* spends spring and fall sailing 7-night Columbia/Snake River itineraries roundtrip from Portland calling at Bonneville Dam, Hells Canyon, Washington's wine country and Oregon's beaches. On May 13 a 10-night cruise from Seattle to Juneau positions the ship for three- and four-night cruises out of Whittier cruising College Fjords, Columbia Glacier and a call at Valdez. Sept. 3 returns the ship to its river cruise.

Spirit of Columbia makes early spring and late fall seven-night roundtrip cruises from Seattle into Canada's scenic Inside Passage followed by a 10-night repositioning cruise May 4th from Seattle to Juneau. From May 14 to Sept. 17 the ship offers 7-night Alaska Inside Passage cruises between Juneau and Ketchikan, cruising Glacier Bay and calling at Skagway, Haines, Sitka and Wrangell.

The Scoop

The shallow-draft *Spirit of Alaska* was refurbished extensively in 1995, which got rid of most of her former ugly duckling features. The *Spirit of Columbia* was extensively rebuilt from the hull up in a style intended to suggest a national-park lodge, with a generous use of wood. Since there's no elevator on either vessel, mobility-impaired travelers should consider booking the line's *Spirit of '98* instead, which has an elevator (although no cabins designated for the disabled) and cruises some of the areas these ships do. While the per diem prices may seem high for these simple vessels, the product is so successful that the company does not need to discount or make any special two-for-one offers.

Insider Tips

Five Good Spots to Stake Out

1. A seat on the sheltered amidships covered area on Bridge Deck on the *Spirit of Alaska* or on the warm Sun Deck on the *Spirit of Columbia* that gives a view to both port and starboard.

2. A dining room seat by the windows so you can see wildlife sightings on either side of the vessel; the best whale sightings almost always seems to happen at mealtimes.

3. A forward seat in the Glacier View/Riverview Lounge in order to view glaciers, rivers and other points of interest.

4. A vantage point on the Bow Viewing Area to chat with a visiting ranger or photograph a whale.

5. An Upper or Bridge Deck cabin with doors that open directly onto the Great Outdoors when a wildlife-spotting opportunity arises (or a nicotine addict has to have a cigarette).

Five Good Reasons to Book These Ships

1. The tireless and enthusiastic young American crew.
2. You never have to put on a tie.
3. You can sit anywhere you wish at mealtime.
4. You can walk or jog around the Upper Deck area as many times as you wish with no obstructions to slow you down.
5. You can go places in the Inside Passage or along the Columbia River that few if any other ships visit.

Five Things You Won't Find On Board

1. Breakfast in bed.
2. A blackjack table that takes real money.
3. A self-service laundry.
4. An intimate little hideaway lounge away from the other passengers.
5. Anywhere for children to stay or play.

ALASKA SIGHTSEEING/
CRUISE WEST

SPIRIT OF ALASKA
SPIRIT OF COLUMBIA

Registry	U.S.
Officers	American
Crew	American
Complement	21
GRT	97
Length (ft.)	143
Beam (ft.)	28
Draft (ft.)	7.5
Passengers-Cabins Full	82
Passengers-2/Cabin	78
Passenger Space Ratio	NA
Stability Rating	Fair
Seatings	1
Cuisine	American
Dress Code	Casual
Room Service	No
Tip	$10 PPPD pooled among staff incl. bar

Ship Amenities

Outdoor Pool	0
Indoor Pool	0
Jacuzzi	0
Fitness Center	Yes
Spa	No
Beauty Shop	No
Showroom	No
Bars/Lounges	1
Casino	No
Shops	1
Library	Yes
Child Program	No
Self-Service Laundry	No
Elevators	0

Cabin Statistics

Suites	3
Outside Doubles	24
Inside Doubles	12
Wheelchair Cabins	0
Singles	0
Single Surcharge	Yes
Verandas	0
110 Volt	Yes

ALASKA SIGHTSEEING/ CRUISE WEST

⚓⚓⚓⚓

SPIRIT OF DISCOVERY

On Miner's Night the bartenders and dining room servers get down and dirty with raunchy red long johns, toy revolvers and popguns, and painted-on whiskers, which are especially funny on the females. While all the vessels in this line have a high degree of bonding among the passengers, Spirit of Discovery seems particularly sociable.

Miner's Night aboard Spirit of Discovery *leads to crew high jinks.*

Built in 1976 for now-defunct American Cruise Line and named the *Independence*, perhaps because of the bicentennial spirit we all had that year, this shallow draft coastal vessel went through a stint as the *Columbia* before being renovated and renamed by AS/CW in 1992. A favored spot on the ship whether at sea or in port is the trim, open Bow Viewing Area, the place to be to sip late afternoon cocktail in Ketchikan sunshine or watch for humpback whales in Glacier Bay. A colorful information bulletin board with pictures and details about the cruising area is changed daily. Cabins are compact but attractively furnished, and there is a gift shop with books, maps and logo sweatshirts and windbreakers.

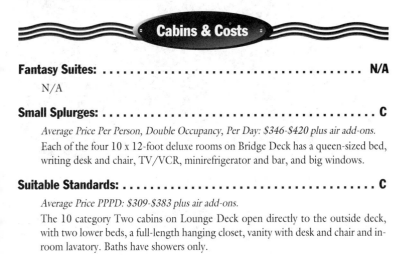

Cabins & Costs

Fantasy Suites: . . . . **N/A**

  N/A

Small Splurges: . . . . **C**

Average Price Per Person, Double Occupancy, Per Day: $346-$420 plus air add-ons.
Each of the four 10 x 12-foot deluxe rooms on Bridge Deck has a queen-sized bed, writing desk and chair, TV/VCR, minirefrigerator and bar, and big windows.

Suitable Standards: . . . . **C**

Average Price PPPD: $309-$383 plus air add-ons.
The 10 category Two cabins on Lounge Deck open directly to the outside deck, with two lower beds, a full-length hanging closet, vanity with desk and chair and in-room lavatory. Baths have showers only.

Bottom Bunks: . . . . **D**

Average Price PPPD: $279-$353 plus air add-ons.
The category Four cabins with upper and lower berths, because they are forward on the Main Deck, are curved from the contours of the hull, eight-and-a-half feet at the widest point and narrowing toward the bathroom, which has a shower only. There is a view window, but no chair, and the lavatory is located in the cabin rather than in the bath.

The Routes

Spirit of Discovery begins the season on April 13 with a 10-night northbound cruise from Seattle to Juneau with a Glacier Bay visit and calls at Ketchikan, Wrangell, Sitka, Skagway and cruising Tracy Arm. A season of 7-night cruises between Juneau and Ketchikan with calls at Skagway, Haines, Sitka, Wrangell and a cruise of Glacier Bay continue through Sept. 10. A 10-night return to Seattle preceeds a series of 7-night cruises from Portland on the Columbia River until the end of October visiting Bonneville Dam, Snake River and Hells Canyon, Hood River, Washington's wine country and Oregon's beaches.

The Scoop

These cruises, while fascinating, are fairly pricey (*Spirit of Discovery* per diems are higher than some of the line's other ships), and optional shore excursions carry an additional cost. But the food and camaraderie on board are excellent, and it's pleasant to stand on the Bow Viewing Area with no nautical machinery to stumble over. If you want to make new friends and see some wildlife, this may be the ship for you.

Tlingit teenagers from Ketchikan come aboard Spirit of Discovery *to talk about local culture and crafts.*

Insider Tips

Five Special Things About This Ship

1. The two single cabins, which may be booked at a flat rate rather than a singles' surcharge.

2. The food, especially the peanut butter pie and the Dungeness crab.

3. On northbound Alaska cruises only, the riveting evening talk about Tlingit culture by Native American Joe Williams, along with songs and dances by teenagers from his extended family in Ketchikan.

4. The wall of floor-to-ceiling windows in the Glacier View Lounge.

5. The sign-up sheet for passengers who wish to be awakened for wildlife sightings or the Northern Lights.

SPIRIT OF DISCOVERY ⚓⚓⚓

Registry	U.S.
Officers	American
Crew	American
Complement	21
GRT	94
Length (ft.)	166
Beam (ft.)	37
Draft (ft.)	7.5
Passengers-Cabins Full	84
Passengers-2/Cabin	82
Passenger Space Ratio	NA
Stability Rating	Fair
Seatings	1
Cuisine	American
Dress Code	Casual
Room Service	No
Tip	$10 PPPD pooled among staff incl. bar

Ship Amenities

Outdoor Pool	0
Indoor Pool	0
Jacuzzi	0
Fitness Center	Yes
Spa	No
Beauty Shop	No
Showroom	No
Bars/Lounges	1
Casino	No
Shops	1
Library	Yes
Child Program	No
Self-Service Laundry	No
Elevators	0

Cabin Statistics

Suites	0
Outside Doubles	43
Inside Doubles	0
Wheelchair Cabins	0
Singles	2
Single Surcharge	Yes
Verandas	0
110 Volt	Yes

⚓⚓⚓⚓⚓
SPIRIT OF ENDEAVOUR

We remember this ship as Clipper Cruise Line's Newport Clipper, first of the trio of small, U.S.-flag ships that brought a warm, fresh American style to cruising in the 1980s. Since then, it's served through a couple of incarnations (including one company that painted it with lots of pink) but AS/CW spent most of a year refurbishing it, and it looks great again.

The low, sleek, yachtlike lines of the new *Spirit of Endeavour* mark a different shape and profile from the line's other taller, boxier vessels. Cabins, more luxurious than on the other ships, are fairly similar, with three slightly larger ones in the top category, and all of them contain TV/VCRs. Most cabins boast large view windows, especially nice in Alaska; only the four forward cabins on Main Deck have portholes instead. The bathrooms are identical throughout the ship, quite compact with shower but no tub. All the cabins on the Upper Deck and the four aft cabins on the Lounge Deck open directly to the outside—nice when it's sunny but a little annoying if it's raining. The dining room has wide windows so you won't miss the scenery during mealtimes, and both it and the lounge have been lushly refurbished with plenty of oak, teak and marble, as well as all new fabrics. There is no elevator aboard.

The Brochure Says

"Our newest ship...features a variety of comfortable staterooms, all with windows or portholes."

Translation

Cabins are slightly larger than on some of the other vessels in the line, and you can see the scenery from them.

Cabins & Costs

Note: Prices quoted are the published brochure rates per passenger, double occupancy, per day.

Fantasy Suites: . . . . N/A
N/A

Small Splurges: . . . . B+
Average Price Per Person, Double Occupancy, Per Day: $496-$607, depending on sailing date, plus air add-ons.
There are three deluxe cabins, each with a pair of twin beds inside converting to a queen-sized bed on request. There is a long counter on the desk/dresser with chair, a mini-refrigerator and a pullman upper berth for an optional third occupant. Wardrobes are the same size as in the other cabins. Deluxe cabins measure roughly 10 x 15 feet.

Suitable Standards: . . . . B+
Average Price PPPD: $385 to $532 depending on season and category, plus air add-ons.
All the remaining cabins on the ship are 13 feet x 8 feet four inches, but prices and categories vary. Basically, they contain twin beds (some but not all convert to queen-sized so check when booking), a standard size desk/dresser with chair and adequate double-door wardrobe.

Bottom Bunks: . . . . B+
Average Price PPPD: $360 to $470, depending on sailing date, plus air add-ons.
These four bottom-priced cabins have portholes instead of view windows, and a slight narrowing toward the bow of the vessel with a small desk/dresser and shelves along the window wall. The twin beds cannot be put together to make a queen-sized bed.

The Routes

Spirit of Endeavour cruises Alaska's Inside Passage between mid-April and mid-September, with add-on overland options that can extend your holiday to eight-, 13- or 17-night packages. The ship cruises between Seattle and Juneau, sailing Desolation Sound, the Inside Passage, Misty Fjords and Glacier Bay, and calling in Ketchikan, Petersburg and Sitka.

The Scoop

The newest vessel in this rapidly-growing fleet offers the same warm, friendly service, tasty meals and environmentally-oriented cruising, with the added plus of a sleeker, more elegant interior and silhouette.

Five Good Reasons to Book This Ship

1. To call at rarely visited Petersburg, a town that's more like the real Alaska than tourist-filled Skagway or Sitka.

2. To visit your captain (he or she will welcome you) on the bridge.

3. To sample the line's cornmeal pistachio cookies.

4. To lounge about in the elegant lounge.

5. To get near enough to Admiralty Island to watch for bears through your binoculars.

SPIRIT OF ENDEAVOUR ♨♨♨♨

Registry	U.S.
Officers	American
Crew	American
Complement	32
GRT	99
Length (ft.)	207
Beam (ft.)	37
Draft (ft.)	8
Passengers-Cabins Full	107
Passengers-2/Cabin	102
Passenger Space Ratio	NA
Stability Rating	NA
Seatings	1
Cuisine	American
Dress Code	Casual
Room Service	No
Tip	$10 PPPD pooled among staff incl. bar

Ship Amenities

Outdoor Pool	0
Indoor Pool	0
Jacuzzi	0
Fitness Center	No
Spa	No
Beauty Shop	No
Showroom	No
Bars/Lounges	1
Casino	No
Shops	1
Library	Yes
Child Program	No
Self-Service Laundry	No
Elevators	0

Cabin Statistics

Suites	0
Outside Doubles	51
Inside Doubles	0
Wheelchair Cabins	0
Singles	0
Single Surcharge	175%
Verandas	0
110 Volt	Yes

ALASKA SIGHTSEEING/ CRUISE WEST

⚓⚓⚓

SPIRIT OF GLACIER BAY

The littlest and plainest vessel in the overnight fleet, the Spirit of Glacier Bay has a tougher style than the other "soft adventure" vessels and the capability of cruising into remote inlets and out-of-the-way places. We could imagine it dedicated to more rugged adventure and expedition sailing, and, since it offers the least expensive of AS/CW's cruises, it might attract younger people who want to experience Alaska in a more active fashion.

Small-ship fans who gravitate toward the *Spirit of Glacier Bay*, the smallest overnight vessel in this small-ship fleet, should know it's also the slowest, cruising at only 10 to 11 knots. But its size gives it unique access to wilderness inlets and closeup views of glaciers. The top category cabins usually sell out first on this ship because they have windows. The lounge is forward, with banquette seating and view windows, and the dining room is aft on the same deck, with four cabins in between. Since it has only three passenger decks, space is at a premium.

INSIDER TIP

Claustrophobes should avoid all cabins on the Lower Deck on this ship because they have portlights (small portholes high up in the cabin that offer no view and only a minimum amount of light) instead of windows. Because they're over the engine room, they're also noisy.

Cabins & Costs

Fantasy Suites: . . . . **N/A**

N/A

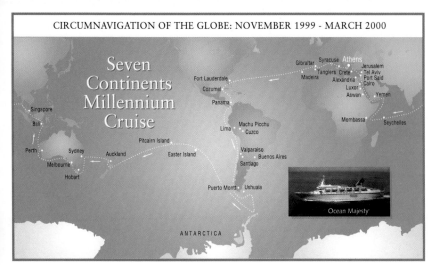

Quark Expeditions' original *Erich Graf*

RCCL's *Legend of the Seas* has an 18-hole miniature golf course.

Oasis pool on Celebrity Cruises *Galaxy*

Suitable Standards: C

Average Price Per Person, Double Occupancy, Per Day: $417 plus air add-on.
With a double bed or two lower beds (that crowd it a bit in this 8-by-10-foot
space), these basic category A cabins offer a lavatory actually in the bathroom
instead of the sleeping area (but a shower that sprays over the entire bathroom).
Opt for cabins 309 or 310 which are set apart and have views from two sides. There
are also two single cabins on the upper deck.

Bottom Bunks: . . . . D

Average Price PPPD: $287 plus air add-on.
The largest number of cabins on this ship are 13 category B cabins with two lower
berths and a portlight (see "Insider Tip," above) wedged into a 6-by-10 foot space.
These are so small you have to go out in the hall to change your mind, so we'll call
them Unsuitable Standards.

INSIDER TIP

*One of the writers, a card-carrying claustrophobe, once had the misfortune
of bunking in a cabin like this with a rival cruise line; if you're stuck with
one, try turning on the bathroom light and pulling the shower curtain
across the doorway so you can pretend it's a window.*

The Routes

The *Spirit of Glacier Bay* makes spring and fall three- and four-night cruises from Seattle into the San Juan Islands. During the summer the ship offers three- and four-night
cruises from Whittier into Prince William Sound, cruising College Fjords and Columbia
Glacier and calling at Valdez.

The Scoop

As the smallest, plainest and oldest overnight ship in the fleet, the *Spirit of Glacier Bay*
(or SGB, as the crew calls it) doesn't always get the proper respect. Built in 1971 as the
New Shoreham I, it was one of Luther Blount's first no-frills vessels for American Canadian Caribbean Line. But there are two appealing upscale cabins, 309 and 310, plus two
much-in-demand single cabins, 301 and 302. The doughty little vessel can go almost
anywhere, including not only lots of places the big ships can't go, but even a few nooks
and crannies the other AS/CW vessels can't visit. While remodeling goes on, the SGB is
still not up to the modest glamour of her bigger sisters.

Insider Tips

Five Good Reasons to Book This Ship

1. To cruise where nobody else can.

2. It's a little less expensive than the other overnight vessels in the fleet.

3. To sleep in one of "The Condominiums," a pair of freestanding cabins on the aft
   end of the upper deck, with one picture window facing aft and one facing the side.

4. The prime rib of Angus beef roasted on a bed of rock salt.

5. The new Washington's Island Discoveries itinerary.

SPIRIT OF GLACIER BAY · ⚓⚓⚓

Registry	**U.S.**
Officers	**American**
Crew	**American**
Complement	**21**
GRT	**97**
Length (ft.)	**125**
Beam (ft.)	**28**
Draft (ft.)	**6.5**
Passengers-Cabins Full	**57**
Passengers-2/Cabin	**54**
Passenger Space Ratio	**NA**
Stability Rating	**Fair**
Seatings	**1**
Cuisine	**American**
Dress Code	**Casual**
Room Service	**No**
Tip	**$10 PPPD pooled among staff incl bar**

Ship Amenities

Outdoor Pool	**0**
Indoor Pool	**0**
Jacuzzi	**0**
Fitness Center	**Yes**
Spa	**No**
Beauty Shop	**No**
Showroom	**No**
Bars/Lounges	**1**
Casino	**No**
Shops	**1**
Library	**Yes**
Child Program	**No**
Self-Service Laundry	**No**
Elevators	**0**

Cabin Statistics

Suites	**0**
Outside Doubles	**12**
Inside Doubles	**13**
Wheelchair Cabins	**0**
Singles	**2**
Single Surcharge	**Yes**
Verandas	**0**
110 Volt	**Yes**

⚓⚓⚓⚓⚓
SPIRIT OF '98

We watched her sail into Ketchikan looking tiny and top-heavy, even a little ungainly, compared to a big cruise ship, which was approaching the dock from the south, but as she got closer, she whizzed around the end of the pier and into her little inside spot while the other ship seemed to be standing still.

Passengers on the bow of Spirit of '98 *get close in to shore.*

We first saw this ship, now the flagship of Alaska Sightseeing/Cruise West, back in 1984 in St. Thomas, when it was the newly built *Pilgrim Belle* for now-defunct American Cruise Line. As the *Colonial Explorer*, it sailed for also-defunct Exploration Cruise Line, then was briefly the *Victorian Empress* for Canadian-flag St. Lawrence Cruises.

A replica of a Victorian riverboat, the *Spirit of '98* is much more appealing than you might expect, with fairly spacious cabins furnished in reproduction Victorian antiques, good dresser and closet hanging space and large, if rudimentary, bathrooms with shower. Only the lavish owner's suite (see "Fantasy Suites," below) has a bathtub. Like the other vessels of the line, the *Spirit of '98* has only one major lounge where the passengers gather, although there is a smaller, quieter area called Soapy's Parlour aft off the dining room, where the bar is rarely if ever manned.

EAVESDROPPING

"I hate to go home," sighed an Arizona woman on the last morning of her cruise. "This has been the most wonderful trip of my life—beyond my wildest expectations."

INSIDER TIP

This is usually the most popular ship in the fleet, so if you want to sail aboard, book as early as possible or put yourself on a waiting list in case there's a cancellation.

Cabins & Costs

The Small Splurge cabin nomination for the Spirit of '98*—the category one cabins on Main Deck forward.*

Fantasy Suites: . . . . **A**

Average Price Per Person, Double Occupancy, Per Day: $747 plus air add-on.

The Owner's Suite is a lavish 552-square-foot apartment set all by itself on the topmost Sun Deck behind the navigation bridge, with big windows on three sides for optimum viewing. The living room has a sofabed, loveseat, two chairs, end tables and coffee table, as well as a full built-in entertainment center, wet bar stocked with complimentary drinks and a game and dining table with four chairs. A separate bedroom has a king-sized bed, and the green marble bath contains a tub/shower combination. This cabin is the only one on the ship that has full room-service privileges, even at dinner, as well as complimentary beverages, including bar drinks, and cabin hors d'oeuvres service nightly.

Small Splurges: . . . . B

Average Price PPPD: $518 plus airfare add-on.

We particularly like the category One cabins all the way forward on Main Deck, because they're spacious with very little foot traffic passing by. You do hear the engines, but not with a deafening roar, just a quiet steady throb. Bigger than most of the other cabins, this pair narrows with the curvature of the ship's hull. There's a queen-sized bed, covered with a handsome dark-green-and-black-striped quilted spread and a clutch of lush pillows, including bolsters, in case you want to lie down and read in bed.

A three-drawer nightstand on either side, along with two drawers built in under the bed and a large wooden armoire, provides generous hanging and wardrobe space for anything you'd carry on a weeklong cruise. A desk, reading lamp, mini-refrigerator, TV/VCR and two chairs round out the furnishings, and the bath, large but basic, has a big shower, lavatory and toilet. A small basket of toiletries is also presented.

Suitable Standards: . . . . B

Average Price PPPD: $471, plus airfare.

Category Two and category Three cabins open onto outer decks, and have big windows, twin or queen-sized beds, chairs, closet and spacious bathroom. Furnishings are virtually identical to those described above.

Bottom Bunks: . . . . B

Average Price PPPD: $364 plus airfare add-on.

A pair of category Five cabins on the Upper Deck have upper and lower berths, along with a built-in deck and chair, closets and bath with shower, not bad at all for minimum accommodations. They open directly onto the outdoor deck.

DID YOU KNOW?

Kevin Costner as Wyatt Earp was aboard to film the final scene of the Western of the same name; you can see his autograph, along with those of other cast and crew members, on the life ring displayed near the dining room entrance (look at the area where eight o'clock would be on a clock face).

The Routes

The *Spirit of '98* spends the summer—from mid-May through mid-September cruising on seven-night itineraries between Seattle and Juneau, with calls in Ketchikan, Sitka, Skagway, Haines and Wrangell, plus cruising through Glacier Bay and Tracy Arm. During October and November the vessel sails from San Francisco on three- and four-night cruises of the wine country with visits to Napa Valley and Sacramento's Old Town.

ALASKA SIGHTSEEING/
CRUISE WEST

CHAMPAGNE TOAST

When the time comes to disembark, all the officers and crew line up at the end of the gangway to say a personal goodbye, and only the most reserved passengers settle for a 'thank you' and handshake. Most of them exchange hugs and addresses, and take photos of each other.

Waitresses serenade passengers aboard the **Spirit of '98.**

The Scoop

This is a classy "soft adventure" with a roster of affluent and intelligent passengers, many of them taking a first cruise, who selected the vessel for its historic character and up-close-and-personal looks at Alaska. The American crew is young, energetic and enthusiastic, the food and service are quite good, and there's really nothing to complain about except the utilitarian, less-than-lavish bathroom facilities—and they're not THAT bad. *Spirit of '98* is a real winner for anyone who wants to travel through southeast Alaska in comfort and style.

Insider Tips

Five Special Spots On Board

1. The forward viewing area on lounge deck, great for spotting orcas and bald eagles.

2. The giant checkerboard aft on Bridge Deck, good for a group game of checkers or chess.

3. Soapy's Parlour, a quiet hideaway for reading aft of the dining room where nothing ever happens in the daytime unless someone comes in to swap a videocassette.

4. The Klondike Dining Room, with big windows and tables for six, and open seating that allows you to sit where and with whom you please.

5. The Grand Salon with its small, appealing bar, Continental breakfast and cocktail hour hors d'oeuvres buffet, cozy and crowded with small tables, chairs and sofas for chatting, reading, card-playing or catching up on correspondence.

Five Good Reasons to Book These Ships

1. You can open the cabin windows.
2. The 10-night cruises begin or end in Seattle.
3. It's the only vessel in the line that has an elevator.
4. You can lounge in the sun or shade on the Sun Deck, feet propped against the rail, watching the gorgeous scenery along the Inside Passage.
5. Settle into the Owner's Suite in luxurious comfort (see "Fantasy Suites,").

Five Things You Won't Find On Board

1. Kevin Costner—at least not this year. (See earlier "Footnote.")
2. A library with hardback best-sellers.
3. A stuffy attitude.
4. A key to lock up your cabin.
5. A high crew-to-passenger ratio.

ALASKA SIGHTSEEING/
CRUISE WEST

SPIRIT OF '98   ♨♨♨♨

Registry	**U.S.**
Officers	**American**
Crew	**American**
Complement	**26**
GRT	**96**
Length (ft.)	**192**
Beam (ft.)	**40**
Draft (ft.)	**9.3**
Passengers-Cabins Full	**101**
Passengers-2/Cabin	**98**
Passenger Space Ratio	**NA**
Stability Rating	**Fair**
Seatings	**1**
Cuisine	**American**
Dress Code	**Casual**
Room Service	**No**
Tip	**$10 PPPD pooled among staff incl bar**

Ship Amenities

Outdoor Pool	**0**
Indoor Pool	**0**
Jacuzzi	**0**
Fitness Center	**Yes**
Spa	**No**
Beauty Shop	**No**
Showroom	**No**
Bars/Lounges	**1**
Casino	**No**
Shops	**1**
Library	**Yes**
Child Program	**No**
Self-Service Laundry	**No**
Elevators	**1**

Cabin Statistics

Suites	**1**
Outside Doubles	**48**
Inside Doubles	**0**
Wheelchair Cabins	**0**
Singles	**0**
Single Surcharge	**Yes**
Verandas	**0**
110 Volt	**Yes**

AMERICAN CANADIAN CARIBBEAN LINE, INC

"The Small Ship Cruise Line"

461 Water Street, Warren, RI 02885
☎ (401) 247-0955, (800) 556-7450
www.accl-smallships.com

History

Captain Luther Blount of Blount Marine in Warren, Rhode Island, founded ACCL, "the small ship cruise line," more than 30 years ago. He grew up in a fishing family and when he was 17, influenced by reading Gifford Pinchot's book *To the South Seas,* set out for the Galapagos as part of the crew aboard a 30-foot yacht. "We never got there—the boat got shipwrecked—I don't know how my folks ever let me go." The energetic New England octogenarian (when we first interviewed him by phone in 1989, he said, "I'm 74 but I only look 58") built his own three vessels, plus several that sail at present for Alaska Sightseeing/Cruise West. His offbeat itineraries demand "a good sea boat that can't draw over six feet, and it has to go through the Erie Canal so the top has to fold down flat." His ships also have a stern swimming platform with steps to get in and out of the water, a mini-sailboat for passenger use in the Caribbean, a motorized skiff to take passengers ashore when the bow landing feature is not used (see below) and a glass-bottom boat to let passengers view underwater life.

—Inventor of the bow-landing ramp; the vessel noses into shore and opens a forward ramp, allowing passengers to walk from the ship directly onto land. Inventor of the retractable pilot house, which folds down to allow the vessel to sail under low bridges such as those on the Erie Canal.

Concept

To create ships that can offer a maximum of 100 passengers a chance to go where larger vessels can't, to provide a casual onboard ambience so passengers and crew get to know each other well, and to take people on "real adventures close to home," including to the Erie Canal, Belize and Guatemala, Costa Rica, Nicaragua, Honduras, Trinidad and Tobago, the Orinoco, and a cruise between New Orleans and Chicago. The line says it's destination-oriented rather than ship-oriented.

Signatures

The unique bow-landing ramp and retractable pilot house, plus extremely shallow drafts, allow the ships to go under low bridges, into shallow waters and disembark passengers almost anywhere.

A BYOB (Bring Your Own Bottle) policy, because Blount doesn't believe in making money off a bar. The cruise line provides soft drinks and snacks, but passengers who want a cocktail or glass of wine have to bring their own.

Gimmicks.

After a passenger takes nine cruises with ACCL, his 10th cruise is free. This alone keeps 'em coming back year after year, comparing notes on how near they are to their freebie.

Who's the Competition

In the Caribbean, Blount's vessels compete (only slightly) with Clipper Cruises. Their type vessel and cruise experience is unique in these waters.

EAVESDROPPING

Captain Luther Blount: "I haven't gone whole hog in borrowing a lot of money and getting in the hole by trying to do too much, (and) I haven't tried to be the biggest guy on the lot." He makes it a point of pride to build a new ship only when he can do it without borrowing money. His Mayan Prince debuted in 1992, the Niagara Prince in 1994, and the new Grande Caribe debuted in June 1997 with Grande Mariner due in mid-1998.

Who's Aboard.

Couples and singles, most of them in the golden years beyond retirement, with an aversion to dressing up, gambling, hanging around bars and watching floor shows. Instead, they enjoy getting close-up looks at exotic parts of our own hemisphere. They love swimming and snorkeling (although none of them would make the *Sports Illustrated* swimsuit issue), exploring archeological ruins and visiting remote primitive villages, and all of them look forward to their free 10th cruise with the company.

Who Should Go

Basically, the people who are aboard, plus middle-aged couples who'd like to go snorkeling in Belize, cruising the Erie Canal or bird-watching in Trinidad.

Who Should Not Go

Young couples and singles, families with small children (or teenagers, for that matter) or anybody who wants to live it up.

INSIDER TIP

The ships do not permit any passengers under 14 years of age.

The Lifestyle

Very casual, just as Captain Blount intends. No need to ever dress up, or even change clothes between the day's excursion and the evening's dinner unless you really want to. The closeness between passengers and crew that the boss advocates is nearly unavoidable, since these vessels are quite compact with a paucity of public space. Basically there's a dining room and a nearby lounge, and that's it except for open decks. Passengers sit where they wish at large informal tables in the dining room and food is served family-style, so everybody gets to know everybody pretty quickly, if only from passing the salt. Despite the absence of a bar, cocktail hour is diligently observed every night before dinner, with mixers and nibbles in abundance. The bottle-owners write their names on their bottles and stow them in the lounge between cocktail hours. Smoking is permitted only on the deck on the ships. Entertainment, when it occurs, may be a folkloric company on shore or a musician brought on board at a port of call. Or a passenger may play the piano or do birdcalls. Some shore excursions are free, some sold at a modest charge from $15-$30.

Wardrobe

Very casual, anything you'd wear to the Kmart, but polyester with elastic waistbands is very popular. These passengers are people who aim at practicality, traveling light and skipping wrinkles—they are not interested in being fashion plates. However, the men may don a tie or bolo (string tie) and the women put on a dress or pantsuit on a special evening. There is one very sophisticated couple we know who love these cruises and do like to dress up, so there are exceptions.

Bill of Fare   C

It's American home cooking served family-style, and the quality relies heavily on what chef is in charge, but even if one of the less talented is in the galley, there's always plenty you will like. Once in a while a beach barbecue is scheduled, and coffee and snacks are available 24 hours a day. One special treat if you're in cabins near the galley is to smell the coffee brewing and breakfast cooking early in the morning.

EAVESDROPPING

"The best thing about these ships," says a handsome La Jolla matron who sails them regularly, "is that you can go barefoot all the time."

Discounts

On designated sailings a 5 or 10 percent discount may be offered.

INSIDER TIP

The big sellouts—available on a first-come first-served basis—are positioning and exploratory cruises, which are offered at a flat rate of $125 a day per person to a limited number of passengers (usually 12) who dine with the crew. Call ☎ (800) 556-7450 for dates and details.

The Bottom Line

ACCL delivers just the sort of unpretentious, friendly and adventuresome cruise it promises, and the price is right. Loyal repeaters cite the casual lifestyle, the friendliness of the other passengers and the fact the vessels can go where nobody else can is the main reasons they continue to book. One regular calls the trips "senior citizen camping at sea."

⚓⚓⚓⚓

GRANDE CARIBE
GRANDE MARINER
MAYAN PRINCE
NIAGARA PRINCE

In Guatemala, bouncing along a dirt road in the back of a banana truck on one of ACCL's offbeat excursions, we stopped by the roadside and bought a fresh heart-of-palm, a huge chunk four feet long and big around as an elephant foot, for about 50 cents, but when we presented it to the ship's chef—whose forte seemed to be blueberry muffins and chocolate chip cookies—he studiously ignored our plea to let us make it into a salad for dinner. Later we heard a suspicious splash that we suspect was our heart-of- palm being tossed from the galley window.

While the four ships are not identical, they are quite similar to each other with comparable furnishings (functional) and decor (no-nonsense). Our first cruise with them was also our only cruise in tiny inside cabins; we had one each. Shirley is claustrophobic and had to leave the bathroom light on all night with the shower curtain pinned across the open doorway to pretend it was a window with a street light outside, and Harry went into hibernation in the soothing darkness, sleeping some mornings until nearly noon.

The cabins we're talking about are the ones we call "the terrible 20s," the tiny bottom-category forward cabins on the lowest deck with numbers in the 20s.

The ship layouts are simple—a Sun Deck on top with the pilot house, top category cabins and deck space, a Main Deck with more cabins, the galley, dining room and lounge, and the lower deck on some ships with crew quarters and "the terrible 20s."

The Brochure Says

"We at ACCL have been offering the traveling public 'adventure' cruises for 30 years, but we've done so with certain self-imposed restrictions. We believe in challenging trips, but never at the expense of your well-being, your wallet or your general comfort and peace of mind."

Translation

This is Captain Blount speaking bluntly—as is his wont—to his passengers. On the back page, there is also a paragraph that begins, "American Canadian Caribbean Line believes in honesty, reliability and good business ethics." You get a very strong sense of honor, decency and character with this line.

DID YOU KNOW?

When Princess Cruises objected to the proposed name of Mayan Princess for Blount's new ship, he promptly announced, "The ship will undergo a sex change operation." It was christened Mayan Prince. The original plan to name the next ship **Grand Prince** *was scuttled for the same reason due to Princess' 104,000-ton megaship* **Grand Princess** *and it became the* **Grande Caribe**.

Cabins & Costs

Fantasy Suites: . . . . **NA**
Are you kidding?

Small Splurges: . . . . **C-**
Average Price Per Person, Double Occupancy, Per Day: $205 plus airfare.
We'd recommend springing for the biggest cabins you can afford on these ships. The Sun Deck amidships cabins are usually the costliest but not always the biggest so check the brochure diagrams carefully. Dimensions and furniture arrangements are given. Cabins on the *Niagara Prince* measuring 12 feet by eight feet are the largest in the fleet, along with the cabins aboard the *Mayan Prince*, which come in at 11 feet by eight. They have two lower beds (some of which can be made into a double berth if the request is made at the time of booking), picture windows, a closet, a couple of stools and a dresser, as well as a very compact bath with a European-style hand-held shower which (if you don't handle it right) will drench the entire bathroom.

Suitable Standards: . . . . **C**
Average Price PPPD: $185 plus airfare.
Main Deck outside cabins are perfectly acceptable, but we wouldn't recommend the inside ones unless you're interested in hibernating. You'll find the usual two lower

beds, perhaps a desk/dresser and stool, a closet and the compact bathroom with European hand-held shower.

Bottom Bunks: . . . . F

Average Price PPPD: $122 plus airfare.

We told you about "the terrible 20s," but there's one cabin on the *Mayan Prince* that's even cheaper, the A Cabin. It's beside the galley, which means an early morning wake-up from the minute the chef starts rattling those pots and pans. It's also somewhat smaller than even "the terrible 20s" and we can't in good conscience recommend it.

The *Grande Caribe* spends winters in Panama cruising between Balboa and Colon on 12-day itineraries. In spring the ship sails the intracoastal waterway between Florida and Rhode Island and in summer it cruises the Erie and Saguenay Canals.

The *Grande Mariner* is expected to join the fleet sometime in 1998. Schedules are yet to be announced.

The *Mayan Prince* sails the Caribbean in winter also visiting the Orinoco River and Venezuelan Islands as well as Panama, Nicaragua, Honduras and Belize. In summer the ship sails to Erie Canal and Saguenay, then moves to Massena, Labrador and Newfoundland.

The *Niagara Prince* makes fall foliage cruises between New Orleans and Nashville, followed by a winter season in Belize, Roatan, Barrier Reef and Guatemala. In spring the vessel cruises between New Orleans and Chicago and them moves to New England in mid-summer and to the Great Lakes and Canals of America (between Buffalo and Warren) in late summer.

DID YOU KNOW?

In fine print under the description of each cruise is the note: Every effort will be made to follow the published itinerary—wind, weather, tide and the good Lord providing. ACCL reserves the right to change, omit or add stops, change the route or consume extra days.

While we have a tremendous admiration for Captain Blount and his practical, no-ripoff approach to cruising, we have to caution readers that these ships are not for everybody. If you don't like mixing and mingling, you may not be happy aboard. You get to know everybody pretty well because there's nowhere to get away from them but in your cabin. You need to be footloose (or barefoot) and fancy free, able to take schedule changes or little annoyances in your stride. And look, at these prices, if you're a happy camper, you can earn your free cruise in no time.

Insider Tips

Five Gathering Points

1. The Lounge, where passengers stash their booze, names neatly written on the bottles, and there's usually somebody who suspects somebody else has been sampling his stash. Pretzels, cheese puffs and potato chips are in good supply.

2. The Dining Room, where passengers may dine on a single seating (where the timing is usually the same as early seating on other ships) and the crew dines at the second seating.

3. The Sun Deck, the place to stand to see the sea, where a stretch of tarpaulin may serve as shade because it's "low bridge, everybody down" on some sailings.

4. The Pilot House, where passengers are permitted to visit a couple at a time (it's too small for any more people than that) and see "who's driving the boat."

5. The bow-landing ramp, the entrance and exit in many ports.

Five Good Reasons to Book These Ships

1. The above-mentioned honor, decency and character.

2. To buy nine cruises and get the 10th one free.

3. To see the Americas first.

4. The price is right.

5. On the *Niagara Prince* in most cabins, the windows open.

Five Things You Won't Find On Board

1. A swimming pool.

2. A bar.

3. A casino.

4. A ventriloquist.

5. Sequins.

GRANDE CARIBE ♾ ♾ ♾ ♾

Registry	U.S.
Officers	American
Crew	Amer & Panamanian
Complement	18
GRT	98.4
Length (ft.)	182
Beam (ft.)	38
Draft (ft.)	6'6"
Passengers-Cabins Full	100
Passengers-2/Cabin	100
Passenger Space Ratio	NA
Stability Rating	Fair to Good
Seatings	1
Cuisine	American
Dress Code	Casual
Room Service	No
Tip	$8 - $10 PPPD

Ship Amenities

Outdoor Pool	0
Indoor Pool	0
Jacuzzi	0
Fitness Center	No
Spa	No
Beauty Shop	No
Showroom	No
Bars/Lounges	1
Casino	No
Shops	0
Library	Yes
Child Program	No
Self-Service Laundry	No
Elevators	0

Cabin Statistics

Suites	0
Outside Doubles	50
Inside Doubles	0
Wheelchair Cabins	0
Singles	6
Single Surcharge	175%
Verandas	0
110 Volt	Yes

AMERICAN CANADIAN CARIBBEAN LINE, INC.

MAYAN PRINCE   ⚓⚓⚓

Registry	U.S.
Officers	American
Crew	Amer & Panamanian
Complement	18
GRT	98.4
Length (ft.)	169
Beam (ft.)	38
Draft (ft.)	6'8"
Passengers-Cabins Full	92
Passengers-2/Cabin	90
Passenger Space Ratio	NA
Stability Rating	Fair to Good
Seatings	1
Cuisine	American
Dress Code	Casual
Room Service	No
Tip	$8 - $10 PPPD

Ship Amenities

Outdoor Pool	0
Indoor Pool	0
Jacuzzi	0
Fitness Center	No
Spa	No
Beauty Shop	No
Showroom	No
Bars/Lounges	1
Casino	No
Shops	0
Library	Yes
Child Program	No
Self-Service Laundry	No
Elevators	0

Cabin Statistics

Suites	0
Outside Doubles	44
Inside Doubles	1
Wheelchair Cabins	0
Singles	6
Single Surcharge	175%
Verandas	0
110 Volt	Yes

NIAGARA PRINCE · ↯↯↯↯

Registry	U.S.
Officers	American
Crew	American
Complement	17
GRT	99
Length (ft.)	177
Beam (ft.)	40
Draft (ft.)	6'9"
Passenger-Cabins Full	88
Passengers-2/Cabin	84
Passengers Space Ratio	NA
Stability Rating	Fair to Good
Seatings	1
Cuisine	American
Dress Code	Casual
Room Service	No
Tip	$8–$10 PPPD

Ship Amenities

Outdoor Pool	0
Indoor Pool	0
Jacuzzi	0
Fitness Center	No
Spa	No
Beauty Shop	No
Showroom	No
Bars/Lounges	1
Casino	No
Shops	0
Library	Yes
Child Program	No
Self-Service Laundry	No
Elevators	0

Cabin Statistics

Suites	0
Outside Doubles	40
Inside Doubles	2
Wheelchair Cabins	0
Singles	6
Single Surcharge	175%
Verandas	0
110 Volt	Yes

AMERICAN CANADIAN CARIBBEAN LINE, INC.

AMERICAN HAWAII CRUISES & LAND VACATIONS

30 Robin Street Wharf, New Orleans, LA 70130
☎ (800) 765-7000
www.cruisehawaii.com

Dress aboard is casual during the daytime, as here during a deck hula lesson.

History ·

The only ocean going U.S.-flag ship, the *Independence* of American Hawaii Cruises, was designed by Henry Dreyfuss and built in 1951 at Bethlehem Steel in Quincy, Massachusetts. It started as a transatlantic liner for American Export Lines of New York, carrying such famous passengers as President Harry S Truman, King Saud of Saudi Arabia, Rita Hayworth, Walt Disney, Alfred Hitchcock and Ernest Hemingway.

But the arrival of transatlantic jets in the 1960s changed ocean travel, and the ship fell into hard times. The formerly dignified *Independence* was chartered by a New York travel company called Fugazi, painted in garish Pop Art colors that featured a sunburst with Bette Davis eyes, and sent sailing as a one-class "funship" for a new kind of cruising in which passengers paid for their meals restaurant-style. That lasted for about 20 minutes before the ship was laid up in Baltimore, Maryland, in 1969.

In 1974, C.Y. Tung, a Hong Kong shipping magnate, bought the *Independence* and sister ship *Constitution* for his Atlantic Far East Lines and renamed the pair *Oceanic Independence* and *Oceanic Constitution* under the Monrovian flag. This act decommissioned the ships, meaning they lost their U.S.-flag status when they were acquired by a foreign owner. (Tung had also been the owner of Cunard's great liner *Queen Elizabeth*, predecessor of the *QE2*, when she burned and sank in Hong Kong harbor in 1972.)

The *Independence* got in a couple of years of cruising before she was laid up in Hong Kong with the *Constitution*, which never cruised under her new name.

In 1979, a reorganization within the C.Y. Tung family created a New York-based company called American Global Lines Inc., which acquired the pair of ships and, after a special act of Congress signed by President Carter, allowed the vessels to be recommissioned with the U.S. flag to enable them to cruise in the Hawaiian Islands. The *Independence* started sailing again in 1980, and Princess Grace of Monaco returned to christen the *Constitution* in 1982 at the shipyard in Taiwan where it was refurbished and sent back into service. The *Constitution* was retired in 1996.

Delta Queen Steamboat Company bought American Hawaii Cruises in 1993 and a year later renamed the joint company American Classic Voyages, which is traded on NASDAQ.

Concept. . . . .

Under American Classic Voyages, the *Independence* has been extensively renovated—they term it "reinvented"—to emphasize the culture and traditions of Hawaii in the decor, food, activities and shore excursions aboard.

Signatures . . . .

An Hawaiian teacher called a Kumu is aboard every sailing to talk about traditional culture, tell stories and demonstrate dances, and the famous Bishop Museum of Honolulu has helped set up a floating museum exhibit of Hawaiiana.

Gimmicks. . . . .

Orchids, orchids everywhere, along with other fresh tropical foliage, decorate the ships. A Hawaiian "word of the day" is printed on the daily program, and passengers can learn Hawaiian crafts from weaving a ti leaf lei to playing the ukulele.

Who's the Competition . . . .

Nobody, really, because the foreign flag vessels who cruise around the Hawaiian islands—among them Princess, Holland America and Royal Caribbean—have to begin or end their cruises in a non-U.S. port such as Papeete, Tahiti or Ensenada, Mexico, because of an archaic cabotage law popularly called the Jones Act. There was once, very briefly, a competing U.S.-flag company called Aloha Pacific Cruises, which brought the refurbished *Monterey* into Honolulu in 1988, but that company, hit with a flurry of lawsuits and other charges from American Hawaii, soon went into bankruptcy and the ship was laid up, then later sold to Star-Lauro, an Italian cruise company, now sailing as Mediterranean Shipping Cruises.

DID YOU KNOW?

One of the charges, ironically, was that the Monterey, which had never been decommissioned, should not be permitted to use the U.S. flag since some of her renovations were made in a foreign shipyard; this was strange coming from a company who had renovated its decommissioned vessels in Taiwan and needed an act of Congress to recommission them under the U.S. flag.

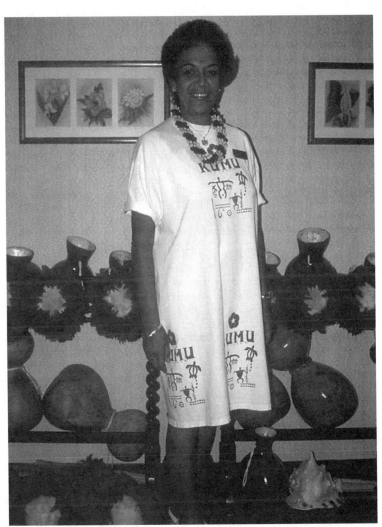

American Hawaii emphasizes the culture and traditions of the islands; a Kumu or Hawaiian teacher and storyteller such as Pua Lani Kauila, pictured here, is aboard every sailing.

Who's Aboard. . . . .

An interesting mix of families with young children, honeymooners, middle-aged couples, singles and retirees. When we were aboard recently, there were several affinity groups from businesses, churches or civic clubs in the southeast. Residents of Hawaii also get special cruise-only rates when sailings aren't filled.

Who Should Go . . . .

More first-time visitors to Hawaii should experience the islands first by sea rather than spending a week on a package in Waikiki or Maui. Aboard ship, they can sample the best of four islands easily without flying between them or packing and unpacking. Also, families with children will find a cruise can usually save them money in the long run.

Who Should Not Go . . . .

Anyone looking for a live-it-up, Las Vegas-style cruise with lots of gambling and glitzy entertainment; American Hawaii does not have casinos and fog-and-laser production shows. It doesn't even permit smoking except on deck.

The Lifestyle . . . .

Casual best describes the daytime ambience. Naturally, with a port-intensive cruise, there are a large number of shore excursions available, from a helicopter flight over Kilauea Volcano to tropical garden and macadamia nut farm tours. Passengers dine at assigned tables on one of two meal seatings. In port lunches and dinners are usually served open seating, which means passengers arrive during a set time period and are shown to a table.

DID YOU KNOW?

The ride aboard is smooth, without vibration and motor noise, because it's operated by steam turbines.

Wardrobe. . . . .

The dress is casual on every night aboard except for the captain's welcome-aboard cocktail party and dinner, to which passengers are requested to wear semi-formal dress, usually interpreted as a jacket and tie for men, a dress or pantsuit for women. On deck and ashore in the daytime, shorts and T-shirts are acceptable most places except posh restaurants. There are always one or two nights that call for aloha wear (otherwise, why visit that muu muu factory?)

Bill of Fare. . . . . B+

We think the food has improved tremendously under the new ownership. The accent is now on Pacific Rim cuisine that incorporates more fresh foods made from island ingredients whenever possible. Breakfast offers all those familiar Honolulu hotel favorites, from fresh tropical fruits to macadamia nut pancakes, from Hawaiian Spam steak (yes, *that* Spam; it's very popular in Hawaii) to Portuguese sausage. Lunch always features an authentic Hawaiian plate lunch, the sort served by little cafes in Hilo, including teriyaki beef with two scoops of rice and a macaroni-potato salad. But finicky eaters may also opt for Thai papaya-shrimp salad, a baked island fish or a paniolo (Hawaiian cowboy) burger with taro chips or curly fries. At the food court buffet lunch upstairs, you can hit the deli counter for an order-your-own sandwich if the regular hot, cold or grill items don't tempt you. Dinners offer two appetizers (perhaps Kona crab cakes or seared sashimi), two soups (wild mushroom or won ton), two salads, four main dishes (perhaps fresh Hawaiian fish, roast turkey, grilled New York steak or seared sea scallops) and a separate menu of desserts.

The Ohana Buffet is like a food court with various food stations from a deli counter for a choose-your-own sandwich to a hot area with carvery roasts.

CHAMPAGNE TOAST

One very good American Hawaii idea more ships should emulate is the use of professional entertainers to amuse passengers waiting in the terminal to board the ship. In this case, Hawaiian musicians, singers, dancers and storytellers present a lively preview of the cruise to come.

Showtime C

Entertainment aboard is a blend of Hawaii and the mainland U.S., with both hula and line dancing classes, Big Band and Blue Hawaii theme sailings and the Newlywed/Not So Newlywed game following a Hawaiian standup comic. Movie screenings in the theater, a passenger talent show, or dancing under the stars—there's always something to do.

Discounts . . . .

An early booking discount knocks down brochure prices; children 18 or younger sharing a cabin with two full-fare adults get special deals.

The Bottom Line

An authentic Hawaiian experience is what American Hawaii wants to offer its passengers, and it seems to be doing a very good job of it. It has integrated music, food, culture, history and traditions such as "talk story," in which the Kumu, or teacher, relates island myths and legends. The ship is charming in its new guise, the food delicious, the all-American staff friendly and the scenery spectacular as you sail around the islands.

★ ★ ★
INDEPENDENCE

Before it became our 50th state, Hawaii was our myth, our sweet sugar-and-pineapple candyland, with romantic popular songs such as "Blue Hawaii" and "Sweet Lelani" on the radio bringing crashing surf and sinuous hula rhythms into our living rooms. In those magical days, the lush landscape of Hawaii was our secret garden, and we sailed in fantasy on glistening white steamships to palatial pink hotels on golden beaches, to the ports of paradise.

If you haven't been aboard the *Independence* in the last couple of years, you've missed the big makeover—pots of fresh orchids and birds of paradise everywhere, showy lobby carpets with tropical floral border, bare wood floors and bamboo and wicker period furniture, balcony windows that open to the outside, bars with old movie posters and Cadiz shell lampshades, a free jukebox with all-Hawaiian melodies. There's even hallway carpeting with small swimming whales headed toward the bow of the ship, so if you follow the pattern, you're walking forward.

From a practical point of view, the renovation has improved the traffic flow tremendously with the new aft deck stairs, and added six lavish solarium suites on Bridge Deck. One big change is the opening up of the formerly enclosed ocean liner areas to create more of an indoor-outdoor lanai atmosphere.

Between The Lines

The Brochure Says

"Created by legendary American designer Henry Dreyfuss and built in 1951, this classic ship features a full array of 50 different configurations of fully-appointed suites, staterooms and cabins.... Cabins, though similar in size and amenities, may vary within each category."

Translation

Back in the days of three-class ships, cabins came in all shapes and sizes, and that's what you'll find aboard. The bathrooms in particular on some of the cheaper cabins may remind you of the old Navy term "head." Some of the tiniest cabins on the lower decks make us remember the tearful bride complaining at the desk that there wasn't room in their cabin for both her luggage and her new husband. You should always book the highest category you can afford on this ship.

INSIDER TIP

Go easy buying aloha tropical wear; what looks hot on Oahu doesn't always work back home in Omaha.

Cabins & Costs

Hawaiian decor dresses up the cabin interiors.

Fantasy Suites: .... A

Average Price Per Person, Double Occupancy, Per Day: $450 plus airfare for the Boat Deck suites, $379 plus airfare for the solarium suites.

A clutch of new AA suites on the *Independence's* Bridge Deck and AAA suites on the Boat Deck provide from 300 to 575 square feet of space. Solarium suites have high ceilings with skylights and windows that open, best for passengers who like to see starlight and sunrises; they can't be darkened completely. The larger Boat Deck suites have separate living and sleeping rooms. All are prettily turned out with original Hawaiian art, Hawaiian quilts and fabrics, and most should offer you a double or queen-sized bed.

Small Splurges: .... **A**

Average Price PPPD: $335 plus airfare.
We particularly like some of the A category deluxe suites with separate sitting and sleeping rooms and big windows to the view. The new furnishings are in beautiful florals and pastels, and the carpeting repeats a traditional basketweave pattern.

Suitable Standards: .... **B**

Average Price PPPD: $292 plus airfare.
Opt for an outside double standard and you'll find a window or porthole, bathroom with shower and, in many, a sofa that converts to a single berth and a fold-away single berth, more comfortable than they sound.

Bottom Bunks: .... **D-**

Average Price PPPD: $159 plus airfare.
Cheapest are the inside category G budget cabins (the ones that made the bride tearful, see "Translation," above), with upper and lower berths. The last refurbishment added attractive furnishings but didn't increase the size.

INSIDER TIP

Suites and newly added cabins are more apt to have real beds inside than the original cabins, many of which were furnished with a sofa that makes into a single berth and a second berth that folds out from the wall. But look, if Grace Kelly and Cary Grant could sleep on those, you should be able to.

The Routes

The *Independence* sets out from Honolulu's Aloha Tower every Saturday, has a day at sea, calls at Kauai, spends an overnight in Maui, Hilo and Kona on the Big Island.

The classic 1950s ocean liner offers a wonderful introduction to Hawaii.

The Scoop

Sailing the classic 1950s ocean liner from one island to the next provides the best possible introduction to Hawaii. But even old hula hands still get a thrill seeing the town of Lahaina from the sea or cruising past the rugged contours of Molokai. The way the *Independence* sparkles from its last renovation dramatically improves an already good product. Our only caveat is to try to stay out of the very cheapest inside cabins; spend a little bit more to get some space.

Insider Tips

Five Happy Havens

Wood floors and koa wood doors open onto open-air lanais from the lounges, a cultural exhibit created by the Bishop Museum ornaments each lounge.

1. The signature Kama'aina Lounge, or living room, has koa wood doors that open onto open-air lanais on both sides; a cultural exhibit created by the Bishop Museum is the focus.

2. The redesigned deck areas greatly improve traffic flow.

3. The Commodore's Terrace is a handsome glass-walled room with two gold-and-royal-blue sofas with gold stars and gold fringe like a commodore's uniform; the carpet is dark blue with gold stars.

4. The Ohana Buffet is set up like a food court with various food stations—a deli counter for a choose-your-own sandwich, a grill for hot dogs and hamburgers, a fruit juice area, a cold area with salads, a hot area with carvery roasts and side dishes and a dessert area.

5. The Hapa Haole Bar is reminiscent of old downtown Honolulu, filled with movie stills and posters from films shot in Hawaii, tacky Cadiz shell lampshades and a free jukebox with only Hawaiian songs.

The Hapa Haole Bar, reminiscent of old downtown Honolulu, sports movie stills, a jukebox and shell lamps.

Five Good Reasons to Book This Ship

1. To see Hawaii from the sea like the first Polynesian settlers did; these days there's virtually no inter-island boat service—everyone commutes by air.

2. To immerse yourself in a real Hawaiian experience with no Don Ho, Tahitian *tamare* or plastic grass skirt in sight.

3. To go resort-shopping if you want to come back and stay awhile; the ships stop in almost all the popular beach areas so you can pick out your beach and hotel for the next visit.

4. To visit four of Hawaii's islands without endlessly sitting around in airports waiting an hour for a 20-minute commuter hop, not to mention having to divulge your weight every time you check in for a flight.

5. To sightsee at your own pace by booking one of nearly 50 shore excursions, arranging for a rental car on every island to do your own touring or just walking around in the ports.

Five Things You Won't Find On Board

1. A casino.

2. Smoking areas anywhere inside the ship.

3. Bathtubs in standard cabins.

4. A Jacuzzi.

5. A library.

INDEPENDENCE ★★★

Registry	U.S.
Officers	American
Crew	American
Complement	315
GRT	30,090
Length (ft.)	682
Beam (ft.)	89
Draft (ft.)	26.5
Passengers-Cabins Full	1165
Passengers-2/Cabin	802
Passenger Space Ratio	37.51
Stability Rating	Good to Excellent
Seatings	2
Cuisine	Pacific Rim
Dress Code	Hawaiian casual
Room Service	No
Tip	$8.75 PPPD, 15% automatically added to bar check

Ship Amenities

Outdoor Pool	2
Indoor Pool	0
Jacuzzi	0
Fitness Center	Yes
Spa	No
Beauty Shop	Yes
Showroom	Yes
Bars/Lounges	3
Casino	No
Shops	Yes
Library	No
Child Program	Yes
Self-Service Laundry	Yes
Elevators	4

Cabin Statistics

Suites	32
Outside Doubles	171
Inside Doubles	188
Wheelchair Cabins	3
Singles	20
Single Surcharge	160-200%
Verandas	0
110 Volt	Yes

AMERICAN HAWAII CRUISES

AMERICAN WEST STEAMBOAT COMPANY

601 Union Street, Suite 4343, Seattle, WA 98101
☎ *(206) 292-9606, (800) 434-1232*

Queen of the West *sails the Columbia River from Portland, Oregon.*

History ·

Brand-new American West Steamboat Company had some delays with its first boat, the 165-passenger paddlewheel steamer *Queen of the West*. Technical problems with its hydraulic system and paddlewheel were adjusted before the end of the first season. The new U.S.-flag cruise line is headed up by Seattle's Bob Giersdorf, whose eight-ship Exploration Cruise Line folded in 1988 after a financial dispute with investor Anheuser-Busch led to a declaration of bankruptcy and a dispersal of the fleet to other cruise companies. Giersdorf was also president of Glacier Bay Tours and Cruises and Yachtship Cruise Line until early 1996, when he sold the 49-passenger catamaran *Executive Explorer* and the

36-passenger *Wilderness Explorer* to Juneau-based Goldbelt, Inc., an Alaskan Native American corporation.

—The first overnight sternwheeler to operate on the Columbia river since 1917.

Concept . . . .

The boat follows an "American West" theme with historical material, nightly entertainment and complimentary escorted motorcoach shore excursions "to reflect the elements of the rich past of the historic Columbia, Snake and Willamette river regions."

Signatures . . . .

Showboat-style entertainment nightly. The big red three-story paddlewheel. A 45-foot bow ramp for shore access.

Gimmicks. . . . .

All shore excursions are included in the price of the cruise.

Who's The Competition? . . . .

The only other riverboat-type vessel in the Pacific Northwest is Alaska Sightseeing/Cruise West's *Spirit of '98*, a more contemporary looking vessel, and the small expedition vessels from Special Expeditions and Alaska Sightseeing/Cruise West that cruise along the Columbia and Snake in the spring and fall. For a real head-to-head competition between paddlewheelers, the *Queen of the West* would have to be in the heartland of America along the mighty Mississippi and take on those three paddlewheel champions from Delta Queen Steamboat Company, the *Delta Queen* (a former Westerner herself), *Mississippi Queen* and *American Queen*—but those ladies don't seem to have a hankering to head west.

Who's Aboard. . . . .

Most of the passengers are older couples 55 to 75, many from the east and midwestern U.S., but there's usually a sprinkling of young-to-middle-aged Americans as well as families with teenagers.

Who Should Go . . . .

Anyone who has an overwhelming desire to see America close-up and learn the history and culture of the Pacific Northwest from shipboard historian Alden Jencks.

Who Should Not Go . . . .

The vessel is not appropriate for babies and small children, because there are no child-care programs or playrooms on board.

The Lifestyle and Wardrobe . . . .

Casual to informal wardrobe is the rule as well as layered clothing for spring and fall because of temperature changes, and walking shoes for deck and shore excursions. They prefer gentlemen don a jacket, with or without tie, for the captain's welcome aboard party. Meals are served in a single seating. Shore excursions specified in the itinerary are included in the fare. There are no telephones aboard for ship-to-shore calls; they should be made from the daily shore stops. Smoking is limited to outer deck areas only, and the vessel does not have medical service, laundry service, dry-cleaning or a beauty or barber shop. All these services are available ashore.

Bill of Fare . . . . B+

The food aboard is well-prepared by an American chef who figures he rustles up 550 meals a day with all desserts and baking from scratch. Hot rolls are prepared fresh for lunch and dinner every day, and he takes on fresh local seafood frequently, with fresh salmon the first night out, followed on subsequent evenings by items such as fresh scallops, halibut and steamer clams. One of his lunch specialties is a luscious smoked pork sandwich from a tenderloin he lightly smokes on board. Heart-smart and vegetarian offerings are on every menu, and he uses all fresh produce and dairy products. Menu items include fresh clam chowder, Dungeness crab cakes, Washington state rack of lamb, Tillamook cheese, Oregon pears, Walla Walla sweet onions, fiddlehead ferns and Northwest fresh berries. Each breakfast features a special of the day— blintzes with Oregon berries, western omelette, Idaho potatoes with poached eggs and bacon, salmon frittata, French toast stuffed with cherries or smoked salmon with poached eggs on a bagel.

Showtime . . . . B+

Nightly entertainment is provided by entertainers who come aboard from shore, plus a resident three-piece band and a singer/pianist who belts out singalong ballads and blues in the Paddlewheel Lounge. The most popular evening combines close-up magic tricks by card sharp Matt "Maverick" Burton along with an Oregon trail music-and-narration by Dallas McKennon, one of the stars of TV's "Daniel Boone" series. Country/western musicians, "Golden Oldies" singers, a "Best of Broadway" musical evening and a 10-piece Big Band for dancing come aboard one evening each cruise.

Discounts . . . .

Special occasion group rates covering birthdays, 25th and 50th wedding anniversaries, family reunions and holiday getaways for groups of 10 or more qualify for group rates. With 15 paid staterooms in a group, a complimentary stateroom is provided. Early booking discounts are also offered.

⚓⚓⚓⚓

QUEEN OF THE WEST

She's sailing the Columbia River, not the Mississippi, but a first glimpse of the Queen of the West with her tootling calliope, gold-flanged black smokestacks and bright red paddlewheel would remind most cruise buffs of the venerable Delta Queen Steamboat Company in New Orleans, something the western competition does not seem averse to.

Cabins & Costs

All 73 suites and staterooms are outsides, some with private verandas. There are nine price categories from a single top-category owner's suite down to the lowest priced pair of value staterooms (slightly smaller than the others with a single lower bed, pulldown upper berth and small sitting area). A choice of beds from twins, doubles, queens to twins that can convert to a queen is available; baths have showers only. All rooms have view windows, and all but two have inside corridor entries. The two Vista View Deck Suites on the topmost deck adjacent to the captain's quarters and wheelhouse open directly onto the deck, each with its own fenced "front porch." Prices range from $135 to $563 per person, double occupancy, based on a seven-day sailing.

The Routes

The *Queen of the West*'s itinerary is a major attraction, with cruises of seven nights in length and a route that goes roundtrip from Portland along the Willamette River to the Columbia, then through the Columbia Gorge National Scenic Area to the Hood River, where passengers get off for a rail excursion on the Mount Hood Scenic Railway. Visits include Pendleton's Underground city plus a shopping stop at the Pendleton Woolen Mills, Happy Canyon and the Nez Perce Historical Museum. Other highlights include a cruise along the Snake River, Maryhill Museum, Columbia Gorge Discovery Center,

Coldwater Ridge Interpretive Center and the Forest Learning Center, plus wine-tasting and Fort Clatsop.

The Scoop

Queen of the West (and a sister ship planned for a future debut) bring a classy riverboat operation to the northwest without slavishly copying the Delta Queen Steamboat product. Cabins are spacious and prettily furnished, public areas are large and hallways wide, and the crew young and friendly. So far, surprisingly, much of the clientele has come from distant rather than nearby cities.

Insider Tips

Five Special Places

1. The top deck area with the Calliope Bar & Grill, covered with heavy plastic curtains in inclement weather, serves early bird continental breakfast, 24-hour coffee and fresh fruit, frozen yogurt, jumbo hot dogs and hot fresh popcorn.

2. The Paddlewheel Lounge overlooks the churning red wheel from a stunning, glass-walled aft area.

3. The Lewis & Clark Dining Room with hot fresh rolls served the minute you sit down for your lunch or dinner.

4. The Columbia Showroom with its big windows, long bar at one end and small dance floor.

5. The railed deck areas all around the ship, ideal for river-watching except for a few bitterly cold days in winter and early spring.

Five Reasons to Book This Ship

1. To meet Cincinnatus from the old "Daniel Boone" TV series.

2. To go jet-boating in Hell's Canyon.

3. To sample the foods and wines of the Pacific Northwest.

4. To play the steam calliope.

5. To buy a plaid wool shirt on sale at the Pendleton Woolen Mills.

Five Things You Won't Find Aboard

1. Assigned meal seatings.

2. A casino.

3. A gym.

4. A beauty shop.

5. An ash tray in any of the public rooms or cabins; smoking is permitted only on outside decks and verandas.

QUEEN OF THE WEST   ⚓⚓⚓⚓

Registry	U.S.
Officers	American
Crew	American
Complement	41
GRT	NA
Length (ft.)	230
Beam (ft.)	50
Draft (ft.)	NA
Passengers-Cabins Full	163
Passengers-2/Cabin	146
Passenger Space Ratio	NA
Stability Rating	Unrated
Seatings	1
Cuisine	American
Dress Code	Casual
Room Service	No
Tip	$7-$8 PPPD

Ship Amenities

Outdoor Pool	0
Indoor Pool	0
Jacuzzi	0
Fitness Center	No
Spa	No
Beauty Shop	No
Showroom	No
Bars/Lounges	3
Casino	No
Shops	1
Library	Yes
Child Program	No
Self-Service Laundry	No
Elevators	1

Cabin Statistics

Suites	6
Outside Doubles	67
Inside Doubles	0
Wheelchair Cabins	0
Singles	0
Single Surcharge	150%
Verandas	23
110 Volt	Yes

BERGEN LINE

405 Park Avenue, New York, NY 10022
☎ *(212) 319-1300, (800) 323-7436 (reservations), (800) 666-2374 (brochures)*
www.bergenline.com

The 490-passenger **Kong Harald,** *built in 1993, sails year-round for Norwegian Coastal Voyages, marketed by Bergen Line.*

Bergen Line represents a group of shipping companies in Norway that offers a variety of coastal and canal cruises, ferry services and summer expeditions to Spitsbergen.

Its best-known product is **Norwegian Coastal Voyages**, which operates 11 working coastal steamers year-round along the 1250 nautical miles between Bergen in the south and Kirkenes in the north, the so-called *Hurtigruten* or Quick Route. While the practical Norwegians get on and off board to travel from Point A to Point B, foreign travelers—Americans, Canadians, Mexicans, Germans, British, Spanish, Japanese, Swiss and Austrians—board the ships for the spectacular scenery along the route and the chance to get acquainted with Norwegians following their line of work. Schoolchildren, midwives, mail, cargo and commuters sail between ports and islands along the route.

The ships sail year-round, but the number is always set at 11. When a new ship comes on line, as the *Kong Harald* (above) did in 1993, celebrating the 100th birthday of the cruises, an old ship is retired. Among the newest vessels added are the 480-passenger *Polarlys*, the 490-passenger *Nordkapp* and the 490-passenger *Nordnorge*. The new, bigger vessels also increase the fleet capacity by 25 percent to 4477 passengers. More than half the fleet has been built since 1993.

There are 32 ports of call on the northbound segment, and the same 32 on the southbound segment, in case you missed anything the first time.

While summer is the most popular season with tourists, many people enjoy the off-season sailings, even in winter, when the periods of darkness may run from Nov. 21 through Jan. 23. Winter is the best time for spotting the Aurora Borealis.

The Midnight Sun shines 24 hours a day north of the Arctic Circle between mid-May and Aug. 1.

A variety of 11-, 12- and 16-day air/sea programs are available, at prices ranging generally between $2000 and $3500 per person, double occupancy, depending on cabin choice and season. Rates do include round-trip airfare from New York with add-on fares from other cities. You can choose between new ships, newer generation ships or traditional ships. All cabins have private bathroom facilities except category D on the traditional ships.

Retired vessels from Norwegian Coastal Voyages are not sent to the breakers as a rule, but go into other cruise service. The 179-passenger *Nordstjernen*, for instance, has been offering **Arctic Adventure** sailings from Oslo or Tromso to Spitsbergen the past several summers. While most cabins on board have private bathroom facilities, a few lower categories have wash basins in the cabin and the toilet and shower down the hall. Arctic Adventure cruises have double outside cabins with two lower berths and bath with toilet and shower costing around $3140 per person, double occupancy, including round-trip airfare from New York. An eight-day cruise-only program in the same cabin costs $1689 per person, double occupancy. Simpler quarters, whether inside cabins, upper and lower berths or cabins with wash basin only are somewhat cheaper.

Bergen Line also is North American sales representative for **Silja**, **Color Line** and **Scandinavian Seaways** ferries and the historic vessels that sail the Gota Canal. (See "Alternative Cruises, Canal Sailings," page 66.)

CANAVERAL
CRUISE LINE, INC.

751 Third Avenue, New Smyrna Beach, FL 32169
☎ (904) 427-6892

Stunning Bahamian sunsets are a treat for cruise passengers.

History ....

The *Dolphin IV* was purchased from Dolphin Cruise Line by Kosmas Shipping Corporation in July 1995, and was repositioned to Port Canaveral for two-day cruises to the Bahamas as part of a weeklong Florida land/sea package. Kosmas named its new line Canaveral Cruise Line Inc.

243

★ ★
DOLPHIN IV

The most delicious things on the ship are the breadsticks, which disappear all too quickly from the breadbaskets. At the captain's table (where we joined an astonishingly large group of 19) the captain is given his own personal basket of them, from which no one had the audacity to swipe one. After making the breadsticks disappear, the captain entertained his guests with after-dinner magic tricks with coins and cigarettes.

The ship, built in 1955 as the *Zion* for Zim Israel Line, was turned into the *Amelia de Mello* for Lisbon-Canary Islands service in 1966, laid up in 1971, sold to a Greek company in 1972 and renamed *Ithaca*, then sold again in 1979 to operate as the *Dolphin IV* under a joint agreement between Ulysses Cruise Line and Paquet. In 1984, Dolphin Cruise Line was formed to operate the vessel, which made three- and four-day cruises to the Bahamas out of Miami. At present, it makes short cruises from Port Canaveral to Grand Bahamas Island.

Cabins & Costs

Fantasy Suites: . . . . **N/A**

N/A

Small Splurges: . . . . **C-**

Average Price Per Person, Double Occupancy, Per Day: $238 cruise-only.

There are some modest suites on the ship, five of them on the topmost passenger deck and four of them on the deck below the major public areas. Suites 500 and 501 are rather cramped, with double beds against the wall on one side and a sofa, coffee table and closet so close together you have to clamber over the coffee table to put clothes in the closet or sit on the sofa. Suites 513 and 515 are a little larger, but the view is partly obstructed from hanging lifeboats. In all the suites, the sofa makes into a bed, but we can't imagine how it opens up—there's no room.

Suitable Standards: . . . . D

Average Price PPPD: $198 cruise-only.
Most of the cabins are just big enough for two lower beds, a dresser and bathroom with shower, but some also have upper berths.

Bottom Bunks: . . . . D-

Average Price PPPD: $105 cruise-only.
The lowest-priced are inside cabins with upper and lower berths, five of them deep down into the ship and forward, where the ride is bumpier.

The Routes

The vessel sails from Port Canaveral to Grand Bahamas Island on two-night cruises, sold as part of a land package that also includes three days in Orlando theme parks and two days at the beach.

The Scoop

It's a high-density ship with long lines for buffets, for teatime, or any other time food is set out. Still, it has a pleasing personality, and the large numbers of first-time cruisers aboard always seem to be having a wonderful time. We do hope the new owners will refurbish the deck areas, which really need work. The teak is badly worn and oil-spotted. And the self-service buffet, which is tucked into a niche just inside from the pool area, is laid out very inefficiently, forcing the lines to circle the room and come back out the same narrow door. At breakfast, they add a second outdoor buffet on deck that cuts down some on the traffic.

Insider Tips

Five Favorite Places

1. The main lounge has a large metal dance floor and chrome-framed tub chairs that supplement long banquettes around the outside perimeters.

2. The library, with locked cases of books, a strip mirror wall and movable chairs, doubles as a film-screening room.

3. The casino, with one roulette wheel, three blackjack tables, a Caribbean stud table and 71 slots.

4. Two small plunge pools surrounded with tiny blue tiles ornament the aft end of the public rooms deck.

5. A disco buried deep in the bowels of the ship has a shiny, sunken dance floor and mirrored posts.

DOLPHIN IV ★★

Registry	**Panama**
Officers	**Greek**
Crew	**International**
Complement	**285**
GRT	**13,007**
Length (ft.)	**501**
Beam (ft.)	**65**
Draft (ft.)	**26**
Passengers-Cabins Full	**670**
Passengers-2/Cabin	**588**
Passenger Space Ratio	**22.12**
Stability Rating	**Good**
Seatings	**2**
Cuisine	**Continental**
Dress Code	**Traditional**
Room Service	**No**
Tip	**$8.50 PPPD**

Ship Amenities

Outdoor Pool	**1**
Indoor Pool	**0**
Jacuzzi	**0**
Fitness Center	**No**
Spa	**No**
Beauty Shop	**Yes**
Showroom	**Yes**
Bars/Lounges	**2**
Casino	**Yes**
Shops	**1**
Library	**Yes**
Child Program	**Yes**
Self-Service Laundry	**No**
Elevators	**1**

Cabin Statistics

Suites	**9**
Outside Doubles	**208**
Inside Doubles	**77**
Wheelchair Cabins	**0**
Singles	**0**
Single Surcharge	**150%**
Verandas	**0**
110 Volt	**Yes**

ᗀ Carnival®

3655 NW 87 Avenue, Miami, FL 33178
☎ (305) 599-2600, (800) CARNIVAL
www.carnival.com

Carnival designer Joe Farcus stands amid the flash and dazzle of his lobby.

History . . . .

"The most popular cruise line in the world," as the slogan goes, was founded by Ted Arison, who had sold an air-freight business in New York in 1966 and headed back to his native Tel Aviv to retire. According to Arison's son Micky, now chairman and CEO of Carnival, his father never intended to go into cruising, but once he was back in Israel, he took over the management of a struggling charter cruise operation and turned it into a success.

When that vessel, a ship called *Nili*, was returned to the Mediterranean because of the owner's continuing financial difficulties, Arison had several cruises booked but no ship. As Micky tells it, "Ted heard the *Sunward* was laid up in Gibraltar, so he called (Norwegian shipping executive) Knut Kloster and said, "You've got a ship, I've got the passengers, we could put them together, and we'd have a cruise line.' So in effect, they started NCL (Norwegian Cruise Line) that way."

When that partnership dissolved in 1972 after some disagreement between the principals, Arison went out and bought the *Empress of Canada*, renamed it *Mardi Gras* and started Carnival Cruise Lines. The line's first sailing with 300 travel agents aboard ran aground. There was nowhere to go but up.

By mid-1998, Carnival Cruise Lines will have a dozen ships in service with two more 100,000-ton giants due in the near future, the *Carnival Triumph* in 1999 and the *Carnival Victory* in 2000. Parent company Carnival Corporation also owns all or part of three other cruise lines, Holland America, Windstar and Seabourn. Carnival also owns 30 percent of the British-based cruise and tour company Airtours. Founder Arison, an intensely private billionaire and philanthropist, has retired to Israel but still keeps an active eye on the company. *Mardi Gras* and *Carnivale* have also retired from the fleet; both were sold to Greek-owned Epirotiki Lines.

In 1997, Carnival Corporation and its British affiliate Airtours acquired a majority of Costa Cruises, and Carnival's Windstar subsidiary bought the *Club Med 1* to add to its fleet of motor/sail vessels.

Carnival went public in 1987 and is traded on the New York Stock Exchange.

—The largest cruise line in the world, based on the number of passengers carried.

—Claims the largest staff of trained and qualified youth counselors in the industry (80 full-time employees) to handle some 100,000 kid cruisers a year.

—First cruise line to build a dedicated performance stage in the show lounge (*Carnivale*, 1975).

—First cruise line to use TV commercials on a saturation schedule during the network news hour around the country (1984).

—Pays off a $1,065,428.22 "MegaCash" jackpot to two cruisers from Alaska (aboard the *Jubilee*, March 1994).

—Introduced the first-ever 100,000-ton cruise ship, the *Carnival Destiny*, in November 1996.

—Announced a first-ever Vacation Stores concept to sell Carnival Corp. cruises in retail malls and other high-traffic shopping areas beginning in early 1998.

Concept. . . . .

The fledgling company took off when Arison and a young vice president of sales and marketing named Bob Dickinson created a new concept. They cut prices and added casinos and discos to attract more passengers. By loosening the traditional structure of the cruise market with its formality and class distinctions, they created the "Fun Ships" concept for a vast new cruise audience, a segment of the population that had never cruised before. The company calls itself a "contemporary product" aimed at a mass market, and the cruises are meant to tap the fantasy element to stimulate passengers rather than soothe them, turning the ship into a theme park for adults. Carnival's architect, Joe Farcus, the Michael Graves of the cruise industry, says, "The ships give people a chance to see something they don't in their ordinary lives...Instead of sitting in a theater watching, they're in the movie."

EAVESDROPPING

"Carnival is Wal-Mart, value-oriented for Middle America, for the masses, and it always meets their expectations," cruise industry analyst Jim Parker told the Miami Herald in a 1993 interview.

Signatures . . . .

Carnival's distinctive winged funnel painted in bright red, white and blue is instantly recognizable in warm water ports all over the Caribbean and Mexico, as well as Alaska. Chosen originally as a design statement, the funnel, which vents the smoke off to each side, surprised everyone when it actually worked.

Almost as recognizable is the bright blue corkscrew slide into the amidships pool on every "Fun Ship."

Splashy, fog-and-laser shows with contemporary pop music and spectacular dancing are a regular feature aboard Carnival ships; the bigger the ship, the bigger the show.

DID YOU KNOW?

Carnival's ship designer Joe Farcus, famous for his splashy "entertainment architecture," got his start with the line when a Miami architectural firm he worked for was contracted to go to Greece in 1975 to turn the Empress of Britain into the Carnivale. When Farcus' boss got sick and no one else in the office was free to go, the young architect got the job, and the rest, as they say, is history.

Gimmicks . . . .

Carnival's unique "vacation guarantee" program promises nervous first-time cruisers satisfaction or their money back. Here's how it works—if the passenger is unhappy with his cruise experience, he can disembark in the first non-U.S. port of call and get back the remainder of the cruise price plus an economy air ticket back home. The guarantee is in place throughout 1998.

Smiling waiters in tropical colors circulate around the decks on embarkation day with trays of Technicolor drinks in souvenir glasses, which first-time cruisers sometimes accept without realizing they have to pay for them. And kids in the $1 million virtual reality entertainment complex aboard the *Holiday* can activate the high tech games by using their passenger I.D. cards; they don't need to go get money from Mom or Dad, once the initial use has been approved.

Who's the Competition. . . . .

In the Caribbean, Carnival competes with Royal Caribbean and Norwegian Cruise Line for under-40 couples and singles in the seven-day market and goes head-to-head with both in the mini-cruise market out of Miami and Los Angeles, as well as competing with Premier Cruises out of Port Canaveral. The line still perceives land-based resorts as its primary competition, and exerts a lot of effort to entice first-time cruisers. Dickinson himself says the former competitors are all "moving upscale" and leaving the field to Carnival and what he flippantly calls "the bottom feeders," low-budget cruise lines with old ships.

Who's Aboard.

Despite the line's early reputation for swinging singles' party ships, Carnival attracts a broad spectrum of passengers from newlyweds to families with small children to middle-aged couples to retirees. About 60 percent are first-time cruisers, down from 80 percent in the 1980s, and some 23 percent have taken a Carnival cruise previously, up from nine percent in the 1980s.

Families comprise a large part of the line's mini-cruise business.

Who Should Go

Families with children and teenagers will find plenty of diversions for the kids aboard, but there's also a well-thought-out Camp Carnival program with youth counselors that divides them into four age groups—toddlers 2–4, intermediates 5–6, juniors 9–12 and teens 13–17. They'll find playrooms stocked with games and toys, a full program of daily activities at sea including special aerobics classes and karaoke parties, a kiddies' pool tucked away on its own deck area and the trademark slide at the adult pool (see "Signatures"). Baby-sitting is usually available as well.

Plus: Anyone who likes to spend a weekend in Atlantic City, Nassau or Las Vegas, anyone who wants to show off some new clothes and stay up late dancing, or anyone who adores glittering high-rise resorts.

Who Should Not Go

People whose favorite cruise line was Royal Viking; early-to-bed types; or anyone allergic to twinkle lights and neon.

The Lifestyle

About what you'd expect if you've seen the Kathy Lee Gifford commercials—you know, "If they could see me now..." (Gifford says that when she auditioned for the job she almost didn't get it; she was sixth down on the list of performers they wanted to see.)

While the ships are glitzy, they are also very glamorous if you like bright lights and shiny surfaces, and the humor and whimsy Joe Farcus brings to the designs comes closer to *gee-whiz*! than *omigod*! The casinos and the spas are among the biggest at sea, the disco stays open very late, there's often an X-rated midnight cabaret adult comedy show, singles get-togethers, honeymooner parties, around-the-clock movies on the in-cabin TV set, plenty of fitness classes, trapshooting, shuffleboard, knobby knees contests, ice carving demonstrations, bridge and galley tours and all the other usual shipboard folderol.

INSIDER TIP

No passengers under 18 years of age are permitted to travel without a parent or adult guardian, and new I.D. cards issued to every passenger, including youths, flags a bar computer to report an underage wanna-be drinker.

Wardrobe . . . .

While Carnival ships are a bit less dressy than more traditional lines, many of the passengers look forward to dressing up on the one to two formal nights a week, when formal dress or a dark suit is suggested. You will see more sequins and tuxedos those nights than sport coats without a tie. The pattern is usually two formal nights, two informal nights (the line suggests sport coat and tie for men) and three casual nights that call for resort wear. For daytime, almost anything goes (or almost nothing, if you opt to sunbathe in the secluded upper deck topless sunbathing area). To go ashore in the Caribbean, Mexico or Alaska, casual, comfortable clothing and good walking shoes are best. Don't forget to take a sun hat and sunblock.

Bill of Fare . . . . .B+

From a predictable mainstream seven-day menu rotation on its ships featuring Beef Wellington and Surf 'n Turf several years ago, the line has made some changes in its menus after finding a 300 percent increase in the number of vegetarian entrees ordered and a 20 percent rise in chicken and fish. Fewer than half the passengers order red meat these days, says Carnival's food and beverage director; a popular fresh fish "catch of the day" is now offered on every dinner menu.

That's not to say Beef Wellington and Surf 'n Turf have disappeared—they haven't—but rather that menus have moved a little closer to the cutting edge without scaring diners with huitlacoche mushrooms or fermented soybean paste; "Fun Ship" fans will still encounter those ubiquitous theme nights (French, Italian, Caribbean and Oriental) and flaming desserts parade, and children can order from their own special menus of familiar favorites.

Three-quarters of all the passengers opt for buffet breakfast and lunches rather than going to the dining room to their assigned seating, so a much wider range of casual, self-service options has been added, from a 24-hour pizzeria to across-the-fleet salad bars, hot daily breakfast and lunch specials, made-to-order pasta stations and spa cuisine. Table service has been upgraded in the buffet areas as well.

All the shipboard dining rooms are smoke-free on Carnival. You can breakfast in bed and order simple menu items such as sandwiches and fruit and cheese 24 hours a day from room service. Throughout the fleet, Carnival has introduced Seaview Bistros, casual evening eateries open from 6 to 9:30 p.m. daily that offer pasta, steaks, prime rib, grilled chicken, salads and desserts, along with a daily special. These offer an interesting alternative to the more formal dining room service.

Showtime. . . . . **A+**

Lavishly costumed, fully professional entertainment as good as (often better) than you'd see in Las Vegas is one of the line's hallmarks. The company produces its own musical shows in-house with high-tech lighting, sound and special effects. Different shows are featured on different ships (much as the Broadway shows on Norwegian Cruise Line ships vary from one vessel to another) so if you're a fan of big production shows, you'll want to cruise them all sooner or later.

Three different live bands and a piano bar are usually playing around the ship in the evening, along with a steel drum or calypso band on deck at midday in the Caribbean.

Except on the Alaska sailings, which carry a naturalist, the only lecturers you'll run across on the "Fun Ships" are the people who tell you where to shop.

Discounts . . . .

Deduct up to $1200 per cabin from the listed brochure rates if you book early. Savings amounts are reduced over time based on demand, so earliest bookings get the lowest rates. Some restrictions apply.

Following Princess' lead, Carnival initiated a cruise financing program in which a designated bank will lend passengers the cruise fare, which they later repay on an installment plan.

Members of AARP (American Association of Retired Persons) get a $200 discount on Alaska cruises or on voyages of 10 days or longer.

The Bottom Line

Carnival is not just for party-time singles any more. The new generation of sleek megaliners that began with the *Fantasy* in 1990 and continues through the *Ecstasy, Sensation, Fascination, Imagination, Inspiration, Elation* and *Paradise,* are real crowd-pleasers. The gigantic *Carnival Destiny* has expanded Carnival's audience into new age and economic groups with an even broader appeal than the other vessels.

While the public areas pulse with their abstract sensory stimulation, fiber optics, neon, Tivoli lights, state-of-the-art stagecraft and virtual reality machines, there are a few quiet areas to get away from it all—in the massage rooms, the indoor whirlpool spas, the top deck jogging track or the outdoor deck wings aft behind the indoor Lido Deck bar. Cabins are adequate in size and comfortably free of glitz, with all-day movies and room service, although not so cushy you'll spend your whole cruise there rather than hitting the bars and casino.

On the other hand, if you want a quiet, relaxing cruise, better book another cruise line, because these are the "Fun Ships." While they're not to our own particular cruising taste—we find it hard to spend more than three or four days aboard before the color, lights and pinging slot machines get to us—most Carnival passengers think they've died and gone to heaven. For flat-out fun-and-games cruising, nobody does it better.

★ ★ ★ ★ ★
CARNIVAL DESTINY
CARNIVAL TRIUMPH*

Our first glimpse of the gigantic Carnival Destiny came on a visit to Italy's Fincantieri shipyard when we stood on the decks of the Destiny and looked across to Princess' Grand Princess, also under construction in the same yard. The next time we saw her was on her debut in Miami, when designer Joe Farcus said, "We wanted to put into the ship everything we've learned in the past, to make it the ideal cruise ship." Joe feels that the ship illustrates entertainment architecture and is really a city at sea. He has deliberately created an urban environment because he believes most people choose a city for their holiday.

The $400 million Carnival ship carries 2642 passengers based on two to a cabin, but with Carnival's increasing family business and the number of third and fourth berths available, the average number of passengers aboard is expected to be around 3000 a cruise. Overall, the line claims a 107 percent occupancy rate, based on two passengers in a cabin.

The ship has the first-ever three-deck showroom with state-of-the-art technical facilities from laser lighting to an orchestra pit with an elevator so the musicians can be raised to the stage or lowered to the pit at the push of a button. A huge spa and fitness center 30 percent larger than the 12,000-square-foot facilities on the Fantasy-class ships and a Sun & Sea Lido restaurant not only serves 8,000 pizzas a week from its 24-hour food station, but also features an Italian trattoria, a deck grill, salad bar and mixed-menu buffet.

Four glass elevators serve the nine-deck atrium with a showy fiber optic cityscape covering the full nine decks simulating skyrockets exploding. "It's a show you can enjoy going up and down in the elevator," says designer Farcus modestly.

Three adult swimming pools are on deck (plus a kids' wading pool) with swim-up bars, a sliding sky dome roof and a 15-foot platform and waterslide. On our sailing, even these fantastic pools played second fiddle to the very popular Jacuzzis.

Piano bar fans appreciate the Apollo Bar, where every table has its own microphone and spotlight for singing along, controlled, fortunately, by the piano bar host from a central console.

A series of stained glass windows created by Venetian artist Luciano Vistosi line Destiny's Way, the enclosed promenades, and the two dining rooms have dramatic window walls.

The Brochure Says

"More Stately Staterooms. On every Carnival "Fun Ship," the staterooms are larger than those of any other cruise lines'. On the *Carnival Destiny*, they're even larger."

Translation

Aw, c'mon fellas, how could you let your brochure writer get away with this vague hyperbole? What staterooms are larger than what? In all categories on just some? If you're really proud of your stateroom sizes, you should publish them in your brochure the way many other lines, including Celebrity, Crystal, Disney, Princess and Radisson Seven Seas do.

EAVESDROPPING

At the introductory press conference, one European reporter asked if the 124-foot-wide Carnival Destiny will be going through the Panama Canal, which is 110 feet wide. "We could do it only once," quipped line president Bob Dickinson.

Fantasy Suites: . . . . A

Average Price Per Person, Double Occupancy, Per Day: $400 plus airfare.
Eight sensational suites with granite entry, granite desk/dresser, separate living area with sofa and chairs, and bedroom, dressing room, big Jacuzzi tub, huge windows, and private veranda.

Small Splurges: . . . . B+

Average Price PPPD: $293 plus airfare.

Lido Deck category, 10 ocean view balcony cabins have twin beds which convert to king-size, love seat and coffee table, TV, cabinet with safe, mirrors with makeup lights, good storage spaces, and bath with shower.

Suitable Standards: . . . . **B+**

Average Price PPPD: $279 plus airfare.

The majority of the standard outside doubles on the ship have private verandas, at a price only slightly higher than for those without. Twin beds convert to queen-sized, and there's a leather sofa, wall-mounted TV, chair, stool, coffee table, desk/dresser covered with glittery gold plastic laminate, a larger closet, big shower in pink tile bathroom, and plenty of storage space.

A standard outside cabin without veranda aboard the **Carnival Destiny.**

Bottom Bunks:

Average Price PPPD:$232 plus airfare.

An inside cabin with upper and lower berths, wall-mounted TV, desk/dresser, chair, and bath with shower.

The Routes

Carnival Destiny sails on alternating eastern and western Caribbean itineraries, calling at San Juan, St. Croix and St. Thomas on the eastern sailings, at Playa del Carmen/Cozumel, Grand Cayman and Ocho Rios on the western sailings.

The Scoop

While designer Farcus seems to have restrained his exuberance somewhat on this vessel, it's proving very successful with a wider range of passengers than Carnival's normal roster. The line continues its appeal to first-time cruisers, and a ship like this one should satisfy any doubting Thomas or Tina who thinks cruises might be boring. Whether you wanna dance or watch some expert dancers in a show, wanna play paddle tennis or watch sports on a big screen TV in the All Star Bar, wanna relax in the sunshine by the pool or concentrate energies on the jackpots in the Millionaire's Club Casino, you'll find what you're looking for here.

Five Fantastic Places

1. Down Beat Bar, our own favorite for its larger-than-life musical instruments around the walls and the musical notes carpeting and decorations. The base of the cocktail tables and barstools are trumpets, the barstools are perched atop black clarinets and there's a golden French horn over the bandstand.

2. The Onyx Room is below the disco, and the light patterns from the bottom of the disco's dance floor illuminate the onyx and granite room with its fluted dark green columns.

3. The Grecian urn themes in the Apollo piano bar, along with the Grecian key pattern on the carpet and mosaics created from motifs on pottery in Greek museums.

4. The 15,000-square foot Nautica Spa, a real health club for people looking for a serious workout.

5. The celestial ceilings in the dining rooms, with cloud sky panels and tivoli "stars" in the skies and more spacious dining tables than previous Carnival ships.

Five Good Reasons to Book This Ship

1. A new safety feature places the lifeboats level with the deck so passengers can board them in an emergency without first waiting for them to be lowered.

2. To see yourself on video screens all around the disco as you dance.

3. To watch fantastic live productions in the Palladium show room with its three decks of height plus another deck for flying scenery and performers on and off the stage.

4. To dine in the casual Seaview Bistro on evenings when you've been ashore all day and don't feel like dressing for the dining room.

5. To be able to get off the ship and fly home, getting back the rest of your cruise fare, if you don't like your cruise. It's called a "vacation guarantee" and is good through all of 1998.

CARNIVAL DESTINY
CARNIVAL TRIUMPH*

★★★★★
★★★★

Registry	**Panama**
Officers	**Italian**
Crew	**International**
Complement	**1050**
GRT	**101,000**
Length (ft.)	**892**
Beam (ft.)	**116**
Draft (ft.)	**27**
Passengers-Cabins Full	**3400**
Passengers-2/Cabin	**2642**
Passenger Space Ratio	**38.22**
Stability Rating	**Good**
Seatings	**2**
Cuisine	**Contemporary**
Dress Code	**Traditional**
Room Service	**Yes**
Tip	**$7.50 PPPD, 15% automatically added to bar checks**

Ship Amenities

Outdoor Pool	**4**
Indoor Pool	**0**
Jacuzzi	**7**
Fitness Center	**Yes**
Spa	**Yes**
Beauty Shop	**Yes**
Showroom	**Yes**
Bars/Lounges	**11**
Casino	**Yes**
Shops	**4**
Library	**Yes**
Child Program	**Yes**
Self-Service Laundry	**Yes**
Elevators	**18**

Cabin Statistics

Suites	**48**
Outside Doubles	**758**
Inside Doubles	**515**
Wheelchair Cabins	**20**
Singles	**0**
Single Surcharge	**150-200%**
Verandas	**418**
110 Volt	**Yes**

CARNIVAL CRUISE LINES

★★★
CELEBRATION
HOLIDAY
JUBILEE

At the 1985 debut of the Holiday, first of this trio of then-new ships, we recall being vastly amused because the piano bar in Rick's Cafe American was literally a piano-shaped bar with black-and-white keys all the way round the bar area. But what seemed avant-garde in 1985—a whimsical late-night buffet inside a Danish bus permanently parked in a lounge, the grotto with an undulating blue "undersea" ceiling, the flashy Reflections discotheque—was only a modest forecast of the wonders to come from the imagination of Carnival's designer, Joe Farcus.

Covered promenade decks—here aboard the Jubilee—take passengers from bar to casino to disco.

These ships were the first to introduce a wide starboard "boulevard" with the casino and lounges on port side; the earlier *Tropicale* has a more traditional center casino flanked by enclosed promenades on either side. In fact, this trio forecasts many of the design features of the later Fantasy class, with veranda cabins forward on a top deck, then a Lido deck with amidships pool, two interior decks with lounges, dining rooms and showroom, then below them, all the other passenger cabins.

These are also the vessels that discreetly offered an "Adults Only, No Jogging, Top-Optional Sunbathing" deck, and pioneered the line's recycling separation of garbage.

EAVESDROPPING

An excited family group boarding the Holiday was cautioned by one of their party, "Now remember, everybody needs to take a Valium." We hope she meant dramamine.

The Funnel Bar & Grill aboard the Jubilee *carries through a fanciful and bright nautical cafe theme.*

The Brochure Says
"Enjoy. What's your idea of fun?"

Translation
Take your pick—an average day at sea offers you 14 eating opportunities (including two late-night buffets), eight screenings of the day's feature film on the cabin TV, six exercise sessions, bingo, Knobby Knees Contest, trivia quiz, disco, passenger talent show, sing-along piano bar, Newlywed and Not-So-Newlywed game, calypso, pool games, trap-shooting, ice-carving demonstration, poker games, skin-care demonstration and shopping opportunities, plus all the bars and lounges, the evening production show and late-night cabaret or comedy show and the casino.

Fantasy Suites: .... B

Average Price Per Person, Double Occupancy, Per Day: $315 plus airfare.
Each ship has 10 Veranda Deck suites with sliding glass doors that lead to private
balconies, separate sitting area with L-shaped sofas that can make into an additional
bed, elegant wood cabinetry, large TV set, twin beds that convert to king-sized, a
slightly larger than standard bathroom with tub and shower and a walk-in closet.

Small Splurges: C

Average Price PPPD: $224 plus airfare.
The Empress Deck category Nine outside doubles are just one deck down from the
dining rooms, show lounge and shops, and two decks down from the casino, disco
and other lounges. If you run back and forth a lot and are too impatient to wait for
the elevator, the convenience might be worth the slightly higher tariff. Otherwise,
the size and furnishings are identical to all the other standard cabins. See "Suitable
Standards," below.

Suitable Standards: C

Average Price PPPD: $215 plus airfare.
You'll find twin beds that can convert into a king-sized bed, wall-mounted TV set,
corner table, chair, two stools, desk/dresser, closet, bath with large shower.

Bottom Bunks: .... D

Average Price PPPD: $187 plus airfare.
The cheapest cabins are in category One on the two lowest cabin decks, 19 of them
altogether, with upper and lower berths, wall-mounted TV, chair, stool, desk/
dresser with drawers, closet and bath with shower.

INSIDER TIP

*Prices listed under Cabins and Costs (above) are based on seven-day fares.
Three-day cruises will run slightly higher per day, four-day cruises slightly
lower.*

The *Celebration* sails every Friday year-round from New Orleans to the Western Caribbean, calling in Tampa, Grand Cayman and Playa del Carmen/Cozumel. You can also
depart from Tampa on Sundays.

The *Holiday* makes three- and four-day cruises out of Los Angeles to Ensenada, Mexico; the three-day sailing leaves Fridays and the four-day sailing, which also visits Catalina
Island, leaves Mondays. During the Christmas holidays, the ships will make 10- and 11-
day Mexico Resort cruises, with departures Dec. 19 and 29, 1997 and Jan. 9 and 19,
1998.

The *Jubilee* makes seven-day sailings out of Los Angeles to the Mexican Riviera, leaving every Sunday and calling in Puerto Vallarta, Mazatlán and Cabo San Lucas. In the
summer of 1998, the *Jubilee* replaces the *Tropicale* in Alaska, with Hawaii cruises in
spring and fall.

The Scoop

While not as shiny as when they were brand-new, these vessels are holding up pretty well; the age shows primarily in deck and cafeteria areas where the natural teak is spotted from food spills. Housekeeping aboard is generally good.

The buffet meal service has been expanded beyond the original closet-sized pantries to add a big salad bar that holds Continental breakfast makings in the mornings. Despite the gimmicks, they have a more nautical feeling than the newer ships, especially in the Lido Deck bar and grill rooms with resin-covered wood tables decorated with period luggage tags and other cruise memorabilia, coils of rope, the suggestion of a tugboat and a big red, white and blue funnel in the middle of the room. Best of all, the fleetwide alternative dining options have also been installed.

Insider Tips

Five Fun Places

1. The Speakeasy Lounge on the *Jubilee* with its fire-engine red piano, wrought iron spiral stairs to the casino above, brick walls adorned with Prohibition-era auto posters, low-hanging pool hall lights and ceiling with faux skylights.

2. The *Jubilee's* Smuggler's Lounge with cargo-net ceilings, corrugated tin walls and burlap-covered bales and shiny oil drums lying around.

3. The *Jubilee's* Churchill's library with several suits of armor, a massive pseudo-stone fireplace with a baronial air and wood paneled walls.

4. The Trolley Bar on the *Celebration's* Bourbon Street enclosed promenade, with its vintage trolley and New Orleans-style sidewalk cafe.

The million-dollar entertainment center aboard the Holiday *features games galore, including virtual reality.*

5. The *Holiday's* million-dollar entertainment complex (replacing the Blue Lagoon grotto) with virtual reality machines, a teen disco, ice cream/pizza parlor, motorcy-

cle and car racing video machines, dozens of video games and R360, a strap-in aerial machine that spins around 360 degrees.

Five Good Reasons to Book These Ships

1. The fun and games (see "Translation").

2. The high-quality entertainment, especially on the *Holiday* with its high-tech shows such as "Here's Hollywood" and "Broadway!"

3. To play MegaCash, the biggest slot jackpots at sea.

4. To enroll the kids in Camp Carnival.

5. To check out the virtual reality games on the *Holiday*.

Five Things You Won't Find On Board

1. Smoking in the dining rooms.

2. Those little stainless steel closets where the buffet hot foods used to be served; now there are two snack bars and a pizzeria plus Seaview Bistros.

3. Single cabins.

4. A cinema.

5. A passenger with nothing to do.

CARNIVAL CRUISE LINES

CELEBRATION ★★★
HOLIDAY ★★★
JUBILEE ★★★

Registry	**Liberia**
Officers	**Italian**
Crew	**International**
Complement	**670**
GRT	**47,262**
Length (ft.)	**733**
Beam (ft.)	**92**
Draft (ft.)	**24.7**
Passengers-Cabins Full	**1896**
Passengers-2/Cabin	**1486**
Passenger Space Ratio	**31.80**
Stability Rating	**Good**
Seatings	**2**
Cuisine	**Contemporary**
Dress Code	**Traditional**
Room Service	**Yes**
Tip	**$7.50 PPPD, 15% automatically added to bar checks**

Ship Amenities

Outdoor Pool	**3**
Indoor Pool	**0**
Jacuzzi	**2**
Fitness Center	**Yes**
Spa	**Yes**
Beauty Shop	**Yes**
Showroom	**Yes**
Bars/Lounges	**6**
Casino	**Yes**
Shops	**4**
Library	**Yes**
Child Program	**Yes**
Self-Service Laundry	**Yes**
Elevators	**8**

Cabin Statistics

Suites	**10**
Outside Doubles	**437**
Inside Doubles	**279**
Wheelchair Cabins	**15**
Singles	**0**
Single Surcharge	**150-200%**
Verandas	**10**
110 Volt	**Yes**

★★★★★

ECSTASY
ELATION*
FANTASY
FASCINATION
IMAGINATION
INSPIRATION
PARADISE*
SENSATION

"All I can say is, Wow!" sang spokeswoman *Kathy Lee Gifford in the Carnival commercials, and passengers walking for the first time into these ships with their soaring seven-deck atriums, glass elevators and moving sculptures are saying the same thing—except for an occasional, "Oh my God!" from those who pretend to more refined tastes.*

On the Fantasy, the huge clear-glass skylight in the dome ceiling seven decks above drenches the atrium with natural light during the daytime, but as dusk approaches, the room is suffused with color from miles of neon tubing that circle every level of the space. The effect is strangely impressive, but disorienting, something like walking into a giant jukebox. If you don't like the color, hang around for a while and it will change.

This is no place like home.

Toto, I don't think we're in Kansas any more.

Are you listening, Elvis? Las Vegas is alive and floating.

The *Fantasy*-class ships are all virtually identical in superstructure and deck plan, but each is dramatically different inside. We find ourselves doing a lot of standing by the rail looking down, both inside from the upper atrium levels down into the lobby, watching the glass elevators glide up and down, and outside from the upper decks down into the amidships pool deck with its acres of bronzing bodies in all shapes and sizes, at kids (and adults) trying out the bright blue water slide, at the impromptu dancers in bathing suits who always begin to gyrate on deck when the band comes out on the raised stage.

The 12,000-square-foot Nautica spas with their large whirlpool spas and well-equipped gyms are among the best at sea.

On the topmost deck is a rubberized jogging track, then down one deck on Veranda Deck is the huge Nautica spa with one of every exercise machine known to man, 26 suites with private verandas and on the aft deck, a sunbathing area and pool with two Jacuzzis.

One deck down on Lido is a large glass-walled self-service cafe with indoor and outdoor dining and the amidships pool area with its stage. In the evenings, the casual Seaview Bistro serves dinners for passengers who don't want to dress for the dining room.

The Promenade Deck and Atlantic Deck contain most of the bars, lounges, showrooms and dining rooms, along with a galley on Atlantic Deck that makes the aft dining room a you-can't-get-there-from-here proposition. Directly behind that dining room is the teen club and children's playroom, and on the deck just above, the wading pool, all completely removed from the adult areas of the ship. Forward on the same deck is a second dining room, a small lounge and library, the atrium, shops and the main level of the showroom. One deck up on Promenade is the showroom balcony, the atrium, a vast casino on port side and an enclosed "avenue" on starboard side with sidewalk cafes and bars, another lounge and a disco, then still another lounge and a cabaret showroom aft.

The remainder of the cabins are on four decks below Atlantic; the base of the atrium with the ship lobby and information desk is one deck down on Empress. Three banks of elevators and three sets of stairs access the cabins.

These are "get up and get out and have fun" ships; the cabin TV runs the same daily feature over and over in any 24-hour period, and with only a minimal library of books, you mustn't expect to snuggle down and read.

CHAMPAGNE TOAST

On the Imagination, *the exquisite hand-set mosaics in Venetian glass sparkling with bits of gold-leaf-covered glass are framed in gilded wood to cover tabletops and inset in the granite floors. And don't overlook (as if you could) the gilded, bosomy Sphinxes staring down from the walls around the upper atrium levels.*

Between The Lines

The Brochure Says

"The best vacation on land or sea! Children have plenty to do on a 'Fun Ship' cruise. Relax on acres of sun-splashed decks. Kick up your heels to one of our many live bands. Pamper yourself with our Nautica Spa program. Our attentive staff will wait on you 24 hours a day. Savor a fabulous array of food from around the world. We bet you'll have a great time in the largest casinos at sea. Enjoy lavish Las Vegas-style entertainment."

Translation

Every sentence is accompanied by a picture making the intent very clear—"Children" are eating pizza with a youth counselor serving them and no hovering parents in the background. "Relax" shows rows of sunbathing bodies holding flower-garnished drinks. "Kick up" depicts a pair of sedate middle-aged couples doing what kids today call close-dancing, meaning they're dancing while holding each other in their arms, like people over 50 do sometimes. "Pamper" shows shapely young bodies, mostly female, on gym machines with smiling male instructors. "Our attentive staff" is a waiter serving breakfast in bed to a happy couple. "Savor" shows a table of six-plus passengers (the table edge is cropped, but a six-top is standard on these vessels). "We'll bet" is a croupier at the roulette wheel with a lot of happy couples, all of whom seem to think they're winning. "Enjoy lavish Las Vegas-style entertainment" depicts a bevy of chorines in pink feathers and towering headdresses. Altogether, it's Cruising 101 Illustrated for first-timers.

INSIDER TIP

Sometimes passengers are so hypnotized by the dazzle that they just stand there staring indecisively at the elevator buttons, the buffet selections, the ice cream dispensing machine, the coffee dispensing machine, lost in space or reverie. You may have to nudge them to move them along.

DID YOU KNOW?

There are 226 slot machines, 23 blackjack tables, three craps tables, two roulette wheels and a giant wheel in the Crystal Palace Casino on the Ecstasy.

EAVESDROPPING

Designer Joe Farcus says passengers should feel romance, excitement and the anticipation of boarding a new ship, "and when they come on board, I don't want them to be disappointed; when they leave, I want them to feel they got more than they expected."

Cabins & Costs

Fantasy Suites: .... A

Average Price Per Person, Double Occupancy, Per Day: $315 plus airfare.

The *Fantasy*-class ships have some of the best veranda suite buys at sea, with 28 Upper Deck veranda suites and 26 Veranda Deck demi-suites. But opt for the top— one of the Upper Deck suites with separate sitting area is big enough for entertaining and furnished with an L-shaped sofa, two chairs, coffee table, cocktail table, built-in wood cabinetry that includes a mini-refrigerator, glassware and TV with VCR, and a teak-floored private veranda with lounger, two chairs and a small table. The bedroom area has twin beds that can convert to queen-sized bed and marble counter desk/dresser with five drawers. The bath is fairly large with a marbleized counter, inset porcelain sink, Jacuzzi tub and tile walls and floor. There's an entry with walk-in closet, one full-length and two half-length hanging spaces, shelves and a large safe.

Fantasy-class suites like this veranda suite on the **Imagination** *are good buys.*

Small Splurges: .... A

Average Price PPPD: $287 plus airfare.

The demi-suites on Veranda Deck have twin or queen-sized beds, big windows, private veranda with two chairs and a table, sitting area with sofa, table and chair and a bath with tile shower. Some have partially obstructed views due to hanging lifeboats.

Suitable Standards: .... B

Average Price PPPD: $215 plus airfare.

Carnival's standard cabins are consistent throughout this class, 190 square feet with twin beds that convert to queen-sized, dark gray carpeting thinly striped in bright colors, an armchair and matching stool, a built-in corner table, wall-mounted TV set and desk/dresser with four drawers. The closets have one enclosed and one open full-length hanging space plus shelves. The tile bath has a big shower, a counter around the sink and a glass-doored medicine cabinet.

Bottom Bunks: .... D

Average Price PPPD: $187 plus airfare.

The lowest category cabins are insides with upper and lower berths placed perpendicular to each other, considerably smaller than the standards (the brochure calls them "cozy"), similar closet space and a tile bath with shower. There are only nine of these on each ship, plus 28 more with upper and lower berths in higher price categories than are slightly roomier.

EAVESDROPPING

Carnival president Bob Dickinson: "We say we're 'Fun Ships'; we're not trying to be Royal this or Platinum that. People don't want to spend their vacations with the Queen Mum."

The Routes

The *Ecstasy* sails from Miami every Friday on three-day cruises to Nassau and every Monday on four-day cruises to Key West and Playa del Carmen/Cozumel.

The *Fantasy* sails every Thursday and Sunday from Port Canaveral on three- and four-day cruises calling in Nassau; the four-day sailing also visits Freeport.

The *Fascination* cruises the Southern Caribbean on year-round itineraries leaving San Juan every Saturday and calling in St. Thomas, St. Maarten, Dominica, Barbados and Martinique.

The *Imagination* sails every Saturday from Miami to the Western Caribbean, calling in Playa del Carmen/Cozumel, Grand Cayman and Ocho Rios.

The *Inspiration* sails every Sunday from San Juan into the Southern Caribbean, calling in St. Thomas, Guadeloupe, Grenada, St. Lucia and Santo Domingo, Dominican Republic.

The *Sensation* sails Saturdays from Miami calling at San Juan, St. Thomas and St. Maarten.

The new *Elation* will sail from Los Angeles every Sunday to the Mexican Riviera, beginning March 20, 1998. Ports of call include Puerto Vallarta, Mazatlán and Cabo San Lucas. This is the first time Carnival has positioned one of the Fantasy-class ships on the west coast.

The *Paradise* itinerary has not yet been announced.

The Scoop

These ships come to life at night when the dramatic colors and lighting are highlighted against the many glass surfaces. They are tactile (touch the surfaces of the chairs, tables, walls and floors on *Imagination*), aural (changing sounds of nature—the surf, rain, wind and chirping birds—wash by on *Sensation's* Sensation Boulevard) and intensely visual (fiber optics and neon panels "jump off" the walls as passengers walk by on the *Sensation*).

Elsewhere in this book, we call the *Fantasy* a lava lamp for the 1990s, but we mean it in a fond sense. This series of ships is constantly amazing and amusing, thanks to the ingenuousness and genius of Joe Farcus, whose own innocence and clarity of image keep them from being vulgar.

Are they gaudy? Sometimes. Do they tread dangerously close to maxing out? Perhaps. But they can match the much-praised pair of Crystal ships in marble, crystal and glove leather, dollar for dollar, ton for ton. Whether they strike you as glitzy or glamorous depends on your own individual taste, but they're never boring. Carnival delivers precisely what it promises, and if you've seen its advertising, you should already know whether it's the right cruise line for you.

Insider Tips

Five Fabulous Spaces

1. The Old Curiosity Library aboard the *Imagination* boasts replicas of Bernini's altar columns from St. Peter's in Rome along with genuine and reproduction antiques to give the atmosphere of an antique shop.

2. Also on the *Imagination*, the classy Horizon Bar & Grill with its 24-hour pizzeria (also serving calzone, Caesar salad with or without grilled chicken and garlic bread), jukebox, elegant cast aluminum chairs, granite and aggregate floors, Matisse-like hand-painted fabric tabletops under resin, fresh flowers, cloth napkins and silverware already on the tables and lots of drinkable wines by the glass.

3. Diamonds Are Forever on the *Fascination* is a James Bond take on a disco, with fiber optic diamonds on the walls and ceilings, tabletops that glitter with handset "diamonds", and carpets woven with diamond shapes; the black granite floor and banquette bases emit smoke/fog at night when the disco is going full blast. It's hot, hot, hot!

4. The Universe show lounge aboard the *Fantasy*, which in the words of one passenger "looks like it's ready to blast off" with its carpet covered with comets and swirling ringed planets, its black upholstery flocked with tiny, intensely bright metallic microchips in red, blue, silver and gold, and its ability to turn from a gigantic stage with a 33-foot turntable in the center to a ballroom closed off by a wall of beveled gold mirrors with a sunken orchestra pit that rises to eye level.

5. The 12,000-square-foot Nautica spas on every ship with Steiner of London beauty services from facials to aromatherapy and massage, an abundance of state-of-the-art exercise machines facing a glass wall overlooking the sea, sauna and steam rooms, fully mirrored aerobics room and big twin Jacuzzis lit by the sun through an overhead skylight.

Five Off-the-Wall Places

1. Cleopatra's Bar on the *Fantasy*, patterned after an ancient Egyptian tomb, with stone floor, hieroglyphics on the walls, gilded sarcophagi and full-sized seated and standing Egyptian gods and goddesses. In the center of the room is a glossy black piano bar, and as random laser lights spotlight details around the room, you half expect to hear a chorus of "My Mummy Done Ptolemy."

2. Cats Lounge on the *Fantasy*, inspired by the set for the musical of the same name, with oversized tin cans and rubber tires, bottle cap and jar lid tabletops, and walls

lined with soap and cereal boxes; you enter through a giant Pet milk can and the band plays atop a giant rubber tire laid on its side.

3.   Touch of Class piano bar on the *Sensation*, entered through a doorway framed by hands with long red fingernails; the same supporting hands cup the barstool seats (making for some funny images from the back when the stools are filled) and support cocktail tables, while the walls are covered with ceramic tile handprints.

4.   The movie star mannequins spotted all around the *Fascination*, from Vivien Leigh and Clark Gable standing by the faux fireplace in the Tara Library to Bette Davis sitting in a corner booth of the Stars Bar with her ubiquitous cigarette, amid delightful Al Hirschfeld drawings under glass on the tops of the small white cafe tables. Passengers stand in line to photograph each other hugging a movie star; it's a big hit.

5.   The Rhapsody in Blue bar aboard the *Inspiration* with its rippling blue fabric ceiling and Manhattan-deco upholstery.

Five Good Reasons to Book These Ships

1.   To have fun in an unintimidating, relaxed atmosphere without worrying about picking up the wrong fork or wearing the wrong clothes.

2.   To try to win a million dollars.

3.   To eat, drink, gamble, dance and watch movies all night long if you want to; it's your vacation.

4.   To show the snapshots of the ships to your neighbors back home "so they can see you now..."

5.   To get married on board (the line can arrange it) and spend your honeymoon at sea, all for less than a formal church wedding at home would probably cost; call Carnival's Bon Voyage Department at ☎ *800-WED-4-YOU* for details.

Five Things You Won't Find On Board

1.   Lavish gift toiletries, even in the suites; all you get is a sliver of soap.

2.   A table for two in the dining room.

3.   A lot of books in the library.

4.   A cruise director who spells Knobby Knees (as in the contest) with a "k"; every program we've seen calls it "Nobby Knees."

5.   An atrium sculpture that doesn't move; some of them are inadvertently hilarious.

ECSTASY	★★★★★
ELATION*	★★★★★
FANTASY	★★★★★
FASCINATION	★★★★★
IMAGINATION	★★★★★
INSPIRATION	★★★★★
PARADISE*	★★★★★
SENSATION	★★★★★

Registry	**Panama**
Officers	**Italian**
Crew	**International**
Complement	**920**
GRT	**70,367**
Length (ft.)	**855**
Beam (ft.)	**104**
Draft (ft.)	**25' 9"**
Passengers-Cabins Full	**2594**
Passengers-2/Cabin	**2040**
Passenger Space Ratio	**34.49**
Stability Rating	**Good**
Seatings	**2**
Cuisine	**International**
Dress Code	**Traditional**
Room Service	**Yes**
Tip	**$7.50 PPPD, 15% automatically added to bar checks**

Ship Amenities

Outdoor Pool	**3**
Indoor Pool	**0**
Jacuzzi	**6**
Fitness Center	**Yes**
Spa	**Yes**
Beauty Shop	**Yes**
Showroom	**Yes**
Bars/Lounges	**5**
Casino	**Yes**
Shops	**3**
Library	**Yes**
Child Program	**Yes**
Self-Service Laundry	**Yes**
Elevators	**14**

Cabin Statistics

Suites	**28**
Outside Doubles	**590**
Inside Doubles	**402**
Wheelchair Cabins	**20**
Singles	**0**
Single Surcharge	**150-200%**
Verandas	**54**
110 Volt	**Yes**

CARNIVAL CRUISE LINES

★★★
TROPICALE

When Ted Arison announced in 1978 that he was ordering his line's first brand-new ship, the 36,674-ton Tropicale, 20,000 tons was considered large for a cruise ship. The wisdom of the day was that he'd never fill it. (Today the Tropicale is the smallest ship in the fleet.)

When it was delivered in 1982, he further confounded industry insiders by taking it out of the Caribbean and positioning in on the west coast for Mexican Riviera cruises out of Los Angeles. It wasn't very long until the vessel was operating at 100 percent-plus capacity.

The smallest ship in Carnival's fleet, the *Tropicale* has a new homeport, Inchon, South Korea, and a new parent company, Carnival Cruises Asia, a joint venture with South Korea's Hundai Merchant Marine Division, The ship will target the growing Asian cruise market.

Some of the details on the *Tropicale* reflect design styles of older vessels, and again may have been influenced by the *Festivale*. The dining room, for instance, is on a lower deck with no windows, making it an awkward three-deck climb up to the show lounge, which is forward on Empress Deck.

At the same time, it modestly forecasts some of the bells and whistles that would distinguish the later new ships—the Exta-Z disco with its glass dance floor lit from below, the swimming pool with a slide leading down into it, the distinctive split T-shaped funnel that vents the smoke off to each side.

Cabins are modular, virtually the same size in all categories except for the slightly larger top deck veranda suites.

Cabins & Costs

Fantasy Suites: . . . . **B**
Average Price Per Person, Double Occupancy, Per Day: NA.

The veranda suites with private balconies are best, especially if there's scenery on your side of the ship. The suites contain twin beds that convert to king-sized in a separate sleeping area, with a comfortable sitting area as well. There is a pulldown upper berth and a sofa that makes into a bed, in case you want to take two additional family members along. The private veranda has a couple of chairs, the bath has a tub, and a low room divider separates sleeping and sitting areas. It could work as a family suite, especially since the kids (or adult occupants) would pay only $599 apiece for the cruise.

Small Splurges: . . . . NA

There's nothing that really qualifies; all the rest of the cabins are standards, and prices change only according to the deck and whether the cabin is inside or outside (Carnival calls the latter Ocean View cabins).

Suitable Standards: C

Average Price PPPD: NA

Upper Deck outsides in category Eight offer windows and twin beds that convert to king-sized beds. A corner table, wall-mounted TV set, chair and desk/dresser with drawers, closet and bath with shower are what you get. Eleven cabins have been modified for the physically challenged and provide 32.5 inch-wide doors.

Bottom Bunks: C

Average Price PPPD: NA

A few bottom-price insides with upper and lower berths are on the *Tropicale* with furnishings similar to all the other ships in the fleet. The good news is they're larger than on most other vessels, the bad news is there are only nine of them.

The Routes

The *Tropicale* will cruise North Asia in summer and relocate to South Asia in winter, visiting ports in China and Japan.

The Scoop

The ship is in very good condition except for some worn natural teak decking that appears to be gradually being replaced.

Since the *Tropicale* is the line's smallest ship, it was a logical choice to check out the new itinerary. The downside, of course, is the lack of a retractable glass roof over the pool and sunbathing area for sometimes inclement Asian weather, but there are wind baffles that shelter the central area.

The enclosed promenades on each side of the casino make a comfortable and attractive place to sit. It's certainly cheerful enough with its school bus yellow and black chairs and floor squares, inset with a Mondrian-pattern carpet in primary colors on the floor and walls, along with plastic-topped tables in red, yellow, blue and purple. In Asia the lighting level will be intensified to create the brighter environment Asians prefer, and elaborate buffets will offer dishes representing all the major cuisines of the continent.

Insider Tips

Five Fun Spots

1. Chopstix, a dazzling piano bar that was added to the ship in a remodeling, has table-tops bordered with piano keys, a carpet sprinkled with musical notes, arches that are neon-lit piano keys, and a black piano covered with piano keys and encircled with black barstools.

2. The Boiler Room Bar & Grill, with its deliberately exposed pipes painted in rainbow colors and industrial-looking tables of brushed chrome with a bottle of catsup sitting on each; this is where the buffet breakfasts and lunches are served.

3. The Tropicana Lounge with its sofas and long curved banquettes in a dark batik print shot through with gold threads and a Picasso-print carpet; the stage doubles as a raised dance floor.

4. The Paradise Club Casino, where the most comfortable barstools on the ship are—where else?—in front of the slot machines.

5. The Exta-Z Disco, with a glass floor lit from underneath with bright bands of neon plastic high-backed banquettes piped in shocking pink, chrome chairs and tables and Tivoli lights.

TROPICALE ★★★

Registry	**Liberia**
Officers	**International**
Crew	**International**
Complement	**550**
GRT	**36,674**
Length (ft.)	**660**
Beam (ft.)	**85**
Draft (ft.)	**23' 1"**
Passengers-Cabins Full	**1400**
Passengers-2/Cabin	**1022**
Passenger Space Ratio	**35.88**
Stability Rating	**Fair to Good**
Seatings	**2**
Cuisine	**Asian /Western**
Dress Code	**Traditional**
Room Service	**Yes**
Tip	**$7.50 PPPD, 15% automatically added to bar checks**

Ship Amenities

Outdoor Pool	**3**
Indoor Pool	**0**
Jacuzzi	**0**
Fitness Center	**Yes**
Spa	**No**
Beauty Shop	**Yes**
Showroom	**Yes**
Bars/Lounges	**5**
Casino	**Yes**
Shops	**4**
Library	**No**
Child Program	**Yes**
Self-Service Laundry	**Yes**
Elevators	**8**

Cabin Statistics

Suites	**12**
Outside Doubles	**312**
Inside Doubles	**187**
Wheelchair Cabins	**11**
Singles	**0**
Single Surcharge	**150-200%**
Verandas	**12**
110 Volt	**Yes**

CARNIVAL CRUISE LINES

Celebrity Cruises, Inc.

5201 Blue Lagoon Drive, Miami, FL 33126
☎ (305) 262-6677, (800) 242-6374
www.celebrity-cruises.com

A passenger volunteer assists executive chef Walter Lauer in a cooking demonstration.

History

The Greek-based Chandris Group, founded in 1915, began passenger service in 1922 with the 300-ton *Chimara*, and by 1939 had grown to a 12-ship family-owned cargo and passenger line. In the post-World War II years, the company acquired a number of famous cruise liners, most of which have been retired. Under the Fantasy label, the company operated the *Amerikanis* mainly for the European market and retired the *Britanis*.

In April 1989, Chandris formed Celebrity Cruises with the intention of creating an upscale division with a premium cruise product. The *Meridian*, a massive makeover of the classic liner *Galileo Galeilei*, debuted in April 1990, followed the next month by the all-new *Horizon*. In April 1992, sister ship *Zenith* followed.

In October of that same year, Chandris formed a joint venture with Overseas Shipholding Group (OSG), a large publicly-held bulk-shipping company, and entered into the next expansion phase, ordering three 70,000-ton ships to be constructed by Joseph L. Meyer in Papenburg, Germany. The first of these, the innovative *Century*, debuted at the end of 1995, followed in the fall of 1996 by sister ship *Galaxy* and *Mercury* in late 1997. The *Meridian* was to be sold in October 1997 to Metro Holdings of Singapore.

In mid-1997, Royal Caribbean Cruise Ltd. acquired Celebrity Cruises under a cash/stock merger arrangement, but plans are to continue Celebrity's operation under its own name as a separate entity.

—Chandris introduced the fly/cruise concept in the Mediterranean in the early 1960s.

—Pioneered fly/cruise packages in the Caribbean in 1966.

—Celebrity pioneered affiliations with land-based experts from London's three-star Michelin restaurateur Michel Roux to Sony Corporation of America to create innovative onboard products and programs.

Concept. . . . .

Celebrity from its beginning has aimed at presenting the highest possible quality for the best price, and offers luxury service and exceptional food with a very solid value for the money spent. These stylish ships illustrate the decade's new values—luxury without ostentation, family vacations that don't just cater to the kids and close-to-home getaways that provide pure pleasure.

Celebrity's celebrity came in part from its exceptionally good food, created and supervised by Guide Michelin three-star chef Michel Roux; here, a whimsical touch adorns a buffet dish at lunchtime.

Signatures . . . .

Perhaps the single best-known feature of this fleet is its superlative cuisine, created and supervised by London master chef Michel Roux, a longtime *Guide Michelin* three-star chef, who takes a hands-on approach, popping in for surprise visits to the ships, training shipboard chefs in his own kitchens and sending key supervisory personnel for regular culinary check-ups.

Gimmicks

The Mr. and Mrs. icebreaker game. At the beginning of each cruise, a man and a woman on board are chosen to represent Mr. and Mrs. (*Horizon, Zenith, Mercury, Century*). During the cruise, passengers are encouraged to ask individuals if they're the Mr. and Mrs. selected, and the first to find them gets a prize. In the meantime, everyone gets acquainted. Anyone for musical chairs?

Who's the Competition

In its brief seven years of service, Celebrity has managed to virtually create a class of its own by providing a product priced competitively with Princess and Holland America but with a level of food, and sometimes service, that approaches Crystal Cruises. Previously, the line limited its itineraries to Caribbean and Bermuda sailings, but has expanded to include Alaska and Panama Canal sailings, and may enter the Mediterranean in the future.

Who's Aboard

Young to middle-aged couples, families with children, and, on certain early-season Bermuda sailings from southeastern ports, groups of senior citizens from Florida retirement communities who request early sitting dinners that start at 5:30 instead the normal 6 or 6:30 p.m. In winter season, Celebrity attracts some European and French Canadian passengers as well. Although the line is only seven years old, it has many frequent cruisers with double-digit sailings.

Who Should Go

Anyone looking for a good value for the money; discriminating foodies who will find very little if anything to complain about; families with children; couples of all ages. When the line was first introduced in 1990, Al Wallack, then Celebrity's senior vice president for marketing and passenger services, had several suggestions: "People who are joining country clubs but not necessarily the most expensive or exclusive country club on the block;" passengers of the former Home Lines and Sitmar ships who did not merge into Princess and who like "ships that look like ships, ships that have a European quality."

Who Should Not Go

Anyone who calls for catsup with everything or after perusing the menu asks the waiter, "But where's the surf and turf?"

The Lifestyle

Upscale without being pretentious, sleek and fashionable without being glitzy, the Celebrity ships offer a very comfortable seven-day cruise that is outstanding in the areas of food, service and surroundings. Evenings aboard are fairly dressy, with jacket and tie for men requested on both formal and informal nights; only casual nights suggest a sports shirt without jacket. Meals are served at assigned tables in two seatings.

Book a suite and you get all-day butler service; take the kids along during holiday and summer sailings and you'll find well-trained youth counselors on board. Ladies looking for a dancing partner will find social hosts on many sailings.

Evenings the ships present musical production shows and variety shows (except when they are docked in Bermuda, which does not permit professional entertainment other than live music on cruise ships in port), recent feature films, and duos or trios playing for dancing or listening in small lounges around the ships. Daytimes bring popular culinary demonstrations by the executive chef, arts and crafts lessons, trapshooting, napkin folding, golf putting, lectures on finance or current affairs, a trivia quiz, basketball, exercise classes and bingo.

Wardrobe. . . . .

A seven-night cruise normally schedules two formal nights, in which the line suggests "both men and women may prefer more dressy attire, such as an evening gown for women and a tuxedo or dress suit for men." In our experience aboard the line's ships, a cocktail dress or dressy pants suit for women and a dark suit or blazer with tie will be acceptable. There is also a tuxedo rental service aboard the *Zenith*.

Two nights are designated informal, and men are asked to wear a jacket and tie, women a suit or dress, and three casual nights when a sport shirt and slacks are acceptable for men, dresses or pantsuits for women.

Daytime wear is casual, with good walking shoes a must. Bermuda-bound passengers in spring and fall should take a jacket or sweater, hat or scarf, for going ashore; there's often a cool breeze blowing.

A rolling cart of wines available by the glass serves the buffet restaurants.

Bill of Fare . . . . .A+

Celebrity's executive chef, Vienna-born Walter Lauer, who goes from one ship to another constantly checking quality, describes it as "creating something new, where you can't cook everything in advance. Here there is the chance to do something new, more of the high standards in cuisine." One example: All the stock for soups is made from scratch on board rather than using prepared bases as many cruise kitchens do.

Lauer's mentor, Michel Roux, says, "The most important thing is to have a very good quality product and to rely on cooking skill more than the richness of the product." Fresh ingredients cooked to order figure prominently, and the menus are changed every six months.

Basically, the idea of serving simple but sophisticated dishes prepared from fresh ingredients as close as possible to serving time was revolutionary in the basic banquet/hotel catering kitchens of big cruise ships. But it succeeds splendidly. Usually if we find two or three dishes a meal that tempt us we're happy, but we could cheerfully order one of everything straight down the menu on these ships.

For lunch you might find a vegetable pizza or minestrone to start, then a main-dish salad of romaine with Mediterranean tabouli, hummus and pita bread garnished with garlic chicken; a piperade omelet with ham, tomatoes, peppers and onions; broiled ocean perch; roasted chicken with Provencale potatoes; spaghetti with fresh tomato sauce; grilled calf's liver with bacon and onions.

Dinner could begin with New England clam chowder or a pasta tossed with cilantro, oregano, ancho chile and fresh cream; a low-fat version of coquilles Saint-Jacques on vegetable tagliatelle; a pan-seared darne of salmon; roast lamb with garlic, thyme, fresh mint and olive oil with country roasted potatoes; broiled lobster tail or prime rib of beef. The dessert menu always includes one lean and light suggestion, along with fruit and cheese, pastries, ice creams and sorbets and a plate of showcase sweets presented to each table by the waiter, who describes them in mouth-watering detail. Vegetarian menus are offered at every lunch and dinner.

A substantial 24-hour room service menu, gala midnight buffets, Caribbean barbecues on deck, continental breakfast in bed, late morning bouillon and afternoon tea are other meal options during a typical cruise.

Lunchtime buffets are reminiscent of Impressionist paintings, with displays of fresh fruits and vegetables, woven baked baskets holding bread and wonderfully crunchy homemade breadsticks, fresh and crisp salads, a huge display of fresh vegetables, a rolling cart of wines by the glass, cold and hot main dishes and plenty of desserts.

A variety of entertainment from production musicals to, as here, classical string quartets in the **Horizon's** *Centrum.*

Showtime. . . . . A

The production musical shows have a lot of verve and are well-performed and well-costumed; they follow the usual musical revue formats with salutes to Broadway and/or Hollywood, but with fresh looks at vintage shows such as *Hair* and *Jesus Christ Superstar.* Variety performers, musical soloists and duos and a Caribbean band round out the evening entertainment. Daytimes are chock-a-block with games, movies, lectures and exercise classes. The new *Century* and *Galaxy* introduce still more technological marvels from rooms with "video wallpaper" to a nightly light-and-sound spectacular.

Discounts . . . .

Special advance purchase fares save up to 45 percent for passengers who book well ahead of time; ask a travel agent for details.

The Bottom Line

In today's world with value for the vacation dollar so important, it's comforting to sail with a cruise line that delivers high-quality food and service on a stylish ship at moderate prices. We sense welcome and commitment from every employee, even the cleaning crew who polish the brass and chrome and the deck crew who pick up dirty dishes and wet towels more promptly than on many ships. All the ships in the line have our highest recommendation for quality for the money.

★ ★ ★ ★ ★
CENTURY
GALAXY
MERCURY*

During the inaugural sailing of these "ships of the future"—a joint venture between Celebrity and Sony Corporation of America—we found ourselves wandering around the decks trying to decipher this brave new world. There were the very appealing intimate game booths for two or more in the Images Lounge, three high-back booths with very expensive built-in game screens on tabletops. While we never quite got the hang of them, a young couple in the booth next door was bent intently over the screen, playing with great concentration when we first saw them, then later, when we checked in again, they looked up at each other from the game and began kissing passionately. We wanted what they had, but apparently it was a different game.

Celebrity's chairman John Chandris calls his trio of babies "the ships I've always wanted to build...ships for the next century" and tags them super-premium, saying they are for "discriminating consumers who demand the highest quality experience at the best possible value." There are a lot of exciting new features on board. Take the state-of-the-art spa with its hydro-pool underwater "air beds" to give the body a weightless sensation and jets of water that provide neck massages as well as another spa area with jets of water at different heights that are similar to a standup Jacuzzi. Along with the usual hydrotherapy and thalassotherepy is a seagoing first—a mud, steam and herbal treatment called rasul. All the AquaSpa programs can be booked in advance with a travel agent.

A lounge called Images on the *Century* utilizes "video wallpaper," hundreds of changeable, custom-designed backgrounds that can be punched up on a wall-sized video display system to change the room's ambiance from

CELEBRITY CRUISES

tropical palms to low-light jazz club to sports bar or wine cellar, whatever background fits the activity of the moment. Around one end is a series of interactive gaming booths big enough to seat several people at a time. For showtime, there's a Broadway-style theater with row seating, orchestra pit and four-deck fly loft for scenery. A glazed dome in the Grand Foyer changes in a slow transition from dawn to daylight to sunset to night, when astronomically correct "stars" appear in the dome "sky." Sony Corporation of America has created exclusive interactive guest services, touch-screen information kiosks, in-cabin entertainment systems, telephonic video service and special teleconferencing equipment for meetings. The *Galaxy* offers a warmer ambience without as much emphasis on technology, but never fear, it's all here.

The Brochure Says

"Welcome to the new *Century*, a vessel that recaptures the golden age of cruising blended with modern sophistication."

Translation

Perhaps too much emphasis was initially put into the joint venture between Celebrity and Sony. While we think passengers will certainly note the two dozen technological additions from Sony, they will be even more impressed by the elegant dining room, theater, casino, Michael's Club and the Crystal Room nightclub than electronic gadgetry.

Fantasy Suites: . . . . A

Average Price Per Person, Double Occupancy, Per Day: $928 including airfare.
A pair of lavish penthouse suites measuring 1173 square feet offer a private veranda with its own outdoor hot tub, a living room, dining room, butler's pantry and 24-hour butler service, master bedroom with walk-in closet, living room with wet bar and entertainment center and a guest powder room supplementing the marble bath with spa tub.

Small Splurge: . . . . A

Average Price PPPD: $656 including airfare.
The eight Royal Suites are spacious inside although the private verandas are fairly narrow. The living rooms have sofa and two chairs, dining table with four chairs and a separate bedroom. Museum "art boxes" in each suite displays themed pieces of art; the suite we saw featured African carvings.

Suitable Standards: . . . . B+

Average Price PPPD: $371 including airfare.
A typical cabin is furnished with a queen-sized bed under a large window with a striped Roman shade, a marble-topped desk/dresser, two armchairs, a cocktail table, TV set, minibar and big hinged mirror covering shelves and a safe in the wall behind it. The bathroom has a very large white tile shower (chairman John Chandris is very big on spacious shower stalls) with excellent shower head, marble counter and lots of storage.

Bottom Bunks: .... B

Average Price PPPD: $268 including airfare.

All the cabins contain safes, minibars, hair dryers, direct dial telephones and color TV sets, and the smallest is 171 square feet. The bottom units still contain two lower beds that can convert to a queen-sized bed, bath with spacious shower and all the amenities listed above.

The Routes

The *Century* sails alternating Eastern and Western Caribbean itineraries from Fort Lauderdale every Saturday. The Eastern Caribbean sailing calls in San Juan, St. Thomas, St. Maarten and Nassau, while the Western Caribbean program visits Ocho Rios, Grand Cayman, Cozumel and Key West. The *Galaxy* spends the summer in Alaska on an Inside Passage Itinerary and winters in the Deep Caribbean, sailing Saturdays from San Juan calling at Catalina Island (Dominican Republic), Barbados, Martinique, Antigua and St. Thomas. The ship also makes seasonal Panama Canal transits.

The *Mercury* cruises the Western Caribbean in winter, sailing every Sunday from Fort Lauderdale, and cruises Alaska Inside Passage in Summer. When she debuts November 2, 1997, the ship will offer seven-night western Caribbean itineraries visiting Key West, Cozumel, Grand Cayman and Calica. In spring she repositions to Alaska for the summer and then returns to the Caribbean in the fall.

The amidships pool on the Resort Deck of Century.

The Scoop

The suites aboard are lovely, well worth the splurge—and having your own private veranda means you can skip the deck sunbathing. Note, however, that the *Galaxy* and *Mercury* have three times as many verandas as the *Century*. Dining rooms aboard these vessels are as elegant as the cuisine and there are a lot of alluring little lounges for romantic getaways. The spa facilities are first-rate and the theater is state of the art for cruise ships. Even the towels are 100% cotton. With the elaborate interactive cabin TV service a passenger never has to leave his cabin.

CELEBRITY CRUISES

Images Lounge on the **Century** *features sports-bar-type video walls plus one-on-one electronic game booths.*

Insider Tips

Five Good Reasons to Book These Ships

1. The exceptional AquaSpa from Steiners with an elaborate program of beauty and spa appointments that can be booked from home before the cruise via your travel agent.

2. To enjoy some of the best cuisine at sea, including ice cream made on board.

3. To play video games almost anywhere and use interactive cabin TV service to order food, watch pay-per-view movies or wager on a few hands of video poker.

4. To dine in the elegant two-deck Grand Restaurant on the *Century* that evokes the dining room from the *Normandie*.

5. To watch a production show in a theater where there are no bad sightlines.

Five Favorite Spots

1. The dazzling casino, designed by California's Louis Periera, with its swirling gold ceiling and a carpet with a pattern of cherries and fanned cards.

2. Cigar aficionados will appreciate Michael's Club, a smoking room where a resident cigarmaker turns out Cuban- style stogies.

3. John McNeece's sensational theater complete with "floating" walkway entrances and an orchestra pit.

4. The sleek art deco nightclubs reminiscent of Radio City's Rainbow room.

5. The popular little cafe bar called Tastings, where you can sip a cappuccino while you check out the other passengers going by.

Five Things You Won't Find Aboard

1. Obstructed sightlines in the showroom; the view is perfect from every seat.

2. Visitors.

3. Pets.

4. A golf cart at the simulated golf links.

5. As many verandas on the *Century* as on the *Galaxy*.

CENTURY ★★★★★

Registry	**Liberia**
Officers	**Greek**
Crew	**International**
Complement	**843**
GRT	**70,606**
Length (ft.)	**807**
Beam (ft.)	**105**
Draft (ft.)	**25**
Passengers-Cabins Full	**2056**
Passengers-2/Cabin	**1750**
Passenger Space Ratio	**40**
Stability Rating	**Excellent**
Seatings	**2**
Cuisine	**Contemporary**
Dress Code	**Traditional**
Room Service	**Yes**
Tip	**$9 PPPD, 15% automatically added bar checks. Suites tip Butler $3 PPPD**

Ship Amenities

Outdoor Pool	**2**
Indoor Pool	**0**
Jacuzzi	**4**
Fitness Center	**Yes**
Spa	**Yes**
Beauty Shop	**Yes**
Showroom	**Yes**
Bars/Lounges	**4**
Casino	**Yes**
Shops	**2**
Library	**Yes**
Child Program	**Yes**
Self-Service Laundry	**No**
Elevators	**9**

Cabin Statistics

Suites	**52**
Outside Doubles	**517**
Inside Doubles	**320**
Wheelchair Cabins	**8**
Singles	**0**
Single Surcharge	**150–200%**
Verandas	**61**
110 Volt	**Yes**

GALAXY
MERCURY*

★★★★★
★★★★★

Registry	**Liberia**
Officers	**Greek**
Crew	**International**
Complement	**900**
GRT	**77,713**
Length (ft.)	**852**
Beam (ft.)	**105**
Draft (ft.)	**25**
Passengers-Cabins Full	**2209**
Passengers-2/Cabin	**1930**
Passenger Space Ratio	**40.2**
Stability Rating	**Excellent**
Seatings	**2**
Cuisine	**Contemporary**
Dress Code	**Traditional**
Room Service	**Yes**
Tip	**$9 PPPD, 15% automatically added bar checks. Suites tip Butler $3 PPPD**

Ship Amenities

Outdoor Pool	**3**
Indoor Pool	**0**
Jacuzzi	**5**
Fitness Center	**Yes**
Spa	**Yes**
Beauty Shop	**Yes**
Showroom	**Yes**
Bars/Lounges	**8**
Casino	**Yes**
Shops	**5**
Library	**Yes**
Child Program	**Yes**
Self-Service Laundry	**No**
Elevators	**10**

Cabin Statistics

Suites	**50**
Outside Doubles	**613**
Inside Doubles	**302**
Wheelchair Cabins	**7**
Singles	**0**
Single Surcharge	**150-200%**
Verandas	**220**
110 Volt	**Yes**

★★★★★
HORIZON
ZENITH

Revisiting a ship you've known from its birth is sort of like being a godparent to a child and watching it grow up. The first time we saw the Zenith, at the Joseph L. Meyer shipyard in Papenburg, Germany, she was unprepossessing, a huge brooding structure of dark red steel with bare stairways, dangling wires and cords. Then, at her inaugural sailing in 1992, she was an elegant beauty decked out in expensive if understated finery, and when we saw her again not long ago she was prettier than ever, lovingly polished and primped within an inch of her life.

The **Horizon's** *Rendezvous Lounge is a popular before-dinner cocktail spot.*

The *Horizon* and *Zenith* are very similar sister ships, with a few modifications on the interior of the *Zenith*—an expanded health club, a much larger forward observation lounge and 10 more passenger cabins (including two additional suites), giving her a higher gross registry tonnage than the *Horizon*. The children's playroom was moved to a higher deck on the *Zenith*, and the topmost deck's Mast Bar eliminated, along with Fantasia, the teen center ice cream and juice bar, which is replaced by a meeting room on the *Zenith*. The *Zenith* also has warmer colors and more woodwork in its decor.

Because most of the cabins aboard are modular design, insides and outsides are virtually identical in size (around 172 square feet) and furnishings, with the cabin's deck position determining the price.

INSIDER TIP

In the back of the balcony, tall barstools around a tall table look inviting to latecomers to the shows, but those seats don't swivel and are clumsy to get into and out of; move on down to a regular seat, but avoid the front row of balcony seats where the wooden balcony rail is right at eye level.

Between The Lines

The Brochure Says

"At Celebrity Cruises our objective is a simple one, present an incomparable cruise experience aboard ships of uncompromising style and sophistication."

Translation

The care and attention to detail goes beyond the design and decor into every part of the service. A cadre of personable and well trained waiters and cabin stewards are at your service and food and entertainment are far above the norm. An outstanding cruise for the money.

Cabins & Costs

Fantasy Suites: . . . . **A-**

Average Price Per Person, Double Occupancy, Per Day: $613 including airfare in the Caribbean.

The two top suites, called Royal Suites on the *Zenith* and Presidential Suites on the *Horizon*, are 510 square feet with separate sitting room (the one we like has caramel leather sofas and chairs), glass dining table with four chairs, wood and marble counter, TV set and big windows; the bedroom has twin or king-sized beds, walk-in closet with generous storage space and built-in safe, and a second TV set. The marble bathroom is not large but does have a Jacuzzi bathtub. And there's butler service, hot cabin breakfasts if you wish, fresh fruit replenished daily and a welcome bottle of champagne.

Small Splurges: . . . . **A-**

Average Price PPPD: $499 including airfare in the Caribbean.

Deluxe suites, 18 on the *Horizon* and 20 on the *Zenith*, have two lower beds or a king-sized bed, sitting area with two chairs or loveseat and chair, glass table, large window and small TV, as well as a long marble-topped desk/dresser with chair. The bathroom is very like the one in the bigger suites (see "Fantasy Suites" above). Perks: Butler service, terrycloth robes, hot breakfasts served in-cabin, fresh fruit, a welcome bottle of champagne.

An outside deluxe cabin aboard the Zenith.

Suitable Standards: . . . . B

Average Price PPPD: $356 including airfare in the Caribbean.
Most standard cabins measure 172 square feet and have two lower beds or a double, two chairs, table, window, large built-in desk/dresser, TV set and bath with shower. Four outside wheelchair-accessible cabins on each ship have generous bedroom and bathroom space for turning, a big shower with fold-down seat, extra-wide doors and ramp access over the low bathroom sill.

Bottom Bunks: . . . . B

Average Price PPPD: $268 including airfare in the Caribbean.
The cheapest insides are also 172 square feet with two lower beds or a double, two chairs, table, TV, wide dresser and bath with tile shower and white Corian self-sink and counter. A vertical strip of mirror on the wall where a window would be lightens and brightens the space. Some have third and fourth fold-down upper bunks.

The Routes

The *Horizon* replaces the *Meridian* in Bermuda for the summer of 1998, with weekly Sunday sailings from New York and other East Coast cities. The itinerary is a new one with calls at both Hamilton and King's Wharf. In winter *Horizon* makes 10- and 11-night Ultimate Caribbean cruises from Fort Lauderdale calling at a variety of ports depending on the sailing date.

The *Zenith* sails every summer Saturday from New York to Bermuda, and in winter offers nine Panama Canal itineraries for 10 to 16 nights.

The Scoop

When the line was introduced, executives were careful not to over-hype the new product and bombard the public with extravagant promises. Instead, they let the product speak for itself, and it did—in volumes. Early passengers commented that they had not expected so much for the price, and Celebrity's reputation grew quickly among knowledgeable cruise passengers looking for a good buy.

After sailing aboard all the line's ships, we find very little to criticize, other than the captain's formal parties with their tepid, watery, premixed cocktails; and we often wish, in dining rooms aboard other ships, we had one of Celebrity's menus facing us instead.

Insider Tips

Five Great Spaces

1. The shipshape navy-and-white nautical observation lounges high atop the ships and forward, America's Cup on the *Horizon* and Fleet Bar on the *Zenith*. Lots of wood and brass trim and snappy blue chairs with white piping around the edges.

2. The self-service cafe, with two indoor and one outdoor buffet line with an inviting array of dishes at breakfast and lunch, waiters on hand to carry passengers' trays to the tables, and a rolling wine cart of vintages available by the glass at lunchtime. The floors are wood and tile, the seats a pretty floral pattern.

3. Harry's Tavern, named for former company president Harry Haralambopoulos, is a small Greek taverna decorated with a mural depicting a Mexican fountain splashing under Greek trees occupied by South American parrots on a Tuscan hillside.

4. The elegant Rainbow Room on the *Zenith*, with its cabaret/nightclub ambience, wood-toned walls, gently curved bar, raised seating areas and blue leaf-patterned upholstery.

5. The show lounge offers optimum sightlines in most areas, with seven seating levels on the two decks facing the large raised stage; multimedia projections and high-tech lighting design enhances the well-costumed shows.

Five Good Reasons to Book These Ships

1. Because they may very well be the best restaurant in Bermuda this summer.

2. Because they represent perhaps the best value for the money in the whole world of cruising.

3. Because they take service seriously.

4. Because there's an excellent health center where you can work off the calories.

5. Because the whole family can experience a top-quality cruise experience without mortgaging the farm.

Five Things You Won't Find On Board

1. Hot breakfasts served in standard cabins; you only get it in suites.

2. Private verandas.

3. Permission to bring your own alcoholic beverages aboard for cabin consumption; the brochure spells this out as a No-No. You're expected to buy your drinks on board. (Other cruise lines permit passengers to use personal supplies while in the privacy of their cabins.)

4. A hungry passenger.

5. A cinema. Movies are shown daily on the cabin television.

HORIZON
ZENITH

★★★★★
★★★★★

Registry	**Bahamas**
Officers	**Greek**
Crew	**International**
Complement	**642**
GRT	**46,811**
Length (ft.)	**682**
Beam (ft.)	**95**
Draft (ft.)	**24**
Passengers-Cabins Full	**1752**
Passengers-2/Cabin	**1354**
Passenger Space Ratio	**34.57**
Stability Rating	**Good**
Seatings	**2**
Cuisine	**Contemporary**
Dress Code	**Traditional**
Room Service	**Yes**
Tip	**$9 PPPD, 15% automatically added bar checks. Suites tip Butler $3 PPPD**

Ship Amenities

Outdoor Pool	**2**
Indoor Pool	**0**
Jacuzzi	**3**
Fitness Center	**Yes**
Spa	**Yes**
Beauty Shop	**Yes**
Showroom	**Yes**
Bars/Lounges	**4**
Casino	**Yes**
Shops	**4**
Library	**Yes**
Child Program	**Yes**
Self-Service Laundry	**No**
Elevators	**7**

Cabin Statistics

Suites	**20**
Outside Doubles	**513**
Inside Doubles	**144**
Wheelchair Cabins	**4**
Singles	**0**
Single Surcharge	**150-200%**
Verandas	**0**
110 Volt	**Yes**

CELEBRITY CRUISES

CLIPPER

7711 Bonhomme Avenue, St. Louis, MO 63105
☎ *(314) 727-2929, (800) 325-0010*
www.ecotravel.com/clipper

Nantucket Clipper *passengers spot a whale off the coast of Massachusetts.*

History . . . .

Founded in 1982 in his native St. Louis by travel entrepreneur Barney A. Ebsworth, who also founded Intrav tour company, Clipper Cruises owns and operates two small ships, the 138-passenger *Yorktown Clipper* and the 100-passenger *Nantucket Clipper*, both U.S. flag vessels built in Jeffersonville, Indiana. The company was acquired by Intrav in April 1997.

The first ship on line was the 104-passenger *Newport Clipper*, which introduced the line's signature Colonial South cruises in 1984. That vessel was subsequently sold and now sails as *Spirit of Endeavour* for Alaska Sightseeing/Cruise West.

A third ship, the *Clipper Adventurer*, will join the fleet in April 1998, in Europe. A remake of the Russian research vessel *Admiral Lazarev*, the 121-passenger vessel will carry an A-1 Super Ice Class rating for Northwest Passage, Spitsbergen and Antarctic itineraries.

The other two ships cruise the waterways of North and Central America from Alaska to Costa Rica, the Caribbean to New England, with an emphasis on local culture, art, history and swimming and snorkeling off the side of the ship, depending on the cruising region.

Concept . . . .

Clipper uses small, shallow-draft vessels to explore America's waterways, tying up in small, out-of-the-way ports as well as urban areas in walking distance of the sightseeing. The line prides itself on being "a thoughtful alternative to conventional cruising," stressing substance over slickness, naturalist and lecture programs over musical productions and bingo and sneakers over sequins.

Clipper president Paul H. Duynhouwer likes to point out the misconceptions about adventure cruising—"Elitist, expensive, far away and long are common misconceptions," he says. Clipper, on the other hand, makes soft adventure trips that are as short as seven days and more affordable than many of the exotic journeys other lines offer.

Signatures . . . .

Clipper was one of the early providers of golf theme cruises but these days is concentrating more on soft adventure sailings.

Open-seating meals served by friendly young Americans, many of them just past college-age, are prepared by chefs trained at the famous Culinary Institute of America in Hyde Park.

Gimmicks. . . . .

Clipper Chippers—warm chocolate chip cookies served at teatime and other times.

Who's the Competition . . . .

While Clipper offers a fairly unique product because of the scope of its itineraries, it does compete somewhat with Special Expeditions in Alaska, Costa Rica, Panama and Mexico's Sea of Cortez, as well as rivaling American Canadian Caribbean Line in the Virgin Islands in winter. And the all-American style of its food and service, as well as an emphasis on lesser-visited ports and cruising areas, competes with Alaska Sightseeing/Cruise West in Alaska. With its new *Clipper Adventurer*, it can compete with the other expeditioners in the polar regions.

Who's Aboard. . . . .

Couples and singles past 40, many from the South and Midwest, dominate the passenger list. What the passengers have in common is an interest in history, culture and nature, and a desire to learn more about the world around them. They are destination-oriented rather than pleasure-driven, and would show little interest in a casino or production show, even if Clipper were to offer them. Most represent household incomes of over $70,000 with substantial discretionary income.

Who Should Go . . . .

We think more younger couples would enjoy the ship as much as their elders, the same people who would take a bicycling tour through a wine region or stay in bed-and-breakfast establishments. Also, Clipper would appeal to people who have taken package tours or bus tours because they feel safer being escorted around but are tired of all that regimentation, packing and unpacking.

Who Should Not Go . . . .

Families with young or restless children, because there are no places on these ships for them to get away; everyone congregates in one large indoor lounge more suitable to quiet adult activities. Because the ships have no elevators, they are not appropriate for travelers who require wheelchairs or walkers to get around.

The Lifestyle . . . .

Single-seating meals with no assigned tables allow passengers to get acquainted more easily than on large ships, and many of the Clipper crowd find they have a great deal in common. Most days the vessels are in port for all or part of the day, with a range of organized excursions and suggestions for on-your-own activities. Naturalists and lecturers are scheduled frequently to talk about special features of the ports of call, and if there is any entertainment, it is apt to be someone from shore performing folk songs or playing jazz.

Wardrobe . . . .

Day dress is casual but in the East Coast preppy or country club style, with topsiders, golf pants, plaid Bermuda shorts and such. Zippered windbreakers, soft hats rather than billed caps and sensible shoes are worn ashore. While there is no specific dress code, passengers usually dress up a bit for dinner, and men will sometimes wear jacket and tie.

Bill of Fare . . . . .B+

As mentioned above, chefs from the Culinary Institute of America are responsible for preparing the excellent contemporary American cuisine on board. We've found the food uniformly good and the menus consistent in their appeal and variety. Half-portions can be ordered for people with small appetites and "light" dishes are offered on every menu. Much of the food is prepared with fresh ingredients from scratch—including homemade crackers served with the day's soups.

DID YOU KNOW?

A free 21-minute video is available for loan from Clipper for any potential passenger who'd like a closer look at the vessels and the life aboard them. Rather than using models as most cruise lines do, the video features actual Clipper passengers. Call ☎ (800) 325-0010 to borrow a copy.

The Bottom Line

These are rewarding and enjoyable cruises, with as many surprises and delights to be discovered in the Great Lakes as in Costa Rica or in Annapolis as in Panama's Darien jungle. The cruises are especially delightful when a passenger is following a subject of particular interest—whether Civil War history, great art museums, Native American legends and lore, snorkeling or restored historic rail cars on a combination cruise/train journey. Soft Adventure sailings will be on tap when the *Clipper Adventurer* joins the fleet. Some excellent American rail/cruise tours are offered in conjunction with the luxurious American Orient Express.

⚓⚓⚓⚓⚓
NANTUCKET CLIPPER
YORKTOWN CLIPPER

A cruise along the coast of Maine brings back indelible memories of a lunchtime when a humpback whale mother swam by, her nursing calf clinging to her, lazily flapping her white fins in a backstroke wave just outside the dining room windows. On other days, we'd search out the lobster pound in every port, and feast on fresh steamed one-and-a-quarter pounders, promising each other it was in lieu of dinner—and then dinner was always so tempting we'd eat it anyhow.

The *Nantucket* and the *Yorktown Clippers* have four passenger decks reached by stairs; there are no elevators. Topmost is the Sun Deck, with lounge chairs and good observation points; it doubles as an outdoor dining venue from time to time, and, on the *Yorktown Clipper*, also has four passenger cabins. The Promenade Deck, as its name implies, is wrapped all around by a covered promenade, and cabins on this deck open directly to the outdoors, a boon except when it's raining. Lounge Deck has a forward observation lounge and an outdoor bow area in front of that, along with passenger cabins, some opening into an inside hallway, others at the aft end opening to the outdoors. Main Deck is where the dining room is located, along with additional passenger cabins. All cabins are outsides with windows or portholes.

Between The Lines

The Brochure Says

"Lifestyle on board is casual and unregimented. The crowds, commercial atmosphere and hectic activities so often associated with conventional cruise ships are nowhere to be found on Clipper. Your fellow travelers are likely to remind you of the members of your own country club."

Translation

None needed; it's a very precise description of the lifestyle and passengers.

Cabins & Costs

Fantasy Suites: . . . . **NA**

Nothing on board really qualifies for this category.

Small Splurges: . . . . **B**

Average Price Per Person, Double Occupancy, Per Day: $492 plus airfare.
The category six outside double staterooms are the most expensive digs aboard, primarily because of being slightly larger with more desirable deck locations. Like all the other Clipper cabins, they contain twin beds, bath with shower, desk/dresser with chair plus windows rather than portholes.

Suitable Standards: . . . . **C**

Average Price PPPD: $328 to $438, plus airfare.
Same as the above (see "Small Splurges") except slightly smaller, the category Two, Three, Four and Five cabins are very similar but vary slightly in price. The category Fives have twin beds in an L-configuration with a bit more floor space, while the others have the two beds parallel to each other with a small desk/dresser in between. All three categories have bath with shower only and windows instead of portholes.

Bottom Bunks: . . . . **C**

Average Price PPPD: $290 plus airfare.
The lowest-priced cabins on board are forward on the lowest passenger deck and have portholes instead of windows. Otherwise, each contains twin beds arranged parallel to each other with a small desk/dresser and chair in between. Baths have shower only.

The Routes

The *Yorktown Clipper* spends winter in Costa Rica, Panama, the Orinoco and the Caribbean, then travels through the Panama Canal to the Sea of Cortez. Summer is spent in British Columbia and Alaska, and autumn in the waterways of the Pacific Northwest and Northern California.

The *Nantucket Clipper* sails from St. Thomas around the "yachtsman's Caribbean" in winter, then spends spring along the East Coast, cruising the Antebellum South, Colonial America and Chesapeake Bay. In summer the ship heads for New England and the St. Lawrence River, then into the Great Lakes. In September the ship makes several fall foliage sailings from new York.

While the prices could be regarded as slightly higher than average—and there's no early booking discount advertised—the value is there. The vessels are comfortable, attractively decorated and always spotlessly clean, although when the ship is full, the lounge sometimes feels crowded. In a few areas they visit—notably off the coast of Maine—the shallow draft causes more ship motion than some passengers might like. The other downer is getting from the Promenade Deck cabins, which open onto a covered deck, down to the dining room when it's raining. But the food, service, itineraries and overall experience are so delightful that little annoyances about space or rain in the face seem minuscule. We like these ships very much.

Five Favorite Places

1. The tasteful Dining Room, just about everyone's favorite hangout three times a day, plus when it doubles as a cinema after dinner some evenings and the crew makes a batch of fresh popcorn.

2. The Observation Lounge, where passengers socialize, listen to lectures, play cards and games, write letters and do needlepoint, is prettily decorated in pastels and subdued pale tones. This is where the chocolate chip cookies are served at teatime.

3. The Promenade Deck, good for getting in a mile walk if you don't mind counting double-digit laps.

4. The bow observation area, a good place to watch for Alaska wildlife or denizens of the Darien jungle, also where you might sip a cup of hot coffee or glass of iced tea.

5. The Sun Deck, where you sit in lounge chairs and observe the scenery, is also the place where a New England clambake may be dished up.

Five Good Reasons to Book These Ships

1. To get delightful rail/sea travel packages around the U.S. and into Mexico.

2. To vacation in a smoke-free atmosphere; smoking is not allowed inside the ships.

3. To enjoy some genuinely warm and friendly American service and delicious American food.

4. To cruise some unusual and interesting waterways, including the Great Lakes, the St. Lawrence Seaway, the Sea of Cortez, the Orinoco River and Intracoastal Waterway.

5. To meet other people around the same age who share the same interests.

NANTUCKET CLIPPER   ⚓⚓⚓⚓

Registry	U.S.
Officers	American
Crew	American
Complement	32
GRT	95
Length (ft.)	207
Beam (ft.)	37
Draft (ft.)	8
Passengers-Cabins Full	102
Passengers-2/Cabin	102
Passenger Space Ratio	NA
Stability Rating	NA
Seatings	1
Cuisine	American, contemporary
Dress Code	Casual
Room Service	No
Tip	$9 PPPD

Ship Amenities

Outdoor Pool	0
Indoor Pool	0
Jacuzzi	0
Fitness Center	No
Spa	No
Beauty Shop	No
Showroom	No
Bars/Lounges	1
Casino	No
Shops	1
Library	Yes
Child Program	No
Self-Service Laundry	No
Elevators	0

Cabin Statistics

Suites	0
Outside Doubles	51
Inside Doubles	0
Wheelchair Cabins	0
Singles	0
Single Surcharge	150%
Verandas	0
110 Volt	Yes

YORKTOWN CLIPPER ⚓⚓⚓⚓⚓

Registry	**U.S.**
Officers	**American**
Crew	**American**
Complement	**40**
GRT	**97**
Length (ft.)	**257**
Beam (ft.)	**43**
Draft (ft.)	**8.5**
Passengers-Cabins Full	**138**
Passengers-2/Cabin	**138**
Passenger Space Ratio	**NA**
Stability Rating	**NA**
Seatings	**1**
Cuisine	**American, contemporary**
Dress Code	**Casual**
Room Service	**No**
Tip	**$9 PPPD**

Ship Amenities

Outdoor Pool	**0**
Indoor Pool	**0**
Jacuzzi	**0**
Fitness Center	**No**
Spa	**No**
Beauty Shop	**No**
Showroom	**No**
Bars/Lounges	**1**
Casino	**No**
Shops	**1**
Library	**Yes**
Child Program	**No**
Self-Service Laundry	**No**
Elevators	**0**

Cabin Statistics

Suites	**0**
Outside Doubles	**69**
Inside Doubles	**0**
Wheelchair Cabins	**0**
Singles	**0**
Single Surcharge	**150%**
Verandas	**0**
110 Volt	**Yes**

Unrated
CLIPPER ADVENTURER

The 121-passenger *Clipper Adventurer* joins the line April 9, 1998, in Lisbon, Portugal. A massive makeover of a Russian ice class research vessel, the *Admiral Lazarev*, the ship is being converted in Scandinavia under the supervision of Captain Hasse Nilsson, who holds several records in Arctic cruising.

The ship is 295 feet long, 4575 tons, with a 17-foot draft. It carries eight zodiac landing craft. All cabins are outsides with two lower beds and private baths. Meals are single seating and the service staff is American. The ship will also have an observation lounge, bar, library, sauna, gym and beauty salon.

The vessel will make its inaugural voyage around the Iberian Peninsula for 10 days, calling in Madeira, the Canary Islands, Casablanca, Tangier, Gibraltar and Seville. As the summer progresses, the *Clipper Adventurer* will visit Western Europe, Scandinavia, Russia, Greenland, the Atlantic Coast from Halifax, Nova Scotia to Port Everglades, Florida, the Amazon and Brazil, and Antarctica.

Club Med® Cruises

40 West 57th Street, New York, NY 10019
☎ (212) 977-2100, (800) 453-7447
www.clubmed.com

The same emphasis on watersports as in the land clubs can be found aboard the Club Med ships with their marine platforms.

NOTE: The *Club Med 1* was sold to Windstar Cruises and leaves the Club Med fleet in March, 1998.

History . . . .

The vacation phenomenon that is Club Med started in the summer of 1950 in a small tent village on the island of Mallorca and has grown to more than 100 all-inclusive vacation villages around the world. In February 1990 the company introduced the first of two five-masted sailing ships, the *Club Med 1*, built by France's Société Nouvelle des Ateliers et Chantiers du Havre, the yard that also constructed the three Windstar sailing ships. Similar to the Windstar ships but larger, and also with computer-trimmed sails, the Club Med ships are sleek, handsome vessels carrying 376 passengers.

—At 14,745 tons, a length of 617 feet and a draft of 16.5 feet, they are the world's largest sailing ships.

Concept . . . .

To offer a cruise vacation aboard a motor/sailing ship in "unparalleled comfort and elegance" with a relaxed atmosphere that "fosters freedom, intimacy and camaraderie."

Signatures . . . .

Some 64 to 77 GOs, *gentils organisateurs,* or "congenial organizers," as in the Club Med land resorts, operate as a sort of freewheeling social staff aboard each ship.

Gimmicks. . . . .

Usually once a cruise there's a shoreside lobster picnic lunch, along with a water-skiing exhibition by the GOs.

Who's the Competition . . . .

While the Club Med vessels are similar to those of Windstar, the lifestyle aboard differs because of the very strong presence of the GOs, who function as cheerleaders, entertainers and quasi-passengers. The end result is part-cruise, part-Club Med land village experience. Therefore, the real competition Club Med ships face is from Club Med land resorts.

Who's Aboard. . . . .

Young to middle-aged singles and couples, families with children over 10 (kids under 10 are no-nos), watersports enthusiasts, honeymooners, and destination-oriented young vacationers primarily from Europe and North America.

Who Should Go . . . .

Anyone young at heart who enjoys sun, sand, surf and sails, who has a sense of adventure, a dislike of formality but an appreciation for luxurious, if unpretentious, accommodations and surroundings.

Who Should Not Go . . . .

Children under 10.

Mrs. Pritchard, author James Thurber's quintessential cruiser: "If you travel much on cruise ships you are bound, sooner or later, to run into Mrs. Abigail Pritchard. She is not one woman, but many; I have encountered at least fifteen of her." Mrs. Pritchard, who appreciates Cunard, would be confused at the absence of a professional cruise staff, the lack of dress code and the babel of different languages with French predominating.

The Lifestyle . . . .

There is no assigned seating for meals. A variety of indoor and outdoor, self-serve and full-service restaurants are on board, plus the Hall Nautique, a watersports marina that can be lowered astern when the ship is at anchor. Daily ports of call are visited by passengers who shuttle ashore by tender to go to an island beach or shops or restaurants.

Wardrobe. . . . .

Daytime dress is casual aboard ship and on shore, and topless sunbathing is popular aboard with both passengers and female GOs. Bathing suits and coverups are the most common daytime garb. While recent

Club Med brochures show a formally dressed couple on deck, we can't recall seeing anyone wearing black tie on our cruise. "Stylish resort attire" is what is requested for evening, and a jacket without tie on men, a long skirt or silk slacks on women is about as dressy as it gets normally.

Bill of Fare . . . . B

An open-air snack bar, self-serve restaurant for breakfast and lunch plus a full-service restaurant for lunch and dinner offer meal choices for French-accented cuisine. A complimentary table wine is served at both lunch and dinner in generous quantity, with a wine list available offering premium wines for purchase. The cooking when we were aboard was more Continental than nouvelle. A room service menu offers additional choices at a surcharge—smoked fish, caviar and sandwiches.

Showtime . . . . D

As in the land Club Meds, the GOs perform a lot of the entertainment, lip-syncing to records and donning funny hats with the same enthusiasm Judy Garland and Mickey Rooney used to put into their shows in grandpa's barn in the old MGM movies. Sometimes a steel band from shore comes aboard.

Discounts . . . .

Land/cruise combination packages can save money when purchased as a package, but the cruise line does not routinely offer discounts.

The Bottom Line

With *Club Med 1* sold to Windstar Cruises, which are negotiating to buy *Club Med 2*, the chances seem slim that Club Med Cruises will continue. If *Club Med 2* is not sold, there is the possibility it could be moved from the Pacific to the Mediterranean to replace *Club Med 1*.

★★★
CLUB MED 1
CLUB MED 2

Her first captain, Alain Lambert, loves the Club Med 1. *"She's like a fish, just like a fish when she's running. She's lovely. She puts her nose in the water, she likes the water."* Her maximum list is two percent but he can control it from one degree to five degrees. *"If I have sportive passengers, I can put it five degrees."* The combination of sails and engine saves seven tons of bunker fuel a day. Twenty tons are consumed in the average day. The ship makes 14 knots under motor and sail with favorable winds, and he can raise or lower the sails in one-and-a-half minutes. *"She's very stable."*

Waterskiing demonstrations are performed by Club Med's GOs.

Instead of a professional cruise staff, pursers, hotel managers, entertainers and such, the cruise is run by a team of 64 to 77 energetic young men and women from various parts of the French-speaking world called GOs (for *gentils organisateurs*) who seem to be having more fun than anybody. Rather than hotel staffers in the traditional sense, they function as quasi-guests, taking part in the same activities with the guests. When they're not water-skiing or leading passengers in songs and dances, they're sunbathing by the pool or rehearsing lip-sync songs for shows. The chief purser/hotel manager is called the *chef de village*, or head of the village, and he may spend more time polishing his mono waterski technique than his hotel-keeping skills, while the ship's doctor may spend his days checking out scuba equipment to the passengers if no one is ill.

INSIDER TIP

Newlyweds on the Club Med ships get a bottle of sparkling wine, two bar coupons, two T-shirts and a VIP gift basket, plus a cocktail party with the chef de village. Honeymooners must be spending one week or longer aboard, must travel within three months of their wedding, must present their marriage certificate when checking in and should request the gift package when booking.

The Brochure Says

"On the eight elegant decks of this luxurious 600-foot ship, everything has been carefully, lovingly prepared for your complete comfort and pleasure. State-of-the-art nautical technology assures the smoothest sail on the Seven Seas while taking advantage of every energy-saving breeze."

Translation

The only problem is, you'll have to get up early in the morning to experience it since the ships tend to spend most of each day in port with the sails furled.

Note: Club Med Membership and initiation fees not included in these fares.

Fantasy Suites: . . . . **NA**

There is nothing on board that fits this category.

Small Splurges: . . . . **A**

Average Price Per Person, Double Occupancy, Per Day: $425 including airfare from California in French Polynesia.
Suites (two measuring 321 square feet each on the *Club Med 1*, five measuring 258 square feet each on the *Club Med 2*) containing the same basic furnishings as standards (see "Suitable Standards," below) are also available.

Suitable Standards: . . . . **A**

Average Price PPPD: $350 including airfare from California in French Polynesia.

All the *Club Med* cabins are outsides with portholes rather than windows and measuring 188 square feet, with white walls, mahogany trim, twin beds that can be made into a queen-sized bed and space module bathrooms that are trim and sleek with excellent pulsating shower heads. Some 23 cabins have a third upper berth. Furnishings include a long dresser/desk with six drawers, a mirror wall, wide counter, built-in TV set fitted into a wooden base (most of the programming is in French) and a hotel-type folding suitcase rack. Niceties include attractive art, reading lights over the beds, hair dryers, terrycloth robes, fresh fruit in each cabin and Club Med label toiletries. A stocked mini-refrigerator and minibar carry price lists for the contents. Except for continental breakfasts, room service carries a charge.

Bottom Bunks: . . . . **NA**

There are no accommodations that fit this category.

INSIDER TIP

You have to join Club Med with a nonrefundable, one-time-only initiation fee when booking your cruise and pay an annual membership fee. Think of it as just another port tax.

EAVESDROPPING

"A real babble tower," is the way one of the Club Med executives described their 64 GOs that come from all over the world.

The Routes

Club Med 1 is scheduled to spend the winter of 1997–1998 in the Caribbean, sailing from Fort-de-France, Martinique on seven night itineraries through late February or early March. *Club Med 2* sails in French Polynesia. Length of sailings varies from three to seven nights with land package combinations available.

The Scoop

While more emphasis has been placed on English-speaking personnel aboard the ships, these cruises still favor French-speaking passengers. Passengers have to hustle to get to the best deck chairs, watersports gear and barstools ahead of the GOs. While the ships are lovely in every way, the food perfectly acceptable and the wines drinkable, we find the bar prices extremely high and some of the GOs irritating. Club Med ships are primarily for the young at heart who want a casual, active holiday, or anyone who had the time of their lives at summer camp. The *Club Med 1* leaves the fleet in March 1998. *Club Med 2* was based in Tahiti year-round as this book goes to press.

CLUB MED 1 ★★★

Registry	Bahamas
Officers	French
Crew	International
Complement	178
GRT	14,745
Length (ft.)	617
Beam (ft.)	66
Draft (ft.)	16
Passengers-Cabins Full	399
Passengers-2/Cabin	376
Passenger Space Ratio	39.21
Stability Rating	Good to Excellent
Seatings	1
Cuisine	French
Dress Code	Casual elegance
Room Service	Yes
Tip	No tipping

Ship Amenities

Outdoor Pool	2
Indoor Pool	0
Jacuzzi	1
Fitness Center	Yes
Spa	Yes
Beauty Shop	Yes
Showroom	No
Bars/Lounges	5
Casino	Yes
Shops	1
Library	Yes
Child Program	No
Self-Service Laundry	No
Elevators	2

Cabin Statistics

Suites	2
Outside Doubles	186
Inside Doubles	0
Wheelchair Cabins	0
Singles	0
Single Surcharge	130%
Verandas	0
110 Volt	Yes

CLUB MED CRUISES

CLUB MED 2   ★★★

Registry	**Bahamas**
Officers	**French**
Crew	**International**
Complement	**214**
GRT	**14,983**
Length (ft.)	**617**
Beam (ft.)	**66**
Draft (ft.)	**16**
Passengers-Cabins Full	**521**
Passengers-2/Cabin	**392**
Passenger Space Ratio	**38.22**
Stability Rating	**Good to Excellent**
Seatings	**1**
Cuisine	**French**
Dress Code	**Casual elegance**
Room Service	**Yes**
Tip	**No tipping**

Ship Amenities

Outdoor Pool	**2**
Indoor Pool	**0**
Jacuzzi	**1**
Fitness Center	**Yes**
Spa	**Yes**
Beauty Shop	**Yes**
Showroom	**No**
Bars/Lounges	**5**
Casino	**Yes**
Shops	**1**
Library	**Yes**
Child Program	**No**
Self-Service Laundry	**No**
Elevators	**2**

Cabin Statistics

Suites	**5**
Outside Doubles	**191**
Inside Doubles	**0**
Wheelchair Cabins	**0**
Singles	**0**
Single Surcharge	**130%**
Verandas	**0**
110 Volt	**Yes**

COMMODORE CRUISE LINE
Western Caribbean–Yucatan

4000 Hollywood Boulevard, South Tower, Suite 385, Hollywood, FL 33021
☎ *(954) 967-2100, (800) 237-5361*
www.commodorecruise.com

History . . . .

In mid-1995, a financial group headed by Jeffrey I. Binder bought Commodore Cruise Line from its owners, Finnish-based EffJohn International, for $33.5 million, which included the line's two ships, *Enchanted Seas* and *Enchanted Isle*.

This transaction, plus Cunard's acquisition of the former *Crown Dynasty*, now Norwegian Cruise Line's *Norwegian Dynasty*, marked the end of EffJohn's longtime cruise operations in North America which at one time or another had included Bermuda Star Line (which was merged with Commodore in 1989) and Crown Cruise Line. Only the EffJohn-owned, NCL-operated *Leeward* remains

The two vessels are very likely the most-named passenger ships in the world. They started life as the *Brasil* and *Argentina* for New York-based Moore-McCormack Lines in 1958 in South American service. The *Brasil* became the *Volendam* and the *Argentina* the *Veendam* for Holland America in 1972, but after a year of service were laid up and subsequently the former *Argentina* was chartered out to Agence Maritime International, which, for some mysterious reason, renamed her *Brasil*, according to Arnold Kludas in *Great Passenger Ships of the World, Volume 5*. After that, things get even more confusing, but according to our reckoning, *Enchanted Seas* has had 12 names, *Enchanted Isle* 10. Two of them came out of waffling when Bermuda Star Line couldn't decide between *Bermuda Queen* and *Queen of Bermuda*, announcing first one and then the other, and later, on the same ship, Commodore was going to call her *Enchanted Odyssey* but decided it sounded too much like Royal Cruise Line's ships. (See "Did You Know," below.)

After a brief stint as a Russian hotel (*Hotel Commodore*, moored on the Neva River in St. Petersburg), the *Enchanted Isle* was returned to service in the Caribbean in 1995. The *Enchanted Seas* was leased to World Explorer Cruises in 1996 to become the *Universe Explorer*. (See World Explorer Cruises page 923).

COMMODORE CRUISE LINE

DID YOU KNOW?

1958	Brasil	1958	Argentina
1972	Volendam	1972	Veendam
1975	Monarch Sun	1974	Brasil
1977	Volendam	1975	Veendam
1984	Island Sun	1976	Monarch Star
1986	Liberté	1978	Veendam
1987	Canada Star	1984	Bermuda Star
1988	Bermuda Queen	1990	Enchanted Isle
1988	Queen of Bermuda	1994	Hotel Commodore
1990	Enchanted Odyssey	1995	Enchanted Isle
1990	Enchanted Seas		
1996	Universe Explorer		

Concept. . . . .

Commodore aims "to provide top quality service to the markets we serve," according to the line's chairman and CEO, Fred A. Mayer. The budget-priced cruises sail from New Orleans year-round.

Signatures. . . . .

A distinctive line logo features the gold braid sleeve insignia of a commodore.

Gimmicks. . . . .

In 1993-4, the line used a distinctive jazzy, neon-bright campaign called, "Tell Reality to Take a Hike," with some of the most innovative cruise brochure graphics in the industry. It was a shade more hip than the ships. In 1995 they went back to slimmer, more conservative brochures.

Who's the Competition . . . .

Since the ship sails from New Orleans year-round, the line compete head-to-head with Carnival's Tampa/New Orleans sailings as well as Norwegian Cruise Line's Texaribbean cruises out of Houston.

Who's Aboard. . . . .

Lots of first-time cruisers drawn by the low prices and port-intensive itineraries. When we were aboard during the summer, there was an even mix of families with children, young and middle-aged couples and a good sprinkling of singles who seemed to have a grand time.

Who Should Go . . . .

People looking for a casual, moderately-priced getaway to the Western Caribbean.

Who Should Not Go . . . .

Veteran cruisers fussy about food and service.

The Lifestyle . . . .

Generally, things follow a traditional medium-sized cruise ship pattern, with self-service breakfasts and lunches available as well as dining room meals. A cruise staff leads fun and games, and helps with the evening's entertainment. This line is noted particularly for theme cruises and social hosts.

Wardrobe . . . .

Plan to dress on the casual side of traditional. Two formal nights a week would find some men in tuxedos or dinner jackets but more in suits or sport jackets with tie. Women, as usual, can get by with just about anything except shorts.

Bill of Fare C

The passengers generally don't complain about the food (but some self-styled gourmets might). Portions are generous and service is usually friendly if not always proficient. The self-service buffet meals—breakfast, lunch and tea—were less appealing than the dining room meals. Generally dinners offer a couple of appetizers plus fruit juices, several soups, a couple of salads and four main-dish choices, including a Lite Cuisine selection. Desserts are showy, on the rich and elaborate side.

> ### NO NOs
> *Shorts, tank tops and bare feet are not permitted in the dining room.*

Showtime C

Evening musical and variety shows are supplemented with lots of cruise staff-led fun and games, from horse racing and bingo to audience participation lip sync shows, line dancing lessons, trapshooting and wine and cheese parties.

Discounts . . . .

Early booking discounts require a $200 per person deposit or a full payment 90 days prior to the confirmed sailing date. The second passenger gets a 50% discount. Discounts are applied only to the first two full-fare adults per stateroom and are not applicable to groups.

The Bottom Line

The ships have fairly spacious cabins, many with third and fourth berths good for families with children. The relatively deep draft means they ride well, an asset in the sometimes-rough Gulf of Mexico. Although the ships are generally clean and attractively furnished, they're on the basic side. But hey, at these prices what's not to like? With discounts in economy season (August, September, late November and early December) a couple can cruise a week for only $498 apiece.

COMMODORE CRUISE LINE

COMMODORE CRUISE LINE

★ ★
ENCHANTED ISLE

Here and there on this ship, you can still glimpse a touch of the original vessel, or at least the Holland America version, with wood paneling, old wooden dressers with recessed vanity areas, etched glass folding panels to close off a bar area and bits of odd architectural details in the self-service cafes.

There are as many dissimilarities as similarities on this ship which has been through so many name and design changes through the years. The cinema deep down in the ship was turned into a disco. Cabin configurations, however, are virtually the same with high density passenger numbers vis-a-vis the open deck space and public room areas.

Between The Lines

The Brochure Says

"Fine food is part of Commodore's unique New Orleans heritage. Only a cruise line that sails from the gastronomical capital of America can give you dining that puts the love of fine cuisine in every bite."

Translation

Brennan's famous New Orleans restaurant is the inspiration for a special breakfast on each cruise.

Cabins & Costs

Fantasy Suites: . . . . **NA**

There are no cabins aboard that would qualify in this category.

Small Splurges: . . . . **C**

Average Price Per Person Double Occupancy Per Day: $228 plus air add-ons.

The cabins are called deluxe suites and have a double bed, sitting area, desk/dresser with drawers, nightstands, good closet space and large tiled bathroom. The room is spacious and light. Some of the cabins in this category have old wooden dressers that look as if they date from Holland America days.

Suitable Standards: C

Average Price PPPD: $209 plus air add-on.

Since the ship was built in the days before modular cabins, don't expect any two standards to be exactly alike. Many have portholes and most are fairly spacious, with two lower beds (some can be put together into a queen-sized bed, others should be specified as twins or double bed when booking), desk/dresser with drawers, fair closet space and in designated cabins, there is a tub in the bathrooms.

Bottom Bunks: . . . . D

Average Price PPPD: $142 plus air add-ons.

Category 11 insides have upper and lower berths but are fairly spacious. They're not very luxurious, but then they're not very expensive either.

The Routes

The *Enchanted Isle* sails every Saturday from New Orleans, calling in Playa del Carmen and Cozumel, Grand Cayman and Montego Bay.

The Scoop

Prices are quite moderate, with some cabins coming at under $150 a day per person, double occupancy. Work in all the discounts and it can cost less than $75 a day per person double occupancy.

If you're a first-time cruiser, don't anticipate a ship that looks like, say, the ones in Carnival's TV ads or the ones you loved on "The Love Boat." This is an old ship and it shows its age in some spots on deck and in the cheaper cabins on the lower decks. There's a lot of sound seepage between cabins as well. But it has a deep draft and rides fairly smoothly in rough seas, and the air conditioning was overhauled a couple of years ago and should still be working O.K. Look, this vessel achieved a record 107 per cent occupancy in the past year.

Insider Tips

Five Social Spots

1. The observation lounge high atop the ship with a row of windows facing forward, a piano bar and late-night cabaret shows. Tub chairs, cocktail tables, a small bar with three stools and a large round center sofa furnish it.

2. The Monte Carlo casino is spacious but looks as if it's made up of several smaller rooms.

3. The Grand Lounge has some vintage wood paneling and a marble dance floor along with some murky upholstery on the banquettes and chairs and lots of columns which spoil the sightlines during shows.

4.   Barnacle's Bar in the Bistro (try to say that three times real fast!) on the *Enchanted Isle* is a popular gathering spot for daytime drinks (and checking out the singles action).

5.   Neptune's Disco on the *Enchanted Isle* replaced the cinema so now they project movies on the back wall of the disco.

Five Good Reasons to Book This Ships

1.   The prices are very modest, as low as any you'll find anywhere these days—even based on published brochure prices, before any discounting and dealing!

2.   To be able to sail from New Orleans.

3.   To find low-priced cabins big enough for a family of four to move around in (so long as you avoid the really small ones down on Dolphin Deck).

4.   To sample some theme cruises from Mardi Gras to Country and Western, Jazz, even Polka (left over from the days of the *Boheme!*)

5.   To see how well they used to build ships in Pascagoula, Mississippi.

Five Things You Won't Find Aboard

1.   A self-service laundry.

2.   A parking problem if you drive to New Orleans; Commodore has secured parking at $32 for the full cruise but you need to make arrangements when you book the cruise.

3.   A wallflower; two or more dancing hosts are on every sailing to make sure unaccompanied females get a chance to dance.

4.   A promenade deck that goes all around the ship.

5.   An 18-year-old without an accompanying adult sharing the cabin.

ENCHANTED ISLE ★★

Registry	**Panama**
Officers	**European/American**
Crew	**International**
Complement	**350**
GRT	**23,395**
Length (ft.)	**617**
Beam (ft.)	**84**
Draft (ft.)	**28**
Passengers-Cabins Full	**840**
Passengers-2/Cabin	**729**
Passenger Space Ratio	**32.09**
Stability Rating	**Good**
Seatings	**2**
Cuisine	**International**
Dress Code	**Traditional**
Room Service	**Yes**
Tip	**$8.50 PPPD, 15% automatically added to bar check**

Ship Amenities

Outdoor Pool	**1**
Indoor Pool	**0**
Jacuzzi	**1**
Fitness Center	**Yes**
Spa	**No**
Beauty Shop	**Yes**
Showroom	**Yes**
Bars/Lounges	**6**
Casino	**Yes**
Shops	**2**
Library	**Yes**
Child Program	**Yes**
Self-Service Laundry	**No**
Elevators	**3**

Cabin Statistics

Suites	**4**
Outside Doubles	**286**
Inside Doubles	**77**
Wheelchair Cabins	**2**
Singles	**6**
Single Surcharge	**150-200%**
Verandas	**0**
110 Volt	**Yes**

COMMODORE CRUISE LINE

COMMODORE CRUISE LINE

C O S T A *Italian Style* C R U I S E S

80 Southwest 8th Street, Miami, FL 33130
☎ *(305) 358-7325, (800) 462-6782*
www.costacruise.com

Costa's distinctive bright yellow stack with a blue "C" is seen in many Mediterranean and Caribbean ports.

History . . . .

The founding company of Miami-based Costa Cruises was Costa Crociere of Genoa, which started back in 1860 with a family business that imported olive oil from Sardinia, refined it and exported it all over Europe. When patriarch Giacomo Costa died in 1916, his sons inherited the family business and bought a freighter to transport their oil themselves. By 1935 they had eight freighters.

They started passenger service after World War II with the 12,000-ton *Anna "C"* cruising between Genoa and South America. A fleet of three others was added in just four years—the *Andrea "C"*, *Giovanna "C"* and *Franca "C"*.

COSTA CRUISES

The first new ship came in 1957–58 when Costa constructed the 24,000-ton *Federico "C"*, now sailing as Dolphin's *SeaBreeze*. In 1959 they moved the *Franca "C"* to Florida and entered seven-day Caribbean cruising. It wasn't long before their entire fleet began spending winters in the Caribbean.

In 1997 Carnival Corporation and its British affiliate Airtours bought a majority interest in Costa, primarily to take advantage of Costa's strong presence in Europe. At press time Carnival had no plans for major changes on the Costa vessels but will divest the company of the *Costa Playa* and the *Mermoz*.

With one of the youngest fleets in the Caribbean, Costa markets tropical cruises in winter and Mediterranean cruises in summer.

—Introduced three- and four-day cruises to the Bahamas from Miami (*Anna "C"*, 1964).

—Based a cruise ship in San Juan and began the first air/sea program between the U.S. mainland and Puerto Rico (*Franca "C"*, 1968).

—Launched "Cruising Italian Style" with toga night parties (*CostaRiviera*, 1985).

DID YOU KNOW?

Costa's Bianca "C", originally built as La Marseillaise for a French shipping company, burned and sank at the mouth of the harbor in St. George, Grenada, in 1961. You can still see the statue Costa erected in the harbor to commemorate the kindness and hospitality of the Grenadians, who took the 725 passengers and crew into their homes for two days until a rescue vessel could arrive. The statue depicts Christ of the Depths, and is a copy of the original statue in Portofino, Italy, dedicated to scuba divers. One crew member and two passengers died as a result of the fire, and another crew member was never accounted for.

Concept . . . .

"Italian Style by Design," Costa explains as "a product that combines the sophisticated elegance of a European vacation with the fun and spirit of the line's Italian heritage."

Signatures . . . .

The distinctive bright yellow stack with a blue "C" and a blue band across the top makes a Costa ship easily recognizable in any port in the world, especially on the new ships, with their clusters of three narrow vertical yellow stacks.

The use of "C" (meaning Costa) following the ship's name in earlier days and the present use of the ship's name following the Costa name in one word, as in *CostaClassica*, emphasize the fact that this was until recently a family-owned, family-run company.

The piazza, or town square, comparable to the lobby in a major hotel, is the heart of every Costa ship.

Gimmicks . . . .

Roman Bacchanal, better known as "toga night," has progressed from a fairly primitive form—passengers tying on sheets taken from their beds—to a very sophisticated routine—ready-made togas handed out by cruise staffers who also pass around gilded laurel wreaths and such. From its very inception it's been wildly popular with North American passengers (they don't usually do it in Italy but offer a Venetian Carnival night instead). It used to be that on masquerade night, you often cringed in embarrassment if you had put on a costume and were one of the few—on toga night, you're embarrassed if you're wearing street clothes because you're very conspicuous. It's usually held the last night of the cruise, simplifying the what-to-wear question for people who pack before dinner. Also, at least one cruise director warns reluctant toga-wearers, "No sheet, no eat."

On Toga Night, almost every passenger dons one of the costumes, partly because it happens the last night aboard, when you've packed most of your clothes, but also because at least one cruise director threatens, "No sheet, no eat."

Who's the Competition . . . .

Costa used to face a lively competition from Sitmar and Home Lines, both Italian cruise lines that are now defunct, but doesn't really have to duke it out with Princess, despite Princess owning the former Sitmar ships; they appeal to different people.

Because of the stylish new hardware both lines have, we'd say Costa and Celebrity might compete in the Caribbean, since both are major names on the east coast. But in the Mediterranean, Costa dominates the upper price market, Epirotiki the lower price market. That's the reason Carnival bought them.

Who's Aboard . . . .

Costa has always attracted a large segment of cruisers from the northeastern U.S., especially those with an Italian-American heritage. In both the Caribbean and Europe, French and Italian passengers are numerous. Young to middle-aged couples, young families, retirees and often three generations from the same family may all be seen cruising Italian style.

Who Should Go . . . .

More young couples, especially anyone wearing an Armani label, would love the newest Costa ships, because they have the same spare elegance with their chic Italian furniture and uncluttered cabins. Opera fans will enjoy the bigger-than-life dining rooms with their strolling musicians and La Scala-painted murals that change by the evening from a medieval street to an Italian garden. Anyone who wants to travel in Europe with more Europeans than fellow Americans. Anyone who never said "Basta!" ("Enough!") to pasta.

Who Should Not Go . . . .

Cunard first-class transatlantic passengers who might find the energy and noise level a little high; anyone who dislikes pasta and pizza; anyone unwilling to don a toga when everyone else on board does; anyone who doesn't want a multi-cultural experience on a European itinerary or can't stand to hear shipboard announcements broadcast in five languages.

The Lifestyle . . . .

Traditional cruise programs with an Italian accent characterize the Costa ships, with the usual dress code requests, two meal seatings, and a full onboard and shore excursion activities program. Lavish spas imitating Roman baths are on board the newer ships, and the pool decks encourage spending all day outside with cocoon cabana chairs, sidewalk-cafe tables and chairs, splashing fountains and lounge chairs with pale blue-and-white striped cushions. Overall, there's a lighthearted good humor on these ships, especially when a lot of unflappable Italians are aboard.

Because of the number of Europeans aboard in summer, Costa adds an American hostess program to perform as special liaison for the English speakers on board, usually a minority on European sailings.

Wardrobe. . . . .

Costa says it would like its passengers to wear on gala evenings tuxedos or dark suits for gentlemen, evening gowns or cocktail dresses for ladies; there is at least one gala evening a cruise. On other evenings, men wear sports coats and slacks, ladies resort attire. In the daytime, casual resort wear is in order, including light cotton clothing and swimwear. Don't worry about toga nights if one is scheduled (they don't usually do it in Europe); the cruise staff delivers the costumes.

Bill of Fare. . . . . B+

Meals are served at two seatings, with early or main seating at noon for lunch and 6:15 p.m. for dinner, and late or second seating at 1:30 p.m. for lunch, 8:30 p.m. for dinner. All dining room breakfasts and occasional lunches are designated open seating, which on these ships mean any passenger may arrive within a set time and be seated at whatever table has space. It's not unusual on the larger *Classica* and *Romantica* to find a queue forming 15 or 20 minutes ahead of time; some Costa passengers always seem to be worrying needlessly about when their next meal is arriving.

Food and service are usually good to excellent, with a captain or maitre d'hotel always willing to toss a salad or pasta especially for you at tableside. While the chef may be an Austrian and the waiters Croatian or Honduran instead of Italian, the spirit is there. "They're all Italians at heart," says Costa's president.

Whoever's in the kitchen, we've found the pastas generally outstanding, along with vegetarian eggplant dishes, flambé shrimp, breadsticks, salads, cheeses, fresh fruits, grilled veal chops and pasta-and-bean soups. Less successful on most ships are the pizzas (with the notable exception of the *CostaRiviera*, which has a fine pizzeria on board), some of the meats and the desserts. We particularly miss the Italian-style gelati that has been replaced with American commercial ice creams on several ships.

A fresh fish "catch of the day" is sometimes on display on a decorated cart at the entrance to the dining room on the *CostaClassica* and *CostaRomantica*.

Showtime . . . . **B-**

Because passengers on board speak several languages, Costa ships rely more on musical programs or variety performers including magicians, jugglers and acrobats rather than comedians or production shows that need an English-language narrative. The production shows we have seen aboard are produced by a British company and are handsomely costumed and well-choreographed but seem dated beside some of the state-of-the-art shows coming out of Carnival, Princess and RCI these days.

Films are shown on cabin TV sets throughout the day and evening on an alternating basis, and a late-night disco promises to keep going until the wee hours. Live music for listening or dancing is performed throughout the ships before and after dinner. In Europe, a small company of opera singers may be brought aboard to entertain for the evening.

Discounts . . . .

Passengers who book 90 days ahead of time get early booking discounts.

The Bottom Line

Costa has been through several ups and downs in the past few years, as in 1992 when U.S. advertising and marketing executives for Costa attempted to abandon the very successful "Cruising Italian Style" concept for a new EuroLuxe label heralding the debut of the *CostaClassica*, proclaiming "a standard of elegance, entertainment and personal service so unprecedented, there wasn't even a name for it until now—EuroLuxe." While the new ship was dramatic and dazzling with its bare marble floors and sleek, stark ambience, its debut was marred by passengers who complained they had been promised plusher surroundings and more pampering from the service staff than they were getting.

But a change of U.S. executives and a return to the Italian-style theme led to a quick recovery, and by the time sister ship *CostaRomantica* was introduced a year later, most passengers took the marble floors in stride.

Since it's the number one line sailing in Europe today, with the new Carnival ownership, costa should be around a long time.

Costa offers a good, middle-of-the-road traditional cruise with an Italian accent—you should have a lot of fun aboard if you like Italian-American food and have an easygoing sense of humor.

★ ★ ★ ★
CostaAllegra
CostaMarina

When the CostaMarina was new, we had two magazine story assignments to cover it, and through a series of mishaps had to chase the ship all around the Mediterranean, from Ibiza to Barcelona to Madrid to Tunis for three days, arriving in Tunisia just after Saddam Hussein had invaded Kuwait, only to be greeted by two machine-gun wielding teenagers who studied our U.S. passports muttering, "Bush, Bush," to each other, then turned us over to the Tunisian police to be interrogated. By the time we got aboard the CostaMarina, she was the most wonderful and welcoming ship we'd ever seen, and our fondness for her exists to this day.

The *CostaMarina* was the first of the pair to debut, in the summer of 1990, an extensive rebuilding from the hull up designed by Italian architect Guido Canali. The same architect designed the *CostaAllegra*, which was built in 1992 on an existing hull. The result is a pair of high-tech, midsized ships that are cost-efficient and trim but without a lot of extra flourish and furbelows. This is not to say they're not attractive—on the contrary, they are extremely handsome, even whimsical—but they're not traditional. They have a trim, clean, almost austere design that lets the bones, the very skeleton of the ship, show through here and there.

The stern is cropped off in a vertical wall of glass which looks strange from outside but makes a lot of sense when you're sitting inside in the dining room or lounge looking out through all that glass. We recommend them to anyone who doesn't want to sail aboard one of today's megaships, but particularly to those younger passengers, Europeans and Americans, who have no preconceived notions of what a ship should look like.

Venetian "canals" run along the pool deck of the **CostaMarina** *between the whirlpool and the swimming pool.*

Between The Lines

The Brochure Says

"Sophisticated, stylish and architecturally stunning, the *m/v CostaAllegra* is a timeless masterpiece of color, light and water with an irrepressible Italian soul."

Translation

While the language is a bit effusive, we agree.

Cabins & Costs

Fantasy Suites: . . . . **A**

> *Average Price Per Person, Double Occupancy, Per Day: $551 in Europe including airfare from New York.*
> On the *CostaAllegra* only, three forward-facing Rousseau Grand Suites offer a private veranda, separate living room with white sofa wrapped around two walls, wet bar, big portholes looking forward and mirrored walls. In the bedroom is a queen sized bed and wood-toned walls, with a marble bathroom with toilet and bidet,

Jacuzzi tub and separate stall shower, and a walk-in closet with dressing room area. The total space is 376 square feet.

Small Splurges: .... B+

Average Price PPPD: $549 in Europe including airfare from New York.

On the *CostaMarina*, eight deluxe outside staterooms with verandas just big enough for two lounge chairs also have a folding wood wall that can separate bedroom from living room. The bedroom has a queen-sized bed and the living room a pull-down berth and a sofa that can be made up as a bed, making room for two additional passengers. Bathrooms have a chic black-and-white tile floor and a Jacuzzi tub.

Suitable Standards: .... B+

Average Price PPPD: $437 in Europe including airfare from New York.

Most outside cabins aboard *CostaAllegra* in Category 7 on Gauguin deck have twin beds that can convert to queen-sized, two large portholes covered with solid shade and sheer curtains, walls covered in fabric wall hangings, a long desk/dresser with eight drawers plus a combination safe, color TV with remote control, three-drawer nightstands, bathroom with a futuristic round shower of clear curved plexiglass, gray marble counter with basin, big mirrors, good lighting and built-in hair dryer. The size is adequate but hardly generous at 156 square feet.

Bottom Bunks: .... C-

Average Price PPPD: $265 in Europe including airfare from New York.

Category One inside cabins include some designated for disabled passengers (only on the *CostaAllegra*) with upper and lower berths; the others contain one lower bed, as well as furnishings similar to outside standards, including desk and chair. (See "Suitable Standards," above.) Inside cabins measure only 146 square feet.

INSIDER TIP

Playing the cabin radio is a good cover for your own in-cabin conversations, somewhat like a '50s spy movie.

The Routes

From May to September the *CostaAllegra* makes a variety of Baltic and Scandinavian cruises, some of them to the Norwegian fjords and Spitsbergen. There are two repositioning sailings from Genoa to Amsterdam and a series of seven-night autumn cruises in Spain and Portugal.

CostaMarina does seven-day cruises out of Copenhagen to the Baltic and Scandinavia, then moves to Genoa for a series of Mediterranean cruises.

The Scoop

These ships are especially well-designed for younger passengers, with considerable space devoted to spa, gym and disco. Particularly in Europe, we notice a number of young families, mostly Italian, with small children. There is a children's program and dedicated children's center on board the *CostaAllegra*; a meeting room on the *CostaMarina* is turned over to children when necessary.

Food and service in the dining rooms on both ships are quite good, with tableside service; here, aboard the **CostaMarina.**

Food and service in the dining rooms as quite good, with some tables for two available.

In tropical climates, the great expanses of glass mean some parts of the ship—notably the disco and spa—get uncomfortably warm by late afternoon despite the air conditioning. A less-structured daily program is offered in Europe, where passengers have a laissez-faire attitude. Sightlines are not very good in the showrooms, but the entertainment is not always riveting anyhow.

The real pleasure of these ships is the fresh design, the open and inviting decks and public rooms and the ease with which even first-time cruisers can find their way around.

COSTA ALLEGRA ★★★★

Registry	Liberia
Officers	Italian
Crew	International
Complement	450
GRT	30,000
Length (ft.)	615
Beam (ft.)	84.5
Draft (ft.)	27
Passengers-Cabins Full	1066
Passengers-2/Cabin	810
Passenger Space Ratio	37.03
Stability Rating	Good
Seatings	2
Cuisine	Italian
Dress Code	Traditional
Room Service	Yes
Tip	$8.50 PPPD, 15% automatically added to bar checks

Ship Amenities

Outdoor Pool	1
Indoor Pool	0
Jacuzzi	2
Fitness Center	Yes
Spa	Yes
Beauty Shop	Yes
Showroom	Yes
Bars/Lounges	7
Casino	Yes
Shops	Yes
Library	Yes
Child Program	Yes
Self-Service Laundry	No
Elevators	4

Cabin Statistics

Suites	3
Outside Doubles	219
Inside Doubles	186
Wheelchair Cabins	8
Singles	0
Single Surcharge	150%
Verandas	3
110 Volt	Yes

COSTA CRUISES

CostaMarina   ★★★★

Registry	Liberia
Officers	Italian
Crew	International
Complement	395
GRT	25,000
Length (ft.)	571.5
Beam (ft.)	84.5
Draft (ft.)	27
Passengers-Cabins Full	1025
Passengers-2/Cabin	772
Passenger Space Ratio	32.38
Stability Rating	Good
Seatings	2
Cuisine	Italian
Dress Code	Traditional
Room Service	Yes
Tip	$8.50 PPPD, 15% automatically added to bar checks

Ship Amenities

Outdoor Pool	1
Indoor Pool	0
Jacuzzi	2
Fitness Center	Yes
Spa	Yes
Beauty Shop	Yes
Showroom	Yes
Bars/Lounges	7
Casino	Yes
Shops	Yes
Library	Yes
Child Program	Yes
Self-Service Laundry	No
Elevators	8

Cabin Statistics

Suites	8
Outside Doubles	180
Inside Doubles	173
Wheelchair Cabins	0
Singles	0
Single Surcharge	150%
Verandas	8
110 Volt	Yes

COSTA CRUISES

★★★★★
CostaClassica
CostaRomantica

The CostaClassica, first of the two new ships, got off to a bad start because some former executives misled travel agents and potential passengers by tagging the new ship "EuroLuxe," creating the expectation of a plush Crystal-style ship rather than an austere but handsome contemporary Italian design. Expecting "luxury, elegance and sumptuousness," as the dictionary defines luxe, one disgruntled passenger looked at the bare marble floors and muttered, "The luxe stops here."

The dining rooms change their looks when they change their background scenery, painted by a La Scala Opera House designer.

CRUISING IS GOOD.
CRUISING *Italian Style*
IS *Magnifico!* [SM]

Awarded 5 stars by Fielding's Cruise Guide.

nly Costa, Europe's *#1* cruise line, gives you a taste of Italy in the Eastern and Western Caribbean. You'll enjoy authentic Italian cuisine, warm Italian hospitality and Italian-inspired theme nights. Cruise for 7 nights on the breathtaking CostaVictoria or the elegant CostaRomantica both sailing Sundays from Ft. Lauderdale. Or sail one of 6 ships on 7-to 16-night cruises to the Eastern or Western Mediterranean, North Cape/Fjords, Baltic & Russia or Transatlantic. Also ask about our 2-night **Free Europe*** package available after most sailings.

For reservations, see your Travel Agent
or call 1-800-33-COSTA, ext. 925,
for a brochure or $9.95 video.

C O S T A C C R U I S E S
Italian Style

Yorktown Clipper, Willemstad, Curacao

Norway Sky Deck pool

French Country Waterways' *Horizon II* navigates a lock.

These sister ships are sleek and stylish with marble, tile, brass, polished wood, fountains and sculptures. So much hard surface lends a cool rather than warm ambience.

The ships have an angular bow, a boxy midsection and a rounded stern, with a vertical cluster of bright yellow funnels aft balanced by a forward glass-walled circular observation lounge set atop an all-glass deck housing the Caracalla Spa and amidships pool.

Two stairwells with bare stone floors and no risers provide the main vertical traffic flow through the ship, and on busy occasions like the lifeboat drill, sounds like changing classes at Woodrow Wilson Junior High.

Decks are handsome and well-designed. One pool is amidships, a second one aft, along with two Jacuzzis and several levels of teak decking for sunbathing.

Between The Lines

The Brochure Says

"Created for those with a sense of adventure and an appreciation for style…(with) Italian hospitality, European charm and American comforts."

Translation

You can expect to find pasta and pizza; a cabin with TV, radio, hair dryer and safe; and a charming waiter who may just as likely come from Riga or Rijeka as Roma.

Cabins & Costs

Fantasy Suites: . . . . **A+**

Average Price Per Person, Double Occupancy, Per Day: $646 in Europe including airfare from New York.

Among our very favorite suites at sea are the 10 veranda suites on each ship, particularly those on the *Romantica* named for operas. Each is 580 square feet with private veranda, living room with burled brierwood furniture, a kidney-shaped desk, a small round table, two tub chairs and a long sofa; a separate bedroom with queen-sized bed, elegant wood dresser with round brass-framed mirror; floor-to-ceiling white window shades operated electronically, gauzy white undercurtains and a tied-back sheer green curtain at the windows; large whirlpool bathtub, stall shower and double lavatories in a wide counter. Butler service, minibar, terry-cloth robes and reclining deck chairs on the veranda. Romantic? Yes!

Small Splurges: . . . . **A**

Average Price PPPD: $603 in Europe including airfare from New York.

Mini-suites, on the *Romantica* only, measure 340 square feet and contain a couch, two chairs, desk and chair, floor-to-ceiling windows, queen-sized bed, single trundle bed, bath with Jacuzzi tub, stall shower and double lavatories. Butler service, minibar and terrycloth robes.

Suitable Standards: . . . . **B+**

Average Price PPPD: $503 in Europe including airfare from New York.

More spacious than on many ships, the standard outside cabins measure 200 square feet and contain two lower beds, most of which convert to queen-sized; a few designated cabins have fixed queen-sized beds only. White marble counters and built-in hair dryers are in all bathrooms, hanging and storage space is generous and the room has a dresser and a sitting area with two chairs and a table. Several inside cabins (cheaper than the price above) are designated wheelchair-accessible with extra-wide doors, bathrooms with pulldown shower seats and generous turning space.

The lowest-priced inside cabins on the CostaRomantica can sleep up to four in style and comfort.

Bottom Bunks: . . . . **C**

Average Price PPPD: $374 in Europe including airfare from New York.
The cheapest cabins aboard are insides with a lower bed and upper berth, with two chairs, small table, dresser, TV set and bath with space-age shower. There are only six on each ship and they are sometimes assigned to staff. The next category up has two lower beds and is only marginally higher in price.

The Routes

The *CostaClassica* sails from May through October with a series of seven-day cruises from Venice calling at five Greek islands.

The *CostaRomantica* in winter makes alternate Eastern and Western Caribbean cruises out of Fort Lauderdale, calling at San Juan, St. Thomas, St. John, Serena Cay/Casa de Campo and Nassau on the eastern itinerary; and on the western itinerary calls at Key West, Playa del Carmen/Cozumel, Ocho Rios and Grand Cayman. The ship then sails across the Atlantic to spend the summer in Europe doing seven-day cruises from Genoa calling at Naples, Palermo, Tunis, Palma de Mallorca, Barcelona and Marseilles.

The Scoop

The "Italian by Design" theme emphasizes the architecture and decor of the ships and stresses Costa's Italian heritage, but most of the Italian waiters are gone, replaced over the years by other Europeans, many from the newly independent eastern countries and some of whom are still awkward with English.

Furnishings aboard are beautiful, with one-of-a kind high-style Italian chairs set about here and there like pieces of art.

In the dining room, despite the dangerous marble floors, meals are served on Limoges china and double-skirted Pratesi linen tablecloths while strolling musicians play. The food is most often very good.

Many standard cabins on the *Classica* have large wooden room dividers that steal floor space without adding any useful storage area; a better bet for couples are the cabins with fixed queen-sized beds and no room divider, the same size as the others but they seem much bigger.

Insider Tips

Five Easy Places

1. With a pool, an Italian sidewalk cafe, beach cabanas with striped blue-and-white curtains, a striking blue marble "Trevi" fountain and a thrust overhead runway from the jogging deck above overlooking all the action, it's La Dolce Vita time.

2. The heart of each ship is the piazza—on the *Classica* the Piazza Navona, on the *Romantica* the Piazza Italia—where everyone seems to gather, with an all-day- and-evening bar and lounge and music for dancing before and after dinner.

3. The dining rooms aboard change its looks on special evenings when the staff unfurls background scenery to turn it into an Italian garden or medieval city, ancient Pompeiian villas or Renaissance town; the backgrounds are painted by a scenic designer for the La Scala Opera House in Milan.

4. The big open-air cafe aft on each ship is covered with a sweeping white canvas awning and furnished with apple green wicker chairs and marble-topped tables, just like the Via Veneto.

5. The glass-walled discos high atop the ship and forward, like see-through flying saucers, double as observation lounges in the daytime.

CostaClassica   ★★★★★

Registry	Liberia
Officers	Italian
Crew	International
Complement	650
GRT	54,000
Length (ft.)	723.5
Beam (ft.)	101
Draft (ft.)	25
Passengers-Cabins Full	1766
Passengers-2/Cabin	1300
Passenger Space Ratio	41.53
Stability Rating	Good
Seatings	2
Cuisine	Italian
Dress Code	Traditional
Room Service	Yes
Tip	$8.50 PPPD, 15% automatically added to bar checks

Ship Amenities

Outdoor Pool	1
Indoor Pool	0
Jacuzzi	2
Fitness Center	Yes
Spa	Yes
Beauty Shop	Yes
Showroom	Yes
Bars/Lounges	8
Casino	Yes
Shops	Yes
Library	Yes
Child Program	Yes
Self-Service Laundry	No
Elevators	8

Cabin Statistics

Suites	10
Outside Doubles	438
Inside Doubles	216
Wheelchair Cabins	6
Singles	0
Single Surcharge	150%
Verandas	10
110 Volt	Yes

COSTA CRUISES

CostaRomantica ★★★★★

Registry	Liberia
Officers	Italian
Crew	International
Complement	650
GRT	54,000
Length (ft.)	723.5
Beam (ft.)	101
Draft (ft.)	25
Passengers-Cabins Full	1782
Passengers-2/Cabin	1356
Passenger Space Ratio	39.82
Stability Rating	Good
Seatings	2
Cuisine	Italian
Dress Code	Traditional
Room Service	Yes
Tip	$8.50 PPPD, 15% automatically added to bar checks

Ship Amenities

Outdoor Pool	1
Indoor Pool	0
Jacuzzi	4
Fitness Center	Yes
Spa	Yes
Beauty Shop	Yes
Showroom	Yes
Bars/Lounges	8
Casino	Yes
Shops	Yes
Library	Yes
Child Program	Yes
Self-Service Laundry	No
Elevators	8

Cabin Statistics

Suites	16
Outside Doubles	462
Inside Doubles	216
Wheelchair Cabins	6
Singles	0
Single Surcharge	150%
Verandas	10
110 Volt	Yes

COSTA CRUISES

★ ★
COSTARIVIERA

We were aboard this ship in January 1986, when then-Costa president Howard Fine introduced toga night by donning a handsome, custom-made red Roman centurion costume and a gold helmet with stiff red brush and marched through the dining room giving an imperial wave. "Cruising Italian Style" was the theme, and the then-new CostaRiviera, a massive makeover of the Marconi, was being introduced in the Caribbean. Howard's presidency lasted another year or two, "Cruising Italian Style" was axed in favor of "EuroLuxe" in 1992 and the CostaRiviera turned briefly into the kiddie cruise ship American Adventure in 1993-94. But everything that goes around comes around, and they're all back—"Cruising Italian Style," CostaRiviera, toga night—all except Howard.

Until the *CostaMarina* entered the scene in 1990, the *CostaRiviera* was the closest thing to a "new" (read made-over) ship the company had, but when it joined then-Costa president Bruce Nierenberg (co-founder of Premier Cruises) in a project to create American Family Cruises, this was the ship AFC got. With both *CostaMarina* and *CostaClassica* in place, the *CostaRiviera* didn't look so shiny any more. But with the demise of AFC in late 1994, the *CostaRiviera* sailed back to Genoa, was quickly refitted into a more-adult vessel and put out into the European cruise market. Fuzzy Wuzzy's Den and the Rock-O-Saurus Club turned into the dignified Vienna Ballroom, and Sea Haunt, formerly for ages 8 to 12, became a computer center.

The Brochure Says

"The *CostaRiviera* is embarking on a limited number of sailings to some of the most unforgettable places on earth. Casablanca. Barcelona. Funchal. Lanzarote. Exotic destinations to faraway places on a ship that's as comfortable as your own backyard."

Translation

While we never had the luxury of a steamship in our backyard, we can agree that the *CostaRiviera* is comfortable and low-key, unpretentious and good for families. And this winter's Canary Islands and North Africa cruises out of Genoa look like fun.

Cabins & Costs

Fantasy Suites: . . . . **N/A**

There are no accommodations on board that fit this description.

Small Splurges: . . . . **C-**

Average Price Per Person, Double Occupancy, Per Day: $468 in the Canary Islands including airfare from New York.

The top accommodations are in category Nine, an upper deck of cabins that was added on Amalfi Deck when the ship was extensively renovated in 1985, but take care making a choice—some of these are much larger than others, and many have views partly or totally obstructed by hanging lifeboats. All have twin beds or a queen-sized bed; specify which you want when booking. Some of the larger ones may have as many as three additional bunks for children from the American Family Cruises days. Baths have showers only, and closet space is usually adequate.

Suitable Standards: . . . . **C-**

Average Price PPPD: $418 in the Canary Islands including airfare from New York.

Capri Deck category Seven cabins also have two lower beds or a queen-sized bed, and most offer fold-down third and fourth berths as well.

Bottom Bunks: . . . . **D**

Average Price PPPD: $324 in the Canary Islands including airfare from New York.

The lowest-priced category of inside cabins provides upper and lower berths and baths with shower; they're pretty basic.

The Routes

The *CostaRiviera* offers 10-night sailings from Genoa to Egypt and Israel between April and October, calling at Naples, Catania, Alexandria, Port Said, Ashdod, Limassol, Rhodes, Kithera and Sorrento. This itinerary alternates with 10-night Canary Islands cruises, also from Genoa, calling at Barcelona, Casablanca, Tenerife, Funchal and Malaga. The ship also makes five Black Sea cruises from Genoa on 11-night itineraries, Istanbul, Yalta, Odessa, Varna, Mykonos, Yithion and Sorrento. In winter the ship cruises the Canary Islands.

The Scoop

This ship had some hard use during its days as the *American Adventure*, with as many as 500 or more kids aboard at a time. The density is intense, with 972 lower-bed spaces and 833 additional upper berths. But this plethora of cabins with two or even three additional berths can be a boon for the budget-minded. Among the specialty areas on board are a teen center, a two-level cinema, a small pizzeria, a fairly large beauty shop, a fitness center and a computer center. The addition of new soft furnishings throughout and TVs in all the cabins adds to the comfort factor.

Insider Tips

Five Focal Points

1. The Bella Napoli Pizzeria, which in our fond memory serves up the best made-to-order pizza at sea.

2. The Grand Prix Bar with its cushiony couches and chairs makes a grand place to meet friends for a drink before dinner; a long drinks-and-espresso bar along one side gives it the congeniality of an Italian town square.

3. In the Galleria Via Veneto you'll find the shopping, all the treasures from Milan, Florence and Venice as well as worldwide duty-free buys.

4. Portofino Restaurant provides a few tables for two along the sides of the room near the windows, but most are bigger round tables for six or eight; "Mangia, mangia!" ("Eat, eat!")

5. The La Scala Showroom is structured with a lot of sofa-like theater row seats, comfortable and with fair sightlines to the stage, as well as a covey of tables and chairs down front on the sides and center.

Five Good Reasons to Book This Ship

1. The aforementioned Canary Islands, Egypt and Black Sea itineraries.

2. To set out across the desert from Alexandria to see Cairo and the great pyramids at Giza.

3. If you want to shoehorn a family of five in one cabin, *CostaRiviera* has the berths.

4. The Bella Napoli Pizzeria.

5. To follow the Road to Morocco.

CostaRiviera ★★

Registry	Liberia
Officers	Italian
Crew	International
Complement	535
GRT	31,500
Length (ft.)	700.9
Beam (ft.)	94.1
Draft (ft.)	28.3
Passengers-Cabins Full	1805
Passengers-2/Cabin	972
Passenger Space Ratio	32.4
Stability Rating	Good
Seatings	2
Cuisine	Italian
Dress Code	Traditional
Room Service	Yes
Tip	$8.50 PPPD, 15% automatically added to bar checks

Ship Amenities

Outdoor Pool	1
Indoor Pool	0
Jacuzzi	3
Fitness Center	Yes
Spa	Yes
Beauty Shop	Yes
Showroom	Yes
Bars/Lounges	5
Casino	Yes
Shops	Yes
Library	Yes
Child Program	No
Self-Service Laundry	No
Elevators	6

Cabin Statistics

Suites	0
Outside Doubles	299
Inside Doubles	178
Wheelchair Cabins	0
Singles	0
Single Surcharge	150%
Verandas	0
110 Volt	Yes

COSTA CRUISES

★ ★ ★ ★ ★
CostaVictoria

Our first sailing aboard this gorgeous new ship was in the company of 500 Brazilians who literally danced all night—or at least until long after we turned in. While it meant Portuguese was added to the already four-language ship announcements, it also lent a lively energy and some very brief bathing suits to shipboard life.

The 1950-passenger *Victoria* introduces a new generation of ships for Costa, repeating some of the same bare-bones design features from the early *CostaClassica* and *CostaRomantica*, including the uncarpeted marble stairways and comfortable if austere cabin designs. There are, mysteriously, no private balconies even in the top-category suites, a strange omission these days when they're so wildly popular, but there are panoramic mini-suites with solid floor-to-ceiling glass walls.

The most splendid space on the vessel is the breathtaking Concorde Plaza, designed by noted Swedish designer Robert Tilborg. The forward, glass-walled lounge fills four full deck areas in a cool, contemporary fashion, with a generous, even prodigal, use of space. A waterfall cascades against the back wall behind the bandstand, an all-glass elevator offers a dramatic alternative to the curving stairways that connect the upper areas, and a sleek bar is set against a glass window wall with a captain's-eye view of the sea ahead.

But all the lounges are beautiful, and the top decks are appealing for swimmers, sunbathers and readers alike. A splendid spa with indoor pool also deserves high marks.

The debut of the *CostaVictoria* was slightly delayed when the shipyard, Germany's Vulkan Group's Shichau Seebeckwerft, underwent financial problems that culminated in a bankruptcy filing. This also eliminated the anticipated sister ship *CostaOlympia*, which remained an unfinished hull until acquired by Norwegian Cruise Line in mid-1997.

COSTA CRUISES

An expansive pool deck appeals to sunbathers.

Between The Lines

The Brochure Says

"This boldly sophisticated cruise ship is setting new standards of excellence with its avant-garde design, opulent meeting and entertainment areas and exquisitely appointed accommodations."

Translation

We agree. On the interior, this is one of the handsomest cruise ships to debut in the last decade. Carnival certainly got a good buy when the fleet includes a ship like this.

The Capriccio Bar is decorated in elegant shades of celery, sienna and gold.

COSTA CRUISES

Cabins & Costs

Fantasy Suites: . . . .**A**

Average Price Per Person, Double Occupancy, Per Day: $674 in Europe including airfare from New York.

Top accommodations on board are five suites, each configured slightly differently, all with sitting and dining areas, whirlpool bath, separate shower, mini-refrigerator and pulldown or Murphy beds for additional family members.

The mini-suites aboard CostaVictoria, *with small sitting area with art deco dresser and oval mirror, are priced at $617 a day per person, double occupancy.*

Small Splurges: . . . .**A**

Average Price PPPD: $617 in Europe including airfare from New York.

The 14 mini-suites are lovely, with queen-sized beds covered in a green-and-beige striped bedspread with a big floral tapestry wall in lieu of a headboard. A large sitting area includes a small curved sofa and two chairs with matching tapestry. A built-in wooden wall cabinet houses a large-screen TV set, a minibar and refrigerator. A glass art deco dressing table with a large oval mirror that swivels and four curved drawers below, along with a huge walk-in closet and dressing room and a marble bathroom with whirlpool tub make this a grand getaway.

Suitable Standards: . . . . **B+**

Average Price PPPD: $517 in Europe including airfare from New York.

Standard outside cabins, depending on the deck, have either an outsized porthole or a large window, and twin beds, most of which can be made into queen-sized beds. There is plenty of hanging and drawer space for garments, even in the smallest cabins.

A standard outside cabin with large porthole costs more than $500 a day per person, double occupancy, in Europe.

Bottom Bunks:. . . . . B

Average Price PPPD: $384 in Europe including airfare from New York.
The inside cabins are very similar to the outsides except smaller, and bathrooms have shower only. Six larger insides are designated for handicapped with two bathrooms, the regular modular design and a second accessible for wheelchairs. The price on these insides is somewhat higher than that listed above.

The Routes

The *CostaVictoria* cruises the Greek Islands and Turkey on seven-day roundtrip itineraries out of Venice in Summer, calling at Katakolon, Kusadasi, Volos and Piraeus (for Athens). In winter the ship sails alternate eastern and western Caribbean itineraries from Ft. Lauderdale, calling at San Juan, St. Thomas, St. John, Casa de Campo and Nassau on the eastern program, and visiting Key West, Playa del Carmen, Cozumel, Ocho Rios and Grand Cayman on the western itinerary.

The Scoop

Costa continues to produce some of the sleekest and most sophisticated ships at sea, most appealing, perhaps, to younger Americans or first-time cruisers who don't have fixed ideas about what a ship should look like. The experience aboard, especially in Europe, is a multilingual, multinational one, so if you tense up when you can't understand what someone at the next table is saying, you should book a Princess cruise instead.

COSTA CRUISES

Five Favorite Places

1. The Capriccio Bar with terrazzo walls covered in Chagall-like murals in celery green, sienna and gold, colors that are repeated harmoniously throughout the ship in various textures and patterns.

2. A pretty little chapel, rare on ships these days when religious services are relegated to the cinema or meeting rooms, with wood-toned walls and comfortable blue seats.

3. Very spacious meeting rooms with handsome furniture, blue ultrasuede chairs, big glass or wood tables, screens and moving walls.

4. The Concorde Plaza, with a carpet in Mondrian patterns in sand, brick and a couple of beiges with black, sand-colored leather club chairs, a grand piano and accent chairs in brick red ultrasuede.

5. The Orpheus Lounge and Grand Bar is the *piazza* (meeting place) on this ship, with ecru floral upholstery, circular banquettes and small chrome cocktail tables. Javanese batik prints offer contrasting upholstery on other chairs.

Five Reasons to Book This Ship

1. The friendly Italian maitre d'hotels and dining room captains.

2. The very good pasta, breadsticks and *bruschetta*.

3. The large number of reasonably priced wines, including half-liter carafes of house red and white for only $5 each.

4. The Portobello Market, a section of the lounge where the shops set out special bargains on days at sea.

5. The show "Cinemagique" with its silent-movie, pie-in-the-face opening.

A pair of bright and airy dining rooms have a sophisticated evening look with strolling musicians.

Five Things You Won't Find Aboard

1. A real library; instead you get a printout of the books available in English (237 of them) from the front desk.

2. Brief announcements in English only; instead you're treated all day long to lengthy speeches in four or five languages, one after the other.

3. Topless sunbathing; there is a rule against it, despite this being a European cruise line.

4. Toga nights in Europe, because, as cruise director Nick Wier says, "Roman night when you have a ship full of Romans doesn't make any difference."

5. A private balcony.

CostaVictoria   ★★★★★

Registry	**Liberia**
Officers	**Italian**
Crew	**International**
Complement	**800**
GRT	**76,000**
Length (ft.)	**824**
Beam (ft.)	**105.5**
Draft (ft.)	**13**
Passengers-Cabins Full	**2250**
Passengers-2/Cabin	**1950**
Passenger Space Ratio	**38.9**
Stability Rating	**Good**
Seatings	**2**
Cuisine	**Italian**
Dress Code	**Traditional**
Room Service	**Yes**
Tip	**$8.50 PPPD, 15% automatically added to bar checks**

Ship Amenities

Outdoor Pool	**3**
Indoor Pool	**1**
Jacuzzi	**4**
Fitness Center	**Yes**
Spa	**Yes**
Beauty Shop	**Yes**
Showroom	**Yes**
Bars/Lounges	**9**
Casino	**Yes**
Shops	**Yes**
Library	**Yes**
Child Program	**Yes**
Self-Service Laundry	**No**
Elevators	**12**

Cabin Statistics

Suites	**20**
Outside Doubles	**555**
Inside Doubles	**389**
Wheelchair Cabins	**6**
Singles	**0**
Single Surcharge	**150%**
Verandas	**0**
110 Volt	**Yes**

COSTA CRUISES

CRYSTAL
C R U I S E S

2121 Avenue of the Stars, Los Angeles, CA 90067
☎ *(310) 785-9300, (800) 446-6620*

An expansive amidships pool and raised whirlpool is surrounded by plenty of sunbathing area.

History . . . .

Los Angeles-based Crystal Cruises did the cruise line equivalent of coming from 0 to 60 in six seconds. Founded in 1988 by century-old NYK (Nippon Yusen Kaisha), one of the largest transportation companies in the world, the Japanese-financed company set up a long and elaborate program of introducing to the United States a new ship that was still two years away from completion.

The line's first ship, the 960-passenger *Crystal Harmony*, was built in the Mitsubishi shipyard in Nagasaki, Japan, and made its debut in Los Angeles in July 1990, to great critical acclaim. A sister ship, the *Crystal Symphony*, built in Finland's Kvaerner-Masa Yard, made its debut in New York in May 1995.

—First line to offer two alternative dinner restaurants to all passengers at no surcharge (*Crystal Harmony*, 1990).

DID YOU KNOW?

Interestingly, this very upscale line deliberately chose as godmothers for its ships actresses that are better-known for popular television series than for feature films or theater, Mary Tyler Moore for the Crystal Harmony *and Angela Lansbury for the* Crystal Symphony.

Concept

From its inception, Crystal set out to define "luxury" by trying to provide the best of everything—food, entertainment, service and shipboard accommodation—and to offer "warm and personal service in an elegant setting." They say, "The line provides sophisticated travelers and experienced cruisers with an intimate and luxurious cruise experience."

Signatures

The turquoise seahorses on the Crystal stacks have become a recognized logo in most of the great ports of the world, and that particular shade is carried through on logo caps and T-shirts and other Crystal souvenir merchandise.

In the lobby of each ship is a "crystal" piano made of lucite, along with bronze-colored statuary, a waltzing couple on the *Harmony* and a pair of ballet dancers on the *Symphony,* and waterfalls with crystal cut-glass cylinders and Tivoli lights.

Gimmicks

Using costly Louis Roederer Cristal Champagne for special occasions like christenings.

Extension telephones in the bathrooms.

Who's the Competition

In its brief five years of cruising, Crystal has garnered an enviable reputation for service and overall quality, so that it virtually stands alone at the head of its class. It would have rivalled the former Royal Viking Line, and we do note some passenger and crew crossover from Cunard's *Royal Viking Sun.* It also attracts veterans of Princess and Holland America, as well as Seabourn and Sea Goddess.

Who's Aboard

Most of the passengers are successful couples between 40 and 70, with a sprinkling of older singles who enjoy the gentleman host program aboard. Very few of the passengers are Japanese, but those who do sail represent the upper strata of independent travelers rather than group tourism. Some 90 percent of the line's passengers are 45 and up with a median age of 60, and 80 percent are married. Of the line's total passengers, nearly half have traveled with Crystal before. A recent passenger list shows guests from the United States (primarily California), Canada, Saudi Arabia, Japan, Australia, Hong Kong, Mexico, Switzerland, Brazil, Germany and Belgium.

Who Should Go . . . .

Younger passengers and upscale first-time cruisers who will enjoy the excellent entertainment, the high quality of food and service and the only pair of Caesars Palace casinos at sea.

Who Should Not Go . . . .

Anyone who doesn't like to dress up and socialize.

The Lifestyle . . . .

These ships offer one of the finest versions of classic, traditional, luxury ship cruises available, with a fairly formal dress code and assigned dining at two seatings but with two alternative restaurants available most evenings as well by advance reservation. Lavish surroundings, pampering service, excellent housekeeping and superlative dining keep the same passengers coming back again and again. Daytime activities are frequent and fascinating, shore excursions very well handled and evening entertainment top-notch.

Wardrobe . . . .

Dressy, dressy, dressy. We're frequently carry-on people with only a little luggage, but we always check a large bag when we're flying to board a Crystal ship. Daytimes and shore excursions can be casual, but the passengers are almost always attired in smart casual, or casual elegance (what the Crystal handbook calls "country club attire.") Evenings, women wear cocktail dresses or dressy pantsuits for informal (what some lines now are calling "semi-formal") nights, while men don jacket and tie; on formal nights, women wear evening gowns (we saw as many long gowns as short ones on the inaugural of the *Symphony*) and men don tuxedos or dark business suits.

Bill of Fare . . . . A

Creative contemporary cuisine, much of it prepared to order, comes out of the Crystal galleys, which are under the direction of executive chef Toni Neumeister, former executive chef for Royal Viking Line. A dinner menu will carry suggestions for a full menu recommended by the chef, a lighter fare menu giving the calorie, fat and sodium counts, a vegetarian menu and cellar master wine suggestions by the glass or by the bottle. Traditionally, you can choose from three or four appetizers (perhaps tempura fried softshell crab with red pepper aioli), two or three soups (maybe a chilled tomato soup with goat cheese quenelles), three salads, a nightly pasta special (such as fusilli with zucchini, garlic, olive oil and onions) and four main dishes (say, seared fresh ahi tuna steak, crisp baby hen, grilled tournedos of beef tenderloin Rossini or roasted Scandinavian venison loin) plus a vegetarian option such as a baby eggplant stuffed with ratatouille. The dessert roster runs to five desserts (maybe a tarte Tatin with vanilla ice cream or a souffle Grand Marnier) plus a cheese trolley and various frozen desserts. A little silver tray of freshly made petits fours always arrives with the coffee service.

But that's only the dining room. There are also two alternative restaurants with special evening menus, one Italian and one Asian (Chinese on the *Symphony* and Japanese on the *Harmony*) and a wonderful assortment of casual buffet lunch choices from an elegant spread of cold seafoods and meats and hot dishes in the Lido Cafe to our favorite gardenburger, pizza, grilled hot dogs or hamburgers on deck. There's also an ice cream bar where the treats are free, of course.

Showtime. . . . . A

The entertainment is dazzling, with highly professional productions that are constantly updated, along with prestigious lecturers, concerts, cabarets and game shows. Lecturers include names such as journalist and author Pierre Salinger, ship historian Bill Miller, novelist Judith Krantz and former Los Angeles mayor Tom Bradley. Production shows are gorgeously costumed (some of the hand-beaded wardrobe pieces cost as much as $10,000 each) and beautifully choreographed and performed. The line's entertainment director, Peter Johnson, scored quite a coup with the first-ever authorized seagoing production of Rodgers and Hammerstein music called "Some Enchanted Evening." Social hostess Teri Ralston also performs some of the numbers from her many Broadway shows.

Discounts . . . .

Crystal's new Milestone Levels program rewards frequent cruisers with free cruises, air upgrades, shipboard credits and cabin upgrades, based on the number of cruises taken. And unlike airline frequent flyer miles, the total number of cruises continues to mount up after awards are claimed, never going back to zero.

Members of the Crystal Society (previous cruisers with the line) get a 5 percent discount with no advance booking deadline. If you book a future cruise while you're aboard one of the ships, you get a discount of $250 to $500 per person, and your travel agent gets her full commission as well. Pay in full six months ahead of sailing time and you get an additional 5 percent discount.

The Bottom Line

There are only two possible criticisms demanding luxury cruisers could make—the two seating dining and the shortage of really generous closet space on very long sailings such as the full world cruise. To the first, we'd point out that you could book the alternative restaurants for 7:30 or order dinner in your cabin for those nights when you didn't want to dine at your assigned table. To the second, we'd suggest if you're taking a really long cruise and you like to dress up, book as high a cabin category as you can, say one of the penthouses or penthouse suites.

The Crystal ships are for those who want—and are willing to pay for—the very best in a traditional big-ship sailing experience.

★ ★ ★ ★ ★ ★

CRYSTAL HARMONY
CRYSTAL SYMPHONY

The highly successful Crystal ships have had only a few gaffes in their career—and our favorite is the Viennese Mozart Tea, which used to be presented as one of the highlights of the cruise. On the inaugural of the Crystal Harmony in 1990, it was dazzling, with a string trio and all the waiters decked out in white wigs, gold lame frock coats and vests, long white stockings and slippers—visualize Tim Curry as Mozart in the film Amadeus and you get the picture. On our next outing aboard the Harmony in 1993, the procedure had gotten routine, and the Viennese Mozart tea on that sailing had only three of the waiters (the ones who looked as if they'd drawn the losing straws) garbed in white wigs and partial costumes, but wearing loafers and white tennis socks. The Manila Strings trio were only two, wearing their ordinary daytime garb of white pants and shirts. (The third musician was missing, Harry pointed out, because Mozart didn't write for guitar.) On the inaugural of the Crystal Symphony, there were no white wigs, gold lame vests and knee breeches in sight, just the table of elegant cakes and pastries. The wigs had caused near-revolution in the ranks of waiters, as had the costumes, so the whole fancy-dress thing was written off.

This elegant pair of ships with their sleek, graceful lines offers a lot of sensational cabins with private verandas, a plethora of posh public rooms and an easy-to-get-around layout. The public areas are concentrated on the top two decks and two lower decks with most of the cabins in between. An amidships pool deck is sheltered enough with its sliding glass roof and glass side windows that it provides a cozy sun-trap even on a cool Alaska day. By limiting the major "avenues" to one rather than both sides of a deck, the traffic flows neatly without sacrificing space that could be devoted to a shop or bar. Craftsmanship is meticulous aboard both these ships. Comfortable cruising speed is 16 to 17 knots, but the *Crystal Symphony* on its inaugural was averaging 20 between New York and Bermuda.

The Brochure Says

"From the moment you step aboard the gleaming white jewels known as *Crystal Harmony* and *Crystal Symphony*, you will feel you have arrived at a very special place and have been warmly embraced as part of the Crystal family."

Translation

They're serious about this, folks. There's something called The Crystal Attitude, a service philosophy that is a part of the intensive training each employee goes through, with motivational tapes and videos and classes for upper echelon employees in notable hotel schools like L'Ecole Hotelier in Switzerland and Cornell Hotel School. Crystal has the highest crew return factor of any cruise line, with more than 70 percent re-enlisting.

Fantasy suites like the Crystal Penthouse with veranda aboard the **Crystal Symphony** *are sought after by big spenders.*

Fantasy Suites: . . . . **A+**

Average Price Per Person, Double Occupancy, Per Day: $1306–$1843 with some airfare included.

The most lavish quarters aboard are the Crystal penthouse suites, each measuring 948–982 square feet, with large sitting room, dining area, private veranda, wet bar, big Jacuzzi tub with ocean view, separate master bedroom with king-sized bed, big walk-in closets and a guest bath. There's butler service, of course.

Small Splurges: . . . . **A+**

Average Price PPPD: $790 to $1260 with some airfare included.

Eighteen penthouse suites with verandas that measure a total of 491 square feet and 44 penthouses with verandas that measure 367 square feet are spacious and prettily furnished. Butler service is offered in all the penthouses, along with complimentary bar, cocktail hour canapes, and in-room dining with dishes that can be ordered from the dining room or either alternative restaurant.

Suitable Standards: . . . . A+

Average Price PPPD: $541–$689 with some airfare included.
The deluxe stateroom with private veranda is the most numerous of the cabin categories on board, with 214 cabins (on the *Symphony*) each measuring 246 square feet, with a private veranda, king-sized bed, loveseat sofa, chair, built-in desk/dresser with plenty of storage space, a safe, mini-refrigerator, TV/VCR, plus a large closet with built-in shoe rack and tie rack, and a marble bathroom with tub/shower combination, double sinks and two hair dryers. Seven staterooms for the disabled are available on the *Symphony*, four on the *Harmony*.

Bottom Bunks: . . . . A

Average Price PPPD: $367 for the Harmony *insides with some airfare included.*
Inside cabins on the *Crystal Harmony* and outside cabins without verandas on the *Crystal Symphony* are the lowest-priced digs aboard. The latter number 202, and some have restricted views due to hanging lifeboats. The insides on the *Harmony* measure 183 square feet and have two lower beds, remote control TV/VCR, full bath with tub and shower, mini-refrigerator, safe, small sofa and chairs with desk/dresser and coffee table. You're not slumming here.

The Routes

The *Crystal Symphony* begins 1998 with a 101-day Around-the-World cruise departing Los Angeles Jan. 14 and ending in London April 25. Overnight stays include Honolulu, Hong Kong, Ho Chi Minh City, Bangkok and Singapore. The ship then offers a series of summer sailings in Western Europe and the Baltic through July, along with early spring and late summer itineraries in the Mediterranean and Black Sea. In November and December *Crystal Symphony* cruises the Caribbean and Mexican Riviera with Panama Canal transits.

The *Crystal Harmony* spends January through May with several South American sailings, then some Caribbean/Panama Canal/Mexican Riviera programs before repositioning for a summer season in Alaska's Gulf, sailing between Vancouver and Anchorage. In the autumn, *Crystal Harmony* sails the Pacific Rim and Orient, as well as Australia and New Zealand. *Crystal Harmony* makes its first-ever sailing along the west coast of South America, departing Nov. 30, 1997, for 14 days between Valparaiso, Chile, to Acapulco. The sailing will offer an optional overland tour to Machu Picchu.

The Scoop

While the ship's interior is handsome and dignified, the real sense of the luxury comes not from eye-grabbing architecture but rather fine attention to detail—items such as the Wedgwood teacups in the Palm Court at teatime, Riedel hand-blown wine glasses in the Prego Restaurant, Villeroy & Boch china and Frette linens in the dining room, goose down pillows in each cabin, the designs on the Bistro plates and cups. Passengers are treated like adults rather than children at summer camp. Every crew member is warm friendly and efficient, and the service aboard is superlative. Big-ship cruising doesn't get any better than this.

Five Spectacular Spots

1. The Palm Court, a sunny, airy winter garden with wicker chairs and ceiling fans, potted palms and a harpist playing for tea.

2. The Avenue Saloon, the "in" bar on board (you can always tell the "in" bar because that's where the officers and the entertainers hang out) with its wood floors and Oriental rugs, green leather bar rails and movable stools.

3. Caesars Palace At Sea, a truly classy shipboard casino operation that actually (in the Vegas style) gives free drinks to players.

4. The spectacular Crystal Spa and Salon on the top deck with lots of glass windows, aerobics area, gym with lots of machines, sauna, steam and massage.

5. The elegant Prego Restaurant aboard the *Symphony*, the Italian alternative dining option, with its red-and-white striped pillars and high-backed blue armchairs tied with red tassels and cord, the very essence of a classy Venetian restaurant.

The Palm Court is a favorite lounge for relaxing on the **Crystal Harmony.**

Five Good Reasons to Book These Ships

1. To tell all your friends about your cruise.

2. To show off your wardrobe and jewelry.

3. To be pampered by a happy staff who have the best crew accommodations at sea plus their own gym and Jacuzzi.

4. Cabin telephones with voice mail, and bathroom extension phones.

5. To have a private veranda, which will change your whole picture of luxury cruising.

Five Things You Won't Find On Board

1. Portholes; all the outside cabins have windows.

2. Anyone inappropriately dressed on formal night.

3. A bad attitude or discouraging word.

4. A lot of children, even though there's a youth and teen area provided.

5. A really unhappy passenger.

CRYSTAL HARMONY ★★★★★★

Registry	**Bahamas**
Officers	**Norwegian/Japanese**
Crew	**International**
Complement	**545**
GRT	**49,400**
Length (ft.)	**791**
Beam (ft.)	**104**
Draft (ft.)	**24.6**
Passengers-Cabins Full	**1010**
Passengers-2/Cabin	**960**
Passenger Space Ratio	**51.45**
Stability Rating	**Good to Excellent**
Seatings	**2**
Cuisine	**Contemporary**
Dress Code	**Traditional**
Room Service	**Yes**
Tip	**$10 PPPD, 15% automatically added to bar check**

Ship Amenities

Outdoor Pool	**2**
Indoor Pool	**1**
Jacuzzi	**2**
Fitness Center	**Yes**
Spa	**Yes**
Beauty Shop	**Yes**
Showroom	**Yes**
Bars/Lounges	**7**
Casino	**Yes**
Shops	**4**
Library	**Yes**
Child Program	**Yes**
Self-Service Laundry	**Yes**
Elevators	**8**

Cabin Statistics

Suites	**62**
Outside Doubles	**399**
Inside Doubles	**19**
Wheelchair Cabins	**4**
Singles	**0**
Single Surcharge	**115 - 200%**
Verandas	**260**
110 Volt	**Yes**

CRYSTAL CRUISES

CRYSTAL SYMPHONY ★★★★★

Registry	**Bahamas**
Officers	**Norwegian/Japanese**
Crew	**International**
Complement	**530**
GRT	**50,000**
Length (ft.)	**781**
Beam (ft.)	**100**
Draft (ft.)	**24.9**
Passengers-Cabins Full	**1010**
Passengers-2/Cabin	**960**
Passenger Space Ratio	**52.08**
Stability Rating	**Good to Excellent**
Seatings	**2**
Cuisine	**Contemporary**
Dress Code	**Traditional**
Room Service	**Yes**
Tip	**$10 PPPD, 15% automatically added to bar check**

Ship Amenities

Outdoor Pool	**2**
Indoor Pool	**1**
Jacuzzi	**2**
Fitness Center	**Yes**
Spa	**Yes**
Beauty Shop	**Yes**
Showroom	**Yes**
Bars/Lounges	**7**
Casino	**Yes**
Shops	**4**
Library	**Yes**
Child Program	**Yes**
Self-Service Laundry	**Yes**
Elevators	**8**

Cabin Statistics

Suites	**64**
Outside Doubles	**416**
Inside Doubles	**0**
Wheelchair Cabins	**7**
Singles	**0**
Single Surcharge	**115 - 200%**
Verandas	**278**
110 Volt	**Yes**

CUNARD

555 Fifth Avenue, New York, NY 10017-2453
☎ *(212) 880-7500, (800) 5-CUNARD*
www.cunardline.com

Cunard's posh Royal Viking Sun *with its swim-up bar on pool deck is one of the topmost luxury vessels at sea.*

History . . . .

"I want a plain but comfortable boat, not the least unnecessary expense for show," Samuel Cunard instructed the Scottish shipyard that built his 1154-ton wooden paddlewheel steamer *Britannia* in 1840. And when it set out on its maiden voyage from Liverpool to Halifax and Boston on July 4, with 63 passengers, 93 crew members and a cow to supply fresh milk on the voyage, the conservative businessman from Nova Scotia was more concerned about his cargo—he had a lucrative contract to carry Her Majesty's mails and dispatches across the Atlantic twice a month—than his passengers.

DID YOU KNOW?

One of the Britannia's early passengers was novelist Charles Dickens, who sailed the North Atlantic through severe gales in January 1842, describing his feelings tersely as, "Not ill, but going to be." His cabin contained "a very thin flat quilt, covering a very thin mattress, spread like a surgical plaster on a most inaccessible shelf," and the dining room was "not unlike a gigantic hearse with windows in the sides."

That same year, Cunard quadrupled his fleet, eventually cutting down crossings from the usual six weeks of that era to two weeks.

DID YOU KNOW?

"Going to sea is a hardship," wrote one early Cunard executive in response to a query as to why the ships did not provide napkins in the dining room. "The Cunard Company does not undertake to make anything else out of it, and if people want to wipe their mouths at a ship's table, they could use their pocket handkerchiefs."

In its 157-year history, Cunard has operated more than 190 ships, including the famous *Queen Mary* and *Queen Elizabeth*, who saluted each other in the mid-Atlantic as their paths crossed. They transported 4000 people a week between the U.S. and U.K.

In the late 19th and early 20th centuries, the Cunarders carried hundreds of thousands of immigrants from Europe to the U.S., and during World War II carried troops to and from Great Britain.

*Cunard's **Mauretania** is remembered today with a striking 16-foot model displayed aboard the **QE2** complete with lighted portholes.*

But the 1920s and 1930s were the heyday of ocean liners. Cunard's legendary *Mauretania* with its four red-and-black stacks and lavish wood-paneled, plaster-ceilinged public rooms, ruled the waves through the twenties. The *Queen Mary* was star from the thirties to the waning days of transatlantic crossings in the sixties, with guests such as the Duke and Duchess of Windsor, in perpetual, glittering exile with their 75 suitcases and 70 trunks; Noel Coward; Rex Harrison; Rita Hayworth; Richard Burton; and Elizabeth Taylor.

DID YOU KNOW?

After 31 years of service, the Queen Mary *was retired in 1967, exactly a decade since the number of transatlantic travelers crossing by air first outnumbered those crossing by sea. The* Queen Mary *is today a landmark moored at the city of Long Beach, California, serving as a hotel and tourist attraction.*

Samuel Cunard would probably not be surprised at the size and diversity of his company's present fleet—five seagoing ships ranging from the 1500-passenger *QE2* to the deluxe little 116-passenger *Sea Goddess* ships—but he would probably be astonished to find that people book passage by sea not by necessity but for the sheer pleasure of traveling slowly, emulating those shadowy companions of another day who enjoyed an infinite supply of the one travel luxury we lack—time.

DID YOU KNOW?

Cunard had been a wholly owned company of London-based Trafalgar House, PLC, since 1971. The company was acquired in 1996 by Kvaerner.

—First company to take passengers on regularly scheduled transatlantic departures (*Britannia*, 1840).

—Introduced the first passenger ship to be lit by electricity (*Servia*, c. 1881).

—Introduced the first twin-screw ocean liner (*Campania*, 1893).

—Introduced the first steam turbine engines in a passenger liner (*Carmania*, 1905),

—Introduced the first gymnasium and health center aboard a ship (*Franconia*, 1911).

—Introduced the first indoor swimming pool on a ship (*Aquitania*, 1914).

—First cruise line to introduce an around-the-world cruise (*Laconia*, 1922).

—Held the record from 1940 to 1996 for the largest passenger ship ever built (*Queen Elizabeth*, 1940).

—The only cruise company to sail regularly-scheduled transatlantic service year-round (*Queen Elizabeth 2*).

DID YOU KNOW?

"Getting there is half the fun," was an ad slogan Cunard came up with in 1956 to promote its transatlantic crossings against the new competition from jet aircraft.

Concept...

In the wide diversity of Cunard ships, the flagship *Queen Elizabeth 2* stands alone, providing an around-the-world cruise, regular transatlantic crossings and warm-water cruises.

The highly rated *Royal Viking Sun* and the prestigious *Vistafjord* offer very good quality food, service and accommodations at sea for the most demanding and sophisticated travelers.

Cunard's ultra-deluxe little *Sea Goddess* ships are among our very favorite vessels, because they give passengers the sense of sailing on their own private yachts.

Signatures...

The distinctive red-and-black funnel that has characterized Cunard ships since the *Britannia* in 1840 has not been affixed to the *Royal Viking Sun* and the pair of *Sea Goddess* ships. The *Sun* retains the red RVL sea eagle, and the *Sea Goddess* ships carry a golden goddess.

The dark hull of the *QE2* is a modern-day version of the standard Cunard North Atlantic black as opposed to the white hulls more typical of cruise ships.

The Cunard lion, rampant, wearing a crown and holding a globe in his paws, first appeared in 1880 when the company went public; according to ship historian John Maxtone-Graham, rival sailors disparagingly called it "the monkey wi' the nut."

Serving caviar and champagne in the surf is an eye-catching Sea Goddess tradition; here, passengers and crew wading at Jost van Dyke in the British Virgin Islands.

Gimmicks...

Serving caviar from the blue two-kilo tins is a trademark/gimmick aboard the *Sea Goddess* ships, where it adorns the serve-yourself appetizer table at cocktail time and is fetched ashore by waiters in black tie and swim trunks on beaches in the Caribbean.

The Cunard Incentives Collection offers Cunard logo key chains, T-shirts and tote bags to groups rewarding their employees. Companies can also charter the ship's Princess Grill for special programs.

Who's the Competition. . . . .

A unique vessel, the *Queen Elizabeth 2* has no real competition except herself, because of the intense love/hate relationship her passengers accord this most famous and most misunderstood vessel. They complain about signs of aging or inconveniences aboard the ship, then scream when things are changed. Every other year like clockwork, when the ship comes out of drydock in late autumn, something or other on board doesn't work. They complain to each other, rage to the media and threaten lawsuits—then book passage again the next time they're going to take a cruise.

Cunard's purchase of the *Royal Viking Sun* eliminated much of the direct competition facing *Vistafjord*; now the pair competes with the Crystal ships. *Sea Goddess*, almost always mentioned in the same breath with *Seabourn*, is also like Radisson Seven Seas' *Song of Flower* or the Silversea ships since the beverages service on board is complimentary on all of them.

Who's Aboard . . . .

Perhaps the broadest possible spectrum of passengers is aboard one of the short segments of the *QE2's* world cruise, everyone from the very rich penthouse passengers to the Miss Marples in the more modest digs, who are signed up for the full cruise, and the transients taking a segment, a mix of middle-aged, middle-income couples and upscale singles and families. The Panama Canal transit and the transpacific segment between Los Angeles and Honolulu always sell out.

Older couples and singles, most of them North Americans with an upper-range income, are typically aboard *Royal Viking Sun*, while the *Vistafjord* usually draws a more cosmopolitan and slightly younger crowd, a mix of North Americans, British and Germans.

Sea Goddess attracts almost exclusively couples who have money or want people to think they do and who may or may not be married.

Who Should Go . . . .

Everyone who loves ships and cruising should make a transatlantic crossing at least once on the *QE2* to experience the tremendous difference between crossing and cruising. Families with children will also find *QE2* a good ship because of its nursery overseen by two professional British nannies and a special high tea (which correctly used means a light supper, not English-style afternoon tea) for kids at 5:30.

Anyone who loves luxury and can afford it should book one of the *Sea Goddess* ships, preferably in the Caribbean or Mediterranean, to be pampered with caviar and champagne around the clock as if it's your own private yacht. And aging baby boomers who've done well in business should reward themselves by sampling the *Royal Viking Sun* or *Vistafjord* to see if that's how they want to vacation when they retire.

Who Should Not Go . . . .

Cunard has its own style, sophisticated and British accented, where dress codes and tradition are important. Older singles, especially women who want organized activities, would not enjoy the laisser-faire lifestyle aboard Sea Goddess ships, nor would the hyperactive mass-market Caribbean crowd understand the *Royal Viking Sun* or *Vistafjord*.

The Lifestyle . . . .

Because the lifestyle aboard Cunard vessels, unlike those of other cruise lines, varies depending not only on the ship but also the type of sailing—transatlantic, world cruise, warm-weather cruising—we'll describe it with each individual ship.

Wardrobe. . . . .

The Cunard ships call for a fairly dressy wardrobe. The exception, interestingly enough, is on a transatlantic crossing, when many businessmen, particularly Europeans, will wear a dark suit that doubles as business wear rather than a tuxedo. On the crossings, every night except first and last are formal.

Day wear aboard the ships is smart casual or "country club" garb. On informal nights, especially on the *Royal Viking Sun*, some of the men wear madras jackets with bright linen pants in what we think of as a preppy or southeastern resort look.

It is noted in the fine print that "women prefer evening or cocktail dresses, or other formal attire, and gentlemen wear black tie or dark suit. On informal evenings, regular cocktail dresses for women, and jacket and tie for men are the norm."

Bill of Fare. . . . . .A+ to B

The *QE 2* recently introduced the A La Carte Menu in the Queens Grill Restaurant, the top grill room for penthouse, suites and deluxe cabin passengers. Cunard's corporate executive chef Rudi Sodamin promises 24 appetizers and 20 entrees every night, much as a top-rated shoreside restaurant would do. Choices include Truffle Foie Gras, Creamy Lobster Bisque, Whole Dover Sole and Prime Filet Steak flamed in brandy, with Chocolate Souffle Chantilly for dessert.

The *Royal Viking Sun* and *Vistafjord* have good to excellent cuisine, with some dishes cooked to order and a pleasurable range of choices, including the option to order special meals. Wine lists are outstanding on both ships. *Sea Goddess* cuisine and service have always been superlative, even their deck buffet dishes.

Cuisine Report Card:

A+ *Sea Goddess, Royal Viking Sun*

A *Vistafjord*

Showtime. . . . . B+

Cunard entertainment, while hewing to a general pattern, varies according to the size of the ship's show lounge facilities. The classic stars—*Royal Viking Sun* and *Vistafjord*—follow a traditional format of musical production shows and variety acts by magicians, ventriloquists, puppeteers and comedians, as well as audience-participation game shows such as Liars Club and Team Trivia. There's usually a dance team (yes, Velez and Yolanda live!) who perform on variety nights and teach dance classes during the daytime to groups or in optional private lessons. On the *Sea Goddess* ships, entertainment consists primarily of the passengers socializing with each other or dining alone in their suites, so except for a musical group that plays nightly for dancing, or a late-night cabaret artist, there is usually not much happening.

The *QE2* presents a full range of entertainment, especially on the world cruise, with gala balls, famous lecturers and entertainers, notable orchestras and big bands, authors signing their books and karaoke nights in the pub.

Discounts

Cunard gives a 20 percent early booking discount to passengers who book and place a deposit on a cabin 120 days before sailing. Passengers who become members of the World Club for repeaters receive additional perks and privileges.

The Bottom Line

With the current policy of dropping some of its less-upscale vessels, and acquiring rather than building ships, Cunard has set itself apart from the other major cruise lines who are introducing new builds almost annually. With five ships, Cunard is outnumbered by many lines these days.

★★★★★
Queen Elizabeth 2

The storm seemed to spring full-blown from nowhere on the late May New York-to-Southampton crossing in 1987, buffeting the ship for 16 hours with hurricane-strength winds up to 50 miles an hour, registering Force 10 on the Beaufort scale and leaving in its wake smashed dishes and glassware, spilled vases and planters, granite lounge tables crumbled like cookies and overturned grand pianos looking like fallen elephants. A friend in a nearby cabin woke suddenly with icy water splashing across his chest and feared he had been thrown overboard, but it was only the pitcher of ice water his stewardess had thoughtfully placed on the table by his bed the night before.

The *QE2* has changed its dining rooms to single seatings despite retaining the assignments by cabin category—Grill Room class, meaning passengers booked in cabins that are assigned to dine in the Queens, Britannia and Princess Grills in categories Q1 through P2, and the Caronia and the Mauretania Dining Room class for the rest of the ship.

Built as a two-class turbine steamer in Brown's Clydebank yard in 1967 and 1968, the *QE2* set out on its maiden voyage to the Canary Islands Dec. 23, 1968, prior to the official delivery of the vessel to the line. A fault developed in the turbines along the way and the ship was returned to the builder. Since the passenger accommodations were still unfinished, Cunard refused to accept delivery of the ship on the planned date of Jan. 1, 1969, and the ship made its actual maiden voyage May 2, 1969, from Southampton to New York.

The classic ocean liner retooled its engines from steam turbine to diesel in 1987, and some of the crew say the plumbing has never worked right since. The most massive renovation since the engine retooling took place was in late 1994, when 850 bathrooms were remodeled and most of the public rooms and deck spaces changed and/or relocated—"cosmetically the biggest renovation ever done to the *QE2*," according to Commodore John Burton-Hall—and set up a howl from unhappy passengers who complained of unfurnished cabins, bad plumbing and "exploding toilets" which reverberated throughout the world media for a month.

Less drastic but even more noticeable is the 1996 refit that cut total passenger numbers by nearly 200. The intention is to create a single standard of luxury throughout the fleet, with single meal seatings in all dining room. The cabins eliminated were the smallest inside cabins on the lower decks, now relegated to crew cabins or storage areas.

Life aboard the *QE2* could be compared to living in a self-contained seagoing city with its own post office and city hall (the bureau), its own police force (on-board security, both uniformed and plainclothes), its own public library with a fulltime professional librarian, its own pub, five restaurants, a movie theater, a shopping mall, a travel agency (shore excursions and tour office), eight bars, a bookstore, a computer center, casino, photo shop, florist, daily newspapers, gymnasium, spa, beauty salon, barber shop, 40-car garage, kennel, hospital with operating room, a private club (Samuel Cunard Key Club), casino, laundromat, video rental shop, a sports center and bank. Even the staff demeanor is more serious and businesslike than on a cruise ship.

DID YOU KNOW?

Deja vu *all over again? "Hindsight suggests that Cunard was overly optimistic in setting out with a shipload of full-fare passengers, and a not-quite-finished refit...where some passengers complained of unfinished staterooms, erratic air conditioning and leaking water pipes, making newspaper headlines and TV and radio newscasts around the world..."*

from the authors' Cruise Views
column, Los Angeles Times,
July 12, 1987

NO-NOs

Who shouldn't go on the QE2*? Anyone who dislikes large ships—you take a lot of long hikes getting around on this ship; young couples and honeymooners, because there are not a lot of young couples aboard.*

Between The Lines

The Brochure Says

"Sumptuous single seating dining awaits in *QE2's* enhanced restaurants."

Translation

No more main and second seatings for the Miss Marples in their modest digs—everybody gets a single seating now that the ship has retired some of those tiny, over-the hill cabins on the lower decks.

Fantasy Suites: . . . . **A**

Average Price Per Person, Double Occupancy, Per Day: $1597 on a world cruise segment, including airfare.

Any of the 31 penthouse suites except #8184 (the only one without a private veranda) would do well, although some of them overlook lifeboats as well as the sea. Each has lounge chairs and table in the veranda, king-sized bed, sofa and two chairs, built-in desk/dresser, good storage space, mini-refrigerator, safe and bathroom with toilet, bidet, deep tub and double sinks. You'll dine in the elegant Queens Grill with its own private cocktail lounge on treats such as fresh grilled Dover sole, fresh lobster and fresh foie gras by request, and from the breakfast menu, shirred eggs with caviar and cream, along with a rolling cart of more than a dozen kinds of marmalade.

Small Splurges: . . . . **A**

Average Price PPPD: $957 on a world cruise segment, including airfare.

Ultra-deluxe outside cabins in category P1 are spacious and comfortable, nicely furnished in rich dark blue and beige fabrics, with sofa and chairs, a long desk/dresser in wood, a big walk-in closet, a bath with tub, mini-refrigerator and terry-cloth robes, plus plenty of storage space. You dine in the Princess Grill, a red candybox of a room with small tables and an intimate atmosphere. Both the Princess and Britannia Grills have recently improved menus and food preparation.

Suitable Standards: . . . . **C+**

Average Price PPPD: $635 on a world cruise segment, including airfare.

Standard outside cabins in the C categories are not identical or even similar, and the size is the luck of the draw. But all are refurbished with attractive fabrics and colors and a renovated bathroom. Figure on twin beds and, in Category C4, a shower instead of those lovely long, deep tubs. You'll dine in the Caronia restaurant after cocktails, if you like, in the Crystal Bar, which serves the Princess Grill, Britannia Grill and Caronia. We found the food and service in the Caronia better than we recall from the old Columbia first-class restaurant although the room itself is less dramatic.

Bottom Bunks: . . . . **C**

Average Price PPPD: $391 on a world cruise segment, including airfare.

A cabin with two lower beds and bath with shower located amidships on a lower deck is the least expensive cabin for two; remember that *QE2* also has a number of single cabins. All the dining rooms on the ship carry the same basic menus, but the service, quality of preparation and availability of special order dishes may vary from one to another. The Mauretania features single meal seatings following the November 1996 refit.

The *QE2* sets out this year in January on her around-the-world cruise, sailing from New York to Los Angeles, then on to the Pacific and Asia, Australia, Singapore, Vietnam, India, Japan and Southern Africa, West Africa, the Iberian Peninsula and back to Southampton and New York. Altogether she visits 76 ports.

The rest of the year the ship makes a series of transatlantic crossings between the U.S. and U.K., interspersed with warm-water cruises to Bermuda and the Caribbean.

The Scoop

While her newest scheduled renovation reduces the number of berths, the *QE2* will never be a perfect luxury cruise ship because she serves too diverse a group of passenger types and nationalities to offer one consistent across-the-board product. Aboard the world cruise, her entertainment is ambitious, particularly with renowned lecturers and soloists from the world of politics, media, music, theater and film, but the musical production shows still leave something to be desired, primarily because there's no venue devoted exclusively to them. Two decks of advanced spa areas, including a full thalassotherapy area, plus an indoor pool, make the ship a good destination for fitness-oriented travelers no matter what the climate in the area cruised. "We're looking for the over-40s professional people who know the meaning of quality service, style, people who want the best, whether it's in food or entertainment or sheer relaxation," says cruise director Brian Price. But despite the frequent intrusion of "cruise" activities, the ship retains the atmosphere of a transatlantic liner with places to go and things to do rather than the aimless fun-and-games ambience of a pure cruise ship.

Insider Tips

Five Recent Changes On the Ship

1. The Cunard history and artifacts exhibits along the Heritage Trail, with a four-panel mural of Cunard history in the Midships Lobby, a striking 16-foot model of the 1906 *Mauretania* with lights glowing from each porthole, and menus and silver serving pieces from the much-loved 1948 *Caronia*, nicknamed the Green Goddess for her unusual green livery.

2. Passengers who don't want to dress up for the dining rooms may opt most evenings for a seven-course buffet dinner in the Lido Cafe where the attire is informal resort evening wear. But if you plan to visit other areas of the ship during the evening you must adhere to the dress code of the evening.

3. The greatly enlarged Lido self-service buffet restaurant, which replaces an indoor/outdoor pool area that was rarely used; it has a sliding glass dome roof, pale wood floors and neon cove lighting and can seat 500 passengers at a time for breakfast, lunch, children's high tea and midnight buffet. A stairway leads down to the Pavilion, a new glassed-in casual buffet adjacent to the pool deck serving early Continental breakfast and lunchtime hot dogs, hamburgers, steak sandwiches and vegetarian specials.

4. The former Midships Bar has been replaced by the elegant little Chart Room, an intimate lounge where singer/pianists perform sophisticated music of Porter and Gershwin.

5. The already excellent library has been expanded into two rooms, one staffed with a professional librarian who checks out books and videotapes to passengers free of charge, the other a bookshop that sells volumes about ships and the sea plus an ever-changing collection of books written by lecturers sailing aboard.

Five Off-the-Wall Things to Do

1. Try and find the dog kennels.

2. Try and find the nursery.

3. If you're dining in the Queens Grill, make a special dinner order of bubble and squeak or baked beans on toast.

4. Go to karaoke night at the pub and see if you can sing "Moon River" without hitting a single note on key. (It isn't easy, but a dear little English lady in a Miss Marple frock did it one night when we were aboard.)

5. Enter the table tennis competition against the keen British and Australian players.

Five Good Reasons to Book This Ship

1. Because she's the *QE2* and there's no other ship in the world like her.

2. To shop at the chic new Cunard-label sportswear shop that replaced Harrod's.

3. To earn Cruise Miles (like frequent flyer miles) for discounts or future free cruises.

4. To walk through the wonderful self-guided Heritage Trail chockablock with 150 years of Cunard artifacts and history; it's riveting for anyone who loves ships.

5. To take the shortest and cheapest possible segment of a world cruise (Ensenada to Honolulu every January); ask your travel agent since it's not promoted in the brochures.

Five Things You Won't Find On Board

1. A little entrance stage into the Caronia dining room to show off your evening finery.

2. The private lounge that used to distinguish the Princess Grill; now everyone has before-dinner drinks in the large Crystal Bar.

3. That indoor swimming pool under the sliding dome roof has gone; in its place, a 500-seat buffet restaurant that one disgruntled passenger said "looks like a big cafeteria." Funny, that's exactly what it's supposed to be. Anyhow, there's another indoor pool in the spa down on Deck 7.

4. Access to all the bars and lounges; one is a private key club for world cruise passengers only, another the Queens Grill bar, accessible only to passengers who dine in the Queens Grill.

5. A dinky little dance band—the *QE2* prides itself on its 15-piece dance orchestra.

QUEEN ELIZABETH 2 ★★★★★

Registry	**Britain**
Officers	**British**
Crew	**International**
Complement	**1015**
GRT	**70,327**
Length (ft.)	**963**
Beam (ft.)	**105**
Draft (ft.)	**33**
Passengers-Cabins Full	**1620**
Passengers-2/Cabin	**1500**
Passenger Space Ratio	**46.88**
Stability Rating	**Good to Excellent**
Seatings	**1**
Cuisine	**Continental**
Dress Code	**Traditional**
Room Service	**Yes**
Tip	**Included; 15% automatically added to bar checks**

Ship Amenities

Outdoor Pool	**2**
Indoor Pool	**2**
Jacuzzi	**4**
Fitness Center	**Yes**
Spa	**Yes**
Beauty Shop	**Yes**
Showroom	**Yes**
Bars/Lounges	**6/2**
Casino	**Yes**
Shops	**Yes**
Library	**Yes**
Child Program	**Yes**
Self-Service Laundry	**Yes**
Elevators	**13**

Cabin Statistics

Suites	**34**
Outside Doubles	**576**
Inside Doubles	**144**
Wheelchair Cabins	**4**
Singles	**27**
Single Surcharge	**175-200%**
Verandas	**34**
110 Volt	**Yes**

★★★★★★
ROYAL VIKING SUN

England's Princess Anne hosted a gala benefit on the ship's pre-inaugural in December 1988, while it was moored in Greenwich in the middle of the River Thames. Dress instructions were precise: Men were to wear proper black tie attire and women were to wear modest gowns with long sleeves, and no one could photograph the Princess Royal except when she was presenting an award. Shirley noted that actress Joan Collins was appropriately modestly garbed. But la-di-da, you'd never believe what London's cafe society showed up wearing! One striking-looking woman had on a long skirt, all right, but it was totally see-through over the tiniest micro-mini we'd ever been exposed to, and another had on a long dress cut down to expose her cleavage—in the back. Still, the gala was a big success, with the princess dancing in the disco until well past midnight, and the London society types hanging in until nearly dawn. That's probably the latest that disco was ever open!

This extremely spacious ship with its graceful lines introduced the first swim-up bar at sea, as well as the first croquet court seen in many years. She's a quiet, smooth-riding ship. Rubber-mounted engines virtually eliminate vibration, and extra-heavy cabin insulation shuts out extraneous noise. Cabins are large and each includes rheostat light controls on the dressing table and bed lamps, a hairdryer, personal safe, terry-cloth robes and TV with VCR. Dining is at an assigned table on a single seating, and the spa is operated by Golden Door Spa at Sea. The clubby wood-paneled Oak Room was to have had a wood-burning fireplace, but the Coast Guard prohibited it; now it glows from a cool red light buried in its ersatz logs. The sophisticated ship's tenders are air-conditioned with rest rooms in case there's an extra-long ride to shore.

The Brochure Says

"Sail for 104 days or as few as 15—indulging in your wanderlust for as long as you wish with the added option of staying in one of the world's great hotels."

Translation

This ship was made for cruising with really spacious cabins you could move into for a month or more.

Fantasy Suites: . . . . **A+**

Average Price Per Person, Double Occupancy, Per Day: $952 to Bermuda including air-fare.

Any of the penthouse suites would make a fantasy holiday; the Owner's Suite is the most expensive but also most often booked first. Fortunately there are 10 penthouses, each 488 square feet with its own private veranda, floor-to-ceiling windows, separate living room with sofa and chairs, TV/VCR, walk-in closet, big bathroom with tub, stall shower and extra vanity; bedroom with TV/VCR, desk/dresser, lots of built-in cabinetry, personal safe, stocked bar, mini-refrigerator and butler service. The Owner's Suite, if you're curious, is twice as large with two bathrooms and two glass bay windows and a double-sized veranda; the price is available "on request."

Small Splurges: . . . . **A+**

Average Price PPPD: $750 to Bermuda including airfare.

The A Deluxe staterooms make a splendid splurge, at 362 square feet big enough for modest entertaining. You'll have twin beds that can be converted to king-sized, sitting area with curved leather sofa, handsome dark wood and glass cabinetry, large marble bathroom with deep tub and shower, and separate water closet with its own marble washbasin and telephone.

Suitable Standards: . . . . **A**

Average Price PPPD: $418–$473 to Bermuda including airfare.

Standard outside doubles are 191 square feet and have either bathtub or tile shower, along with large windows, twin beds, a loveseat, chair, table and corner cupboard for the TV set. Two outside cabins on Scandinavia Deck are designated singles, and there are four wheelchair-accessible cabins.

Bottom Bunks: . . . . **B**

Average Price PPPD: $359 to Bermuda including airfare.

There are 25 inside cabins measuring 138 square feet each, with two lower beds, large closet, desk/dresser with chair, TV/VCR, and bath with tub/shower combination or shower only.

The *Royal Viking Sun* sails Jan. 6 from San Francisco for a 104-day Around-the-World cruise, visiting French Polynesia, Tonga, Fiji, Australia, Indonesia, Hong Kong, Vietnam, Cambodia, Thailand, Singapore, Andaman Islands, India, Sri Lanka, Oman,

Jordan, Egypt, Israel, the Western Mediterranean, the Azores and Bermuda before arriving in Fort Lauderdale April 21. Segments are available.

The ship cruises to Bermuda roundtrip from Fort Lauderdale in May, then goes to Europe for various northern Europe, western and eastern Mediterranean itineraries.

Royal Viking Sun *can claim, if not the first croquet court at sea, certainly the first in many years.*

The Scoop

The ship offers the same seamless service in which things materialize just before you realize that's what you want, as well as the same genuine warmth and hospitality of the crew, the fine cuisine, the Scandinavian stewardesses who always remember to fill the ice bucket at 5 p.m. The *Royal Viking Sun* provides one of the finest cruise experiences available at any price.

Five Great Spaces

1. The Midnight Sun Lounge, lively throughout the day and evening with its big glass windows facing aft; this is where you play team trivia, listen to cabaret entertainers and classical artists and have pre-lunch Bloody Marys.

2. The Norway Lounge, where you can take early morning stretch classes, watch evening production shows and dance with gentleman hosts.

3. The dining room has big glass windows all around and a spiral staircase leading down from the Compass Rose room above; this is where you enjoy beautifully served, well-prepared meals.

4. The Stella Polaris Room, high up and forward with a 180-degree view, serves an elegant afternoon tea and makes a quiet hideaway for pre-dinner cocktails.

5. The romantic 60-seat Venezia Restaurant, serving Italian dinners to passengers who reserve this alternative dining option in advance.

Five Good Reasons to Book This Ship

1. To enjoy some of the best food and service available anywhere on land or sea.

2. To take an around-the-world cruise that calls in such exotic ports as Broome, Australia; Ujung Padang, Indonesia; Ho Chi Minh City, Vietnam; Aqaba, Jordan; Sharm El Sheikh, Egypt; and Dubrovnik, Croatia.

3. To spend a Scandinavian Christmas at sea with gingerbread houses, caroling children and fragrant fresh Christmas trees all over the ship.

4. To swim in one of the few lap pools at sea, conveniently located just outside a splendid spa and fitness center.

5. To take a cabin with private veranda and eat breakfast every morning by the sea.

Five Things You Won't Find On Board

1. A caddy in the golf simulator; you can, however, play Pebble Beach, and there is usually a golf pro aboard.

2. A concessionaire who'll take cash except in the Casino; you are requested to charge beauty, massage and photo services and gift shop items.

3. A children's play area, although there is a children's program when enough kids are aboard, as during the Christmas cruise.

4. A nightly midnight buffet; late-night snacks are usually served instead except on designated occasions.

5. A chance to get out of shape; the Golden Door Spa at Sea is on hand with as many as 10 exercise classes a day.

ROYAL VIKING SUN ★★★★★

Registry	**Bahamas**
Officers	**Norwegian**
Crew	**International**
Complement	**460**
GRT	**38,000**
Length (ft.)	**673**
Beam (ft.)	**95**
Draft (ft.)	**23**
Passengers-Cabins Full	**843**
Passengers-2/Cabin	**766**
Passenger Space Ratio	**49.60**
Stability Rating	**Good to Excellent**
Seatings	**1**
Cuisine	**Contemporary**
Dress Code	**Traditional**
Room Service	**Yes**
Tip	**Included, 15% automatically added to bar check**

Ship Amenities

Outdoor Pool	**2**
Indoor Pool	**0**
Jacuzzi	**1**
Fitness Center	**Yes**
Spa	**Yes**
Beauty Shop	**Yes**
Showroom	**Yes**
Bars/Lounges	**3**
Casino	**Yes**
Shops	**1**
Library	**Yes**
Child Program	**Yes**
Self-Service Laundry	**Yes**
Elevators	**4**

Cabin Statistics

Suites	**19**
Outside Doubles	**338**
Inside Doubles	**25**
Wheelchair Cabins	**4**
Singles	**2**
Single Surcharge	**125-140%**
Verandas	**141**
110 Volt	**Yes**

★★★★★★
SEA GODDESS I
SEA GODDESS II

When we asked the founder of Sea Goddess back in 1984 how he came up with the basic concept, an expensive and luxurious alternative to the usual sea vacation, Helge Naarstad, a handsome young Norwegian businessman, said, *"I sat down and made a list of all the things I myself would like to do on a cruise."* What Helge and his beautiful wife Nini like is, quite simply, the best of everything.

The little extras that you can take for granted aboard Sea Goddess include a special afternoon tea and grandly themed afternoon fruit-and-cheese buffets.

Well, setting out to create your own ideal vacation and give your passengers the best of everything does not necessarily guarantee a profit margin, certainly not when you're the first on the block to come up with such an unusual idea. So a financially troubled Sea Goddess was acquired by Cunard Line in 1986, which had the wisdom not to change a thing, including the legendary largesse with champagne and caviar. All the alcoholic and nonalcoholic beverages consumed on board (except special-order wines) are included in the basic fare, as are the tips for the exceptionally fine staff. As the forerunner of the super-deluxe small ships, the *Sea Goddesses* are good but far from ideal, something their designers, Pettar Yran and Bjorn Storbraaten, would readily admit. The duo has created the interiors for virtually all the ships in this class—Seabourn, Silversea, *Song of Flower*—and acknowledge that each subsequent ship got design refinements they learned from doing the previous one. Cabins are comfortable but not particularly large, closet space is sparse and bathrooms are strictly mainstream rather than upscale-sybaritic as on the Seabourn class vessels. But all in all, these are among only a handful of our very favorite ships at sea.

The Brochure Says

"For connoisseurs, accustomed to indulging their sense of adventure, the twin Sea Goddesses offer the ultimate yachting experience in a sophisticated atmosphere."

Translation

This is a Rorschach test. Read it and you'll know if you're right for Sea Goddess and Sea Goddess is right for you.

Two suite-rooms combine for a small splurge.

Fantasy Suites: . . . . **NA**

All the accommodations on board are suites.

Small Splurges: .... A

Average Price Per Person, Double Occupancy, Per Day: $1,392 plus airfare, all tips and beverages included, in the Mediterranean.

You can either opt for a suite-room or a suite. The latter is two suite-rooms, and would represent a splurge. In 410 square feet you get two entry halls, two full baths, a his and a hers, a large sitting room with two sofas and table and lots of built-in cabinetry, a bedroom with queen-sized bed, and a study or smaller sitting room with two chairs and large windows.

Suitable Standards: .... A

Average Price PPPD: $938 plus airfare, all tips and beverages included, in the Mediterranean.

The suite-rooms are the standard outside doubles in these ships; there are 58 of them with about 205 square feet each. They contain an entry, bath with tub and shower, sitting area with sofa and chair, coffee/dining table, built-in cabinetry, mini-refrigerator, entertainment center, TV/VCR and stocked bar. The bedroom has a queen-sized bed, night tables, picture windows and vanity counter with stool and drawers. Closet space is adequate but not generous.

Bottom Bunks: .... NA

See "Suitable Standards," above.

The Routes

Sea Goddess I and *II* sail all over the world, alternating schedules that include the Caribbean, the Mediterranean, Northern Europe, Greek Isles, the Middle East, Southeast Asia and the Orient.

The Scoop

The bathrooms and closets could be larger and the suites could have a private veranda, but there's little else we would change about these wonderful ships. They're not stuffy and not pretentious. Extra little surprises may include meals created by famous chefs (who just might be aboard to cook them for you), wine-tasting with famous vintners and unique shore excursions called Sea Goddess Exclusives. These ships fulfill the fantasies of sybaritic couples of all ages, but singles may find them frustrating.

SEA GODDESS I ★★★★★
SEA GODDESS II ★★★★★

Registry	**Norway**
Officers	**Norwegian/European**
Crew	**International**
Complement	**89**
GRT	**4,250**
Length (ft.)	**344**
Beam (ft.)	**47**
Draft (ft.)	**14**
Passengers-Cabins Full	**116**
Passengers-2/Cabin	**116**
Passenger Space Ratio	**36.63**
Stability Rating	**Good**
Seatings	**1**
Cuisine	**Contemporary**
Dress Code	**Traditional**
Room Service	**Yes**
Tip	**Included**

Ship Amenities

Outdoor Pool	**1**
Indoor Pool	**0**
Jacuzzi	**1**
Fitness Center	**Yes**
Spa	**No**
Beauty Shop	**Yes**
Showroom	**No**
Bars/Lounges	**3**
Casino	**Yes**
Shops	**0**
Library	**Yes**
Child Program	**No**
Self-Service Laundry	**No**
Elevators	**1**

Cabin Statistics

Suites	**58**
Outside Doubles	**0**
Inside Doubles	**0**
Wheelchair Cabins	**0**
Singles	**0**
Single Surcharge	**175-200%**
Verandas	**0**
110 Volt	**Yes**

★★★★★
VISTAFJORD

The suite life: Every day at noon, Martina brings another big basket of fresh fruit swathed in cellophane and tied with a ribbon, "like an Easter basket, no?" she says, even if you haven't opened the one from yesterday yet. And every day at 5:30, she arrives with a silver tray of canapes—a bit of caviar or goose liver pâté, a shrimp with a feathery sprig of fresh dill, a curl of smoked salmon, strawberries dipped in chocolate, to go with the cocktails you can mix in your own wet bar. If you want to lunch on your private veranda, you can order from a room-service menu or from the lunch menu from the dining room (always arranged on your bar in its own leather cover every morning). You can soak in a private hot tub on the veranda as you watch the sun go down, or relax in your private sauna, just off the living room in one of the two most lavish suites at sea, PH 1 and PH 2 on the Vistafjord.

Expect excellent food from executive chef Kurl Winkler and his staff, who turn out luscious beauties such as these.

The *Vistafjord* was introduced in 1973, eight years after her sister ship *Sagafjord*, now sailing as the Saga Holidays' *Saga Rose*, and the pair sailed for Norwegian American Cruises before being acquired by Cunard in 1983. The ship is unique for its almost equal mix of North American, British and German passengers, plus a sprinkling of other Europeans, a few Australians and an occasional passenger or two from Asia. The passenger list is usually made up of 50 to 70 repeaters, and many of the Germans and British who sail regularly have become friends over the years. The *Sagafjord* left the Cunard fleet in 1996.

DID YOU KNOW?

On an average 14-day cruise, the Vistafjord *serves 13,000 pounds of meat, 75 pounds of Russian caviar, 36,000 fresh eggs, 1800 quarts of ice cream and 13,690 bottles of beer.*

Between The Lines

The Brochure Says

"High atop the ship, *Vistafjord's* new glass-enclosed penthouse suites become a 'box seat' for the grandest views of sea and sky that cruising has to offer."

Translation

From these glass perches and big private balconies, you can even look down on the captain when he's on the bridge wing.

Cabins & Costs

The lavish new duplex penthouses include a private veranda with outdoor whirlpool plus an en suite private sauna and two marble bathrooms.

Fantasy Suites: .... **A+**

Average Price Per Person, Double Occupancy, Per Day: $1242 in the Mediterranean including airfare.

Two penthouse duplex suites were added during the last refit, each of them 827 square feet with a glass window wall forward on the upper level that gives a captain's-eye view of the scenery ahead, and a huge private veranda with natural teak decking, a hot tub and plenty of room for a cocktail party. A private sauna, tiled shower and separate large marble and tile bath is also upstairs. Inside the big living room are two sofas and two easy chairs in dark green, an oval coffee table, wet bar with stocked liquor cabinet and mini-refrigerator, an entertainment center with color TV/VCR and CD player with a full stock of CDs and new hardback books, a deluxe Scrabble set, a Nordic Track treadmill. Outside, a forward private deck covered in royal blue astroturf looks down on the bridge wings. A spiral staircase leads down to the bedroom with its own private veranda and a large bath with Jacuzzi tub, double basins, toilet and bidet.

Small Splurges: . . . . **B+**

Average Price PPPD: $617 in the Mediterranean including airfare.

The Category B outside doubles with private veranda on Sun Deck have marble bathrooms with tubs, king-sized beds and mirrored dressing table, mini-refrigerator, TV/VCR, personal safe and terry-cloth robes.

Suitable Standards: . . . . **B**

Average Price PPPD: $444 in the Mediterranean including airfare.

Category H outside double cabins have twin beds in a fairly small cabin, a chair, dresser/desk, marble bathroom (some with tub and shower, some with shower only). There are a number of single cabins available in various price ranges, including some with private veranda.

Bottom Bunks: . . . . **B**

Average Price PPPD: $425 in the Mediterranean including airfare.

With the refurbishment, even the lowest-priced inside category J cabins are prettily furnished with the new marble bathrooms (some have tub and shower, some shower only) and two lower beds, plus desk/dresser, chair, adequate closet space, TV/VCR, robes and safe.

DID YOU KNOW?

The Vistafjord *is "The Love Boat" of Europe; it starred in the German TV series "Traumschiff"–"Dreamboat"–as well as the 1983 Jon Voight/Millie Perkins feature film,* Table for Five. *Kevin Costner played a small role in that film before he was famous.*

The Routes

The *Vistafjord* makes a lazy, easy circuit through the world's warm waters, starting in the Caribbean in January, moving to South America in early February, then across the Pacific to Tahiti and back. She crosses the Atlantic in April for a summer of Mediterranean and Northern Europe cruises, covers the North Cape and Iceland in July, the Black Sea and the Holy Land in the autumn, then sails back into the Caribbean in time for Christmas.

The Scoop

This is a classic, traditional vessel with nothing harsh, glitzy or noisy, no hard edges, and a staff and crew that have worked together for a long time. The recent renovation brings her into the forefront of traditional luxury ships, but a few areas still need improvement, primarily the food and service in the Lido Cafe, which is still not large enough for the numbers of people who use it. The overflow people take their breakfast trays into the ballroom and risk getting food all over the expensive carpeting and upholstery. With just a little more effort and a larger staff, this ship could rival its running mate *Royal Viking Sun*.

Insider Tips

Five Favorite Places

1.   Tivoli, a romantic 40-seat Italian restaurant on the balcony above the nightclub, serves as an alternative to the dining room by advance reservation; the food is delicious.

2.   The North Cape Bar, intimate and evocative, in gray and taupe with a finely meshed black spiderweb pattern in the upholstery and putty leather barstools along the rosewood bar.

3.   The library, with its comfortable dark green leather sofas, Oriental rug, mahogany and glass bookcases, gold drapes with knotted ropes and tassels, is very clubby but rich-looking, as is the adjoining writing room with black and gold fabric on the chairs and a pair of computers on writing tables in the corner.

4.   The pale and elegant Garden Lounge, all in ivory and very light green, with tile-topped tables, bleached wood walls, sage and ivory-striped silk curtains with rope ties.

5.   The dining room is leafy green with wood-framed chairs covered in green and gold striped silk, the carpet green with pale pink flowers, and lots of tables for two in the room.

Five Good Reasons to Book This Ship

1.   The new penthouse suites high atop the ship are the most sybaritic at sea; nothing else can equal them.

2.   It's a classy and classic ship with a Continental flair.

3.   The traditional Bavarian Brunch, with aquavit and beer, sausages and sauerkraut, roast suckling pig and German potato salad, served once on every cruise; the crew always feasts on one as well.

4.   To take an exotic winter cruise such as the Los Angeles-to-Papeete itinerary in March that calls in Hawaii, American Samoa and the Cook Islands before arriving in Tahiti.

5.   To dine on Chef Karl Winkler's salmon with horseradish crust in the dining room or sample the splendid Zuppa Valdostana in the Tivoli restaurant.

VISTAFJORD ★★★★★

Registry	**Bahamas**
Officers	**Norwegian**
Crew	**European**
Complement	**379**
GRT	**24,492**
Length (ft.)	**628**
Beam (ft.)	**82**
Draft (ft.)	**27**
Passengers-Cabins Full	**730**
Passengers-2/Cabin	**679**
Passenger Space Ratio	**36.07**
Stability Rating	**Good to Excellent**
Seatings	**1**
Cuisine	**Continental**
Dress Code	**Traditional**
Room Service	**Yes**
Tip	**Included, 15% automatically added to bar check**

Ship Amenities

Outdoor Pool	**1**
Indoor Pool	**1**
Jacuzzi	**1**
Fitness Center	**Yes**
Spa	**Yes**
Beauty Shop	**Yes**
Showroom	**Yes**
Bars/Lounges	**3**
Casino	**Yes**
Shops	**Yes**
Library	**Yes**
Child Program	**No**
Self-Service Laundry	**Yes**
Elevators	**6**

Cabin Statistics

Suites	**16**
Outside Doubles	**254**
Inside Doubles	**33**
Wheelchair Cabins	**6**
Singles	**71**
Single Surcharge	**150%**
Verandas	**34**
110 Volt	**Yes**

DELPHIN SEEREISEN

Postfach 10 04 07 Offenbach/Main, Germany, 63004
☎ *[01149] (699) 840-3811*

The dolphin logo at the bottom of the ship's pool indicates its worldwide warm-weather itineraries.

History . . . .

This large German travel company has a long-term lease (through the year 2001) on the newly refurbished *Delphin*, the former *Kazakhstan II*, owned by Lady Lou/Sea Delphin Shipping Ltd., Malta, which is marketed almost exclusively to German-speaking passengers.

★★★★
DELPHIN

The Russian ships we saw in the 1980s in various ports of the world always looked faintly threatening with that red flag and gold hammer-and-sickle on the stack. And inside they were utilitarian with a no-nonsense, no-tipping staff that could get grumpy at times. But after the breakup of the U.S.S.R., the Ukrainians, notably Black Sea Shipping, controlled the majority of the newer passenger ships, and with Western-based joint venture travel firms, they upgraded the fleet to world-class standards, managing at the same time to keep the prices down in many cases.

The *Delphin* is the former *Kazakhstan II*. After a 1994 renovation in Bremerhaven, the ship has turned into a real dazzler—spotlessly clean and very elegant, but with a certain charming period quality (the cocktail of the day is a Sidecar, something few American bartenders under 60 have ever heard of).

The Brochure Says

"Mehr Komfort, mehr Spass, merh Erlaben: Den gestiegenen Anspruchen der Gaste entspricht die neu schiff mit einem Erlebniskonzept, das ganze Schiff umfasst."

Translation

"More comfort, more fun, more adventure: the enriching fulfillment the guests talk about with the new 'ship' with only one concept idea, that the whole experience on board is a total delight."

Cabins & Costs

Fantasy Suites: . . . . **A**

Average Price Per Person, Double Occupancy, Per Day: $370 plus airfare.
The top suites are #1010 and 1011, very large suites with living room, dressing room and separate bedroom, pale green carpets, curved sofa and two chairs plus several pale wood chairs and a small TV set, then another small TV set and a lot of storage in the dressing room, then a bedroom with twin beds and a chest in between, plus a marble bath with several colors of marble arranged in a mosaic pattern, a bathtub and separate stall shower.

Small Splurges: . . . . **B**

Average Price PPPD: $325 plus airfare.
Junior suites such as # 1014 are very spacious cabins with double bed, sofa, table, chair and two dressers, plus plenty of storage and a built-in hair dryer. The bathroom is tile with shower only.

Suitable Standards: . . . . **A**

Average Price PPPD: $281 plus airfare.
Category I cabins are outside doubles with lots of space, twin beds, a wooden armoire and wooden dresser and a tile bath with shower.

Bottom Bunks: . . . . **C**

Average Price PPPD: $118 plus airfare.
The lowest-priced inside category is S, with two lower beds, dresser and chair and tile bath with shower.

The Routes

The *Delphin* spends the first part of 1998 in the South Pacific, then cruises in Europe and the Mediterranean for the summer and fall before heading back to the tropical seas.

The Scoop

The main problem is the extremely steep stairs around the vessel, which require concentration for older passengers ascending or descending them. The shipboard announcements are made only in German, and the daily program printed only in German, but most members of the staff speak English as well as German. The upside is that the prices for very nice, newly redecorated inside cabins hover down near the $100-a-day mark on long cruises.

Insider Tips

Five Gemütlich Spots

1. The Sky Club Disco, the ship's nightclub, on the topmost desk, reclaimed deck area to make this big handsome room with lavender carpet and lavender upholstery and leather tub chairs and a long, glamorous, curved marble bar, glass dome, wood dance floor and DJ booth.

2. The Boat Deck, covered in natural teak with a sheltered overhang, ping-pong tables, a mosaic tile swimming pool with a blue tile dolphin in the bottom, a children's wading pool, white plastic tables and chairs and a long curved pink marble bar.

3. The Delphin Lounge, a gorgeous room with golden yellow upholstery on chairs and banquettes, a navy and yellow carpet, a small splashing fountain in the room's center, tub chairs and banquette sofas and lovely art.

4. The Grand Salon music bar with its parquet wood floor, bar with black leather swivel stools, tub chairs and curved banquettes.

5. The Lido Bar serves a buffet for continental breakfast and lunch, with white wicker tub chairs made cushy with handsome upholstered cushions and booth banquettes along the window walls on both sides.

Five Good Reasons to Book This Ship

1. It's one of the most elegant vessels sailing today.

2. It literally sails around the world in a leisurely pattern without repeating a port to anywhere the sun is shining.

3. You can be a loner without offending anyone by simply saying you don't speak the language.

4. You can visit the South Seas, China, Burma, Papua New Guinea and Arabia this winter.

5. You can learn German by ear, talking with Germans, which is much easier than trying to read it.

DELPHIN ★★★★

Registry	**Malta**
Officers	**Ukrainian**
Crew	**Western European**
Complement	**250**
GRT	**16,214**
Length (ft.)	**512**
Beam (ft.)	**72**
Draft (ft.)	**19**
Passengers-Cabins Full	**554**
Passengers-2/Cabin	**464**
Passenger Space Ratio	**34.94**
Stability Rating	**Good**
Seatings	**1**
Cuisine	**International**
Dress Code	**Traditional**
Room Service	**Yes**
Tip	**$5 PPPD**

Ship Amenities

Outdoor Pool	**1**
Indoor Pool	**0**
Jacuzzi	**0**
Fitness Center	**Yes**
Spa	**No**
Beauty Shop	**Yes**
Showroom	**Yes**
Bars/Lounges	**8**
Casino	**No**
Shops	**2**
Library	**Yes**
Child Program	**In Summer**
Self-Service Laundry	**No**
Elevators	**2**

Cabin Statistics

Suites	**2**
Outside Doubles	**129**
Inside Doubles	**107**
Wheelchair Cabins	**3**
Singles	**0**
Single Surcharge	**130%**
Verandas	**0**
110 Volt	**No**

DELTA QUEEN
STEAMBOAT
COMPANY

Robin Street Wharf, 1380 Port of New Orleans Place, New Orleans, LA 70130
☎ *(504) 586-0631, (800) 543-7637*
www.deltaqueen.com

A New Orleans jazz band parades around the dining rooms on special evenings.

History . . . .

In 1890, 28-year-old Gordon C. Greene bought his first riverboat, the 150-foot-long *H.K. Bedford*, and married Mary Becker, who began working alongside him in the pilot house. Later Captain Mary B. Greene, one of the few women to earn both a pilot's and a master's license on the river, was often in command of Greene Line's new *Greenland*, which carried passengers to the 1904 St. Louis World's Fair as well as handling the company's more profitable freight hauling. In the 1930s Greene Line added a steamboat for passenger cruises when diesel towboats took away their freight business.

After World War II, Gordon's son Tom paid $46,000 for the historic *Delta Queen*, built in 1926 to cruise California's Sacramento delta, and had it crated up and barged through the Panama Canal to the Mississippi; it began overnight passenger service in 1947.

In 1976, the company launched the new *Mississippi Queen*, and the *American Queen* made its debut in June 1995.

The three-vessel fleet enjoys a high year-round occupancy rate, 93 to 96 percent a year. The 106-year-old company, which also owns American Hawaii Cruises, is traded on NASDAQ under the corporate name American Classic Voyages.

—*Delta Queen* is the only National Historic Monument that travels at eight miles an hour (riverboats measure in miles instead of knots).

—*Mississippi Queen* was designed by James Gardner, co-designer of Cunard's *Queen Elizabeth 2*.

—*American Queen* is the only vessel in history to be christened with a giant bottle of Tabasco pepper sauce. The 21.3 gallons of spicy sauce went into the Mississippi, "but we were told it wasn't a large enough amount to endanger the fish," says a spokeswoman.

Concept. . . . .

The line intends to provide a warm, sincere, all-American experience with generous dollops of river scenery and history, a friendly and mostly young American crew, a 19th-century ambience and, according to former line president Jeffrey Krida, "good solid American food, hearty American fare with some regional dishes as the boats go through the country."

Signatures . . . .

A steam-powered calliope that can be heard for five miles up and down the river signals a Delta Queen steamboat's arrival and departure. The bright red paddle wheel tosses up drops of water that hang and glisten in the sunlight for a moment before falling back into the yellow-brown, mud-colored river. "Riverlorians," historians who give passengers infinite details about the route, scenery and river, are aboard every sailing.

Two long-standing traditions are the annual steamboat race between the *Delta Queen* and the *Belle of Louisville* at Kentucky Derby time and the Great Steamboat Race between the *Mississippi Queen* and the *Delta Queen* that recreates the famous contest between the *Natchez* and the *Robert E. Lee*. Book well ahead to be aboard one of these coveted sailings.

DID YOU KNOW?

When the Delta Queen looked as if it would be banned for its wooden superstructure by federal SOLAS (Safety of Life At Sea) legislation in 1973, Congress granted it a nick-of-time reprieve at the end of what was to have been its last voyage.

Gimmicks . . . .

Mike Fink Day with its "floozie" competition and seafood buffet is a crowd-pleaser, along with Calliope Capers, when each passenger has an opportunity to play the steam calliope on deck. While the vessels have no casinos, real money is bet on Steamboat Races, bingo and Dollar Bill Drawings, where each passenger signs a bill and puts it in a winner-take-all pot.

INSIDER TIP

Don't call them ships; these are boats.

Who's the Competition. . . . .

Delta Queen Steamboat enjoys a unique niche because of its Midwestern river itineraries and very popular vessels, although some other small U.S. flag companies such as Alaska Sightseeing/Cruise West with the *Spirit of '98* and the *Queen of the West* from American West Steamboat Company also offer river cruises aboard steamboat replicas in the Pacific Northwest and Alaska. In Canada, little St. Lawrence Cruise Lines provides replica steamboat cruises on the St. Lawrence and Ottawa Rivers aboard the *Canadian Empress.*

Who's Aboard . . . .

Delta Queen is frank about concentrating on over-50 passengers, saying it doesn't need younger passengers or families with children to fill the boats, since the entertainment would have to be changed to appeal to a under-50 crowd. Some 70 percent of all its passengers are cruise veterans, many of them also Alaska cruisers. The average passenger age is 64, and there are a fair number of singles, mostly female. Some 26 percent of Delta Queen Steamboat's passengers come from California and the Pacific Northwest; three percent come from Europe, Australia and New Zealand.

Who Should Go . . . .

Anyone, especially foreigners who want to get in touch with the real American heartland; people who like banjoes, sing-alongs and respectful young waiters and waitresses who always have a minute to chat; anyone who loves to tour stately homes and gardens; and travelers who want what the line calls "security, safety and predictability." (We were aboard the *Delta Queen* during the 1992 Los Angeles riots and had trouble imagining such a disturbance that could be threatening our residence as we cruised languidly along the Ohio River.)

Who Should Not Go . . . .

Small children or restless teenagers, although a bright, history-oriented preteen might have a wonderful time. Wheelchair-users should book only the *Mississippi* or *American Queens*, which have elevators, and avoid the *Delta Queen*, which does not.

> ## INSIDER TIP
>
> *With so many repeat passengers sailing, you can count on new itineraries to sell out completely within a few days of being announced.*

The Lifestyle . . . .

Steamboating is an amiable blend of down-home Americana, a history tour and a visit to Grandmother's house or a favorite Victorian bed-and-breakfast with plenty of books, games and puzzles. Self-service snacks can be found around the ship between the copious meals, and singing along to old songs, while not required, usually happens anyhow.

The river itself turns out to be as beguiling a sight as a campfire or clouds drifting overhead. Here and there white cranes, said to be reincarnated old riverboatmen, sit on the broken snags of a half-submerged tree trunks, watching the boats go by in the sunlight. But when a fog comes up, they fly from one snag to the next, resting on each until they are certain the pilot has seen them and knows to keep clear of the tree that could puncture the hull of his boat.

The boats tie up frequently at ports of call, historic small towns or cities where passengers can usually walk to points of interest if they don't want to spring for the optional shore excursions.

Dress is casual by day, only slightly more dressy in the evenings, although many men don jacket and tie for the captain's dinner. The two larger boats have two assigned meal sittings, while the *Delta Queen* has only one.

There are no casinos aboard any of the boats, although they may stop along the river near a moored casino boat so passengers can get off to gamble if they wish.

Wardrobe. . . . .

The dress code could be described as "clean and decent" with comfortable shoes and casual wear during the daytime and something only slightly fancier for the evenings. Trips ashore during the warmest months call for lightweight cotton or linen fabrics. Since there is a small swimming pool aboard the *Mississippi* and *American Queens*, a bathing suit might also be in order.

> ## INSIDER TIP
>
> *Since the boats do not travel more than 12 miles away from shore at any time, there is no doctor or nurse required to be on board.*

Bill of Fare. . . . . **B+**

Breakfasts with a southern accent include grits, ham and hot breads, along with fancier New Orleans brunch fare such as eggs Benedict and eggs Sardou. Lunches offer light fare such as a New Orleans fried shrimp poor boy sandwich as well as more substantial dishes such as braised short ribs with vegetables. The normal dinner menu offers three appetizers, two soups, two or three salads and five main dishes, including a Heart Smart main dish and/or vegetarian offering, along with beef, chicken and fish. The vessels' hot breads and desserts are particularly delicious, and portions are medium to large. Special diets can be arranged at time of booking, and some simple dishes not listed on the menu may also be requested from the servers if you don't find what you want in the usual fare.

Between meals, you can help yourself to a great hot dog (with cooked or raw onions, sauerkraut, chili sauce and other condiments) from a rolling cart on deck near the outdoor bar aboard the *Mississippi* and *American Queens* or a basket of freshly popped corn in the indoor bar on all three boats, along with soft ice cream, fresh lemonade, and 24-hour iced tea and hot coffee.

INSIDER TIP

If you're boarding one of the boats in New Orleans and have your own or a rental car along, you can park free in a covered shed at the Robin Street Wharf, where passengers embark.

Showtime . . . .

Quartets perform barbershop or Broadway melodies, soloists belt out cabaret numbers and banjo players, pianists, riverboat gamblers, harpists and clog dancers may appear at any time. A church gospel choir is sometimes brought aboard for a rousing evening of music, and Mark Twain has been known to show up on stage in his white linen suit with a few well-chosen remarks. Many on-board activities are passenger-generated, from making and flying kites to lessons in Victorian parlor crafts.

Discounts . . . .

Early booking discounts from 10 to 15 percent are offered on certain sailings for passengers booking and making a deposit six months in advance. Some discounted air add-ons can also be booked in conjunction with a Delta Queen Steamboat sailing. Passengers who book a 7-night or longer sailing and book with deposit at least 8 months in advance in an "E" category stateroom or higher get free roundtrip airfares.

INSIDER TIP

On these early-to-bed vessels, pre-lunch Bloody Mary specials are apt to be put out at 10:30 a.m., cocktail hour starts at 4:30 p.m. and the Night Owls Club gathers for "late night entertainment" at 10 p.m.

The Bottom Line

These very popular cruises draw a number of repeat passengers who enjoy the low-key excursions into the heart of America and are willing to pay somewhat higher tariffs than on a typical Caribbean cruise. The end product, however, is so unique that it cannot be compared to any other cruise.

To sit and watch the paddle wheel turning on a genuine historic steamboat is one of the joys of river cruising.

With the new *American Queen* in place, this line is operating at the peak of its form. Over the last 10 years, we've watched "steamboating" evolve into a precise and polished vacation that just seems to get better and better for that spectrum of Americans—and we don't feel it should be limited to over-50s—who like Dixieland jazz and sing-alongs, kite flying and calliope music, and get misty-eyed when they hear "God Bless America."

⚓⚓⚓⚓⚓
AMERICAN QUEEN

On the good ship Serendipity you can go back to a magical summer afternoon in childhood, discovering hidden treasures in Grandmother's parlor, swinging in a creaky wooden porch swing, drinking tart-sweet lemonade and stealing an extra cookie when no one's looking. We barely managed to resist the temptation to take a book and lie stomach-down on the cool, polished hardwood floors to read. The atmosphere is so beguiling that we don't even mind the two meal seatings. Big family dinners in the South always had two seatings, adults first and children and some of the meal preparers later. Country roads can take you home on water as well as land.

The biggest steamship on the river doesn't feel like a behemoth when you're aboard, although the 89.3-foot width—21 feet more than the *Mississippi Queen*—gives the *American Queen* a vast sense of space. So counterbalancing the spaciousness and grandeur of the dining room with its tall gold-framed mirrors, crystal chandeliers and tables set comfortably apart are a number of smaller, more intimate spaces such as the pretty little Captain's Bar off the dining room, the Gentlemen's Card Room and the Ladies' Parlor. Screened-in porches with wicker chairs are spotted at intervals around the boat.

A plus or minus, depending on the weather, is that many of the cabins open directly onto the outer decks rather than an interior hallway.

INSIDER TIP

Those A-category cabins 403 and 404 on Observation Deck with private screened porches look more appealing than they really are on a hot day, when the breeze is blocked by cabins on either side. It's cooler to sit out on the open deck.

Between The Lines

The Brochure Says

"…entire towns will turn out to celebrate her arrival…the *American Queen* is the most elaborate paddle-wheeler ever."

Translation

She looks like a gigantic floating wedding cake, except that instead of a bride and groom placed atop the cake, there are two black metal smokestacks with fancy "feathered" tops that sit 109 feet above the river and an all-glass wheelhouse with rococo birdcage trim situated between them. The folks will gather to watch, because in order to pass under some of the lower bridges, the captain has to flatten the smokestacks and lower the wheelhouse. One bridge is so low, the riverlorian says, that the captain, controlling the vessel from a wing bridge, has to get down on his knees to clear it.

Cabins & Costs

Fantasy Suites: .... **A**

Average Price Per Person, Double Occupancy, Per Day: $589 plus airfare. (See "Discounts" above.)
Any of the AAA suites can transport you back to the golden days of steamboating, but we especially like the Mississippi Queen suite, # 352, very ornate with a queen-sized bed with carved headboard, bath with tub and shower, a vanity mirror trimmed in Venetian glass beading, velvet and brocade draperies over the hanging

closet that look just like the draperies Scarlett O'Hara turned into a new dress in *Gone With The Wind*, and a small private balcony overlooking the paddle wheel.

Small Splurges: .... A

Average Price PPPD: $425 plus air add-ons. (See "Discounts" above.)
An A Outside Superior cabin has a lot of space inside; several even have private screen porches (which overlook the promenade so are not really secluded). You'll have one or two easy chairs, a dresser, queen or twin beds, French doors to the deck, big windows and mirrors, adequate storage space, and spacious bath with tub and shower.

Suitable Standards: .... B+

Average Price PPPD: $359 plus air add-on. (See "Discounts" above.)
The standard outside doubles, including seven of the nine wheelchair-accessible cabins, have big bathrooms with black-and-white mosaic tile floors, twin beds in an L-configuration, sometimes a wicker chair, a desk and highboy with drawers and beautiful period wallpaper. There are also eight cabins designated singles.

Bottom Bunks: .... C+

Average Price PPPD: $249 plus airfare add-ons.
The lowest-priced inside cabins are cozy but livable accommodations on the Promenade Deck, with twin beds placed close together because the room is narrow. The wallpaper is elegant, and there's a handsome old-fashioned dresser, a chair and a bathroom with black-and-white mosaic tile floor and shower only.

The Routes

American Queen starts the year with a series of Dixieland Festival roundtrip sailings from New Orleans in January, followed by Big Band cruises in February and March, then heads north into the heartland for summer sailings from St. Paul, Cincinnati, St. Louis and Pittsburgh.

The Scoop

We think this is one of the best see-America cruises possible, especially recommended for foreign visitors who want a genuine American experience instead of a theme park ersatz America. While the line concentrates on marketing to the over-50 group, we could see a family with bright 10- to 12-year-olds really grooving on this cruise, despite the absence of video games and flashy entertainment. The ship is delightful for anyone who enjoys bed-and-breakfast establishments, but the food, entertainment and privacy are even better. It's worth every penny of the fairly pricey tariff!

Insider Tips

Five Evocative Places

1. The Front Porch, a glassed-in, air-conditioned porch with wicker rocking chairs, carefully painted to look well worn on the seat and along the arms, with old-fashioned game tables, much-read copies of Tom Swift and Bobbsey Twins books, and help-yourself lemonade and cookies.

2. The Gentleman's Cardroom with green velvet sofas, a stuffed bear, a miniature billiards table, and a stereopticon with naughty French postcards.

3. The Ladies' Parlor with its Victorian furniture and painted screens, a morning glory Victrola with round Edison wax cylinder recordings, a big table with a Ouija board on it and a screen porch with wicker chairs.

4. The Mark Twain Gallery, opulent, cool and dark, a perfect Victorian parlor with its Tiffany stained glass lampshades, bookcases and busts, and fringed lampshades. On either side, glass windows look down into the airy, sunlit dining room below, inspired by the grand restaurants aboard 19th-century steamboats.

5. The Grand Saloon, with a balcony level of private boxes entered by doors labeled for such luminaries as Ralph Waldo Emerson and Harriet Beecher Stowe, a wooded stage with footlights and a main floor with banquettes, marble-topped tables and Victorian chairs.

Five Off-the-Wall Things to Do On Board

1. Drop a penny into the coin-operated stereopticon in the Gentleman's Card Room to flip through an innocently naughty set of turn-of-the-century French postcards.

2. Sit down in the Ladies' Parlor with a couple of friends and ask the Ouija board some questions.

3. Hang out in the engine room with the amiable engineers and watch the pair of 1932 steam engines salvaged from a submerged barge in Mississippi propel the bright red paddlewheel. (Get there from a marked doorway in the Engine Room Bar.)

4. Earn a Vox Calliopus certificate by playing five consecutive notes on the steam calliope when the daily program lists Calliope Capers.

5. Go fly a kite you've made yourself from the aft Calliope Bar aboard, but watch out for that kite-eating bridge near Oak Alley Plantation.

Five Good Reasons To Book This Boat

1. It's more fun than visiting your favorite aunt.

2. The yummy bread pudding with caramel sauce.

3. To have a serious chat with Mark Twain.

4. To enjoy the ambience of an antiques-filled bed-and-breakfast without having to tiptoe around.

5. To sit in the Engine Room Bar watching the red paddlewheels churning and sing "Proud Mary"…"big wheel keep on turning …"

DELTA QUEEN STEAMBOAT COMPANY

AMERICAN QUEEN ⚓⚓⚓⚓⚓

Registry	U.S.
Officers	American
Crew	American
Complement	170
GRT	3,707
Length (ft.)	418
Beam (ft.)	90
Draft (ft.)	8.5
Passengers-Cabins Full	436
Passengers-2/Cabin	436
Passenger Space Ratio	NA
Stability Rating	Excellent
Seatings	2
Cuisine	American
Dress Code	Casual
Room Service	Yes
Tip	$10 PPPD, 15% automatically added to bar checks

Ship Amenities

Outdoor Pool	1
Indoor Pool	0
Jacuzzi	0
Fitness Center	Yes
Spa	No
Beauty Shop	Yes
Showroom	Yes
Bars/Lounges	2
Casino	No
Shops	1
Library	Yes
Child Program	No
Self-Service Laundry	Yes
Elevators	2

Cabin Statistics

Suites	24
Outside Doubles	144
Inside Doubles	54
Wheelchair Cabins	9
Singles	8
Single Surcharge	150-175%
Verandas	29
110 Volt	Yes

⚓⚓⚓⚓⚓
DELTA QUEEN

You can arrange to cheer (and put money on) two famous races during a nine-day cruise if you can be aboard the Delta Queen for the annual steamboat race with the Belle of Louisville (one-and-a-half hours for 12 miles), then add on a visit to the Kentucky Derby three days later (two minutes for a mile-and-a-quarter). The year we did it was 1992, concurrent with the Los Angeles riots, and it was hard to imagine someone might be burning our house down while we were relaxing in the friendly, slow-moving heartland. P.S.: Our place was still standing when we got back home after the derby, so our only losses were on the hosses.

This is a genuine National Historic Landmark listed on the National Register of Historic Places, the only national monument that steams along at eight miles an hour. It took an act of Congress to keep her in business (see "Footnote" under "History"). She's slow-moving, far from spacious (the dining room doubles as the show lounge and lecture hall) and hasn't the most luxurious accommodations on the river (those belong to her newer sister *American Queen*) but love and devotion from her dedicated fans have kept her afloat since 1948 and no one had better murmur about retiring her.

DID YOU KNOW?

They say the ghost of Mary "Ma" Greene still haunts the Delta Queen. If so, better avoid the bars, since Ma was a strict teetotaler and would never let liquor be served on board during her lifetime. The first time they installed a bar after her death, the steamboat was forcefully rammed by a barge which surprised officers noted was named the Mary Greene.

The Brochure Says

"Walk the decks where a princess or a president may have strolled before you. Immerse yourself in the inspiring beauty, nostalgic adventure and captivating history that so wonderfully exemplify the grand American tradition of Steamboatin'."

Translation

Famous previous passengers, many of them remembered with brass plaques fitted to the doors of the cabins they occupied, include Princess Margaret, Lady Bird Johnson, Jimmy Carter, Van Johnson, Helen Hayes and opera stars Roberta Peters and Jan Peerce.

Cabins & Costs

Fantasy Suites: . . . . **B+**

Average Price Per Person, Double Occupancy, Per Day: $589 plus air add-ons. (See "Discounts" above.)

The AAA Outside Superior Suites, a pair of posh cabins all the way forward on the Sun Deck with queen-sized beds, sitting area, big mirrors, bath with tub and shower and doors that open right onto the deck. There are two others, slightly smaller, down on Cabin Deck aft, that would do in a pinch.

Small Splurges: . . . . **B**

Average Price PPPD: $425 plus air add-ons. (See "Discounts" above.)

Next best are the pair of AA Outside Luxury Suites located aft on Sun Deck with queen-sized bed, windows, a chair, a desk and bath with shower.

Suitable Standards: . . . . **C**

Average Price PPPD: $359 plus air add-ons. (See "Discounts" above.)

All the cabins aboard are outsides, so in this category we'll look at some of the mid-range outside doubles, leaving the bottom-priced outsides for the category below. You should generally expect twins or double bed, mirror and bath with shower. Chairs are at a premium in these small cabins, but the decor is attractive and you won't suffer.

Bottom Bunks: . . . . **C**

Average Price PPPD: $155 plus air add-ons.

The very cheapest cabins aboard are the category F outside staterooms with extra-wide lower bed and upper berth. The cabins themselves are narrower than the others on board (which can be very narrow indeed; people were smaller or less demanding in the 1920s). Anyhow, the downside is, there's a partly obstructed river view; just open the door and wander down the deck to improve it. Tain't no big thang.

The Routes

The *Delta Queen* celebrates special winter Dixie Fest and Big Band cruises with guest stars Pete Fountain, the Dukes of Dixieland, Bob Crosby and the Bobcats, the Ink Spots and the Tommy Dorsey Orchestra aboard one or another sailing. February finds her sailing more Dixie Fest jazz cruises out of New Orleans, followed by spring pilgrimages through the Old South. An April Kentucky Derby cruise between Memphis and Cincinnati is followed by Wilderness and Crossroads itineraries.

The Scoop

The food is delicious, the entertainment down-home but amusing, and all cabins are outsides, many of them opening directly onto the deck. Antiques decorate the few public rooms aboard, and porch swings and rocking chairs invite passengers to sit awhile on deck, watching the river go by, living in the rhythms of the 19th century. This is the only authentic period riverboat making overnight cruises in the United States.

Insider Tips

Five Big-Easy Places

1. The Orleans Room on Main Deck fills triple duty as dining room, show lounge and lecture hall, but its wide windows, plank floor, pressed-tin ceiling and lace curtains set the mood of an earlier time.

2. The steam calliope, which, depending on your hearing, is a great boon or a great nuisance, trills out tunes as the boat goes up and down the river; passengers also get a turn at playing it.

3. The Forward Cabin Lounge is where passengers gather for afternoon tea or late-night (we hesitate to say "midnight" since it's usually much earlier) buffet amid handsome antique furniture.

4. The Grand Staircase, made of handcrafted of oak, teak, mahogany, Oregon cedar and other hardwoods, is accented with Tiffany stained glass and brass appointments.

5. The Texas Lounge, where spicy Cajun Bloody Marys are on special at 10:30 a.m., hot fresh popcorn is always available, and singalongs are frequent.

DELTA QUEEN ⚓⚓⚓⚓⚓

Registry	U.S.
Officers	American
Crew	American
Complement	75
GRT	3,360
Length (ft.)	285
Beam (ft.)	58
Draft (ft.)	8.5
Passengers-Cabins Full	174
Passengers-2/Cabin	174
Passenger Space Ratio	NA
Stability Rating	Excellent
Seatings	2
Cuisine	American
Dress Code	Casual
Room Service	No
Tip	$10 PPPD, 15% automatically added to bar checks

DELTA QUEEN STEAMBOAT COMPANY

Ship Amenities

Outdoor Pool	0
Indoor Pool	0
Jacuzzi	0
Fitness Center	No
Spa	No
Beauty Shop	No
Showroom	No
Bars/Lounges	1
Casino	No
Shops	1
Library	No
Child Program	No
Self-Service Laundry	No
Elevators	0

Cabin Statistics

Suites	6
Outside Doubles	87
Inside Doubles	0
Wheelchair Cabins	0
Singles	0
Single Surcharge	175%
Verandas	0
110 Volt	Yes

⚓⚓⚓⚓⚓
MISSISSIPPI QUEEN

The first time we went steamboatin' was aboard the Mississippi Queen, and we were thrilled to have our own tiny screened porch overlooking the river. We immersed ourselves in stories about Big Al the alligator, who when he smoked under the river created fog to bother the captains above, and the cranes, the souls of reincarnated boatmen, who appeared to show captains where the underwater snags (logs) were. It was a wonderful introduction to the romance of American travel.

*A hoop-skirted hostess aboard the **Mississippi Queen** greets passengers.*

On the other hand, until her recent reincarnation as a proper sister ship to the elegant *American Queen*, we were not particularly fond of the somewhat glitzy *Mississippi Queen*.

The Brochure Says

"...unlike early steamers, she features a pool on the Sun Deck, a beauty salon, a movie theater and elevators, as well as climate-controlled staterooms with steamboat-to-shore telephones."

Translation

This boat is for people who want to go steamboatin' on a cruise ship.

Delta Queen Steamboat Company

Fantasy Suites: .... A

Average Price Per Person, Double Occupancy, Per Day: $589 plus air add-ons. (See "Discounts" above.)

There are four Superior Veranda Suites, the top digs on the *MQ*, with twin beds that convert to king-sized or a fixed queen-sized bed, depending on the cabin, along with sitting area with sofa bed, bathroom with tub and shower, and a private veranda. If you book 401 or 402, you're adjacent to the wheelhouse with a steamboat captain's view; if you book 274 or 275, your veranda overlooks the paddle wheel.

Small Splurges: .... B

Average Price PPPD: $425 plus air add-ons. (See "Discounts" above.)

Again, we'd go for a suite with veranda, perhaps one of the Deluxe Veranda Suites on Texas Deck, with twin beds plus a day bed to sleep a third person, a big walk-in closet, bath with tub and shower and a small private veranda.

Suitable Standards: .... B

Average Price PPPD: $394 plus air add-ons. (See "Discounts" above.)

The predominant cabin configuration on board is the category B Deluxe Veranda Stateroom. There are 68 of them, all with small private verandas, windows, a chair, a dresser, bath with shower and closet.

Bottom Bunks: .... D

Average Price PPPD: $155 plus air add-ons.

There are only eight of the very cheapest cabins, the category F Inside Staterooms, which have a lower bed, upper berth, bathroom with shower and a dresser. But all cabins have been handsomely redecorated in Victorian furniture, fabrics and wallpaper.

In the winter, the *Mississippi Queen* sails from New Orleans on Big Band cruises, followed by Spring Pilgrimage sailings through the Old South, then Kentucky Derby cruises and in summer, Wilderness and Crossroads itineraries on the Arkansas, Tennessee and Cumberland Rivers.

The Scoop

What the *Mississippi Queen* offers that the *Delta Queen* doesn't is elevators, a swimming pool, Continental breakfasts served in the cabin, telephones and individual climate controls in the cabin, a movie theater, a self-service hot dog stand and ice cream bar, a sauna and fitness room, shuffleboard, hot hors d'oeuvres before dinner and a cage of pet birds in the lobby. With the glitz all gone and the decor brought up to speed with the new *American Queen*, the *Mississippi Queen* steams right along with her sister boats.

Insider Tips

Five Favorite Places

1. The Paddlewheel Lounge has two-deck-high windows facing the churning red wheel; passengers sit, transfixed, watching the water like flames in a fireplace.

2. The Forward Cabin Lounge with its baroque bird cages and chirping finches doubles as lobby and shore excursions office.

3. The Calliope Bar, forward on the top deck, is the place to gather in the open air and listen to the ridiculously ornate gilded steam piano tootling out Stephen Foster songs from the balcony above or help yourself to a hot dog with all the trimmings from a rolling cart.

4. The Grand Saloon with its chandeliers and bay windows is the gathering spot after dinner for music from Dixieland to blues, Big Band sounds for dancing to tunes from Broadway.

5. The Sun Deck, with its swimming pool, shuffleboard and sunny lounging chairs is the place to be on a warm summer day.

Five Good Reasons to Book This Boat

1. It's a great introduction to the heartland of America.

2. The chocolate-peanut butter pie.

3. Steve Spracklen, a former student of pianist Eubie Blake, playing an evening of ragtime.

4. Waving at the people who line up along the river just to see her pass by, including whole classes of grade-school children.

5. To toodle when your turn comes on the steam calliope and be heard five miles up and down the river.

Five Things You Won't Find Aboard

1. Seasickness—the ride is quiet and smooth.

2. Speed measured in knots; on the river it's measured in miles per hour.

3. A children's program.

4. A casino.

5. A TV set in your cabin.

MISSISSIPPI QUEEN ⚓⚓⚓⚓⚓

Registry	U.S.
Officers	American
Crew	American
Complement	165
GRT	3,364
Length (ft.)	382
Beam (ft.)	68
Draft (ft.)	8.5
Passengers-Cabins Full	458
Passengers-2/Cabin	414
Passenger Space Ratio	NA
Stability Rating	Excellent
Seatings	2
Cuisine	American
Dress Code	Casual
Room Service	Yes
Tip	$10 PPPD, 15% automatically added to bar checks

Ship Amenities

Outdoor Pool	1
Indoor Pool	0
Jacuzzi	1
Fitness Center	Yes
Spa	No
Beauty Shop	Yes
Showroom	Yes
Bars/Lounges	2
Casino	No
Shops	1
Library	Yes
Child Program	No
Self-Service Laundry	Yes
Elevators	2

Cabin Statistics

Suites	26
Outside Doubles	109
Inside Doubles	72
Wheelchair Cabins	1
Singles	0
Single Surcharge	175%
Verandas	94
110 Volt	Yes

DISNEY CRUISE LINE

210 Celebration Place, Suite 400, Celebration FL 34747-4600
☎ *(407) 939-3500 (offices), (407) 566-7000 (information)*
www.disney.com/disneycruise

Kids aboard the **Disney Magic** *enjoy 15,000 square feet of play area in the Oceaneer Club. More than 200 activities are available for children.*

History . . . .

The Walt Disney Company had long been associated with cruising through lines such as Premier's Big Red Boats, which offered Disney World packages in combination with three- and four-day cruises from nearby Port Canaveral. Many of the general public, in fact, erroneously believed the Big Red Boats were owned and operated by Disney, so much so that when the new Disney Cruise Line was formed in June 1994, some of our readers called to ask what Disney was going to do with its other cruise line.

The key executives for the Disney Cruise start-up were all veterans of the cruise industry, many of them from Crystal Cruises, including line president Art Rodney, marine/hotel operations Erling Frydenberg and entertainment director Cliff Perry.

The *Disney Magic*, the line's first ship, makes its bow March 12, 1998, followed in December 1998 by sister ship *Disney Wonder*.

Concept.

The intention, as stated in early press releases from the line, is "to bring Disney Magic to the sea for the ultimate vacation by combining the hallmarks of Disney creativity, style and service to offer unparalleled adventures and never-ending enchantment on every deck, and in every stateroom, creating a memorable vacation experience for adults and children alike." Romantic getaways for adults—promised but not delivered by earlier child-oriented lines like now-defunct American Family Cruises—are high on the agenda at Disney, with honeymooners being targeted as a major market.

Signatures.

The Mouse is very much in evidence around Disney Cruise Line, with his silhouette head and ears ingrained in the company logo and on the twin stacks of the ship. The line also has land packages at Disney World to round out a full week with the three- and four-day cruise programs.

Disney owns its own private island in the Bahamas for shipboard beach days, Disney's Castaway Cay, the 1000-acre, uninhabited former Gorda Cay in the Abaco Islands.

Disney has also constructed its own cruise terminal at Port Canaveral, a $27 million, art deco-designed facility.

Gimmicks.

Disney classic and first-run films will be screened on board the ship on every sailing, and the theater will incorporate scenes from Disney musical productions such as "Beauty and the Beast" into the live stage shows.

Goofy is suspended from a rope-and-platform rig painting the name on the ship.

A gilded Steamboat Willie in the brochure commemorates the Mouse's first movie; he's wearing a sou'wester and wrestling with a ship's wheel. On the lower right corners of each brochure page is an animation cel of Mickey and a life ring; if you flip the pages quickly, you see Mickey spinning around.

Who's the Competition

The competing cruise lines sailing from Port Canaveral, at least in their public utterances, have welcomed the new competitor from the get-go, figuring logically that the Disney label would bring a lot of new first-time cruisers into the area and they could get both the Disney overflow and the bargain-seekers looking for a cruise price lower than Disney's. Also sailing from Port Canaveral are Cruise Holding/Premier's *Oceanic*, Carnival's *Fantasy* and Royal Caribbean International's *Nordic Empress*.

Who's Aboard

Just about everybody, at least at the beginning, according to veteran travel agents, who say early cruises were already sold out with extensive wait lists by mid-1997. The intended market includes families with small children, honeymooners and couples without children. President Art Rodney estimates 60 percent families and 40 percent couples, including the honeymoon market. Couples can arrange their wedding at the Disney World wedding chapel, then cruise for their honeymoon.

Children can enjoy hands-on learning in the Oceaneer Lab.

Who Should Go . . . .

First-time cruisers leery of experimenting with an unknown product will find reassurance with the familiar patterns of the Walt Disney Company. The intent is to make the package experience a seamless transition from land to sea or vice versa, using the same coded card key at both the hotel and aboard the ship, providing motorcoach transport with entertainment between venues and handling luggage from airport to ship to resort and back to airport without the passenger having to carry it.

Who Should Not Go . . . .

It takes a sharper crystal ball than we've got to predict the audience for a ship that has not sailed by the time this book goes to press, but we'd suggest only those die-hard curmudgeons who hate Disneyland, Disney World, Mickey Mouse and children should avoid the *Disney Magic.*

The Lifestyle . . . .

The traditional cruise experience is enhanced with some typical Disney touches in the 15,000 square feet devoted to children, with constant attention to ages 3 to 17 between 9 a.m. to 1 a.m. with more than 200 activities available. Special adults-only areas and programs range from spa pampering to wine-tasting, and Beat Street, an area restricted after 8 p.m. to passengers 18 or over, includes three music-and-dance venues offering rock and country in one lounge, a piano bar in a second and an improvisational comedy club in a third.

Wardrobe.

The line suggests passengers pack lightly and carry primarily casual, informal resort wear, shorts, slacks, sundresses, jeans and tops along with a sweater or jacket for cool evenings or overzealous air conditioning. They suggest leaving jewelry and black tie apparel at home, bringing only a jacket for men and a dress or pantsuit for women for the evening you dine in Lumiere's, the dressy restaurant aboard.

Bill of Fare.

The ships will feature three restaurants on board with assigned seating, the Animator's Palate, Lumiere's and an island-themed eatery. Only Lumiere's requires dressing up a bit; the other two are totally casual. However, restaurants and tables are assigned for two meal seatings, main and second. Travel agents should request your preference when making the initial booking.

An alternative dinner restaurant called Palo is open nightly for adults only.

An alternative dinner restaurant called Palo is available for dining between 6 and 11 p.m. nightly, but does require reservations (taken on board) and restricts diners to those 18 or over. A service charge of $5 is added to take care of gratuities, but the meal itself is free.

Casual breakfasts and lunches are served in both Lumiere's and the island restaurant, plus an indoor/outdoor meal service at Topsider Buffet for breakfast and lunch. Children's menus are offered in all the restaurants, and an informal buffet dinner is available for children who take part in the supervised programs during dinner hours.

Showtime.

The line plans to screen Disney films in the Ship's Buena Vista Theater and present three live Broadway-type shows with music and special effects in a state-of-the-art shipboard theater. For sports fans, a special

ESPN Skybox presents nonstop action, and teens will find their own teen lounge with tunes, films and socializing areas.

Beat Street, restricted to passengers 18 and over after 8 p.m., offers standup comics in Offbeat lounge, live music from rock 'n roll to country and western in Rockin' Bar "D", and a singalong piano bar in Sessions they say will remind you of the Carlyle Hotel in New York.

Expect, overall, the same lavish production values and painstaking attention to detail you get at the other Disney venues. With the endless resources of Walt Disney Productions available, there seems no end to the entertainment possibilities aboard these ships.

Discounts . . . .

Early booking discounts of up to $700 a cabin for a seven-day package or $500 a cabin for a three- or four-day cruise are available on most sailings. Blackout dates not available with early booking discounts are April 6 through March 3 and Dec. 18 through 31, 1998.

The Bottom Line

All will be revealed.

DISNEY CRUISE LINE

Unrated
DISNEY MAGIC
DISNEY WONDER

The ships are massive, some 85,000 tons each, which would have made them the world's largest cruise ships only a couple of years ago. Both are built at Fincantieri Shipyards in Italy, and one red-letter day in the line's brief history was in April 1997, when the bow construction for the *Disney Magic* was towed 100 miles from the Trieste yard to another Fincantieri yard near Venice to be joined up with the stern.

The sister ships are both scheduled to debut in 1998, *Disney Magic* in March and *Disney Wonder* in December. The *Disney Magic* is homeported in Port Canaveral, Florida. The ships carry 1760 passengers, based on two to a cabin, but with the great amount of family business anticipated (60 percent of the total passengers, line president Art Rodney estimates) the number on board most sailings will probably be nearer the maximum capacity of 2400. Officers are European, as is hotel and dining staff, with American cruise staff and child counselors. There is no casino aboard, and smoking areas are strictly limited on the vessel.

The ship's two stacks are painted red with a white silhouette of Mickey Mouse's head, the line's logo, on each. The two top decks contain the two-level Topsider Buffet for casual breakfasts and lunches, the Palo adult restaurant, two swimming pools (one designated adults only), sports deck and fitness center, a teen lounge and Mickey's Pool and waterslide for children. A bandstand and stage for dancing are also on the open decks.

Lumiere's restaurant features a large "Beauty and the Beast" mural.

There are three restaurants aboard the vessel, plus a fourth, adults-only alternative restaurant called Palo which is available for candlelight dinners by reservation only; you make reservations after you board the ship. Of the three assigned-seating restaurants, Lumiere's with its "Beauty and the Beast" wall mural requests a slightly dressier wardrobe in the evening than the others. Animator's Palette provides a unique light show for its diners, who find the restaurant totally black-and-white when they enter. Colors begin to appear around the room as you dine on California cuisine, and by the end of your meal, you're sitting amid a room filled with dazzling colors. And a tropical restaurant rounds out the trio. In a unique move, Disney has decreed that all passengers will dine in all three restaurants by moving groups of passengers along with their waiters nightly from one dining room to the next.

The 875 passenger cabins are located on six of the eleven decks; 44 percent of them have private verandas. Some family suites are available that can sleep four or five people, and the top-priced suites can handle up to seven.

Some 15,000 square feet of space devoted to kids' facilities, plus the cinema which screens Disney features, are located on Deck 5, while Deck 4 has Animator's Palate restaurant, the Walt Disney showroom, shops and Studio Sea, a lounge featuring entertainment for the whole family. Beat Street, on the other hand, is an entertainment facility limited to those over 18 in the evenings. It's located on Deck 3, along with the Lumiere and island restaurants and the Promenade Lounge.

The Brochure Says

"A land and sea adventure you'll never forget. In seven unforgettable days, on one incredible vacation, with spectacular entertainment, unique dining experiences and enchanting adventures that only Disney could create, a new kind of magic unfolds on a ship inspired by the glorious ocean liners of the past."

Translation

We don't want to alarm you first-timers out there by suggesting you're going to take a cruise. No, you're signing up for a Disney vacation, part of which includes an evocative boat ride on the water somewhat longer than the Pirates of the Caribbean.

Fantasy Suites . . . .

Average Price Per Person, Double Occupancy, Per Day: $491 including airfare for 7-day resort/cruise package.

The two Royal Suites are the most posh accommodations aboard, with around 1000 square feet of luxury, a large private veranda, and space to sleep seven comfortably. Additional passengers travel for $919 apiece for the full cruise. A pair of two-bedroom suites are slightly less expensive with 899 square feet, two-and-a-half bathrooms, separate living room with dining table, wet bar, walk-in closets, TV with VCR, whirlpool tub and private veranda.

Small Splurges. . . . .

Average Price PPPD: $434 including airfare for a 7-day resort/cruise package.

One-bedroom suites can sleep a family of four or sometimes five in 591 square feet with a large separate living room with dining table and sofa that converts to a double bed, a pull-down bed, large veranda, two bathrooms, walk-in closet, wet bar and TV set with VCR.

Suitable Standards. . . . .

Average Price PPPD: $282 including airfare for a 7-day resort/cruise package.

Outside cabins without private verandas are located on several decks, and contain sleeping facilities for at least three guests, with some offering a fourth berth as well. Baths have tub and shower, and there is an in-room safe, remote-control color TV set, hair dryer, phone and hotel-type minibar.

Bottom Bunks ....

Average Price PPPD: $189 including airfare for a 7-day resort/cruise package.
Inside cabins are larger than on many ships, with 173 square feet of space that sleeps three. A queen-sized bed or twin beds plus a sofa that converts into a single bed are standard furnishings, along with a privacy divider, a bathroom with tub and shower and all the other amenities listed above under Suitable Standards.

Animator's Palette provides an ever-changing light show for its diners.

The Routes

The *Disney Magic* sails from Port Canaveral on three- and four-day sailings that can be combined with four- and three-day Disney resort vacations at Disney World to make a seven-day package. The ship calls in Nassau and at Disney-owned Castaway Cay in the Bahamas, the latter an uninhabited 1000-acre island with a half-mile of beach and a full range of watersports and beach activities for families, plus a mile-long, adults-only beach.

| DISNEY MAGIC | Unrated |
DISNEY WONDER	Unrated
Registry	NA
Officers	European
Crew	European and American
Complement	945
GRT	85,000
Length (ft.)	964
Beam (ft.)	106
Draft (ft.)	25.3
Passengers-Cabins Full	2400
Passengers-2/Cabin	1760
Passenger Space Ratio	48
Stability Rating	NA
Seatings	2
Cuisine	Contemporary
Dress Code	Casual/Traditional
Room Service	Yes
Tip	$8.50 PPPD, 15% automatically added to bar checks

Ship Amenities

Outdoor Pool	3
Indoor Pool	0
Jacuzzi	4
Fitness Center	Yes
Spa	Yes
Beauty Shop	Yes
Showroom	Yes
Bars/Lounges	6
Casino	No
Shops	2
Library	NA
Child Program	Yes
Self-Service Laundry	No
Elevators	12

Cabin Statistics

Suites	104
Outside Doubles	537
Inside Doubles	234
Wheelchair Cabins	12
Singles	0
Single Surcharge	NA
Verandas	385
110 Volt	Yes

DISNEY CRUISE LINE

DISNEY CRUISE LINE

DOLPHIN CRUISE LINE

P.O. Box 025420, Miami, FL 33102-5240
☎ (305) 358-5122, (800) 222-1003
www.dolphincruise.com

History

Dolphin Cruise Line came about through a marketing agreement in 1979 between Peter Bulgarides, who formed Ulysses Cruise Line, and Paquet to operate the *Dolphin IV*. That agreement was terminated in 1984, and Dolphin Cruise Line was born to handle the ship.

A second ship, the former *Star/Ship Royale* from Premier Cruises, was acquired in 1989, and renamed the *SeaBreeze*, and when Admiral Cruises was disbanded by its parent company Royal Caribbean Cruise Line in 1992, Dolphin acquired the former *Azure Seas*, which it named *OceanBreeze*. The latter ship had been based in Los Angeles for more than a decade, making highly successful three- and four-day cruises to Baja California.

For three years, the company operated its trio of vessels, using the *Dolphin IV* for short cruises to the Bahamas and the other two for seven-day Caribbean sailings. In August 1995, Dolphin sold its *Dolphin IV* to Kosmas Shipping Group, Inc., a Florida-based company (see Canaveral Cruise Line, page 243).

In 1996, Dolphin acquired the former *Festivale* from Carnival which became the *IslandBreeze*, and in 1997, Dolphin joined a new corporate entity, Cruise Holdings Ltd., who also own Seawind Cruise Line and Premier Cruise Line. At some point in the near future, the three may be marketed under a new corporate name.

Concept

Dolphin feels it established itself as a leader in the three- and four-day cruise market early on by providing quality and value, as well as offering "quality service and gourmet dining" on all of its ships. The vintage Dolphin vessels still carry details from their ocean liner days such as teak decks, wood paneling, etched glass and polished brass. Under Cruise Holdings the intention is to continue to offer lower-priced cruises than major mass-market operators and to emphasize its classic, vintage fleet.

DOLPHIN CRUISE LINE

Signatures

The distinctive blue dolphin on the ships' white stacks makes an easily recognized and identified logo.

On-board weddings were popularized by Dolphin and frequently take place on the ships.

Gimmicks

Kids get a treat that Mom and Dad might envy—a trip to the bridge to meet the captain. They go in a group with the youth counselors on board.

Who's the Competition

Dolphin has long been a leader in the budget cruise arena and competes primarily in the price-driven market that also includes Commodore Cruise Line and Regal Cruises.

Who's Aboard

A great many first-time cruisers, family groups, singles, couples, many passengers in their 20s and 30s.

Who Should Go

Anybody who wants to sample a cruise to see what it's all about without having to make a big commitment in time and money.

Who Should Not Go

Fussy veteran cruisers will not like the very long lines that form anywhere food is being arranged, served or set out.

EAVESDROPPING

A man standing in line at tea time watching several family members heaping plates with cakes and sandwiches shakes his head in mock dismay and says, "I'm gonna hafta get some new springs for my car before I can drive the five of them back home."

The Lifestyle

Dolphin tries to work in as many special activities as possible. The usual daily pattern always offers plenty of chances to eat, plus as many as eight shore excursions in port. Sports and exercise classes, movies, ping pong, dance classes, beauty salon demonstrations, napkin folding, fruit and vegetable carving, pool games, horseracing, tours of the navigation bridge, Name That Tune, captain's cocktail party, shore excursion sales, dance music, game shows led by the cruise director, a deck party under the stars, ice carvings, midnight buffet, disco and night-owl movie— and that's just one day! Children's programs offer a variety of options from kite flying to talent shows and treasure hunts. The atmosphere on board is friendly, even ebullient, because people worried about whether they were going to have a good time realize they're having a great time.

Wardrobe

Generally, they expect men to wear at least a jacket and tie for formal nights; a lot of men bring tuxedos or dinner jackets. They do not permit shorts in the dining rooms after 6 p.m. On evenings designated semi-formal, they also expect men to wear a jacket. On Tropical and Casual dress code nights, almost anything goes.

Bill of Fare . . . . **B**

Dolphin has always impressed us with the quality and quantity of its embarkation day buffets when many more-expensive cruise lines are doling out sandwiches. Breakfast buffets on the pool deck usually include bacon, eggs, potatoes, French toast, fruit and pastries. Dinners are fairly predictable hotel banquet-type meals, but the homemade breadsticks are delicious and there are always a lot of rich, elaborate desserts that seem to please the multitudes. Menus rotate on a fixed basis and are changed "every couple of years." Midnight buffets are especially big on the three- and four-day sailings, with a themed version scheduled every night, Italian Buffet, Fruit Buffet and Farewell Buffet, plus the Magnificent Buffet on four-night sailings. There's usually a diet dish on every lunch and dinner menu.

Showtime . . . . **C**

The sailings offer a lot of audience participation games including "The Newlywed and Not-So-Newlywed Game," along with disco and casino action, male nightgown competitions and cash bingo, as well as mini-musical revues, variety shows and karaoke contests. The ship's orchestras play quite well for dancing.

Discounts . . . .

Ask your travel agent.

● The Bottom Line ●

These are good economy-priced ships for first-timers who want to spend a week sampling popular Caribbean ports in a casual atmosphere. The staff is friendly and the food tasty, and the ships are kept very clean. The only vessel we felt badly needed some deck maintenance was the *Dolphin IV*, which the line has sold but continues to operate for the new owners.

★ ★
ISLANDBREEZE

The former *Festivale* from Carnival was built in 1961 as the *Transvaal Castle* for Union Castle Lines. It carried mail and passengers between Southampton and Durban, South Africa, then was transferred to South African Marine Corporation and renamed Vaal. Carnival bought it in 1977, and Dolphin acquired it from Carnival in 1996. The *IslandBreeze* is long and sleek with ocean liner lines and vestiges of its previous decor, including a remarkable art deco-style steel stairway, but don't expect a classic cruise ship. This is basic but attractive. It has a lot of sunbathing deck, two swimming pools aft and a small wading pool forward. Most of the cabins are fairly spacious, although more than half of them are insides. The dining room, typical of vessels from this vintage, is amidships on a lower deck without windows.

Lounges can get crowded when the ship is full, but you can usually find stretch-out room on deck.

Between The Lines

The Brochure Says

"The proof is in the pudding. It's also in the passion fruit Caulis, the crispy roast duckling and the broiled lobster tail."

Translation

You can pig out on this ship.

Cabins & Costs

Suites aboard IslandBreeze have private verandas and cozy sitting areas.

Fantasy Suites: C

Average Price Per Person, Double Occupancy, Per Day: $313 plus airfare.
Ten suites with private verandas have twin beds that can be converted to queen-sized, plus a sitting area with sofa that makes into a third bed. The bathroom has a tub.

Small Splurges: C

Average Price PPPD: $270 plus airfare.
Two forward-facing cabins on Veranda Deck are the biggest accommodations on board, larger even than the more expensive veranda suites. Both have queen-sized beds.

Suitable Standards: .... D

Average Price PPPD: $242 plus airfare.
The basic standards are similarly priced whether inside or out. You'll need to specify whether you want twin beds or a queen-sized or double, since they're not convertible. In many, the sink is in the main cabin rather than in the bathroom.

Bottom Bunks: . . . . **D**

Average Price PPPD: $155 plus airfare.

There are only a handful of cabins in the lowest-priced category, all insides with upper and lower berths and all on lower decks. Again, you can expect the sink in the main cabin rather than in the bathroom.

The *IslandBreeze* sails from Santo Domingo on two different itineraries, one visiting Barbados, St. Lucia, Guadeloupe, St. Maarten and St. Thomas, the other visiting Curaçao, Caracas, Grenada, Martinique and St. Croix.

For the price, *IslandBreeze* offers a good getaway—an interesting itinerary on a vintage vessel that still looks like a ship.

Five Favorite Gathering Places

1. The Veranda Deck pool, where everyone pulls their sun loungers into a circle like wagon trains around a campfire.

2. The Gaslight Club Casino and Cafe, where a darkish period feeling prevails, is flanked by two enclosed promenades.

3. The Fanta-Z Disco with its mirrored ceiling and lighted dance floor that blinks in rhythm with the music.

4. The Copacabana Lounge, a vivid parrot carpet and bamboo bentwood chairs lend a tropical look, enhanced by a sunshine-bright ceiling.

5. The Tradewinds Lounge, all rattan tub chairs and ceiling fans; you half-expect to see Peter Lorre in a fez peering from behind a potted palm.

Five Good Reasons to Book This Ship

1. To travel aboard a vintage ship built for ocean crossings.

2. To walk up and down that magnificent steel staircase.

3. To meet the (man, woman) of your dreams at the singles' party (it does happen sometimes).

4. To book one of the modestly priced, fairly sizable cabins with third and fourth berths for the kids.

5. To sail with her around the southern Caribbean.

Five Things You Won't Find On Board

1. A card room.

2. A gym with a view.

3. A cabin designated wheelchair-accessible.

4. A whirlpool spa

5. A hot breakfast from room service.

DOLPHIN CRUISE LINE

ISLANDBREEZE ★★

Registry	**Bahamas**
Officers	**Greek**
Crew	**International**
Complement	**612**
GRT	**31,793**
Length (ft.)	**760**
Beam (ft.)	**90**
Draft (ft.)	**32**
Passengers-Cabins Full	**1400**
Passengers-2/Cabin	**1146**
Passenger Space Ratio	**33.31**
Stability Rating	**Good**
Seatings	**2**
Cuisine	**Continental**
Dress Code	**Traditional/Casual**
Room Service	**Yes**
Tip	**$9 PPPD, 15% automatically added to bar checks**

Ship Amenities

Outdoor Pool	**3**
Indoor Pool	**0**
Jacuzzi	**0**
Fitness Center	**Yes**
Spa	**No**
Beauty Shop	**Yes**
Showroom	**Yes**
Bars/Lounges	**4**
Casino	**Yes**
Shops	**2**
Library	**Yes**
Child Program	**Yes**
Self-Service Laundry	**No**
Elevators	**4**

Cabin Statistics

Suites	**10**
Outside Doubles	**250**
Inside Doubles	**306**
Wheelchair Cabins	**0**
Singles	**0**
Single Surcharge	**150%**
Verandas	**10**
110 Volt	**Yes**

DOLPHIN CRUISE LINE

★ ★ ★
OCEANBREEZE

"We've never been on a cruise before," the young couple confided as they stood by the rail holding hands in the sunset. "Now we're going to save up for a longer one—14 days at least." He went on to say that he works as a mechanic for a municipal bus system; his wife bags groceries at a chain supermarket. Two chic and pretty African-American women who work for the post office were flirting with a Fijian bar steward, and a young punk rocker with purple hair spent most of his port time feeding the sea gulls perched on the ship's rail.

DID YOU KNOW?

One question we've been asked over the years is about timing—how we happened to get into the field of cruise writing 15 years ago before it was generally realized cruising would become a major industry. The answer is easy. The passage above was written on the Azure Seas back in 1981, showing that cruising is for everyone, not just the rich or retired.

A very young Queen Elizabeth II christened this ship as the *Southern Cross* in 1954, when it made the Australia/New Zealand run from Great Britain. It featured several design innovations, including the placement of the funnel and engines at the aft end and the elimination of cargo holds; both features have become commonplace on nearly every passenger ship constructed since. The ship was laid up in Southampton in 1971, then sold to a Greek company in 1973 to be refitted as a cruise vessel named *Calypso*. She sailed the Mediterranean for five years, primarily with British vacation package tourists aboard, then was sold in 1980 to Eastern Steamship Lines and renamed *Calypso I*. In 1981, she was sold to the company's West Coast associates, Western Steamship Lines, named the *Azure Seas* and began sailing on three- and four-day cruises out of Los Angeles to Ensenada, Mexico. Eastern and Western Steamship Lines merged to become Admiral Cruises in 1986, which was subsequently acquired by Royal Caribbean Cruises and disbanded in 1992.

Still handsomely maintained, the *OceanBreeze* shows more than a bit of her art deco background as well as a touch of glitter and glamour from recent makeovers. Cabins are larger than on many ships in this price and age range.

Between The Lines

The Brochure Says

"It's impossible to be bored on board. There's so much to do on a Dolphin ship that you can stay busy around the clock and never do the same activity twice."

Translation

Try it, you'll like it.

Cabins & Costs

Fantasy Suites: .... B+

Average Price Per Person, Double Occupancy, Per Day: $299 plus airfare.
One of the 12 new penthouse suites they added on Boat Deck during a recent refit is called the owner's suite, and faces forward for a great view. With two big rooms—a living room with sofa and chairs, coffee table, minibar and TV, and a bedroom with queen-sized bed and plenty of storage, plus a bath with tub and shower—it's large enough to live in. The sofa makes into a double bed if you want to bring the kids along to share.

Small Splurges: .... B

Average Price PPPD: $270 plus airfare.
The spacious Category 2 double outside cabins on Barbizon Deck are bigger, cheaper and more private than the pricier category 1 cabins on Atlantis Deck, a promenade deck where you have people going past your window all the time. Most have two lower beds or double, and many have a third pulldown berth. The bath has shower only.

Typical outside cabin aboard OceanBreeze

Suitable Standards: .... B

Average Price PPPD: $256 plus airfare.
The Category 3 outside double cabins on Caravelle and Dolphin Decks are adequate, although if you worry about motion sickness, we'd suggest avoiding the ones on Caravelle Deck, which are all forward from the dining room. A deck lower they're amidships for a smoother ride. Most of these have two lower beds but some of the choicest locations—# 239-244—have double beds instead and are near the elevators. Your bathroom will have a shower instead of a tub.

Bottom Bunks: C

Average Price PPPD: $155 plus airfare.
The cheapest cabins aboard are the Category 10 inside doubles on Emerald Deck, and there are only two of them. They have two lower beds or a double and a shower in the bathroom.

The Routes

The ship sails year-round into the Panama Canal as far as Gatun Lake and back out. Montego Bay is home port, with pre- and post-cruise packages for Jamaica available as add-ons. Calls include Cartagena, the San Blas Islands of Panama and Puerto Limon, Costa Rica.

The Scoop

A graceful and dignified ship, the *OceanBreeze* offers a good, medium-priced vacation at sea for first-time cruisers or anyone who wants to get away for a few days. The itinerary includes the Caribbean, Central and South American ports for country collectors.

Insider Tips

Mayfair Lounge aboard OceanBreeze

Five Unforgettable Places

1. The elegantly refurbished two-deck casino with its art deco brass railings and light fixtures.

2. The Cafe Miramar, where buffet breakfasts and lunches are served and late-night cabaret shows sometimes happen.

3. The Mayfair Lounge with its wicker furniture, potted palms and ceiling fans evokes the past. Sunlit during the day, the bay windows offer pleasant sea views; softly lit at night with a pianist playing, it's an appealing spot for a quiet rendezvous.

4. On the other hand, the Rendezvous Show Lounge glitters and sparkles with the evening's main entertainment, which you watch from comfortable swivel tub chairs upholstered in a tight red-and-blue check that looks mauve from a distance. Don't sit behind a post or you'll miss some of the show.

Library aboard OceanBreeze is a comfortable retreat after excursions ashore.

5. The hard-to-find library has always been one of our favorites because it doesn't get much through traffic; books are locked in wood-and-glass bookcases and there are plenty of comfortable dark blue chairs and sofas.

Five Things You Won't Find On Board

1. TV sets in cabins that are not suites.

2. Windows in the dining room.

3. Windows in the disco—it's below the waterline.

4. Cabins designated wheelchair-accessible.

5. A passenger that knows the difference between a boat and a ship.

DOLPHIN CRUISE LINE

OceanBreeze ★★★

Registry	Liberia
Officers	Greek
Crew	International
Complement	400
GRT	21,486
Length (ft.)	604
Beam (ft.)	78
Draft (ft.)	29
Passengers-Cabins Full	980
Passengers-2/Cabin	776
Passenger Space Ratio	28.00
Stability Rating	Good
Seatings	2
Cuisine	Continental
Dress Code	Traditional/Casual
Room Service	Yes
Tip	$9 PPPD, 15% automatically added to bar check

Ship Amenities

Outdoor Pool	1
Indoor Pool	0
Jacuzzi	1
Fitness Center	Yes
Spa	No
Beauty Shop	Yes
Showroom	Yes
Bars/Lounges	3
Casino	Yes
Shops	2
Library	No
Child Program	Yes
Self-Service Laundry	No
Elevators	1

Cabin Statistics

Suites	12
Outside Doubles	226
Inside Doubles	150
Wheelchair Cabins	0
Singles	0
Single Surcharge	150%
Verandas	0
110 Volt	Yes

★ ★ ★
SeaBreeze

The only mystery we kept bumping into was a sign in the main lobby, near the purser's desk, that said Pictures From An Exhibition. How classy, we said, perhaps an art show, an art auction is behind that locked door, or a lounge that presents classical music in the afternoons. The space was shown and neatly labeled in the deck plan bracketed by a pair of restrooms, with nothing more to illuminate it. Finally, the moment came when the doors were unlocked and open. It was the ship photographer's display of the passengers arriving, shaking hands with the captain, coming down the gangway in port and posing in formal clothing on a dress-up night, perhaps the first time since the prom or the wedding pictures. Pictures From An Exhibition. Yes.

The *SeaBreeze* was built as Costa's *Federico C* in 1958 as a two-class ship, then became Premier's *Royale* in 1984. Dolphin acquired her in 1989. There are nine passenger decks, with cabins located on all but two, the topmost deck, where there is a buffet setup, and the bottom most, where the disco is located. During its ownership of the vessel, Premier increased the density both by adding cabins in former deck areas and adding third and fourth berths, so that almost any cabin you book is likely to have additional overhead bunks. The idiosyncratic cabin layout means the configuration of the cabins varies; some have twin beds, some double beds, some bathrooms have tub and shower, some shower only.

CHAMPAGNE TOAST

To the hotel manager of the SeaBreeze, who not only keeps a superbly clean ship but who won't let passengers take their buffet breakfast and lunch trays from the cafe into the adjacent air-conditioned show lounge to eat. There's a sign on the door: No food permitted inside. That's the way it should be–If you want air conditioning, eat lunch in the dining room. If you want a buffet, eat it outdoors on the sunny or shaded deck. But don't spill your food and drink all over the lounges.

Between The Lines

The Brochure Says

"Everyone wants their money's worth, especially on vacation. After all, it's hard to enjoy yourself if you think you're spending too much, too often, and with too little in return. That's why so many cost-conscious travelers cruise with Dolphin. For starters, most everything's included in one low price."

Translation

The appeal is to first-time cruisers, reminding them that many more things are included in the basic fare on ships than they are accustomed to in resort hotels.

The dining room of the SeaBreeze, a very attractive, budget-priced ship.

Cabins & Costs

Fantasy Suites: .... **B+**

Average Price Per Person, Double Occupancy, Per Day: $249 plus airfare.
Seven suites on board are spacious, pretty rooms with king-sized bed, sitting area with sofa and chair, and a long built-in desk/dresser, along with two windows.

If you get B4, you'll have a view forward, a tile bath with tub and a frosted window in the bathroom, the last really rare on ships.

Small Splurges: .... **B**

Average Price PPPD: $213 plus airfare.
Category 2 outside superior cabins are fairly spacious, some of them (# D8, for example) with built-in cabinetry from the 1960s, lovely old coatracks fitted onto the cabin walls with pull-out hangers, brass temperature gauges made in Milan with all the instructions in Italian, left over from the *Federico C* days. We like the cabin despite its obstructed view and its two additional overhead berths.

Suitable Standards: . . . . **C**

Average Price PPPD: $195 plus airfare.
Category 4 cabins are outsides on the lower passenger decks with two lower beds or a double bed (specify which one you want when booking), bathrooms with shower and portholes instead of windows.

Bottom Bunks: . . . . **D**

Average Price PPPD: $142 plus airfare.
The very cheapest cabins on board are two very tiny Category 11 inside cabins with upper and lower berths forward on Isolde Deck, the lowest deck with passenger cabins. (The only one lower is the Juliet Deck, where the disco is located.)

The Routes

The *SeaBreeze* sails every Sunday form Miami to the Western Caribbean, visiting Playa del Carmen/Cozumel, Montego Bay and Grand Cayman.

The Scoop

When we were last aboard the *SeaBreeze*, we were tremendously impressed at how clean and fresh she looks, especially given her age and her background as a veteran of the children's crusades over at Premier, when she was the *Royale*. Frankly, this ship is kept more spic-and-span than a lot of fancy new vessels built in the 1980s. It's a good economy-priced vessel for first-timers who want to sample the Western Caribbean in a non-intimidating atmosphere.

Insider Tips

Five Special Places

1. The Water Music Whirlpool, a trio of Jacuzzi pools surrounded by rows of plastic loungers, is on the aft end of the Boheme Deck.

2. The Prelude Bar is an intimate little lounge with very comfortable swivel rattan barstools, a varnished teak floor and latticework walls, plus lots of healthy fresh green plants.

3. The Casino, with some rare five-cent slot machines among the 99 one-armed bandits, plus four blackjack tables, one Caribbean stud and one roulette.

4. Royal Fireworks Lounge, wide rather than deep, with curved sofas, wood tables, blue and mauve chairs and an oval dance floor in wood parquet.

5. The Carmen Lounge, a show lounge filled with swivel tub chairs in rose or sage, round wooden cocktail tables, bar with eight stools, and very poor sightlines.

Five Good Reasons to Book This Ship

1. The price is right.

2. To go snorkeling in Cozumel.

3. To climb Dunn's River Falls in Jamaica.

4. To be one of the displays at Pictures From An Exhibition.

5. You could get married on board—and sail away on a wonderful honeymoon. Have your travel agent contact the Wedding Coordinator at Dolphin to find out about five different wedding packages from $275 to $750.

SEABREEZE ★★★

Registry	**Panama**
Officers	**Greek**
Crew	**International**
Complement	**400**
GRT	**21,000**
Length (ft.)	**605**
Beam (ft.)	**79**
Draft (ft.)	**29**
Passengers-Cabins Full	**1100**
Passengers-2/Cabin	**840**
Passenger Space Ratio	**25.00**
Stability Rating	**Good**
Seatings	**2**
Cuisine	**Continental**
Dress Code	**Traditional/Casual**
Room Service	**Yes**
Tip	**$9 PPPD, 15% automatically added to bar check**

Ship Amenities

Outdoor Pool	**1**
Indoor Pool	**0**
Jacuzzi	**3**
Fitness Center	**Yes**
Spa	**No**
Beauty Shop	**Yes**
Showroom	**Yes**
Bars/Lounges	**3**
Casino	**Yes**
Shops	**2**
Library	**No**
Child Program	**Yes**
Self-Service Laundry	**No**
Elevators	**2**

Cabin Statistics

Suites	**7**
Outside Doubles	**253**
Inside Doubles	**160**
Wheelchair Cabins	**0**
Singles	**1**
Single Surcharge	**150%**
Verandas	**0**
110 Volt	**Yes**

ESPLANADE TOURS

581 Boylston Street, Boston, MA 02116
☎ (617) 266-7465, (800) 426-5492

Exotic Bali is one of the most popular dream ports for dedicated travelers.

Esplanade Tours of Boston is the North American marketing representative for Noble Caledonia Ltd. and Spice Island Cruises.

In cooperation with Noble Caledonia, Esplanade markets the newly acquired *Oceanic Odyssey*, the former *Oceanic Grace* from Oceanic Cruises, on expedition cruises in India, the South Pacific and the Far East. The ship carries 115 passengers and was built in Japan in 1989.

Spice Island Cruises operates the *Bali Sea Dancer*, the former *Illiria*, on three- and four-day cruises out of Bali.

Esplanade also markets the *MS Regency* on seven-night Nile sailings from Luxor.

★ ★ ★ ⚓⚓⚓⚓
BALI SEA DANCER

Bali has a way of softly and sweetly dictating its own terms. Tourism is the main industry here, and Bali is expert at it. It is street theater raised to an exquisitely detailed level, and everyone has to play. This is no place for a cynic, or even a pragmatist. It is a well-worn island, lush and green, most of it lovingly terraced and sculpted so often over the centuries that there is probably no inch of landscape that has not been rearranged a dozen times.

The *Bali Sea Dancer*, built as the *Illiria* in Italy in 1962, is quite pretty, long and low with yachtlike lines, a short wide funnel and a lot of wood and polished brass. The food aboard is tasty, with fresh fruit, big hearty breakfasts and—the culinary highlight—a big Dutch/Indonesian *rijsttafel*, the traditional Dutch planter's feast of rice topped with meats, seafood, vegetables, sauces, coconut and pickled and spiced side dishes. The Indonesian crew is fluent in English, eager to serve and always remembers your name and favorite libation.

• Between The Lines •

The Brochure Says

"On shore there's even more to see and do. Dive the exquisite reefs with our onboard Dive Master. Or you can snorkel or just paddle about in the crystal clear waters. A number of enthralling cultural tours are offered at each destination. And each stop promises to be handicraft heaven for the shoppers amongst you."

Translation

Not only is it a lovely ship to cruise the waters of Indonesia aboard, but look at everything you can do in the ports of call.

Cabins & Costs

Fantasy Suites: . . . . **N/A**
N/A

Small Splurges: . . . . **B**
Average Price Per Person, Double Occupancy, Per Day: $310 plus airfare.
A couple of deluxe cabins with floral bedspreads and matching easy chairs, wooden nightstand and bathroom with tub and shower are the most spacious and comfortable quarters aboard.

Suitable Standards: . . . . **C**
Average Price PPPD: $220 plus airfare.
All the cabins on the ship are on the small side; the outside mid-category doubles have two lower beds (some also with a third berth), a three-drawer wooden cabinet and a vanity stool, two hanging closets and a large tile bathroom almost as big as the bedroom, with shower, makeup mirror and storage for toilet articles.

Bottom Bunks: . . . . **C**
Average Price PPPD: $150 plus airfare.
The nine inside cabins are actually larger than many of the outside cabins, and contain the same furnishings as the Suitable Standards described above.

The Routes

The *Bali Sea Dancer* sails on Fridays for a three-day cruise to Komodo, home of the famous Komodo dragons, and Badas, Sumbawa, to see the buffalo races. A four-day cruise adds the unspoiled island of Lombok to the itinerary.

The Scoop

This is a comfortable, well-riding ship with more class and luxury than you would expect to find in short-cruise vessels going out of Bali. It is highly recommended for people who enjoy expedition cruises as well as people looking for a warm-weather, watersports-oriented holiday.

Insider Tips

Five Easy Places

1. The library, one of the most charming at sea, displays reproductions of Greek art, and has a small ornamental fireplace, sofas, chairs, wooden game tables and writing tables, as well as a good collection of books about nature, geography and wildlife.

2. The pool deck has a buffet setup at one end, a sheltered area for chairs and tables; the pool is fairly large with a wide wooden rim that provides extra seating.

3. The Ikat Lounge has a small wood dance floor, six columns that support the ceiling wrapped in tree-trunk-like material, wood coffee tables, chairs and sofas and arrangements of fresh tropical flowers.

The Ikat Lounge is a relaxing place to unwind after dinner.

4. The reception area and purser's square are furnished with comfortable leather chairs and hassocks, wood walls with a rubbed satiny finish; glass-and-wood French doors open to the deck.

5. The Orchid Dining Room has very attentive service but can get crowded when the ship is full.

Five Good Reasons to Book This Ship

1. To see a Komodo dragon.

2. To dive the reefs.

3. To sample some of the delicious cuisine of Indonesia.

4. To sail from Bali on three- and four-day cruises, just right to add onto a land visit.

5. To watch the buffalo races in Badas.

Five Things You Won't Find On Board

1. A casino.

2. A large gym; the tiny one on board has a treadmill, two stationary bikes and an adjacent sauna.

3. A level cabin floor at either end of the ship.

4. A good view from the forward observation deck; the curve of the bow inhibits looking ahead.

5. A fire in the library's fireplace.

BALI SEA DANCER ★★★, ⚓⚓⚓

Registry	**Indonesia**
Officers	**Indonesian**
Crew	**Indonesian**
Crew	**90**
GRT	**4.000**
Length (ft.)	**329.5**
Beam (ft.)	**47.6**
Draft (ft.)	**16.3**
Passengers-Cabins Full	**150**
Passengers-2/Cabin	**146**
Passenger Space Ratio	**27.39**
Stability Rating	**Good**
Seatings	**1**
Cuisine	**International**
Dress Code	**Casual**
Room Service	**Yes**
Tip	**$4 PPPD**

Ship Amenities

Outdoor Pool	**1**
Indoor Pool	**0**
Jacuzzi	**0**
Fitness Center	**Yes**
Spa	**No**
Beauty Shop	**Yes**
Showroom	**No**
Bars/Lounges	**1**
Casino	**No**
Shops	**1**
Library	**Yes**
Child Program	**No**
Self-Service Laundry	**Yes**
Elevators	**0**

Cabin Statistics

Suites	**2**
Outside Doubles	**62**
Inside Doubles	**9**
Wheelchair Cabins	**0**
Singles	**0**
Single Surcharge	**150%**
Verandas	**0**
110 Volt	**No**

★ ★ ★ ★
OCEANIC ODYSSEY

The ship itself looks like a cross between Sea Goddess and Seabourn, with a yachtlike sleekness and a gleaming white finish. And the owners admit that the 116-passenger Sea Goddess ships were the image they had in mind when the project began, except that they wanted to have a bigger ship that would carry the same number of passengers. So they went for a gross registry tonnage of 5050 tons, compared with Sea Goddess's 4260 and Seabourn's 10,000. (Seabourn carries 212 passengers.)

Cabins are spacious and modular, all almost precisely the same size, except for a suite measuring 363 square feet, and are laid out forward and amidships on four decks, with public areas aft on the same four decks. Above is a Sun Deck with jogging track. And there's also a gymnasium, two saunas, swimming pool and Jacuzzi.

Between The Lines

The Brochure Says

"The atmosphere is more akin to a private yacht than a cruise ship."

Translation

An elegant small ship with single meal seating and spacious cabins, the *Oceanic Odyssey* will feel like your own personal yacht.

Cabins & Costs

Fantasy Suites: . . . . **A**

Average Price Per Person, Double Occupancy, Per Day: NA.

While all cabins aboard are suites, one of them is much larger, with 363 square feet of space. It has spacious sitting area, separate bedroom, generous wardrobe space and luxurious bath.

Small Splurges: . . . . **A**

While all the cabins are the same general size and rated at the same value in the brochures, eight of them, the cabins on Deck 6 numbered 601-608, have private balconies, worth making a play for.

Suitable Standards: . . . . **A**

Average Price PPPD: $325 plus airfare; price varies widely depending on season, destinations and length of cruise.
On this all-suites ship, the 56 cabins measure 191 square feet each and contain a choice of twin or queen-sized beds, loveseat, chair and table, built-in desk/dresser with wide counter and TV set with VCR, generous use of mirrors and wood paneling, fairly good closet space, a minibar, mini-refrigerator, vanity, terry-cloth robes, toiletries and safe. The marble-trimmed bathroom has a Japanese-style tub, short and deep; if you're tall, you'll sit with your knees tucked under your chin.

Bottom Bunks: . . . . **NA**

See Suitable Standards, above.

The Routes

The *Oceanic Odyssey* begins in November with a 14-day voyage through the Java Sea from Singapore to Bali, followed by a 15-day cruise from Bali to Australia's Barrier Reef and Cairns. For Christmas holidays the ship sails around Australasia, followed by a New Zealand coastal voyage. In early spring the ship makes a 19-day expedition sailing from New Zealand to Fiji. When not deployed in long cruises, the ship will follow similar short itineraries in Indonesia similar to the *Bali Sea Dancer.*

The Scoop

This lovely ship, which is virtually unknown in the Untied States, deserves a look-see from veteran cruisers who love exotic ports and small luxury vessels.

OCEANIC ODYSSEY　★★★★

Registry	NA
Officers	European
Crew	Indonesian
Complement	70
GRT	5,050
Length (ft.)	336
Beam (ft.)	50
Draft (ft.)	13
Passengers-Cabins Full	115
Passengers-2/Cabin	114
Passenger Space Ratio	44.29
Stability Rating	Good
Seatings	1
Cuisine	Continental
Dress Code	Traditional
Room Service	NA
Tip	NA

Ship Amenities

Outdoor Pool	1
Indoor Pool	0
Jacuzzi	1
Fitness Center	Yes
Spa	No
Beauty Shop	Yes
Showroom	No
Bars/Lounges	3
Casino	No
Shops	1
Library	Yes
Child Program	No
Self-Service Laundry	No
Elevators	1

Cabin Statistics

Suites	57
Outside Doubles	0
Inside Doubles	0
Wheelchair Cabins	1
Singles	0
Single Surcharge	NA
Verandas	8
110 Volt	Yes

EUR☉CRUISES
INCORPORATED

303 West 13th Street, New York, NY 10014
☎ *(212) 691-2099, (800) 688-EURO*

St. Xavier in St. Petersburg is visited on **Kristina Regina** *cruises.*

History . . . .

EuroCruises is the largest North American marketer of ships to Europe, representing ships, ferries, riverboats and canal barges that are owned and operated by various European companies. In 1998 it also offers Fred. Olsen Line sailings to Asia and South America.

For North Americans looking for a particularly European experience, often on smaller, simpler vessels than today's glittering megaliners, Bjarne "BJ" Mikkelsen and Maria Conte can help. They focus on European ships that sail in European waters, with an emphasis on the Baltic Sea and St. Petersburg as destinations, as well as the Black Sea. They also market year-round sailings in the Red Sea, expeditions to Iceland and Russia's Arctic, and river cruises on the Danube, Volga, Moselle and Rhine, as well as canal sailings on Sweden's historic Gota Canal. For information on river and canal cruises, see Alternative Cruises, (page 66).

Among the most unusual cruises the company represents are the ice-breakers *Nordbris* and *Polarstar*, which cruise to polar bear country in Spitsbergen on four- and seven-night cruises. The *Nordbris* carries 38 passengers, the *Polarstar* 25.

For North Americans traveling around Northern Europe, EuroCruises also markets the splashy ferries of Scandinavian Seaways and Viking Line, which offer year-round service between major capitals such as St. Petersburg, Helsinki, Copenhagen, Stockholm, Oslo, Tallinn and Riga.

★ ★ ★
AUSONIA

She's laid out and ready for sun and fun, with a lighthearted Italian lilt, and she sails along the sparkling Turquoise Coast of Turkey and to the citrus-scented island of Cyprus, where the roadways are lined with cypress trees so dense they form a tunnel, and the "typical local lunch" we sampled consisted of 20 different hot and cold dishes.

Grimaldi Cruises' *Ausonia*, fourth in the line to carry this name, was built in Italy's Monfalcone yard in 1956–57 for Adriatica SAN as a three-class ship and put into Trieste-Beirut service before her long career as a popular Mediterranean cruise ship. Her most recent makeover was in 1991.

The vessel is literally all decked out for Mediterranean sunshine, with her expansive aft pool decks on two levels, both surrounded with plenty of teak deck as well as cooler, shaded areas with tables and chairs. The interior is clean and comfortable with adequate if not exactly cutting-edge decor. Eight passenger decks include five with cabins on them and elevators to most but not all passenger sleeping areas. A single public-room deck has the dining room, show lounge, library, disco, shops, bars and card room packed into the space.

Between The Lines

The Brochure Says

"A truly all-inclusive holiday, all meals, à lá carte luncheons and dinners, afternoon tea with pastries, complimentary red wine (in carafe) at lunch and dinner, Captain's Welcome Cocktail, movie shows, dancing every evening to the orchestra, nightly entertainment, Piano Bar, Disco until early hours, deck games, swimming pool, card room, safe for your valuables, library, deck chairs, gymnasium, Jacuzzi."

Translation

Veteran cruisers take far too much for granted. It takes a page of copy like this, obviously aimed at first-time cruisers, to realize what a good deal we really get. And hey, did you notice the *vin ordinaire c'est inclus?*

Cabins & Costs

Fantasy Suites: .... B

Average Price Per Person, Double Occupancy, Per Day: $280 plus airfare.

There are six junior suites on board named for Italian composers, of which we'd tout the Verdi and Donizetti, forward on the Bahia Deck, over the others amidships two decks down on Delphi, because they have a better view. What you get is a two-room suite with living room—sofa, chairs, coffee table, built-in cabinetry and chests—a bedroom with two lower beds, nightstand and closets, and a bathroom with tub. Naturally, they include the Le Club perks described below (see Five Good Reasons to Book This Ship).

Small Splurges: C

Average Price PPPD: $250 plus airfare.

Category 9 cabins have two lower beds, a tub in the bathroom, a minibar, the Le Club extras, a banquette, TV, and desk/dresser with chair.

Suitable Standards: C

Average Price PPPD: $200 plus airfare.

An outside double with two lower beds, nightstand, bath with shower, and sometimes a fold-down third berth, plus a bathroom with shower.

Bottom Bunks: .... D

Average Price PPPD: $167 plus airfare.

The cheapest digs on this ship are the four-berth insides, spacious as a Scandinavian ferry (which means, not very). Cabins do have a private bath with shower.

The Routes

The *Ausonia* perambulates around the Mediterranean between late March and late October, calling, depending on itinerary, in France, Spain, Italy, Greece, Egypt, Israel, Cyprus, Turkey, Tunisia, Morocco, Malta, Sardinia, Corsica and Syria.

The Scoop

When you get down to where the hoi polloi sleeps, the price is reasonable and your fellow travelers are almost certainly young stay-up-late types. You'll be subjected to the usual five-language announcements, but they publish a daily program in English and perhaps you'll enjoy meeting the Continental crowd.

Insider Tips

Five Special Spots

1. The big Jacuzzi pool, aft on the Bahia Deck, is usually full of kids and young people—but this ship draws a lot of young people anyhow.

2. The Ball Room Majorca is the largest lounge on board; this is where the dancing girls come on and kick 'em high.

3. The disco goes on until the wee small hours with a lot of great (and not so great) bodies gyrating; the junior officers show up here.

4. The free-form pool and shallow-water surround on Athena Deck is a great place to lie in cool water while sunbathing.

5. The cozy Lounge Venezia is a good place to meet for a quiet drink.

Five Good Reasons to Book This Ship

1. Honeymooners and seniors get a discount off the published rate.

2. Because it's Italian; there are two meal seatings for that pasta, fashionably late, the early at 7 p.m., the late at 8:45.

3. Because it goes to some of the most exotic ports in the Med—Limassol, Casablanca, Antalya, Latakia, Alexandria, Tangier and Tartous.

4. Because you can book a Le Club cabin and get a bonus bottle of Italian champagne (a.k.a. Spumante) and fresh fruit daily.

5. Because in the European fashion (without those dreary cabotage laws) you can get on and off in any of several ports, completing a seven-day cruise from whichever city you prefer.

Five Things You Won't Find On Board

1. The certainty of a call at Capri; if the weather doesn't permit anchoring and tendering, the ship goes on to Naples instead.

2. Good sightlines in the show lounge—if you sit in the back during the dance routines, you'll see only the t and not the a.

3. A crew member who doesn't speak at least a little English—except maybe down in the engine room.

4. A casino; Italians don't want Italian-flag ships offering gambling in Italian waters.

5. A wheelchair-accessible cabin; companionways are steep and passageways narrow on this vintage vessel.

AUSONIA   ★★★

Registry	**Italy**
Officers	**Italian**
Crew	**Italian**
Complement	**220**
GRT	**13,000**
Length (ft.)	**523**
Beam (ft.)	**70**
Draft (ft.)	**17.5**
Passengers-Cabins Full	**550**
Passengers-2/Cabin	**497**
Passenger Space Ratio	**26.15**
Stability Rating	**Good**
Seatings	**2**
Cuisine	**Italian**
Dress Code	**Informal**
Room Service	**No**
Tip	**N/A**

Ship Amenities

Outdoor Pool	**1**
Indoor Pool	**0**
Jacuzzi	**1**
Fitness Center	**No**
Spa	**No**
Beauty Shop	**Yes**
Showroom	**Yes**
Bars/Lounges	**3**
Casino	**No**
Shops	**1**
Library	**Yes**
Child Program	**No**
Self-Service Laundry	**No**
Elevators	**1**

Cabin Statistics

Suites	**6**
Outside Doubles	**140**
Inside Doubles	**101**
Wheelchair Cabins	**0**
Singles	**3**
Single Surcharge	**140%**
Verandas	**0**
110 Volt	**No**

★ ★ ★
AZUR

We think of the Azur in the same fond terms we remember the longtime "Follies" show girl who triumphantly belts out "I'm Still Here" in the musical. We were aboard during her Paquet period in the early 1980s when the French cruise company was trying to build a U.S. market. They were so anxious they even offered a bacon and eggs breakfast and American coffee on board—and you know how the French hate that.

The *Azur*, which sails under the Azur-Bolero Cruises banner these days, was built as the deep-sea ferry *Eagle* in France in 1970–71 for P & O's ferry division, and in 1975 went over to Nouvelle Cie de Paquebots for ferry service out of Marseilles, when she was renamed *Azur*. She was rebuilt as a cruise ship in 1981, when cabins were added to her car-carrying decks, most of them obviously insides, which is why she has more inside than outside cabins. She sailed for Paquet until 1987, when she went over to Chandris Fantasy Cruises and was renamed *The Azur*, dropped out of sight for a while and then resurfaced later in the early 1990s when she was put out to charter under Classical Cruises, EuroCruises and other banners. With seven passenger decks, five of them carrying cabins, she's a fairly dense vessel but has all the traditional cruise ship niceties from the early 1980s, from cinema to playroom, two swimming pools and two major lounges. They suggest men wear a jacket and tie and women a cocktail dress to dinners. And like her passengers, the *Azur* looks spiffy these days.

The Brochure Says

"The 750-passenger vessel is made for leisurely cruising. It offers spacious cocktail bars, lavish midnight buffets, and a host of onboard program activities including aerobics, karaoke and casino gambling."

Translation
See how with-it we are—even offering karaoke.

Cabins & Costs

Fantasy Suites: . . . . **N/A**
   N/A

Small Splurges: . . . . **N/A**
   N/A

Suitable Standards: . . . . **C+**
   Average Price Per Person, Double Occupancy, Per Day: $195 plus airfare.
   The cabins are all fairly comparable, with all the outside standards similar in size and
   furnishings. Two lower beds, a desk/dresser with chair, perhaps a second chair and
   coffee table if you've booked one of the pricier categories. The top-priced cabins
   have tub/shower combinations, all others have shower only.

Bottom Bunks: . . . . **C**
   Average Price PPPD: $111 plus airfare.
   The cheapest inside double cabins are fairly spacious with two lower berths (and
   some quads with two uppers as well) and have similar furnishings to the Suitable
   Standards, above.

The Routes

The *Azur* cruises the Greek Islands and Eastern Mediterranean roundtrip from Venice
most of the summer, with a couple of longer repositioning spring and fall cruises to and
from Genoa, plus winter sailings in the Canary Islands, Egypt and North Africa.

The Scoop

It's a good buy for cruisers watching their budgets. Even the lowest-priced inside cabins have two lower beds and enough room to change your mind. The itinerary is good,
with some beach and shopping time worked in, not always common on seven-day Greek
Islands sailings, and an added bonus is cruising through the Corinth Canal.

Insider Tips

Five Special Places

1. The Lounge Deck swimming pool is a bit larger than the Sun Deck swimming pool,
    but the fact that there are two pools will brighten your Mediterranean cruise.

2. A really proper cinema with a balcony and rows of theater seats on a raked level
    makes the Rialto Cinema a favorite.

3. The casino, of course, on this Panamanian-flag vessel with Greek officers and no
    Machiavellian Italian rules to get in the way

4. The Tahiti Lounge with its wicker chairs and tropical laziness is a combination
    disco, bar and buffet cafe.

5.   The Azur show lounge with its reflective ceiling and swivel tub chairs is where you see the entertainment.

Five Good Reasons to Book This Ship

1.   The airfare is included from New York with some good add-on package rates from other cities.

2.   A seven-day roundtrip Greek Isles sailing from Venice with eight ports of call plus cruising the Corinth Canal and a technical call in Bari, where they don't let you get off the ship.

3.   To visit the blue caves of Zakynthos.

4.   To play squash at the only squash court at sea—now that the *Seawind Crown* removed hers.

5.   The cabins are relatively spacious for a Mediterranean cruise ship in this price range.

Five Things You Won't Find On Board

1.   A shop or bar that takes U.S. dollars; you spend Italian *lira* on this ship.

2.   A private veranda.

3.   A lunch without pasta.

4.   A bad sport—not with squash, volleyball, ping pong, trap shooting, gymnasium and bodybuilding center available.

5.   Late-night hunger; you get a midnight buffet followed an hour later, at 1 a.m., by pizza and a snack.

AZUR ★ ★ ★

Registry	Panama
Officers	Greek
Crew	International
Complement	325
GRT	15,000
Length (ft.)	466
Beam (ft.)	72
Draft (ft.)	20
Passengers-Cabins Full	770
Passengers-2/Cabin	661
Passenger Space Ratio	22.69
Stability Rating	Good
Seatings	2
Cuisine	Italian
Dress Code	Informal
Room Service	Yes
Tip	N/A

Ship Amenities

Outdoor Pool	2
Indoor Pool	0
Jacuzzi	0
Fitness Center	No
Spa	No
Beauty Shop	Yes
Showroom	Yes
Bars/Lounges	5
Casino	Yes
Shops	1
Library	Yes
Child Program	Yes
Self-Service Laundry	No
Elevators	3

Cabin Statistics

Suites	0
Outside Doubles	146
Inside Doubles	180
Wheelchair Cabins	0
Singles	93
Single Surcharge	160–170%
Verandas	0
110 Volt	No

★★★
BLACK PRINCE

We still remember being stunned by the watersports platform on the stern of the Black Prince *that was added in the 1987 refit. That was ahead of Seabourn's collapsible wire mesh swimming pool but after Sea Goddess's more modest watersports platform.*

Fred. Olsen Cruise Lines' *Black Prince*, a favorite of the British cruise market, was built in Germany in 1966, and boasts not only one of the earliest watersports marina platforms but also the biggest—60 feet long when it's all in place. The Marina Park extends from the stern when the ship is at anchor to allow passengers to swim in a collapsible wire mesh pool with teak decking around it, or sail, water-ski or windsurf off a watersports platform. It's used most frequently in the Canary Islands or in quiet Mediterranean and Caribbean bays away from shipping traffic.

The *Black Prince* has seven passenger decks, with cabins concentrated on four of them. The main public room deck is anchored with a lounge at either end and restaurants amidships.

The Brochure Says

"These days there are all sorts of holidays to choose from. Beach holidays and city holidays, cultural holidays and holidays crammed full of activities. But there's one break that combines them all and does it without you having to check in and out of countless hotels, jump on and off planes, trains and automobiles. It's a cruise."

Translation

None necessary.

Cabins & Costs

Note: Unlike North America, European lines' published rates are their actual prices.

Fantasy Suites: .... **N/A**
N/A

Small Splurges: .... **B**
Average Per Person Double Occupancy Per Day: $347 plus airfare.
There are four larger-than-average deluxe double outside on the topmost Marquee Deck, attractively decorated, with two lower beds, a new in-house video system and bath with tub and shower.

Suitable Standards: .... **B**
Average Price PPPD: $240 plus airfare.
Outside cabins with two lower beds may mean two real beds, one bed and one sofa, or one bed and one Pullman bed that folds into the wall. These cabins have bath with shower only. There are also "family cabins" with a double bed, one lower and one upper berth; a wide range of inside and outside singles; and the possibility of creating a two-room suite out of certain adjoining cabins on Marina Deck.

Bottom Bunks: .... **C**
Average Price PPPD: $157 plus airfare.
The little inside three-berth cabins are the low man on the *Black Prince* totem pole, with two lower beds and one upper berth. There is also fairly limited wardrobe space in the lower category cabins.

The Routes

The *Black Prince* sails to South America for a 37-night voyage leaving Dover January 17 and calling in Barbados, Trinidad, Devil's Island, and several Brazilian Amazon ports. The ship also cruises the Canary Islands in winter. Eastern and western Mediterranean itineraries and Northern Europe sailings round out the summer schedule. Early booking discounts are offered.

The Scoop

This is a sparkling clean, very sophisticated ship with a dedicated following in the United Kingdom. Cruises average 12 to 30 days in length, and discounts are offered for two back-to-back sailings as well as early bookings. The main problem we find is that most of the cabins don't offer a lot of wardrobe space, although the ship will store your "trunks and suitcases" down the hall in special closets for you.

Insider Tips

Five Favorite Principalities

1. The Aquitaine Lounge, a place to slip away and read in the daytime or sip before-dinner cocktails to piano music.

2. Neptune Lounge is where the evening entertainment happens with all those chorus girls, plus daytime fun and games when one of them just might be calling bingo.

3. The Video Lounge, where you can watch a movie on video (if you must).

4. The Marquee Restaurant is a top deck sidewalk cafe under canvas where you can breakfast or lunch alfresco.

5. The Sauna Deck, to steam out your aches, get a massage, exercise or have your hair done.

Five Good Reasons to Book This Ship

1. So you can become a member of the Fred. Olsen Cruise Lines Club and get perks on future sailings.

2. To take a games theme cruise, a whole sailing built around lots of Scrabble, Clue and Trivial Pursuit.

3. To visit the Canary Islands, Morocco or the Amazon for a little winter sunshine.

4. If you're over 62, you get a five percent senior discount; if you book certain soft sailings, you'll get 10 percent off.

5. To sail with the Norwegians to Norway.

Five Things You Won't Find On Board

1. Free 24-hour room service; there's a small fee for cabin service.

2. Ashtrays in the ship's indoor restaurant; smoking is not permitted there.

3. A visitor; *Black Prince* security systems do not permit them.

4. U.S. dollars; all accounts are run in pounds sterling.

5. Sloppy dressers; a jacket and tie are required for informal evenings, a dark suit or dinner jacket for formal evenings.

BLACK PRINCE   ★★★

Registry	**Norway**
Officers	**Norwegian**
Crew	**Filipino**
Crew	**200**
GRT	**11,209**
Length (ft.)	**460**
Beam (ft.)	**70**
Draft (ft.)	**19**
Passengers-Cabins Full	**433**
Passengers-2/Cabin	**395**
Passenger Space Ratio	**28.37**
Stability Rating	**Good**
Seatings	**2**
Cuisine	**International**
Dress Code	**Traditional**
Room Service	**Yes**
Tip	**$7 PPPD**

Ship Amenities

Outdoor Pool	**1**
Indoor Pool	**1**
Jacuzzi	**1**
Fitness Center	**Yes**
Spa	**No**
Beauty Shop	**Yes**
Showroom	**Yes**
Bars/Lounges	**3**
Casino	**Yes**
Shops	**2**
Library	**Yes**
Child Program	**No**
Self-Service Laundry	**No**
Elevators	**2**

Cabin Statistics

Suites	**0**
Outside Doubles	**149**
Inside Doubles	**33**
Wheelchair Cabins	**2**
Singles	**31**
Single Surcharge	**120%**
Verandas	**0**
110 Volt	**No**

★★★★
BLACK WATCH*

The first cruise we ever took, in what seems like eons ago, was aboard one of the Royal Viking ships in the days before the "stretch" (when the ship was cut in half and a new midsection of additional cabins and public space inserted). We cruised in Alaska, and thought it was the most magical vacation anyone could possibly have. Now, some 200 cruises later, we still do.

The *Black Watch* is the former *Star Odyssey/Royal Viking Star*, comfortably midsized, and carrying around 750 passengers. Cabins are built in the modular style, so all except the suites are about the same size with similar furnishings, and the prices differ only by the deck you choose.

Cabins & Costs

Fantasy Suites: . . . . **A**

Average Price Per Person, Double Occupancy, Per Day: $468 plus air fare in Europe.
The three owner's suite apartments with private veranda have separate bedroom and sitting room, small veranda, large bath and walk-in closet. Twin or queen-sized beds, voluminous storage space, a graceful living room with sofa, several chairs and coffee table, adequate for entertaining, a bathroom with tub and shower, TV/VCR, hair dryer and mini-refrigerator provide all the comforts of home.

Small Splurges: . . . . **B**

Average Price PPPD: $320 plus air fare in Europe.
There are about three dozen of the JS suites spread around the ship. These are comfortable cabins with picture windows, sitting areas with sofa, chair and coffee table, bathroom with tub and shower, TV, hair dryers and mini-refrigerator.

Suitable Standards: . . . . **B**

Average Price PPPD: $216 plus air fare in Europe.

Cabins are built on a modular plan, so all are about the same size with the same furnishings; the major difference is which deck you're on and whether you're amidships, forward or aft. The F category deluxe outside staterooms on the Coral Deck are typical, with portholes rather than windows, bathroom with tub and shower (in a few cases, shower only—ask when booking if it's important), TV and hair dryer.

Bottom Bunks: .... **B**

Average Price PPPD: $191 plus air fare in Europe.

The lowest-priced category is I, a deluxe inside on the lowest passenger deck with two lower beds, bath with shower only, hair dryer and TV set, as well as a desk/dresser with chair, another chair and table, large closet.

The Routes

The *Black Watch* cruises through the Middle East to Asia January to the end of March, followed by European sailings from Dover.

The Scoop

A lot of money was spent both on the cosmetic and the behind-the-scenes upgrading and updating of this vintage vessel. If anything, the makeovers have turned it into a more sophisticated vessel, particularly in the public rooms and bars, where there is more and longer cocktail service than there used to be. Older couples and singles in particular will find this ship offers an appealing, traditional cruise of the same high quality they used to enjoy on Royal Viking and Royal Cruise Line.

Insider Tips

A handsome bar adjacent to the show lounge is where regulars congregate.

Five Favorite Spots

1. The Panorama forward observation lounge with its wide windows and swivel leather chairs where you can sit transfixed by the view all day long.

2. The Seven Seas Lounge and Terrace replaces what we used to call the morning bar, because everybody used to gather there about 11 or so with Bloody Marys and sing along to the pianist's popular melodies.

3. The bar adjacent to the show lounge with rose tapestry sofas and tub chairs, oval marble tables and a long bar with swivel leather stools where the regulars congregate before dinner.

4. The fitness area with enclosed gym and sauna on the top deck.

5. The deck area mini-galley.

BLACK WATCH* ★★★★

Registry	Norway
Officers	Norwegian
Crew	Filipino
Complement	410
GRT	28,000
Length (ft.)	676
Beam (ft.)	83
Draft (ft.)	24
Passengers-Cabins Full	821
Passengers-2/Cabin	775
Passenger Space Ratio	36.12
Stability Rating	Good
Seatings	2
Cuisine	International
Dress Code	Traditional
Room Service	Yes
Tip	$7 PPPD

Ship Amenities

Outdoor Pool	1
Indoor Pool	0
Jacuzzi	3
Fitness Center	Yes
Spa	Yes
Beauty Shop	Yes
Showroom	Yes
Bars/Lounges	6
Casino	Yes
Shops	2
Library	Yes
Child Program	No
Self-Service Laundry	Yes
Elevators	5

Cabin Statistics

Suites	54
Outside Doubles	279
Inside Doubles	33
Wheelchair Cabins	4
Singles	48
Single Surcharge	120%
Verandas	9
110 Volt	Yes

EUROCRUISES, INC.

★ ★ ★
BOLERO

As the Starward, *she was the first ship built especially for cruising in the Caribbean; the only ship sailing year-round ahead of her was the* Sunward I, *which had been repositioned from the Mediterranean.*

The last of the old Norwegian Cruise Line "white ships" to bite the dust, the former *Starward*, has become the *Bolero* for Azur-Bolero Cruises, and began service with the Christmas cruise at the end of 1995. *Starward* was also the first of the trio of new-builds for Norwegian Cruise Line between 1968 and 1971.

Cabins & Costs

Fantasy Suites: C

Average Price Per Person, Double Occupancy, Per Day: $282 plus airfare.
Not really fantastic, but adequate unto the need—the ship's six outside deluxe suites. A separate sitting area can be curtained off from the sleeping area, and has a sofa that can be made into a bed, chairs, desk/dresser, coffee table, mini-refrigerator, and a big double closet with plenty of storage. The white tile bathrooms have tub, bidet and a long sink counter.

Small Splurges: C

Average Price PPPD: $263 plus airfare.
Two other similar suites amidships on a lower deck have a double bed and sitting area with a convertible sofa bed and lounge chair.

Suitable Standards: . . . . D

Average Price PPPD: $206 plus airfare.
The basic cabin has two lower beds, a window, a small nightstand with drawers, a tiny desk, a shelf in the window and a curtain rather than doors covering the hanging closet space, which allows only about 12 inches of free space before a built-in

cabinet underneath begins. The bathroom has a shower only, and an open two-shelf unit for toiletries.

Bottom Bunks: .... **D**

Average Price PPPD: $135 plus airfare.
A few really small cabins with upper and lower berths can be found forward on the lowest passenger deck, and some of them are outsides with portholes, but a tight squeeze to get into.

The Routes

Bolero spends the winter season cruising the Canary Islands, Red Sea, Italy, Egypt, Greece and Israel, then repositions for summer and fall Eastern Mediterranean sailings.

The Scoop

The *Bolero* has very small cabins with very thin walls, and was built on the premise that in the Caribbean everyone will spend the whole day ashore anyhow. Perhaps the same thing happens in the Med. The ship is probably best for young couples; on our sailing, one-third of the entire passenger list was on a honeymoon, making this a real love boat.

Insider Tips

Five Special Spots

1. The cozy bar on the topmost deck overlooking the amidships swimming pool.
2. The amidships pool with tile surround, white plastic cafe chairs and loungers, sheltered with glass wings and partly covered overhead.
3. A second, aft swimming pool and sun lounging area and an adjacent buffet cafe.
4. A small, chic amidships lounge below the buffet cafe deck is near the casino and an intimate spot to meet for a drink.
5. The dining room has mostly tables for four, six, eight and 10, but a few for two are set so close together they might as well be a four.

Five Good Reasons to Book This Ship

1. Despite the small cabins with thin walls, the vessel itself is clean and well-decorated.
2. It sails to the Canary Islands, the Red Sea, Italy, Israel, Greece and Egypt.
3. Some special fares through EuroCruises.
4. It's very handsomely decorated and small enough to find your way around easily.
5. To eavesdrop on your neighbors through the thin walls; we learned a lot about the private life of a certain football star and his wife in the cabin next door.

Five Things You Won't Find On Board

1. Good traction on an early morning jog; the decks can get slippery when wet.
2. Good sightlines in the show lounge.
3. Single cabins.
4. A self-service laundry.
5. An unwelcome breeze on the covered pool deck.

BOLERO ★★★

Registry	**Bahamas**
Officers	**Italian/Greek**
Crew	**International**
Crew	**315**
GRT	**16,107**
Length (ft.)	**525**
Beam (ft.)	**75**
Draft (ft.)	**22**
Passengers-Cabins Full	**938**
Passengers-2/Cabin	**766**
Passenger Space Ratio	**21.02**
Stability Rating	**Good**
Seatings	**2**
Cuisine	**International**
Dress Code	**Traditional**
Room Service	**Yes**
Tip	**N/A**

Ship Amenities

Outdoor Pool	**2**
Indoor Pool	**0**
Jacuzzi	**0**
Fitness Center	**Yes**
Spa	**No**
Beauty Shop	**Yes**
Showroom	**Yes**
Bars/Lounges	**3**
Casino	**Yes**
Shops	**3**
Library	**Yes**
Child Program	**Yes**
Self-Service Laundry	**No**
Elevators	**4**

Cabin Statistics

Suites	**7**
Outside Doubles	**216**
Inside Doubles	**160**
Wheelchair Cabins	**0**
Singles	**0**
Single Surcharge	**160–170%**
Verandas	**0**
110 Volt	**Yes**

★★
FUNCHAL

It's difficult to think of the Funchal as a Scandinavian vessel because of its name and long Portuguese associations. But the Swedish officers and Portuguese staff do their best to remind you of both countries on this Panamanian-registry ship.

The *Funchal* from Fritidskryss has been around for a while but was extensively refurbished in 1991. Along with the former *Vasco de Gama*, this is the cruise ship long associated with Portugal's George Potamianos, who calls himself "a passionate lover of real ships." Built in Denmark in 1961, the veteran ship has a lot of character, can feed all the passengers at a single seating in the two dining rooms and even includes an overnight and city tour in Gothenburg on Spitsbergen and North Cape itineraries. A recent $2 million refurbishment has upgraded cabins and public rooms.

Between The Lines

The Brochure Says
"The *Funchal* is appointed in the simple, modern style preferred by Europeans."

Translation
Don't expect fancy.

Cabins & Costs

Fantasy Suites: . . . . **N/A**
   N/A

Small Splurges: . . . . **C**
   Average Price Per Person, Double Occupancy, Per Day: $341 plus airfare.

An outside double cabin the company calls a suite (there are five of them) with two lower beds can be had.

Suitable Standards: . . . . D

Average Price PPPD: $270 plus airfare.

There are a variety of double outside cabins on the *Funchal* with various bed arrangements—doubles, two lowers and a Combi, with extra Pullman berths. The cabins are small, and a few have shared bathroom facilities, so double check the status before booking.

Bottom Bunks: . . . . D

Average Price PPPD: $131 plus airfare.

Oddly enough, the cheapest cabins aboard are not those singles with shared facilities, but rather the inside doubles with upper and lower berths and private bath on a bottom deck.

The Routes

Probably the two most popular itineraries in summer for the *Funchal* are the Spitsbergen run and the North Cape. The former is an 18-night roundtrip out of Gothenburg and the latter a 12-night cruise.

The Scoop

Basically an expedition vessel in itinerary, the *Funchal* still hews to traditional cruise patterns such as dressing up for dinner even in the high Arctic. Dr. Ian Fleming (no, not James Bond's creator) is a popular onboard lecturer on the subject of Arctic geology and Nordic cultures. Think expedition—perhaps Special Expeditions with its Swedish officers —to get a handle on these cruises.

Insider Tips

Five Happening Places

1. The cozy Porto Piano Bar reminds us of the singalong piano bar on the Orient Express trains, both the VSOE and the Nostalgic Istanbul OE.

2. The bow deck with its tables and chairs and great views of the fjords and ice pack.

3. The *Funchal's* cabins are concentrated on five of the six passenger decks.

4. The Portuguese serving staff presents both à la carte and buffet offerings in the single-seating dining rooms.

5. The promenade decks are protected, ideal for passengers heading far above the Arctic Circle.

Five Good Reasons to Book This Ship

1. To go to Spitsbergen and look for polar bears.

2. To glory in the beauty of the Norwegian fjords.

3. To take advantage of very good transatlantic air rates offered by EuroCruises.

4. To sing along in that happy piano bar.

5. To get a free overnight in Gothenburg; as they used to say in vaudeville, second prize is two free nights in Gothenburg.

FUNCHAL ★★

Registry	**Panama**
Officers	**Swedish**
Crew	**Portuguese**
Complement	**165**
GRT	**10,000**
Length (ft.)	**500**
Beam (ft.)	**63**
Draft (ft.)	**18**
Passengers-Cabins Full	**467**
Passengers-2/Cabin	**424**
Passenger Space Ratio	**23.98**
Stability Rating	**NA**
Seatings	**2**
Cuisine	**Continental**
Dress Code	**Informal**
Room Service	**No**
Tip	**N/A**

Ship Amenities

Outdoor Pool	**1**
Indoor Pool	**0**
Jacuzzi	**0**
Fitness Center	**No**
Spa	**No**
Beauty Shop	**Yes**
Showroom	**Yes**
Bars/Lounges	**2**
Casino	**Yes**
Shops	**1**
Library	**Yes**
Child Program	**No**
Self-Service Laundry	**No**
Elevators	**2**

Cabin Statistics

Suites	**5**
Outside Doubles	**129**
Inside Doubles	**58**
Wheelchair Cabins	**0**
Singles	**33**
Single Surcharge	**110%**
Verandas	**0**
110 Volt	**No**

Unrated
KRISTINA REGINA

The *Kristina Regina*, from a family-owned Finnish company, carries a maximum of 189 passengers on a vessel with 381 berths. Still, there's not a lot of space per passenger, even with the smaller payload. The vessel is laid out in the Scandinavian ferry concept, with revenue-producing bars and restaurants and duty-free shopping getting priority space while passenger sleeping accommodations are small and sparse.

Cabins are located on all the passenger decks, many of them in the bow, while the more stable amidships area is almost totally given over to officer and crew housing and "backstage" facilities. The topmost deck has sunbathing space and a few cabins, while the next down boasts an aft cafe and two forward bar/lounges, one with a dance floor. Two restaurants, a children's play area and a hairdressing salon are on the next deck. Below that is a deck given over mostly to passenger cabins except for a large duty-free shopping area and a sizable multipurpose hall that could be devoted to groups and conventions.

Note that there is no swimming pool aboard, but a small sauna is wedged into the bow on the lowest passenger deck. They claim five "allergy cabins" but no wheelchair-accessible facilities, and the passenger-to-crew ratio is very small.

On the plus side, there is a single meal sitting, the food is good, port lecturers are usually expert, the ship docks close to the center of the city, and shore excursions are sometimes included in the basic fare.

EuroCruises on certain sailings will get a guaranteed confirmation on an inside or outside cabin at a rock-bottom fare but hold off assigning the actual cabin number and deck until shortly before departure.

Cabins & Costs

Fantasy Suites . . . . **N/A**
  N/A

Small Splurges . . . .
  Average Per Person Double Occupancy Per Day: $477 including airfare.
  The Luxe category offers five cabins with queen-sized beds, mini-refrigerator, bath-room with toilet and shower, telephone and music channels in 129 square feet.

Suitable Standards . . . .
  Average Price PPPD: $399 including airfare; $231 for the guarantee rate (see above).
  Several mid-range categories for standard cabins end up with very much the same configuration, two beds, small bathroom with shower, portholes and a nightstand with stool.

Bottom Bunks . . . .
  Average Price PPPD: $333 including airfare.
  The lowest-price accommodations on board include some inside cabins with upper and lower berths and some insides and outsides with two lower beds.

The Routes

The *Kristina Regina* sails itineraries from three to 10 days out of Helsinki to St. Peters-burg, the Baltic capitals and the Norwegian fjords. Both *Kristina Regina* and her smaller sailing mate, *Kristina Brahe*, make special opera cruises to Savolinna, Finland.

Insider Tips

Five Good Reasons to Book This Ship

1. It gives you a chance to visit Vilnius in Lithuania on an overnight excursion.
2. You can save money on a cabin guarantee deal.
3. You can sample a popular Finnish cocktail called Diesel, vodka and black licorice over ice.
4. You can learn to tango Finnish style.
5. You can learn to speak Finnish.

KRISTINA REGINA — Unrated

Registry	Finland
Officers	Finnish
Crew	Finnish
Complement	NA
GRT	3,878
Length (ft.)	325'
Beam (ft.)	48.7'
Draft (ft.)	16.2'
Passengers Full	381
Passengers 2/Cabin	200
Passenger Space Ratio	19.39
Stability Rating	Fair
Seatings	1
Cuisine	Continental
Dress code	Informal
Room service	No
Tip	NA

Ship Amenities

Outdoor Pool	0
Indoor Pool	0
Jacuzzi	0
Fitness Center	Yes
Spa	No
Beauty Shop	No
Showroom	No
Bars/Lounges	4/3
Casino	No
Shops	Yes
Library	No
Child Program	No
Self-Service Laundry	No
Elevators	0

Cabin Statistics

Suites	0
Outside Doubles	105
Inside Doubles	33
Wheelchair Cabins	0
Singles	0
Single Surcharge	Yes
Verandas	0
110 Volt	No

ALASKA'S
Glacier Bay™
TOURS AND CRUISES

520 Pike Street, Suite 1400, Seattle, WA 98101
☎ (206) 623-7110, (800) 451-5952
www.glacierbaytours.com

Glacier Bay Tours and Cruises guarantees you'll spot a whale in Icy Strait or your money back.

History . . . .

Glacier Bay Tours and Cruises is a spin-off from Seattle entrepreneur Robert Giersdorf's now-defunct Exploration Cruise Lines, which operated eight vessels when it went into bankruptcy in 1988 after a legal dispute with investor Anheuser-Busch. Giersdorf retained his wholly owned, 49-passenger catamaran *Executive Explorer* and Glacier Bay Lodge from the previous company, and added the leased 36-passenger *Wilderness Explorer* in 1992. In 1995, he also founded American West Steamboat Company, introducing the 165-passenger replica paddle-wheel steamer *Queen of the West*, cruising the Columbia River out of Portland.

In early 1996, Giersdorf sold Glacier Bay Tours and Cruises and Yachtship Cruise Line to Juneau-based Goldbelt, Inc., an Alaska Native American Corporation, as a turnkey operation, retaining previous staff and crew. At that time, Goldbelt purchased the *Wilderness Explorer.*

A new vessel, the 80 passenger *Wilderness Adventurer,* the former *Caribbean Prince,* was introduced in 1997 for six-night "soft adventure" sailings from Juneau.

Concept. . . . .

The company offers a variety of "soft adventure" and "active adventure" sailings in Alaska and British Columbia that emphasize "wholesome meals" and "modest accommodations." Wilderness excursions such as sea kayaking and naturalist walks to see flora and fauna are promoted over shipboard entertainment and cuisine. Because Native Americans own the company, there is a active attempt to serve as "stewards of the environment."

Signatures . . . .

Bow landing access for passengers when the vessel comes ashore.

Some 18 to 20 two-person sea kayaks are carried on board both the *Wilderness Adventurer* and the *Wilderness Explorer*, and use of the kayaks is included in the base fare.

Off-vessel groups are limited to 12, out of sight and sound of each other, when exploring ashore, due to National Park and National Forest regulations.

Gimmicks. . . . .

Whale-spotting in Icy Strait, summer home of many humpback whales, is guaranteed or you get your money back from the cruise portion of the trip when you book the one-night Glacier Bay Extravaganza tour.

> ### CHAMPAGNE TOAST
>
> *Port charges are included in the basic fare rather than added on, a forecast of a change today's cruise companies are making.*

Who's the Competition? . . . .

Quite obviously, Alaska Sightseeing/Cruise West, Special Expeditions, and, to a lesser extent, Clipper Cruises. Much depends on the following of loyal passengers for each line, along with the ability to book charter groups for some soft sailing dates. A major difference here is that, unlike Alaska Sightseeing and Special Expeditions, Glacier Bay's *Executive Explorer* charges for its shore excursions rather than including them in the base fare.

Who's Aboard. . . . .

Older North American couples and singles from 55 to 75 used to predominate the passenger lists, but as they add more active adventures, passengers get younger and younger.

Who Should Go . . . .

Anyone interested in getting a close-up look at Alaska, going sea kayaking or observing Alaskan wildlife.

Who Should Not Go . . . .

Families with small children, since there's nowhere on these small vessels for them to play; anyone who decided to take a cruise after watching a Carnival commercial.

The Lifestyle . . . .

Aboard the *Wilderness Adventurer* and the *Wilderness Explorer*, the life-style is simple, family-style and dress-down, in a few words. Accommodations are basic—even the brochure describes them as "modest"—and food is served family-style with sack lunches issued for shore excursions. With no fashion police on board, you can wear anything decent you like, but carry a change of clothes in case you get splashed kayaking.

The more lavish *Executive Explorer* has compact but plush staterooms with picture windows, twin or queen-sized beds, and color TV sets, and Native American artworks displayed throughout the vessel. Mealtimes as well are aimed at fussier passengers who like a little creature comfort, with plate service rather than family-style service.

Meals are served at a single open seating on all three vessels, meaning passengers may sit where and with whom they please rather than at an assigned table.

As for entertainment, don't expect much beyond what you provide yourself, except for an occasional crew show or visiting lecturer or musician from shore.

Gratuities are pooled and divided among the staff.

Wardrobe . . . .

Glacier Bay Tours and Cruises recommends that passengers dress in layers, suggesting a combination of shirt, sweater, jacket and raincoat or rain poncho so you can add or subtract items as the weather changes. Wool slacks and medium-weight sweaters are termed "ideal" but you'll also see plenty of jeans and sweatshirts along. For footwear, to supplement the ubiquitous jogging shoes, they suggest you take hiking boots, rubber boots or treated water-resistant shoes for walking on outside decks, hiking in the rainforest or kayaking. (If you forget something, don't worry; they also sell specialty clothing aboard the ships.) If you're booking the *Executive Explorer*, you may want to throw in a dressier outfit for one or two evenings.

Discounts . . . .

Early booking nets up to $300 discount per couple, depending on the booking date. If a lower price is offered after you make your booking, they will adjust the price and refund the difference, except on those occasional cruises sold at a special price to Alaska residents.

The Bottom Line

With small vessels, unregimented dining room seating, American officers and crew and a serious approach to Alaska's environmental concerns, Glacier Bay Tours and Cruises offers a good alternative choice to a traditional big-ship cruise for a person who doesn't want to dress up, be entertained by professional performers, gamble or indulge in long, fancy meals or midnight buffets.

Passengers gather on the bow to watch a waterfall.

Going Ashore

As the name suggests, Glacier Bay Tours and Cruises has more than a passing interest in Glacier Bay National Park. The Juneau-based company is owned by Goldbelt, Inc., a Native American corporation, and is an authorized concessionaire of Glacier Bay National Park. One of its nonfloating properties is the estimable Glacier Bay Lodge, where passengers can book a stay before or after their cruise for sportfishing programs, sea kayaking and one-day whale-watching, wildlife and glacier cruises.

A two-day Kodiak Adventure Tour ($1168 per person, double occupancy from Juneau, $774 from Anchorage and $944 from Fairbanks) includes roundtrip flight to Kodiak, overnight, a cultural morning tour and visit to the National Wildlife Refuge Center and a flightseeing expedition to look for the famous Kodiak brown bear. If weather permits, the chopper may land so you get an even closer look.

EXECUTIVE EXPLORER

We first boarded this ship in San Diego, far from the glaciers that define her terrain these days, when she was in between an attempt at cruising the Hawaiian Islands and an effort to cruise Baja California in the late 1980s. In both cases, the seas were too rough for her shallow twin hulls, but she's been smooth-riding and happy in the sheltered Inside Passage for years now.

The 49-passenger *Executive Explorer* has twin hulls, a tall profile and squared-off aft, lending her a distinctive if somewhat clumsy profile, but inside everything is prettily arranged and decorated. Cabins, while not large, are very cushy, especially in the two forward Vista Deluxe cabins. All are outsides with view windows. Both forward lounge and aft dining room also have big windows so you don't miss any wildlife while you're eating or socializing. Her small size enables her to get into narrow channels more easily, and an open top deck makes a good vantage point for scenery-watchers and photographers.

Between The Lines

The Brochure Says

"The exclusive catamaran design enables the *Executive Explorer* to cruise faster than other small U.S. flag ships. We've designed the cruise itinerary so you visit more ports and attractions, have more time in port, see more glaciers, more stunning scenery, more fascinating communities, and more wildlife."

Translation

At a top cruising speed of 18 knots, this catamaran does move faster than the clumsier, boxier vessels that make up the rest of this line as well as the two main competitors, but speed never guaranteed good wildlife spotting nor a smooth ride on this vessel when it gets out into exposed waters. The itinerary for both ports and cruising areas, however, is top-of-the-line. Take plenty of warm clothing; you'll spend a lot of time on deck.

Cabins & Costs

Fantasy Suites: . . . . **N/A**
N/A

Small Splurges: . . . . **B+**
Average Price Per Person, Double Occupancy, Per Day: $487 plus airfare.
Top digs are the two window-walled Vista Deluxe cabins forward on Upper Deck, with built-in window seat, queen-sized bed, enclosed water closet with shower, lavatory in the cabin and hanging closet. All cabins have color TV sets, VCRs (with free videotapes available for screening) and stocked mini-refrigerator.

Suitable Standards: . . . . **B+**
Average Price PPPD: $428 plus airfare.
The category A and AA cabins are fairly similar, with the AAs slightly larger (and slightly more expensive). Both have twin beds that convert to queen-sized, two view windows, desk dresser with mirror, enclosed water closet with shower, lavatory in the cabin and hanging closet. The AAs also have an easy chair. Some cabins in both categories have pull-down berths for third and fourth passengers. All cabins have color TV sets, VCRs (with free videotapes available for screening) and stocked mini-refrigerator.

Bottom Bunks: . . . . **B+**
Average Price PPPD: $387 plus airfare.
The sole category B cabin, # 306, has upper and lower berths, two windows, small chest with drawers, water closet with shower, lavatory in the cabin and hanging closet. This cabin is primarily recommended for single passengers, who pay 175 percent of the per-person double occupancy price. All cabins have color TV sets, VCRs (with free videotapes available for screening) and stocked mini-refrigerator.

The Routes

The *Executive Explorer* cruises on six-day itineraries between Juneau and Ketchikan, with calls in Petersburg, Sitka, Skagway and Haines, and cruising Tracy Arm Fjord, Glacier Bay, Sergius Narrows, Wrangell Narrows and Misty Fjords. The season runs from mid-May through mid-September.

The **Executive Explorer** *cruises close to glaciers.*

The Scoop

This is one of the most interesting and offbeat ships in Alaska, and the pleasures of cruising with fewer than 50 people in relatively plush surroundings cannot be underestimated. An American crew offers friendly, attentive service and the food is tasty. The shore excursions are optional on this vessel, the only one of the line's ships that offers organized in-town tours. However, passengers can strike out on foot or by cab on their own if they prefer. We do feel, even if the fares do include port taxes, that the cabins are overpriced. But so are the competition's, and passengers still seem willing to pay them. We can only suggest early booking for discounts and a tough travel agent to negotiate the real price as compared with brochure price.

EXECUTIVE EXPLORER ⚓⚓⚓⚓

Registry	**U.S.**
Officers	**American**
Crew	**American**
Complement	**18**
GRT	**98**
Length (ft.)	**98.5**
Beam (ft.)	**36**
Draft (ft.)	**8**
Passengers-Cabins Full	**55**
Passengers-2/Cabin	**49**
Passenger Space Ratio	**N/A**
Stability Rating	**Fair**
Seatings	**1**
Cuisine	**American**
Dress Code	**Casual**
Room Service	**No**
Tip	**$8–$12 PPPD pooled among staff**

Ship Amenities

Outdoor Pool	**0**
Indoor Pool	**0**
Jacuzzi	**0**
Fitness Center	**No**
Spa	**No**
Beauty Shop	**No**
Showroom	**No**
Bars/Lounges	**1**
Casino	**No**
Shops	**1 (small)**
Library	**Yes (small)**
Child Program	**No**
Self-Service Laundry	**No**
Elevators	**0**

Cabin Statistics

Suites	**0**
Outside Doubles	**25**
Inside Doubles	**0**
Wheelchair Cabins	**0**
Singles	**1**
Single Surcharge	**175%**
Verandas	**0**
110 Volt	**Yes**

⚓⚓⚓
WILDERNESS ADVENTURER

New to the fleet, the little *Wilderness Adventurer* is the former *Caribbean Prince* from American Canadian Caribbean Line, carrying 80 passengers. Typical of these small adventure vessels, it has bow landing capacity, meaning passengers can walk down a gangway directly onto the beach or island. Unlike the line's similar *Wilderness Explorer*, all cabins have two lower beds. A small lounge forward and an amidships dining room are the only enclosed public rooms aboard, along with an observation deck in front of the wheelhouse and a covered deck aft of the wheelhouse.

Between The Lines

The Brochure Says

"The *Wilderness Adventurer*...introduced to Alaska 'soft adventure' cruising in 1997."

Translation

"Soft adventure" means a true wilderness trip rather than a port-to-port cruise, with a special circumnavigation and stops ashore at Admiralty Island National Monument, home to the world's largest concentration of brown (or grizzly) bears, as well as a thousand nesting bald eagles. At the same time, it's a gentler, more ship-oriented experience than the "active adventure" cruises aboard the line's *Wilderness Explorer*.

Cabins & Costs

Fantasy Suites: . . . .**N/A**
    N/A

Small Splurges: . . . . **C**
    Average Price Per Person, Double Occupancy, Per Day: $382 plus airfare.

The AA cabins on Sun Deck are the top lodgings aboard this fairly simple vessel. At least they're big enough in which to change your mind, with a double bed or two lower beds (and an occasional third pulldown berth), picture window and compact bath with shower.

Suitable Standards: . . . . C-

Average Price PPPD: $346 plus airfare.

The dozen A category cabins are located on the same deck with the lounge and dining room, a convenience for passengers who want to be close to the action. We would hesitate to recommend cabin A 201 to anyone but early risers, however, because it's also smack against the galley, where the pots and pans start rattling early in the morning. Each of these cabins has two lower beds that can convert to double, a reasonable amount of turning-around space and a compact bathroom with toilet, shower and lavatory.

Bottom Bunks: . . . . D-

Average Price PPPD: $313 plus airfare.

Please, please, we beg of you, spring for the extra few bucks to book one of the A or double AA cabins if you're claustrophobic or at all particular about where you sleep. The seven B category cabins (six on the lowest deck, one adjacent to the wheelhouse on the Sun Deck) in the lowest price category are so small the beds almost overlap and cover more than half the total area, leaving very little floor space. These six cabins also have portlights set up high inside instead of windows, which means you may have a little daylight but no views.

The Routes

The *Wilderness Adventurer* makes six-night cruises roundtrip from Juneau with an emphasis on "soft adventures" for moderately active, outdoor-oriented passengers. The vessel spends more time cruising and exploring than docked ashore, spending two days cruising Glacier Bay (most cruise ships spend only one day there) as well as sailing around Admiralty Island, cruising in search of humpback whales at Point Adolphus and Icy Strait, sailing along the bays and inlets of Frederick Sound for additional wilderness wildlife spotting and cruising Tracy Arm Fjord. Sea kayaks and other launches are aboard to take passengers in for closer looks, as well as some bow landings that let passengers walk ashore from the ship.

The Scoop

As has the *Caribbean Prince*, this vessel was been well cared for by its owner-builder Luther Blount, so it underwent very few changes in its transition to *Wilderness Adventurer*.

Insider Tips

Five Good Reasons to Book This Ship

1. If you want to spend more time in Alaska's wilderness than in overcrowded towns.

2. Because your port tax is included rather than added on as a surcharge.

3. To spend two full days in Glacier Bay, twice as long as anybody else cruising Alaska.

4. To go sea kayaking at no extra charge.

5. To take a guided hike with a maximum of 12 people.

Five Things You Won't Find Aboard

1. A children's program, or any place for small children to play.

2. A self-service laundry.

3. A doctor; the ship is always within 12 miles of land.

4. A beauty salon; if you want to get your hair done, you're on the wrong ship.

5. A bingo game.

WILDERNESS ADVENTURER ⚓⚓⚓

Registry	U.S.
Officers	American
Crew	American
Complement	19
GRT	89
Length (ft.)	156.6
Beam (ft.)	38
Draft (ft.)	6.5
Passengers-Cabins Full	80
Passengers-2/Cabin	78
Passenger Space Ratio	N/A
Stability Rating	Fair to Good
Seatings	1
Cuisine	American
Dress Code	Casual
Room Service	No
Tip	$8–$12 PPPD pooled among staff

Ship Amenities

Outdoor Pool	0
Indoor Pool	0
Jacuzzi	0
Fitness Center	No
Spa	No
Beauty Shop	No
Showroom	No
Bars/Lounges	1
Casino	No
Shops	1 (small)
Library	Yes (small)
Child Program	No
Self-Service Laundry	No
Elevators	0

Cabin Statistics

Suites	0
Outside Doubles	32
Inside Doubles	6 (w/port light)
Wheelchair Cabins	0
Singles	0
Single Surcharge	175%
Verandas	0
110 Volt	Yes

⚓⚓⚓
WILDERNESS EXPLORER

The *Wilderness Explorer* is Glacier Bay's most basic vessel, aimed at adventurers who want an active, outdoors exploration of Alaska and won't fuss because the cabin has upper and lower berths instead of twin beds or a queen. You can paddle your kayak in pristine waters and still come home to a hot, wholesome meal at the end of the day. Cabins are small and few of them have windows, only portlights high up in the wall that let a bit of light in but don't give you a view. The top deck has an open observation area forward of the pilot house and a covered deck aft, with the ship's only deluxe cabin in between. (We suspect this used to belong to the captain, but now it's sold to paying passengers.) There's a small lounge forward and dining room amidships on the middle deck, with both crew and passenger cabins wedged into the lower deck.

Kayaking off the Wilderness Explorer.

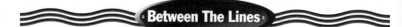

Between The Lines

The Brochure Says

"These *Wilderness Explorer* cruises are geared for the active, outdoor-oriented person who really wants to experience nature in ways that no other Alaska cruise or tour can deliver."

Translation

While everybody talks about offering "a real Alaska wilderness experience," this ship delivers more day-to-day opportunities than most. The line calls the vessel a "Cruising Base Camp," promising that you'll spend all day off the vessel in active adventures, coming back on board mainly to eat and sleep.

Cabins & Costs

Fantasy Suites: .... **C**

Average Price Per Person, Double Occupancy, Per Day: $264 plus airfare on a five-day cruise.

Don't imagine this as anything approaching a traditional cruise ship suite, but rather as the only fairly large, comfortable space on this ship, even if it does have upper and lower berths. It also has two windows, a pearl beyond price on this vessel. The bathroom, like all the others aboard, has a shower/toilet combination that can leave a lot of residual water around if you don't plan your activities in the right order.

Small Splurges: .... **C**

Average Price PPPD: $252 plus airfare on a five-day cruise.

This has to be a record—the only time we've ever used the word "splurge" in conjunction with a cabin with upper and lower berths. But this is an unusual vessel and a special sort of cruise, and the price is much lower than the line's other ships. What you get for your splurge is a AA cabin with a picture window on the main deck with the lounge and dining room. The bad news is, there are only three of them.

Suitable Standards: .... **D**

Average Price PPPD: $246 plus airfare on a five-day cruise.

Now we're getting basic—these cabins are on the bottom deck with a portlight (a small sort of skylight high up in the wall that you can't see out of) instead of window or porthole. Upper and lower berths, of course, and the same bathroom described above. Spring for the AA category above if you can.

Bottom Bunks: .... **D**

Average Price PPPD: $232 plus airfare on a five-day cruise.

Don't ask. The three B-category cabins have the aforementioned portlight but are smaller than the A category above—each of them has part of its area donated to stairway adjacent to the wall, so you'll be able to hear footsteps of both passengers and crew bounding up and down.

The Routes

The *Wilderness Explorer* offers cruises that last for two, three, four and five nights. The two shorter ones still provide a day and a half in Glacier Bay with a kayaking day and hiking trips. On the three-night cruise, you'll also visit Pt. Adolphus, summer home of the humpback whales, and the Inian Islands. On the four-night itinerary, you'll spend two full days in Glacier Bay National Park, one full day at Pt. Adolphus and the Inian Islands, and have three full days of kayaking, hiking and nature explorations, plus a cruising day in Tracy Arm Fjord. The five-day program adds a full day exploring Tracy Arm by kayak, hiking and other launch vessels. Depending on your cruise, you'll board in Juneau or fly to Glacier Bay Lodge to begin.

The Scoop

This is an ideal cruise for the active traveler who has no interest in sitting on deck with binoculars in hand but would rather be out there in the midst of things doing and seeing. The flexibility allows those who are pressed for time to get in a little Alaskan adventuring, or to take several mini-cruises throughout the season instead of one longer one. If you've cruised before, you have to remind yourself that this is a very basic vessel offering a comfortable bunk, a hot shower and a home-cooked meal you don't have prepare yourself. What you get in exchange is a lot of Alaska up-close.

The dramatic ice flow at Margarie Glacier comes from the Fairweather Mountain Range, the highest coastal mountain range in the world.

WILDERNESS EXPLORER   ⚓⚓⚓

Registry	U.S.
Officers	American
Crew	American
Complement	13
GRT	98
Length (ft.)	112
Beam (ft.)	22
Draft (ft.)	7.6
Passengers-Cabins Full	36
Passengers-2/Cabin	36
Passenger Space Ratio	N/A
Stability Rating	Fair
Seatings	1
Cuisine	American
Dress Code	Casual
Room Service	No
Tip	$8–$12 PPPD pooled among staff

Ship Amenities

Outdoor Pool	0
Indoor Pool	0
Jacuzzi	0
Fitness Center	No
Spa	No
Beauty Shop	No
Showroom	No
Bars/Lounges	1
Casino	No
Shops	1 (small)
Library	Yes (small)
Child Program	No
Self-Service Laundry	No
Elevators	0

Cabin Statistics

Suites	0
Outside Doubles	4
Inside Doubles	14 (w/ port light)
Wheelchair Cabins	0
Singles	0
Single Surcharge	175%
Verandas	0
110 Volt	Yes

GLACIER BAY TOURS AND CRUISES

HAPAG-LLOYD

Gustav Deetjen Allee 2-6, Bremen D 28215, Germany
☎ *011-49-421-350-0333 or (800) 551-1000 (for* Bremen*), (800) 334-2724 (for* Europa*)*

The *Bremen* may also be booked through Radisson Seven Seas Cruises,
☎ *(800) 333-3333.*

Expedition cruising offers close-ups of nature.

History . . . .

Hapag-Lloyd represents a merger between two legendary German shipping and cruise lines, Hamburg-Amerika or HAPAG (an acronym for Hamburg-Amerikanische Packetfahrt Actien-Gesellschaft), which was founded in 1856, and North German Lloyd, which began service between Germany and America in 1858 aboard the *Bremen*. The two companies merged in 1931, and today concentrate most of their activities in cargo-carrying. They presently operate two ships named after North German Lloyd's classic Blue Riband winners *Bremen* (in 1929) and *Europa* (in 1930) and recently purchased Hanseatic Tours, which owns the *Hanseatic,* The 15,000-ton *Columbus* was expected to enter service for the company during the summer of 1997. The German-built ship will be marketed primarily to German-speaking passengers.

487

—Built in 1990 the first new expedition ship to debut in 16 years, *Frontier Spirit*, now *Bremen*.

★★★★★   ⚓⚓⚓⚓⚓

BREMEN

On remote Micronesian atolls such as Lamotrek in the state of Yap, supply barges are the only large seagoing vessels many of the villagers have ever seen, and as we were sailing in on the Frontier Spirit *in 1990 early one Sunday morning, the chief's young son ran to his father and shook him awake, crying, "Papa, papa, an island is coming!"*

The *Bremen* began life as Salen-Lindblad's *Frontier Spirit*, and later SeaQuest's *Frontier Spirit*, the first new expedition ship to be built in 16 years when it debuted in 1990 under the command of the well-known expedition captain, Heinz Aye, master of Society Expeditions' *World Discoverer* for so many years. The ship was financed by a consortium of owners that included Salen-Lindblad, Hapag-Lloyd, Mitsubishi and Japan's shipping giant NYK, which also owns Crystal Cruises, and built by Mitsubishi in their Kobe shipyard. It carries a Super Ice-Class rating, the highest possible, and an impressive array of environmentally friendly features from refrigerated garbage compactors and glass-grinders to incinerators and bilge oil separators that skim off the waste oil to incinerate and return the water to the bilge. But the vessel's luxury details are equally impressive, with private verandas, a self-service laundry room, a separate heated drying room that can dry out wet sneakers overnight, minibars and mini-refrigerators in every cabin, along with remote-control color TV sets and built-in hair dryers.

EAVESDROPPING

"The old-timers said, "don't want so much luxury,'" one Salen-Lindblad executive told us after the first sailing. "They call me and say, 'Why do we need so many forks and knives? Why does dinner take so long?'"

Between The Lines

The Brochure Says

"The popular *MS Bremen* offers passengers a special combination of exploration capability and luxurious accommodations not found on other ships."

Translation

A really luxurious, state-of-the-art expedition ship, the *Bremen* is rivaled only by the newer, perhaps even more luxurious expedition ship *Hanseatic* from Radisson Seven Seas Cruises, also owned by Hapag-Lloyd. Frequently both ships may be booked through Radisson Seven Seas.

DID YOU KNOW?

Captain Heinz Aye has circled the globe 33 times and made more than 60 voyages to the Antarctic, as well as claiming dozens of major seagoing expedition "firsts."

One of the fantasy suites aboard the Bremen.

Cabins & Costs

Fantasy Suites: . . . . A

Average Price Per Person, Double Occupancy, Per Day: $1000 including airfare and gratuities.

There are two suites with verandas aboard, the only two accommodations on the topmost pool deck, one decorated in aqua, the other in rose. Each contains twin beds that can be made into a queen-sized bed, separate sitting area with curved sofa and two chairs, a desk and built-in cabinetry, a bath with tub/shower combination and wide counter with two wash basins.

Small Splurges: .... A

Average Price PPPD: $883 including airfare and gratuities.
Almost as nice are the standard outside doubles with veranda, 16 cabins on Deck 6. (Cabins 615, 616, 617 and 618 are slightly smaller than the others.) Each has a small veranda with two chairs and a table, a sitting area with two chairs inside, plus a desk and built-in cabinetry and bath with shower. Wardrobe space is generous.

Suitable Standards: .... A

Average Price PPPD: $502 to $742 including airfare and gratuities.
All the remaining cabins on board are outside doubles divided into cabin categories that depend on deck location for the price.

Two are designated wheelchair-accessible with ample turning space and a ramp for the bathroom doors. Each has twin or queen-sized beds, writing desk, two chairs, bath with shower and generous wardrobe. All cabins and suites also contain color TV, minibar/refrigerator and hair dryer.

Bottom Bunks: .... NA

There are no cabins in this category on this ship.

The Routes

The *Bremen* sails in winter to Morocco and the Canary Islands en route to South America's east coast, then south to the Falklands, South Georgia and the Antarctic. In summer the ship sails on various European itineraries.

The Scoop

The passenger complement is international, but German-speaking travelers are the most numerous, along with North Americans.

The ship is extremely comfortable with state-of-the-art technical and environmental niceties, even a helipad on the top deck. It carries inflatable Zodiac landing craft for exploring in remote areas.

Insider Tips

Five Favorite Places

1. A main lounge with bar and comfortable conversational groupings of sofas and chairs serves as location for the nightly cocktail hour.

2. High atop the ship and forward is a glass-walled observation lounge that also serves as a lecture room, with a wide range of projection equipment, rows of blue banquettes on four levels along with fixed round tables and blue and chrome tub chairs that can be moved.

3. An expansive deck area with swimming pool, a rarity among expedition ships.

4. A small gym contains lifecycles, weights and other equipment and is adjacent to a large sauna.

5. A quiet library off the main lounge with beige leather chairs, long tables covered with recent magazines and newspapers in several languages and reference and paperback books.

BREMEN ★★★★★, ♨♨♨♨

Registry	**Bahamas**
Officers	**German**
Crew	**International**
Complement	**94**
GRT	**6,752**
Length (ft.)	**366**
Beam (ft.)	**56**
Draft (ft.)	**16**
Passengers-Cabins Full	**185**
Passengers-2/Cabin	**164**
Passenger Space Ratio	**41.17**
Stability Rating	**Good**
Seatings	**1**
Cuisine	**Continental**
Dress Code	**Casual**
Room Service	**No**
Tip	**Included in fare**

Ship Amenities

Outdoor Pool	**1**
Indoor Pool	**0**
Jacuzzi	**0**
Fitness Center	**Yes**
Spa	**No**
Beauty Shop	**Yes**
Showroom	**No**
Bars/Lounges	**3**
Casino	**No**
Shops	**1**
Library	**Yes**
Child Program	**No**
Self-Service Laundry	**Yes**
Elevators	**2**

Cabin Statistics

Suites	**2**
Outside Doubles	**80**
Inside Doubles	**6**
Wheelchair Cabins	**0**
Singles	**0**
Single Surcharge	**120–160%**
Verandas	**18**
110 Volt	**No**

HAPAG-LLOYD

Unrated
EUROPA

This ship, built in 1982 and refurbished in 1990, is an extremely popular super-luxury vessel among German-speaking passengers but scarcely known in North America. The 37,012-ton vessel carries 600 passengers and 300 multinational crew members, along with German officers, and a passenger space ratio of 61, among the highest in the industry. This means passengers aboard have lots of space to stretch out on deck, in the clothing-optional sunbathing areas or in the public rooms.

Formal and "correct" in the German sense, the ship excels in cuisine and service, is beautifully furnished and spotlessly clean. *Europa* spends the year cruising around the world on longer itineraries that please its upscale European clientele. Entertainment and activities on board are geared to them; there's no casino.

There are three swimming pools, a health club, sauna and massage facilities and library.

Seabourn Spirit at Santorini

Aerobics class on Royal Caribbean

Outside looking in on RCCL's *Splendor of the Seas*

Snorkeling off of Clipper Cruise Line's *Nantucket Clipper* in the Virgin Islands

HOLLAND AMERICA LINE

300 Elliott Avenue West, Seattle, WA 98119
☎ (206) 283-2687, (800) 426-0327
www.hollandamerica.com

String trios play for teatime and after dinner, as here, aboard the **Statendam.**

History . . . .

One of the oldest and most distinguished of the cruise lines, Holland America was founded in 1873 as the Netherlands-America Steamship Company, a year after its young co-founders commissioned and introduced the first ship, the original *Rotterdam*, a 1700-ton iron vessel. The new ship left the city it was named for on Oct. 15, 1872, and spent 15 days sailing to New York on its maiden voyage. It carried eight passengers in first class and 380 in steerage. Only a few years later, because all its sailings were to the Americas, it became known as Holland America Line.

—A leading carrier of immigrants to the United States, Holland America transported nearly 700,000 between 1901 and 1914 alone; a steerage fare cost $20.

—After World War II, when middle-class Americans began touring Europe in large numbers, HAL concentrated on offering moderately priced tourist-class service with two medium-sized ships that carried 836 tourist class passengers and only 39 first-class passengers.

—The line introduced educational and pleasure cruises to the Holy Land just after the turn of the century, and in 1971, suspended transatlantic sailings in favor of cruise vacations.

—The first line to introduce glass-enclosed promenade decks on its ocean liners.

—First line to introduce a full-service Lido restaurant on all its ships as a casual dining alternative.

—First cruise line to introduce karaoke, a sort of high-tech singalong (on the *Westerdam* in 1990).

—Through its subsidiary Westours, Holland America retains a strong tour profile in Alaska, and with another subsidiary company, Windstar, offers small-ship sailing vacations in Costa Rica, the Caribbean and Mediterranean.

—In 1989, Carnival Cruise Lines acquired Holland America and its affiliated companies, but retains HAL's Seattle headquarters and separate management.

Concept. . . . .

With its slogan "A Tradition of Excellence," Holland America has always had a reputation for high quality and giving full cruise value for the money, along with a strong program of security and sanitation. Since its acquisition by Carnival, the line has worked to upscale its product and sees itself now firmly entrenched in what is called the "premium" segment of the cruise industry, a notch up from mass-market lines such as Carnival but not in the highest-priced luxury segment.

The line welcomes three new ships to the fleet—the new *Rotterdam VI* in September 1997, and two additional 65,000-ton ships in 1999, bringing the line total to 10.

HAL defines its premium status with such details as adding suites with private verandas to its four newest ships, *Statendam, Maasdam, Ryndam* and *Veendam*, along with more elaborate spas and advanced technology showrooms. The new vessels have also been designed to handle both short and long cruises equally well, with generous closet space and more-spacious staterooms.

There's also a strong undercurrent of "politically correct" behavior, consistent with its Pacific Northwest base, from specially packaged, environmentally safe cabin gift toiletries to taking a stand against the proposed Alaska aerial wolf-hunting program several years ago. The company also makes frequent, generous contributions to Alaskan universities and nonprofit organizations such as the Alaska Raptor Rehabilitation Center in Sitka.

Signatures ....

A "No Tipping Required" policy means that while tips are appreciated by crew members, they cannot be solicited. However, very few passengers disembark without crossing more than a few palms with silver.

The line's long-standing tradition of hiring Indonesian and Filipino crew members and training them in its own Jakarta hotel school results in consistently high-quality service.

The continuing use of museum-quality antiques and artifacts from the golden days of Dutch shipping adds dignity and richness to the ship interiors.

The classic ship names, taken from Dutch cities, are always repeated in new vessels, with the present *Statendam* and *Maasdam* each the fifth to bear the name, the *Veendam* the fourth, the *Nieuw Amsterdam, Noordam* and *Ryndam* the third namesakes, and the *Westerdam* the second in the line with that name. The new *Rotterdam VI* reflects its sixth incarnation in its name.

Holland America's distinctive logo is painted on the funnels of its ships.

Gimmicks.

The ubiquitous Holland America bag, a white canvas carry-all embellished with the company's logo and names of all the ships, can be glimpsed all over the world. Each passenger on each cruise is given one of these, so you can imagine how many frequent cruisers manage to amass. They're washable and last forever. "It's the single best investment we ever made," said one HAL insider.

Passport to Fitness, a folded card that has 48 separate areas to get stamped as the holder completes a qualifying activity, from the morning walkathon to aerobics class or a volleyball game. The prizes vary by the number of stamps, but are usually a Holland America logo item such as a T-shirt, cap or jacket. (We heard one eager-to-win passenger ask the librarian to stamp her passport for checking out a book about sports.) Theme cruises, too, continue to proliferate, with '50s sock hops, Big Band Music, Country Music, Improv at Sea and a $25,000 Grand Bingo Jackpot Cruise on tip for 1998.

Five Special Touches

1. Beautiful red plaid deck blankets.

2. Toiletries in each cabin wrapped in replicas of period Holland America posters and advertising art.

3. Museum-quality ship and seafaring artifacts in special display cases, along with antique bronze cannons and figureheads.

4. Fresh flowers flown in from Holland all over the ship.

5. Trays of mints, dried fruits and candied ginger outside the dining room after dinner.

Who's the Competition

Princess is the closest head-on competitor, vying to be top dog in the Alaska cruise market. The two lines can claim the two largest land tour operators, HAL's Westours and Princess's Princess Tours. For the past couple of years, Princess has had more ships in Alaska than Holland America, but Westours claims more tour departures. In the Caribbean, Celebrity Cruises is a major competitor with Holland America. HAL is also in the league to compete in the premium market with Princess for senior couples and singles.

Who's Aboard.

While the Alaska market is attracting more and more younger cruisers and families, Holland America's basic passengers can still be defined as middle-aged and older couples who appreciate solid quality in food, surroundings and service.

Perhaps the most interesting are those who sail on the line's world cruises, many wealthy, set-in-their-ways dowagers who cruise together year after year, throwing lavish cocktail parties and luncheons and competing to see who brings the most gorgeous gowns (and the most agreeable rent-a-male escorts).

Who Should Go

More younger couples and families should be aboard Holland America's shorter sailings, especially to Alaska, where the line excels in the scope and variety of its land/cruise packages. Single women and families with children will find HAL is thinking of them—youth counselors coordinate activities for each age group, from an ice cream sundae party for the 5-to-8 set to teen disco parties and contests, and social hosts to dance with unattached women on all cruises 14 days or longer. Physically challenged passengers will find suitable accommodations on board all the new ships, plus extra assistance from the attentive staff, who also lavish special care and attention on the elderly and small children.

Who Should Not Go . . . .

Young swinging singles looking to boogie all night or meet the mate of their dreams.

Nonconformists.

People who refuse to dress up.

The Lifestyle . . . .

A surprising amount of luxury and pampering go on aboard these ships, with string trios (two of them usually work each ship now) playing at teatime, white-gloved stewards to escort you to your cabin when you board, vases of fresh flowers everywhere, bowls of fresh fruit in the cabins, and most of all, what the Dutch call *gezellig*, a warm and cozy ambiance, defined with curtains in the cabins that can separate the sleeping area from the sitting area, friendly Dutch officers and caring Indonesian and Filipino crew members, who make it a point of pride to remember your name.

In Alaska, naturalists and longtime Alaska residents are always among the lecture staff. Kodak ambassadors are on board designated cruises to assist passengers with photo problems and show examples of good slide photography from the area. Movies are shown at three or four daily screening times, as well as on cabin TV, and shore excursions emphasize sightseeing and flightseeing, with float-plane and helicopter glacier flights, kayaking, raft trips and visits to cultural (Native American) areas and historical city tours.

Half Moon Cay, HAL's new private island, formerly the uninhabited Bahamian Island called Little San Salvador, serves as a new port of call on Caribbean sailings. The island debuts in time for the 1997-98 holiday sailings, with beach facilities, watersports, nature walks, souvenir shopping, children's playground and tram tours.

Wardrobe . . . .

Dress code follows a traditional pattern, with a week usually calling for two formal nights (and they do dress up on these ships, even in Alaska), two informal nights when men are expected to wear a jacket but a tie is usually optional, and three "elegantly casual" nights with no shorts, T-shirts, tank tops, halter tops or jeans permitted. During the daytime, comfortable, casual clothing—jogging outfits, shorts or slacks, T-shirts, bathing suits and cover-ups—are adequate deck wear.

Holland America consistently produces some of the most attractive buffets at sea; here, breakfast aboard the Maasdam.

Bill of Fare... A

"Genteel tradition" is important to Holland America, from a chime master who announces dinner to the Indonesian bellman in the bellboy outfit (similar to the doormen in white at the Peninsula Hotel in Hong Kong) who holds open the doors between the Lido buffet and the deck for every passenger.

Holland America consistently produces some of the tastiest and most appealing buffets at sea, from the lavish Dutch-style breakfasts to wonderfully varied luncheons. In addition to a full hot-and-cold buffet in the Lido restaurants, chefs on deck will grill hot dogs and hamburgers to order, serve up make-your-own tacos, stir-fry to order and pasta of the day, plus a very popular make-your-own-ice-cream-sundae counter with a bowl of homemade cookies.

Because of the scope and popularity of the buffet service, dining room breakfast and dinner are served open seating, which means you can arrive within a specified time and sit with whom you wish.

Dinner menus have grown increasingly sophisticated. A typical dinner might include six appetizers (among them warm hazelnut-crusted Brie with apple and onion compote and French bread, bay shrimp coupe with cocktail sauce, smoked king salmon with horseradish cream and herb crostini), two soups (one may be five-onion cream with frizzled onions), three salads (including field greens with smoked duck, Asian pears and toasted pecans), six entrees, from a low-calorie, low-fat sauteed Alaskan snapper teriyaki or fresh halibut with asparagus and lemon pepper mashed potatoes to a Parmesan-crusted chicken breast or a grilled New York steak with baked Idaho potato and onion rings. A cheese and fresh fruit course follows, then a choice of four desserts plus pastry tray, ice creams and frozen yogurts, and sugar-free desserts.

Chocoholics will adore the Chocolate Extravaganza late show, served once during each cruise as a midnight buffet.

Children's menus offer four standard entrees—hamburger and fries, hot dog, pizza or chicken drumsticks—plus a nightly chef's special, perhaps beef tacos, fish and chips or barbecued ribs. The more urbane kid may prefer to order from the regular menu.

CHAMPAGNE TOAST

Holland America serves Seattle's famous Starbucks coffee on board all its ships; on the big new liners—Statendam, Maasdam, Ryndam and Veendam—after-dinner espresso is complimentary in the Explorer's Lounge.

Showtime . . . . .B+

A more sophisticated level of production shows was introduced recently, with each ship featuring its own specially tailored programs. On the line's long cruises and world cruises, headliner entertainers such as Rita Moreno, Roy Clark, Victor Borge and Vic Damone, plus noted lecturers and even a Las Vegas-style ice skating spectacular, may show up on the program.

Discounts . . . .

Early booking savings can take off 10 to 20 percent for passengers who book and make a deposit on a specified timetable, which may mean anything from one to six months ahead of time. Passengers who book earliest get the lowest prices, and if a new money-saver is introduced after they book, their fare will be adjusted on request and verification. Past passengers also get added discounts and special mail offers on certain cruises.

The Bottom Line

This is an extremely high-quality product with good fulfillment for the money, one that keeps getting better. As much as anybody in the business, Holland America delivers what it promises.

Officers are Dutch, with a no-nonsense attitude about safety and seamanship. The lifeboat drill is thorough and explicit, and cleanliness and sanitation are of an extremely high standard.

When we gave Shirley's parents their first cruise a few years ago for an anniversary gift, Holland America was the line we chose—and they're still saying it was the best vacation they ever had.

★ ★ ★ ★ ★
MAASDAM
RYNDAM
STATENDAM
VEENDAM

The Dutch, or more precisely the Netherlanders, have lent their name to some decidedly unglamorous expressions—in Dutch, Dutch treat, Dutch uncle, Dutch courage. Over the years, they have given us cozy and cliché images of dowager queens in sensible shoes, herrings, Hans Brinker, Gouda and Edam cheese, windmills and respectable burghers staring out at us from museum walls and cigar boxes.

But these ships are not apple-cheeked little Dutch girls in wooden shoes and stiff white bonnets. They're sophisticated and very elegant women of the world who know who they are and what they're doing.

The newest HAL ships are ideal for long cruises, with spacious cabins, each with its own sitting area, and generous closet and drawer space. A variety of lounges, public rooms and outdoor spaces offer enough entertaining alternatives to ensure that passengers won't get bored.

A 26-foot Italianate fountain ornaments the three-deck lobby of the *Statendam,* and a slightly smaller version of the same also decorates the *Ryndam* lobby, while the *Maasdam*'s centerpiece is a monumental $350,000 green glass sculpture created by Luciano Vistosi of Murano, Italy, that looks as though it's made from Superman's kryptonite. The *Veendam* also has a towering Vistosi glass sculpture in the lobby called "Jacob's Ladder."

From the gangway level, a graceful curved stairway and an escalator (convenient but unusual aboard ships) take passengers up one deck to the front office and lobby, the bottom level of the three-deck atrium. Each ship shows off a $2 million art collection, along with dazzling two-deck theaters and showy glass-walled dining rooms, sizable spas and expansive deck areas.

CHAMPAGNE TOAST

For the charming artwork created for the Maasdam by whimsical Danish artist Bjorn Windblad, especially in the beauty salon, where his mural of the "Judgment of Paris" (when the handsome youth Paris had to choose the most beautiful of the Greek goddesses) is accompanied by Windblad's handwritten note wishing that all the salon's clients will leave feeling like Aphrodite, the winner.

Between The Lines

The Brochure Says

"Floating resorts, our ships are our own private islands, destinations in themselves, offering everything you'd expect in a great resort on land. Fine dining. Dazzling entertainment. Activities galore. When was the last time you paid so little for so much?"

Translation

Holland America seems to be looking to appeal to a new group of passengers, younger, more resort-oriented people who may not have cruised before, by accenting entertainment, cuisine, price and variety. The previous emphasis on overall cruise value and 125 years of service is still underscored as well.

Cabins & Costs

The lavish owner's suite aboard the **Maasdam.**

Fantasy Suites: . . . . **A+**

Average Price Per Person Double Occupancy Per Day: $759 plus airfare in the Caribbean.

The penthouses on Navigation Deck, one on each ship, are huge—1123 square feet—ideal for entertaining with a living room with wraparound sofa, four chairs, big screen TV; a large private veranda, dining table that seats eight, butler pantry; separate bedroom with queen-sized bed, built-in dressing table and walk-in dressing room lined with closets. The marble bathroom has double sinks, a whirlpool tub, a steam bath/shower combination and separate water closet with bidet; there's even a custom-tiled guest bath.

Small Splurges: . . . . A

Average Price PPPD: $366 plus airfare in the Caribbean.
A deluxe outside double with private veranda in categories A or B measure 284 square feet and have a sitting area with sofa that can be converted into a third bed, a TV with VCR, minibar and a refrigerator, as well as a whirlpool bath. Both categories are identical, but the As are one deck higher than the Bs.

Suitable Standards: . . . . B

Average Price PPPD: $269 plus airfare in the Caribbean.
Each large outside double contains twin beds that can convert to queen-sized, a sitting area with sofa and chair, a desk/dresser with stool, coffee table, hair dryer, safe, large closet, and bath with tub/shower combination. Six wheelchair-accessible cabins, outside doubles with shower only, are also available.

Bottom Bunks: . . . . B

Average Price PPPD: $222 plus airfare in the Caribbean.
Even the cheapest cabins on the luxurious vessels are pretty good. Inside doubles are 187 square feet with sitting area sofa and chair, twin beds that can convert to queen-sized, a desk/dresser with stool, coffee table, hair dryer, safe, and a four-door closet. Bathrooms have showers only, and a floral privacy curtain between beds and sitting area.

The Routes

The *Statendam*'s itinerary includes 10-day roundtrip Southern Caribbean sailings from Fort Lauderdale, followed by a repositioning cruise to Alaska through the Panama Canal, then summer-long seven-day Inside Passage cruises from Vancouver that call in Ketchikan, Juneau and Sitka.

The *Maasdam* makes 10-day Panama Canal transits between Acapulco and Fort Lauderdale, then offers a transatlantic crossing to Europe, followed by a summer of Mediterranean and Northern Europe itineraries.

The *Ryndam* makes a winter series of 10-day Southern Caribbean cruises through mid-April from Fort Lauderdale, then repositions to Alaska through the Panama Canal before starting a summer season of seven-day Glacier Route sailings between Vancouver and Seward, calling in Ketchikan, Juneau, Sitka and Valdez. In September the ship is scheduled to return through the canal to the Southern Caribbean to resume its 10-day programs.

The *Veendam* makes a series of seven-day Caribbean itineraries roundtrip from Fort Lauderdale that alternate between the Eastern and Western Caribbean in winter and cruises Alaska in summer. Three special Solar Eclipse sailings are scheduled in February.

The Scoop

A musical production show aboard the Statendam *illustrates HAL's younger, more energetic style that has emerged with the newest class of ships.*

Traditionalists as well as luxury-loving passengers should like these vessels, which gleam with softly burnished wood and brass, with the added zing of dramatic showrooms that are themed from Dutch masterpieces by Vermeer, Rembrandt, Rubens and Van Gogh.

While the decorous gentility will attract well-heeled older passengers, there's enough spark and energy to appeal to upscale younger couples and singles as well. Almost anyone should feel at home aboard, especially if home were a palatial mansion with a smiling staff.

The message these newest Holland America ships seem to be sending is that the company is aiming in the direction of other luxurious large-ship companies, such as Crystal Cruises. Both hardware (the new ships) and software (the food, service and ambience) just keep on improving on this very fine line.

Insider Tips

Five Spectacular Places

1. The striking two-deck Rotterdam dining rooms on all the ships have a magnificent entry stairway ideal for making a grand entrance, window walls on three sides and a ceiling covered with a thousand frosted Venetian glass morning glories.

2. The Crow's Nest top deck observation lounges, especially on the *Maasdam* with its Alaska-themed decor of craggy granite "mountains" and silvery freeform fiber optic tubing that suggests waterways and fjords, with cross-cut wood slabs covering floors, bars and tabletops. On the *Ryndam*, designer Joe Farcus has taken the theme another step, with crackle-glass "glaciers" as flooring and a ceiling of glass cylinders cut at different angles like glacial ice surfaces.

3. The sumptuous and subdued Rembrandt show lounge on the *Maasdam* is like walking into a tasteful, 17th-century drawing room full of fluted mahogany columns, Delft tiles and upholstery fabrics in red and blue shot through with gold threads.

4. The full promenade decks on all the ships, covered in teak and lined with classic wooden deck loungers, invite you to stretch out in the shade with a good book.

5. The handsome covered Lido Deck pool area with its retractable sliding glass dome (ideal in Alaska's changeable climate), playful dolphin sculptures, spas and children's wading pools.

Five Good Reasons to Book These Ships

1. Sunbathers will like the blue terry-cloth covers fitted to the loungers, much more comfortable for wet or oiled bodies than the usual plastic strips or removable cushions.

2. Buffets galore for nibbling and noshing, from an ice-cream-sundae bar to a make-your-own taco stand, free hot fresh popcorn at the movie matinees in the theater, the Chocolate Extravaganza late-night buffet, the hot hors d'oeuvres at cocktail time in the Crow's Nest, the Royal Dutch Tea, and a glass of fresh carrot juice from the juice bar in the Ocean Spa.

3. A good workout, from the Passport to Fitness program (see Gimmicks, above) to a jog around the *Statendam* or a fast game of deck tennis on the *Ryndam* or *Maasdam*, with some aerobics, massage, sauna and steam treatments in the expansive Ocean Spa with its Stairmasters, treadmills, bicycles and free weights.

4. You'll have plenty of closet and drawer space to store your wardrobe, no matter how much you've over-packed.

5. The romantic little piano bars on board each ship, especially the *Maasdam's* elegant candy box of a room with rich gold and crimson curtains swagged from the ceiling like a pasha's tent.

MAASDAM ★★★★
RYNDAM ★★★★
STATENDAM ★★★★
VEENDAM ★★★★

Registry	**The Netherlands**
Officers	**Dutch**
Crew	**Indonesian/Filipino**
Complement	**571**
GRT	**69,130**
Length (ft.)	**720**
Beam (ft.)	**101**
Draft (ft.)	**25**
Passengers-Cabins Full	**1613**
Passengers-2/Cabin	**1266**
Passenger Space Ratio	**54.60**
Stability Rating	**Good to Excellent**
Seatings	**2**
Cuisine	**International**
Dress Code	**Traditional**
Room Service	**Yes**
Tip	**No Tipping Required**

Ship Amenities

Outdoor Pool	**2**
Indoor Pool	**0**
Jacuzzi	**2**
Fitness Center	**Yes**
Spa	**Yes**
Beauty Shop	**Yes**
Showroom	**Yes**
Bars/Lounges	**8**
Casino	**Yes**
Shops	**5**
Library	**Yes**
Child Program	**Yes**
Self-Service Laundry	**Yes**
Elevators	**8**

Cabin Statistics

Suites	**29**
Outside Doubles	**485**
Inside Doubles	**148**
Wheelchair Cabins	**6**
Singles	**0**
Single Surcharge	**150%**
Verandas	**200**
110 Volt	**Yes**

★★★★
NIEUW AMSTERDAM
NOORDAM

In May 1984, two new ships, the Noordam and Sitmar's Fairsky (now Princess Cruises' Sky Princess), each made a debut cruise from Los Angeles to the Mexican Riviera a week apart along the same familiar route down to Puerto Vallarta and back. Cruise writers who were aboard both sailings had spirited arguments back and forth about which ship was prettier, the innovative Fairsky, the last big steamship to be built, or the solid, well-crafted and traditional Noordam. There was no decision, no winners or losers, although proponents of each went away certain their arguments had prevailed.

A tile surround on the aft swimming pool aboard the Noordam *keeps sunbathers cool.*

The *Nieuw Amsterdam* debuted in 1983, the first new ship for Holland America in nearly quarter of a century, and, like her identical sister *Noordam* a year later, was built in France's Chantiers d'Atlantique yard. Despite some noticeable vibration in certain areas, the ships are classy, traditional and comfortable, with museum-quality artifacts relating to sailing and the sea handsomely displayed.

All the cabins are relatively large with plentiful wardrobe space, from the minimum-priced insides to the deluxe staterooms with sitting areas. There are no large suites or private verandas. Outside cabins have windows on Main Deck and above; the portholes begin on A Deck and get more view-restrictive on B and C Decks. Inside cabins mark the imaginary "window" with fabric draperies that are always closed.

Once on board, passengers relax almost instantly in the spacious public rooms and tasteful, subdued decor. There's no glitz or jingle-jangle to bring in a jarring note, and the smiling, soft-spoken serving staff of Indonesians and Filipinos do nothing to break the mood. A few pockets of activity shelter night owls—the Horn Pipe Club on the *Nieuw Amsterdam*, the Pear Tree on the *Noordam*—but most passengers turn in fairly early.

The Brochure Says

"Attentive Filipino and Indonesian crew members offer gracious 'Five-Star' service, expecting no reward beyond your smile of thanks—because Holland America sails under a 'tipping not required' policy."

Translation

Note it does not say, Tipping not permitted. If you wanted to press the issue, you could claim tipping is not required on any cruise ship, but very obviously the passenger is expected to supplement the low base salaries on most major vessels with a tactfully "suggested" tip. Holland America does not permit its employees to "suggest" or even "hint" about a tip; instead, they simply provide excellent service the entire time you're aboard the ship, so that only a churl would even consider disembarking without dispensing some largesse.

INSIDER TIP

Happy Hour in the Crows Nest on the Noordam *is from 4:45 to 5:45 and from 7 to 8 p.m., with the first drink at the regular price and subsequent ones at half-price. Drinks are accompanied by a generous assortment of hot and cold hors d'oeuvres.*

Fantasy Suites: C

Average Price Per Person, Double Occupancy, Per Day: $311 plus airfare in the Caribbean. While there are no really big elegant suites aboard, the top category A cabins offer a great deal of comfort if not space. The wood furnishings are dark and polished, and all accommodations contain a king-sized bed, sitting area with sofa-bed, armchair, table, desk and double windows, as well as mini-refrigerator, closets with good storage space and bathroom with tub/shower combination. The down side is that every window in the A category cabins has a partially obstructed view from hanging lifeboats. The part you'll see through your window is only the top half, which still lets you see some of the sea.

Small Splurges: . . . . B

Average Price PPPD: $282 plus airfare in the Caribbean.

We'd recommend opting for a B or C rather than an A category on these ships, because you'll get the same or even more space, along with tub and shower and sitting area, and may not, depending on deck location, have to look out over hanging lifeboats. The best B cabins are 114 and 115 on Boat Deck, oversized quarters with double bed, and our favorite C cabins are those forward on Boat and Upper Promenade Decks with a captain's-eye view of the sea ahead. On the Boat Deck, cabins #100–103 are wheelchair-accessible quarters with bathroom grip rails, shower seat and low-hanging closet rack.

An inside cabin on the **Noordam** *is spacious and comfortable; notice the curtains that suggest a window may be behind them.*

Suitable Standards: . . . . B

Average Price PPPD: $264 plus airfare in the Caribbean.

If you could nail down one of two E category Large Outsides (cabins E 711 or 716) you'd find a very big cabin with twin beds, large TV, long desk counter, leather headboards, and plenty of storage; these two cabins are almost double the size of the others in this category. The others are also OK, just not so big.

Bottom Bunks: . . . . C+

Average Price PPPD: $207 plus airfare in the Caribbean.

All the lowest-priced inside cabins have two lower beds and are the same size with the same furnishings as most of the other cabins aboard, including color TV, but on a lower deck (C Deck) and forward. You can negotiate an even lower fare with a Y or Z Inside Guarantee, meaning HAL selects your cabin for you.

ANNOYANCES

This is really nit-picking, but the friendly, polite servers stand and chat with well-meaning passengers in the dining room, asking questions about their families and home towns, slowing down the service to a crawl sometimes.

INSIDER TIP

One of the best views of the stage is from the five rows of black leather theater seats in the center back of the main level of the show lounge, where latecomers are often put.

On the balcony level of the show lounges, late arrivals have to sit on the outer edges away from the railing in tables and chairs arranged in conversational groupings, and they do just that–make conversation while the show is going on at a volume that competes with the performers.

The Routes

The *Nieuw Amsterdam* introduces a new series of South American sailings in January and spends summer in Alaska on an Inside Passage seven-day roundtrip itinerary out of Vancouver, calling in Juneau, Sitka and Ketchikan. In the fall of 1997, the ship sails from Vancouver to Asia on a series of Grand Orient and Pacific voyages that visit China, Japan, South Korea, Vietnam, Indonesia and Australia.

The *Noordam* also makes seven-day Western Caribbean sailings in winter, sailing from Tampa and calling in Grand Cayman, Santo Tomas de Castilla in Guatemala, Playa del Carmen and Cozumel, with a summer seven-day Glacier Route in Alaska between Vancouver and Seward, calling in Juneau, Sitka, Ketchikan and Valdez.

The Scoop

While more than 10 years old, both ships are kept remarkably clean in the traditional Holland America shine-and-polish style. Where the age and wear shows is on the few outer deck areas covered with astroturf, with spots, splotches and patches all too apparent. Inside, however, housekeeping is of the sort our mothers used to describe as, "You could eat off the floor."

We like the glass bowls of fresh fruit in the cabins and batik bedspreads with matching privacy curtains, one of the cozy touches the Dutch call *gezellig*, as well as the comfortable places to sit all around the ship with antiques, ship models and old maps to study.

Insider Tips

Five Favorite Spots

1. The Crow's Nest, elegantly cozy forward observation lounges with hot hors d'oeuvres at cocktail time and piano music throughout the evening, as well as period ship models in plexiglass cases.

2. The Lido, where the art of the buffet comes to life; not only does everything look good enough to eat, but it really is. And you can make your own ice cream sundaes for dessert.

3. The Explorer Lounge on the *Nieuw Amsterdam*, with a wall lined with wooden ship figureheads holding lamps; this is where the Rosario Strings play after dinner while bar waiters offer espresso, cappuccino and liqueurs—on a tab, of course.

4. The Ocean Spa on both ships, with massage rooms, saunas, gym with bikes, rowing, treadmills and weights, and just outside, the pool and spas.

5. The broad natural teak deck all around both ships on Upper Promenade, with sheltered, covered reading spots and rows of traditional wooden deck loungers reminiscent of ocean-liner days.

Off-the-Wall

For the birds: The Partridge Bar on the *Nieuw Amsterdam* displays large paintings of peacocks on its back wall.

Five Good Reasons to Book These Ships

1. A tempting range of food opportunities, from light and healthful menus and sugar-free desserts to make-your-own-taco or ice-cream-sundae stations.

2. Hot, fresh popcorn served for movie matinees (but not evening screenings) in the theater.

3. The Dutch figures in traditional costume in the glass cases at the entrance to the Lido restaurant.

4. The broad expanse of Lido Deck in natural teak with fresh water swimming pool, wading pool and splash surround, only steps away from the hot dog/hamburger grill and the outdoor Lido Bar.

5. The classic Holland America tote bag, free to every passenger on every sailing.

Five Things You Won't Find On Board

1. A well-stocked library; if you want to read a current best-seller, bring it yourself.

2. A free self-service laundry; you pay $1 to wash your clothes, but soap and the dryer are free.

3. A bathroom mirror reflection in the designated handicap cabins if you're in a wheelchair; you can easily roll the chair under the sink rim, but can't see your reflection once you're there.

4. Private verandas.

5. A good view of the stage from every seat in the two-deck show lounge, especially in the balcony; you'll have to search to find a good spot from which to see everything.

HOLLAND AMERICA LINE

NIEUW AMSTERDAM ★★★★
NOORDAM ★★★★

Registry	**The Netherlands**
Officers	**Dutch**
Crew	**Indonesian/Filipino**
Complement	**566**
GRT	**33,930**
Length (ft.)	**704**
Beam (ft.)	**89**
Draft (ft.)	**25**
Passengers-Cabins Full	**1378**
Passengers-2/Cabin	**1214**
Passenger Space Ratio	**27.94**
Stability Rating	**Good**
Seatings	**2**
Cuisine	**International**
Dress Code	**Traditional**
Room Service	**Yes**
Tip	**No tipping required**

Ship Amenities

Outdoor Pool	**2**
Indoor Pool	**0**
Jacuzzi	**1**
Fitness Center	**Yes**
Spa	**Yes**
Beauty Shop	**Yes**
Showroom	**Yes**
Bars/Lounges	**8**
Casino	**Yes**
Shops	**3**
Library	**Yes**
Child Program	**Yes**
Self-Service Laundry	**Yes**
Elevators	**7**

Cabin Statistics

Suites	**0**
Outside Doubles	**411**
Inside Doubles	**194**
Wheelchair Cabins	**4**
Singles	**0**
Single Surcharge	**150%**
Verandas	**0**
110 Volt	**Yes**

Unrated
ROTTERDAM VI

The predecessor of this new ship was one of our all-time favorite vessels, the classy and classic *Rotterdam*, in service for Holland America from 1959 until her retirement in the fall of 1997. She was one of the true grande dames of the sea, and it will take a lot more than technology, bells and whistles to replace her.

The new *Rotterdam*, the new flagship for the fleet and sixth to carry this name for HAL, is built especially for world cruising, according to the line, and so, hardly surprising, is scheduled for a 97-day Grand World Voyage in January. First, however, the ship is scheduled to sail an initial season in Europe in late 1997 before arriving in Fort Lauderdale for a few warm-weather cruises. From here, the ship sets out on a Panama Canal transit to Los Angeles to begin the world voyage, an echo of the 29 around-the-world cruises the previous *Rotterdam* made. A series of summer European cruises will follow.

The cruise leaves Los Angeles Jan. 19, and sails to Hawaii, Fiji, New Zealand, Australia, Papua New Guinea, Philippines, Hong Kong, Vietnam, Brunei, Malaysia, India, Seychelles, Kenya, Mauritius, Reunion, South Africa, Tristan de Cunha, Argentina, Uruguay, Brazil and Trinidad before arriving in Fort Lauderdale on April 24 and New York City on April 26.

The ship itself is much larger than its predecessor at 62,000 tons and carrying 1316 passengers. The topmost decks have plenty of sports and sunning areas, with a sliding dome cover over an amidships pool, a traditional Holland America design feature. A pair of paddle tennis courts and a large sun lounging area are aft on Sports Deck with the Crow's Nest Bar, another HAL signature, forward as observation lounge.

On Lido Deck forward is the Ocean Spa with a sizable gym facing the sea through glass windows, an aerobics area and a juice bar. A beauty salon, treatment rooms for massage and facials, and steam room and saunas are adjacent. On the amidships deck, sheltered by the sliding dome roof, is a pool, wading pool and pair of whirlpool spas, a terrace grill for hot dogs and hamburgers cooked to order, and a terrace bar. Aft is the expansive Lido self-service restaurant with two serving lines and indoor and outdoor seating.

Another swimming pool is located aft on Navigation Deck. The most expensive suites, all with private verandas, are also located on Navigation Deck, with additional private balcony cabins one deck lower on Verandah Deck. The public rooms are located on Upper Promenade Deck and Promenade Deck. A two-deck show lounge called the Queens Lounge is forward, with the double-deck, glass-walled La Fontaine Restaurant aft. In between are the casino, a series of shops, the library and puzzle corner, cinema, ship's lobby and the popular Ocean Bar, another HAL trademark. An alternative dining area called Odyssey Restaurant is amidships on Promenade Deck.

Three lower decks of cabins, both insides and outsides, are below the main public rooms, as are self-service launderettes, hospital facilities and staff offices. The lower promenade deck has a full, around-the-ship teak promenade, still another HAL feature.

Standard cabins are all fairly spacious, with two lower beds that can be converted to queen-sized, a tile bathroom with tub and/or shower. The smallest are the bottom-priced insides at a generous 192 square feet, while outside doubles are 196 square feet.

Big spenders will appreciate Navigation Deck, except for an aft pool and sunbathing area dedicated entirely to suites. The most opulent are four penthouses featuring oversized whirlpool tubs in the bathroom, separate living room and bedroom, private veranda, minibar, refrigerator, TV with VCR, dressing room and sofa bed that can sleep an additional passenger. The 36 other suites are 575 square feet each, with similar furnishings and amenities to the penthouses. What should be especially appealing to passengers who want to enjoy upscale digs and are willing to pay well for them is the Suites Lounge, located amidships among all the suites, which will serve as a private lounge and meeting area.

Social hosts will be aboard for dancing and socializing with single women travelers.

ROTTERDAM VI   Unrated

Registry	The Netherlands
Officers	Dutch and European
Crew	Indonesian/Filipino
Complement	700
GRT	62,000
Length (ft.)	778
Beam (ft.)	NA
Draft (ft.)	NA
Passengers-Cabins Full	1655
Passengers-2/Cabin	1316
Passenger Space Ratio	47.11
Stability Rating	NA
Seatings	2
Cuisine	International
Dress Code	Traditional
Room Service	Yes
Tip	No tipping required

Ship Amenities

Outdoor Pool	2
Indoor Pool	0
Jacuzzi	2
Fitness Center	Yes
Spa	Yes
Beauty Shop	Yes
Showroom	Yes
Bars/Lounges	10
Casino	Yes
Shops	3
Library	Yes
Child Program	Yes
Self-Service Laundry	Yes
Elevators	12

Cabin Statistics

Suites	40
Outside Doubles	500
Inside Doubles	118
Wheelchair Cabins	23
Singles	0
Single Surcharge	120–200%
Verandas	162
110 Volt	Yes

HOLLAND AMERICA LINE

★★★★
WESTERDAM

Built in Papenburg, Germany, by Meyer Werft as the Homeric *for now-defunct Home Lines, the* Westerdam *was, until the new* Rotterdam VI, *Holland America's largest ship, thanks to a "stretching" from the same shipyard in 1989. How do you stretch a ship? Very, very carefully. Cut through the superstructure with acetylene torches, then check to make sure all the units have been completely severed by running a piano wire along the cut from top to bottom. Drop in a prefabricated midsection, then put it all back together again.*

The distinctive Sun Deck pool area with its sliding glass roof and enclosed glass-walled veranda offers optimum comfort both in Alaska's cool climate and the Caribbean when it gets hot and muggy. The same walls and roof that let in the sun and keep out the rain also hold in the air conditioning.

Nine passenger decks, two separate self-service buffet restaurants, two outside swimming pools, a two-deck showroom and a number of lounges keep the 1494 passengers well dispersed around the ship, while a wood-and-plexiglass dome with special lighting brightens the lower-deck dining room.

Perhaps a little less formal than the line's other ships, the *Westerdam* offers some competitive prices on seven-day cruises. The Big Apple teen disco and video center make this a good ship for families.

HOLLAND AMERICA LINE

Between The Lines

The Brochure Says

"The *Westerdam* may be the best value in the Caribbean...and she sails into the new season with exciting new amenities: a new Sports Bar with ESPN, expanded Spa and Fitness Center, and for the kids, the action of Club HAL."

Translation

The line keeps polishing and improving their ships as they see a younger clientele and more families with children coming aboard.

Cabins & Costs

Fantasy Suites: . . . . B+

Average Price Per Person, Double Occupancy, Per Day: $478 plus airfare in the Caribbean.

The five top suites on board are located on Lower Promenade Deck amidships, the traditional place for the most expensive cabins on classic vessels because the ride is smoother. Larger than two standard cabins, each of the suites has a separate bedroom with two lower beds that can convert to king-size, a living room with sofa bed that can sleep an additional two persons, as well as several comfortable upholstered chairs, a bathroom with tub and shower and some handsome cabinetry.

Small Splurges: . . . . B

Average Price PPPD: $283 plus airfare in the Caribbean.

Deluxe double cabins in C category are long rooms with separate sitting area which has sofa and matching chair, plus a sleeping area that can be set off with curtains that close. The entry hallway is lined on one side with two closets, on the other with tile bathroom with tub/shower combination. A desk/dresser with stool and a coffee table round out the furnishings.

Suitable Standards: C

Average Price PPPD: $226 plus airfare in the Caribbean.

Standard outside cabins with two lower beds are somewhat smaller than the deluxe, without the sofa and sitting area, and bathrooms have shower only. There is a desk/dresser with good storage drawers and a mirror over and stool underneath.

Bottom Bunks: . . . . **C**

Average Price PPPD: $199 plus airfare in the Caribbean.

The cheapest standard inside cabins, which are N category, have two lower beds that can convert to queen-sized bed, a nightstand, desk/dresser, TV set and bath with shower only, but are surprisingly spacious for bottom-of-the-line. However, there are only nine of these, so don't expect to nab one right off the bat. You may have to move up a grade or two on a popular cruise, but HAL has always been good about upgrading passengers when space permits.

The Routes

The *Westerdam* cruises the Eastern Caribbean in winter from Fort Lauderdale on seven-day itineraries, calling at San Juan, St. John, St. Thomas and Nassau. In fall she makes a series of Canada/New England cruises before returning to the Caribbean.

The Scoop

While the *Westerdam* is the only vessel in the fleet not built from the hull up by Holland America, she still has been rebuilt to fit almost seamlessly into the fleet. (A hint: If you're looking for her "stretch" marks, begin in the smaller dining room addition amidships on Restaurant Deck, the Bookchest library on Promenade Deck, the self-service laundries on Upper Promenade and Navigation Decks or the Veranda Deck and restaurant on Sun Deck.)

A very good value for the money, *Westerdam* provides bigger-than-average cabins and a sense of comfort throughout.

Insider Tips

Five Favorite Places

1. The beautiful Veranda restaurant with live music during luncheon and tea is one of the prettiest self-service cafes at sea; there's a second Lido Cafe two decks below.

2. The amidships Veranda pool area adjacent, with a sliding glass dome so you can sit comfortably in a lounge chair, loll in the Jacuzzi or swim in the heated pool even on a chilly day.

3. The 127-seat Admiral's Terrace balcony overlooking the main stage has some good sightlines for the evening's entertainment, but late arrivals have to stand to see the show. The 680-seat Admiral's Lounge below provides big, cushy theater-type seats and couches and is probably a better bet.

4. The volleyball and paddle tennis courts on Sports Deck, covered at the sides and top with nets, get a good workout on short cruises.

5. The 17th-century bronze cannon, cast in Rotterdam in 1634, once defended a Dutch admiral's warship, then lay at the bottom of the sea for 300 years until a Dutch fisherman dragged it up in his nets.

Five Good Reasons to Book This Ship

1. It sails to some of the most popular ports in the Eastern Caribbean—San Juan, Puerto Rico; Nassau, Bahamas; and St. Thomas and St. John in the U.S. Virgin Islands.

2. To try and find the seams from the "stretch," which added 130 feet in length, 13,872 more gross registry tons and capability for 494 more passengers.

3. Because four laps on the all-around-the-ship Upper Promenade Deck make one mile.

4. Because for the price range the cabins are unusually spacious.

5. The little hideaway Saloon with a Victorian accent and singalong piano bar.

Five Things You Won't Find On Board

1. Private verandas.

2. An indoor swimming pool.

3. A single cabin.

4. Skimpy cabins for wheelchair users; designated mobility impaired, cabins E002, D068, J021 and D087 are all on upper decks with plenty of extra turning space.

5. A long walk to an elevator; with four locations along each deck, it's an easy stroll to a lift.

WESTERDAM ★★★★

Registry	**The Netherlands**
Officers	**Dutch**
Crew	**Indonesian/Filipino**
Complement	**639**
GRT	**53,872**
Length (ft.)	**798**
Beam (ft.)	**104**
Draft (ft.)	**25**
Passengers-Cabins Full	**1833**
Passengers-2/Cabin	**1494**
Passenger Space Ratio	**36.04**
Stability Rating	**Good to Excellent**
Seatings	**2**
Cuisine	**International**
Dress Code	**Traditional**
Room Service	**Yes**
Tip	**No tipping required**

Ship Amenities

Outdoor Pool	**2**
Indoor Pool	**0**
Jacuzzi	**2**
Fitness Center	**Yes**
Spa	**Yes**
Beauty Shop	**Yes**
Showroom	**Yes**
Bars/Lounges	**8**
Casino	**Yes**
Shops	**3**
Library	**Yes**
Child Program	**Yes**
Self-Service Laundry	**Yes**
Elevators	**7**

Cabin Statistics

Suites	**5**
Outside Doubles	**495**
Inside Doubles	**252**
Wheelchair Cabins	**4**
Singles	**0**
Single Surcharge	**150%**
Verandas	**0**
110 Volt	**Yes**

IVA'RAN
Lines
Since 1925

111 Pavonia Avenue, Jersey City, NJ 07310-1755
☎ (201) 798-5656, (800) 451-1639

Aboard Ivaran's **Americana** *is a surprisingly spacious pool and deck area.*

History ·

The distinguished freighter-cruise company Ivaran Lines began in 1925, but its freight-carrying vessels started way back in 1902. The company's funnels bear a white "C" on a field of red for its founder, Norwegian-born Ivar Anton Christensen, who signed himself Ivar An. Christensen. Over the years, the company has had a number of notable executives, include Anders Wilhelmssen, co-founder and co-owner of Royal Caribbean Cruises Ltd., who was made general manager of Ivaran in 1950.

The *Americana*, hands-down the most luxurious of the cargo-carrying passenger ships, was built in Korea by Hyundai Heavy Industries and made its maiden voyage in 1988. It remains the world's only container/cruise vessel. Ivaran had the option to build two more, but the Korean authorities refused to grant export license when the options were declared, and the building of any similar vessels was put on hold indefinitely.

The vessel sails from ports in the southeastern United States to ports along the Atlantic coast of South America, selling both full voyages of some 53 days and segments of five or more days. One reason the *Americana* is an exceptional vessel is because it carries 88 passengers, whereas the usual freighter takes a maximum of 12 passengers. That's because of a ruling that any seagoing ship with more than 12 passengers has to have a doctor aboard. The line also has a more traditional, new 12-passenger cargo ship *San Antonio*, with six single and three double cabins, a small dining room, lounge, bar and conference room.

—Operates the world's only container/cruise vessel (*Americana*, 1988).

Concept...

The *Americana* is a hybrid, a small luxury cruise ship riding atop a workaday cargo vessel.

Signatures..

The white C on the red stack.

Gimmicks..

A Norwegian dinner is served once during each cruise, making the officers particularly happy, since otherwise they have to eat the same continental menu the passengers do.

Who's the Competition................................

Nobody at all, because there's no other comparable vessel in passenger service today. Purists sniff that the *Americana* is too luxurious for a freighter, which suits us just fine.

Who's Aboard..

On our sailing, while there were some younger people—a California psychiatrist and his wife in their early 40s, two young Norwegian men, the captain's 16-year-old daughter—most passengers are singles and couples past retirement age, one a sprightly retired priest from New York near 90. There's no maximum age limit like most freighters have because the *Americana* carries a doctor.

Who Should Go ....

The *Americana* represents a good travel buy for the right kind of passenger—including veterans of freighter travel, for example, who are beyond the age limit set by some freighters with no doctors. Other candidates are single passengers tired of paying surcharges for occupying a cabin alone—Americana has a number of single cabins that cost little more than the per-person, double-occupancy rate—and anyone who hankers to write The Great American Novel. The late Alex Haley wrote most of his books aboard freighters.

Who Should Not Go ....

Mobility-impaired travelers will find there are no wheelchair-accessible cabins, although there is an elevator for the passenger decks. But the long steep gangway from the dock is difficult to negotiate.

No families with children, because there's nowhere for children to play.

Anyone who needs a cruise staff to keep him or her entertained.

The Lifestyle . . . .

Since there may be as many as nine days at sea between port calls, the ambiance on board takes on a long-cruise flavor, with groups of two or three chatting quietly together in the lounge, others reading on the spacious sunny deck or in the quiet, well-stocked library, still other swimming in the deck pool, working out in the gym or screening a feature film on the ship's video system or their own in-cabin VCR. In port, optional shore excursions are sometimes available. The cruise experience of posh cabins and dining room service is expanded with an easygoing freighter ambiance and the unpredictability of arrival and departure times.

Wardrobe . . . .

Casual clothing is acceptable on the vessel and in the ports in the daytime, but the passengers like to dress up a little on special evenings such as the captain's welcome aboard party. On many evenings men are requested to wear jacket and tie in the public areas after 6 p.m. Don't forget a bathing suit; there's a pool and Jacuzzi on board. And bring good walking and deck shoes. Forty cubic feet of baggage is permitted aboard for each passenger.

Bill of Fare C

Meals are served in one seating, with large buffet breakfasts and lunches, and sit-down dinner service with a choice of two soups, three main dishes (one is always a reliable grilled steak with baked potato) and several desserts. Homemade pastries and baked goods are particularly nice, but since the galley is five decks below the passenger dining room, most of the hot dishes have been waiting in the finishing kitchen on a steam table.

Showtime . . . . N/A

Unlike regular cruise ships, the *Americana* has little in the way of organized shipboard activities, only an occasional after-dinner program of Trivial Pursuit, dancing to recorded music, blackjack, or entertainment brought on from shore, such as a lively samba group. Although there are six slot machines on board, we never saw anyone playing them.

Discounts . . . .

Passengers sailing a full southbound or northbound voyage may discount 5 percent on cruise only fares, and Fly/Sail passengers may discount 5 percent on that package.

The Bottom Line

Because it is primarily a cargo vessel, the *Americana* does not have stabilizers, so the ride, while not uncomfortable, is less smooth than on many new cruise vessels, with a little more vibration discernible in some parts of the ship. You'll have to climb up and down a very steep gangway in port, although once you reach the passenger decks, there is an elevator. Regulations vary in ports; don't expect to be permitted to casually stroll around during loading and unloading operations.

★ ★ ★
AMERICANA

Most people have only a day in a port of call such as Santos, South America's busiest port, a two-hour drive away from the continent's largest city, São Paulo. But those of us aboard the Americana, *a passenger-carrying cargo ship, have two whole days to explore the area while our vessel is loading and unloading some of 1120 containers of automobile parts or animal hides. Another two days is spent in Buenos Aires, perhaps taking on canned corned beef and taking off coffee beans. Since all containers look alike, we're never sure which one holds what.*

The same designers that did the Sea Goddess and Seabourn ships created the interiors for the *Americana*. The passenger areas cover six decks, with three decks of cabins connected by a graceful center staircase with curved chrome railings. Both public rooms and cabins are elegantly decorated and extremely comfortable; you won't be roughing it on this vessel!

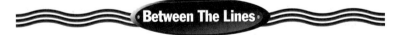

Between The Lines

The Brochure Says

"If you watch enough of the Late, Late Show, your image of dining aboard a freighter will be that of Humphrey Bogart or Clark Gable sitting at a wooden table in the crew's mess as the stew is served during a South China Sea storm. It's fun to watch, but we don't think that's quite the kind of adventure you have in mind."

Translation

Roughing it at sea aboad the *Americana* is like camping-out in a $500,000 motorhome. Despite its being a cargo-carrying vessel the ship's expansive cabins, dining and other accoutrements make this a truly deluxe cruise.

Cabins & Costs

Fantasy Suites: . . . . **A**

Average Price Per Person, Double Occupancy, Per Day: $327 including international air-fare and hotel stay in Buenos Aires.
The two top suites aboard are called the Americana Suite and the Presidential Suite, but also sometimes referred to as the owner's suites, presumably because they overlook the containers, surely a view only an owner could love. The suites—really apartments—have an entry foyer, a large living room with sofa, two chairs, coffee table, lots of windows, separate bedroom and one and a half baths, as well as two TV/VCRs and two minibars.

Small Splurges: . . . . **A**

Average Price PPPD: $285 including international airfare and hotel stay in Buenos Aires.
The deluxe suites with big private balconies are like the standard cabins (see Suitable Standards, below) but have the outside area with two lounging chairs facing aft on a painted green deck.

Suitable Standards: . . . . **A**

Average Price PPPD: $251 including international airfare and hotel stay in Buenos Aires.
Standard double cabins measure 258 square feet, with king-sized or twin beds, sofa and chair in a sitting area, two built-in desks with chairs, five closets and plenty of enclosed shelf space, a refrigerator and minibar, TV and VCR, combination safe, hair dryer, fresh fruit, fresh flowers and a welcome-aboard bottle of champagne. Each large bathroom has a tub/shower combination and bidet, as well as plenty of storage shelves in the mirrored medicine cabinets and a lavish gift kit of toiletries.

Bottom Bunks: . . . . **B**

Average Price PPPD: $207 for an inside, $251 for an outside, including international air-fare and hotel stay in Buenos Aires.
Singles get a break on the *Americana* because the company has installed 8 outside and 12 inside singles and priced them at a flat rate with no surcharge. Singles measure 133.5 square feet and contain a bed that makes into a sofa for daytime, a coffee table, chair, built-in desk/dresser, TV/VCR, bath with shower and adequate closet space.

The Routes

The *Americana* goes from New Orleans to South America on 53-day roundtrip sailings, usually calling at Houston; Rio de Janeiro and Santos, Brazil; and Buenos Aires, Argentina, on the southbound route; and Sao Francisco or Paranagua/Itajai, Santos and Rio de Janeiro, Salvador de Bahia, Brazil; Puerto Cabello, Veracruz and Altamira, Mexico, on the northbound itinerary. Passengers may book the full cruise or only the northbound or southbound portions, along with a package that includes airfare and hotel stays in New Orleans or Buenos Aires.

The Scoop

The *Americana* is best for self-reliant people with good sea legs who don't require constant entertainment and diversion, especially singles who want to avoid punishing surcharges and couples who want big, lavish cabins at moderate prices. Because cargo scheduling takes priority, potential passengers must be flexible about departure and arrival dates and ports of call. The housekeeping and service aboard are outstanding, and tipping is not required. Friendly South American staffers fluent in English call passengers by name and know each one's drink preferences within a day or two. The Norwegian officers are always around at mealtime and in the evenings to socialize, and the navigation bridge is open at all times to passengers. If you fit the profile of a freighter passenger, this vessel has our highest recommendation.

Five Sociable Spots

1. The Neptune Lounge has a white piano, a bar with six or eight stools, a long row of windows, fixed round tables and nicely upholstered sofas and chairs.

2. The teak sports and pool deck has a bar (that is rarely open), a pool, Jacuzzi and shower, shuffleboard court, lots of lounge and regular deck chairs and round tables bolted down.

3. Glass-doored bookcases, leather sofas and chairs and leather-topped tables make the library a good place for reading or playing cards.

4. The dining room has double glass doors and two rows of tables set for five or six places each; meals are served at a single open seating with a long center buffet used for food service at breakfast and lunch, for appetizer and cheese displays in the evening.

5. The large gymnasium has mirrored walls and an array of exercise equipment.

Five Good Reasons to Book This Ship

1. It has niceties freighters don't always offer—a gift shop, beauty shop, masseuse, sauna and self-service laundromat with ironing boards.

2. To get an in-depth look at the east coast of South America.

3. To write or read The Great American Novel.

4. To be treated like an individual rather than a number.

5. To get away from it all.

Five Things You Won't Find On Board

1. A singles surcharge.

2. A children's program; this ship is inappropriate for small children.

3. A cabin designated wheelchair-accessible; the ship is not appropriate for mobility-impaired passengers.

4. Tips. There's no tipping required.

5. Age limits.

AMERICANA ★★★

Registry	**Norway**
Officers	**Norwegian**
Crew	**South American**
Complement	**53**
GRT	**19,500**
Length (ft.)	**578**
Beam (ft.)	**85**
Draft (ft.)	**32**
Passengers-Cabins Full	**102**
Passengers-2/Cabin	**84**
Passenger Space Ratio	**NA**
Stability Rating	**Good**
Seatings	**2**
Cuisine	**Continental**
Dress Code	**Casual**
Room Service	**No**
Tip	**No Tipping**

Ship Amenities

Outdoor Pool	**1**
Indoor Pool	**0**
Jacuzzi	**1**
Fitness Center	**Yes**
Spa	**No**
Beauty Shop	**Yes**
Showroom	**No**
Bars/Lounges	**1**
Casino	**No**
Shops	**1**
Library	**Yes**
Child Program	**No**
Self-Service Laundry	**Yes**
Elevators	**2**

Cabin Statistics

Suites	**10**
Outside Doubles	**22**
Inside Doubles	**0**
Wheelchair Cabins	**0**
Singles	**20**
Single Surcharge	**None**
Verandas	**4**
110 Volt	**Yes**

MEDITERRANEAN SHIPPING
C R U I S E S

420 Fifth Avenue, New York, NY 10018
☎ *(212) 764-4800, (800) 666-9333*

History . . . .

This Italian line began as Flotta Lauro (Lauro Fleet) but was little-known in the United States until the 1985 terrorist attack on the *Achille Lauro* off Egypt when an American passenger was killed. Later, the company changed its name to StarLauro Cruises.

In 1990, Mediterranean Shipping Company, part of the giant Swiss shipping group MSC, purchased StarLauro, which at that time was sailing the *Achille Lauro* and the *Angelina Lauro,* and shortly afterward purchased the *Monterey,* formerly a U.S. flag vessel operated by short-lived Aloha Pacific Cruises in Hawaii, which immediately became the company's flagship. Mediterranean Shipping operates more than 40 cargo liners around the world.

The ill-fated *Achille Lauro* sank off the Horn of Africa in 1994 (see "Where Are They Now?" page 123) and the *Angelina Lauro* was retired from the fleet. Replacing them are the former *Cunard Princess,* now the *Rhapsody,* and the former *EnricoCosta,* now the *Symphony.*

In 1996, they changed the company name from StarLauro to Mediterranean Shipping Cruises and began more active promotion in the North American market.

In 1997, MSC purchased the *Star/Ship Atlantic* from Premier Cruise Line for $70 million and renamed her *Melody.* The ship's Caribbean debut under her new name is in January 1998.

MEDITERRANEAN SHIPPING CRUISES

529

★ ★ ★
MELODY*

Our first surprise aboard Star/Ship Atlantic *was that the ice cream parlor was filled with more adults than children, many of them seniors on special discounts, spooning up the make-your-own sundaes with obvious delight. Next door in the pub not much was happening.*

Built in 1982, the former *Atlantic* is a durable vessel with high passenger density, thanks to those 452 upper berths in the cabins. A sliding plexiglass roof over the amidships terrace and pool makes the area comfortable year-round. Passenger activity is concentrated on the Pool Deck and Lounge Deck with most of the cabins and the dining room below. A group of cabins is also located forward on Lounge Deck, and a children's play area is aft on the deck below Lounge Deck with its own kiddies' pool outside.

The new *Melody* made her European debut in June 1997, and winters in the Caribbean.

The Brochure Says

"We are delighted to be able to offer the American public a Caribbean program onboard a magnificent ship like to *Melody* with a classic Italian atmosphere."

Translation

The ship, built for now defunct Home Lines, returns to its Italian roots.

Fantasy Suites: . . . . **C**

Average Price Per Person, Double Occupancy, Per Day: $236 in the Caribbean.

The largest accommodations on board are the apartment suites, which have a sitting room with sofa-bed and TV set and a bedroom with queen-sized bed, enough space for a family of four. While not huge, these are twice the size of the suites in the next category down, and have bathrooms with tub.

Small Splurges: C
Average Price PPPD: NA.
Demi-suites have queen-sized bed or two lower beds plus third and fourth upper berths. Both have sitting area, TV sets and bathroom with tub.

Suitable Standards: C
Average Price PPPD: NA.
Outside cabins are about the same size but on a lower deck. A few have one upper berth for a third child, but most have two lower beds or a queen-sized bed plus two or even three additional berths, sitting area, TV and bathroom with tub. Four outside cabins are designated wheelchair-accessible.

Bottom Bunks: . . . . D
Average Per Person Per Day, Quad Occupancy: $60 in the Caribbean.
The cheapest cabins are insides with four berths and bathroom with shower only.

The Routes

The *Melody* enters the Caribbean in January 1998, offering 11-night cruises from Fort Lauderdale into the Yucatan, Jamaica and Santo Domingo. Following the sailing of April 11, the ship returns to Europe for a summer of sailings from Genoa to Capri, Sicily, Tunisia and Spain.

The Scoop

As the *Melody*, the ship retains its former density and so offers good budget cruise options in the Mediterranean and the Caribbean. We'll be glad to see the lovely pool areas aft and amidships filled with adults again after a long session of kiddie cruises for Premier.

Insider Tips

Five Favorite Spots

1. The Sunrise Terrace, formerly an observation lounge, has been turned into a cafe with ice cream tables and chairs and two buffet service lines leading into it from the terrace.

2. The Galaxy Restaurant with its dome overhead serves meals at assigned tables in two seatings.

3. Club Universe is a handsome room where shows are presented, along with port talks, bingo and the captain's cocktail party; don't sit behind one of the big posts, however, or you'll miss some of the show.

4. The casino has a roulette table, craps table, six blackjack tables and lots of slots.

5. The Calypso Pool is aft on the pool deck, surrounded by a natural teak deck, a lot of lounge chairs, a couple of whirlpools and a small bandstand.

MELODY*   ★★★

Registry	**Liberia**
Officers	**Italian**
Crew	**International**
Complement	**535**
GRT	**35,143**
Length (ft.)	**671**
Beam (ft.)	**90**
Draft (ft.)	**25**
Passengers-Cabins Full	**1550**
Passengers-2/Cabin	**1098**
Passenger Space Ratio	**32**
Stability Rating	**Good**
Seatings	**2**
Cuisine	**Italian**
Dress Code	**Traditional**
Room Service	**Yes**
Tip	**$9 PPPD**

Ship Amenities

Outdoor Pool	**2**
Indoor Pool	**1**
Jacuzzi	**1**
Fitness Center	**Yes**
Spa	**No**
Beauty Shop	**Yes**
Showroom	**Yes**
Bars/Lounges	**5**
Casino	**Yes**
Shops	**2**
Library	**Yes**
Child Program	**Yes**
Self-Service Laundry	**Yes**
Elevators	**4**

Cabin Statistics

Suites	**6**
Outside Doubles	**371**
Inside Doubles	**178**
Wheelchair Cabins	**4**
Singles	**14**
Single Surcharge	**125%**
Verandas	**0**
110 Volt	**Yes**

★★★
MONTEREY*

When Aloha Pacific Cruises brought back the classic Monterey in 1988, she sailed triumphantly into Honolulu in the morning, echoing the images of the 1930s "boat day" with welcoming bands and hula dancers at the Aloha Tower, and orchids dropped from a helicopter to the cheering passengers on deck. Unfortunately, it went downhill from there, with ruinous charges and countercharges involving competitor American Hawaii and an underfinanced venture operated by cruise-line amateurs. After making only a few cruises around the islands, Aloha Pacific declared bankruptcy and the Monterey was laid up in Honolulu and sold to the highest bidder more than a year later.

The American-built ship, launched at Sparrows Point Shipyard in 1952 as the *Free State Mariner*, was renovated handsomely, if sparely, in 1988, following stringent guidelines from the U.S. Coast Guard. When Mediterranean Shipping acquired the ship, it made only nominal changes, since the refit had been so recent. It even retained the Hawaiian-accented deck names.

As on many ships of that vintage, the cinema, disco and gymnasium are located below the passenger decks deep in the bowels of the ship. A tiny casino, not a part of the ship previously, is adjacent to the disco. The restaurant and passenger cabins are located on the Aloha Deck, while the Maile Deck, one deck above, has the majority of the cabins plus a small forward sun lounging area.

Cabins are located forward on the Promenade Deck, with bars and lounges, library, card room, swimming pool and outdoor cafe amidships and aft. The Promenade runs three-quarters of the way around the ship, but above on the Boat Deck, walkers and joggers have a full around-the-ship track. Aft on the Boat Deck is the self-service cafe. The topmost deck is dedicated to table tennis, volleyball and other sports activities.

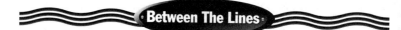

The Brochure Says

"The *Monterey* takes you to the most historic cities in the Mediterranean—in the ultimate Italian style."

Translation

I'll meet you in Captain Cook's Bar for a mai tai, Guido.

NOTE: All prices are approximate and are calculated per person, double occupancy, per day.

Fantasy Suites...

Average Price Per Person, Double Occupancy, Per Day: $409 including airfare from New York.
Two royal suites are located amidships on Promenade Deck, more than twice the size of other outside cabins. There's a separate sitting area, a bedroom and bathroom with tub. Soft furnishings (bedspreads and curtains) are attractive, but the cabin walls are still as austere as before.

Small Spluges ....

Average Price PPPD: $340 including airfare from New York.
Deluxe outside cabins on the Boat, Promenade and Maile Decks have twin beds, sitting areas and desk/dresser combinations. Cabin size and furnishings vary from deck to deck.

Suitable Standards...

Average Price PPPD: $313 including airfare from New York.
One peculiarity of U.S. built ships from the 1950s are the folding bed/sofas that, while well-upholstered and perfectly comfortable, look like bunks. Some of the outside and inside double cabins offer these.

Bottom Bunks ....

Average Price PPPD: $227 including airfare from New York.
Inside cabins with two berths may mean uppers and lowers in some instances, so clarify before you book.

The *Monterey* spends part of 1998 out of service while being refitted to comply with SOLAS regulations. Her normal cruising venues are the eastern and western areas of the Mediterranean.

MONTEREY* ★★★

Registry	**Panama**
Officers	**Italian**
Crew	**International**
Complement	**280**
GRT	**21,061**
Length (ft.)	**565**
Beam (ft.)	**80**
Draft (ft.)	**29.4**
Passengers Full	**638**
Passengers 2/Cabin	**600**
Passenger Space Ratio	**35.10**
Stability Rating	**Good**
Seatings	**2**
Cuisine	**Continental/Italian**
Dress code	**Traditional**
Room service	**Yes**
Tip	**$8.50 PPPD**

Ship Amenities

Outdoor Pool	**1**
Indoor Pool	**0**
Jacuzzi	**2**
Fitness Center	**Yes**
Spa	**No**
Beauty Shop	**Yes**
Showroom	**Yes**
Bars/Lounges	**3**
Casino	**Yes**
Shops	**3**
Library	**Yes**
Child Program	**Limited**
Self-Service Laundry	**No**
Elevators	**2**

Cabin Statistics

Suites	**4**
Outside Doubles	**159**
Inside Doubles	**96**
Wheelchair Cabins	**0**
Singles	**0**
Single Surcharge	**140–150%**
Verandas	**0**
110 Volt	**Yes**

★ ★ ★
RHAPSODY*

We were aboard the QE2 with members of the cruise staff the day the news came of the sale of the Cunard Princess to Mediterranean Shipping, and we saw how dearly beloved the ship that we always considered one of Cunard's ugly ducklings was to staffers who worked aboard her. A pall fell over the conversation, and everyone sighed and stared down into their drinks.

A veteran warm-weather ship, the *Rhapsody* has its top decks devoted to sunbathing, jogging, paddle tennis, splashing (the pool is a bit small for swimming) and soaking in a Jacuzzi. The children's pool is nearby, so parents can keep an eye on the kids.

Cabins are located primarily on the three lowest passenger decks, with a few top-category accommodations forward on the two public rooms decks, Five and Six. The Six Deck has the showlounge, small casino and Eight Bells indoor and outdoor center, bar and dance floor with more sunbathing aft, while the Five Deck aft is where the self-service Outrigger Cafe is located. A cinema and indoor lounge are adjacent, with the dining room amidships.

The Brochure Says

"The superb hospitality, congenial atmosphere and reasonable rates make the *Rhapsody* ideal for cruising to the diverse Mediterranean destinations."

Translation

Comfortable and unintimidating, the *Rhapsody* is that increasingly rare favorite, a midsized vessel that still looks like a ship.

Cabins & Costs

Fantasy Suites . . . .

Average Price Per Person, Double Occupancy, Per Day: $333 plus air add-on.
The two category 1 suites on the Five deck are next to the restaurant and elevators and relatively spacious, with king-sized bed, sitting area and long desk/dresser with storage.

Small Splurges. . . . .

Average Price PPPD: $272 plus air add-on.
Mini-suites are really more like deluxe cabins, almost half the size of the suites but offer twin or double beds, sitting area and adequate closet space.

Suitable Standards. . . . .

Average Price PPPD: $245 plus air add-on.
Outside doubles with twin beds have a corner nightstand, a desk/dresser with stool and bathroom with shower.

Bottom Bunks . . . .

Average Price PPPD: $127 plus air add-on.
Inside doubles have two lower beds, even in the bottom category, so if you're not claustrophobic, you could consider booking an inside and saving a little money.

The Routes

The *Rhapsody* sails from Genoa on an 18-night cruise to Rio de Janeiro on Nov. 15, followed by a series of short sailings between Rio and Santos (for São Paolo) and around Brazil until March, when the ship returns to Europe for the summer.

RHAPSODY* ★★★

Registry	**Panama**
Officers	**Italian**
Crew	**International**
Complement	**350**
GRT	**16,850**
Length (ft.)	**541**
Beam (ft.)	**76**
Draft (ft.)	**19**
Passengers Full	**950**
Passengers 2/Cabin	**790**
Passenger Space Ratio	**21.32**
Stability Rating	**Good**
Seatings	**2**
Cuisine	**Continental/Italian**
Dress code	**Traditional**
Room service	**Yes**
Tip	**$8.50 PPPD**

Ship Amenities

Outdoor Pool	**1**
Indoor Pool	**0**
Jacuzzi	**2**
Fitness Center	**Yes**
Spa	**No**
Beauty Shop	**Yes**
Showroom	**Yes**
Bars/Lounges	**5**
Casino	**Yes**
Shops	**2**
Library	**Yes**
Child Program	**Limited**
Self-Service Laundry	**No**
Elevators	**2**

Cabin Statistics

Suites	**22**
Outside Doubles	**234**
Inside Doubles	**129**
Wheelchair Cabins	**0**
Singles	**0**
Single Surcharge	**140–150%**
Verandas	**0**
110 Volt	**Yes**

★★★
SYMPHONY*

The former EnricoCosta began life as the Provence, built for South American service in 1951, when ships rather than planes were the best way to travel a great distance. In the early days, the ship carried three classes of passengers—actually four, because third class was divided into third class with cabins and the cheaper third class with dormitories. In 1965, after several years of chartering the vessel, Costa purchased it and renamed it the Enrico C, which later became EnricoCosta.

The two topmost decks are dedicated to Mediterranean fun-in-the-sun, with three swimming pools, one on the Sun Deck and two below on the Lounge Deck. The outdoor Sun Restaurant is also on the top deck. The Lounge Deck houses most of the remaining public areas aboard, from the forward Riviera Lounge, the larger amidships Alassio Lounge, as well as the photo shop, card room, beauty shop and boutiques.

A cozy tavern is aft on the Promenade Deck, along with a number of the ship's cabins; below that on the Restaurant Deck, the Positano Restaurant fills the amidships area with a few more cabins, the chapel and the cinema aft.

Three more decks, Amalfi, Bordighera and Capri, are below, with cabins both fore and aft but, on the lower two decks, the forward contingent and the aft contingent are divided with no pass-through corridors.

• Between The Lines •

The Brochure Says

"Passengers from around the world appreciate the *Symphony's* aura of the golden age of luxury ocean liners. They have found that the seven-night cruises on the newly appointed *Symphony* recreate the nostalgia of yesterday offering an unequalled travel experience."

Translation

She's 46 years old, well-traveled and just had a face-lift. What's not to like?

Cabins & Costs

Fantasy Suites ....**N/A**

N/A

Small Splurges. ....

Average Price Per Person, Double Occupancy, Per Day: $272 plus air add-ons.
The 20 outside twins (or doubles) on the Promenade Deck are the largest and most luxurious accommodations aboard. Besides the twin or double bed (specify which when booking) you'll find a chair, desk/dresser and window, and, in some, a nightstand.

Suitable Standards. ....

Average Price PPPD: $160 plus air add-ons.
The outside twins on the other decks have similar furnishings, but sizes vary widely from deck to deck. Twin or double beds are available in some categories.

Bottom Bunks ....

Average Price PPPD: $88 plus air add-ons.
The least-expensive cabins for two are the inside two-berth accommodations on the Capri and Bodighera Deck, but a family or group of friends might look into the cheapest of all, the inside four-berth cabins on the Capri Deck. Since there are only three of them, they may be used for staff or entertainers. There's enough room to sleep a quartet if they left their instruments outside.

The Routes

Now that *Melody* has come on line to replace *Symphony* on summer European sailings, the *Symphony* will be based year-round in South Africa. Itineraries vary, as do cruise lengths, but most sailings go from Durban or Cape Town. Some call at Mozambique or Mauritius.

SYMPHONY* ★★★

Registry	**Italy**
Officers	**Italian**
Crew	**International**
Complement	**300**
GRT	**16,495**
Length (ft.)	**577'**
Beam (ft.)	**72'**
Draft (ft.)	**24.6**
Passengers Full	**750**
Passengers 2/Cabin	**632**
Passenger Space Ratio	**26.34**
Stability Rating	**Fair**
Seatings	**2**
Cuisine	**Continental/Italian**
Dress code	**Traditional**
Room service	**Yes**
Tip	**$8.50 PPPD**

Ship Amenities

Outdoor Pool	**3**
Indoor Pool	**0**
Jacuzzi	**0**
Fitness Center	**Yes**
Spa	**No**
Beauty Shop	**Yes**
Showroom	**Yes**
Bars/Lounges	**4**
Casino	**Yes**
Shops	**3**
Library	**Yes**
Child Program	**Limited**
Self-Service Laundry	**No**
Elevators	**2**

Cabin Statistics

Suites	**0**
Outside Doubles	**159**
Inside Doubles	**157**
Wheelchair Cabins	**0**
Singles	**0**
Single Surcharge	**140–150%**
Verandas	**0**
110 Volt	**No**

NORWEGIAN°
CRUISE LINE

7665 Corporate Center Drive, Miami, FL 33126
☎ *(305) 436-4000, (800) 327-7030*
www.ncl.com/ncl

The sports bar on the **Norwegian Wind** *underscores NCL's emphasis on active and theme cruises.*

History...

Norwegian Caribbean Lines was founded in 1966 by Knut Kloster and Ted Arison (see Carnival Cruises, History, above) to create casual, one-class cruising in the Caribbean in contrast to the more formal, class-oriented tradition of world cruises and transatlantic crossings. That partnership soon broke up, however, leaving Kloster to begin a rapid expansion of the line while Arison went off to found Carnival Cruise Lines.

NCL's first ship was the *Sunward*, but the fleet soon grew to include the *Starward* (1968), *Skyward* (1969), *Southward* (1971) and, also in 1971, a replacement for the original *Sunward* called *Sunward II* (the former *Cunard Adventurer*).

But the real coup came in 1979 when the Kloster family bought French Line's *France*, which had been laid up in Le Havre for five years, made a major rebuilding to convert the former ocean liner into a cruise ship and renamed her *Norway*. From her debut in 1980, she was the flagship of the line, and the other four vessels came to be called "the white ships" for their white hulls that contrasted sharply with the dark blue hull of the *Norway*. (All the original "white ships" have been retired from the fleet, the last in September 1995.)

In 1984, Kloster Cruise Limited, the parent company of Norwegian Cruise Line, bought Royal Viking Line, promising to make minimal changes to the highly respected company. Two years later, Kloster changed the Norwegian registry of the RVL ships to Bahamian, then a year after that closed down the long-time San Francisco headquarters and moved the entire operation to Florida.

In 1987, the former Norwegian Caribbean Lines changed its name to Norwegian Cruise Line with an eye to long-range marketing of Alaska, Bermuda and European cruises, and in 1989 acquired San Francisco-based Royal Cruise Line. This time, however, Kloster left the company in San Francisco with most of its executive roster intact.

The dismantling and sale of RVL happened in the summer of 1994, with the flagship *Royal Viking Sun* and the Royal Viking name, logo, past passenger list and general goodwill sold to Cunard, who promptly (but only briefly) named their new division Cunard Royal Viking Line (see Cunard, above). The *Royal Viking Queen* was soon transferred over to Royal Cruise Line and renamed the *Queen Odyssey*. Two earlier RVL ships, *Royal Viking Star* and *Royal Viking Sea*, also went to Royal to become *Star Odyssey* and *Royal Odyssey*.

In 1996, Royal Cruise Line was dismantled, the *Crown Odyssey* becoming NCL's *Norwegian Crown*, the *Queen Odyssey* becoming *Seabourn Legend* and the *Star Odyssey* becoming the *Black Watch* for Fred. Olson Lines. The *Royal Odyssey* was put up for sail but in 1997 was taken into the fleet as the *Norwegian Star*.

In the late 1980s, Knut Kloster began taking a less active role in the company in order to pursue his dream of building the world's biggest passenger ship, the 250,000-ton, 5600-passenger *Phoenix World City*. Despite its detractors who say the project's dead, the giant ship may still be a viable possibility, pending funding. Recently, Westin Hotels signed on as hotel manager for the newly named *America World City: The Westin Flagship*, but funding was still not set at press time.

—First national air/sea packages (1973).

—First year-round Western Caribbean itinerary (*Southward*, 1975).

—First computerized reservation system (1974).

—The first three- and four-day cruises to the Bahamas incorporating a private island beach day (1977).

—First line to restage hit Broadway musicals aboard cruise ships; the *Norway*'s first production was "My Fair Lady."

—The official cruise line of the National Basketball Association, the Basketball Hall of Fame and the National Football League Players Association; NCL presents a number of sports theme cruises throughout the year.

—First cruise line to broadcast live NFL and NBA games live aboard its ships.

Signatures . . . .

Norwegian Cruise Line has decided to emphasize its Norwegian character and is in the process of changing the names on most of its ships to reflect this, for instance, the *Seaward* will become the *Norwegian Sea*, the *Dreamward* the *Norwegian Dream*, etc. The image they market is of clean, crisp, well-maintained ships, safe and secure under the leadership of Norwegian officers.

Theme cruises—especially the annual *Norway* jazz festival, now in its 15th year, and the sports theme cruises that are aboard all the ships.

The "Dive-In" program—the first and perhaps most successful of the watersports packages found on cruise ships—combines onboard instruction and equipment rentals with shore excursions to snorkel and dive spots. A Sports Afloat T-shirt is given to participants in designated activities who accrue seven tickets by the end of the cruise.

Gimmicks . . . .

The line's former award-winning advertising campaign, built around a sexy young couple who look like they might star in lingerie or perfume ads and the slogan, "It's different out here," has been abandoned. The campaign itself was great, but the ads were barking up the wrong mast, because once they got the viewer's attention they failed to deliver the sales message.

Who's the Competition . . . .

The main competitors in all its cruising areas (now that Carnival has entered Alaska) are the ships owned by Kloster's old nemesis Arison and the rapidly growing Royal Caribbean International. The *Norway*, unique in the otherwise modern fleet because of her history as the famous ocean liner *France*, may soon be upscaled for a more discerning clientele.

Who's Aboard . . . .

A lot of sports-oriented young couples from the heartland, yuppies and baby boomers, jazz fans for two weeks every autumn on the *Norway*; people who want to see a Broadway show without actually having to set foot in Times Square.

Who Should Go . . . .

Young couples and singles looking for a first-time cruise; music fans who'll enjoy not only the two-week annual jazz festival but the annual blues festival and two country music festivals; comedy aficionados for the summer comedy cruise; rock 'n rollers for the '50s and '60s cruise; Big Band devotees for the November sentimental journey; and fitness buffs for the annual fitness and beauty cruise each fall aboard the *Norway*.

Young families who will appreciate NCL's "Kids Crew" program for kids 3 to 17, with special kids-only activities onboard and ashore.

They're divided into four different age groups: Junior Sailors, 3–5; First Mates, 6–8; Navigators, 9–12; and teens, 13–17.

Who Should Not Go.

In the words of Executive Vice President Bruce Nierenberg, "Price-driven passengers" and "the T-shirts-and-sneakers Las Vegas crowd."

The Lifestyle

"Elegant, yes; stuffy, never," was the way they described themselves a couple of years ago, and it's fairly apt. NCL's ships offer traditional cruising, with themed sailings (see Who Should Go, above), international themed dinners several times a sailing, live music on deck, and something going on around the ship every minute. Not long after boarding, passengers are offered free spa demonstrations, free casino lessons, a rundown on the children's program for the week, a free sports and fitness orientation, dive-in snorkeling presentation and as many as three singles parties—one each at 8 p.m. for college-aged spring break celebrants and over-30 singles (a Big Band dancing session is usually scheduled at the same time for the over-50s set), plus a third at 11:30 for any singles that couldn't find a friend at the first two parties.

In other words, you'll stay busy aboard—and that's before the dozen or so shore excursions offered in each port of call!

Wardrobe

NCL calls for less-stringent dress codes than its Caribbean competitors, good news for guys who hate to wear ties. A seven-day cruise usually calls for two formal outfits, two informal outfits and a "costume" for a theme country/western or Caribbean night if you wish. Short cruises schedule one formal night and two informal nights. Formal garb is described by NCL as "cocktail dresses or gowns for the ladies and the men wear a jacket and tie or tuxedo." On informal nights, "just about anything but shorts is fine." For daytimes, take along some exercise clothing, bathing suits, shorts, T-shirts and sandals, plus light cotton clothes and walking shoes for going ashore. NCL also reminds passengers not worry about clothes—if they forget something, they can buy anything they need in the shipboard shops.

Bill of Fare. . . . . B+

The food is big-ship cruise fare with some new cutting-edge options.

New menus, nine months in the making, have recently been introduced fleet-wide. The dinner menu includes three cold appetizers, a hot appetizer, three soups, a salad, five main dishes, one of which is fish, along with a vegetarian entree, a spa cuisine menu under 800 calories with nutritional breakdowns for each dish and a wide range of deserts offered nightly. Dinners are served in two assigned seatings at assigned tables, with first seating 6 or 6:30 p.m. and second seating 8 or 8:30 p.m.

For lunch, passengers choose from four appetizers and salads, three soups, a three-course spa cuisine menu, a cold entree, a vegetarian entrée and three hot dishes including a sandwich, a pasta and a meat or chicken dish.

An alternative restaurant called Le Bistro, on board the most of the lines's vessels, requires an advance reservation and a tip to the waiter but makes no surcharge for the food. The cuisine is Italian/Continental, and there are plenty of intimate tables for two or four.

Showtime . . . . A

NCL was the first cruise line to create a buzz about its onboard entertainment, presenting shipboard versions of popular Broadway shows from "My Fair Lady" to the popular revivals "Grease" and "Crazy For You." In addition to the Broadway shows, each ship presents a song-and-dance "Sea Legs Revue" as well as variety performers on other evenings.

A new "Riverdance" segment highlights the Sea Legs revue.

Also aboard: Q and A sessions with sports stars, several different lounges offering live music for dancing, art auctions, games, dance lessons, and pop psychology lectures about astrology or fashion colors.

Discounts . . . .

NCL's Leadership Fares deducts from 25 percent up, depending on sailing date and ship on a year-round basis. Children under 2 sail free; a maximum of two adults and two children per cabin is the limit for this offer.

The Bottom Line

These are good, moderately-priced traditional cruises that will particularly appeal to first-time cruisers, honeymooners, couples, families and singles up to the outer perimeters of Baby Boomdom. Filled with nonstop activities, music, very professional entertainment and sports-themed programs for watching or doing, NCL is never boring for middle-of-the-road mainstreamers.

Management hints 1998 passengers aboard the *Norway* and *Norwegian Crown* may see some upscale developments on board for more discerning veterans as well.

NORWEGIAN CRUISE LINE

★★★★
NORWAY

Ship buffs and historians know the Norway was built in 1962 as the France, the last of the great French Line fleet that also included the Ile de France and the Normandie. While the last major makeover added two additional decks that thickened her sleek line, she's still one of the most beautiful vessels at sea. She makes us think of the 1954 film The French Line with Jane Russell and a lot of U.S. Olympic athletes working out down by the indoor pool area, which has been remodeled lots of times since then but still looks glamorous. While most people visualize Jane Russell leaning against a shock of hay eyeing a baby-faced Billy the Kid in The Outlaw, our favorite shipboard film is Gentlemen Prefer Blondes, filmed aboard the Ile de France in 1953 with her co-star Marilyn Monroe.

The sybaritic Roman Spa aboard the Norway.

On our most recent *Norway* visit the ship looked very clean and spiffy from a recent makeover—she could rival any Hollywood star in number of facelifts, and she's only 34. Over the years, new luxury cabins and penthouses have been added, each with big windows or private balconies overlooking the sea. But because of the ship's vintage, the original cabins come in all shapes and sizes rather than the neat, identical modules you find on new ships. It's worth spending some extra time studying the deck plan and cabin specifics to be sure you're getting the sort of cabin you want.

The heart of the ship is the International Deck with its enclosed promenade most of the way around on both sides, like fashionable boulevards lined with sidewalk cafes and elegant boutiques. Two separate dining rooms, remnants of the two-class ocean liner days, are divided by the galley in a you-can't-get-here-from-there arrangement, and cabins are dispersed throughout the 10 passenger decks in random configuration.

Even from a distance (she usually lies at anchor in her ports of call) you can recognize her twin stacks and dark blue hull.

Between The Lines

The Brochure Says

"Ever since her launch as the *SS France*, she has been hailed for her plush splendor and architectural marvels. Now, after the finishing touches of a three-year, $60 million refurbishment...she has emerged with her classic features intact: the hand-laid tile mosaics, art deco murals, marble statuary, teak rails, two-story Broadway theater, and the magnificent Club Internationale ballroom."

Translation

The real joy of cruising on the *Norway* for a ship buff is to recreate some of the glory and nostalgia from an ocean liner, even a liner-come-lately like the *France*. In many of the cabins, touches remain from the original; some bathrooms still have the 1960s plumbing fixtures like old-fashioned bathtubs, heated towel racks and tile mosaics. And look for the five antique slot machines on exhibit in the new marble-floored casino, probably not from the original ship but antiques nevertheless. The greatest pleasure is to sail on one of her occasional return voyages to France, where the past is recreated.

INSIDER TIP

Enjoy the free ice cream from Sven's Ice Cream Parlor on the International Deck; passengers used to have to pay for it because, as one staffer said back then, "Otherwise it would be full all day with people eating ice cream." There was no crowd when we sampled some at 3 p.m. on a hot afternoon last spring—we were the only customers.

Cabins & Costs

Fantasy Suites: . . . . **A**

Average Price Per Person, Double Occupancy, Per Day: $778 including airfare.
While we admire the original two-bedroom, two-bath grand suites on Viking Deck (Jerry Lewis always occupied one of them when he was the headline entertainer on

a cruise), today's luxury-loving passengers would probably prefer one of the two new owner's suites forward on the top deck. Each has its own wrap-around terrace; a living room with leather sofa and chairs, desk, tape/CD deck, large TV, fully stocked bar, marble table, built-in cabinetry, and plenty of room for entertaining; a bedroom with queen-sized bed, big walk-in closet, marble bath with Roman tub, marble floor, separate stall shower and powder room; and concierge service.

Small Splurges: . . . . A

Average Price PPPD: $392 including airfare.

The junior suites on Pool Deck are marvelously light, bright rooms with three big picture windows, two lower, queen-sized or king-sized beds, sitting area with sofa and chair, dressing table with make-up lights and good mirror, mini-refrigerator, tub and shower, and concierge service.

This standard outside double cabin aboard the **Norway** *is actually a bit more spacious than some in that category.*

Suitable Standards: C

Average Price PPPD: From $300 to $321, including airfare.

Cabins vary widely, with the four standard outsides and one superior inside categories more or less falling into the standard cabin range. Each has a bed arrangement that sleeps two people in some fashion in lower beds, a bath with tub or shower, a chair, dresser, TV set and table. If you don't mind an inside, O88 has a lot of room, twin beds, two dressers, two chairs and a table.

Bottom Bunks: . . . . F

Average Price PPPD: $228 in category N, $256 in category K, including airfare.

The category N inside doubles with upper and lower berths are the bottom-of-the-line on the *Norway*, and the one we looked at recently—V 248—we could not recommend, even to the most forgiving first-timer. A tiny space with a stool, TV set, single bed and overhead bunk, with fresh carpeting and upholstery but an original bathroom with shower only and the smell of bad drains. We'd suggest spending another $190 each for the week and take a category K inside such as A 023 with a double bed and upper pulldown (making it workable even for roommates who want separate beds), chair, dresser, TV set and bath with shower only. Management hopes to eliminate some of these cabins from the market if a new upscale program is instituted.

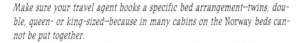

The Routes

The *Norway* will spend the summer season of 1998 in Europe between April and October. Several cruises will sail around France from Marseilles to Le Havre and a number of Mediterranean and Northern European itineraries. Since some of the sailings are under charter and some marketed primarily in Europe, anyone who wants to sail this classic ocean liner in Europe should rush to a travel agent and make arrangements as soon as possible. In winter the ship sails from Miami every Saturday, anchoring off St. Maarten, St. John, St. Thomas and Great Stirrup Cay, the line's private island in the Bahamas, for a beach day.

The Scoop

It's important for a potential passenger, especially an ocean liner aficionado, to make a clear mental distinction between the *Norway* in the Caribbean and the *Norway/France* in Europe. In its previous incarnation the ship offered superb first-class food and service that rivaled the three-star Michelin restaurants of France on crossings in the 1960s. The line recaptures some of this ambiance on its European sailings. Hopefully, even in the Caribbean the ship will recapture a bit of this elegance.

Insider Tips

Five Lovely Locales

1. The Club Internationale looks like the kind of nightclub Nick and Nora Charles would have frequented, except perhaps for the tuxedoed mannequin seated at the player piano and those gesso gods of the sea in the side niches. Elegant green and gold silk tapestry covers the banquettes and chairs, and original light fixtures from the 1960s still adorn the walls and ceilings.

2. The Champs Elysees on starboard side and Fifth Avenue on port side are almost as grand as the originals, enclosed promenades that let you saunter past shop windows glittering with jewelry, crystal, perfumes and sequinned gowns, even a fur shop, and a sidewalk cafe where you can sit down in white wrought-iron chairs for a drink.

3. The sybaritic spa compound built around the ship's indoor pool, operated by Steiner of London, a 6000- square-foot Roman spa with hydrotherapy baths, steam rooms, saunas and aquacise pool with spa treatments sold individually or part of a package, plus a 4000-square-foot health and fitness center, basketball court and jogging track.

4. The charming children's playroom called Trolland on the *Norway*, still has its original fairy-tale wall mural from the *France*; three youth counselors are always aboard, but the number swells to seven during holiday sailings and summer.

5. The Saga Theatre is a proper theater with its comfortable row seats and balcony, just the place to watch Gershwin's "Crazy For You," to catch Arturo Sandoval during the jazz festival or the Shirelles singing "Dedicated to the One I Love" during a '50s and '60s theme cruise with great rock 'n roll era names.

Five Good Reasons to Book This Ship

1. To look for details from the original *SS France*. Where to start: The first-class dining room was the one now called the Windward, amidships on Atlantic Deck with its magnificent staircase for grand entrances; its original name was the Chambord Restaurant.

2. Because there's no extra charge for all that jazz—you can hear the world's greatest jazz musicians gathered together for concerts and impromptu jam sessions all over the ship at any hour of the day or night during the two-week annual autumn jazz festival.

3. To win a free T-shirt with seven vouchers proving you took part in seven "In Motion on the Ocean" fitness and sports activities.

4. You can claim you've sailed on the world's longest cruise ship.

5. To enroll in a full spa program and get The Body Beautiful at the Roman Spa; each October there's a fitness and beauty cruise with top Olympic athletes and experts in fitness, health and beauty.

Five Things You Won't Find On Board

1. A gangway down to the dock in most ports of call; passengers usually go ashore by tender, since the ship docks only in Miami.

2. A bad sport.

3. That nice couple you met on deck the other day; the ship is so big you'll want to get names and cabin numbers from anyone you'd like to see again.

4. A cabin designated single, although there are a lot of teeny-tiny ones that should be.

5. A self-service laundry (but can you imagine all the rich and famous who crossed the Atlantic on the *France* running down and washing their undies themselves?).

NORWAY ★★★★

Registry	**Bahamas**
Officers	**Norwegian**
Crew	**International**
Complement	**900**
GRT	**76,049**
Length (ft.)	**1035**
Beam (ft.)	**110**
Draft (ft.)	**34.5**
Passengers-Cabins Full	**2548**
Passengers-2/Cabin	**2032**
Passenger Space Ratio	**37.42**
Stability Rating	**Excellent**
Seatings	**2**
Cuisine	**Contemporary**
Dress Code	**Traditional**
Room Service	**Yes**
Tip	**$9 PPPD, 15% automatically added to bar checks**

Ship Amenities

Outdoor Pool	**2**
Indoor Pool	**1**
Jacuzzi	**3**
Fitness Center	**Yes**
Spa	**Yes**
Beauty Shop	**Yes**
Showroom	**Yes**
Bars/Lounges	**4**
Casino	**Yes**
Shops	**9**
Library	**Yes**
Child Program	**Yes**
Self-Service Laundry	**No**
Elevators	**11**

Cabin Statistics

Suites	**165**
Outside Doubles	**473**
Inside Doubles	**423**
Wheelchair Cabins	**9**
Singles	**0**
Single Surcharge	**150-200%**
Verandas	**58**
110 Volt	**Yes**

NORWEGIAN CRUISE LINE

★★★★
NORWEGIAN CROWN

Notes from the inaugural sailing, 1988: The overwhelming first impression is a feeling of total luxury, a relaxed sense of being in the best of all possible worlds where only pleasant things can happen to you. It's a world of marble, polished granite, glove leather, meltingly soft suede, gleaming brass.

Christened in 1988 as the *Crown Odyssey*, the ship turned into the *Norwegian Crown* almost overnight in 1996.

The glittering lounges and intimate bars, comfortable cabins and attractive dining room create an upscale ambience that should please most NCL passengers very well. Especially appealing is a state-of-the-art cinema on board. The new South American itineraries offer some exciting cruise possibilities.

Between The Lines

The Brochure Says
"We like to think of it as extremely southern hospitality."

Translation
From Patagonia to Rio de Janeiro and the Chilean fjords, the ship sets out to show you South America.

Cabins & Costs

Fantasy Suites: . . . . **A**

Average Price Per Person, Double Occupancy, Per Day: $643 plus airfare in South America. The Owner's Suite apartments with private verandas are named for their decor; Sandringham and Balmoral, for instance, follow a Scottish theme with lace curtains, plaid carpeting and darkish upholstered furniture, while Portofino has a lot of white and Bel Air an art deco look with lots of black. Each is about 615 square feet with separate living room, bedroom and dressing room, two sofas and a dining table with four chairs, TV/VCR, whirlpool tubs in the bathroom, a queen-sized bed and plenty of storage.

The bay window suites on the **Norwegian Crown** *are worth a small splurge.*

Small Splurges: .... A

Average Price PPPD: $486 pus airfare in South America.

The S1 suites with bay windows let in a lot of light and give a bit of a view in three directions (and sometimes into the edge of the bay window cabin next door when the shades are open). Push buttons raise and lower the shades automatically from the bedside, and a pair of tub chairs flank a glass cocktail table in the bay, while a six-foot marble-topped desk/dresser provides four big storage drawers on each side. Twin or queen-sized beds, marble nightstands and mirror with lucite wall fixtures dominate the sleeping area. There are two closets, each with full-length and half-length hanging areas, built in drawers and shoe storage, a white tile bathroom with marble-faced tub/shower combination and marble sink counter.

Suitable Standards: .... B

Average Price PPPD: $364 plus airfare in South America.

All the deluxe outside doubles (there are apparently no standard cabins on the ship; all are deluxe inside or outside doubles) are around 165 square feet with two lower beds, nightstand with drawers, desk/dresser with chair, a second chair and table, generous closets and bath with shower (some have bathtubs as well). Four are designated suitable for wheelchairs and have shower only.

Bottom Bunks: .... C+

Average Price PPPD: $293 plus airfare in South America.

An L Category inside with two lower beds has a desk/dresser, two chairs and bathroom with shower plus generous closet space.

The Routes

The *Norwegian Crown* sails in South America on 14-day itineraries in winter. Ports include Buenos Aires, Montevideo, Puerto Madryn, Port Stanley, Ushuaia, Punta Arenas,

Puerto Chacabuco, Puerto Montt, Lima and Santiago, with cruises around Cape Horn, through the Beagle Channel, the Strait of Magellan, Chilean Fjords and the Moraleda Canal. Optional shore excursions include Machu Picchu and a fly-over of the Antarctic Peninsula with pre- and post-cruise options. In spring and fall the ship cruises to Bermuda from Port Canaveral and in summer sails from New York to Bermuda. Canada/New England and Colonial America cruises are also offered in spring and fall.

The Scoop

The former *Crown Odyssey* was a custom-designed vessel built just for Royal Cruise Line loyals by the two people who knew them best, Richard Revnes and Pericles Panagopoulos. And it still attracts a lot of Royal Loyals who are health- and image-conscious but also want to have fun with a little dancing, sharing cocktail chatter and taking an occasional whirl in the casino.

Insider Tips

Five Good Reasons to Book This Ship

1. "She's the most incredibly stable ship I've ever worked on," says Captain Sverre Sovdnes.
2. There are always at least four dance hosts aboard every cruise.
3. NCL spends more for food on this ship than the others in the fleet.
4. The tableside cooking at lunch and dinner.
5. The regional dishes and drinks in the new menus that reflect the area being cruised.

NORWEGIAN CROWN ★★★★

Registry	**Bahamas**
Officers	**Norwegian**
Crew	**International**
Complement	**470**
GRT	**34,250**
Length (ft.)	**614**
Beam (ft.)	**92.5**
Draft (ft.)	**23**
Passengers-Cabins Full	**1240**
Passengers-2/Cabin	**1052**
Passenger Space Ratio	**32.55**
Stability Rating	**Excellent**
Seatings	**2**
Cuisine	**Contemporary**
Dress Code	**Traditional**
Room Service	**Yes**
Tip	**$9 PPPD, 15% automatically added to bar checks**

Ship Amenities

Outdoor Pool	**1**
Indoor Pool	**1**
Jacuzzi	**4**
Fitness Center	**Yes**
Spa	**Yes**
Beauty Shop	**Yes**
Showroom	**Yes**
Bars/Lounges	**6**
Casino	**Yes**
Shops	**3**
Library	**Yes**
Child Program	**No**
Self-Service Laundry	**No**
Elevators	**4**

Cabin Statistics

Suites	**90**
Outside Doubles	**322**
Inside Doubles	**114**
Wheelchair Cabins	**4**
Singles	**0**
Single Surcharge	**150-200%**
Verandas	**16**
110 Volt	**Yes**

NORWEGIAN CRUISE LINE

★★★★★ NORWEGIAN DREAM (DREAMWARD) NORWEGIAN WIND (WINDWARD)

NOTE: Both ships undergo a name change in early 1998 following a major lengthening of the vessel.

> *It was the water curtain on the* Norwegian Dream *that really grabbed attention. On the inaugural sailing, we sat in the front row scribbling notes about traffic "flow" and "splashy" production numbers while watching a dazzling revue staged behind a unique curtain of water. A Gene Kelly-lookalike splashed about in* Singin' in the Rain, *marine creatures frolicked* Under the Sea *and not a drop of water fell on the front row. The water spurts from below like fountains or drizzles from above like rain, and the big finale incorporated fireworks, fog and film clips of Esther Williams swimming with cartoon characters Tom and Jerry.*

How do you make a big ship that looks like a little ship into an even bigger ship? The answer is, you cut it in half and insert a new 130-foot prefabricated midsection. The operation is called a "stretch." NCL's *Dreamward* and *Windward* carried 1246 passengers. Their new incarnations *Norwegian Dream* and *Norwegian Wind* will carry about 1750 passengers in a total of 875 cabins plus additional passengers in third and fourth berths. This includes a clutch of new super-suites and 248 new cabins. Particularly useful for families are the 78 cabins with connecting doors, which lets the kids sleep nearby rather than underfoot. Also new: an additional three-tiered dining room, a new casino, spa, children's play area, cigar-and-cordials room, business and conference center, coffee shop and shopping gallery.

The Brochure Says

"By day, you can avail yourself of the fitness center, basketball court, jogging track, golf driving net, and aerobics classes. At night, the ship pulls out all the stops. First, an extraordinary meal. Then, live music. Dancing. Comedy. Parties. A Broadway musical. And if you just feel like hanging out, there's a Sports Bar & Grill, where broadcasts from the NFL, NBA, and ESPN International are beamed in live."

Translation

We're ready for the young and the restless, and double-dare anyone to get bored aboard.

A suite aboard the **Norwegian Wind.**

Fantasy Suites: . . . . A

Average Price Per Person, Double Occupancy, Per Day: $628 plus air add-on in Alaska.
Six 350-square-foot grand deluxe suites with concierge service face forward on three decks for a captain's-eye view of the world. The living room is sumptuously furnished with a brocade sofa and three chairs, a long desk and dresser with eight drawers and glass coffee table. In the bedroom, you can choose either twin or queen-sized beds. The bathroom has tub and shower, and additional perks include a mini-refrigerator and a private safe.

Small Splurges: . . . . B

Average Price PPPD: $514 plus air add-ons in Alaska.
Penthouses with private balconies are 175 square feet inside plus a veranda that is large enough for two chairs and a table. A separate sitting area with love seat and chairs, floor-to-ceiling windows, twin or queen-sized bed, private safe, TV set, mini-refrigerator and concierge service are included.

Suitable Standards: . . . . B

Average Price PPPD: $314 plus air add-ons in Alaska.

Standard outside staterooms are virtually identical in size (160 square feet) and furnishings—sitting area and twin or queen-sized bed, TV set, built-in cabinetry—with the price varying according to deck location. "I'd advise clients to book one of the lower-category outsides," one travel agent told us, "because the differences in deck and amenities isn't that much." Accordingly, we'd recommend the D category outsides; get any lower on the totem pole and you're facing partial or full obstruction from hanging lifeboats. Six wheelchair-accessible cabins have shower seat and hand rails plus spacious turn-around room and no sills to impede the wheels.

Bottom Bunks: C

Average Price PPPD: $236 plus air add-ons in Alaska.

The lowest-priced cabins aboard are category L inside double cabins with two lower beds in 150 square feet of space. Needless to say, you shouldn't expect a sitting area with sofa.

INSIDER TIP

If you want to book a category A outside cabin and value your privacy, opt for those on Atlantic Deck instead of Promenade Deck. While Promenade Deck is considered posh by old-time cruisers, it also means the joggers and strollers are walking around the deck outside your windows day and night, while on Atlantic deck only the gulls and flying fish can look in while the ship's at sea.

The Routes

After her "stretch" the *Norwegian Dream* will spend most of the year in Europe and the Mediterranean on 12- and 13-day itineraries. Then she offers a short winter season in the Caribbean.

In winter, the *Norwegian Wind* sails from San Juan on Caribbean cruises in winter and spends the summer in Alaska.

The Scoop

This is a very special pair of ships, stylish enough for frequent travelers but accessible to first-time cruisers as well. They offer everything an active young passenger might want. While the cheaper cabins are not as spacious as you might wish, they're a lot bigger than many NCL cabins used to be. Snobs should have their travel agent book one of a dozen proposed new supersuites with private elevators.

Insider Tips

Five Fabulous Places

1. The sunbathing deck, not acres of Astroturf lined with sunbathers sprawled everywhere, but lounge chairs arranged in a series of teak terraces separated by low wooden planters filled with clipped boxwoods, rather like an amphitheater.

The aft pool deck aboard the **Norwegian Dream** *has terraced sunbathing.*

2. The new swim-up pool bar to be added during the "stretch".

3. The big forward Observation Lounge doubles as a late-night disco with marble dance floor and a pair of electronic route maps that show the ship's itineraries.

4. Le Bistro, a 76-seat specialty restaurant with no surcharge, only a request for advance reservations and a tip for the waiter afterwards. It's a good place for a quiet dinner for two, perhaps celebrating a romantic occasion, or a place to get together with other new friends.

5. The 150-seat Sun Terrace dining room, three levels set high atop the ship and aft, facing a wall of windows to the sea, and one deck below, The Terraces, 282 seats on several levels that also overlook the sea through an expanse of glass with a huge undersea mural on the back wall.

The Sun Terrace dining rooms aboard the **Norwegian Dream** *and* **Norwegian Wind** *offer sweeping views to the sea.*

NORWEGIAN DREAM ★★★★★
NORWEGIAN WIND ★★★★★

Registry	Bahamas
Officers	Norwegian
Crew	International
Complement	614
GRT	45,000
Length (ft.)	754
Beam (ft.)	94
Draft (ft.)	22
Passengers-Cabins Full	2500
Passengers-2/Cabin	1750
Passenger Space Ratio	25.71
Stability Rating	Good
Seatings	2
Cuisine	Contemporary
Dress Code	Traditional
Room Service	Yes
Tip	$9 PPPD, 15% automatically added to bar checks

Ship Amenities

Outdoor Pool	2
Indoor Pool	0
Jacuzzi	3
Fitness Center	Yes
Spa	Yes
Beauty Shop	Yes
Showroom	Yes
Bars/Lounges	8
Casino	Yes
Shops	4
Library	Yes
Child Program	Yes
Self-Service Laundry	No
Elevators	7

Cabin Statistics

Suites	74
Outside Doubles	624
Inside Doubles	164
Wheelchair Cabins	13
Singles	0
Single Surcharge	150-200%
Verandas	74
110 Volt	Yes

★★★★
NORWEGIAN DYNASTY

We loved all three of the former Crown ships, but are dizzy with confusion as they keep changing lines and names. This ship is an ideal size, elegantly decorated, with good food and entertainment. The only problem is, a lot of people never heard of it, which is understandable.

The pretty oval pool is surrounded by a Palm Beach-style deck with comfy loungers and umbrella-shaded tables.

The Norwegian Dynasty, previously known as the *Crown Dynasty*, the *Cunard Dynasty* and the *Crown Majesty*, is one of three ships built between 1990 and 1993 for Palm Beach-based Crown Cruise Line, owned by the Scandinavia-based Effjohn Group. But the owners sold two of the vessels to Asian shipping interests, leaving only the *Crown Dynasty*, which has undergone more personality changes than the movie heroine in *Three Faces of Eve.*

The newest incarnation, according to NCL management, will feature the line's popular Sports Bar & Grill, Dive-In program and Broadway entertainment.

Between The Lines

The Brochure Says

"Intrepid travelers have sailed Alaska's glorious Inside Passage since the 1800s... (but) we think you'll find (this ship) a considerable improvement over the paddle-wheelers of that time... You may be deep in the heart of the wilderness. But you certainly won't be roughing it."

Translation

It's all happening here, on a lovely ship that you share with fewer than 800 fellow passengers.

Cabins & Costs

Fantasy Suites: .... **B+**

Average Price Per Person, Double Occupancy, Per Day: not available.
Top digs are 10 suites with about 350 square feet of area each, with teak-decked private balconies, separate sitting areas, mini-refrigerator and extra-large closets. (Two other suites have extra-large sitting areas with bay windows instead of private balconies if you prefer.) The two lower beds can be converted to one double, and the bath has a shower only.

Small Splurges: .... **B+**

Average Price PPPD: not available.
The seven extra-large forward cabins on Deck Six give you a captain's-eye view of the sea through big angled glass windows, two beds that can be put together for a double, two chairs, cocktail table, dresser/desk and chair. These are about the same size as the Fantasy Suites above, but without the veranda.

Suitable Standards: .... **B**

Average Price PPPD: not available.
Standard outside doubles are available on three decks, average 140 square feet with two lower beds that can convert to a double, remote-control color TV, safe, mirrored built-in dresser/desk, satellite telephone and bath with shower.

Bottom Bunks: .... **C**

Average Price PPPD: not available.
The two lowest-category cabins would be so rare to be able to book—they're like the loss leader in a supermarket ad—that we might as well recommend the next category up, a 132-square-foot inside double with two lower beds, TV, telephone and bath with shower.

The Routes

The *Norwegian Dynasty* cruises Alaska for the summer of 1998, followed by a possible relocation to Asia in the fall for seasonal exotic sailings.

The Scoop

While big enough to give a sense of stability, the *Norwegian Dynasty's* public rooms and lounges have an intimate ambience, so passengers can socialize easily. And its staterooms, while not overly spacious, are comfortable and handsomely furnished. There's something for everyone aboard this clean, pretty ship.

Insider Tips

Five Super Spaces

1. The drop-dead gorgeous five-deck atrium with its spiral staircase and trompe l'oeil mural of Italian colonnades with blue skies and clouds beyond, and down at the very, very bottom on a parquet floor, a white piano.

2. The Palm Beach-style deck with comfy loungers covered in blue-and-white striped mattresses, matching umbrellas to shade the tables and pretty oval pool.

3. The Rhapsody Lounge showroom with wood-backed banquettes in dark pink and purple tapestry fabric and matching carpet.

4. The surprisingly lavish Olympic Spa that offers seaweed body wraps, massages, body-composition analysis, makeup and hair styling and full beauty salon services.

5. The Marco Polo Cafe, the casual buffet-service restaurant with wicker chairs and a sunny tropical atmosphere.

NORWEGIAN CRUISE LINE

NORWEGIAN DYNASTY ★★★★

Registry	**Bahamas**
Officers	**Norwegian**
Crew	**International**
Complement	**320**
GRT	**20,000**
Length (ft.)	**537**
Beam (ft.)	**74**
Draft (ft.)	**18**
Passengers-Cabins Full	**856**
Passengers-2/Cabin	**800**
Passenger Space Ratio	**25**
Stability Rating	**Fair to Good**
Seatings	**2**
Cuisine	**Contemporary**
Dress Code	**Traditional**
Room Service	**Yes**
Tip	**$9 PPPD, 15% automatically added to bar check**

Ship Amenities

Outdoor Pool	**1**
Indoor Pool	**0**
Jacuzzi	**4**
Fitness Center	**Yes**
Spa	**Yes**
Beauty Shop	**Yes**
Showroom	**Yes**
Bars/Lounges	**6**
Casino	**Yes**
Shops	**Yes**
Library	**Yes**
Child Program	**Yes**
Self-Service Laundry	**No**
Elevators	**4**

Cabin Statistics

Suites	**12**
Outside Doubles	**268**
Inside Doubles	**120**
Wheelchair Cabins	**4**
Singles	**0**
Single Surcharge	**150-200%**
Verandas	**10**
110 Volt	**Yes**

★★★★

NORWEGIAN MAJESTY

In the dining room of the ship when it was the Royal Majesty, when we are ushered to our table, three pretty young women already seated there are stunned; we suspect they expected the other two seats to be occupied by handsome young men. We think of them later as Thelma and Louise and Louise, very nice women from a southern state, three pals, one of them married and two single, on their very first cruise, and they expect more romance and adventure than is reasonable. Fortunately, we have a flirtatious waiter who fills some of the gap.

A white piano is the centerpiece of the **Norwegian Majesty's** *marble lobby.*

It's an elegant ship with some of the most distinctive fabrics and carpeting we've seen anywhere, along with a generous use of wood that lends a warm ambience.

Cabins are located on six of the nine passenger decks, with a top-deck sunning area, below which is the pool and spa area. Deck 5 is where most of the public rooms are located, starting from the forward observation deck and lounge and moving back through a series of small rooms that double as meeting areas when a conference is on board and bars, card rooms and such when there's no group. Amidships is the lobby area, directly below the casino, and the dining room is aft. The show room is conveniently located one deck above the dining room, making it an easy progression from dinner to entertainment.

The Brochure Says

"Trust us, even a few days will do more to rejuvenate your spirit than a whole year's worth of weekends back home."

Translation

More and more travelers are taking short cruise getaways several times a year.

Fantasy Suites: .... A

Average Price Per Person, Double Occupancy, Per Day: NA.

Two royal suites are the top digs aboard, two large separate rooms with floor-to-ceiling bay view windows, a living room with paisley sofa, coffee table, two chairs, glass dining table with four chairs and long built-in granite counter, and a bedroom with queen-sized bed, covered in a paisley print bedspread, nightstands, desk/dresser with chair, TV/VCR, minibar, safe, hair dryer, ironing board, bathrobes and 24-hour butler service. There's also a marble bath with long tub and a big walk-in closet/dressing room with good hanging storage.

Small Splurges: .... A

Average Price PPPD: NA.

The 14 deluxe suites have twins or queen-sized beds, a granite-topped, built-in desk and dresser with blue tweed chair, a granite-topped nightstand with four drawers, a big window in the bedroom side and a sliding fabric panel in strips of beige fabric that can be pulled across the room to separate the bedroom from the sitting area. The latter has a large sofa and two chairs, plus a wood-and-glass coffee table. A built-in wood console has TV/VCR and underneath is a wooden cabinet with glassware and minibar. In the marble bathroom is a tub, sink with marble counter and big mirror with good makeup lights, a built-in hair dryer, shower over the tub and complimentary toiletries. There is a glass bay window in the sitting area, and the artwork in the cabin consists of three pleasant watercolors.

Suitable Standards: .... B

Average Price PPPD: NA.

The outside standard cabins are very attractive because of the elegant fabrics used throughout the ship. You can request queen-sized, double or twin beds, and also get a picture window, color TV, safe, hair dryer and ironing board (ingeniously built into a dresser drawer). The bath is adequately sized with shower only, and there's also a pair of nightstands with drawers, a desk/dresser with chair and a closet with two full-length hanging spaces and one half-length hanging space with four drawers under, quite adequate for a week's cruise. Four cabins are designated wheelchair-accessible.

Bottom Bunks: .... **B**

Average Price PPPD: NA.
Even the lowest-priced inside doubles have two lower beds, and a handsome mirror wall where the window would be successfully presents the illusion of light and space, brightening the room inside. There's a nightstand with drawers, a desk/dresser with chair, bath with shower only, adequate closet and wall-hung TV set. Some of these cabins have upper berths as well.

The Routes

Norwegian Majesty makes three- and four-day cruises to Mexico during the winter season. In spring the ship repositions to Boston for seven-night round-trip sailings to Bermuda during the summer.

The Scoop

This is a classy ship and the prices are right. The deck sunbathing areas are a bit small and can be crowded when the ship is jam-packed full, as it was on one Easter weekend when we were aboard, along with some 200 children.

The *Norwegian Majesty* is one of the rare new ships that offers a full promenade around the ship for inveterate walkers and joggers. Rubberized red matting covers the entire deck, with a special track laid out in green in the center; five laps around is a mile.

It's a good vessel for fitness-conscious people, with plenty of exercise options on board and ashore, including walking tours with cruise staff members.

Insider Tips

Five Special Places

1. The dining room, one of the first nonsmoking cruise dining rooms at sea in 1992, now one of many, has lights bright enough to see but not flat cafeteria lighting, and there is enough sound baffle on the ceiling to reduce the room noise a bit.

2. A really hot gym on board has every imaginable kind of equipment, plus an adjacent exercise room with wood floor, windows, mirrors, barre and sauna.

3. NCL's traditional Sports Bar with museum-like displays of historic athletic equipment and live sports telecasts on big screens.

4. The observatory, with striped red-and-black tub chairs, antique ship models and drawings, a curved wood bar with brass rail and curved glass walls facing forward.

5. The show lounge with some of the most sophisticated entertainment at sea plus lively music on deck in the daytime and all around the ship at night

Five Good Reasons to Book This Ship

1. To take a sports theme cruise.

2. To learn snorkeling so you can enjoy the Dive-In snorkeling adventures offered in ports of call.

3. To sail from Boston to Bermuda in summer.

4. To indulge in the Chocoholic Buffet served once a cruise.

5. To have a romantic evening for two by arranging guaranteed baby-sitting at the information desk 24-hours in advance.

Five Things You Won't Find On Board

1. An opportunity to get hungry, because you'll have lots of chances to pig out from early bird breakfast to midnight buffet.

2. A problem with laundry and dry cleaning since both services are provided.

3. A cruise fare for a child under 2.

4. A moment of silence in the serene-looking lobby with its white piano, white marble floor and potted palms, because just above in the open atrium is the casino with slot machines constantly ringing and pinging.

5. A self-service laundry.

NORWEGIAN MAJESTY   ★★★★

Registry	**Panama**
Officers	**Norwegian**
Crew	**International**
Complement	**500**
GRT	**32,400**
Length (ft.)	**568**
Beam (ft.)	**91**
Draft (ft.)	**20.5**
Passengers-Cabins Full	**1225**
Passengers-2/Cabin	**1056**
Passenger Space Ratio	**30.68**
Stability Rating	**Good**
Seatings	**2**
Cuisine	**Contemporary**
Dress Code	**Traditional**
Room Service	**Yes**
Tip	**$9 PPPD, 15% automatically added to bar checks**

Ship Amenities

Outdoor Pool	**2**
Indoor Pool	**0**
Jacuzzi	**2**
Fitness Center	**Yes**
Spa	**Yes**
Beauty Shop	**Yes**
Showroom	**Yes**
Bars/Lounges	**3**
Casino	**Yes**
Shops	**3**
Library	**Yes**
Child Program	**Yes**
Self-Service Laundry	**No**
Elevators	**4**

Cabin Statistics

Suites	**16**
Outside Doubles	**327**
Inside Doubles	**185**
Wheelchair Cabins	**4**
Singles	**16**
Single Surcharge	**150-200%**
Verandas	**0**
110 Volt	**Yes**

NORWEGIAN CRUISE LINE

★★★
NORWEGIAN SEA

Of all the ships in NCL's fleet, including the now-departed white ships, the former Seaward has been the hardest for us to warm up to, perhaps because of its cool, almost darkish interiors and upper decks, acres of painted metal and indoor/outdoor carpeting instead of teak. But a recent dry-docking that added more pastels, mirrors and art work lightens it up, at least on the inside. Now, if they could do something about that painted metal Promenade Deck surface...

The *Seaward* was turned into the *Norwegian Sea* recently to reflect the line's new emphasis on its Norwegian character. It is a ship for the young and active, with a fitness center, golf driving range, a basketball court and a full, around-the-ship jogging track on promenade deck labeled with arrows so everyone runs or walks in the right direction (counter-clockwise). The Big Apple Cafe serves a lot of breakfasts and lunches for passengers too busy to go down to the dining room. Down on Atlantic Deck is a small children's playroom called Porthole. Traffic flow through the dining room areas moves smoothly along a port side walkway called Park Avenue that links the Four Seasons Dining Room with the Seven Seas Dining Room.

Between The Lines

The Brochure Says

"There are basketball games, aerobics classes, volleyball tournaments, and trapshooting lessons. There's also a golf driving net, a fully equipped fitness center, and a wide-open deck with two beautiful pools.

Translation

With all this happening onboard, you'll have to work hard to squeeze in those fascinating Caribbean island ports every day.

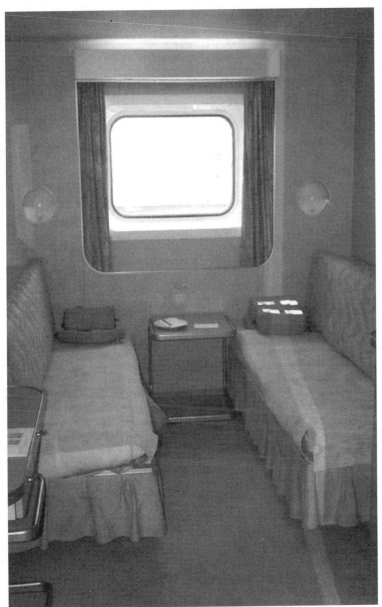

Cabin 4228 is a standard outside double with portholes on the Norwegian Sea; *lifejackets are laid out on the beds on embarkation day.*

INSIDER TIP

There's a tuxedo rental shop aboard if you've forgotten to bring one or don't own formal wear and want to dress up to match your wife's finery.

Cabins & Costs

Fantasy Suites: .... A

Average Price Per Person, Double Occupancy, Per Day: $400 including airfare.
Four Owner's Suites sleep up to five passengers in 280 to 360 square feet, with sitting area with sofa double bed, dining area, separate bedroom, two TV sets, mini-refrigerator and bathroom with tub and shower.

Small Splurges: .... B

Average Price PPPD: $364 including airfare.
Three forward deluxe suites on Norway deck share a captain's eye view of the scenery ahead, along with a sleeping area with two lower beds, sitting area with a sofa that can convert to a bed for an additional occupant, a mini-refrigerator, lounge chair and bath with tub and shower.

Suitable Standards: C

Average Price PPPD: For category E outside doubles, $307 including airfare.
Twin sofa beds with a small table in between, a built-in cabinet tower with desk, four drawers, complimentary bottle of Evian, TV, ice bucket, slender full-length mirror and full hanging cabinet inside, as versatile a storage area as we've seen outside the Hold Everything catalogue. There are also two additional full-length hanging areas on the opposite wall, as well as a bathroom with tile floor, shower and pastel bath fixtures. Cabin described is in category E.

Bottom Bunks: .... D

Average Price PPPD: $238 including airfare.
Six category N cabins with a fairly large lower bed and a pull-down berth that folds up during the day because otherwise there's not enough room to walk between the beds. These cabins might work for two very slender, very close friends. There's also a built-in desk/dresser, a chair, TV set, a small table and a lime green cabinet tower (see Suitable Standards, above). And all cabins are issued a bowl of fresh fruit and a bottle of mineral water.

The Routes

The *Norwegian Sea* offers alternating seven-day Barbados Series and Aruba Series sailings roundtrip from San Juan every Saturday. The Barbados Series calls at Barbados, Martinique, St. Maarten, Antigua, St. John and St. Thomas, while the Aruba Series calls at Aruba, Curaçao, Tortola/Virgin Gorda, St. John and St. Thomas.

The Scoop

While this ship was one of the last to come out of the respected Wartsila shipyard in Finland before its subsequent conversion to Kvaerner-Masa Yard, the construction is not nearly so sturdy. In areas of the deck, you may step on a patch of thin, buckled steel plating under the indoor/outdoor carpet. The ship has been through several major refurbishings to freshen carpeting and upholstery, as well as adding additional suites. (Lavish suites are big-sellers on this line that caters to so many honeymooners.) After a spell of being sentenced to the short-cruise market, which adds so much wear and tear to a ship, she really needed a cosmetic make-over.

Five Dramatic Spaces

1. The Crystal Court two-deck entry lobby with a fountain dripping water down glass pipes, slick white marble squares, wide dark green curved leather benches, plants, a rock garden—a dark, cool contrast to the bright, hot tropics outside.

2. Gatsby's is billed as a wine bar/nightclub, but when we were aboard recently, it was the setting for a small private wedding and luncheon, and showed it could be turned into the most romantic little restaurant at sea. It's pretty dreamy with its tall ladder-back black chairs and round tables, granite floors and white piano.

3. Oscar's Piano Bar, with its very comfortable barstools, could entice a passenger to linger awhile around the curved piano bar, perhaps even join in on a chorus or two.

4. Hallways and landings, an often-ignored part of a ship's decor, here are filled with art, including pretty original water colors, wall hangings and majestic marble and granite, endowing the space with richness.

5. The Pool Deck with its shaded outdoor dining areas lashed with panels of fabric on the sides and ceiling, wood-trimmed tables and woven plastic armchairs.

Five Good Reasons to Book This Ship

1. The Chocoholic Buffet, served once a cruise at midnight, the chocoholic's witching hour, with every fantasy dessert you ever dreamed of.

2. To learn snorkeling with the well-organized, comprehensive Dive-In program.

3. Lickety-Splits ice cream stand, with free cones or dishes of ice cream in four flavors, plus sherbet, frozen yogurt and any toppings you'd like to add; open all afternoon.

4. Le Bistro for alternative dining at no extra charge except a tip for the waiter; an advance reservation is required, however. It's the place to be alone together for a special occasion or a quiet evening, or to get together with new-found friends.

5. To check out the seagoing mall called Everything Under the Sun, with lots of shops and gold chains by the inch.

NORWEGIAN SEA ★★★

Registry	**Bahamas**
Officers	**Norwegian**
Crew	**International**
Complement	**630**
GRT	**42,000**
Length (ft.)	**700**
Beam (ft.)	**96**
Draft (ft.)	**21**
Passengers-Cabins Full	**1796**
Passengers-2/Cabin	**1502**
Passenger Space Ratio	**28.11**
Stability Rating	**Fair**
Seatings	**2**
Cuisine	**Contemporary**
Dress Code	**Traditional**
Room Service	**Yes**
Tip	**$9 PPPD, 15% automatically added to bar checks**

Ship Amenities

Outdoor Pool	**2**
Indoor Pool	**0**
Jacuzzi	**2**
Fitness Center	**Yes**
Spa	**Yes**
Beauty Shop	**Yes**
Showroom	**Yes**
Bars/Lounges	**5**
Casino	**Yes**
Shops	**1**
Library	**Yes**
Child Program	**Yes**
Self Service Laundry	**No**
Elevators	**6**

Cabin Statistics

Suites	**7**
Outside Doubles	**494**
Inside Doubles	**246**
Wheelchair Cabins	**4**
Singles	**0**
Single Surcharge	**150-200%**
Verandas	**0**
110 Volt	**Yes**

★★★★
NORWEGIAN STAR

The first cruise we ever took, in what seems like eons ago, was aboard the Norwegian Star *when it was the* Royal Viking Sea, *in the days before the "stretch" (when the ship was cut in half and a new midsection of additional cabins and public space inserted.) We cruised in Alaska and thought cruising was the most magical vacation anyone could possibly have. Today's first-time cruiser coming aboard the* Norwegian Star, *now 25 years old but almost as classy as ever, will feel the same way.*

The new "Texaribbean Cruise" from Houston is a fresh idea for Caribbean cruisers, along with a convenient nonstop air schedule from most major cities in the West and Midwest. While the ship's density has been mightily increased over the years with third, fourth and even fifth bunks in some cabins to handle the increased numbers of families cruising, you can still find a quiet spot here and there to get away from the crowd. Most of the cabins aboard have a newly installed sofa-bed that sleeps two much more comfortably than you'd expect.

Meals are served in two seatings instead of the previous single seating, but the entertainment aboard is much more sophisticated than it was on the old Royal Viking ships.

Between The Lines

The Brochure Says
"Cozumel, Roatan, Calica, Chichen Itza, Xcaret, Tulum. Need we say more:"

Translation
NCL thinks destinations are an important part of a cruise particularly for young couples and families, and so offers exotic destinations and new places to go and things to do aboard the *Norwegian Star.*

Roving musicians entertain diners on the Norwegian Star.

Fantasy Suites: . . . . A

Average Price Per Person Double Occupancy Per Day: $357 plus air add-on.
The three Owner's suite apartments with private veranda provide separate bedroom
and sitting room, large bath and walk-in closet. Twin or queen-sized beds, voluminous storage space, a graceful living room with sofa, several chairs and coffee table,
a bathroom with tub and shower, terry-cloth bathrobes, TV/VCR, hair dryer and
mini-refrigerator offer all the comforts of home.

Small Splurges: . . . . B

Average Price PPPD: $242 plus air add-on.
There are 31 S3 suites spread around the ship. These are comfortable cabins with
picture windows, sitting areas with sofa, chair and coffee table, bathroom with tub
and shower, TV, hair dryers and mini-refrigerator.

Suitable Standards: C

Average Price PPPD: $178 plus air add-on.
Cabins aboard are on a modular plan with additional berths added to most for more
family sleeping space. The typical outside double has a sofa bed that unfolds into a
queen-sized bed, along with upper and lower berths. Most cabins have tub and
shower but a few have shower only; if it matters, specify preference when booking.
Closet space is adequate but you don't have unlimited hanging space. Lower deck
outside cabins have portholes instead of windows. Generally, we felt the less-expensive category F cabins on Caribbean deck with portholes and no upper and lower
berths seemed more spacious than the deluxe cabins on upper decks with third and
fourth berths.

Bottom Bunks: C

Average Price PPPD: $142 plus air add-on.
The lowest-priced category is J, an inside on the lowest passenger deck with two
lower beds and tub and shower or shower only. The cabins contain a hair dryer and

TV set, along with a desk/dresser with chair, another chair and coffee table, and a closet.

Norwegian Star *passengers enjoy the sunny ambience of the Jacuzzi Deck.*

The Routes

The ship sails Sundays from Houston and visits the Yucatan port facility of Calica for an overnight on Tuesdays. This offers passengers the option of taking a night excursion to Xcaret, a meticulously recreated nature center and Mayan village and folkloric show, or a night on the town in Cancun. A day excursion to Xcaret the next morning can include a chance to swim with dolphins (surcharge). Or you can visit the archeological ruins at Tulum or Chichen Itza. The ship spends all day Wednesday in Cozumel with diving and snorkeling expeditions offered, then sails on to Roatan in the Bay Islands of Honduras for more diving and snorkeling opportunities. Two days at sea allow time to relax on board before the ship docks again in Houston.

The Scoop

We found it difficult to recognize many of the ship's features from the past. Two sports bars have been added, filled with TV monitors broadcasting satellite sports coverage, and plexiglass museum cases housing historic artifacts. An alternative restaurant called The Bistro has been carved out of a corner of the dining room, with its own entrance and a different ambiance from the main room. The casino has been expanded and a new children's facility added. Most of all, the passenger density of the ship has increased tremendously, making it less appealing to the tradition-minded passengers that sailed with now-defunct Royal Viking Line and Royal Cruise Line, but NCL's younger passengers and families should find it just fine. We particularly applaud NCL's decision to base this ship in Houston. In the words of Executive Vice President Bruce Nierenberg, "to take the ship where the people live." This saves Midwest and West Coast passengers heading for the western Caribbean from the chore of dealing with the chaos of Miami International airport and the inconvenient flight schedules into Fort Lauderdale.

Insider Tips

Five Favorite Spots

1. The Top of the Star Bar is a forward observation lounge with wide windows and swivel chairs where you can sit transfixed by the sea views all day long.

2. The Midnight Sun Lounge, under-utilized on the *Royal Viking Sea*, has been turned into an attractive venue for buffet breakfasts and lunches and afternoon tea with potted palms and a winter-garden atmosphere.

3. The Viking Bar & Grill on the aft end of Penthouse Deck still serves hot dogs and hamburgers steps away from the trio of spa pools.

4. The Pool Bar & Pizzeria on Pool Deck proffers hot cinnamon buns at breakfast time, wedges of pizza in late morning and freshly baked chocolate chip cookies at teatime.

5. The pair of Sports Bars, one called Champions, with beer on draught.

Champions sports bar is a popular hangout on **Norwegian Star.**

Five Good Reasons to Book This Ship

1. To fly to Houston and the ship in less than three hours from any U.S. city.

2. To be able to dive and snorkel in some of the world's best dive sites.

3. To enjoy a special Texaribbean dinner that features fried jalapeños stuffed with cheese, chilled avocado soup, and 18 ounce Texas T-bone steak with onion rings and baked potato.

4. To be among the first cruise passengers to visit the fantastic park of Xcaret.

5. The price is right; for the opening season NCL published realistic fares in its brochure rather than inflated ones (deliberately jacked-up printed rates so discounts can be offered across the board).

NORWEGIAN STAR ★★★★

Registry	**Bahamas**
Officers	**Norwegian**
Crew	**International**
Complement	**424**
GRT	**28,000**
Length (ft.)	**676**
Beam (ft.)	**83**
Draft (ft.)	**24**
Passengers-Cabins Full	**1100**
Passengers-2/Cabin	**824**
Passenger Space Ratio	**35**
Stability Rating	**Good**
Seatings	**2**
Cuisine	**Contemporary**
Dress Code	**Traditional**
Room Service	**Yes**
Tip	**$9 PPPD, 15% automatically added to bar checks**

Ship Amenities

Outdoor Pool	**1**
Indoor Pool	**0**
Jacuzzi	**3**
Fitness Center	**Yes**
Spa	**Yes**
Beauty Shop	**Yes**
Showroom	**Yes**
Bars/Lounges	**6**
Casino	**Yes**
Shops	**2**
Library	**Yes**
Child Program	**Yes**
Self Service Laundry	**Yes**
Elevators	**5**

Cabin Statistics

Suites	**54**
Outside Doubles	**299**
Inside Doubles	**61**
Wheelchair Cabins	**4**
Singles	**0**
Single Surcharge	**150-200%**
Verandas	**9**
110 Volt	**Yes**

NORWEGIAN CRUISE LINE

★★★★
LEEWARD

We are struck by how many young male passengers stay aboard the ship watching ESPN in the sports bar rather than going ashore on the idyllic private island with its sandy beaches, barbecue buffet and watersports. Perhaps NCL has stumbled across the answer to the dilemma: Wife wants to take a cruise; husband, accustomed to spending his weekends watching sports on TV, is promised the same thing at sea. Ergo: everybody's happy.

This joint-venture ship owned by Finland's Effjohn International and operated by NCL is far more attractive in total than the sum of its component parts. The size, 25,000 tons carrying 950 passengers, seems ideally human-scale in these days of megaliners, and the decor, evocatively art deco-style, smudges most of the outline of the former Baltic ferry *Sally Albatross.*

Between The Lines

The Brochure Says

"Your heart is saying, 'Go ahead, take a long vacation.' Unfortunately, your schedule is saying, 'Uh-uh, just a few days.' Oh boy, have we got a cruise for you.'"

Translation

As a midsized ship in the three- and four-day market, Leeward offers a more intimate, refreshing change from the big ships of Carnival and RCI.

Cabins & Costs

Fantasy Suites: .... **A**

Average Price Per Person, Double Occupancy, Per Day: $539 including airfare.
A pair of owner's suites, one dubbed the Presidential Suite because George Bush once stayed there, provides large private balconies with outdoor hot tub, living

room spacious enough for a modest party, separate bedroom with two lower beds, picture windows, mini-refrigerator, walk-in closets and bath with tub and shower.

Owner's suites aboard the Leeward *have hot tubs and balconies. They're spacious enough for a party.*

Small Splurges . . . . **A**

Average Price PPPD: $456 including airfare.
Eight deluxe penthouses with small private verandas and living rooms with sofa and large picture window, mini-refrigerator, queen-sized bed in separate bedroom area, wall-mounted TV, and generous storage space.

Suitable Standards . . . . **B**

Average Price PPPD: $293 including airfare in category E.
We deem categories D and E as "suitable," but not categories F and G, outsides with partially or fully obstructed views because of hanging lifeboats. You'll find two lower beds, some sitting areas, and, in many, very handsome black-and-white tile bathrooms with shower. All passengers get a basket of toiletries in the bathroom and a silver dish of fresh fruit in the cabin. Nonsmoking cabins are available on request.

Bottom Bunks . . . . **B**

Average Price PPPD: $213 including airfare.
This quartet of small outsides on Promenade Deck are the lowest-priced accommodations on board. While most of the inside cabins priced slightly higher have two lower beds, these upper and lower berth cabins have a window and a good location just steps away from the open deck.

The Routes

The *Leeward* makes year-round three-day cruises every Friday, with alternate itineraries from Miami to Nassau and Great Stirrup Cay, the line's private island, or from Miami to Key West and Great Stirrup Cay. On Mondays, two alternating itineraries are also offered on the four-day sailing, one roundtrip from Miami to Key West, Cancun and Cozumel, the other roundtrip from Miami to Playa del Carmen, Cozumel and Key West.

The Scoop

All in all, this is a handsome and winning ship. We only wish we couldn't glimpse so much untreated steel superstructure under the cosmetic surface.

Insider Tips

The busy Sports Bar and Grill shows sports events from ESPN.

Five Fabulous Places

1. The Sports Bar and Grill aboard means nobody has to miss any important play of a televised sports event.

2. Gatsby's Piano Bar with angled glass walls, raised curved banquettes and tapestry-covered seating offers a nightclub ambiance.

3. Le Bistro, an alternative restaurant for couples who want to dine alone or with new friends they met aboard.

4. The Stardust Lounge with its entrance that is reminiscent of an art deco movie house.

5. The Four Seasons Dining Room, with a shipboard art deco entrance that reinforces the sense of being at sea.

Five Good Reasons to Book This Ship

1. If you're an art aficionado, you'll find plenty to admire aboard.

2. To dine in one of the two dining rooms that seem no larger than your favorite upscale restaurant.

3. To hang around the Sports Bar and Grill amid museum cases of vintage sports equipment.

4. To enjoy a rousing production of "Pirates of Penzance."

5. To visit the super port of Key West.

LEEWARD ★★★★

Registry	**Panama**
Officers	**Norwegian**
Crew	**International**
Complement	**400**
GRT	**25,000**
Length (ft.)	**524**
Beam (ft.)	**82**
Draft (ft.)	**18**
Passengers-Cabins Full	**1409**
Passengers-2/Cabin	**974**
Passenger Space Ratio	**25.93**
Stability Rating	**Fair**
Seatings	**2**
Cuisine	**Contemporary**
Dress Code	**Traditional**
Room Service	**Yes**
Tip	**$9 PPPD, 15% automatically added to bar checks**

Ship Amenities

Outdoor Pool	**1**
Indoor Pool	**0**
Jacuzzi	**1**
Fitness Center	**Yes**
Spa	**Yes**
Beauty Shop	**Yes**
Showroom	**Yes**
Bars/Lounges	**5**
Casino	**Yes**
Shops	**1**
Library	**Yes**
Child Program	**Yes**
Self-Service Laundry	**No**
Elevators	**4**

Cabin Statistics

Suites	**16**
Outside Doubles	**309**
Inside Doubles	**162**
Wheelchair Cabins	**6**
Singles	**0**
Single Surcharge	**150-200%**
Verandas	**10**
110 Volt	**Yes**

NORWEGIAN CRUISE LINE

NORWEGIAN CRUISE LINE

ODESSAMERICA

Cruise Line of the Czars

170 Old Country Road, Suite 608, Mineola, NY 11501
☎ *(516) 747-8880, (800) 221-3254*

History . . . .

OdessAmerica is North American sales agent for Galapagos Cruise Line and its *Ambasador I*, as well as the *Terra Australis* and *Skorpios*, expedition vessels in Patagonia. In the Mediterranean, OdessAmerica books the *Adriana*, the former *Aquarius*, from Croatia Cruise Lines for Aegean sailings, and in the Indian Ocean represents *Royal Star*, the former *Ocean Islander*, for African Safari cruises. In the Antarctic, OdessAmerica represents Canada's Marine Expeditions. (See Other Cruise Companies for ship descriptions.)

The company also markets a number of Russian and Ukrainian river vessels. (See Alternative Cruises.)

Unrated
ADRIANA

The 4600-ton *Adriana*, built as the *Aquarius* in 1972 and refurbished in 1994, carries 300 passengers on its "Blue Adriatic and Aegean Cruises" for Croatia Cruise Lines, a division of Jadrolinija (see Other Cruise Companies, below). The marketing program, set up with the Croatian National Tourist Office, particularly emphasizes the reopening of the popular port of Dubrovnik, now part of Croatia, for European and North American cruise passengers.

 **Between The Lines**

The Brochure Says
"From the fascinating luxuries of Italy, to the romantic shores and medieval cities of Croatia, to the mysteries of antiquity in Greece and Turkey, OdessAmerica's comprehensive Mediterranean Cruise itineraries present a timeless lesson of history with chapters set in Venetian palaces, Croatian stone-walled cities, Greek theaters, Turkish mosques, charming resorts of Crimea and Roman temples."

Translation
These are port-intensive, destination-oriented cruises.

Cabins & Costs

Fantasy Suites . . . . **N/A**
N/A

Small Splurges . . . . **N/A**
N/A

Suitable Standards . . . . **C**
Average Price Per Person, Double Occupancy, Per Day: $183 plus airfare.
The superior and deluxe staterooms on the Adriana, all of them located on Lyra
Deck, should be interpreted as standard outside doubles with two lower beds and
private bath facility with shower or tub.

Bottom Bunks . . . . **C**
Average Price PPPD: $107 plus airfare.
Inside double cabins are compact but most have two lower beds and bathroom with shower. Some quad insides will sleep four people for $67.50 a day
per person if you like crowds.

The Routes

Cruises sail from Venice to the Aegean and the Adriatic on various itineraries from
seven to 15 days; some call in Korcula and Split as well as Dubrovnik. An eight-day, escorted Croatian land package visiting Zagreb, Opatija, Zadar, Split, Dubrovnik and the
stunning Plitvice Lakes is available for an additional $995 per person, double occupancy.

The Scoop

The vessel and its lifestyle aboard will remind you of other budget Greek Islands cruises with a polyglot of languages, but adding the lure of Croatian ports makes it special for
visitors who have never seen the former Yugoslavia.

Princess Cruises' *Dawn Princess* in Nassau, Bahamas

Royal Caribbean's *Legend of the Seas*

Penguins seen from Abercrombie & Kent's *Explorer* in the Antarctic

Carnival sister ships *Sensation* and *Ecstacy* in Miami

ADRIANA — Unrated

Registry	Croatia
Officers	Croatian
Crew	Croatian
Complement	109
GRT	4600
Length (ft.)	340
Beam (ft.)	45
Draft (ft.)	NA
Passengers-Cabins Full	300
Passengers-2/Cabin	274
Passenger Space Ratio	NA
Stability Rating	NA
Seatings	2
Cuisine	Continental/Croatian
Dress Code	Casual
Room Service	No
Tip	$7 PPPD

Ship Amenities

Outdoor Pool	1
Indoor Pool	0
Jacuzzi	0
Fitness Center	Yes
Spa	No
Beauty Shop	Yes
Showroom	No
Bars/Lounges	3
Casino	No
Shops	1
Library	Yes
Child Program	No
Self-Service Laundry	No
Elevators	1

Cabin Statistics

Suites	0
Outside Doubles	110
Inside Doubles	27
Wheelchair Cabins	0
Singles	0
Single Surcharge	150%
Verandas	0
110 Volt	No

ODESSA AMERICA CRUISE COMPANY (ODESSAMERICA)

★★, ⚓⚓⚓⚓
AMBASADOR I

She's been around in expedition cruises for a long time, and used to sail for Salen Lindblad when it was in business. We used to see her in Piraeus and Dubrovnik and always wondered about the single "s" in her name. We still do.

Built in the former Yugoslavia in 1958, the *Ambasador* has had a long career as an expedition ship. Now registered in Ecuador in order to cruise the Galapagos Islands—only Ecuadorian-flag ships have been permitted to cruise there for the past few years—the ship carries only 86, the maximum permitted because of environmental impact in the islands, instead of the 160 she was built to carry. Spruced up again with some fresh fabrics and new soft furnishings and looking fairly chipper—anyhow, more luxurious than most of the Galapagos vessels—the *Ambasador* affords a comfortable way to go see the Sally Lightfoots and giant tortoises. The ship anchors on most stops and you go ashore by 20-passenger *pangas* (Boston whalers). Dress aboard is casual, but you need cotton shorts and pants, T-shirts, a sweater or windbreaker, walking shoes or sneakers, a swimsuit and a wide-brimmed sun hat, preferably with a string to tie it down.

Between The Lines

The Brochure Says

"With *MV Ambasador I*, an extraordinarily well-equipped, environmentally friendly ship, you can experience all of this without endangering any life forms that make the Galapagos Islands one of the most extraordinary natural environments in the world."

Translation

It's a guilt-free way of enjoying the wilderness without discomfort.

Cabins & Costs

Fantasy Suites: .... **N/A**
N/A

Small Splurges: .... **N/A**
N/A

Suitable Standards: .... **C**
Average Price Per Person, Double Occupancy, Per Day: $435 plus airfare and local taxes.
A deluxe twin-bed cabin on Floreana Deck has floral bedspreads, reading lamps over
the bed, a private bath with shower only, a telephone, radio and dresser.

Bottom Bunks: .... **D**
Average Price PPPD: $209 plus airfare and local taxes.
Some of the inside double cabins are quite small but have private facilities with a
shower, upper and lower berths and small dresser.

The Routes

The *Ambasador I* cruises in the Galapagos Islands year-round.

The Scoop

The cabins are small, the lifestyle casual and the amenities simple, but the reward here
is exploring the unique islands of the Galapagos with excellent guides who take you out
in groups of 20 or fewer. Be prepared for the heat with cool clothing and sunscreen; the
ship provides bottled water to carry ashore with you.

Insider Tips

Five Special Spots

1. The Grand Salon is a large bar and lounge with swivel tub chairs and chrome tables
   where the social life and the lectures are slated because there's nowhere else to go
   but the deck and the dining room.

2. The swimming pool on Sun Deck is a popular favorite in the sizzling equatorial climate of the Galapagos. After an arduous overland trek to the tortoises, a dip in the
   pool is irresistible.

3. The Lido Bar, equally popular for the same reasons and the ice-cold beer or soda
   that's waiting after a hot morning of learning the love life of the lava lizard.

4. There is a small library with materials about the islands, bird guides and such, plus
   a boutique selling souvenirs and sun screen.

5. The restaurant serves all passengers in a single seating, and the cuisine is continental
   with some Ecuadorian specialties such as the fresh local shrimp and the wonderful
   potato cakes called llapingachos covered with cheese and peanut sauce.

Five Good Reasons to Book This Ship

1. To watch the courting displays of the majestic frigate birds.

2. To see the mating dance of the blue-footed booby.

3. To learn the soap-opera ups and downs of the love life of a lava lizard.

4. To wonder how even another marine iguana could love that face.

5. To watch Sally Lightfoot strip (see crabs shed their carapaces).

Five Things You Won't Find On Board

1. A gym or fitness center.

2. Room service.

3. Children under 7 years old.

4. A cabin designated wheelchair-accessible; this ship and the cruise are not suitable for the mobility-impaired because of the amount of tendering that has to be done.

5. An elevator.

AMBASADOR I ★★, ⚓⚓⚓

Registry	Ecuador
Officers	Ecuadorean
Crew	Ecuadorean
Complement	68
GRT	2,573
Length (ft.)	296
Beam (ft.)	43
Draft (ft.)	14.7
Passengers-Cabins Full	160
Passengers-2/Cabin	86
Passenger Space Ratio	29.91
Stability Rating	Fair
Seatings	1
Cuisine	Continental/Ecuadorean
Dress Code	Casual
Room Service	No
Tip	$10 PPPD

Ship Amenities

Outdoor Pool	1
Indoor Pool	0
Jacuzzi	0
Fitness Center	Yes
Spa	No
Beauty Shop	Yes
Showroom	Yes
Bars/Lounges	2
Casino	No
Shops	1
Library	Yes
Child Program	No
Self-Service Laundry	No
Elevators	0

Cabin Statistics

Suites	4
Outside Doubles	40
Inside Doubles	13
Wheelchair Cabins	0
Singles	10
Single Surcharge	120%
Verandas	0
110 Volt	No

★ ★ ★
ROYAL STAR

We always loved this yachtlike ship when it was the Ocean Islander *with its pretty teak decking and tailored interiors. In the Mediterranean, it made a big production out of cruising past Stromboli after dark so we could see the fiery lava from the glowing volcano.*

While the trim decor we recall was replaced with fussier floral fabrics in a 1992 makeover, the deck and pool are holding up fairly well. Suites are spacious and cabins relatively comfortable on all levels. Of the five passenger decks, three have inside and outside cabins. The two top decks contain all the public rooms, the dining room and the sunbathing areas. Generally, you'll find the same facilities the vessel used to offer, from self-service buffet breakfasts and poolside lunches to leisurely meals in the dining room. The emphasis is still on shore excursions in these exotic ports of call.

The Brochure Says

"Aboard this friendly yachtlike vessel you cruise effortlessly amongst a paradise of islands ringed by coral sands and gently lapped by azure waters, where the air is heavy with the scent of spices and the warming breeze barely whispers through the trees."

Translation

It's hot and humid in the Seychelles and along the coast of East Africa.

Fantasy Suites . . . . **B**

Average Price Per Person, Double Occupancy, Per Day: $822 plus airfare.

The President Suite has a huge private veranda and two to three times as much interior space as the other suits and cabins aboard. It's handsomely furnished with desk, bookcases, tables and chairs and living area with separate sleeping and dressing areas.

Small Splurges. . . . . B

Average Price PPPD: $518 plus airfare.
Superior suites (there are eight of them aboard) are much larger than standard outside doubles. Most, however, offer twin beds; only one (# 347) has a double bed, and it's coyly referred to as the Honeymoon Suite.

Suitable Standards. C

Average Price PPPD: $429 plus airfare.
There are five categories of outside double cabins and they vary in size and configuration. Again, most have twin beds with only a small cluster of them, three cabins aft on Pacific Deck, containing double beds. Some cabins provide one or two additional berths.

Bottom Bunks C

Average Price PPPD: $404 plus airfare.
The smallest cabins aboard, hardly surprisingly, are the lowest-priced insides, and most of them have additional pulldown berths. All cabins, including the bottom bunks, have private bathrooms with shower and a telephone.

The Routes

The *Royal Star* cruises to exotic ports of call in Zanzibar, Madagascar, Mauritius, the Seychelles and South Africa, as well as offering overland safari excursions in Kenya. The year-round home port is Mombasa.

The Scoop

This ship has always attracted a strong British following as well as U.S. and Canadian passengers, and with a wraparound African safari package supplementing cruises in the warm blue waters of the Indian Ocean, it represents a good value for a non-fussy traveler.

ROYAL STAR ★★★

Registry	**Bahamas**
Officers	**International**
Crew	**International**
Complement	**130**
GRT	**6179**
Length (ft.)	**396**
Beam (ft.)	**NA**
Draft (ft.)	**NA**
Passengers-Cabins Full	**253**
Passengers-2/Cabin	**220**
Passenger Space Ratio	**38**
Stability Rating	**Fair to Good**
Seatings	**2**
Cuisine	**International**
Dress Code	**Traditional**
Room Service	**Yes**
Tip	**$7 PPPD**

Ship Amenities

Outdoor Pool	**1**
Indoor Pool	**0**
Jacuzzi	**0**
Fitness Center	**Yes**
Spa	**No**
Beauty Shop	**Yes**
Showroom	**Yes**
Bars/Lounges	**3**
Casino	**Yes**
Shops	**1**
Library	**No**
Child Program	**No**
Self-Service Laundry	**No**
Elevators	**1**

Cabin Statistics

Suites	**9**
Outside Doubles	**91**
Inside Doubles	**10**
Wheelchair Cabins	**0**
Singles	**0**
Single Surcharge	**130%**
Verandas	**1**
110 Volt	**Yes**

ORIENT LINES ℠

1510 S.E. 17th Street, Fort Lauderdale, FL 33316
☎ *(954) 527-6660, (800) 333-7300*

The dining room aboard **Marco Polo** *serves the kind of sustenance a weary explorer needs after a day of discoveries.*

History . . . .

British entrepreneur Gerry Herrod has been in the travel and cruise business since he founded Travellers International in the 1970s, which grew to be the largest European tour operator for Americans. He is also former chairman of now-defunct Ocean Cruise Lines and Pearl Cruises; the latter pioneered year-round cruises in the Far East and was among the first ships to visit China. His newest company, Orient Lines, was founded in 1992 and introduced its 800-passenger *Marco Polo* in December 1993.

Herrod is very much a hands-on CEO. During the inaugural of the *Marco Polo*, he was fussing over his ship like a mother hen, prowling the vessel, talking to passengers, fine-tuning details such as lighting and sound levels.

Concept

Herrod calls his product "destinational cruising," and says it is designed for "inquisitive people who want to see something more than Freeport and Nassau but don't necessarily want to go catching butterflies," which we interpret to mean a destination-oriented program of soft adventures. His passengers, he says, like to dress up, eat good food and dance in the evenings after dinner, even when they're in a remote or exotic corner of the world, which he feels differentiates Orient Lines from some of the more solemn expeditioners.

Signatures

The distinctive logo of a stylized wave and a globe symbolizes "the world of Marco Polo."

To bring on board local folkloric performers in as many ports of call as possible.

Gimmicks

Bright red parkas they get to keep are issued to every passenger on the Antarctic cruises. "We need to be able to see them against all that snow and ice," one executive admitted.

Who's the Competition

These days the competition would probably be Radisson Seven Seas' *Hanseatic* and Hapag-Lloyd's *Bremen*, both upscale expedition ships with destination-oriented passengers; Special Expeditions' *Caledonian Star*, the destination-driven Renaissance ships; and the midsized, globe-trotting pair of veteran Princess ships, the *Pacific Princess* and *Island Princess*, with their Pacific and Asia itineraries. In the Aegean, Royal Olympic Cruises, a merger of Sun Line and Epirotiki, has similar prices and itineraries

Who's Aboard

The *Marco Polo* on its longer, more exotic itineraries attracts mostly well-heeled North Americans and British 55 and up. They're a mix of people who've taken land tours along with some cruise veterans. About 80–85 percent are North Americans, most of the rest British or Australian. The Australians, interestingly enough, flock to the seven-day New Zealand cruises because many of them have never been to New Zealand. In the Mediterranean with its short cruises, popular ports and affordable prices, plus group charter business from upscale lines such as Renaissance, Orient is attracting younger passengers than on its Asia, Africa and Pacific itineraries. Young families as well are drawn to the active week-long sailings. In the Antarctic, the ship also draws younger-than-average passengers because prices are lower than on the small expedition ships.

Who Should Go

More younger couples, even honeymooners, will enjoy the affordable new seven-day, island-intensive Mediterranean sailings.

Who Should Not Go . . . .

We can't think of any age group or travel type that wouldn't enjoy the *Marco Polo*, a midsized, affordable ship with its handsome art deco decor, except perhaps a cruise label snob.

The Lifestyle . . . .

Destinations influence the life on board, with a shorter, more port-intensive Mediterranean schedules calling for less formal entertainment. A guest lecture program and local entertainment in each port along with dancing hosts in winter, who act as dance and bridge partners of older women traveling alone, expand the regular program. Menus use local specialties and serve regional wines when in South Africa, Australia and New Zealand, and in summer in the Mediterranean.

We found the onboard pattern follows a traditional cruise style, with formal nights, lectures and activities, and an intensive shore excursions program that even includes some overnight overland journeys. Orient Lines places an emphasis on shoreside excursions and looks for specialty tours not always offered by other cruise lines.

Wardrobe . . . .

Orient Lines says to pack as for any resort destination, suggesting light-weight, easy-to-care-for daytime casual sportswear and good walking shoes for shore visits. Formal attire requests a tuxedo, dinner jacket or dark suit and tie for men, a "party dress or gown of fashionable length" for women. On informal evenings, men are expected to wear a jacket and women a cocktail dress or pantsuit. Casual nights call for dressy sportswear or khakis. Raffles, the alternative restaurant, does not require jackets. Dress is a little more casual on the Antarctic sailings.

Bill of Fare . . . . .A

The food is excellent aboard the *Marco Polo*, just the type of sustenance a weary explorer needs after a day of discovering South Africa or New Zealand. When we were aboard, one dinner started with a salad of lamb medallions on lettuce with vinaigrette and red peppers, followed by a delectable white truffle risotto with sweetbreads and shrimp. The main course was grilled red snapper with puréed white beans and grilled baby zucchini, and dessert featured an old-fashioned apple and raisin pie with vanilla bean sauce and vanilla ice cream.

Executive chef Terence Greenhouse prepares California and continental cuisine, and there is an alternative restaurant called Raffles, open several nights a week, that serves specialty menus based on the region of the world the ship is cruising in. This summer in the Greek Islands, for instance, Raffles menus will feature Italian, Spanish and Mediterranean seafood specialties. Passengers make reservations the same day of the dinners and pay a $15 surcharge which includes unlimited wine with dinner. The same cafe also offers self-service breakfast and lunch dishes. Breakfast may offer scrambled eggs, bacon, sausages, fried potatoes, yogurt, juices, cereals, fruits and pastries. Meals in the dining room are served at assigned tables in two seatings.

Showtime. . . . . B

The dominant entertainment is local and regional troupes brought on board in the various ports—a Zulu dance troupe, Maoris in New Zealand, Australian aborigines, Balinese legong dancers, a Kenyan dance company, and wonderful performers in Cape Town reminiscent of New Orleans parade bands.

To supplement the local talent is a complement of singers and dancers who double as cruise staff and perform musical revues and variety shows. A singer/pianist alternates with a Romanian string trio in the Cafe Concerto.

Discounts . . . .

Early booking discounts take from 5 to 20 percent off the fare for passengers making reservations and a deposit 120 days or more ahead of sailing date. The precise amount depends on the cruise.

The Bottom Line

Herrod is going back to his own travel roots as a land tour operator, building a variety of broader land/sea packages for Orient Line passengers—adding on African safaris, Taj Mahal visits, excursions to Kathmandu or Australia's Ayers Rock and Alice Springs. In the summer of 1996, the vessel made its first Mediterranean sailings, offering seven-day port-intensive cruises in the Greek Islands. Because the company uses many of the key employees from Pearl Cruises, veterans of that line will be welcomed on board by familiar faces.

★ ★ ★ ★
MARCO POLO

It was hard to tell who was enjoying the evening more, the Marco Polo's passengers or the exuberant Zulu dance troupe from the Valley of the Thousand Hills in KwaZulu, which had been brought aboard to entertain us in Durban. Because we had earlier toured Johannesburg on a land excursion with a Zulu guide from the Soweto township named Nicholas, we had more than a passing interest in the traditional dances.

This 800-passenger, midsized ship started life as the *Alexandr Pushkin*, one of five vessels of the same class—the others being the *Ivan Franko, Taras Shevchenko, Shota Rustaveli* and *Mikhail Lermantov*—built in Wismar, East Germany, between 1963 and 1972. An extensive renovation in 1993 turned the 1965 motorship into the glamorous, art deco-accented *Marco Polo*.

Cabins are dispersed among seven of the eight passenger decks, most of which also have public areas on them. The Belvedere Deck is where the main public rooms are located, and it's an easy stroll from the forward show and lecture lounge through the convivial Polo Lounge, past the purser and excursion offices and shops, through the casino, past the library and card room into the self-service restaurant called Raffles and then on to the pool deck aft. The restaurant is located on a lower deck amidships, a health and beauty center on Upper Deck, outdoor Jacuzzis on Sky Deck, and the Charleston Club and an aft sun lounging area on Promenade Deck. A small casino provides roulette, blackjack and slot machines for passengers, most of whom take less interest in gambling than going to enrichment lectures and port talks. A splendid collection of Oriental art and antiques decorates the public areas. Outstanding is a stone Buddha on a glass-and-marble base at the entrance of the dining room, and pair of gold Buddhas above the cruise staff desk.

The *Marco Polo* has an ice-hardened hull, a helipad on the uppermost deck for helicopter take-offs and landings and high-speed launches as passenger tenders; it carries 10 inflatable Zodiac landing craft.

ORIENT LINES

The Brochure Says

"...traveling with around 700 fellow passengers—and even fewer in places like Antarctica—you'll never feel as if you're just part of the crowd. The level of service we provide, both on board and ashore, is every bit as gracious as on a smaller vessel. While at the same time, we can offer the considerable price advantages and seafaring comfort of a larger ship."

Translation

As in "Goldilocks and the Three Bears," the *Marco Polo* is not too large or too small but "juuuuuust right."

Fantasy Suites: . . . . B+

Average Price Per Person, Double Occupancy, Per Day: $410 plus air add-on.
Two deluxe suites, the Mandarin and the Dynasty, are the top digs aboard; both face forward with a captain's eye view of the world. You get a separate living room and bedroom, with a sofa, loveseat, two chairs, two chests, marble counters, a stocked bar that is replenished regularly, a queen-sized bed in the bedroom, generous storage space, robes, a safe and a marble bathroom with tub and shower.

Small Splurges: . . . . B

Average Price PPPD: $265 plus air add-on.
Category A cabins have queen-sized beds, and large seating areas with sofa, chair, stool, coffee table, minibar and double dresser. Cabins in category C and above get robes and safes; suites and A cabins have queen-sized beds and marble bathrooms with tubs as well as showers. We'd suggest going for one of the two Category A cabins amidships on Main Deck; the ones on Sky Deck have partially obstructed views due to hanging lifeboats.

Suitable Standards: . . . . B+

Average Price PPPD: $234 in plus air add-on.
Category C cabins on main deck are fairly spacious, with a large window, twin beds, a wood-toned double dresser with eight drawers and a second smaller dresser with four and a pull-out desk top, handsome furnishings, wall-mounted TV set with remote control, three closets and a bathroom with shower only. All cabins have international direct-dial telephones. Some cabins can accommodate third and fourth passengers in pulldown berths.

Bottom Bunks: . . . . B+

Average Price PPPD: $169 plus air add-on.
The category I inside we saw is large with twin beds, double dresser and chair, while the category H was narrower, also with twin beds and dresser plus a pulldown third berth. Deadlights may be closed in rough seas on the lowest passenger deck.

The Routes

The *Marco Polo* travels to Antarctica in late 1997 and early 1998. From the Antarctic, the vessels sails to Australia and New Zealand with forays into the Java Sea, then on to Singapore. A Passage to India sailing goes from Singapore April 6, followed by an India, Egypt, Israel and Greece repositioning for the summer. In addition to the basic 7-day cruise, the ship offers a variety of air/land/sea packages from 12 to 18 days, some emphasizing Aegean ports, others the Holy Land, the French and Italian Rivieras, and Spain. Prices in "Cabins and Costs" above, are calculated for packages rather than cruise-only tariffs.

The Scoop

Pearl Cruises lives—and with a more luxurious ship! But the *Marco Polo* is not a copy of the *Pearl;* it is a subtler and more upscale rendering of a highly successful, destination-oriented cruise line that specializes not only in cruises in the Far East but all over the globe, including Antarctica. Could all we port-and-country collectors ask for anything more?

Pool deck and outdoor cafe aboard the **Marco Polo.**

Insider Tips

Five Spots to Explore

1. The Charleston Club, a charming spot in the evenings for cocktails and dancing, its tub chairs covered in a confetti-pattern fabric and glass cocktail tables, a curved bar with granite top, swag draperies and pleated paper shades.

2. Raffles, the self-service cafe and evening specialty restaurant with a wood-toned tile floor, glossy blue walls and ceiling, wood chairs with blue/green upholstery, and two buffet feed lines.

3. The Palm Court, with lots of potted palms, wicker and rattan with floral fabrics and marble-topped tables, is where you read or write postcards in the morning and take afternoon tea.

4. The chic black-and-white Casino Bar is faintly art deco with its black-and-white photographs of Fred Astaire and Ingrid Bergman and its intimate atmosphere.

5. The Polo Lounge is the central meeting place with leaf-patterned upholstery and carpet, glass cocktail tables, granite bar with green leather barstools and green swag curtains.

Five Good Reasons to Book This Ship

1. To sail into Cape Town, one of the world's most beautiful harbors, sitting on deck in a traditional Queen Mary-style wooden deck chair.

2. To hit all the highlights of the Greek Islands on 12-day air/land/sea package at a price as low as $1995 per person, double occupancy.

3. To get a free red polar parka you can keep as a perk for booking the lowest-priced Antarctic cruise on the market.

4. To dine on a special menu once each cruise created by London's famous Cafe Royal.

5. To participate in intensive Workshops at Sea on longer sailings, classes that teach you how to photograph icebergs and penguins in the Antarctic or how to capture Mount Kilamanjaro in watercolors while you're cruising off the coast of Kenya.

Five Things You Won't Find On Board

1. Great sightlines in the Ambassador Lounge, because the performance area is almost the same level as the audience and there are lots of posts in between.

2. A hot breakfast from room service; they serve only continental breakfasts in the cabins.

3. Specially designated cabins and some areas of the ship that are accessible for wheelchairs, although there are elevators on board.

4. Anyone who can identify the subject of that statue resembling the late Rudolph Nureyev in an exaggerated balletic pose that stands between the ship's twin exercise rooms in the Health and Beauty Center.

5. A self-service laundry.

MARCO POLO ★★★★

Registry	**Bahamas**
Officers	**Scandinavian**
Crew	**Filipino**
Complement	**350**
GRT	**20,502**
Length (ft.)	**578**
Beam (ft.)	**77**
Draft (ft.)	**27**
Passengers-Cabins Full	**922**
Passengers-2/Cabin	**848**
Passenger Space Ratio	**24.17**
Stability Rating	**Good**
Seatings	**2**
Cuisine	**Contemporary**
Dress Code	**Traditional**
Room Service	**Yes**
Tip	**$8 PPPD**

Ship Amenities

Outdoor Pool	**1**
Indoor Pool	**0**
Jacuzzi	**3**
Fitness Center	**Yes**
Spa	**Yes**
Beauty Shop	**Yes**
Showroom	**Yes**
Bars/Lounges	**5**
Casino	**Yes**
Shops	**1**
Library	**Yes**
Child Program	**No**
Self-Service Laundry	**No**
Elevators	**4**

Cabin Statistics

Suites	**6**
Outside Doubles	**286**
Inside Doubles	**131**
Wheelchair Cabins	**2**
Singles	**2**
Single Surcharge	**125%**
Verandas	**0**
110 Volt	**Yes**

ORIENT LINES

P & O CRUISES

c/o Princess Cruises; 10100 Santa Monica Boulevard, Los Angeles, CA 90067-4189
☎ *(310) 553-1770, (800) PRINCESS*
www.p-and-o.com

Princess Cruises is a North American agent for P & O Cruises' *Arcadia*, *Oriana*, and the *Victoria* (the former *Sea Princess*).

History . . . .

Peninsular and Oriental Navigation Company is the oldest and largest of the British shipping companies, founded in 1837, shortly before Samuel Cunard founded his company. Cunard looked west to America, P&O looked east, first to Spain and Portugal, later to India. The founders of P & O, Arthur Anderson, a one-time Shetland Islands "beach boy" (itinerant worker) and Brodie McGhie Willcox, were serious young men only a few years away from poverty when they invested in their first ship, a small American schooner run aground near Dover which they salvaged. Soon they acquired additional vessels, including the steamer *William Fawcett*, usually credited as being their first passenger ship.

P & O's India-bound passengers in the 1840s had the option of traveling across the Suez overland three decades before the famous canal was built. First-class on P&O was the only socially acceptable way to travel to the raj.

In the 1880s, the *British Medical Journal* recommended sea voyages for health, and by 1898, a P & O poster was advertising a 60-day pleasure cruise to the West Indies.

Not only were generous quantities of food always included on the P & O sailings, but until 1874, unlimited quantities of wine, beer, spirits and mineral water were also included. On Sundays, sailing days and holidays, champagne was also thrown in. In the days before refrigeration, whole barnyards of live animals were taken along to be slaughtered and cooked as needed.

In 1914, P & O merged with British India Company. In 1932, the company had 41 cargo and passenger ships, only three pre-World War I, but in 1939 its ships, including 21 passenger vessels, were requisitioned by the government to serve as armed merchant cruisers and transports. In 1946, there were 13 left; eight had been sunk. Between 1946 and 1950, the government returned the requisitioned hardware to P & O, and in 1960, the first of two new ships debuted, the *Oriana*, followed a year later by the *Canberra*.

—The word "posh," according to popular lore, is said to have originated from the cabin reservation stamped P.O., S.H. for "Port Out, Starboard Home" for passengers traveling between England and India who demanded the coolest staterooms in each direction. Some authorities say that claim is without foundation; others say the word actually came into slang usage from the snobbishness of P&O passengers themselves.

—P & O claims it invented leisure cruising in 1844 when British author William Makepeace Thackery sailed around the Mediterranean on a free ticket to publicize the service and wrote a travel book about his cruise— *From Cornhill to Grand Cairo*—under the pseudonym Michael Angelo Titmarsh. He was not a happy camper—he hated Athens and was often seasick—and because his trip was during the religious holidays of Ramadan, he complained bitterly about missing all the grandly advertised wonders of the East, from the whirling dervishes to the harem at the seraglio in Istanbul.

—One of the three largest cruise lines in the world.

Concept. . . . .

To take English-speaking passengers all over the English-speaking world and beyond, on world cruises, warm-weather getaway cruises and seasonal travels between a home on one continent and one on another.

Signatures. . . . .

Cruising "British style," which appeals to many Anglophiles in North America in addition to the large number of travelers from the United Kingdom.

Gimmicks. . . . .

The children's tea, an early supper served just to kids at 5:30, before the early seating dinner begins.

Who's the Competition . . . .

Naturally the Cunard ships compete head-on with the P & O ships, the difference being that P & O does not participate in active U.S. marketing except through companies such as Princess Tours, while Cunard maintains very active U.S.-based offices.

Who's Aboard. . . . .

Primarily British passengers, but some Americans, Australians, New Zealanders and others; families with children on holiday cruises; singles of all ages.

Who Should Go . . . .

The people that do, plus American and Canadian Anglophiles.

Who Should Not Go . . . .

Anyone who can't mix and mingle with people from another country; any passionately chauvinistic American who thinks everyone else is disadvantaged (much as the British used to feel about the rest of the world).

P & O CRUISES 609

P & O CRUISES

The Lifestyle

Since P & O virtually invented the pleasure cruise, many of the familiar traditions of the genre are practiced aboard these ships, from dress codes to shipboard games.

Wardrobe

We remember being aboard the *Victoria* when it was the *Sea Princess*, and a wealthy Texan showed up on a formal night in a resplendent custom-made outfit, a cowboy tuxedo in white with red patent leather lapels and matching red and white cowboy boots. The irate British at the next table summoned the maitre d'hotel and demanded that the Texan be sent back to his cabin "to change into proper attire." They may run around in frocks and undersized bathing suits and even terry-cloth bathrobes all day long, but when black tie is required in the evening, they're sticklers for correctness.

Bill of Fare ......B

The meal pattern is British rather than American, with kippers, kidneys and finnan haddie on breakfast menus, kedgeree and curries and such for lunch, along with a roast, called a joint. Afternoon tea is much more important than midnight buffet, and high tea (correctly used, the term means a light early supper rather than fancy little sandwiches and scones with cream and jam) a tradition for the children on board. The British like to see the entire array of silverware to be used for the meal arranged in front of them at the beginning. And of course the sweet (dessert) comes before the savory (cheese, marrow or smoked oysters on toast or chicken livers grilled with bacon) that finishes the meal.

Showtime ......B+

Since P & O also invented the amusements that go with cruises—a letter written from before the turn of the century lists "quoits, bull, potato race, egg-and-spoon race, tugs-of-war, skipping contests, thread-needle races"—you can expect a daily quiz, team trivia games, a ship's mileage pool, duplicate bridge, even cricket games. Evenings offer music for dancing, some fairly routine production shows (except on the *Oriana* with its professional theatrical stage) and the usual variety artists from Butlin's.

Discounts

On some cruises early booking discounts on the *Oriana*, *Arcadia* and *Victoria* should be available.

The Bottom Line

"Cruising British style" means less glitz and glamour in the decor but a more traditional shipboard experience. If you wonder what that's about, pick up almost any book by W. Somerset Maugham, who traveled extensively by ship.

★ ★ ★ ★
ARCADIA

It was a unique experience to tour France's Chantiers de L'Atlantique shipyard in late 1988, to see a ship nearing completion that began life as Sitmar's *FairMajesty* and by a stroke of a pen was turned into Princess' *Star Princess* overnight. Now the same ship sails as the *Arcadia* for Princess' parent company, replacing the beloved but aging *Canberra*, retired from the fleet in September 1997. This is the third *Arcadia* to sail for P&O.

Particularly memorable for us was sailing aboard the *Star Princess* inaugural cruise with her godmother, the late Audrey Hepburn, as a fellow passenger.

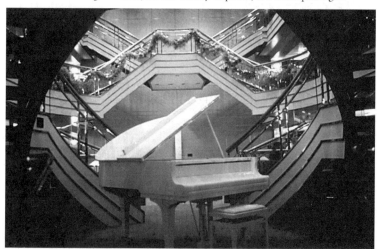

The atrium lobby and piano are framed by a dramatic staircase.

The *Arcadia*, the former *Star Princess*, has one of the best pool-and-sun decks at sea. It runs most of the length of the vessel and stars two large swim-

ming pools spanned by a raised sun deck. The area is filled out by an aft buffet cafe and a forward bar and pizzeria. A three-deck atrium with a stainless
steel kinetic sculpture dominates the amidships area. The very popular cafe
and pastry shop in the lobby is now called Tiffany's.

The spa, beauty salon, gym and massage areas are relegated to below-decks
without windows rather than given a prominent and sunny spot atop the
ship as on many new vessels.

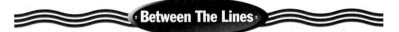

The Brochure Says

"...some of the largest standard staterooms in the industry. Connoisseurs of fine cruising will be dazzled by this modern-day floating resort."

Translation

An apt description. It's hard to think of anything you'd get at a big Caribbean resort
hotel that you can't find on here except for sand between your toes.

Fantasy Suites: . . . . A

*Average Price Per Person, Double Occupancy, Per Day: $1020 on a world cruise seg-
ment.*
The 14 suites are top-of-the-line, measuring 530 square feet. Inside the sliding glass
doors is an open, L-shaped room divided into sitting and sleeping areas with sofa,
two chairs, coffee table, queen-sized bed, nightstands and built-in desk. There's
plenty of closet and storage space, two TV sets, a dressing room with mahogany
built-in dressing table and large mirror, a spacious marble bathroom divided so the
tub, separate shower stall and wash basin can be closed off to let the toilet and second wash basin double as powder room. A mini-refrigerator keeps everything cold.

Small Splurges: . . . . B

Average Price PPPD: $891 on a world cruise segment.
The 36 mini-suites are 370 square feet each, with private veranda, sitting area with
built-in desk and counter as well as sofa and chairs, and a large bath with tub/
shower combination.

Suitable Standards: . . . . A

Average Price PPPD: $387 on a world cruise segment.
All cabins aboard have twin beds that can be rearranged into one queen-sized bed,
walk-in closet and separate dressing area, refrigerator and minibar, guest safe, terry-
cloth robes, hair dryers and color TV. Both outsides (with picture windows) and
insides are the same size—180 square feet. Ten are designated wheelchair-accessible, and these measure 240 square feet with extra-wide doors and no thresholds.

Bottom Bunks: . . . . A

Average Price PPPD: $350 on a world cruise segment.
The cheapest cabins are located forward on Plaza Deck. Furnishings are the same as
"Suitable Standards."

The Routes

Arcadia takes over the *Canberra's* itinerary which usually began with a world cruise the first quarter of the year, followed by various itineraries in Europe and the Caribbean.

The pool deck on the Arcadia *has a very popular waterfall.*

The Scoop

This ship is perfect for warm-weather cruising and a natural magnet for families and younger cruisers so it should perform particularly well for sun-seeking British passengers.

Insider Tips

Five Great Places

1. The deck pools provide a raised sunbathing area flanked by a pool with waterfall and in-pool bar, and a second pool with four whirlpool spas.

2. The Oval on Promenade Deck is a traditional British pub with a cricketing theme.

3. The Horizon Lounge, a circular glass-walled observation lounge above the bridge, doubles as a nightclub after dark. The French shipyard workers called it *Le Camembert* because its round shape reminded them of a cheesebox.

4. Peter Pan's youth center and Decibels teen center get a lot of space, making this a good ship for kids and teens.

5. The Palladium Showlounge is where the resident Stadium Theatre Company performs musicals and plays.

Five Good Reasons to Book This Ship

1. You can spend all day on the pool deck for optimum fun in the sun.

2. It's a great place for kids, who keep busy with supervised activities from 9 a.m. to midnight, plus a kids-only wading pool.

3. To enjoy the traditional British atmosphere of the Century Bar with its array of after-dinner liqueurs.

4. A museum-quality art collection of contemporary works valued at $1 million plus.

5. A night nursery for supervised baby-sitting.

Five Things You Won't Find Aboard

1. The former Characters Bar that served outrageous drinks with funny names; it's been turned into an ice cream bar.

2. Fuddy-duddies.

3. An ocean view from the gym or the beauty salon; they're on a lower deck hidden away for privacy and noise control.

4. The Royal Family tiaras and stomachers in the Crown Jewel shop.

5. A cabin without private facilities now that the *Canberra* has been retired.

ARCADIA ★★★★

Registry	**Britain**
Officers	**British**
Crew	**International**
Complement	**650**
GRT	**63,500**
Length (ft.)	**805**
Beam (ft.)	**105**
Draft (ft.)	**27**
Passengers-Cabins Full	**1650**
Passengers-2/Cabin	**1500**
Passenger Space Ratio	**42.3**
Stability Rating	**Good to Excellent**
Seatings	**2**
Cuisine	**British/Continental**
Dress Code	**Traditional**
Room Service	**Yes**
Tip	**$8 PPPD**

Ship Amenities

Outdoor Pool	**3**
Indoor Pool	**0**
Jacuzzi	**4**
Fitness Center	**Yes**
Spa	**Yes**
Beauty Shop	**Yes**
Showroom	**Yes**
Bars/Lounges	**3**
Casino	**Yes**
Shops	**3**
Library	**Yes**
Child Program	**Yes**
Self-Service Laundry	**Yes**
Elevators	**9**

Cabin Statistics

Suites	**14**
Outside Doubles	**570**
Inside Doubles	**165**
Wheelchair Cabins	**10**
Singles	**0**
Single Surcharge	**NA**
Verandas	**50**
110 Volt	**Yes**

★ ★ ★ ★ ★
ORIANA

We remember the previous Oriana *from the 1960s, but this new one is ever so much lovelier. The drollest touch of British whimsy aboard the* Oriana *turns up in the least expected place, the navigation bridge, where a grandly antlered reindeer head hangs on the wall. It is "Sven the ever-watchful," the captain says, a gift from the mayor of Olden, Norway, which none of the designers would permit in any of the ship's public rooms, so it ended up there. "We've found lots of uses for it," says one officer, "like hanging tinsel from the rack and putting a red nose on it for Christmas."*

The *Oriana* is that increasingly rara avis, a ship that still looks like a ship. Built for the British market and christened in April 1995 by Queen Elizabeth, the newest P&O vessel has a magnificent expanse of teak stern decks, three full-sized swimming pools and the most complete and spacious children's center at sea. It's exhilarating to stand at the stern on an upper deck and gaze down at the vast expanse of natural teak decking on five deck levels, the first four curving gently at both sides in a crescent-shaped ending that allows still more attractive nooks and hideaways for readers, dozers and sunbathers. The full professional theatre has an orchestra pit and flawless sightlines; every seat in the house is good.

Cabins & Costs

Fantasy Suites: . . . . **A**

Average Price Per Person, Double Occupancy, Per Day: $982 on a segment of the world cruise.

Suites with private balconies provide twin beds that can be converted to queen-sized, sofa, cocktail table, five-drawer desk, coffeemaker and generous closet space.

Small Splurges: . . . . **A**

Average Price PPPD: $536 on a segment of the world cruise.

Deck B deluxe doubles with private verandas have two lower beds that can convert to queen-sized, bookshelves, built-in safe, binoculars, robe and slippers, curtains to close off sleeping area from sitting area, and a sofa that can double as a bed for a child.

Suitable Standards: . . . . **A**

Average Price PPPD: $394 on a segment of the world cruise.

All cabins are furnished with twin or double beds, nightstands with drawers, desk/dressers with drawers and large mirrors, mini-refrigerators, combination safes, TV sets with remote control, plentiful closet space, and most bathrooms have tubs as well as showers.

Bottom Bunks: . . . . **B**

Average Price PPPD: $364 on a segment of the world cruise.

The smallest inside doubles are 150 square feet with two lower beds, corner love seat, mirrored cabinets and hair dryers. There are eight designated wheelchair-accessible cabins that measure 257 square feet each.

The Routes

The *Oriana* begins her year with an around-the-world cruise, followed by northern European and Mediterranean itineraries in summer, the Aegean in autumn, and the Canary Islands, Holy Land and Caribbean in winter.

The Scoop

While Princess Cruises are the North American representatives for its parent company, there's no way the *Oriana* could ever be mistaken for a love boat. Strikingly handsome and dignified, this ship is perfect for traditionalists because it looks more like an ocean liner than a floating resort. Young families with small children will really appreciate the extremely good child care facilities and experienced staff. It offers a very British cruise experience that would also be appreciated by American Anglophiles, fans of British country house hotels, experienced cruisers who yearn for proper dress codes and decorum, the return of fancy dress parades and passenger talent shows and enjoy the absence of frenetic onboard revenue pushes from multiple bingo games to art auctions. All in all, the ship has a lot to offer travelers of all ages.

Insider Tips

Five Fantastic Places Aboard

1. Theatre Royal, a full-fledged theatre with rows of red velvet seats and no smoking or drinking inside.

2. Harlequin's, a nightclub with traditional dancing on a large dance floor until midnight, when the disco sound takes over.

3. Lord's Tavern, a cricket-oriented pub that's packed with people at the pre-luncheon hour and decorated with a mural of Lord's Cricket Ground on one wall.

4. Thackeray Room, an elegant library and reading room lined with wood and furnished with handsome tapestry wing chairs and green leather chairs with brass nail studs and floor lamps.

5. The quiet, sedate European-style gaming room, with noisy slots relegated to a soundproofed room next to the pub.

Five Good Reasons To Book This Ship

1. To see the kids fed at a special children's tea at 5:15, after which they can go to the night nursery for free supervised care until 2 a.m.

2. To feast on traditional British breakfasts, complete with kippers, black pudding, fried bread and tinned baked beans.

3. To enjoy some sybaritic beauty treatments in an elegant art nouveau spa.

4. To bask in the limitless acres of teak deck, so nicely laid out that everyone aboard can find his own special spot for sun or shade.

5. To engage in the most dedicated quoits competitions we've ever seen at sea.

ORIANA ★★★★★

Registry	Britain
Officers	British
Crew	British
Complement	760
GRT	69,153
Length (ft.)	850
Beam (ft.)	105
Draft (ft.)	26
Passengers-Cabins Full	1804
Passengers-2/Cabin	1760
Passenger Space Ratio	38
Stability Rating	Good
Seatings	2
Cuisine	British
Dress Code	Traditional
Room Service	Yes
Tip	$8 PPPD

Ship Amenities

Outdoor Pool	3
Indoor Pool	0
Jacuzzi	5
Fitness Center	Yes
Spa	Yes
Beauty Shop	Yes
Showroom	Yes
Bars/Lounges	9
Casino	Yes
Shops	2
Library	Yes
Child Program	Yes
Self-Service Laundry	Yes
Elevators	10

Cabin Statistics

Suites	8
Outside Doubles	477
Inside Doubles	340
Wheelchair Cabins	8
Singles	110
Single Surcharge	NA
Verandas	114
110 Volt	Yes

★★★★
VICTORIA

In the grand tradition of Hollywood films, where a classy, intelligent but plain Jane, usually played by Rosalind Russell, takes off her glasses, lets down her hair and suddenly becomes glamorous, Princess Cruises briefly turned P & O's stalwart Sea Princess (now the Victoria), a sedate British dowager, into a Princess ship in 1987. This move infuriated the British, and after a relative brief whirl in her glamour garments, the Sea Princess returned to the fold. So great and long-standing was their wrath that eight years later the ship was renamed Victoria to erase any confusion in the U.K. that it might be one of those gaudy American Princess ships.

This elegant and classic ship started life as the *Kungsholm* for Swedish American Lines, and was one of the last great ships built by John Brown on the River Clyde. Today the vessel combines a stateliness and solid seaworthiness with the big deck dazzle of a fun-in-the-sun ship. It has a lot of action for active outdoorsy types, two outdoor pools and one indoor one, plus a whirlpool spa, sauna and gym, and a special sports afterdeck with shuffleboard and quoits, table tennis and golf. There are enough bars and lounges on board to visit a different one every day of the week, and several big comfortable reading rooms overlooking the sea. Staterooms are unusually large and beautifully fitted, with enough closet and storage space for a three-month cruise.

• Between The Lines •

The Brochure Says

"Her sleek lines reflect the elegance of her interior. As soon as you step on board, you'll notice a little extra refinement, a touch more style. Wood paneling gleams in the subdued lighting. You'll see fine paintings and delightful floral arrangements everywhere you look. The *Victoria's* small size lets her slip into out-of-the-way ports, and gives you a chance to meet your fellow passengers."

Translation

None needed—well said!

Cabins & Costs

Fantasy Suites: .... A

Average Price Per Person, Double Occupancy, Per Day: $598

Six big suites added during the major refurbishment in 1986 are named for classic P & O ships and have sitting areas, double beds, mini-refrigerators and bathrooms with Jacuzzi tubs.

Small Splurges: .... A

Average Price PPPD: $344

Spacious BA category cabins have sitting area, built-in desk/dresser with stool and mirror, twin or double beds, bathroom with tub.

Suitable Standards: .... B

Average Price PPPD: $259

Many of the standard cabins have two lower berths, one of which folds away during the day to lend more space, while the other can be made up as a sofa. There are some tubs, some showers only in these middle categories. Some 16 inside and outside single cabins are a boon for the solo traveler, so often overlooked in today's new ships or hit with a hefty surcharge for occupying a double cabin alone.

Bottom Bunks: .... A

Average Price PPPD: $212

Bottom category inside cabins on the lowest passenger decks are fairly spacious, fitted out with the lovely wood interiors like the other cabins are, and usually have a desk/dressing table and a chair as well as two lower beds, one of which folds away during the day.

The Routes

The *Victoria* does a series of Caribbean itineraries in winter and them moves to Europe for a summer/fall group of European cruises.

The Scoop

A graceful and elegant classic ship since her days as the *Kungsholm*, the *Victoria* is an antidote to megaliners and glitz. If you're a traditional cruiser who loves polished wood interiors and glass-enclosed promenades, and you subscribe to British understatement, *Victoria* is your ship come in.

Insider Tips

Five Favorite Places

1. Warm wood paneling and finely detailed carpentry show the extraordinary custom work that went into the ship, especially in the International Lounge.

2. The Coral Dining Room is an attractive medium-sized room with two meal seatings and two entrances, one forward and one aft, for anyone who gets mixed up on the way to dinner.

3. The circular bar in the Carib Lounge is a popular gathering spot because the casino is nearby.

4. The International Bar is an intimate place for a drink or two with a very close friend.

5. The Starlight Lounge was our favorite venue for hotly contested Trivial Pursuit games; it helped that if only one table out of the six or eight teams got the right answer, the bar sent over free drinks.

Five Good Reasons to Book This Ship

1. It's a longtime classic and you can tell that by being aboard.

2. It goes to some fascinating places you may not have been before, including Fethiye, Turkey; Mytilene, Greece; Tasacu, Turkey; the Dalmatian Islands (there are not 101 of them); Sinop, Turkey; Cephalonia, Greece; Nesebur, Bulgaria; and Tartous, Syria.

3. Two outdoor pools and one indoor one, plus whirlpool spa, sauna and gym, mean you can work out every day, and a special sports afterdeck provides an out-of-the-traffic area for shuffleboard and quoits, playing table tennis or driving golf balls.

4. Because if you book the right sailing far enough in advance you may be able to take the second person in the cabin along free.

5. Because there's a launderette and ironing room on virtually every deck.

Five Things You Won't Find On Board

1. TV sets in the lower-category cabins.

2. A shortage of closet space.

3. A hot breakfast served in your cabin; only continental breakfasts are offered by room service.

4. A private veranda.

5. A skimpy bathtub; all the cabins with tubs have those great deep British tubs.

VICTORIA ★★★★

Registry	**Britain**
Officers	**British**
Crew	**British**
Complement	**400**
GRT	**27,670**
Length (ft.)	**660**
Beam (ft.)	**87**
Draft (ft.)	**26**
Passengers-Cabins Full	**847**
Passengers-2/Cabin	**722**
Passenger Space Ratio	**38**
Stability Rating	**Good**
Seatings	**2**
Cuisine	**British**
Dress Code	**Traditional**
Room Service	**Yes**
Tip	**$8 PPPD**

Ship Amenities

Outdoor Pool	**2**
Indoor Pool	**1**
Jacuzzi	**2**
Fitness Center	**Yes**
Spa	**No**
Beauty Shop	**Yes**
Showroom	**Yes**
Bars/Lounges	**4**
Casino	**Yes**
Shops	**2**
Library	**Yes**
Child Program	**Yes**
Self-Service Laundry	**Yes**
Elevators	**10**

Cabin Statistics

Suites	**6**
Outside Doubles	**262**
Inside Doubles	**87**
Wheelchair Cabins	**10**
Singles	**12**
Single Surcharge	**NA**
Verandas	**0**
110 Volt	**No**

THE BIG RED BOAT

PREMIER CRUISE LINES

400 Challenger Road, Cape Canaveral, FL 32920
☎ *(407) 783-5061, (800) 327-7113*
www.bigredboat.com

Family cruises aboard the Big Red Boat mean parents spend quality time with kids, but don't have to constantly entertain them because of the plethora of activities and programs.

History ....

Premier Cruise Lines, founded in 1984, got some notice as a cruise line dedicated to families and as the first multi-day cruise ship sailing from Port Canaveral, but it catapulted to attention in November 1985, when it became "the Official Cruise Line of Walt Disney World," selling combination week-long land/sea vacations that allowed passengers to take a three- or four-day cruise and spend the remaining four or three days at Disney World with hotel room, rental car and admissions included in the package.

It was a great idea, first conceived around 1980 or 1981 by Bruce Nierenberg (who also later founded now-defunct American Family Cruises) and Bjornar Hermansen, when both were with Norwegian Caribbean Line (now Norwegian Cruise Line). So it was to NCL they first took the idea of basing a cruise ship in Port Canaveral to take advantage of the nearness of Disney World and tap into some of that rapidly growing leisure travel market. NCL wasn't interested, so in 1983, Nierenberg and Hermansen started up Premier with the backing of the Greyhound Corp. (later to become part of The Dial Corp) of Phoenix, Arizona.

The first ship Premier operated was the *Star/Ship Royale*, the former *Federico C* from Costa, which carried 1050 passengers when all the berths were filled, which they usually were. They bought and renovated the ship for $14 million, painted the hull bright red with orange and yellow trim, and sent it on its maiden voyage in March 1984.

In November 1985, on the heels of the Disney deal, Premier bought the *Oceanic* from Home Lines and made a major conversion that increased the ship's maximum passenger capacity from 1096 to 1800.

Premier acquired the six-year-old *Atlantic*, which became the *Star/Ship Atlantic*, after Home Lines went out of business in 1988. From a maximum of 1167 passengers, the *Atlantic* was remodeled to carry 1600. Later that same year Premier bought the 686-berth *Sun Princess* from Princess Cruises and turned it into the 950-berth *Star/Ship Majestic*, and then sold the *Royale* in January 1989 to Dolphin to become the *SeaBreeze*.

Heading into the 1990s, Premier decided to start calling itself The Big Red Boat, which was picked up instantly by TV-watching children. It also made marketing sense, because it meant instead of calling and requesting a ship by name, the passenger would take whichever Big Red Boat was handy despite the dissimilarities in the fleet.

Carnival Cruise Lines entered into negotiation to buy Premier in April 1991, then in May rescinded the offer. In June, co-founder Nierenberg resigned and sold his stock to Dial Corp. Co-founder Hermansen stayed on, trimming and streamlining company operations until his resignation in June 1992.

In March 1994, the 10-year agreement with Disney came to an end. Disney decided to start its own cruise line, called Disney Cruise Lines, with the first of two new ships scheduled to debut March 12, 1998.

The line operated three vessels until early 1995, when the *Majestic* was leased to CTC, a European cruise operator.

In January 1997, the *Atlantic* was sold to Mediterranean Shipping Cruises to become the *Melody*. In March 1997, Premier Cruise Lines and its one remaining Big Red Boat, the *Oceanic*, was sold to Cruise Holdings, the parent company of *Dolphin* and *Seawind*. Plans were to drydock the vessel for renovation and return it to service as "the Big Red Boat" in October 1997.

Concept . . . .

While other cruise lines, particularly Sitmar, had introduced very good children's programs, nothing anywhere near the scale of Premier's family program had been seen before. Children divided into age groups have their own daily programs as full of activities as the adults', even their own shore excursions, so parents could take the kids on a cruise without having to constantly entertain them, making it a real vacation for everybody.

Signatures . . . .

Bright red hull on the Big Red Boat.

Extensive children's programs that run from 9 a.m. to 10 p.m. with a staff of professionally trained counselors who divide the kids into five age groups. At the end of the scheduled program, baby-sitting is available at a nominal charge. Child care for children ages 2 to 12 is offered on an around-the-clock basis.

The Tasmanian Devil tucks kids in at bedtime—for a fee.

Gimmicks . . . .

Tuck-in bedtime service for kids by one of the costumed characters from Loony Tunes ($10) or a character breakfast in a special dining room ($30 for a family of four).

Chocolate Ship cookies for kids at bedtime.

Who's the Competition

In the short range, it's Carnival, who put its glittering new *Fantasy* into Port Canaveral on three- and four-day cruises. In the long haul, it's the Mouse, of course. Both lines profess to be excited about the Disney cruise ships coming into Port Canaveral in 1998 because they expect them to draw into the area many more potential passengers for everybody.

Who's Aboard

Kids, lots and lots of kids, some 500 or so children on an average summer or holiday cruise. At the same time, the line promotes the romantic aspects of cruising to honeymooners and frequently offers singles and senior citizen specials as well.

Who Should Go

Parents, single parents and grandparents with children. Couples and singles who enjoy being around other people's children.

Who Should Not Go

Anyone who doesn't adore children.

The Lifestyle

A lot of attention is paid to the adults on board, because the line intends to provide a vacation for the whole family, not just the children. Mom and Dad can enjoy a full day working out in the gym, taking a snorkeling tour, signing up for golf lessons, having a massage or beauty treatment at Steiners Beauty and Fitness Salon/Massage, betting on the horse races, attending the captain's champagne reception, gaming in the casino, playing family snowball bingo, hitting a late-night cabaret party before going to the gala buffet at 12:30 a.m. and having some French onion soup and made-to-order omelets between 1 and 3 a.m.

Wardrobe

The garb for these cruises is casual most of the time, although everyone in the family should bring something a little dressy for the captain's party. After dinner, unlike many lines, Premier doesn't mind passengers changing back to casual clothing for the rest of the evening on formal night.

Bill of Fare C

The dinner menu offers three appetizers, three soups, two salads and seven entrees, plus a special children's menu with familiar favorites such as cheeseburgers, chicken nuggets, hot dogs and fish fingers, along with a "health boat" selection that includes cheese pizza, beef kabob, beef and bean burrito and Spaghetti O's. Buffet breakfast and lunch is served in the cafe as well as full-service breakfast, lunch and dinner in the dining room. The Big Dipper ice cream parlor with "make-your-own-sundaes" is open throughout the afternoon. An "America the Beautiful" menu with the Looney Tunes characters strolling around the dining room is usually scheduled the last night of the cruise, with other themed dinners—French, Italian and Caribbean—also on the schedule, depending on the length of the cruise. Meals are served in the dining rooms at assigned tables during two seatings.

Showtime . . . . .B

In addition to daylong activities and shore excursions, evening production shows such as "Legends in Concert" with clones of Elvis, Madonna and the Blues Brothers performing, a Carlos & Charlie's Mexico-themed party, and lots of audience participation, from costumed '50s twist parties and Country Western Jamborees to karaoke contests.

Discounts . . . .

A family reunion plan gives 10 percent off the tariff for the first two guests in each of three cabins with a minimum of 10 people and six full-fare guests. Single parents traveling with one to three children under 17 can take a category 3 through 8 cabin, pay 125 percent of the per person, double occupancy rate, and the kids pay the cheaper third, fourth and fifth guest rate for sharing the same cabin. And seniors (anyone 60 or over) and a guest traveling with them can take 10 percent off the cruise fare during the season (summer and holiday weekends) and 15 percent apiece off during the rest of the year.

The Bottom Line

Premier has always attracted a great many first-time cruisers because it has been selling a vacation package rather than a cruise, with the emphasis on the fun and activities on land and sea rather than on a ship.

Under its new owners, plans were to continue the same service and schedule, but this could change at any time. Have your travel agent check before you book.

★ ★ ★
STAR/SHIP OCEANIC

At the champagne reception, the captain in his neatly pressed white uniform bows and shakes hands formally with a little girl in a ruffled dress and hair ribbons, and Bugs Bunny pads down the corridor to greet an arriving family and pose for snapshots. Inside, at the party, an orchestra plays, and among the many couples are dressed-up little girls dancing with their dads and scrubbed, self-conscious little boys stiffly leading their moms around the floor.

A classic cruise vessel built by Italy's Fincantieri shipyard for now-defunct Home Lines in 1965, the *Oceanic* still has some charming details from the period, including the two free-form Riviera pools and the bright tile floors. The ship is clean and kept in very good shape. The layout puts veranda suites on the topmost deck, a magrodrome sliding glass roof over the amidship pool areas, more cabins aft on the pool deck, a full deck below that of large cabins and suites, then a deck of public rooms. Below that are more cabins and the dining room. When Premier christened the ship in 1986, the godmother was Miss Minnie Mouse.

⋅ Between The Lines ⋅

The Brochure Says
"Bring the family, we'll do the rest."

Translation
Just another reminder that cruise packages are effortless and all-inclusive.

Cabins & Costs

NOTE:

Average per person per day prices below are for three- and four-day cruises; seven-day packages including theme park stays will be less expensive on a per-day basis. The prices are for two full-fare cabin occupants; third, fourth and fifth cabin occupants pay $449–$569 apiece including airfare from some cities for the three-or four-day cruise, depending on the season. Prices could change under the new owners.

Fantasy Suites: . . . . B+

Average Price Per Person, Double Occupancy, Per Day: $399 including airfare.
Eight spacious suites with private verandas high atop the Sun Deck give a great view of the sea as well as having plenty of room for a family of four. There's a king-sized bed plus two other berths, sitting area and bathroom with tub.

Small Splurges: . . . . B

Average Price PPPD: $329 including airfare.
Category 8 suites on the *Oceanic* are large and have a separate sitting area with sofa and chairs, twin or queen-sized bed with room divider and bathroom with tub. Some have room for a third passenger, some a third and fourth. Specify whether you want a double or twin beds. You may prefer the suites on Pool Deck, although slightly smaller, because many of those on Premier Deck have partially obstructed views from hanging lifeboats.

Suitable Standards: . . . . B

Average Price PPPD: $272 including airfare.
Most of the category 5 outside cabins have berths for third, sometimes fourth and fifth passengers, along with a choice of double or twin beds. Bathrooms have tubs and the rooms are fairly spacious and prettily furnished in pastels. Some connecting cabins are available for family groups.

Bottom Bunks: C

Average Price PPPD: $213 including airfare.
The cheapest cabins aboard are 15 category 1 inside cabins with upper and lower berths, quite small and designated for only two passengers.

The Routes

The *Star/Ship Oceanic* sails Friday afternoons from Port Canaveral, arriving in Nassau late Saturday morning and staying at the dockside until past midnight. On Sunday, the ship anchors off Port Lucaya at 9 a.m. and gives you a full day ashore at the beach with lots of things to do. The ship sails at 6 p.m. and arrives back in Port Canaveral early Monday morning.

On Monday afternoons, it sails again with the midweek passengers, spending Tuesday at sea, arriving early Wednesday morning in Nassau with a whole day for shopping and sightseeing, and doesn't sail until after midnight in case you want to check out the local casinos and nightclubs. Thursday the ship anchors off Port Lucaya and arrives back in Port Canaveral Friday morning.

The Scoop

We like a lot about the *Oceanic*—its nice big cabins (well, some of them are!), the lovely pool deck, the cool, darkish public rooms on Lounge Deck that are a good respite from the bright Bahamian sunshine. Kids will like the big play area and supervised wading pool. Some of the former bright yellows, oranges and reds have been subdued into lavenders and burgundies on a recent refit. Now, if that maintenance man could just stay ahead of all those sticky little fingerprints everywhere and the popcorn ground into the carpeting!

Insider Tips

Five Fun Places

1. The Riviera pools on pool deck, a pair of free-form shapes almost touching with blue tile surrounds and shady niches along the sides with tables and chairs.

2. Pluto's Playhouse, a big children's play area with a wading pool outside, bright carpeting, lots of toys and games and children's videos, an arts and crafts center, and jungle gyms.

3. Heroes and Legends, a pub and karaoke club, is a cozy little spot with Victorian decor, frosted glass and big, belly-up bar.

4. Seasport Health Center has a gym with weight room, exercycles and other machines plus a massage room.

5. Starlight Cabaret has a 1960s nightclub look with mushroom-type lights fixed into tabletops, dance floor and bandstand.

Five Off-the-Wall Things For Adults to Do

1. Hit the adults-only karaoke contest in the Heroes and Legends Pub.

2. Have a tequila shooter at the Carlos & Charlie's Party in the Starlight Cabaret.

3. Swim with the dolphins at Port Lucaya; you can have your travel agent book your appointment when you book your cruise.

4. Get in a poker game in the Heroes and Legends Pub.

5. Take golf lessons from the golf pro on board at poolside.

Five Good Reasons to Book This Ship

1. To see what a 1960s ocean liner looked like.

2. To get photographed with Bugs Bunny or have the Tasmanian Devil tuck you in bed at night.

3. To take a cruise and stay on land the rest of the week visiting Orlando theme parks.

4. To get away on a quiet midweek vacation (when there are fewer children on board) at a 15 percent discount if at least one of the two of you is over 60.

5. To enroll the kids in a professionally run children's program tailored specifically for each one's age group.

STAR/SHIP OCEANIC   ★★★

Registry	**Bahamas**
Officers	**Greek**
Crew	**International**
Complement	**565**
GRT	**38,772**
Length (ft.)	**782**
Beam (ft.)	**96**
Draft (ft.)	**28**
Passengers-Cabins Full	**1800**
Passengers-2/Cabin	**1180**
Passenger Space Ratio	**32.85**
Stability Rating	**Good**
Seatings	**2**
Cuisine	**American**
Dress Code	**Traditional**
Room Service	**No**
Tip	**$9 PPPD**

Ship Amenities

Outdoor Pool	**1**
Indoor Pool	**2**
Jacuzzi	**3**
Fitness Center	**Yes**
Spa	**No**
Beauty Shop	**Yes**
Showroom	**Yes**
Bars/Lounges	**6**
Casino	**Yes**
Shops	**2**
Library	**Yes**
Child Program	**Yes**
Self-Service Laundry	**No**
Elevators	**5**

Cabin Statistics

Suites	**65**
Outside Doubles	**190**
Inside Doubles	**335**
Wheelchair Cabins	**1**
Singles	**0**
Single Surcharge	**125%**
Verandas	**8**
110 Volt	**Yes**

PREMIER CRUISE
LINES, INC.

PRINCESS CRUISES®

10100 Santa Monica Boulevard, Los Angeles, CA 90067
☎ (310) 553-1770, (800) PRINCESS (774-6237)
www.princesscruises.com

A new tradition aboard the large Princess ships is to stage the captain's cocktail party in the three-story atrium lobby.

History

While the popular TV series "The Love Boat" catapulted Princess Cruises to worldwide fame, the company had been a household name on the West Coast, at least among cruise aficionados, from the 1960s.

In the winter of 1965-66, Seattle entrepreneur Stan McDonald chartered the 6000-ton *Princess Patricia* from Canadian Pacific Railway and offered cruises along the Mexican Riviera from Los Angeles. From the ship's name came the company name, Princess Cruises. The first season went so well aboard the "Princess Pat," as everyone began to call her, that McDonald soon chartered a newly built Italian ship called the *Italia* and renamed her the *Princess Italia*. In 1968, the *Princess Carla* (the former French Line *Flandre*), then Costa's *Carla C*, was chartered, and in 1971 the *Island Princess* (the only one of these still in the fleet).

Then London-based Peninsular and Orient Steam Navigation Company, better known as P&O (see P & O under Cruise Lines, above), the largest and oldest shipping company in the world, eyed the action and decided to come into the cruise scene with its new *Spirit of London*, which it positioned on the West Coast in the winter of 1972–73 to compete with Princess. There was little competition; McDonald continued to dominate Mexican Riviera cruising, despite one travel writer's comments that aboard the Princess Pat "the standard dessert was canned peaches" and the decor "was on a par with a good, clean $7-a-night room in a venerable but respected Toronto hotel."

So in 1974, P & O acquired Princess Cruises, including its key marketing staff, and set about upgrading the fleet hardware. The *Carla* and *Italia* went back to Costa Cruises in 1974, and the *Island Princess* was purchased outright. P & O's new *Spirit of London* was added to the fleet as the *Sun Princess*, and the *Sea Venture*, sister ship to the *Island Princess*, was acquired to become the *Pacific Princess*.

Things were already going well, but destined to improve even further when TV producer Doug Cramer showed up in 1975 with a new series he wanted to film aboard a cruise ship. *Et voila!* "The Love Boat" was born.

In 1988, continuing its "if you can't beat 'em, buy 'em" strategy, P & O/Princess acquired Los Angeles-based rival Sitmar Cruises, which added three existing ships and one nearly-completed new ship, *Star Princess*, to the fleet, to bring it up to nine vessels.

For most of 1998, there are still nine Love Boats cruising the seven seas, the newest the 109,000-ton giant *Grand Princess*, debuting in the Mediterranean in May and arriving in the Caribbean in early October.

The *Fair Princess*, laid up since October 1995, relocated to Australia to replace P & O's retiring *Fairstar*, and the *Star Princess* moved to parent company P & O to become the *Arcadia*, replacing the retiring *Canbarra*.

—Parent company P & O claims it invented leisure cruising in 1844 when British author William Makepeace Thackery sailed around the Mediterranean on a free ticket to publicize the service and wrote a travel book about his cruise—*From Cornhill to Grand Cairo*—under the pseudonym Michael Angelo Titmarsh.

—One of the three largest cruise lines in the world.

—Offers the largest number of world-wide destinations of any major line.

—First to introduce all outside cabins with a high proportion of private balconies (*Royal Princess*, 1984).

—First major cruise line to introduce multimedia musical shows produced in-house.

—First to install a "black box" recorder on each of its ships for additional safety data in case of an incident at sea.

—Introduced easy-to-use phone cards to make local or long distance calls from anywhere in the world with a push-button phone; the card (good for $20 worth of phone time) was originally developed as a convenience for the Princess crew (sold across the fleet, July 1995).

—TV's "The Love Boat" is still seen in 93 countries and heard in more than 29 languages. The title comes from a book written by a former cruise director named Jeraldine Saunders about her life onboard.

> ### DID YOU KNOW?
>
> *While the* Pacific Princess *is the vessel most associated with "Love Boat" over the years, the pilot episode was actually filmed aboard the original* Sun Princess, *the former* Spirit of London, *now retired from the fleet.*

Concept ·

"It's more than a cruise, it's the Love Boat," a beaming Gavin MacLeod intoned on the Princess commercials.

What does that make you think of? The TV series, of course, with its glamorous, friendly crew, never too busy to intercede in someone's love affair. Luxurious staterooms and elegantly garbed passengers. Nubile nymphs in bikinis. Exotic ports, perpetual sunshine and cloudless blue skies. In other words, the perfect vacation—a cruise.

With its varied fleet of vessels, ranging from the homey, mid-sized 610-passenger *Island Princess* and *Pacific Princess* to the new 1950-passenger Grand Class ships and the 2600-passenger *Grand Princess*, the line feels it offers "something for everyone" from "endless activity" to "total relaxation."

Princess' familiar flowing-haired logo atop the funnel of the **Crown** Princess.

Signatures ·

The line's distinctive stack logo, the "sea witch" with the flowing hair, provides instant identification when a Princess ship is in port. Just as distinctive, but less well known, is the Princess tradition of furnishing each of its new ships with an exquisite museum-quality million dollar-plus art collections from contemporary artists such as Andy Warhol, David Hockney, Robert Motherwell, Frank Stella, Laddie John Dill, Billy Al Bengston, Richard Diebenkorn and Helen Frankenthaler.

On-board pizzerias with special ovens serve up pizzas and calzones cooked to order.

Gimmicks. . . . .

Declaring St. Valentine's Day as Love Boat National Holiday aboard all the line's vessels, with renewal of vows ceremonies in which some 4000 couples participate. The holiday also features a poetry contest and reading, romantic feature films, a Hearts card game tournament and honeymooner and singles parties.

Who's the Competition . . . .

In Alaska, Princess has been competing head-on with Holland America for some years, and usually outnumbers HAL in ships positioned there for the summer. In the Caribbean, HAL is also a main competitor, but Love Boats face some Costa competition for fans of pizza, pasta and Italian waiters.

Who's Aboard. . . . .

Romantic couples of all ages who saw "The Love Boat" on TV; long-time loyals, both couples and singles, over 45; a group of younger couples who've met on board and continue to take vacation cruises together; some families with children, who gravitate toward those ships that have dedicated playrooms and full-time youth counselors; people with glints of gold from head (hair coloring) to toe (gold lamé sandals or ankle bracelets), neck (gold chains) to fingertips (gold pinky rings, a gold lamé tote).

Who Should Go . . . .

Anyone who wants a very traditional cruise experience with a chance to dance and dress up; admirers of avant-garde Pompidou Center architect Renzo Piano, who designed parts of the *Crown* and *Regal Princess*; families whose teenagers like the pizzeria; anyone who loves pasta, pastries and cappuccino; fans of the Cirque du Soleil who'll adore the new avant-garde shows on the big new ships. More younger passengers should be boarding, because Princess is adept at giving them what they want, at least on the big new ships—meals on demand 24 hours a day; a less-structured captain's cocktail party; music for listening and dancing all over the ship; lots of sundeck and water areas with swim-up bars, waterfalls, swimming pools and Jacuzzis; full spa, gym, and beauty services. Families with children now that Princess is welcoming them with open arms.

Who Should Not Go . . . .

Anyone with children under 18 months of age (babies are not permitted on board and children under three are permitted on a limited basis only); anybody who refuses to wear a tie on any occasion; anyone who would answer "Huh?" to the query, "Fourth for bridge?"

The Lifestyle . . . .

Set in the framework of traditional cruises, a day aboard a Princess ship includes a plethora of activities and entertainment, from an exercise class in the gym or a facial in the beauty salon to trivia contests, pool games, bridge classes, aquacise in the ship's pool, indoor and outdoor game tournaments, bingo, golf chipping, feature films in the ship's theater or in the cabin, port lectures, shopping lectures, cooking demonstrations, galley and bridge tours, fashion shows and karaoke singing. Even kids have their own karaoke contests, along with "coketail" parties, coloring contests and ice cream parties.

Many evenings are relatively formal aboard, with passengers wearing their finest clothes and jewelry and Italian or British officers hosting dinner tables, but other nights, such as the traditional London Pub Night, casual wear is prescribed and beer and pub dishes are on the agenda, along with rowdy music hall songs and dances.

Wardrobe . . . .

Princess passengers usually have two formal nights, two or three semi-formal and two or three casual nights during a week. For formal nights, men are requested to wear tuxedos, dinner jackets or dark suits and women cocktail dresses or evening outfits. Semi-formal evenings call for men to wear jacket and tie, women to wear dresses or dressy pantsuits.

On casual evenings, men may wear open-necked sport shirts, slacks and sports outfits; women, slacks, dresses or skirts. Daytime clothing can be quite casual, but coverups over bathing suits are expected for passengers walking through the ship.

Bill of Fare . . . .**B+**

The cuisine aboard Princess ships has changed recently to reflect passenger requests for lighter and more contemporary dishes but still includes many of the previous Continental favorites with an emphasis on Italian dishes. A pasta specialty is featured every day at lunch and at dinner, along with a Healthy Choice menu and vegetarian dishes.

The single most revolutionary restaurant change has been the introduction of the 24-hour Horizon Court food service aboard the new Grand Class ships and introduced retroactively aboard most of the rest of the fleet. Here, buffet food service is available 24 hours a day, plus sit-down dinner service from a bistro menu from 7:30 p.m. to 4 a.m. During this period, there is live music for dancing between courses, and a choice of various appetizers, a soup of the day, salad bar, main dishes from pastas and chicken breasts to steak sandwiches and Southwestern-style pork chops, followed by cheesecake and other desserts. The added attraction here is a casual dress code for families with small children or passengers who don't feel like dressing up for the dining room.

Also in the Horizon Court is a lunch buffet with 12 hot dishes, including a carvery with roasts, pasta dishes, beef stir fry with vegetables, grilled-to-order fish, mussels, pizza squares and fried chicken. A typical menu for the captain's welcome aboard dinner includes a "symphony of three caviars" or a crab quiche with jalapeno chili sauce; a classic capon broth or a hearty lentil puree with herb croutons; an arugula, radicchio and Belgian endive salad with low-fat vinaigrette or a Caesar salad tossed at tableside; rich lobster thermidor or a simple broiled fillet of silver salmon with garlic mashed potatoes. Desserts run the range from ice creams, fruit and cheese to hazelnut chocolate souffle with Armagnac sauce.

While the groaning board midnight buffet has been supplanted by the Horizon Court evening service, the line continues to offer some of its themed late-night presentations such as the champagne fountain and Crepes Suzette, a gala lunch buffet and a deck buffet with dancing on a balmy evening.

Meals are served in two assigned seatings, with dinners somewhere between 6–6:30 p.m. for first seating, 8–8:30 p.m. for second seating. Breakfast and lunch are open seating on the big new ships. Even the smaller *Island Princess* and *Pacific Princess* have an alternative bistro evening restaurant available at more limited hours. Your travel agent should request your seating preference when booking. All Princess dining rooms are smoke-free.

Pizzerias that cook pizzas and calzones to order are aboard most of the line's ships (see Signatures) and the newest vessels have Sundaes, a surcharge ice cream stand selling Haagen-Daz ice cream and sundaes, and the Balcony Grill with hot dogs and hamburgers prepared on deck for sunbathers or swimmers who don't want to go inside.

Wine prices aboard are generally reasonable.

Showtime. . . . . A

Princess pioneered elaborate multimedia shows with film clips projected onto screens beside the stage and pre-recorded "click track" sweetening to swell the musical accompaniment. As other lines began using many of the same techniques, the company started updating its entertainment to include more sophisticated special effects, culminating in the sensational Cirque de Soleil-type entertainments titled "Mystique" and "Odyssea." With a company of 23 performers, including nine European and Asian acrobats, set under the sea with inflatable scenery that literally "grows" in front of your eyes; it's remarkable. These shows at present appear only on board the larger, newer ships.

Big Band music, a splashy new Caribbean revue, a show-biz production called *Let's Go to the Movies*, a lively musical romp called *Pirates*, full lecture program, trivia quizzes, "Baby Boomer" theme nights, stand-up comedians and London Pub Night fill out the fun.

On the Grand Class vessels, big-name entertainers such as Red Buttons, Jack Jones and Fred Travalena are scheduled for some sailings.

Discounts . . . .

The Princess Love Boat Loan was introduced in the spring of 1997 for wanna-be cruisers that prefer to buy a big-ticket item like a cruise the same way they buy cars and furniture, on time with monthly payments. The program lets travel agents refer their Princess cruise clients to a bank that can provide a line of credit in 10 minutes or so. The repayment can be made on a schedule of 24, 36 or 48 months, and the interest on a week-long Caribbean cruise with a 36-month schedule works out to about $1 a day per couple, according to the line.

Love Boat Savers are discounts for early booking, with 50 percent off for second passengers in the same cabin. The lowest fares are for the earliest bookings; discounts may decrease as the sailing date approaches. Discounts vary according to the price and season.

Frequent cruisers who belong to the Captain's Circle are mailed notices on special savings for designated sailings, including deals such as two-for-one buys, 50 percent off for the second passenger in a cabin or free upgrades.

The Bottom Line

Princess prides itself on little extra details that make a cruise more luxurious, such as stocking each passenger cabin with robes to be used during the sailing, a bowl of fresh fruit, CNN on cabin TV sets, complimentary toiletries, pillow chocolates and 24-hour room service.

Housekeeping aboard all the ships is excellent and service generally good, particularly in the dining room where waiters and captains really seem to enjoy taking special orders and preparing tableside dishes such as Caesar salad and Crêpes Suzette.

All in all, these are good cruises for almost everyone except families with infants.

PRINCESS CRUISES

★ ★ ★ ★ ★
CROWN PRINCESS
REGAL PRINCESS

"Euclid alone / Has looked on beauty bare." Edna St. Vincent Millay

The most beautiful ship interior we ever saw was the Crown Princess dome when it was under construction at the Fincantieri shipyard in Italy in early 1990. Architect Renzo Piano walked us through the pristine space that from the outside forms the "dolphin brow" of the ship. Inside it resembles what Piano called "the inside of a whale," with polished, rounded bone-colored ribs arching from ceiling to floor framing wide curved glass windows. As Piano talked about metaphor and magic, we stroked the silky, eggshell finish of the glossy plaster ribs.

When we came back to Europe a few months later to sail on the maiden voyage, the dome was filled with slot machines and potted palms, red leather chairs and cocktail tables. It was never so beautiful again.

This elegant pair of ships were built in Italy's Fincantieri yard. The *Crown Princess* and *Regal Princess* are unmistakable, even at a distance, because of their sloped, dolphin-like brow and strong vertical funnel.

Controversial Italian architect Renzo Piano dislikes too much emphasis on the dolphin-like shape he designed—"A ship is a ship, it's not a dolphin." The vertical funnel, a bold departure from the broad raked funnels on most of the Love Boats, he terms "a frank, clear, strong statement…and it works beautifully, by the way, to take the smoke away."

If an award were given for spacious cabins, these ships would win hands down. Cocktail lounges on board are lovely, as is a wine-and-caviar bar, a patisserie/sidewalk cafe in the lobby, a wonderful shopping arcade and a well-planned show lounge with fairly good sightlines except from the back of the main lounge.

CHAMPAGNE TOAST

On our most recent visit to these ships, the wood bars at eye level that had once sabotaged the observation facility of The Dome had been removed and lower wooden benches put in their places. Now the area really works as an observation lounge; finally, passengers are using it during the daytime as well as after dark.

Between The Lines

The Brochure Says

"Her teak is from Burma, her marble from Carrera, and her fittings were forged by Italian craftsmen in shipyards over 200 years old...a masterpiece of the sea created by one of the world's most gifted architects."

Translation

Just what it says. These ships are the last word in design and decor, luxurious, graceful, stylish and very comfortable, and they whisper about their $200 million-plus price rather than shout it the way Carnival's megaliners do.

EAVESDROPPING

One purportedly cruise-savvy matron to her friend just after boarding, "Don't they have to go three miles out before they can open the bars? I'm sure they do." (P.S.: They don't.)

Cabins & Costs

Fantasy Suites: .... A+

Average Price Per Person, Double Occupancy, Per Day: $837 including airfare on Panama Canal cruises.

Top accommodations are the 14 suites, each with a double-size private veranda large enough for two lounging chairs with a small table between as well as a bigger table with two chairs, ideal for private breakfasts in the sun and sea breeze. A wide wooden doorway divides the living room with its sofa, chairs, tables and mini-refrigerator from the bedroom with its king-sized bed (which has a single mattress top rather than the two divided mattresses one usually gets when two beds are pushed together). Each room has its own TV set. A large dressing room lined with closets and enough storage space for an around-the-world cruise leads to the spacious marble bathroom with separate bathtub and stall shower. The toilet and second lavatory are adjoining, with another door that opens for the living room so it can double as a powder room when you're entertaining.

Small Splurges: .... A

Average Price PPPD: $613 including airfare on Panama Canal cruises.

The category A mini-suites with private veranda are a bit smaller on both balcony and interior, but still very comfortable with bed (twins or queen-sized), sitting area with sofa and chairs, TV, mini-refrigerator, bath with tub and shower and spacious closet space.

A prettily furnished deluxe cabin on the **Regal Princess.**

Suitable Standards: . . . . **A**

Average Price PPPD: $328 including airfare on Panama Canal cruises.
Category GG outside double cabins forward on Plaza Deck provide queen-sized beds and a convenient location, but there are only four of them. All the standards contain amenities usually found only in suites—mini-refrigerators, remote-control TV sets, guest safes and walk-in closets. Baths have showers only. Other standards offer two lower beds that can be made into a queen-sized bed.

Bottom Bunks: . . . . **A**

Average Price PPPD: $267 including airfare on Panama Canal cruises.
Even the lowest category inside double cabin, the N category forward on Plaza Deck (only steps away from the lobby), contains the same amenities and furnishings as the mid-range standards (see "Suitable Standards," above).

The Routes

The *Crown Princess* makes seven-day Gulf of Alaska cruises between Vancouver and Anchorage in summer, and sails the Panama Canal between Fort Lauderdale and Los Angeles in winter.

The *Regal Princess* sails Alaska Inside Passage itineraries in summer and cruises the Panama Canal between San Juan and Acapulco in winter.

The Scoop

This is an exquisite pair of ships, and generally everything runs smoothly. Newly embarking passengers are serenaded by a Filipino string trio and greeted by white-gloved stewards to escort them to their cabins. Everything you need to know is spelled out in the daily "Princess Patter" programs or advance cruise materials mailed ahead of time, making these very good vessels for first-time cruisers. With the improvements in The Dome (see "Champagne Toast"), Piano's vision seems clearer, although a lot of the magnificent view windows between the "whale ribs" are still blocked by slot machines. As for people who worry that there's nothing to do on a cruise, we'd like to take them on a stroll around these ships at almost any hour of the day or night, and they'd never fret again.

Insider Tips

Five Super Places

1. The chic 1930s-style cocktail lounges on promenade deck, the Adagio on the *Regal*, the Intermezzo on the *Crown*, where you half-expect to see Cary Grant at the next table.

2. The Italian garden ambience in the Palm Court Dining Room on the Regal Princess, with its ivy-patterned carpet, pastoral garden murals and pastel rose and teal decor.

3. The Patisserie in the three-deck atriums, the true gathering spot on the ships; you can get cappuccino and espresso all day long, accompanied by freshly baked pastries, and observe the comings and goings of fellow passengers.

4. The Bengal Bar aboard the *Regal Princess* takes you back to the raj with wicker chairs, ceiling fans and a life-sized Bengal tiger, plus some tiger balm—a menu of rare single malt whiskies or a classic Bombay Sapphire gin martini.

5. The Presto Pizzeria on the *Crown Princess* with its Italian food-and-wine print red tablecloths, red-and-white glazed tile walls and natural teak floors, warm and inviting, serving five types of pizzas including vegetarian, plus calzones, garlic focaccio and Caesar salad.

Three Off-the-Wall Things to Do

1. Swim up for a drink at Flipper's pool bar.

2. Converse with the talking elevators, which announce each deck and caution you when you exit to watch your step.

3. Check out the photo of ex-president George Bush on board wearing a *Regal Princess* cap and chatting with Captain Cesare Ditel; you'll find it with other trophies in the corridor between the library and the Stage Door lounge.

Dancing in The Dome on the Regal Princess.

PRINCESS CRUISES

Five Good Reasons to Book These Ships

1. To see the spectacular shows, especially "Mystique," go to the pizzeria afterwards, talk about the performance with other audience members, then watch the stars come in for an after-show snack.

2. To get scuba certification in the New Waves program; the course costs $370 and passengers must sign up ahead of cruise departure or at the very beginning of the cruise.

3. To attend a captain's cocktail party where you don't have to stand in line for ages to shake hands and be photographed with the captain; on these ships everyone circulates throughout the three-deck atrium, drinks in hand, and anyone who wishes to be photographed can pose on the curved staircase for the ship's photographer.

4. To join in some lively passenger game shows including Team Trivia and Jeopardy.

5. To get more spacious cabins for the money than almost anywhere else afloat.

Five Things You Won't Find on Board

1. A gym or spa with sea views.

2. Jogging permitted before 8 a.m.

3. The best seats for the show in the front row; third row from the back, one level up from the main seating area, is better.

4. Locked bookcases; Princess trusts these passengers not to steal books or games.

5. Captain Stubing (although his alter ego, Gavin MacLeod, does show up sometimes).

PRINCESS CRUISES

CROWN PRINCESS
REGAL PRINCESS

★★★★★
★★★★★

Registry	**Liberia**
Officers	**British/Italian**
Crew	**International**
Crew	**696**
GRT	**70,000**
Length (ft.)	**811**
Beam (ft.)	**105**
Draft (ft.)	**26**
Passengers-Cabins Full	**1792**
Passengers-2/Cabin	**1590**
Passenger Space Ratio	**44.02**
Stability Rating	**Good to Excellent**
Seatings	**2**
Cuisine	**Contemporary**
Dress Code	**Traditional**
Room Service	**Yes**
Tip	**$7.75 PPPD, 15% automatically added to bar checks**

Ship Amenities

Outdoor Pool	**2**
Indoor Pool	**0**
Jacuzzi	**4**
Fitness Center	**Yes**
Spa	**Yes**
Beauty Shop	**Yes**
Showroom	**Yes**
Bars/Lounges	**6**
Casino	**Yes**
Shops	**4**
Library	**Yes**
Child Program	**Yes**
Self-Service Laundry	**Yes**
Elevators	**9**

Cabin Statistics

Suites	**14**
Outside Doubles	**604**
Inside Doubles	**177**
Wheelchair Cabins	**10**
Singles	**0**
Single Surcharge	**150-200%**
Verandas	**184**
110 Volt	**Yes**

PRINCESS CRUISES

★ ★ ★ ★ ★
DAWN PRINCESS
SEA PRINCESS*
SUN PRINCESS

It was love at first sight when we walked aboard the Sun Princess, *still under construction in Italy's Fincantieri shipyard. An orchestra was playing, the magnificent marble atrium glowed with polished brass and an Italian barman was handing out cups of freshly made cappuccino. Later, we would see the many unfinished sections of the vessel, but for that one magic moment, it was as if the ship were completed and ready to sail.*

The first of the new Grand Class ships for Princess, the *Sun Princess* at her debut was the largest cruise ship in the world. Eventually she is to be followed by three sister vessels, *Dawn Princess,* which debuted in May 1997; *Sea Princess* in late 1998; and *Ocean Princess* in 1999, plus, of course, the world's largest cruise ship to date, the 109,000-ton *Grand Princess,* debuting in May 1998, in the Mediterranean. The most remarkable thing about the Grand Class ships is that when you're aboard, they really don't seem as large as they are, 77,000 tons and carrying 1950 passengers. Nobody ever seems to be standing in line; even the captain's welcome aboard cocktail party is held in the soaring four-deck central atrium, allowing passengers to enter immediately at any level from any direction. Sunbathing space on deck is generous, and 410 of the cabins have their own private verandas. A full-time gardener tends to the $1 million-plus worth of plants on board.

The Brochure Says

"We're also taking a great Princess tradition and making the ultimate luxury, a stateroom with a private balcony, affordable for everyone. With up to 80 percent of outside accommodations—more than 1500 staterooms—featuring private balconies, these ships truly open up a new world in cruising: Cruising in Grand Style!"

Translation

Princess pioneered the concept of private verandas for more than just penthouse suites when the *Royal Princess* was introduced in 1984. Now, aboard the Grand Class vessels, almost everyone gets a private veranda.

Cabins & Costs

Fantasy Suites: . . . . A+

> *Average Price Per Person, Double Occupancy, Per Day: $478 plus air add-ons in the Caribbean.*
>
> Six spacious aft suites, each measuring between 536 and 754 square feet, with private balcony, separate bedroom, large living room, dining table with four chairs, wet bar, granite counter, big divided bath with stall shower and Jacuzzi tub, dressing room, desk/makeup area in bedroom, two TV sets, mini-refrigerator.

Cabin B310, a mini-suite with veranda, is listed in the brochure prices at around $436 a day per person, double occupancy.

Small Splurges: . . . . A

> *Average PPPD: $436 plus air add-ons in the Caribbean.*
>
> Thirty-two mini-suites are almost as lavish, with private veranda, sitting area with sofa and chair, queen-sized bed, walk-in closet, two TV sets, safe, bathrobes, bath with tub and separate stall shower, and mini-refrigerator.

Suitable Standards: . . . . **A**

Average PPPD: $314 plus air add-ons in the Caribbean.
The least-expensive cabins with private balconies also have twin or queen-sized bed, big closet, desk/dresser with chair, TV and mini-refrigerator.

Bottom Bunks: . . . . **A**

Average PPPD: $186 plus air add-ons in the Caribbean.
The smallest inside doubles are comfortable in size with two lower beds that can convert to queen-sized, desk/dresser, chair, bath with large tile shower and generous storage space.

The Routes

The *Sun Princess* cruises the Western Caribbean in winter on seven-day round-trips from Fort Lauderdale, every Saturday, calling in Princess Cays, Ocho Rios, Grand Cayman and Cozumel. In summer, the ship sails on a Gulf of Alaska itinerary.

The *Dawn Princess* sails the Southern Caribbean from San Juan on seven-day roundtrips leaving every Saturday and calling in Barbados, St. Lucia, Martinique, St. Maarten and St. Thomas. She joins her sister ship in Alaska in summer also sailing Gulf of Alaska cruises.

The Scoop

While the ships and their technology are cutting edge, traditional touches are everywhere—the Wheelhouse Bar with its ship models from the P&O archives, a "museum" of opera costumes (on Sun Princess), vintage movie stills and costumes (on Dawn Princess) in glass cases outside the theater, Queen Mary deck chairs on the natural teak promenade deck, and handsome wood laminates in cabins and public rooms. The deck space is broken up into different levels with free-form "islands" of green Astroturf resembling landscaping. The casino is huge, but is not permitted to dominate the ship. While passengers are aware of where it is, they are not forced to constantly walk through it. The Grand Class ships work extremely well and ride very smoothly.

In Verdi's Pizzeria, a choice of made-to-order pizzas served up hot.

Insider Tips

Five Favorite Spots

1. The elegant pizzerias that resemble a terraced winter garden with verdigris wrought iron trim.

2. The Horizon Court, a gala buffet area serving food 24 hours a day, plus a nightly alternative dinner menu with table service and music for dancing from 7:30 p.m. to 4 a.m.

3. The magnificent Princess Theatre, as professional as anything on Broadway or in the West End, with flawless sightlines from every seat.

4. The Vista Lounge, a second show lounge arranged in a cabaret style, again with perfect sightlines from every seat because of a cantilevered ceiling designed without support posts underneath.

5. The elegant Wheelhouse bar with wood-paneled walls, richly upholstered banquettes and chairs and vintage P&O ship models.

The elegant library aboard **Sun Princess** *has several leather "listening chairs" for music or audio books.*

Five Good Reasons to Book This Ship

1. To be able to dine in the Horizon Court when you don't feel like dressing up for the dining room.

2. To see brilliant entertainment in a professional theater with red plush row seats from the Schubert Theater in Los Angeles.

3. To participate in the New Waves watersports program with a scuba certification course and snorkeling instruction.

4. To enjoy really delicious pizza and calzone baked to order.

5. To try out the "listening chairs" in the library, the sophisticated golf simulator ($20 for 30 minutes, approximately 9 holes at courses such as Mauna Kea) or browse among the millions of dollars worth of specially commissioned art.

DAWN PRINCESS ★★★★★
SEA PRINCESS* ★★★★★
SUN PRINCESS ★★★★

Registry	**Liberian**
Officers	**British/Italian**
Crew	**International**
Complement	**900**
GRT	**77,000**
Length (ft.)	**856**
Beam (ft.)	**106**
Draft (ft.)	**26**
Passengers-Cabins Full	**2270**
Passengers-2/Cabin	**1950**
Passenger Space Ratio	**39.48**
Stability Rating	**Good**
Seatings	**2**
Cuisine	**Contemporary**
Dress Code	**Traditional**
Room Service	**Yes**
Tip	**$7.75 PPPD, 15% automatically added to bar checks**

Ship Amenities

Outdoor Pool	**4**
Indoor Pool	**0**
Jacuzzi	**5**
Fitness Center	**Yes**
Spa	**Yes**
Beauty Shop	**Yes**
Showroom	**Yes**
Bars/Lounges	**7**
Casino	**Yes**
Shops	**7**
Library	**Yes**
Child Program	**Yes**
Self-Service Laundry	**Yes**
Elevators	**11**

Cabin Statistics

Suites	**6**
Outside Doubles	**597**
Inside Doubles	**408**
Wheelchair Cabins	**18**
Singles	**0**
Single Surcharge	**150-200%**
Verandas	**411**
110 Volt	**Yes**

Unrated
GRAND PRINCESS

The 109,000-ton *Grand Princess* at her debut in May 1998, will be the largest cruise ship in the world, a title she will hold until the first of the 130,000-ton behemoths from Royal Caribbean enter the picture in 1999. But Princess intends to impress passengers with much more than size.

The Grand Class vessel offers three state of-the-art showrooms, each offering a different after-dinner entertainment for passengers. Three main dining rooms and a two-level, 24-hour indoor/outdoor restaurant will supplement the more formal meal venues. Additionally, eating options include a pizzeria, an alternative restaurant serving southwestern cuisine, a patisserie, a wine and caviar bar and late-night casual fare in the aft show lounge.

Big spenders will be delighted to find an entire deck of suites that feature "Grand Class Gold" butlers who'll polish your golf clubs, develop film, post mail, book shore excursions, deliver afternoon tea in the suite and arrange for cleaning, laundry, pressing and shoe shines. Fresh-air fiends can look forward to 750 cabins offering private verandas. A virtual reality theater introduces new technology, and a "blue screen" room lets passengers create their own video productions for fun.

The entire upper pool area is enclosed by a retractable magrodome. A chapel for weddings and renewal of vows is on board, along with a 14,000-square-foot casino, a nightclub riding 15 decks above the sea and reached only by a glass-enclosed walkway, a suspended swimming pool and a huge health spa. Wheelchair passengers will find 28 accessible cabins on board.

Too wide to pass through the Panama Canal, the giant ship will debut in Europe with a series of 12-day cruises between Barcelona and Istanbul, calling at Monte Carlo, Florence, Naples/Capri, Venice, Athens and Ephesus. At the end of its Mediterranean summer season, the vessel will relocate to New York for a formal North American debut Sept. 24, prior to beginning her winter season in the Caribbean Oct. 4.

GRAND PRINCESS — Unrated

Registry	Liberia
Officers	NA
Crew	International
Complement	1,150
GRT	109,000
Length (ft.)	935
Beam (ft.)	118
Draft (ft.)	26
Passengers-Cabins Full	NA
Passengers-2/Cabin	2,600
Passenger Space Ratio	41.92
Stability Rating	NA
Seatings	2
Cuisine	Contemporary
Dress Code	Traditional
Room Service	Yes
Tip	$7.75 PPPD, 15% automatically added to bar checks

Ship Amenities

Outdoor Pool	5
Indoor Pool	0
Jacuzzi	9
Fitness Center	Yes
Spa	Yes
Beauty Shop	Yes
Showroom	Yes
Bars/Lounges	18
Casino	Yes
Shops	4
Library	Yes
Child Program	Yes
Self-Service Laundry	Yes
Elevators	14

Cabin Statistics

Suites	26
Outside Doubles	NA
Inside Doubles	NA
Wheelchair Cabins	28
Singles	0
Single Surcharge	150-200%
Verandas	710
110 Volt	Yes

★★★
ISLAND PRINCESS
PACIFIC PRINCESS

We once sailed aboard that most legendary of Love Boats, the Pacific Princess, into the equally legendary city of Casablanca. Play it again, Captain Stubing. It makes you wonder what becomes a legend most. Casablanca looked nothing like the film of the same name, but then the movie was shot on the studio backlot and nothing in it looked like Casablanca anyhow. And there we were on the Love Boat in a cabin that bore no resemblance whatsoever to the palatial accommodations where Lana Turner, Ethel Merman, Stewart Granger, Anne Baxter and all the other gone-but-not-forgotten guest stars lived during their cinematic cruise. Those cabins are on the back lot too, along with Rick's cafe and Paris and the whole thing.

The aft pool deck on **Pacific Princess** *gets a lot of sunbathing action.*

Princess takes very good care of its hardware, and these two dowagers of the fleet have undergone plenty of facelifts over the years. The most recent ones not only introduced new colors and fabrics throughout the cabins and public rooms, but also brought operational and technical systems up to date.

In the showrooms, new tiered floors were added to improve sightlines; casino space was improved and a video arcade added. Cabins were totally refurbished and furnished with TVs, new telephones and hair dryers. Poolside, a new buffet service offers made-to-order omelets and a salad bar.

The Brochure Says

"No ships have been more celebrated in recent times than *Pacific Princess*, the star of the long-running television series 'The Love Boat,' and her twin sister, *Island Princess*. Following the design standard set by our newest ships, these timeless vessels are resplendent with woolen carpets and custom fabrics in tones of aquamarine, rust, burgundy and blue. The stunning showroom offers tiered, banquet seating. There is a gym and casino and new indoor seating for the buffet area."

Translation

Some Princess passengers love these vintage vessels so much they won't let them retire. The interior decoration on the *Crown Princess* and *Regal Princess* turned out so well they decided to go back and add some of its details to the older ships. Good idea!

DID YOU KNOW?

According to Princess President Peter Ratcliffe (try to say that seven times without tripping), the line's most popular dessert is Grand Marnier Soufflé, so the menus during most cruises will offer as many as five different dessert soufflés.

Cabins & Costs

Fantasy Suites: . . . . **B**

Average Price Per Person, Double Occupancy, Per Day: $689-$737 plus air add-on in Africa, Asia.
Two of the four top suites are forward on Promenade Deck with a captain's-eye view; the other two are aft on the same deck. Each contains a separate sitting area with sofa and chairs, coffee table, dining table and chairs, mini-refrigerator and TV set, plus a bathroom with tub and shower and a bedroom with twin beds.

Small Splurges: . . . . **C**

Average Price PPPD: $606-$646 plus air add-on in Africa, Asia.
The mini-suites in A category are a bit smaller but cheaper, and there are nine of them, two facing forward, and seven more aft. All have sitting area with sofa and coffee table, sleeping area with two lower beds, mini-refrigerator, color TV, hair dryer and bathroom with tub and shower.

Suitable Standards: . . . . **D+**

Average Price PPPD: $385-$401 plus air add-on in Africa, Asia.

The standard outside double cabins on these ships are small—there's no getting around that (or much getting around in them)—many of them only 126 square feet. They have a sofa that converts to a bed and a second, recessed lower bed that slides under the sofa/bed. There's also a built-in counter, desk/dresser with stool, TV set, bath with shower and adequate but far-from-generous closet space.

Bottom Bunks: .... **D +**

Average Price PPPD: $333-$347 plus air add-on in Africa, Asia.

The L category inside doubles on Fiesta Deck are really not any smaller than the outside doubles (see "Suitable Standards") and with the same furnishings basically. They just don't have a window or porthole.

The Routes

Both ships cruise exotic itineraries year-round, Europe and the Mediterranean in summer, Africa *(Pacific Princess)* and India *(Island Princess)* in winter. On March 15, 1998, the *Island Princess* makes the line's first-ever world cruise, starting from Rome and winding up in San Francisco May 17. In between, it calls in Greece, Israel, Oman, India, Malaysia, Singapore, Vietnam, Hong Kong, the Philippines, Indonesia, Australia, New Zealand, Fiji, American Samoa and Hawaii. No segments are offered. Pacific Princess offers two new Arctic Circle cruises between Dover and Reykjavik.

The Scoop

While the cabins on these two ships are quite small compared to the rest of the fleet, the intimate quality of life onboard makes up for it for passengers who don't want to travel aboard a megaship. The recent refurbishments totally redecorated them in the style of the newer, more elegant vessels. An appealing range of exotic cruises from 14 to the 64-day World Cruise on the *Island Princess*—a Princess first—will attract Love Boat veterans, especially older couples and singles, who have time and money to go shopping and country-collecting.

Insider Tips

Five Things You Won't Find on Board

1. Self-service laundry.
2. A shortage of bridge tables.
3. A full promenade deck around the ship.
4. A lap swimming pool.
5. A king-size bed.

PRINCESS CRUISES

ISLAND PRINCESS / PACIFIC PRINCESS ★★★ ★★★

Registry	**Britain**
Officers	**British**
Crew	**International**
Complement	**350**
GRT	**20,000**
Length (ft.)	**550**
Beam (ft.)	**80**
Draft (ft.)	**25**
Passengers-Cabins Full	**723**
Passengers-2/Cabin	**610**
Passenger Space Ratio	**31.25**
Stability Rating	**Good to Excellent**
Seatings	**2**
Cuisine	**Contemporary**
Dress Code	**Traditional**
Room Service	**Yes**
Tip	**$7.75 PPPD, 15% automatically added to bar checks**

Ship Amenities

Outdoor Pool	**2**
Indoor Pool	**0**
Jacuzzi	**0**
Fitness Center	**Yes**
Spa	**No**
Beauty Shop	**Yes**
Showroom	**Yes**
Bars/Lounges	**3**
Casino	**Yes**
Shops	**4**
Library	**Yes**
Child Program	**Yes**
Self-Service Laundry	**Yes**
Elevators	**5**

Cabin Statistics

Suites	**4**
Outside Doubles	**234**
Inside Doubles	**67**
Wheelchair Cabins	**2**
Singles	**0**
Single Surcharge	**150-200%**
Verandas	**0**
110 Volt	**Yes**

★ ★ ★ ★ ★
ROYAL PRINCESS

In a simpler, more romantic time back in 1984, the glowing, recently wed Princess Diana christened the Royal Princess, and while the bloom may be off the royalty these days, the Royal Princess is as lovely as ever, proving that class acts last. The inaugural sailing was a media event, with an episode of "The Love Boat" being filmed aboard, as well as a segment of "Lifestyles of the Rich and Famous," starring Connie Stevens (her first cue card read, "Hi, I'm Connie Stevens"), and a number of regional and local TV teams, including a then-little-known host of "AM Chicago" named Oprah Winfrey.

DID YOU KNOW?

Passengers vied with each other on the inaugural cruise through the Panama Canal to work all day for nothing as extras on "The Love Boat," and more passengers were usually inside watching the filming than outdoors watching the canal transit they'd booked the cruise to see.

The *Royal Princess* began as a study design for "the most advanced cruise ship ever built" from the research and design team headed up by Kai Levander at Wartsila in Helsinki, Finland. In a radical design departure for a ship this size, all 600 cabins are outside on upper decks, while the public rooms are located below them, and 150 staterooms have private verandas overlooking the sea.

This was the first ship to introduce private balconies in quantity, adding them to cabins as well as suites and mini-suites. This was also one of the first ships to offer twin beds that could easily be put together into one queen-sized bed. One of the two outdoor swimming pools allows energetic passengers to swim laps instead of just plunge in and get wet. The other is a cluster of pools and whirlpools that is reminiscent of the Crystal pool aboard the *Pacific Princess*.

Circles and curves are a recurring motif—the overlapping large and small circles of the Lido Deck spa pools, the rippling circles of the International Lounge spreading outward from the dance floor, the arc of the double stairway leading down into the dining room and the graceful curved stairways on five aft decks. Recently, a 24-hour food service in the Lido Cafe was added to the ship.

DID YOU KNOW?

Captain Ian Tomkins, who often served aboard the Royal Princess *before his retirement, compared her handling to "dancing with a beautiful lady in a crinoline dress when a Viennese waltz is playing."*

Between The Lines

The Brochure Says

"The five-star *Royal Princess* is one of cruising's most highly acclaimed ships. Not only for her exceptionally sleek and beautiful exterior design but for the multitude of features that truly set her apart. Her series of terraced observation areas both fore and aft, her acres of teak decks and her lavish, floor-to-ceiling windows make her the perfect ship for experiencing an Exotic Adventure."

Translation

Everything you could ever want—this gracious classic ship and exotic itineraries too.

Cabins & Costs

The gala suites aboard the Royal Princess *have large private verandas.*

Fantasy Suites: . . . . **A+**

Average Price Per Person, Double Occupancy, Per Day: $968 in South America, including airfare from the East Coast.

The 806-square-foot Royal and Princess, the pair of penthouse suites aboard the *Royal Princess*, were once the largest suites at sea, and while they may have been eclipsed in size by more recent vessels, they're still among the most posh. The category AA suites contain whirlpool tubs in a huge tiled and mirrored bathroom, sitting room with picture window, separate bedroom with queen-sized bed, a dining table and chairs, TV/VCR, mini-refrigerator, Oriental rugs and original art, plus a big private veranda.

Small Splurges: . . . . A

Average Price PPPD: $633 in South America, including airfare from the East Coast.

Mini-suites with private balcony has twin beds that convert to queen-sized, sitting area with sofa and chairs, balcony with two chairs and a table plus a stretch-out lounger, picture window, bath with tub and shower, dressing area, plenty of closet space, TV and mini-refrigerator.

Suitable Standards: . . . . B

Average Price PPPD: $428 to $471, depending on cabin location, on a South America cruise, including airfare from the East Coast.

An outside double has twin beds that convert to queen-sized, built-in desk/dresser with stool, an easy chair and table, bathroom with tub and shower, color TV and mini-refrigerator. If you want to see the sea from your picture window, stick to categories C, D, E, F, G or GG. One of the twin beds folds into the wall during the day to give more floor space inside the cabin.

Bottom Bunks: C

Average Price PPPD: $385 to $413, depending on cabin category, on a South America Cruise, including airfare from the East Coast.

While there are no inside cabins on the *Royal Princess*, some of the outsides have very limited views because of lifeboats hanging outside—notably, categories JJ, J, K and L, which have windows totally obscured by boats. Still, you'll get enough daylight in to tell day from night and probably enough sky view to get a read on the weather without going out on deck. Otherwise, furnishings and size are identical to the cabins previously discussed (see "Suitable Standards").

INSIDER TIP

Princess restricts the number of wheelchair passengers on this ship. While the staterooms can accommodate a standard wheelchair (22"-23" in width) the bathroom floor rises seven inches above the cabin floor. Public rooms and decks are accessible and some public restrooms are designed to accommodate wheelchairs.

The Routes

For summer, the *Royal Princess* positions to Europe, where she offers 13-day cruises in the Mediterranean and Scandinavia.

In September and October, *Royal Princess* makes 10-day sailings in Canada and New England between Montreal and New York. In late November she repositions to South America for a series of winter sailings.

The Scoop

An elegant ship, the *Royal Princess* presents a seamless blend of classic liner and contemporary cruiser with the best features of each. British officers host dining tables on every cruise, with the kind of first-class courtesy and attention an around-the-world passenger would expect. The natural teak decks provide generous strolling, lounging and games space, and the top deck Horizon Lounge opens up splendid views in three directions. For those passengers with private verandas, one of the most pleasurable parts of a day is to sit in the fresh breezes looking at the ocean, wearing pajamas and robe if you like.

It's hard to find fault with the *Royal Princess*. The Lido Cafe is delightful with its bright tile-topped tables and contemporary patio chairs, now serving food 24 hours a day with no dress code requirement. The new pizzeria is a bonus, and, thankfully, the aft end of Lido Deck has been partially enclosed to get rid of the wind tunnel effect.

Two acres of teak deck delight strollers and loungers on **Royal Princess.**

Insider Tips

Five Elegant Areas

1. The Plaza and Princess Court is a two-deck atrium from the early days of atria, centered with a sculpture called *Spindrift*, a polished arc with soaring birds, waterworn rocks and splashing fountain, and surrounded by cushy chairs and the strains of piano music.

2. The Horizon Lounge with its angled glass window walls overlooks everything to see at sea, but at night turns into a disco, with dancing, a DJ station and projectors and screens around the U-shaped room.

3. The Lido Bar, only steps away from the cluster of pools and Jacuzzis, will always remind us of the late Stewart Granger, who used to order an entire pitcher of Bloody Marys made to his own recipe, then walk around the deck refilling glasses for sunbathing passengers.

4. One of the first top-deck beauty and fitness centers, The Spa is built on Sun Deck between the lap pool and a second, smaller pool with sunbathing platform, and offers massage, sauna, beauty salon and gym.

5. The two acres of teak decks, especially the long sweeping curves of the stern stairways, five beautiful decks of them, that draw the eye inevitably up to the curved stack on top.

Five Good Reasons to Book This Ship

1. She's a classic beauty, perhaps the last of her kind in these days of floating hotels.

2. To have a front-row seat on your own private balcony going through the Dardanelles.

3. To make an entrance—down the curved staircase in the Plaza Foyer, down the stairs into the dining room from the Terrace Room or along the stern deck stairs, which was the setting for Lana Turner's "wedding" to Stewart Granger on "The Love Boat."

4. To have a watery wonderland choice from among three outdoor swimming pools and lots of Jacuzzis.

5. To be able to do your morning walk around a full promenade deck, rarer than ever these days.

Five Things You Won't Find on Board

1. An inside cabin.

2. Everybody up early and out on deck; veranda cabin passengers linger inside until late morning, usually breakfasting on their private balcony.

3. Cabins with shower only; all accommodations have tubs as well.

4. A chance to get hungry; the new Lido Cafe even serves dinner from 5 p.m. to 5 a.m.

5. Prince Charles.

PRINCESS CRUISES

ROYAL PRINCESS ★★★★★

Registry	**Britain**
Officers	**British**
Crew	**International**
Complement	**520**
GRT	**45,000**
Length (ft.)	**757**
Beam (ft.)	**106**
Draft (ft.)	**26**
Passengers-Cabins Full	**1323**
Passengers-2/Cabin	**1200**
Passenger Space Ratio	**37.5**
Stability Rating	**Good to Excellent**
Seatings	**2**
Cuisine	**Contemporary**
Dress Code	**Traditional**
Room Service	**Yes**
Tip	**$7.75 PPPD, 15% automatically added to bar checks**

Ship Amenities

Outdoor Pool	**3**
Indoor Pool	**0**
Jacuzzi	**2**
Fitness Center	**Yes**
Spa	**Yes**
Beauty Shop	**Yes**
Showroom	**Yes**
Bars/Lounges	**5**
Casino	**Yes**
Shops	**4**
Library	**Yes**
Child Program	**Yes**
Self-Service Laundry	**Yes**
Elevators	**6**

Cabin Statistics

Suites	**14**
Outside Doubles	**586**
Inside Doubles	**0**
Wheelchair Cabins	**4**
Singles	**0**
Single Surcharge	**150-200%**
Verandas	**150**
110 Volt	**Yes**

★★★★
SKY PRINCESS

The TSS Sky Princess, *constructed in 1984 in France's CNM shipyard near Toulon as Sitmar's Fairsky, was the last big steam turbine passenger ship to be built, probably the last that will ever be. TSS means turbine steamship, and while steamships are more expensive to operate than motor ships, they also offer a smoother, quieter ride. "She has an underwater body that is a masterpiece," said one of the officers who oversaw her construction. Smooth-riding but unfinished, she had to slip out of the shipyard in the dead of night, according to some crew members aboard at the time, because shipyard workers, fearful of losing their jobs when the project was done, were sabotaging their own work, building things during the daytime and breaking them again at night. The interior finishing was completed on the long crossing from France to Los Angeles.*

A welcome-aboard buffet on the **Sky Princess** *in Alaska.*

Sky Princess was one of the early ships to be decorated by a team of designers, some of them noted for hotel rather than naval architecture. As a result, materials such as silk wall coverings, burled blond wood paneling, marble, Venetian glass and glove leather upholstery (instead of the Naugahyde prevalent then on many cruise ships) and subtle, harmonious shades of beige, gray, pale sage greens and soft rose were introduced into a sea of cheerful Scandinavian woolens in coral, marine blue and bright green. A recent refurbishment has kept the original design features virtually intact.

DID YOU KNOW?

Princess offers a lot of wheelchair-accessible staterooms. Many elevators have Braille call buttons as well as announcements of deck arrivals. Seeing-eye dogs are permitted and hearing and sight impaired passengers will find telephone amplifiers, visual smoke detectors, door knocker sensors and text telephones available by arrangement.

Between The Lines

The Brochure Says

"Passengers looking for comfort and understated elegance need look no further than the *Sky Princess*. Ultra-spacious, her casual, easygoing atmosphere pleases everyone from couples to teens."

Translation

Cabins aboard are larger than on the *Island*, *Golden* or *Pacific Princess*, the decor subtle, and the friendly waiters like to joke with passengers. Children and teens find a lot to like aboard, including three pools, a fully supervised youth and teen center and the pizzeria, of course.

Cabins & Costs

Fantasy Suites: . . . . **A**

Average Price Per Person, Double Occupancy, Per Day: $856 in Australia/New Zealand including airfare from the West Coast.

Book one of the 10 AA category suites and you'll enjoy a private veranda as well as a separate living room with leather loveseat, four leather chairs, glass-and-chrome dining table, long marble-topped desk, stocked minibar and mini-refrigerator and TV. In the bedroom is a queen-sized bed (except Malaga and Amalfi suites, which have twin beds), robe and slippers, marble nightstand with four drawers, a dressing room with marble-topped table, three-way mirror, leather chair, big safe, built-in dressers with six drawers each, and two separate hanging closets with safes in each. The marble bathroom has a deep Jacuzzi tub.

Small Splurges: . . . . **B+**

Average Price PPPD: $692 in Australia/New Zealand including airfare from the West Coast.

Category B mini-suites on the Lido don't have private verandas but they do have picture windows, a bedroom with twin beds and wooden nightstand with two drawers, and a sitting room with long leather sofa, three leather armchairs, desk/dresser with marble inset, color TV, handsome marble lamp with linen shade, cabinet for bar glasses, mini-refrigerator, plenty of good mirrors, two full-length hanging closets with safe, and bath with shower and long marble counter.

Cabin 148 is a Category C outside double.

Suitable Standards: . . . . C+

Average Price PPPD: $361–$437 in Australia/New Zealand including airfare from the West Coast; price varies depending on deck location and whether cabin is inside or outside.

All the standard inside and outside cabins are similar, with twin beds, nightstand, desk/dresser, two chairs, small table, generous closet space and bathroom with shower. Nearly half also have optional pull-down berths for third and fourth occupants. Six cabins are designated wheelchair accessible, including C 207 and C 208, outsides which are slightly larger than standards, with no lip on the doors, a shower with seat and pull bars, a roll-under sink, lower handles on the closets and a low-hanging rod accessible from a wheelchair; very wide inside with three windows.

Bottom Bunks: . . . . C+

Average Price PPPD: $347 in Australia/New Zealand, including airfare from the West Coast.

The category M inside doubles are the least-expensive accommodations on board, but are still fairly spacious and similar to the "Suitable Standards." Two lower beds, TV, very large closets, bath with shower, desk/dresser with chair and a second chair with small table.

INSIDER TIP

Library books must be checked in and out on the Sky Princess, and anyone planning to abscond with an unfinished novel faces a $50 fine added to his cabin account.

DID YOU KNOW?

Don't try this at home! The Love Boat cocktail is a blend of tequila, creme de cacao, Galliano, grenadine and cream.

The Routes

Sky Princess makes 11-night roundtrip cruises to Alaska from San Francisco in summer, then repositions to Asia for a series of Japanese, Singapore and Hong Kong sailings. From mid-January to late March, the ship sails from Australia and New Zealand, after which she relocates to the South Pacific and Hawaii prior to returning to Alaska.

The Scoop

This ship, one of the most elegant at the time of its inaugural sailing in 1984, has held up very well. The top deck indoor spa, including a whirlpool with raised stairs, was one of the first top deck, glass-walled spas; before that, indoor pools and a modest exercise area were usually found on a bottom deck amidships.

Sky Princess is particularly good for families with children because the cabins with upper berths are spacious enough you won't feel cramped and because the child-care and teen programs on board are so well-arranged. The Youth Center is particularly pleasant, with linoleum floor, lie-down sofas and sturdy play tables. The Teen Center has lots of curved banquettes and game tables with industrial lamps overhead and a video game room with six games. The two dining rooms are light and bright with big windows, so if you're lunching during Alaska whale-spotting or Bay of Islands sightseeing, you won't miss much. The buffets on this ship are much more elaborate than most of the others.

Insider Tips

Five Special Spots

1. Veranda Lounge, the venue for dancing before and after dinner, is a lovely room with its swirl marbleized carpet in gray and teal, with teal leather and fabric chairs, teal glass-topped tables with leather trim, sheer Austrian shades at the windows and pale wood walls.

2. The Pizzeria with its black bentwood chairs with red seats, big tile kitchen decorated with faux salamis, cheeses and hams, big round booths big enough for six or eight, and atop every table jars of crushed red pepper and oregano. For people who want a full lunch, a blackboard promotes a soup of the day and a pizza of the day.

3. The Horizon Lounge, an observation lounge with a forward-facing wall of windows, lots of cushy leather chairs in teal and caramel, and squashy cushions in the window ledges for additional seating with a view.

4. A beautiful library with two separate reading rooms, each with deep black leather chairs and wood-paneled walls, along with curved modern desks in wood and black leather for writing diaries or postcards.

5. The intimate little Melody Bar with its long granite bar lined with black leather swivel barstools, burled wood and mirrors on the walls, a perfect hideaway for two.

Five Good Reasons to Book This Ship

1. The Pizzeria for its made-to-order pizza.

2. The big, lavish showroom with its thrust stage where you might see comedian Dick Gold, harmonica virtuoso Harry Bee, the juggling Zuniga Brothers and the Love Boat singers and dancers.

3. To buy some Lladro porcelain in the new Alaska-themed pieces, Eskimos ice-fishing and such; Lladro must sell like crazy on cruise ships if the Spanish are creating whole new groups. What's next? The characters from "The Love Boat"?

4. To compete in the passenger talent show.

5. To experience the smooth ride of the last passenger steamship ever built.

Five Things You Won't Find on Board

1. Alcoholic drinks available for 18-to-21 year-olds in Alaska.

2. Silent elevators—the ones on the *Sky Princess* talk to you.

3. No full promenade deck all around the ship; the green Astroturf-covered walking deck (no jogging) says 11 times around its perimeter is one mile and the textured dark red jogging track above the Sun Deck says 15 laps is a mile.

4. Marble bathroom counters on inside cabins.

5. A cruise without a bingo game.

SKY PRINCESS ★★★★

Registry	**Britain**
Officers	**British**
Crew	**International**
Complement	**535**
GRT	**46,000**
Length (ft.)	**789**
Beam (ft.)	**98**
Draft (ft.)	**25**
Passengers-Cabins Full	**1806**
Passengers-2/Cabin	**1200**
Passenger Space Ratio	**38.33**
Stability Rating	**Good to Excellent**
Seatings	**2**
Cuisine	**Contemporary**
Dress Code	**Traditional**
Room Service	**Yes**
Tip	**$7.75 PPPD, 15% automatically added to bar checks**

Ship Amenities

Outdoor Pool	**3**
Indoor Pool	**0**
Jacuzzi	**1**
Fitness Center	**Yes**
Spa	**Yes**
Beauty Shop	**Yes**
Showroom	**Yes**
Bars/Lounges	**5**
Casino	**Yes**
Shops	**4**
Library	**Yes**
Child Program	**Yes**
Self-Service Laundry	**Yes**
Elevators	**6**

Cabin Statistics

Suites	**10**
Outside Doubles	**375**
Inside Doubles	**215**
Wheelchair Cabins	**6**
Singles	**0**
Single Surcharge	**150-200%**
Verandas	**10**
110 Volt	**Yes**

RADISSON SEVEN SEAS
C R U I S E S

600 Corporate Drive, Suite 410, Fort Lauderdale, FL 33334
☎ *(305) 776-6123, (800) 333-3333*
www.cruisingorg/radisson

Deck meals are served under blue umbrellas on **Song of Flower.**

History . . . .

This hybrid cruise line with three very different ships—what they have in common is superlative quality—came about through a series of marketing agreements. Radisson, of course, is a long-time hotel brand name that entered the cruise industry with the first major twin-hulled cruise vessel, the 354-passenger *Radisson Diamond*, owned by Finland's Diamond Cruise Inc., which debuted in 1992. Seven Seas, acquired by Radisson in January 1997, was a San Francisco-based company marketing the elegant little 172-passenger *Song of Flower*, a Sea Goddess-like ship, and the 188-passenger *Hanseatic*, arguably the most luxurious expedition vessel in the world, is owned by Germany's Hanseatic Cruises, which in turn was acquired by Hapag-Lloyd. The *Bremen*, an equally elegant expedition ship also owned by Hapag-Lloyd, is frequently marketed by Radisson Seven Seas.

The line was launched Jan. 1, 1995, with 500 employees in the Fort Lauderdale-based offices of the former Radisson Diamond Cruise. The line's newest vessel is the 320-passenger *Paul Gauguin*, scheduled to operate year-round in French Polynesia beginning in early 1998.

—First cruise ship to be christened on the stern; it has no discernible bow. (*Radisson Diamond*, 1992, Greenwich, England).

Concept

Radisson Seven Seas says it aims to bring together four ultra-deluxe ships, exotic destinations worldwide and innovative shipboard programming to create four distinct styles of luxury cruising offering excellent service, intimate ambience and strong value for the dollar throughout the fleet.

Signatures

The *Radisson Diamond's* twin hull is an unmistakable sight in every port in the world, warranting at least a double-take if not a "What the hell is that?" Less known but almost equally unique is the ship's policy of using female rather than male servers in the dining room.

Song of Flower is among a handful of luxurious cruise vessels that distinguishes itself by not proffering tabs to be signed; virtually everything on board from bar beverages to tips is included. You pay extra only for laundry, beauty shop services, casino gambling and shop purchases. The distinctive blue lyre on the ship's twin funnels is now the logo for the entire line.

The *Hanseatic* and *Bremen* are notable for their state-of-the-art environment-saving features, including an advanced nonpolluting waste disposal system and a pollution-filtered incinerator that enable them to call in remote and environmentally sensitive areas.

Gimmicks

The *Radisson Diamond's* "An Evening at Don Vito's" is the liveliest and most delicious of all the cruise-line alternative restaurants, with waiters in red aprons singing "O Sole Mio" between serving up bites of everything that comes out of the special Italian kitchen that evening.

A "welcome back" libation greets *Song of Flower* passengers at the gangway when they return from grueling shore excursions—cold lemonade or chilled champagne if it's a hot day in Southeast Asia, hot chocolate, hot buttered rum or mulled wine if it's a cold day in the Black Sea.

A "passenger bridge" on the *Hanseatic* is furnished with ocean charts and radar; in addition, passengers are free to visit the ship's real bridge whenever they wish.

Who's the Competition

The *Hanseatic* faces competition only from its stablemate the *Bremen*, also a state-of-the-art expedition vessel that cruises with a similar mix of Europeans and North Americans. *Song of Flower* was competing mainly with the Sea Goddess ships until the debut of Silversea; now *Silver Cloud* and *Silver Wind*, although somewhat larger, are rivals. Seabourn also provides competition. As for *Radisson Diamond*, that's a different situation entirely; it would seem to compete more with shoreside resorts and tours than other ships, except perhaps its own associate *Song of Flower*. The *Paul Gauguin* takes top-rate luxury cruising into Tahiti to compete with *Club Med 2*. Word of mouth has been the primary factor in attracting more and more passengers to these vessels.

Who's Aboard . . . .

On all the ships, upscale middle-aged couples are the major passengers, along with older singles and younger, baby boomer pairs. *Radisson Diamond* has a number of incentive groups aboard on some sailings—the ship was originally created for that market but has found a huge acceptance from individual travelers as well. *Hanseatic's* luxurious version of soft adventures attracts a more cosmopolitan crowd than the earnest expedition types who like to rough it.

Who Should Go . . . .

People who don't like the idea of having to tip—tips are already included in the fares on all the vessels but passengers may offer additional money for special service at their own discretion.

People who worry about ship motion triggering seasickness should try the smooth-riding, twin-hulled *Radisson Diamond* with its four computer-operated, nonretractable stabilizers that correct pitch and roll after only one degree.

Who Should Not Go . . . .

There are some ship purists who would never set foot on the *Radisson Diamond* because of its boxy shape and twin hulls, and we can understand that reluctance, but it offers one of the finest food and hotel operations at sea, and when you're aboard, you're not really looking at its shape, are you?

The ships reserve the right to limit the number of children on board, but all except very mature teens and well-behaved 10-to-12-year-olds should not be aboard in any case.

The Lifestyle . . . .

What the three ships have in common is a small number of passengers in a relaxed but luxurious atmosphere with impeccable service and very good food. Entertainment, while it is provided, is a minor concern, as are casinos and gift shops, while enrichment lecturers, beauty services, fitness centers and alternative dining options are major on-board pluses.

Tips are included in the basic fares on all the ships, which makes the interrelationship between crew and passenger less forced, and all three provide a single open seating at mealtimes, letting passengers sit where and with whom they please.

Wardrobe . . . .

All the ships are relatively dressy, except that the *Hanseatic* says it wants the penguins to wear the tuxedos, and male passengers are perfectly OK in a dark suit. That's fine, but they also hint that they want him to be in a jacket, not necessarily with a tie, every night. The other vessels are a little more laid-back, with formal night meaning black tie or its equivalent, but casual nights dotted throughout the cruise where no jacket and tie at all are necessary. The *Paul Gauguin*, in keeping with its destinations, is casually elegant.

Bill of Fare. . . . . .A+ to B+

The *Song of Flower* and *Radisson Diamond* outshine the *Hanseatic* a bit in the kitchen, but perhaps that's because they're dealing with a more homogenous passenger list and don't mind pushing the envelope when they've found something really interesting they want people to taste. On the *Radisson Diamond*, passengers are served beautiful meals in the most gorgeous dining room at sea, but when they wish, they can book the alternative dining experience, "An Evening at Don Vito's," a rollicking, finger-licking evening of home-cooked Italian food where you end up sampling a little bit of everything. The *Song of Flower* chefs and waiters are the ones we'd hire to run our own mansion if we were rich and famous.

Cuisine Report Card:

Radisson Diamond A+

Song of Flower A+

Hanseatic B+

Bremen B+

Showtime. . . . . B

Even on the *Hanseatic*, there's life after dinner, what with a quartet playing for dancing and an occasional folkloric troupe showing up to perform esoteric routines they learned from a Peace Corps volunteer. But showtime is not big-time on these smallish ships, and it shouldn't be. We enjoy the singer/dancer foursome that performs on the *Radisson Diamond's* scenery-less stage, as well as the amiable variety artists who double as shore excursion escorts on the *Song of Flower*, but these ships are not Broadway nor were meant to be. They're luxurious hideaways where you might just as soon spend an evening dining with friends or having dinner brought into your cabin and watching a video film.

Discounts . . . .

Early booking bonuses of $250 to $1300 per person off the listed fares are in effect if you book by designated deadlines, and you get another discount if you combine two back-to-back cruises. On *Radisson Diamond*, selected sailings deduct 50 percent of the fare of the second passenger in the cabin, plus adding airfare and free overnights on pre- and post-cruise stays.

The Bottom Line

We can think of no other cruise line that has such dissimilar but very comparable ships. They're all small, intimate and upscale, with flawless European service and excellent food, fascinating itineraries and lavish accommodations. More remarkably, they give you a lot of value for the admittedly top-market prices. Strange bedfellows? Perhaps, but what they have in common is more important than how they are different from each other.

At the end of 1997, another all-new ship, totally unlike the other three, joins the fleet for year-round cruises in the South Pacific. The 320-passenger vessel has 80 cabins with private balconies, and is named *Paul Gauguin*.

★ ★ ★ ★ ★ ⚓ ⚓ ⚓ ⚓ ⚓
HANSEATIC

"Penguins, whales, seals—we can guarantee you'll see them," the captain says cheerfully. On this autumn stopover in San Diego, he's between a successful transit of the Northwest Passage and the beginning of the Antarctic season, and feeling particularly chipper because he believes the Hanseatic, the largest ship ever to make the transit, has established a new time record for it—14 days. We find ourselves remembering not only a much longer transit on a less sophisticated ship a decade before but also the constant wondering about whether we'd make it through at all.

Until the last couple of years, the ship was marketed primarily in Germany and still attracts a mixed bag of Europeans and North American passengers who laud the no-tipping policy, polished European serving staff and open bridge rules that allow passengers access to the navigational bridge at all times. Elegant and luxurious, with spacious cabins and beautifully decorated public rooms, the *Hanseatic* seems almost too lavish for an expedition ship, but who says you have to rough it just because you're going into the wilderness?

⋅ Between The Lines ⋅

The Brochure Says

"After a day of observing penguin rookeries, (a passenger) could ease into the glass-enclosed whirlpool or enjoy a relaxing massage and sauna; perhaps snuggle up with a favorite book from the library, order room service and enjoy the view from the picture window of his spacious stateroom. For guests on Bridge Deck, there's the added luxury of private butler service."

Translation

Wake me when the Northern Lights come on, Jeeves.

Cabins & Costs

Fantasy Suites: .... **A**

Average Price Per Person, Double Occupancy, Per Day: $1044 including round-trip airfare.

There are four deluxe suites aboard, each measuring 475 square feet, with walk-in closet, large sitting area with sofa and chairs, twin or queen-sized beds, dining-height table with chairs and butler service plus other furnishings and amenities listed under "Suitable Standards," below.

Small Splurges: .... **N/A**

It's not necessary to splurge on this ship; the standards are more than adequate.

Suitable Standards: .... **A**

Average Price PPPD: $544 to $850 depending on cabin category, including airfare.

Each accommodation, even the least expensive, has twins or queen-sized bed, a marble bathroom with tub and shower, a separate sitting area with chaise or sofa, TV set with VCR, writing desk, hair dryer, mini-refrigerator stocked with nonalcoholic beverages and generous closet and drawer space. The standards measure 236 square feet.

Bottom Bunks: .... **N/A**

N/A

DID YOU KNOW?

Although the full capacity of the ship is 188, the line claims it never cruises with more than 170 passengers.

The Routes

The *Hanseatic* goes to the ends of the earth—literally. The ice-hardened vessel cruises from the Arctic to the Antarctic, and is as equally at home in Spitsbergen or Patagonia, the Galapagos or the South Georgias. She begins her year in the Antarctic, then sails north.

The Scoop

The *Hanseatic* is an elegant and luxurious ship with rich wood-toned paneling in all cabins and public rooms and spacious staterooms, all outsides with windows or portholes. It's also an extraordinarily tough expedition ship with a 1A1 Super ice class rating, just one notch below the icebreaker classification. A friendly young European staff and a very high crew-to-passenger ratio of one crew member to every 1.4 passengers mean the service is exemplary, and the food, while not cutting-edge contemporary, is quite tasty. A thumbs-up recommendation!

Five Record-Breaking Rooms

1. In the Explorer Lounge with its pretty upholstered, wood-framed tub chairs and leaf-patterned carpet, a quartet plays for dancing before and after dinner, and a pianist accompanies afternoon tea.

2. Darwin Hall is a large and comfortable lecture room that doubles as a cinema; this is where the experts tell you about the local wildlife—and we don't mean pub-crawling.

3. Casual breakfast and lunch buffet service takes place in the Columbus Lounge with its rattan chairs and big windows.

4. The Marco Polo Restaurant manages a miracle—it seats all the passengers at once with every chair near enough to one of the big windows to watch the scenery go by.

5. Passengers have their own "bridge" to monitor the ship's route and progress on ocean charts and a radar monitor in the glass-walled observation lounge with its 180-degree view.

Five Good Reasons to Book This Ship

1. Because they leave the tuxedos to the penguins—male guests need only wear a dark suit for formal nights—but it's still the dressiest expedition vessel afloat, with jackets requested for men every night.

2. Because they supply the parkas and rubber boots you need to go ashore in polar regions; you don't have to go and buy bulky gear you'll probably never use again and figure out how to pack it to get it to the ship.

3. Because they carry 14 Zodiacs to take you ashore or cruising around an iceberg.

4. Because you can travel with the ease of knowing you and your vessel are doing nothing to damage the environment.

5. Because shore excursions are included.

HANSEATIC ★★★★★, ⚓⚓⚓⚓

Registry	**Bahamas**
Officers	**European**
Crew	**International**
Complement	**125**
GRT	**9,000**
Length (ft.)	**403**
Beam (ft.)	**59**
Draft (ft.)	**15.4**
Passengers-Cabins Full	**188**
Passengers-2/Cabin	**170**
Passenger Space Ratio	**52.94**
Stability Rating	**Good to Excellent**
Seatings	**1**
Cuisine	**Continental**
Dress Code	**Informal**
Room Service	**Yes**
Tip	**Included in fare**

Ship Amenities

Outdoor Pool	**1**
Indoor Pool	**0**
Jacuzzi	**1**
Fitness Center	**Yes**
Spa	**No**
Beauty Shop	**Yes**
Showroom	**No**
Bars/Lounges	**2**
Casino	**No**
Shops	**1**
Library	**Yes**
Child Program	**No**
Self-Service Laundry	**No**
Elevators	**1**

Cabin Statistics

Suites	**4**
Outside Doubles	**86**
Inside Doubles	**0**
Wheelchair Cabins	**2**
Singles	**0**
Single Surcharge	**150%**
Verandas	**0**
110 Volt	**No**

Unrated
PAUL GAUGUIN

This luxury ship, debuting Jan. 31, 1998, in year-round service in Tahiti, promises to produce the same excellent food and service that have zoomed the line's other vessels to the top of the charts. The vessel carries 320 passengers in all-outside suites and staterooms, half of them with private balconies.

The itineraries follow a seven-day pattern, with departures from Papeete every Saturday, and calls in Rangiroa, Raiatea, Bora Bora and Moorea. All but Moorea are overnight visits to give passengers a chance to check out local resorts and the interesting, if sometimes sparse, nightlife of French Polynesia.

Shore excursions include jeep safaris, lunches at French country inns, waterfall swims, tours of the Paul Gauguin Museum, snorkeling, diving, water skiing, wind surfing, kayaking, sailing, glass-bottom boat tours, visits to ancient stone temples, parasailing, helicopter sightseeing, horseback riding, outrigger canoe excursions, beach picnics and barbecues and a tour of a South Seas black pearl farm.

The ship is grandly spacious, with the smallest cabins aboard over 200 square feet and penthouses nearly 550 square feet including private balcony space. All the suites provide separate living room and bedroom areas and large marble bathrooms with tub and shower. Terry-cloth robes, hair dryers, mini-refrigerators stocked with soft drinks, personal safes, sofas and TV/VCRs are among the amenities in all passenger cabins.

With seven passenger decks, the vessel has plenty of room for relaxing aboard. The topmost deck has plenty of sunny lounging space and a bar and buffet with tables and chairs. The next deck down has a pool amidships with loungers on teak decking all around it, with a grill room, lounge and outdoor tables aft and suites with private verandas forward. The deck below has mostly deluxe cabins with private verandas, plus the owner's suite forward and the Connoisseur Club lounge aft.

Walk down another deck or two and you come to a pair of restaurants, where two-star Michelin French chef Jean-Pierre Vigator has overseen the menus and recipes. L'Etoile, on deck 5, is a classic, Paris-style restaurant, while La Veranda on deck 6 with its glass walls facing the sea and teak deck surrounds offers a more casual ambiance comparable to the French Riviera.

On deck 6 amidships are the Fare Tahiti information center and bookstore, a boutique, spa and fitness center, and forward are passenger cabins and deck machinery for raising and lowering the Zodiac inflatable landing craft. On deck 5 in addition to L'Etoile, which is aft, are the casino and the Grand Salon show lounge.

The remaining decks house passengers and crew, as well as the hospital and pharmacy and access to the retractable marina where a watersports platform can be raised and lowered when the ship lies at anchor.

Seven-day cruises range in price from a low of $2795 per person, double occupancy (for special inaugural season fares that should be booked before the end of 1997) to a high of $7395 per person, double occupancy, for the owner's suite. Airfare add-ons vary from $150/$250 for West Coast gateways to $350/$450 for east coast gateways. Tips, soft drinks and wines with dinner are all included in the basic fare.

RADISSON SEVEN SEAS CRUISES

PAUL GAUGUIN — Unrated

Registry	**Wallis and Futuna (French Flag)**
Officers	**French/European**
Crew	**International**
Complement	**206**
GRT	**18,800**
Length (ft.)	**513**
Beam (ft.)	**71**
Draft (ft.)	**16.9**
Passengers-Cabins Full	**320**
Passengers-2/Cabin	**320**
Passenger Space Ratio	**59**
Stability Rating	**NA**
Seatings	**1**
Cuisine	**French/Contemporary**
Dress Code	**Casual Elegance**
Room Service	**Yes**
Tip	**Included in fare**

Ship Amenities

Outdoor Pool	**1**
Indoor Pool	**0**
Jacuzzi	**0**
Fitness Center	**Yes**
Spa	**Yes**
Beauty Shop	**Yes**
Showroom	**Yes**
Bars/Lounges	**4**
Casino	**Yes**
Shops	**2**
Library	**Yes**
Child Program	**No**
Self-Service Laundry	**No**
Elevators	**4**

Cabin Statistics

Suites	**19**
Outside Doubles	**142**
Inside Doubles	**0**
Wheelchair Cabins	**1**
Singles	**0**
Single Surcharge	**$995–200%**
Verandas	**0**
110 Volt	**NA**

RADISSON SEVEN SEAS CRUISES

★★★★★★
RADISSON DIAMOND

The first time we ever saw the Radisson Diamond, *the new ship was moored in Tilbury, the Port of London, and right next to her was the long, sleek* Royal Princess. *The effect was like seeing the short wide robot R2D2 from* Star Wars *hanging around with Cary Grant.*

The swimming pool on **Radisson Diamond.**

The *Radisson Diamond* has a unique SWATH design—Small Waterplane Area Twin Hull—with an extra-wide superstructure atop two pontoons. There are four special-design stabilizers, two forward and two aft, inside the well, permanent rather than retractable, and computer-controlled to negate rolling, pitching and heaving. The vessel roll is only one-fifth that of a conventional monohull ship with one-tenth of the noise and vibration levels, the captain says.

Inside, the extra-wide beam gives a great sense of spaciousness. A center atrium with stairs and two glass elevators makes it simple to get around the ship; all the passenger cabins and public rooms are clustered around it. A rubberized, nonskid jogging track, spa, beauty salon, fitness center, golf putting area and driving cage are on the upper-deck areas, and a self-contained watersports marina allows passengers to go water-skiing, windsurfing, sailing or riding wave runners when sea and weather conditions permit.

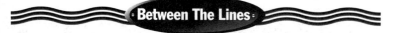

The Brochure Says

"The *Diamond* is truly one-of-a-kind, the only twin-hull passenger vessel in the world. Her innovative design offers you a smooth and stable cruise. This unique configuration allows us to provide our guests with more spacious surroundings than any ship at sea."

Translation

They're so proud of their ship they've got to exaggerate a little. It is innovative and spacious, but not completely unique. There are several twin-hull passenger vessels that have been around longer than the *Radisson Diamond*, although none of the others are quite as large. The 49-passenger *Executive Explorer*, for instance, has been carrying passengers for more than a decade and was still in business when we saw her in Alaska not long ago. And while the *Diamond's* passenger space ratio of 57.33 is impressive, it's still smaller than the *Europa's* 61.68 and the line's own *Paul Gauguin* with a 59.

Fantasy Suites: . . . . **A+**

Average Price Per Person, Double Occupancy, Per Day: $1027 in Europe including airfare from the East Coast.

A hand-painted mural in the style of Henri Rousseau decorates each of a pair of master suites measuring 522 square feet, with a large sitting area with puffy pale blue leather sofa, two chairs, a full-sized desk, mini-refrigerator, fully stocked liquor cabinet and TV/VCR. A king-sized bed has a beige and blue coverlet with greyhounds stitched on it; a sliding etched glass panel can close off the bedroom from the entry hallway and closet area. On the private veranda outside are two chairs and a table. The bathroom has a double basin in a marble counter, separate water closet, stall shower and Jacuzzi tub.

Small Splurges: . . . . **A**

Average Price PPPD: $699 in Europe, including airfare from the East Coast.

Most of the cabins on board have private balconies, and in 243 square feet you'll find queen-sized or twin beds, a sitting area with sofa, chairs and built-in desk, a marble bathroom with tub and shower—short, deep Finnish-style tubs—and TV/VCR, minibar and refrigerator and built-in dresser and storage area.

Suitable Standards: . . . . **A**

Average Price PPPD: $599 in Europe, including airfare from the East Coast.

The third cabin type aboard is the same size as the veranda cabin (243 square feet) but with a larger sitting area instead of the veranda. You'll have a white leather sofa and two chairs, built-in desk and dresser, wide window wall and marble bathroom with tub/shower combination. Two cabins are designated wheelchair-accessible.

Bottom Bunks: . . . . **N/A**
N/A

The Routes

The normal seasonal pattern for the *Radisson Diamond* is a winter in the Caribbean, Panama Canal and Costa Rica, then a repositioning cruise to Europe for a summer of cruising the Mediterranean and Northern Europe.

An art deco-style bar with chrome barstools aboard the **Radisson Diamond.**

The Scoop

We chose to sail on a transatlantic cruise to see how the ship rides in the sometimes-rough Atlantic. At first the sea was smooth, but as we got closer to Portugal it turned choppy. While there was no traditional roll or pitch, the ship would start into a rolling motion, only to have the stabilizers correct it after one degree. We think the motion in rough seas for a passenger walking or standing is similar to standing aboard a moving train.

Despite the ship's unconventional looks, it offers a supremely appealing cruise experience. Our eleven days on the crossing were gloriously relaxing without any ports of call. Why eleven days, you may ask? The ship's maximum comfortable cruising speed is only about 12 or 13 knots; she'd never win the Blue Riband.

Insider Tips

Five Splendid Spots

1.   The Grill, a cluster of several teak-floored rooms with glass walls to the deck on both sides, where buffet breakfasts and lunches supplemented with cooked-to-order

à la carte dishes are served at wooden tables; it turns into Don Vito's most evenings with red tablecloths, singing waiters and a constantly changing Italian menu.

2. In the coolly elegant Club, mushroom-colored leather chairs trimmed in ebony, mirrors and potted palms lend a movie-set 1930s look; you expect to see William Powell and Myrna Loy make an entrance.

3. The most romantic dining room at sea is wide and airy and almost two decks high, with plenty of tables for two against an aft window wall, gilt frame armchairs with striped silk upholstery, art deco pillars and a 1930s frieze of figures, all in tones of copper, silver and bronze. On the evenings when candlelight dinners are served against a background of the fading sunset, it is indescribably lovely.

4. The Windows is a multi-level lounge with ice blue leather furniture, black granite bars and silver and gray barstools, a wide wood dance floor and raised stage with bandstand in front of a window wall; a lavish tea is set out here every afternoon.

5. The Constellation Center, a meeting room and lecture hall with rows of red leather chairs in blond wood frames; this is where art auctions, slide lectures and film screenings (with a big silver punch bowl of hot popcorn) take place.

Five Good Reasons to Book This Ship

1. If you're worried about ship motion that might cause seasickness, the twin hulls prevent pitching and rolling.

2. If you're a claustrophobe worried about ships being confining, check out the extra width and spaciousness.

3. If you enjoy female servers in the restaurant.

4. To squeeze through the Panama Canal with only inches to spare on either side.

5. If you love real Italian home cooking, "An Evening at Don Vito's" trattoria passes around trays of antipasto, followed by platters of lobster risotto, penne with porcini and tomato sauce and tortellini in butter and fresh sage—and those are just the starters. Then comes veal scaloppine with fresh vegetables and a rolling cart of Italian desserts like tirama su and cannoli, all of it served with generous complimentary portions of chilled Soave and Ruffino Chianti.

Five Things You Won't Find on Board

1. A bathtub you can stretch out in; the Finnish tubs are so short that tall bathers end up with their knees under their chins.

2. A place on deck where you can stand and watch the lines cast off; the configuration of the ship doesn't allow a view straight down to the water.

3. A traditional lifeboat drill; instead, passengers are shown where the jackets are stored on deck.

4. A self-service laundry.

5. A children's program.

RADISSON DIAMOND ★★★★★

Registry	**Finland**
Officers	**Finnish**
Crew	**International**
Complement	**192**
GRT	**20,295**
Length (ft.)	**420**
Beam (ft.)	**103**
Draft (ft.)	**23-26**
Passengers-Cabins Full	**354**
Passengers-2/Cabin	**354**
Passenger Space Ratio	**57.33**
Stability Rating	**Excellent**
Seatings	**1**
Cuisine	**Contemporary**
Dress Code	**Traditional**
Room Service	**Yes**
Tip	**Included in fare**

Ship Amenities

Outdoor Pool	**1**
Indoor Pool	**0**
Jacuzzi	**1**
Fitness Center	**Yes**
Spa	**Yes**
Beauty Shop	**Yes**
Showroom	**No**
Bars/Lounges	**3**
Casino	**Yes**
Shops	**1**
Library	**Yes**
Child Program	**No**
Self Service Laundry	**No**
Elevators	**2**

Cabin Statistics

Suites	**2**
Outside Doubles	**175**
Inside Doubles	**0**
Wheelchair Cabins	**2**
Singles	**0**
Single Surcharge	**115-125%**
Verandas	**123**
110 Volt	**Yes**

★★★★★★
SONG OF FLOWER

A frequent question about Song of Flower *is where the name came from. At the beginning, one of the vessel's co-owners was Meiyo Corporation, represented in the person of Miss Tomoko Venada of Kobe, very much a hands-on person whom her devoted crew called Madame. "Serving all western food was Madame's policy," one of her former executive chefs told us, "along with European chefs and serving staff, and she wanted a western rather than Japanese ambience on board...but I usually sneaked in sushi, soba (buckwheat noodles) and California rolls at the midnight buffet." Another of Madame's ideas—not currently in use—was to create glittering formal nights and masquerade parties that involved everyone. So the ship carried formal gowns, dinner jackets and tuxedos that could be rented, altered by an onboard seamstress, and worn on captain's nights. Then for masquerade night, other racks of costumes, wigs, sequins and feather boas were set out for passengers to rummage through and borrow, free, for the evening. It made for a lot of hilarity.*

Song of Flower was commissioned in 1986 as the *Explorer Starship* for now-defunct Exploration Cruise Lines when she was rebuilt in a German shipyard from the hull of a ro-ro (roll-on roll-off) cargo vessel called *Begonia*. In 1989, she underwent another major refurbishment in Norway to become *Song of Flower*, a Japanese/Norwegian joint venture, and, after a February 1990 christening in Singapore, was marketed primarily in Asia for the first year.

But in 1991 the marketing emphasis switched to North America, and the ship began attracting a passenger balance of about half Asian, mostly Japanese, and half North Americans for its summer season in Alaska. In 1993, the ship was repositioned for European sailings in summer, and from that point on the vessel has sailed with predominantly western passengers. The winter cruises in Asian waters were lengthened to appeal to western preferences and varied ports of call were introduced with more of an emphasis on Oriental culture and history than holiday resorts. Now owned by Radisson, the ship carries Scandinavian officers, European hotel staff, British and American cruise staff and entertainers, international crew and a Norwegian flag.

The Brochure Says

"On *Song of Flower* our shipboard staff takes pride in providing you with outstanding service. Enjoy many of life's finer pleasures on your voyage, each one with our compliments...order room service at any hour, cocktails in any lounge, specialty drinks poolside and fine wines to accompany lunch and dinner...all without signing a bill. We try our best to anticipate your needs rather than merely fulfill them."

Translation

You're going to get some of the best service and most relaxing vacation hours you ever spent anywhere, and there's nobody nickel-and-diming you at every turn.

The pool deck on **Song of Flower** *has been retiled in a handsome dark blue with teak facing.*

DID YOU KNOW?

When it is necessary to go ashore by tender, you shuttle aboard the–are you ready?–Tiny Flower.

Fantasy Suites: .... **A**

> *Average Price Per Person, Double Occupancy, Per Day: $1019 including some airfare, tips, beverages, transfers and some shore excursions.*
> The top accommodations on board are two-room, two-bath suites with a living room, separate bedroom with sitting area, color TV and VCR, mini-refrigerator, dressing room, walk-in closet and two baths, one with half-tub and one with shower only. Spacious enough for entertaining, the suites have only one drawback in our eyes—no private veranda.

Small Splurges: . . . . A

Average Price PPPD: $959 including some airfare, tips, beverages, transfers and some shore excursions.

We like the top deck ocean view suites in category B for their private verandas, spaciousness (321 square feet) and full-sized bathtubs. You'll find a queen-sized bed, sofa, three chairs, a desk with four drawers, a small foyer, large closets, stocked minirefrigerator and bar, color TV and VCR, robe and slippers and bath with tub/shower combination.

Suitable Standards: . . . . A

Average Price PPPD: $719 including some airfare, tips, beverages, transfers and some shore excursions.

All the cabins in C, D and E categories are similar, around 200 square feet with twins or queen-sized bed (specify which you want when booking), sitting area, desk/dresser with chair, nightstands, bathroom with half-tub and/or shower, TV/VCR, hair dryer and so on.

Bottom Bunks: . . . . A

Average Price PPPD: $549 including some airfare, tips, beverages, transfers and some shore excursions.

The least expensive cabins aboard are the category F outsides available with twin beds or queen-sized bed (specify which when booking) and bathroom with shower only. You're not exactly slumming in this 183-square-foot cabin with full-length sofa, chair, coffee table, desk/dresser with chair, stocked bar, mini-refrigerator, TV/VCR and double closets.

The Routes

Song of Flower has some of the most fascinating itineraries in the cruise industry, since she spends her winters in Asia and her summers in Europe. She starts the year on Hong Kong-Singapore sailings that visit five ports in Vietnam, then moves on to Burma/Myanmar, Indonesia, more Burma, Borneo, the South China Sea and more Vietnam to round out the winter season. The ship moves to Europe, then spends the summer in the Mediterranean, Baltic and the Norwegian fjords, moves back into the Mediterranean for autumn, then back into Asia in late October.

The Scoop

We've taken three cruises on this ship as the *Song of Flower*, and one earlier as the *Starship Explorer*. The minute we walk aboard, we always experience that warm-and-fuzzy feeling of being home, and say to each other, "She looks better than ever." She's sparkling clean, impeccably run, and just plain fun. It's easy to see why she has so many loyal repeat passengers and has gone from being, "Song of *what*?!" to "Oh, yes, I've heard about *Song of Flower*; they say it's wonderful."

Insider Tips

Five Places You'll Love

1. The dining room, where tables are always set with fresh flowers, the full gamut of silver and the biggest starched white linen napkins at sea; wonderful things arrive on

your plate and waiters never hover but are always there to pull out your chair, unfold your napkin and anticipate every need.

2.	The pool deck cafe is a welcoming blue-and-white haven of deck tables and chairs and big umbrellas, a grill that cooks breakfast bacon and eggs, lunchtime hamburgers and hot dogs to order, plus a cold buffet and made-to-order pasta.

3.	The former casino that has been turned into the alternative Italian restaurants, Angelino's, in the evenings.

4.	The main lounge is where the captain has his cocktail parties, the entertainers perform, the lecturers show slides and the five-piece orchestra plays for dancing. It's done in pastel tapestry upholstery with a bar at the rear, screen and projection equipment and a marble tile dance floor that doubles as a stage.

5.	The library, tucked away behind the main lounge with a spiral staircase connecting it to the deck below, has apricot leather sofas and chairs, wood-and-glass bookcases always unlocked, and plenty of books and videos.

Five Good Reasons to Book This Ship

1.	It's the ideal cruise ship for the 1990s after the excesses of the 1980s—elegant but unpretentious, friendly and accessible, and it provides the kind of pampering people dream about at prices lower than many of its competitors.

2.	A concierge-style shore excursion staff that goes beyond selling tours into helping to arrange independent shore tours for you on an individual basis.

3.	The ease of traveling where everything is included, even airfare, transfers and shore excursions, so you know up front how much your cruise is going to cost.

4.	The ratio of staff to passengers, one crew member to every 1.2 passengers when the ship is full, perhaps the highest in the industry.

5.	To see the walled city of St. Malo, the White Nights of St. Petersburg and the White cliffs of Dover.

Five Things You Won't Find on Board

1.	A self-service laundry.

2.	A sense of regimentation.

3.	Cabins designated wheelchair-accessible; there are elevators aboard.

4.	A lot of glitz and glitter.

5.	Theme cruises.

SONG OF FLOWER ★★★★★★

Registry	Norway
Officers	Norwegian
Crew	International
Complement	144
GRT	8,282
Length (ft.)	409
Beam (ft.)	52.5
Draft (ft.)	15
Passengers-Cabins Full	200
Passengers-2/Cabin	172
Passenger Space Ratio	48.15
Stability Rating	Fair to good
Seatings	1
Cuisine	Contemporary
Dress Code	Traditional
Room Service	Yes
Tip	Included in fare

Ship Amenities

Outdoor Pool	1
Indoor Pool	0
Jacuzzi	1
Fitness Center	Yes
Spa	No
Beauty Shop	Yes
Showroom	Yes
Bars/Lounges	4/3
Casino	Yes
Shops	1
Library	Yes
Child Program	No
Self-Service Laundry	No
Elevators	2

Cabin Statistics

Suites	20
Outside Doubles	80
Inside Doubles	0
Wheelchair Cabins	0
Singles	0
Single Surcharge	125-150%
Verandas	10
110 Volt	No

RADISSON SEVEN SEAS CRUISES

Regal Cruises ™

4199 34th Street, Suite B 103, St. Petersburg, FL 33711
☎ *(813) 867-1300, (800) 270-SAIL*
www.regalcruises.com

The dress aboard Regal Cruises is well-groomed casual.

History

Regal Cruises was founded by executives from Liberty Travel and GoGo Tours in 1993 when the companies acquired the venerable *Caribe I*, "the happy ship" from Commodore Cruises, and turned it into the *Regal Empress* almost overnight. "The world's smallest cruise line" is based in St. Petersburg and is a privately held company.

Concept

While a few longer cruises may be offered, Regal depends primarily on short-term "cruises to nowhere" for first-time cruisers and budget-minded vacationers.

Signatures

Two-day party cruises jamming onboard a capacity quota of the-more-the-merrier types.

Gimmicks

An adults-only spa to keep the kids out; candy bar bingo for the kids; '60s music and theme cruises with waitresses in poodle-cloth skirts.

Who's the Competition . . . .

There's nobody who can match the *Regal Empress's* low, low published brochure rates out of New York or St. Petersburg, Florida.

Who's Aboard. . . . .

A lot of young first-time cruisers, singles and couples and families, party-hearty types who arrive ready for a good time.

Who Should Go . . . .

Just who's aboard, plus a New Yorker or West Coast Floridian who'd like a really low-priced getaway on a lovely old ocean liner with a friendly, if sometimes unpolished, staff.

Who Should Not Go . . . .

Traditional cruise veterans who have specific ideas about wardrobe and behavior; fussy eaters; people who demand top-notch service.

The Lifestyle . . . .

Cramming everything from cruises that's fun or interesting into the format. The line itself calls it "Regal Revelry on the High Seas" on the daily programs. There's a lot going on all day and a plethora of shore excursions, plus mealtimes happening every hour or so.

Wardrobe. . . . .

The line specifies no tank tops or shorts in the dining room, but as often happens with first-time cruisers, they may forget to read the program and so enter in happy ignorance in inappropriate costume and are rarely corrected by the friendly crew, who don't want to hurt any potential tipper's feelings. What Regal Cruises would like to see are people who dress up a little bit for formal nights, even if it's only a jacket without a tie for men. The brochure models, always a tip-off to what the line imagines is right, are studiously casual but well-groomed, shown in polo shirts or sport coats without ties as a rule.

Bill of Fare. C

Feeding times are frequent on the *Regal Empress,* with early-bird coffee at 6 a.m., dining room breakfast 7 to 9 and poolside buffet breakfast 7 to 10 a.m. Lunch open seating buffets on shore days run from 11 a.m. to 1:30 p.m. in the dining room; on days at sea lunch is served later. Teatime with sandwiches and cookies is served at 4 p.m. First seating dinner is at 6 p.m., second seating at 8:15 p.m., and there is usually a midnight buffet.

The food is delivered in generous portions, but during our time aboard did not seem particularly well prepared, especially from the buffets, where meats were dry and tough from being too long on the steam table. We may have hit an off-period, however, because friends (actually, a friend—we don't know that many other people who have ever sailed aboard this ship) says it was acceptable to good during his cruise. A newly added Pietro's Pizza Palace serves pizza, hot dogs and Cuban sandwiches.

Showtime C

The entertainment format follows the usual mass-market cruise pattern: lots of bingo and game shows with the cruise staff, dancing to the ship's orchestra, late-night disco with a DJ and a few variety artists of varying capabilities. The biggest hit aboard is the lip-sync show in which passengers recruited ahead of time double in ship-provided costumes and wigs as, say, Sonny and Cher to mime "I Got You Babe" and suchlike amusements. A new "Hooray for Hollywood" revue salutes movie musicals.

NO NOs

In the show lounge on the Regal Empress, video and flash cameras are not permitted during the performance, the first two rows do not get drink service during the show and there is no smoking permitted in the entire lounge during the show.

Discounts . . . .

They don't really need to offer discounts with their low brochure prices.

The Bottom Line

You get more than you pay for on this line, partly because of the lovely old ship itself, graceful and beautiful in many areas like the library and Mermaid Bar, plus the warm and friendly crew, from the captain and hotel manager down to the ebullient youth counselor and the friendly Filipino crew. It's not a fancy cruise, and isn't meant to be. You're supposed to be ready for a good time or a party-time, and Emily Post ain't nowhere in sight. Let 'er rip!

★★
REGAL EMPRESS

Captain Uwe Bunsen, master of the Regal Empress, *has been at sea for 40 years and was for many years captain of the* Boheme *from Commodore Cruises, which now belongs to the Scientology group, and was 28 times in the Antarctic when he worked for Society Expeditions. But the former* Caribe I *is his favorite ship, and now he's back with her as the* Regal Empress. *"She's still one of the traditional ships, with beautiful design...only the plastic is missing."*

The *Regal Empress*, the former *Caribe I*, was built as the *Olympia* for the Greek Line in 1953 as a two-class ocean liner, making her maiden voyage from Glasgow and Liverpool to New York. In 1974 she was laid up in Piraeus, a victim of the overall cruise malaise brought on by the success of the transatlantic jet planes. In 1981, a German company purchased her and renamed her *Caribe*, but left her laid up in Piraeus, changing the flag from Greek to German. In 1983, with a major refit, she sailed from Piraeus to become the *Caribe I* for Commodore Cruise Lines. Very few changes have been made since she became the *Regal Empress*, so it's a wonderful experience for a ship buff to wander around and spot the beautiful spaces. A recent $3 million refurbishment makes her look spiffy.

Between The Lines

The Brochure Says
"We take pride in our decor, a study in quiet elegance with warm woods, tasteful fabrics and the occasional Art Deco touch. The *Regal Empress* boasts some of the largest staterooms afloat."

Translation
This is a lovely old ship and even the two-day party cruisers to nowhere fall silent when they peek into the elegant library. And for the money, you can get some very nice cabins. (See "Cabins and Costs".)

A classic wood-paneled suite aboard **Regal Empress**; *you could almost imagine Fletcher Christian sleeping here.*

Fantasy Suites: . . . . **B**

Average Price Per Person, Double Occupancy, Per Day: $133 cruise only in the Caribbean.

While not huge nor unrelievedly lavish, there are two suites forward on Upper Deck that call back the grand old days of ocean cruising, even perhaps the captain's quarters on the *Mayflower*, but who's counting? The Admiral Suites forward on upper deck (accept no substitutes; there are other less admirable Admiral Suites on this ship), in particular the Commodore Suite # F, has a lovely wood interior, two rooms with the bedroom separate, windows facing forward, built-in dresser, glass coffee table, hair dryer, fresh flowers, mini-refrigerator, and the sofas in the sitting room convert to beds if you want to put friends or family inside at a reduced rate.

Small Splurges: . . . . **C**

Average Price PPPD: $109 cruise only in the Caribbean.

The category Two deluxe mini-suites with mini-refrigerator, double bed plus two lower berths, sitting area with sofas, two windows and hair dryer are quite acceptable for the price.

Suitable Standards: . . . . **C-**

Average Price PPPD: $101 cruise only in the Caribbean.

A category Four cabin on Upper Deck may have portholes instead of windows, twin beds and an optional upper berth, but you'll also find floral bedspreads, a chair, adequate closets and a bathroom with shower only.

Bottom Bunks: . . . . **C-**

Average Price PPPD: $78 cruise only in the Caribbean.

In one of the lowest cabin categories, 10, in cabin B 24, you can find an inside with two lower beds, two dressers and two closets that will be perfectly adequate for a budget getaway for two.

The Routes

In the winter, *Regal Empress* sails from Port Manatee in St. Petersburg, Florida, on Mexico and Caribbean cruises to Key West, Cozumel and Playa del Carmen on four-, five- and six-day cruises, some including calls in Grand Cayman and Jamaica, and an occasional Panama Canal sailing. In summer, the ship does a number of two-day party cruises out of New York, interspersed with Bermuda, Bahamas and New England/Canada sailings. A 56-night Cruise of the Americas sets out Oct. 23, 1998, from New York City and sails around South America, ending up in St. Petersburg in December.

The Scoop

If the ship looks a little weary around the edges, think a little tenderness. She's had a long, hard life with party-time passengers who don't always appreciate her finer points. But for some impecunious people who would love to get even a tiny taste of what cruising is all about, this is a wonderful entry-level product—so long as you're not a cruise veteran who's just looking for a cheap thrill.

Insider Tips

Five Good Reasons to Book This Ship

1. The price, perhaps the lowest in all cruising today.

2. To poke around and discover some of the lovely little architectural and decorative surprises aboard.

3. If your budget is strapped and you need to get away for a couple of days of R&R.

4. If you'd like to take a cruise to Bermuda on a budget.

5. If you'd like to take a cruise to Cozumel that doesn't cost too much.

Five Beautiful Spaces

1. The Mermaid Lounge, a lovely room with beautiful brass mermaids clinging to the corners of the bar, a brass rail at the feet, of course, and frosted glass "aquarium" windows with mermaids etched on them and light falling down from a clear glass skylight above.

2. Commodore Club, a piano bar adjoining the Mermaid Lounge, small and intimate with two sunken seating areas, an ideal hideaway where you can talk and still hear the music from the lounge next door.

3. The Library, perhaps the most gorgeous library at sea, paneled in dark wood with bull's-eye windows that open, oil paintings, books in glass cases and a rich red patterned carpet on the floor. On the short cruises to nowhere, we suspect nobody ever lingers in this lovely room.

4. The enclosed promenade deck that makes a nice area for reading or chatting or doing needlework. Tables and chairs and potted trees line both sides of the glass-enclosed deck, which also has ping-pong tables, shuffleboard and varnished decking in good shape.

5. The Grand Lounge, the showroom with a big round dance floor in marble, a small bar in one corner, curved floral banquettes all around the room and fair to good sightlines. Drink holders are fitted on the backs of the sofas in front.

Five Things You Won't Find On Board

1. A little kid who can't make his parents happy; if he'll forgo the evening in their company he can get a free after-dinner kids' program in the youth center so his parents can dine alone.

2. Hunger in the afternoon; not only is teatime a "happening thing," but you can scarf down hot dogs, cookies and ice cream from that oh-so-genteel spread.

3. Cabins designated wheelchair-accessible.

4. A passenger without proof of citizenship on most sailings; people don't realize a driver's license doesn't count. You need a passport, a voter registration card or a copy of your birth certificate.

5. Baby-sitting available in cabins; while the child-care program is generous, they will not do in-cabin child care because of insurance liability problems.

REGAL EMPRESS ★★

Registry	**Bahamas**
Officers	**German/European**
Crew	**International**
Complement	**358**
GRT	**23,000**
Length (ft.)	**612**
Beam (ft.)	**80**
Draft (ft.)	**28**
Passengers-Cabins Full	**1180**
Passengers-2/Cabin	**904**
Passenger Space Ratio	**22.5**
Stability Rating	**Good**
Seatings	**2**
Cuisine	**American**
Dress Code	**Traditional**
Room Service	**Yes**
Tip	**$7.50 PPPD, 15% automatically added to bar check**

Ship Amenities

Outdoor Pool	**1**
Indoor Pool	**0**
Jacuzzi	**2**
Fitness Center	**Yes**
Spa	**No**
Beauty Shop	**Yes**
Showroom	**Yes**
Bars/Lounges	**6**
Casino	**Yes**
Shops	**2**
Library	**Yes**
Child Program	**Yes**
Self-Service Laundry	**Yes**
Elevators	**3**

Cabin Statistics

Suites	**7**
Outside Doubles	**224**
Inside Doubles	**128**
Wheelchair Cabins	**0**
Singles	**0**
Single Surcharge	**150%**
Verandas	**0**
110 Volt	**Yes**

RENAISSANCE
CRUISES

1800 Eller Drive, Ft. Lauderdale, FL 33335
☎ *(954) 463-0982, (800) 525-5350*

Renaissance cabins are large enough for entertaining.

History . . . .

Launched in 1989 by the Norwegian-based shipping company Fearnley and Eger, Renaissance began with an innovative idea—to build eight virtually identical 100-passenger luxury ships in a two-year period (actually, it took two-and-a-half years).

Before all the ships were completed, however, Fearnley and Eger foundered, filing for bankruptcy in May 1991, and Renaissance was acquired by a partnership of Italy's Cameli Group and a holding company controlled by Edward B. Rudner, a travel entrepreneur who headed up Certified Tours and had a long association with Alamo Rent-A-Car.

Today, Renaissance sails in the Mediterranean, Northern Europe, the Seychelles and African islands and Indonesia, plus positioning the *Aegean I* in the Mediterranean.

Renaissance has retired the first four ships, *Renaissance I-IV,* but has ordered two 690-passenger vessels *R1* and *R2,* to be delivered in late 1998 and early 1999.

—First company to market a fleet of eight interchangeable ships.

—First cruise line to concentrate its marketing almost exclusively by direct mail to previous cruisers.

—First cruise line to charter a super-luxury airline to ferry passengers nonstop between Los Angeles and Antigua (aboard MGM Grand Air for *Renaissance III*, 1992).

Concept

Renaissance concentrates on destination-oriented seven- and 14-day cruises built around pre- and post-cruise land packages, on-board lecture programs to enrich the passenger's travel experience and in-depth shore excursions. The company describes the ships as having a "private club atmosphere," promoting open seating at mealtimes and the all-outside-suites configuration of the vessels. A shallow draft allows the Renaissance ships to go into ports larger ships must avoid.

Signatures

The repetition of the company name in the ship's names, each followed by its own Roman numeral (and Arabic numbers on the two new vessels) creates a strong identity factor for the line. With emphasis on the brand name rather than an individual ship, Renaissance is free to substitute one vessel for another or shuffle the fleet around when necessary. "Besides," the line's former president Mark Conroy (now president of Radisson Seven Seas) once quipped, "it's impossible to remember eight different names. I can't even remember the Seven Dwarfs."

Gimmicks

Renaissance often sells the destination more than the ship by distributing single-product flyers advertising only one cruise in detail rather than a full cruise brochure, and putting more pictorial emphasis on the scenery and activities at the destination rather than the ship and its lifestyle.

The direct mail brochures touting two-for-the-price-of-one sailings or freebies from roundtrip airfare to African safaris to low-cost upgrades to business class are designed primarily to attract the line's predominantly yuppie/baby boomer audience which can afford to buy whatever cruise it wants but which likes to feel it's getting something for nothing.

Who's the Competition

Nobody really fits into the niche where Renaissance has positioned itself, although there are certain similarities with Sea Goddess in ship size, open meal seatings and the all-suites concept, and with Windstar in a "casual elegance" dress code and day-long visits to beach-oriented islands. While a cursory glance at itineraries might bring some expedition lines to mind, Renaissance is strictly a mainstream "soft adventure" product with no bird-watching or desert hikes.

Who's Aboard

Well-traveled first-time cruisers who are booking for the itinerary rather than the ship; repeat Renaissance veterans who found out they loved the ships as much as the destinations; and bargain hunters who could never resist a two-fer. They're mostly couples, mostly between their late 20s and mid-50s, with an easy camaraderie with fellow passengers.

Who Should Go ....

Anyone who wants to travel to faraway places and be guaranteed a comfortable suite, good to excellent food and a nonregimented on-board life.

Who Should Not Go ....

Families with young children—there's nowhere for the kids to play or get out of the way of the adults; senior singles who'll complain "there's nothing to do"; anyone expecting a big-time gambling and nightlife cruise—the casino is limited to one blackjack table and four slot machines and the entertainment is a musical trio playing for dancing.

The Lifestyle ....

People who like Sea Goddess, Radisson Seven Seas, Seabourn, Silversea and Windstar sailings will immediately be at home with the dine-when-you-wish and sit-where-you-like freedom; the tendency to treat passengers as adults rather than children who have to be constantly entertained and herded about (except during the overland portions, where some organization is essential); and the lack of a regimented dress code.

Wardrobe ....

The dress code calls for "comfortable elegance," meaning no jacket and tie is ever required, although plenty of passengers do dress up in the evening. Resortwear is the operative word—things such as silk shirts, linen pants, gauzy cotton skirts and the like.

Day wear is casual clothing from jogging suits to shorts and T-shirts, whatever is appropriate to the climate and destination.

NO NOs

The line specifically requests that jeans, shorts, T-shirts and tennis shoes not be worn in the dining room at dinner.

Bill of Fare .... A-

The cuisine is contemporary restaurant-style cooking, much of it prepared to order. While simple breakfast and lunch buffets are served on deck for people who don't want to change from their bathing suits, most passengers take all their meals in the dining room. At lunchtime, there is usually an expansive buffet of salads, shellfish, cold meats, sandwiches, breads, cheese and desserts, and guests are also offered a full à la carte menu for hot orders. All-day room service sandwiches are available in the cabins as well as Continental breakfast.

Low-calorie dishes are available every meal, and all dinners provide five main dish choices plus two always-available options, broiled steak with baked potato and a low-calorie, low-fat, four-course meal.

During our three cruises with Renaissance, the food has always been good to excellent, but we have encountered some veterans in port during the past year that felt the quality of food they'd enjoyed on one ship had not been duplicated on a different ship. This may go back to the chef in the kitchen at the time, although a good head of operations should strive to keep things up to par throughout the fleet.

Discounts

Past passengers get enticing two-for-one cruise buys or free airfare and overland package offers constantly in the mail, good if they book by a certain deadline. Groups qualify for discounts, and some frequent-flyer organizations also provide Renaissance discounts. Early bird discounts of $500 are given to passengers who pay in full within five days of booking.

The Bottom Line

On our most recent sailing, we found the basic Renaissance cruise experience that we had enjoyed twice previously still very much intact, with the same care to food and service that we found on earlier sailings. But despite the ships' handsome, spick-and-span interiors, the exteriors and deck areas always look as if they need more spit-and-polish maintenance than they get.

Given the moderate prices for the quality of accommodations, more people should sample Renaissance if they enjoy small-ship, unstructured cruising. Unfortunately, the line is still not as well known as it should be among the travel agent community or the general public.

Unrated
AEGEAN I

The former Aegean Dolphin has become the Aegean I for Renaissance Cruises with sailings in, naturally, the Aegean Sea. But even Renaissance veterans need to be extra-cautious with this one. Accustomed as they are to all-outside cabins on the Renaissance series of ships, they may cheerfully book a "Classic Cabin," "Superior Cabin," or "Deluxe Cabin" without realizing all three categories are in fact inside cabins.

The ship, built in 1974, has been refurbished several times in simple, bright colors, and has a trim line and a low, wide funnel. Typical of its size and vintage, it has a dining room amidships on a lower deck, and a cinema, beauty salon and gym in the very bowels of the vessel. Still, it's fine for travelers who want to get a lot of Greece in a few days.

Cabins & Costs

With eight cabin categories on a 288-cabin ship, there is a wide range of choices and prices. The best lodgings are cabins 501 and 502, which the previous line designated suites, facing forward on the Sun Deck. Oddly enough, there are 14 other cabins in the same price category that are about half the size of 501 and 502. Termed "Renaissance Cabins," they average around $456 a day per person, double occupancy. Coming down a peg or two, the "Premium Cabin" is the lowest-priced outside accommodation at around $314 a day per person, double occupancy. The bottom of the heap is the "Classic Cabin" at $242 a day per person, double occupancy.

The Routes

In addition to the Greek Isles summers, the *Aegean I* offers winter sailings in the Greek Isles, Turkey and Israel, at very low prices that include airfare. Just be careful to heed the warning below.

The Scoop

While we have not been aboard this ship since it became the *Aegean I*, we've had some complaints from previous Renaissance passengers who blithely book what they expect to be a low-priced version of their former cruises without realizing this is a much older ship with much-smaller cabins, many of them inside. Look before you book.

Aegean I — Unrated

Registry	Greece
Officers	Greek
Crew	Greek
Complement	175
GRT	11,563
Length (ft.)	461
Beam (ft.)	67
Draft (ft.)	20
Passengers-Cabins Full	701
Passengers-2/Cabin	576
Passenger Space Ratio	20.07
Stability Rating	NA
Seatings	2
Cuisine	Continental
Dress Code	Traditional
Room Service	Yes
Tip	$5 - $8 PPPD

Ship Amenities

Outdoor Pool	1
Indoor Pool	0
Jacuzzi	0
Fitness Center	Yes
Spa	No
Beauty Shop	Yes
Showroom	Yes
Bars/Lounges	4
Casino	Yes
Shops	1
Library	Yes
Child Program	No
Self-Service Laundry	No
Elevators	2

Cabin Statistics

Suites	16
Outside Doubles	186
Inside Doubles	86
Wheelchair Cabins	0
Singles	0
Single Surcharge	150%
Verandas	0
110 Volt	No

★★★★
RENAISSANCE V–VIII

It was aboard the inaugural cruise of the Renaissance I *that we learned Krakatau is not east of Java, as the old movie title had it, but west of Java and east of Sumatra in the Sunda Straits. We had gone ashore on the hot black volcanic sand to photograph a beach picnic for a* Bon Appétit *article about small luxury cruise ships, and when we uncorked the sweating, chilled bottle of California Chardonnay to pour it into the glasses, half a dozen ragged Sumatran fisherman surrounded us, holding out their own cups for a sample. We wonder how many cruise lines other than Renaissance have put their passengers ashore on the black sand beach at Krakatau.*

The ship layouts are very simple, basically five decks, each with some cabins amidships and forward, and public areas concentrated aft. The lowest passenger deck houses the restaurant, next deck up the lobby and main lounge, next up the piano bar and casino, next up the swimming pool, whirlpool spa and outdoor pool bar, and the topmost the sundeck, forward of the four top category cabins.

Renaissance I, II, III and IV, now retired, were identical sisters, while *Renaissance V-VIII*, all identical to each other, are slightly larger than the first four.

All accommodations on board are suites, but some are more suite-like than others. (See "Cabins and Costs", for more detail.) Tucked away here and there are a small beauty salon, a gift shop, card room, library, sauna and a couple of exercise machines in a makeshift gym area.

The Brochure Says

"...you'll find exciting gaming in the casino, dancing in the lounge and friends to share a cocktail with in the club's Piano Bar. You can browse The Library for a favorite best-seller, or check out the latest video for private, in-suite viewing."

Translation

And all without taking more than 10 steps in any direction.

A standard cabin provides twin beds or queen-sized bed.

Fantasy Suites: . . . . **B+**

Average Price Per Person, Double Occupancy, Per Day: $499 on tour packages including airfare.

The top-priced suites on these vessels are literally on the top and called Owner Suites. They have private verandas, sitting area with sofa, two chairs, cocktail table, mini-refrigerator and desk/dresser with TV/VCR in 250 square feet of space. The bed can be arranged as twins or queen-sized, and there's generous closet space, bathroom and, in some, separate dressing area.

Small Splurges: . . . . **A**

Average Price PPPD: $381 on tour packages including airfare.

The suites on the three central decks are all similar and vary in price depending on the deck. Each has an average of 250 square feet, with separate sitting area with sofa and chairs, bath and plenty of storage space.

Suitable Standards: . . . . **B+**

Average Price PPPD: $318 on tour packages including airfare.

Unless you're set on having a private veranda, we like the restaurant deck suites with the walk-in closets.

Bottom Bunks: .... **N/A**

> There are no accommodations in this category on the Renaissance ships; the cheapest cabins are the suites described under "Suitable Standards," above.

The small casino aboard has one blackjack table.

The Routes

In the first year, the line proudly named just about every sea and continent in the world short of Antarctica, but as realism settled in, based on balance sheets and bookings, the itineraries were narrowed to a few choice spots in the world—the Seychelles and Indonesia in the winter, the Mediterranean and the Baltic in summer. Ask not which ship goes where—they're all more or less alike and it doesn't really matter. Just call and request to be put on their brochure mailing list.

The Scoop

While not quite in the league of Sea Goddess, Seabourn, Silversea and Radisson Seven Seas, Renaissance offers excellent itineraries and a pleasurable on-board experience. Three caveats: The shallow draft of these vessels means sometimes bumpy rides in rough seas. Exercise equipment and self-service buffets sometimes get short shrift on these compact little ships. Last time we were aboard, the buffet filled the space originally designated for the gym and the exercise equipment (both pieces) had been relegated to a covered outdoor area on a lower deck.

But worst of all, the "suggested tipping guidelines" were outrageous the last time we sailed.

INSIDER TIP

You can save money over the brochure price by taking advantage of one of the many discount possibilities. (See "Discounts".)

Insider Tips

Five Favorite Spots

1. The pretty Restaurant has plenty of tables for two, but passengers often want to gravitate to larger tables as they get to know each other, There are also 4s and 6s.

2. The sleek beige piano bar called The Club, where afternoon tea is usually served, card games are played and the casino operates to a piano background.

3. The Lounge is where passengers gather for lectures, cocktails and dancing.

4. The Lobby, a cool, comfortable spot where the information desk is located, convenient for waiting for friends or to cool off after a hot visit ashore.

5. The Library, where books and videotapes can be taken out whenever you wish; all cabins have TV sets with VCR capability.

Five Good Reasons to Book These Ships

1. To go to some of the world's most exotic ports in complete comfort and ease.

2. To be guaranteed an outside suite, no matter how much or how little you pay.

3. To travel in a full, luxurious, well-planned land-and-sea program that is not a bags-in-the-hall-at-6 a.m., everybody-on-the-bus-at-7 package.

4. To have the luxury of dining when and with whom you please instead of being regimented into a set time and table.

5. To get on that repeat passenger mailing list that sends you two-for-one offers.

Five Things You Won't Find on Board

1. A children's program or playroom; the ship is not set up for children.

2. Space for two people at a time in the swimming pool; these birdbath-size waterholes are strictly plunge pools to dip into and get wet.

3. Inside cabins.

4. Wheelchair-accessible cabins, although the vessel does have an elevator.

5. Roulette; the casino consists of one blackjack table and a couple of slot machines.

RENAISSANCE V–VIII ★★★★

Registry	**Liberia**
Officers	**Italian**
Crew	**International**
Complement	**72**
GRT	**4,500**
Length (ft.)	**297**
Beam (ft.)	**50**
Draft (ft.)	**12**
Passengers-Cabins Full	**114**
Passengers-2/Cabin	**114**
Passenger Space Ratio	**39.47**
Stability Rating	**NA**
Seatings	**1**
Cuisine	**Contemporary**
Dress Code	**Traditional /casual**
Room Service	**Yes**
Tip	**$17 - $23 PPPD, 15% automatically added to bar check**

Ship Amenities

Outdoor Pool	**1**
Indoor Pool	**0**
Jacuzzi	**1**
Fitness Center	**No**
Spa	**No**
Beauty Shop	**Yes**
Showroom	**No**
Bars/Lounges	**2**
Casino	**Yes**
Shops	**1**
Library	**Yes**
Child Program	**No**
Self-Service Laundry	**No**
Elevators	**1**

Cabin Statistics

Suites	**57**
Outside Doubles	**0**
Inside Doubles	**0**
Wheelchair Cabins	**0**
Singles	**0**
Single Surcharge	**150%**
Verandas	**12**
110 Volt	**Yes**

ROYAL CARIBBEAN

1050 Caribbean Way, Miami, FL 33132
☎ (305) 539-6000, (800) 327-6700
www.royalcaribbean.com/main.html

The signature Viking Crown Lounge and RCI logo.

History

In 1969, three Norwegian shipping companies, I.M. Skaugen, Gotaas Larsen and Anders Wilhelmsen, founded Royal Caribbean Cruise Line for the purpose of offering year-round seven and 14-day cruises out of Miami. Now owned by Wilhelmsen and the Hyatt Hotels' Pritzger family of Chicago, Royal Caribbean Cruises Ltd. is a publicly traded company on the New York Stock Exchange and the line has been changed to Royal Caribbean International.

The 1997 delivery of *Rhapsody of the Seas* and *Enchantment of the Seas* brought the line's total to 12 vessels. The last Project Vision vessel, *Vision of the Seas*, is due in the spring of 1998, then two gigantic Project Eagle ships, each 130,000 tones will debut in 1999 and 2000.

The most recent development as this book goes to press is a transaction under way to merge Royal Caribbean International and Celebrity

Cruises. Just past its 25th anniversary, RCI is definitely one of a handful of major players in the cruise industry.

—First cruise line to commission three new ships expressly for the Caribbean cruise market, *Song of Norway* (1970), *Nordic Prince* (1971) and *Sun Viking* (1972).

—First cruise line to "stretch" a ship, cutting it in half and dropping in a new midsection, then putting it back together (*Song of Norway*, 1978).

—First cruise line to commission a specially designed ship for three- and four-day cruises (*Nordic Empress*, 1990).

—First seagoing, 18-hole miniature golf course (on *Legend of the Seas*, 1995).

—First cruise line to open shoreside hospitality centers in popular ports where passengers can leave packages, make phone calls, bone up on local shopping or sightseeing, get a cold drink and use toilet facilities (1995).

Concept . . . .

Consistency is the key word here. RCI aims to provide a cruise experience to mainstream, middle-of-the-road passengers that is consistent in style, quality and pricing, with a majority of the ships following a consistent year-round schedule. Rod McLeod, former head of sales and marketing, calls it "the doughnut factor" from a travel agent who once commented that what he liked best about RCI was that all the doughnuts on all the line's ships taste exactly the same.

Signatures . . . .

RCI ships are easily recognized at a distance because of the Viking Crown Lounge, a cantilevered round glass-walled bar and observation lounge high atop the ships projecting from or encircling the ship's funnel; company President Edward Stephan dreamed it up after seeing the Seattle Space Needle.

DID YOU KNOW?

When RCI sold its pair of ships to British-based Airtours last spring, the new owners didn't get to keep the Viking Crown Lounge; the cantilevered signature bars were removed before delivery.

Lounges, bars and restaurants on board are named for Broadway musicals and operettas, sometimes with unintentionally funny results, as with the *Sun Viking's* Annie Get Your Gun Lounge. (That's also a musical that few of today's RCI passengers would remember.)

DID YOU KNOW?

We fantasize over musical titles they haven't yet used on the RCI ships, like a dining room named for Grease or Hair, or a gym called Black and Blue.

Gimmicks . . . .

ShipShape Dollars, given out each time a passenger participates in an exercise or sports activity; with six you get egg roll. Actually, you get egg-yolk yellow T-shirts proclaiming the wearer ShipShape. Passengers compete wildly for them and proudly wear them for years afterward aboard cruise ships of competing lines.

Who's the Competition. . . . .

RCI competes directly with Carnival and Norwegian Cruise Line for Caribbean passengers, but it also vies price-wise with more-upscale lines like Celebrity and Princess. The line's new megaliners have brought in a more glitzy sheen, with flashy gaming rooms created by a Nevada casino designer instead of a ship designer. The company has also gone head-to-head with Carnival in the mini-cruise market in south Florida, pitting its *Sovereign of the Seas* against the neon-throbbing *Fantasy* and glow-in-the-dark *Ecstasy*, and in Los Angeles, where its glitzy *Viking Serenade* is getting some lively competition from Carnival's even glitzier *Holiday* and their upcoming *Elation*.

Who's Aboard . . . .

All-American couples from the heartland between 40 and 60, with new clothes, new cameras and nice manners; families with fairly well-behaved children; two or three 30-something couples traveling together; born-to-shop types who find the line's newer ships with their mall-like galleries familiar and comforting; clean-cut young couples on their honeymoons; single 20-somethings on holiday sharing an inexpensive inside cabin, more often females than males.

Statistically, the median age is a relatively low 42, with a household income from $40,000 to $75,000. One-fourth are repeat passengers, half are first-time cruisers. More Europeans, Australians and Latin Americans are also gravitating to the line. A new advertising campaign aimed at the Hispanic market in Los Angeles and Miami plus splashy introductions of the new ships in Europe should increase the numbers even more.

Who Should Go . . . .

These are ideal ships for first-time cruisers because the staff and the signage instruct and inform without appearing to lecture, putting everyone at ease right away. Also for honeymooners, fitness freaks, sunbathers, big families on a reunion and stressed-out couples who want some time together in a resort atmosphere. Baby Boomers and their juniors 25 to 45 years old will always be warmly welcomed: RCI wants YOU!

Who Should Not Go . . . .

Dowager veterans of the world cruise.

Small ship enthusiasts.

Anyone who dislikes regimentation.

The Lifestyle . . . .

RCI's ships follow a traditional cruise pattern, with specified dress codes for evening, and two meal seatings in the dining room at assigned tables for a minimum of four and a maximum of eight or 10; very few if any tables for two are available. A day-long program of games, activities and entertainment on board is supplemented by shore excursions that emphasize sightseeing, golf and watersports. In the Caribbean, private beach areas at CocoCay in the Bahamas and Labadee in Haiti are beach destinations for swimming and lunch barbecues.

Wardrobe. . . . .

RCI makes it easy for passengers by spelling out dress-code guidelines in the brochure. A normal seven-day Caribbean cruise has four casual nights where sport shirts and slacks are suggested for men, two formal nights where women wear cocktail dress or evening gowns and men wear suits and ties or tuxedos, and one or more theme nights where passengers may don '50s or country/western garb if they wish. During the daytime, comfortable casual clothing—jogging outfits, shorts or slacks, T-shirts, bathing suits and coverups—is appropriate on deck but sometimes not in the dining room.

NO NOs

No bathing suits, even with coverups, are allowed in the dining room at any time. Shorts, jeans and tank tops are not permitted after 6 p.m.

INSIDER TIP

Tuxedos are for rent on board most RCI ships; ask your agent to check when booking if you think you may want to rent one.

Bill of Fare. . . . . B+

Nonthreatening, special-occasion food is produced by an affiliated catering company on a rotating set menu that is similar but not identical on the different ships. There's a wide variety and good range of choices, and the preparation is capable if not inspired. Dinner includes seven appetizers (four of them juices), three soups, two salads, five main dishes and six desserts (three of them ice creams). On a typical day main dishes may include crabmeat cannelloni, sole Madagascar, pork loin au jus, roast duckling and sirloin steak. In addition, a nightly vegetarian menu, a kids' menu and a ShipShape low-fat, low-calorie menu are offered.

Our very favorite from the latter seems tailored to The Ladies Who Lunch—it starts with a shrimp cocktail without sauce, then consommé, hearts of lettuce salad with carrot curls and fat-free dressing, followed by poached fish and vegetables, then rich, sugary Key Lime Pie with a whopping 12 grams of fat per slice.

Except on cruises of 10 days or longer, when cabin occupants can order from set lunch or dinner menus, 24-hour room service is limited to breakfast and cold snacks such as sandwiches, salads and fruit-and-cheese plates. Breakfast and lunch buffets are served in a self-service cafeteria with hot and cold dishes available, and early morning coffee, afternoon tea and midnight buffets fill out the legendary eight-meals-a-day format.

Captain Sealy's menu for kids includes fish sticks, peanut butter and jelly sandwiches, tuna fish, pizza, hamburgers and macaroni and cheese, plus chocolate "ship" cookies. On a recent sailing aboard the *Splendour of the Seas*, we felt the food preparation and presentation had greatly improved.

CHAMPAGNE TOAST

Just like their competitors, RCI bar waiters on embarkation day on Caribbean cruises are hustling around with trays of brightly colored fancy drinks in souvenir glasses, but unlike some of their competitors, they prominently display signs showing the drink price at $4.95 so an unwary first-timer doesn't assume that they're free.

Showtime . . . . A

The major production shows produced by the line, complete with Broadway-style playbills and computerized light cues, are sensational on the bigger ships with their state-of-the-art technical facilities. Passengers entertain each other at karaoke nights, masquerade parades and passenger talent shows, and pack appropriate garb for country/western night and '50s and '60s rock 'n roll night.

Discounts . . . .

The Breakthrough Rate Program promises discounts for early booking.

The Bottom Line

Very nice but overpriced, especially when the line's consistency of pricing puts its older vessels in the same general range as its newer ones. Cabins are small throughout the fleet except in the newest Project Vision ships, but are very quiet in all the newer ships, thanks to modern soundproofing techniques that provide a 42-decibel reduction in the walls and 40 at the door from hallway noise. RCI delivers a consistency across the fleet just as it intends to, even though the ships represent different design groups and sizes.

★ ★ ★ ★ ★

ENCHANTMENT OF THE SEAS*
GRANDEUR OF THE SEAS
LEGEND OF THE SEAS
RHAPSODY OF THE SEAS
SPLENDOUR OF THE SEAS
VISION OF THE SEAS*

They call it "The Ship of Light" and claim it has more glass than any other ship afloat, more than two acres of windows, from the atrium hotel lobby with its soaring glass elevators to a Roman spa with clear crystal canopy that can be opened to the air or covered against temperature extremes. The two-deck dining room walls are glass, the Viking Crown Lounge wrapped around the ship's funnel is almost all glass, and a glass-walled cafe that doubles as observation area is high atop the ship and forward. People who cruise on glass ships should take along their sunglasses.

The six vessels in RCI's Project Vision series, ships that are slightly smaller but considerably faster than the line's giant *Sovereign*, *Monarch* and *Majesty*. They cruise at 24 knots as compared to the usual 20 or less, allowing passengers a longer time in port or shorter transits between ports.

Despite their size, these ships give the impression of intimacy, particularly in the soaring seven-deck Centrum with its glass skylight ceiling, where each deck level has its own small sitting areas, library or cardroom.

The most talked-about feature on the Legend *of the* Seas *and* Splendour of the Seas *are their nine-hole miniature golf courses, the first at sea.*

≈ Between The Lines ≈

The Brochure Says

"At Royal Caribbean we've pioneered some of the greatest advancements in cruising. And nowhere is that more evident than in the innovative design of our newest ships."

Translation

Cabins are a bit bigger than the previous RCI norm, although the one we occupied, called a Larger Outside, begged the question, Larger than what? The ship's extra width—with a 105-foot beam, it's barely slim enough to squeeze through the Panama Canal—gives a greater sense of space throughout the ship. The passenger-space ratio of 38.32 is much higher than on the line's megaships.

≈ Cabins & Costs ≈

Fantasy Suites: . . . . **A+**

Average Price Per Person, Double Occupancy, Per Day: $628 plus airfare in the Caribbean. All prices include port charges.

The 1148-square-foot Royal Suite with its gleaming white baby grand piano is drop-dead gorgeous, from its private veranda to its sumptuous marble bathroom with separate WC and bidet, three wash basins, stall shower and oval Jacuzzi tub. For entertaining, there's a wet bar, mini-refrigerator, full entertainment center with TV, VCR, CD and the rest of the alphabet. Two sofas, two chairs, a glass dining table for four, separate bedroom with king-sized bed, easy chair and super storage space.

Small Splurges: . . . . **A**

Average Price PPPD: $500 each for two, $300 each for four, or $214 each for seven, plus airfare in the Caribbean.

The two family suites, each with two bedrooms, two baths (one with tub and one with shower), private veranda, sitting area with sofa-bed and chair, and a pull-down berth, big enough to sleep seven and certainly comfortable enough for four.

A spacious Category D deluxe outside cabin on **Legend of the Seas** *has sitting area and private veranda.*

Suitable Standards: . . . . C+

Average Price PPPD: $236, plus airfare in the Caribbean.

Category F Larger Outsides provide twin beds that can convert to queen-sized, a sitting area with loveseat, small glass table with a brass wastebasket fitted underneath, nice built-in cabinetry, desk/dresser with three big drawers on one side, three little ones on the other, two nightstands with two drawers each and floral curtains with sheer drapery underneath. A small TV set, closet with one full-length and two half-length hanging areas, safe, full-length mirror and cabinet with shelves above make the basic unit more spacious and comfortable than on most RCI ships. Bathrooms have showers only.

Wheelchair Accessible:

Seventeen cabins from Standard Insides to C category suites are designated accessible for the physically challenged; all are near elevators. Doors are an extra-wide 32 inches across; there are no doorway sills; the bathrooms have shower stalls with stools and grab bars, and both bathrooms and passenger corridors are wide enough for a wheelchair to turn around.

Bottom Bunks: C

Average Price PPPD: $186 apiece for two, $143 apiece for four, plus airfare in the Caribbean.

Even the standard quad insides with two lower and two upper berths have a sitting area with TV and a little space to move around. Storage is adequate, if not overly generous, and you can always take turns sitting on that cute little sofa.

CHAMPAGNE TOAST

For outstanding attention to disabled passengers: the large number of wheelchair-accessible cabins (17); Braille elevator signs; special cabin kits for hearing-impaired passengers with strobe-light door knocker and telephone ringer, mattress-vibrator alarm clock, telephone amplifier and enhancing FM receivers for sound in the show lounge.

The Routes

The *Grandeur of the Seas* sails the Eastern Caribbean year-round from Miami departing Saturdays and calling at Labadee, San Juan, St. Thomas and CocoCay.

The *Legend of the Seas* transits the Panama Canal on 10- and 11- night itineraries in winter, cruises Alaska's Inside Passage on seven-night schedules in summer, visiting Skagway, Haines, Juneau and Ketchikan and offers 10-night Hawaii cruises in spring and fall.

The *Splendour of the Seas* sails the Caribbean from Miami in winter on 10- and 11-night roundtrips, then moves to Europe in the summer.

The *Rhapsody of the Seas* spends the winter making seven-night round-trip cruises from San Juan, calling in Aruba, Curaçao, St. Maarten and St. Thomas; then repositions to Alaska in summer on a seven-night Inside Passage itinerary.

The *Enchantment of the Seas* alternates seven-night Eastern and Western Caribbean sailings from Miami year-round.

Vision of the Seas is scheduled to debut in Europe in May 1998, and after a summer of Mediterranean cruising, reposition for Canada/New England fall foliage cruises, followed by winter Panama Canal transits.

The Scoop

The Project Vision vessels look like moneymakers for the company. They feel like smaller ships than they are, because of the number of intimate areas tucked away here and there.

Cabins are somewhat more spacious than on previous RCI ships—even another 24 square feet is a bonus. A total of 17 staterooms are designated for the disabled. Practical touches like removable coat hangers, some with skirt clips, along with good mirrors and makeup lighting will be appreciated, too.

The six ships are not identical but rather created as three pairs, with *Legend* and *Splendour* slightly smaller than the others. We thought the *Grandeur* particularly splendid for its fine art collection. *Rhapsody* and *Vision* expand the enclosed public space from two full decks to two-and-a-half decks and greatly enlarge the showroom.

Since several different designers created the public areas, there is a pleasurable variety of decorating styles. Deck areas are handsomer than on the line's megaships. There are canvas-shaded seating areas and pools with arcs of water spraying, although the golf course takes up a lot of sunbathing area on the *Legend* and *Splendour*.

We can already hear the cash registers ringing as this formerly conservative company starts crowding Carnival on the outer edges of Glitz World.

Five Fabulous Places

1. A spectacular solarium with a "crystal canopy" sliding roof, pool with water jets and spas, Roman marble floors and walls, fountains, even a convivial marble bar; also there—a full spa, gym and beauty salon, steam baths and saunas.

2. The first 18-hole golf course at sea, in miniature of course, complete with water hazards, sand traps, halogen lights for night play, wind baffles and a clear dome roof in bad weather; reserved tee times, club rentals, $5 a game or $25 for unlimited play throughout the seven-day cruise.

3. The Centrum, the seven-deck, glass-ceilinged heart of the ship with two glass elevators, marble terraces and champagne bar.

4. The two-level dining room, where diners are surrounded by glass walls and a dramatic curving stairway lets well-dressed couples make a dramatic entrance.

5. The theater, the best showroom at sea from an audience point of view because all the seats are good—and comfortable. High-tech professional shows, an orchestra pit and retractable 50-screen video for multimedia productions.

Five Off-the-Wall Fun Facts

1. Sitting in the Viking Crown Lounge on these ships puts you at eye level with the Statue of Liberty.

2. If these two ships sailed through your neighborhood at normal cruising speed, they'd be ticketed for exceeding 30 m.p.h.

3. The steel used in *Legend of the Seas* could build two Eiffel towers.

4. The ships are twice as wide as Rodeo Drive in Beverly Hills, and twice as long and three times as high as the Hollywood sign.

5. Passengers on a seven-day cruise on *Splendour of the Seas* devour 4200 chickens, 2150 bagels, 3065 pounds of watermelons, 600 cases of beer and 383 cases of soda.

Five Good Reasons to Book These Ships

1. If you've always wanted to play miniature golf at sea.

2. If you like translating basic Latin phrases such as those adorning the marble walls of the Solarium—Bene Lava, Omnia Vincet Amor, Genius Loci and Carpe Diem.

3. To enjoy the excellent collection of original art on board, 1939 pieces altogether.

4. To hit the steam room and sauna, Jacuzzi and stand-up Solarium Bar.

5. To stargaze from a special deck with state-of-the-art starwheels that rotate on a "star-time" clock mechanism to show where constellations are in synchrony with real time and place. The cruise staff has been trained to explain it.

Five Things You Won't Find on Board

1. A self-service passenger laundry.

2. A golf cart on the 18-hole course.

3. A bad seat (or a smoking seat) anywhere in the show lounge.

4. A lot of space around your dinner table.

5. Public rest rooms in the Viking Crown Lounge.

LEGEND OF THE SEAS
SPLENDOUR OF THE SEAS

★★★★★
★★★★

Registry	Liberia
Officers	Norwegian
Crew	International
Complement	720
GRT	69,130
Length (ft.)	867
Beam (ft.)	105
Draft (ft.)	24
Passengers-Cabins Full	2076
Passengers-2/Cabin	1800/1804
Passenger Space Ratio	38.32
Stability Rating	Good to Excellent
Seatings	2
Cuisine	Themed
Dress Code	Traditional
Room Service	Yes
Tip	$7.50 PPPD, 15% automatically added to bar checks

Ship Amenities

Outdoor Pool	1
Indoor Pool	1
Jacuzzi	4
Fitness Center	Yes
Spa	Yes
Beauty Shop	Yes
Showroom	Yes
Bars/Lounges	7
Casino	Yes
Shops	4
Library	Yes
Child Program	Yes
Self-Service Laundry	No
Elevators	11

Cabin Statistics

Suites	87
Outside Doubles	496
Inside Doubles	327
Wheelchair Cabins	17
Singles	0
Single Surcharge	150%
Verandas	231
110 Volt	Yes

ROYAL CARIBBEAN
INTERNATIONAL

ENCHANTMENT OF THE SEAS* ★★★★★
GRANDEUR OF THE SEAS ★★★★★

Registry	**Liberia**
Officers	**Norwegian**
Crew	**International**
Complement	**765**
GRT	**74,000**
Length (ft.)	**916**
Beam (ft.)	**105**
Draft (ft.)	**25**
Passengers-Cabins Full	**2076**
Passengers-2/Cabin	**1950**
Passenger Space Ratio	**38.32**
Stability Rating	**Good to Excellent**
Seatings	**2**
Cuisine	**Themed**
Dress Code	**Traditional**
Room Service	**Yes**
Tip	**$7.50 PPPD, 15% automatically added to bar checks**

Ship Amenities

Outdoor Pool	**1**
Indoor Pool	**1**
Jacuzzi	**4**
Fitness Center	**Yes**
Spa	**Yes**
Beauty Shop	**Yes**
Showroom	**Yes**
Bars/Lounges	**7**
Casino	**Yes**
Shops	**4**
Library	**Yes**
Child Program	**Yes**
Self-Service Laundry	**No**
Elevators	**11**

Cabin Statistics

Suites	**87**
Outside Doubles	**561**
Inside Doubles	**327**
Wheelchair Cabins	**17**
Singles	**0**
Single Surcharge	**150%**
Verandas	**231**
110 Volt	**Yes**

RHAPSODY OF THE SEAS
VISIONS OF THE SEAS*

★★★★★
★★★★

Registry	**Liberia**
Officers	**Norwegian**
Crew	**International**
Complement	**765**
GRT	**75,000**
Length (ft.)	**915**
Beam (ft.)	**105**
Draft (ft.)	**25**
Passengers-Cabins Full	**2452**
Passengers-2/Cabin	**2000**
Passenger Space Ratio	**38.32**
Stability Rating	**Good to Excellent**
Seatings	**2**
Cuisine	**Themed**
Dress Code	**Traditional**
Room Service	**Yes**
Tip	**$7.50 PPPD, 15% automatically added to bar checks**

Ship Amenities

Outdoor Pool	**1**
Indoor Pool	**1**
Jacuzzi	**4**
Fitness Center	**Yes**
Spa	**Yes**
Beauty Shop	**Yes**
Showroom	**Yes**
Bars/Lounges	**7**
Casino	**Yes**
Shops	**4**
Library	**Yes**
Child Program	**Yes**
Self-Service Laundry	**No**
Elevators	**11**

Cabin Statistics

Suites	**97**
Outside Doubles	**501**
Inside Doubles	**389**
Wheelchair Cabins	**12**
Singles	**0**
Single Surcharge	**150%**
Verandas	**228**
110 Volt	**Yes**

ROYAL CARIBBEAN
INTERNATIONAL

★ ★ ★ ★

MAJESTY OF THE SEAS
MONARCH OF THE SEAS

One of the most fascinating phenomena of late twentieth-century life is the mall, that vast enclosed emporium of shops, bars, theaters and restaurants that has become a meeting place for teenagers and a weekend and evening destination for the young and upwardly mobile. In a sheltering, climate-controlled environment, surrounded by glittering options for spending money, people get dreamy-eyed and slow-moving. Majesty of the Seas and her sister megaliner Monarch of the Seas remind us a lot of hangin' out at the mall.

Starting with the first ship in this series, the slightly smaller *Sovereign of the Seas*, RCI concentrated on positioning the cabins forward and the public rooms aft so that passengers can make their way vertically from, say the cocktail bars to the dining room to the show lounge to the casino, and horizontally from their cabins to the public areas.

But we would still recommend that a passenger traveling from a modest B deck inside forward cabin to the sports deck area atop the ship aft take along a compass and a brown-bag lunch.

The plus side of big is that the soaring sense of space makes these huge ships especially appealing to first-time cruisers accustomed to hotels and resorts. And you shouldn't get lost too often—a three-dimensional plexiglass ship directory is set in each elevator/stairwell landing to help passengers find their way around.

They're good for kids because of the way the age groups are divided into 5-to-8-year-olds, "tweens" 8 to 12, and teens from 13 to 17. Teens can hang out at their own soft drink bar with its adjacent video games center and even run the special effects and light show in the teen disco.

A whole new subculture of passengers has developed around these megaships. They call themselves Trekkies (after the "Star Trek" TV series) in honor of their own journeys into space.

INSIDER TIP

People in bathing suits should avoid settling into those handsome woven plastic mesh bar seats at the pool bar if they don't want waffle patterns on the back of their thighs when they stand up again.

EAVESDROPPING

"Isn't this something!," gushes a 40ish blonde woman in awe as she enters the Majesty lobby at embarkation. "I'll certainly enjoy this week. You just can't believe it's a ship!"

Between The Lines

The Brochure Says

"Big-city dazzle with its elegant dining rooms...as tall as the Statue of Liberty...unlimited freedom to curl up with a good book, eat all the ice cream you want (and) tell the kids to ship out..."

Translation

It's a big ship but you're going to kick back and have a great time. Head up to the Viking Crown Lounge and fantasize being on eye level with Miss Liberty (only in your imagination, since these ships don't sail into New York). Dazzling, come-hither bright lights and a sense of action draw young and first-time cruisers who know how to have fun. As for good books, see "Insider Tip" below.

For unlimited ice cream, the line's *Nordic Empress* with its own free ice cream bar might be a better bet. But you can certainly tell the kids to ship out, with three child care programs that split age groups between 5 and 8, "tweens" 8 to 12, and teens. The last have their own club and disco called Flashes, created by a line that realizes teens are only a decade or so away from buying cruises for themselves. Attention must be paid.

OFF-THE-WALL

The On Your Toes nightclub/disco on the Majesty of the Seas with its neon signage, optical illusion glass-and-neon entryway and state-of-the-art DJ station strains to send a "with it" message which is sabotaged by the saccharine central sculpture of a pair of ballet dancers.

INSIDER TIP

The elegant library aboard has 2000 books, an impressive number until you realize the ship carries 2354 passengers, presumably leaving 354 people with nothing to read during the cruise. Check out your book ASAP.

CHAMPAGNE TOAST

To the splendid ShipShape Center, open daily from 8 a.m. to 8 p.m., with a padded floor and enough space so aerobics and exercise classes don't have to be scheduled on deck or in one of the lounges, as on many vessels.

Cabins & Costs

The Royal Suite on **Majesty of the Seas** *is a true fantasy suite.*

Fantasy Suites: . . . . A

Average Price Per Person, Double Occupancy, Per Day: $614 plus airfare.
The Royal Suite, #1010 on both ships, provides ideal digs for anyone who wants to entertain in nearly 1000 square feet indoors and out. A separate living room with private veranda, dining table with six chairs, L-shaped sofa and two chairs, wet bar stocked with liquor, soft drinks and snacks and an entertainment center with CDs and VCRs headlines the suite. In the bedroom is a king-sized bed, lovely wood dresser, a marble bathroom with double basins, Jacuzzi tub, stall shower and walk-in dressing area with large safe.

Small Splurges: . . . . B+

Average Price PPPD: $486 per person for first two passengers, $107 per person for third and fourth sharing the suite. Plus airfare.
The Family Suite, #1549 on both ships, has two bedrooms and two baths, adequate sleeping, lounging and wardrobe space for a close family of five, with private veranda, sitting area, master bedroom and bath, and second bedroom with two lower beds, a pulldown berth and small bathroom with shower.

Suitable Standards: C

Average Price PPPD: $250 plus airfare.
F is the predominant category of standard outside double cabins, each with its twin beds in L-shaped configuration, the ends at the L overlapping by 18 inches. In the 127 square feet, you'll find one chair (flip a coin for it), a small TV set, a tripod glass-topped table with a brass wastebasket as its base (we tried to chill champagne

in it but were sternly corrected by a Bahamian stewardess), a built-in cabinet with four drawers, a closet with one full length and two half-height hanging areas plus drawers and a safe and a small tidy tile bath with shower.

Wheelchair Accessible: ....

Two inside category N cabins and two outside category D cabins are designated as physically challenged accessible. They're larger than others in their price category, with good turning room for the wheelchair, and twin beds with pastel covers, along with sofa and chair. The baths have no sills, and provide grab rails by the toilet and in the shower, along with a pull-down plastic seat. Some low hanging closet racks are accessible, but the safe, located on an upper shelf, would be out of reach for someone in a wheelchair.

Bottom Bunks: .... C-

Average Price PPPD: $171 plus airfare.

With the modular cabin design common to new ships, the cheapest digs often offer two lower beds and a bathroom identical to those in higher-priced categories. The bottom-dollar beds are in category Q, insides that measure 114 square feet and are situated well forward on the lowest passenger cabin deck, but hey, they're livable unless you hit a heavy storm, which could toss you out of bed.

DID YOU KNOW?

At the French shipyard a week before delivery of the Monarch of the Seas, a group of American media touring the vessel were bemused to note that in the Ain't Misbehavin' Lounge, the life-sized sculpture of the noted black pianist with his derby hat was labeled Fats Domino instead of Fats Waller.

The Routes

Majesty of the Seas sails year-round, seven-day Western Caribbean round-trips from Miami (Sundays) calling at Playa del Carmen and Cozumel, Grand Cayman, Ocho Rios and Labadee, Haiti, for a beach day.

Monarch of the Seas sails year-round seven-day Southern Caribbean round-trips from San Juan (Sundays) calling at Martinique, Barbados, Antigua, St. Maarten and St. Thomas.

The Scoop

The acres of Astroturf and anodized bronze loungers, glittering shops and glass elevators, leather sofas, potted palms and lobby pianist make the *Majesty* and *Monarch of the Seas* look more like Marriott of the Seas to a purist.

While the cabins and interiors are as spotless as ever, the deck housekeeping is sometimes lax. A well-decked-out lady deserves better than this.

Solid mainstream ships, the *Majesty* and the *Monarch* set out to impress from the moment a passenger boards, just as Carnival does, but they aim for a slightly more sophisticated audience. Only dedicated traditional ship buffs will find much to grouse about here.

Insider Tips

Five Great Space Stations

1. The Centrum, a four-deck lobby with two glass elevators, a two-level marble floor and a pianist, looking for all the world like a Hyatt Regency hotel lobby.

2. Boutiques of Centrum, 10 storefronts in the shopping gallery circled like pioneer wagons around a campfire, each with its own character and line of duty-free products. In the center of it all, a plaza with luggage-brown leather chairs where non-shoppers can sit and wait—just like at the mall.

3. The tri-level show lounge (A Chorus Line on *Majesty*, Sound of Music on *Monarch*) with its curved cantilevered box seats, eye-catching murals and neon entrance signage adds glitz to this fairly conservative line, although kilowatt-wise, it can't compete with the Casino Royale.

4. The spacious Schooner Bar, everybody's favorite piano bar, with a decor that includes plank floors, brass ship lamps, ship models in plexiglass cases and spars and rigging. While the house music is closer to "My Way" than "Blow the Man Down," it's still pretty nautical.

5. The two-deck Windjammer Cafe is open to the sea, with an enclosed cafe forward and a covered, outdoor cafe amidships, sheltered with window walls and a glass dome overhead; unique "waterfall" columns sandwich a cascade that ripples through plexiglass cases and towers of glass blocks.

MAJESTY OF THE SEAS ★★★★
MONARCH OF THE SEAS ★★★★

Registry	Norway
Officers	Norwegian
Crew	International
Complement	822
GRT	73,941
Length (ft.)	880
Beam (ft.)	106
Draft (ft.)	25
Passengers-Cabins Full	2744
Passengers-2/Cabin	2354
Passenger Space Ratio	31.4
Stability Rating	Fair to Good
Seatings	2
Cuisine	Themed
Dress Code	Traditional
Room Service	Yes
Tip	$7.50 PPPD, 15% automatically added to bar check

Ship Amenities

Outdoor Pool	2
Indoor Pool	0
Jacuzzi	2
Fitness Center	Yes
Spa	Yes
Beauty Shop	Yes
Showroom	Yes
Bars/Lounges	8
Casino	Yes
Shops	10
Library	Yes
Child Program	Yes
Self-Service Laundry	No
Elevators	0

Cabin Statistics

Suites	13
Outside Doubles	732
Inside Doubles	445
Wheelchair Cabins	4
Singles	0
Single Surcharge	150%
Verandas	62
110 Volt	Yes

★★★★
NORDIC EMPRESS

Our favorite memory of the Nordic Empress was sitting on our cabin's private veranda late one Saturday night in the summer of 1990 when the then-new ship was docked in Nassau, and watching the equally new Fantasy from Carnival, docked across the way, change colors as its computer-programmed neon tubing strung throughout the vessel shifted from red to blue to fuchsia to lime to pink. The Fantasy, a sort of lava lamp for the 1990s, serves to delineate the differences between the two, the first brand-new ships that had ever been scheduled for profit-generating three- and four-day cruises.

Until then, only the oldest vintage vessels from a line were shoved over into that high-density, high-attrition market once perceived as a one-time-only whoopee cruise for guzzling undergraduates and singles on the make.

Now, suddenly, right before our eyes, the whole scene had changed, and we were witnessing the cruise equivalent of a stare-down confrontation between genteel Melanie Wilkes and flamboyant Scarlett O'Hara.

The *Nordic Empress* actually started on the drawing board as a rather pretentiously named vessel called *Future Seas*, designed expressly for three-and four-day cruises for a now-defunct company called Admiral Cruises, an affiliate of the then RCCL.

Company executives define the differences on the mini-cruise vessels:

—"We try to cram a seven-day cruise into three days."

—More hectic.

—In port daily.

—More steak and lobster, fewer unfamiliar dishes on the menu.

—"Passengers want to eat and drink as much as they would in seven days." (Passengers also spend roughly the same amount of disposable income for on-board extras as they would in seven days.)

—Deck plan must be easy for the passenger to learn and find his way around in a limited time.

Pool deck areas are shaded with canvas umbrellas on the **Nordic Empress.**

The Brochure Says
"A cascading waterfall. Lush tropical plants. The kind of sunlight you never get back home. Wait. This isn't an exotic port. This is your ship. The Centrum Lobby, actually."

Translation
The heart of the ship is a hotel-like lobby that connects to all the passenger decks and so helps passengers learn their way around. (It's no fun when you're on a three-day cruise and can't find your cabin for hours.) The Centrum, as it's called, is drop-dead dramatic, a great place for photographing each other. (It's also a good backdrop for a wedding, if you have romance in mind. See page 59 "Getting Married Aboard".)

CHAMPAGNE TOAST

For their subtle how-to's for first-timers: at the first night's dinner, the waiter, busboy and headwaiter introduce themselves to each table, each explaining what his particular duties are so the uninitiated cruiser doesn't have to worry about which server to summon for a glass of water or a cup of coffee. Cabin stewards greet each arriving guest and point out cabin features, and the welcome-aboard presentation on embarkation day introduces personnel from the ship's shops, sports and fitness program, beauty shop, casino and photography concessions to explain the services and prices, and that there's no charge for being photographed unless you want to buy the finished picture.

Cabins & Costs

Fantasy Suites: .... A

Average Price Per Person, Double Occupancy, Per Day: $616 plus airfare.

The one-bedroom Royal Suite is big enough for entertaining with a wet bar, large dining or conference table, curved sofa and chairs, teak-floored veranda, walk-in closet, Jacuzzi tub, and separate marble-and-glass shower. While the price is about $100 a day more than the owner's suites, the Royal Suite incorporates space from an owner's suite and two standard cabins.

Small Splurges: .... B+

Average Price PPPD: $383 plus airfare.

One of the 56 category C deluxe outside cabins with private balcony, two lower beds which can be arranged as one, a sofa, chair and coffee table, built-in dresser/desk, good reading lamp, built-in vanity table and terry-cloth robes.

Suitable Standards: .... B

Average Price PPPD: $276 plus airfare.

Cabins were designed with women in mind, according the ship designers, who say females comprise 60 percent of all cruise passengers. There's generous counter space in the bathroom, subdued pastel fabrics, floral watercolors and a beauty table with its own makeup lights. H and I category cabins have twin beds that convert to queen-sized, color TV, built-in dresser with stool, one chair, good storage space and small bathroom with shower only.

Bottom Bunks: C

Average Price PPPD: $183 plus airfare.

Q category cabins forward on B deck are the bottom-dollar digs; expect all the standard cabin amenities in a slightly smaller space.

The Routes

Winter: Fridays, three-day roundtrips from San Juan to St. Thomas and St. Maarten.

Winter: Mondays, four-day roundtrips from San Juan to St. Thomas, St. Maarten and St. Croix.

Summer: Three- and four-day cruises from Port Canaveral to the Bahamas.

The Scoop

The *Nordic Empress*, like Carnival's glittering new short-cruise megaships, is attracting a whole new set of first-time cruise passengers of all ages and ethnic backgrounds, a welcome sight in an industry that spent too many years competing for the same narrow stratum of cruise regulars.

This ship offers a gentler, quieter version of the party cruise without soft-pedaling the fun. On Bahamas three- and four-day itineraries, passengers have a full day at the beach on a private island for swimming, snorkeling, sailing and windsurfing with a calypso band and beach barbecue lunch.

The *Nordic Empress* is highly recommended for first-time cruisers of all ages, including families and three-generation groups. It's a good introduction to mainstream cruising.

Five Sensational Spots

1. The Centrum, a nine-deck open atrium with a glass skylight on top, then a waterfall that cascades, sometimes framed in glass or caught up in pools, sometimes splashing free, faced with pink begonias and white marble and a crystal-drop sculpture of a ship's prow, all of it best viewed from the two glass elevators.

2. The two decks of the glass-walled Carmen Dining Room, the first of the nearly one dozen double-deckers now at sea, with a great view of the port as the ship sails away. It's bright and airy for breakfast and lunch, and spectacularly lit at dinnertime when musicians on a raised marble platform serenade diners.

3. The tri-level Casino Royale with 10 blackjack tables, two roulette tables, two craps tables, 40 sit-down poker machines and 220 slot machines is catnip for sporting cats.

4. Kids Connection Playroom has a slide that lets small children fall into a sea of brightly colored plastic balls; there's also a cave-like hidden TV room with carpeted seating levels, great for watching scary videos such as *Jurassic Park*.

5. The Strike Up the Band Showroom in coral tones with white marble and gleaming brass cantilevered curved balcony boxes is lovely to look at, and a wooden thrust stage with splendid turntable and technical equipment offers state-of-the-art stagecraft. The only flaw is the over-exuberance of curved rails in the balcony that limit access and force late arrivals to vault over the railings into their seats.

Five Things You Won't Find on Board

1. The usual blank wall in inside cabins. Where the window would be on an outside cabin, the line has decorated with artwork and vertical fabric and plexiglass strips framing wall sconces.

2. A panoramic ocean view from outside cabins amidships on Mariner Deck (cabins 7100–7652, plus cabins 7032 and 7352) because lifeboats are hanging outside the windows. For the same price, ask your travel agent to book category F cabins well forward or aft to avoid the obstructions.

3. A library or card room.

4. A self-service laundry.

5. Consistently good sightlines in the show lounge; arrive early so you don't have to sit in the balcony.

ROYAL CARIBBEAN INTERNATIONAL

NORDIC EMPRESS ★★★★

Registry	**Liberia**
Officers	**Norwegian**
Crew	**International**
Complement	**671**
GRT	**48,563**
Length (ft.)	**692**
Beam (ft.)	**100**
Draft (ft.)	**25**
Passengers-Cabins Full	**2020**
Passengers-2/Cabin	**1600**
Passenger Space Ratio	**30.35**
Stability Rating	**Good**
Seatings	**2**
Cuisine	**Themed**
Dress Code	**Traditional**
Room Service	**Yes**
Tip	**$7.50 PPPD, 15% automatically added to bar checks**

Ship Amenities

Outdoor Pool	**2**
Indoor Pool	**0**
Jacuzzi	**4**
Fitness Center	**Yes**
Spa	**Yes**
Beauty Shop	**Yes**
Showroom	**Yes**
Bars/Lounges	**6**
Casino	**Yes**
Shops	**3**
Library	**No**
Child Program	**Yes**
Self-Service Laundry	**No**
Elevators	**7**

Cabin Statistics

Suites	**6**
Outside Doubles	**471**
Inside Doubles	**329**
Wheelchair Cabins	**4**
Singles	**0**
Single Surcharge	**150%**
Verandas	**69**
110 Volt	**Yes**

★★★
SONG OF AMERICA

It was a windy but memorable December day in 1982 in Miami when opera star Beverly Sills christened Song of America. It took the durable diva five swings before she broke the bottle of champagne across the bow. Moments before, she had cautioned the crowd of well-wishers not to spill anything on "my carpets—I like to run a tight ship." At the time, Wartsila-built Song of America was the biggest cruise ship ever constructed in Scandinavia, and perhaps the only modern Caribbean ship to boast an ex-president (Jimmy Carter) and his family as passengers on the maiden voyage. The Carters still return periodically, but also travel aboard the Sovereign of the Seas, where Mrs. Carter is godmother.

A deluxe cabin on **Song of America** *with its own sitting area and desk/dresser.*

Unlike this ship's many fervent fans, we dismissed her as Nordic high-tech razzle-dazzle when she was new because of her popsicle interior colors, but in a more recent renovation, some of the original orange cabin furnishings have been muted to beige tones and the former grape-and-raspberry upholstery in the Can Can Lounge and Guys & Dolls Lounge has quieted down as well. It's been some time since the Schooner Bar was introduced and the outdated cinema removed (now that the cabins have color TV sets for video movies) in favor of a conference and meeting area and expanded casino. The soundproofing has been beefed up since the early days as well.

Traditionalists like the long sleek lines compared to today's shoebox shapes, and sunbathers find plenty of room to stretch out on the expansive Compass and Sun Decks. For nightlife, the ship has three spacious lounges for shows, music and dancing, plus the smaller Schooner piano bar.

Between The Lines

The Brochure Says

"We'll do everything, so you have the option of doing nothing. We'll clean up your room (twice a day), cook for you (six times a day), entertain you and take you to faraway places with strange-sounding names."

Translation

A cruise is an easy vacation, because you buy everything in a neat package, even your round-trip airfare and transfers. You have a cabin steward who cleans your cabin twice a day, replacing towels and refilling the ice bucket, and you can eat every couple of hours if you concentrate. Best of all, your cruise ship takes you to exotic spots such as the U.S. Virgin Islands where the inhabitants speak English and welcome U.S. dollars.

Cabins & Costs

Fantasy Suites: . . . . **B**

Average Price Per Person, Double Occupancy, Per Day: $443 plus airfare.
The Owner's Suite, #7000, on Promenade Deck, is double the size of the deluxe outside suites, with sitting area with sofa, chairs and coffee table; mini-refrigerator, color TV, twin beds and an optional third berth, wide desk/dresser, three picture windows and bathroom with tub. On the down side, you're overlooking a public deck area from your picture windows.

Small Splurges: . . . . **C+**

Average Price PPPD: $386 plus airfare.
A deluxe suite in B category, not as lavish space-wise as the Owner's Suite, but comfortable enough, with sofa, chairs, desk/dresser, color TV, separate sleeping area with twin beds and big window, and bath with tub.

Suitable Standards: . . . . **C-**

Average Price PPPD: $271 plus airfare.
The modular cabin design means all standards are virtually identical, with the category and price difference reflected in the deck location. The H category A deck outside doubles have two lower beds (one sofa/daybed and one fold-up twin) except for cabins 3207–3210, 3147–3150 and 3013–3018, all of which have twin beds

that can be put together into a queen-sized bed. Most of these also have a pull-down third berth. All have bathrooms with shower only.

Bottom Bunks: .... **C**

Average Price PPPD: $200 plus airfare.
The B Deck inside doubles in the forward part of the ship, Q category, are the lowest-priced accommodations. Each has two lower beds that can be put together to make a queen-sized bed, a bath with shower, wall-mounted color TV set and a desk/dresser with stool.

> ### INSIDER TIP
>
> *Only about half the cabins on board have twin beds that can be converted to queen-sized beds, so specify your preference when booking.*

The Routes

In winter, *Song of America* cruises the Mexican Riviera on seven-night sailings from Los Angeles, calling at Cabo San Lucas, Mazatlán and Puerto Vallarta. In summer, she sails to Bermuda from New York on seven-night roundtrip itineraries every Sunday.

The Scoop

This long, sleek beauty is one of only three classic non-mega-sized ships remaining in the rapidly-growing RCI fleet, and it has retained its popularity over the years, with some loyals claiming as many as two dozen sailings aboard since its debut.

Because the cabins are on the small side (around 120 square feet for standard doubles), the passenger space ratio is a modest 26.8, but deck areas and lounges are spacious and comfortable, and warm-weather cruisers shouldn't have to spend too much time in their rooms.

Anyone sensitive to cigarette smoke may find, as we do, that although the Viking Crown Lounge with its expansive (and unopenable) glass windows offers dramatic sea and sunset views, it also retains the smell of smoke despite the line's zealous attempts to clean and freshen the air.

Insider Tips

Five Special Spots

1. The cozy Schooner Bar, just the right size on this ship compared to the bigger version aboard the megaliners.

2. The Sun Walk that overlooks the amidships pool deck, which allows you to get in your daily mile or two while checking out the scenic sunbathers below.

3. The 360-degree view from the Viking Crown Lounge, the first one for the line that was wrapped completely around the stack instead of just part of it.

4. The Oriental Terrace and Ambassador Room, two narrower dining ells that branch off the big Madame Butterfly dining room on both port and starboard sides.

5. The Mast Bar on Compass Deck with its 14 barstools that overlook the onboard action.

SONG OF AMERICA ★★★

Registry	**Norway**
Officers	**Norwegian**
Crew	**International**
Complement	**525**
GRT	**37,584**
Length (ft.)	**705**
Beam (ft.)	**93**
Draft (ft.)	**22**
Passengers-Cabins Full	**1552**
Passengers-2/Cabin	**1402**
Passenger Space Ratio	**26.8**
Stability Rating	**Fair**
Seatings	**2**
Cuisine	**Themed**
Dress Code	**Traditional**
Room Service	**Yes**
Tip	**$7.50 PPPD, 15% automatically added to bar checks**

Ship Amenities

Outdoor Pool	**2**
Indoor Pool	**0**
Jacuzzi	**0**
Fitness Center	**Yes**
Spa	**No**
Beauty Shop	**Yes**
Showroom	**Yes**
Bars/Lounges	**7**
Casino	**Yes**
Shops	**2**
Library	**Yes**
Child Program	**No**
Self-Service Laundry	**No**
Elevators	**7**

Cabin Statistics

Suites	**1**
Outside Doubles	**406**
Inside Doubles	**295**
Wheelchair Cabins	**0**
Singles	**0**
Single Surcharge	**150%**
Verandas	**0**
110 Volt	**Yes**

★ ★ ★ ★
SOVEREIGN OF THE SEAS

*In the awesome five-story open lobby, brass-trimmed glass elevators glide
up and down, their gleaming reflections glancing off marble walls. Elegantly
clad guests lean against a brass railing to look far below at a white baby grand
piano where a man in a red coat is playing light classics beside three fountain
pools. Almost every major city has one of these grand hotels with majestic
staircases and soaring, ethereal space. The only difference is, this one is scheduled to sail off into the Caribbean sunset at 5:30.*

The pool deck on Sovereign of the Seas *after embarkation.*

Sovereign of the Seas was the largest ship ever built for cruising when it came
into service in 1988. Like its newer sister ships *Monarch of the Seas* and *Majesty of the Seas*, it has a "bigger than life" theatricality and showy design that
lends excitement. From the moment its mostly youngish, often first-timer
passengers first board, they have the sense of arriving at a major resort. It's
ideal for couples, singles and young families shopping for a Caribbean vacation that just happens to be aboard a cruise ship. A recent $6 million refur-

bishment added greater density and more youth programs for the new minicruise itineraries.

How far does the average passenger have to walk between the show lounge and the midnight buffet on a ship that is almost three football fields long? Theoretically, only a short stroll and a stairway or elevator separate the chorus girls from the cheesecake, because the ship's design concentrates the public rooms aft and the staterooms forward.

In fact, your evening could go something like this: You start at the bottom in your assigned dining room (Gigi is on A Deck and Kismet on Main Deck), then walk up one deck to the casino, to the lower level of the show lounge or the shops, then up another deck if you want to sit in the show lounge balcony or have a quiet drink in Finian's Rainbow Lounge or the champagne bar. Walk up one more deck to catch the late show in the Music Man Lounge, then up another deck to check out the disco. Finally, if you want a nightcap in the Viking Crown Lounge, catch the elevator outside the disco and ride three more decks to the top of the ship. Whew!

DID YOU KNOW?

When this ship was new, we speculated about how many hands a captain can shake at a captain's cocktail party. RCCL set two parties for each of the two dinner seatings, so that the captain had to press the flesh of only 1141 passengers in two shifts, while his second in command was in another lounge handling the other half.

The Brochure Says

"Big. You may wonder if that's what you want in a cruise ship. Won't you get lost just trying to find your stateroom? Not with Royal Caribbean—there's always a staff member who'll point you the right way—or take you there."

Translation

None necessary.

DID YOU KNOW?

When this ship was new, we saw her docked in San Juan as we sailed in on another vessel. The passengers lining the rail wondered aloud what it was, until one man proclaimed, "I know, that's the new Severance of the Seas!"

Cabins & Costs

Fantasy Suites: . . . . **A**
Average Price Per Person, Double Occupancy, Per Day: $583 plus airfare.
The Royal Suite, #1010, some 1000 square feet of luxury, with private veranda, whirlpool tub, living room with wet bar, refrigerator and entertainment center— plus plenty of room for entertaining, and a big walk-in closet with generous storage space and personal safe.

Small Splurges: . . . . **B**

Average Price PPPD: $350–$450 plus airfare.

One of the eight Bridge Deck suites, with large windows, sitting area with sofa and chairs, two lower beds plus a sofa-bed for a third person, mini-refrigerator and bath with tub.

Suitable Standards: . . . . **C**

Average Price PPPD: $286–$298 plus airfare.

In categories F and G, you'll find twin beds in an L-configuration, small tripod brass-and-glass table, one chair, desk/dresser, bath with shower and skimpy storage space in an area approximately 120 square feet.

Bottom Bunks: . . . . **C**

Average Price PPPD: $183 plus airfare.

The Q category inside cabins forward on B Deck are the cheapest on board, with two lower beds in parallel configuration, bath with shower, one chair and dresser.

ROYAL CARIBBEAN INTERNATIONAL

The Routes

The ship makes three- and four-day cruises year-round from Miami to the Bahamas, with a beach day at CocoCay.

The Scoop

We're still not crazy about the vertical stacking that puts the cabins forward and the public areas aft. While it saves long strolls down hallways (unless your cabin is well forward) it still means a lot of stair climbing for impatient passengers who don't want to wait for the elevators.

Families with teenagers will find youth facilities on the *Sovereign* greatly improved.

You'll probably find *Sovereign of the Seas* is like your favorite resort hotel gone to sea, with everything aboard but the golf course; you'll have to book RCI's *Legend of the Seas* or *Splendour of the Seas* for that.

Insider Tips

Five Favorite Space Stations

1. The Centrum, a five-deck atrium with glass elevators, pools and fountains, glittering curved staircases, all dazzle and splash.

2. Touch of Class Champagne Bar, ideal for a romantic early evening glass of the bubbly and a nibble of Camembert amid cushy leather sofas in an intimate step-down sitting room.

3. Boutiques of Centrum, the ship's shopping mall and a veritable town square with its own sidewalk cafe.

4. The new Club Ocean for kids and FantaSeas for teens.

5. The Music Man Lounge, with 76 trombones etched on the windows and three musicians sculpted in metal by the door, presents late cabaret shows and country/ western music on theme nights combining entertainment Lounge and Disco.

SOVEREIGN OF THE SEAS ★★★★

Registry	**Norway**
Officers	**Norwegian**
Crew	**International**
Complement	**808**
GRT	**73,192**
Length (ft.)	**880**
Beam (ft.)	**106**
Draft (ft.)	**25**
Passengers-Cabins Full	**2744**
Passengers-2/Cabin	**2276**
Passenger Space Ratio	**32.15**
Stability Rating	**Good**
Seatings	**2**
Cuisine	**Themed**
Dress Code	**Traditional**
Room Service	**Yes**
Tip	**$7.50 PPPD, 15% automatically added to bar checks**

Ship Amenities

Outdoor Pool	**2**
Indoor Pool	**0**
Jacuzzi	**2**
Fitness Center	**Yes**
Spa	**Yes**
Beauty Shop	**Yes**
Showroom	**Yes**
Bars/Lounges	**8**
Casino	**Yes**
Shops	**3**
Library	**Yes**
Child Program	**Yes**
Self-Service Laundry	**No**
Elevators	**13**

Cabin Statistics

Suites	**12**
Outside Doubles	**722**
Inside Doubles	**416**
Wheelchair Cabins	**6**
Singles	**0**
Single Surcharge	**150%**
Verandas	**0**
110 Volt	**Yes**

★★
SUN VIKING

While the name itself connotes rows of golden Scandinavian gods and god-desses lazily rotating as they turn themselves tan, we think instead of Finnish shipyard workers laboring away in the chill damp of a Helsinki winter morning as they create a fantasy Caribbean cruise ship for the 1970s. A swimming pool—yes!—and no shade to come between the sun and the sunbathers, say the shivering architects.

Everything on the top three decks is centered around a deep oblong pool big enough for modest laps; the decks are swathed in enough robin's egg blue Astroturf to carpet a small stadium. The top three decks stare at that pool and the pair of saunas tucked away just behind it, the Sun Walk looking down from above, and rows of wooden benches like an amphitheater where an audience might applaud a particularly shapely body in a swimsuit. A mural on the sports deck says it all—a 1970s Op Art rendition of a pretty blonde riding a seahorse. You almost expect to see a yellow submarine.

Tidy as the line's ShipShape promotions, the *Sun Viking* offers beige-on-beige rows of cabins and passageways lined with porthole-shaped photographs that look like a Kodak shop window display, some of them faded. As the line's smallest ship, the *Sun Viking* has served as bellwether from the beginning, pioneering new destinations such as Alaska, Europe and now Asia, once the line made the gigantic hurdle to venture beyond the Caribbean.

Between The Lines

The Brochure Says

"...intimate...might have been crossbred with a cozy yacht...generous ratio of staff to passengers..."

Translation

The *Sun Viking* is small enough that it's easy to find your way around and meet fellow passengers, and cabins are about the size you'd find on a very cozy yacht but adequate unto the need, given that dedicated pool deck. The staff is pleasant and friendly, and the ratio of 2.1 passengers to one crew member is better than most ships in this price range.

Cabins & Costs

Fantasy Suites: ....**N/A**

N/A

Small Splurges: .... **C**

Average Price Per Person, Double Occupancy, Per Day: $336 plus airfare.

"Small" is the operative word for almost all RCI cabins, but the category C cabins on Promenade Deck are slightly roomier than most and worth the extra money for the additional storage space, mirrors on the sliding closet doors, a bathtub with shower and the fact that the two of you can sit down on the twin beds without bumping knees. You also get one chair and one hassock.

Suitable Standards: .... **C**

Average Price PPPD: $243 plus airfare.

Inside and outside cabins in the H category are termed Larger Staterooms, meaning larger than a breadbox. Many are interconnecting, making this a possibility for families, and if you pick an amidships location, the ride is smoother.

Bottom Bunks: .... **D**

Average Price PPPD: $200 plus airfare.

Four slim-hipped people could squeeze into one of the budget-priced N category cabins like 746, a quad, with two lower and two upper beds, providing they traveled light and took turns getting up and dressing, then going out of the cabin so the next one could get up and dress. The good news: With four very close friends sharing the space, the rate drops considerably.

INSIDER TIP

Try to get table assignments at one of the tables for four along the window wall in the L-extension of the pretty HMS Pinafore Dining Room for optimum viewing pleasure.

KEELHAUL

We note both a bellstand on board and a printed suggestion sheet saying "Bellboys are tipped when service is rendered." On most lines, cabin stewards lend a hand with baggage without the other hand extended for tips.

The Routes

Sun Viking makes a series of 14- and 15-night sailings—round-trip from Singapore to Indonesia, Malaysia and Thailand; Singapore to Hong Kong with calls in Thailand, Vietnam and China and 13-night cruises between Beijing and Hong Kong that call at five China ports.

The Scoop

As the smallest and oldest vessel in the fleet, the *Sun Viking* is a sentimental favorite with longtime loyal passengers. This also makes it the obvious choice to pioneer new destination areas, since RCI frequent cruisers always want to check out new places, especially when they get frequent-passenger introductory discounts.

Warmer and cozier than the megaliners, *Sun Viking* is making a big success in Asia. Although neither elegant nor deluxe, she's a trim and comfortable ship, and you'll probably love her if you're not a world-class fussbudget.

Best of all, these Asia cruises are great buys, priced, even with roundtrip airfare, not much higher than Caribbean prices aboard the line's other ships.

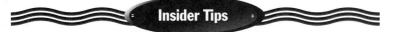

Insider Tips

Five Good Reasons to Book This Ship

1. To take a mainstream American-style cruise in Asia.

2. To enjoy the RCI lifestyle on a more intimate vessel.

3. To get a great perch for sightseeing high atop the ship on the Compass Deck's built-in wood benches.

4. To stake out one of the comfortable barstools in the pretty Merry Widow Lounge with its Tiffany-like stained-glass dome and expanse of shining mahogany bar.

5. To be able to say to new shipboard friends, "I'll meet you in the Annie Get Your Gun."

ROYAL CARIBBEAN
INTERNATIONAL

SUN VIKING ★★

Registry	**Norway**
Officers	**Norwegian**
Crew	**International**
Complement	**341**
GRT	**18,445**
Length (ft.)	**563**
Beam (ft.)	**80**
Draft (ft.)	**22**
Passengers-Cabins Full	**818**
Passengers-2/Cabin	**714**
Passenger Space Ratio	**25.84**
Stability Rating	**Fair**
Seatings	**2**
Cuisine	**Themed**
Dress Code	**Traditional**
Room Service	**Yes**
Tip	**$7.50 PPPD, 15% automatically added to bar checks**

Ship Amenities

Outdoor Pool	**1**
Indoor Pool	**0**
Jacuzzi	**0**
Fitness Center	**No**
Spa	**No**
Beauty Shop	**Yes**
Showroom	**Yes**
Bars/Lounges	**6**
Casino	**Yes**
Shops	**2**
Library	**Yes**
Child Program	**No**
Self-Service Laundry	**No**
Elevators	**4**

Cabin Statistics

Suites	**1**
Outside Doubles	**240**
Inside Doubles	**117**
Wheelchair Cabins	**0**
Singles	**0**
Single Surcharge	**150%**
Verandas	**0**
110 Volt	**Yes**

ROYAL CARIBBEAN INTERNATIONAL

★★★★
VIKING SERENADE

You've come a long way, baby, from your start as a Scandinavian ferry back in 1981, then a stint as the car-carrying Stardancer *in Alaska for Sundance Cruises, the short-lived company operated by Stan MacDonald, founder of Princess Cruises and granddaddy of TV's "The Love Boat." But you kept on truckin' until your fairy godmother RCCL picked you up and dusted you off with a $75 million full-body makeover to turn you into the dazzler you are to-day. Lucky, lucky Los Angeles to have you all to herself alone. Twice a week for 52 weeks all year round, Ensenada here we come!*

Few makeovers have been as startling as the 1991 changeover from the 996-passenger plain-Jane *Stardancer* to the glittering 1514-passenger *Viking Serenade* with 260 new cabins, 144 of them neatly slipped in where the vessel's under-utilized car ferry used to be. And these newest cabins are also the lowest-priced outside doubles (see "Suitable Standards").

You'll find spacious lobby areas, a large shopping center, a big lavish casino and two handsome restaurants featuring theme dinners, everything a first-time cruiser or a weekender would expect. A little neon here, some brass and marble there, and voila, a glamorous weekend getaway at Palm Springs prices.

•Between The Lines•

The Brochure Says

"She's beautiful. She's romantic. And she's always fun.... If we don't see you on deck for coffee and fresh pastries at 6 a.m., *hasta la vista.*"

Translation

You're going to have fun aboard, probably stay up very late, but you'll enjoy some really classy decor aboard this ship.

DID YOU KNOW?

Although Whoopi Goldberg is godmother of the Viking Serenade, *the original vessel, named* Scandinavia, *was christened by actress Liv Ullmann in 1981.*

Cabins & Costs

Fantasy Suites: . . . . **B+**

Average Price Per Person, Double Occupancy, Per Day: $583 plus airfare.
The Royal Suite, # 9566, fills an area that previously held four standard cabins, with a large living room with wet bar and dining area, a TV set with VCR and CD player, a separate bedroom with king-sized bed, a big marble bathroom with oversized Jacuzzi tub, and a walk-in closet.

Small Splurges: . . . . **A**

Average Price PPPD: $403 plus airfare.
We'd opt for one of the five aft suites on Star Deck, which have their own private balconies. These category B quarters, built where the officers' quarters were previously, are a bit bigger than the standard cabins. A great bonus: private sunbathing or reading area away from the sometimes-crowded public decks. They have two lower beds, sitting area with sofa and chairs and plenty of storage space for a short cruise.

Suitable Standards: . . . . **B**

Average Price PPPD: $233 plus airfare.
If you don't mind a porthole instead of a window, you can save money by booking the cheapest outside double cabins, category I on B deck. They're the same size as the other standard cabins on board (around 150 square feet) with modular German-built bathrooms, two lower beds and plenty of storage space.

Bottom Bunks: . . . . **C**

Average Price PPPD: $150 plus airfare.
And that's literally the case with the cheapest digs aboard, the category Q insides with upper and lower bunks. The good part is, you're on Main Deck rather than down in the dungeons somewhere, and the cabin is attractively furnished and ever so slightly larger than some of the more expensive outside doubles across the hall.

INSIDER TIP

Check sailing dates in the brochure to find "value" or "economy" season sailings because prices are somewhat lower than peak season (summer) rates given above.

The Routes

The *Viking Serenade* sails from Los Angeles to Ensenada and back every Monday and Friday, calling at Catalina Island and San Diego on the four-day midweek cruises.

With a 6 p.m. Friday departure and an 8 a.m. Monday arrival it makes a good weekend getaway for southern Californians—so long as they remember to get aboard before 5:30 p.m. and realize they can't disembark until 9:30 or 10 a.m.

Sovereign of the Seas is almost three football fields long.

Crystal Symphony in Alaska

The *Viking Serenade* is handsome, the price is right, and if you've already done Ensenada, you can stay on board and enjoy the pool, spa and sundeck.

Five Hot Hot Hot Spots

1. The Sunshine Bar, the best singles' bar at sea, 50 feet long and dotted with comfortable barstools stretching almost the width of the vessel on the Sun Deck.

2. The Aida Dining Room with its Egyptian art, honey-colored burled wood and marble trim, smaller than the Magic Flute Dining Room one deck above.

3. The Viking Crown Lounge, a combination observation lounge and jazzy disco after dark, was prefabricated in a San Diego shipyard, lifted in one piece (all 144 tons of it) and carefully settled into its allotted space by the funnel during the massive renovation in 1991.

4. The Bali Hai Lounge, with its copper trim, etched glass panels and shiny surfaces, makes a dazzling cabaret and nightclub.

5. The children's playroom with its jumble of brightly colored plastic balls to dive into.

Five Good Reasons to Book This Ship

1. To take a weekend break without going to Las Vegas or Palm Springs.

2. To check out the best bodies as they parade between the swimming pool and the fitness center on Sun Deck.

3. It's the only way to get to Catalina Island, 22 miles across the sea (yes, we know the song says 26, but it's wrong) in peak season and still be assured you have a place to sleep. (Catalina is a port of call on four-day cruises only.)

4. The kids will love it—teenagers because there's a teen club with its own dance floor, DJ booth, video games and cola bar, younger kids for the playroom with pint-sized furniture in Crayola colors.

5. Because actress Whoopi Goldberg is the ship's godmother (she christened the vessel in L.A. in June 1991), and it carries on in her special blend of worldly wise humor and from-the-heart sentiment.

Five Things You Won't Find on Board

1. A car-carrying deck; that was removed in 1991.

2. A bunch of early-to-bed types.

3. Papageno in the Magic Flute Dining Room.

4. The wooden bust of Stan MacDonald that used to grace the Schooner Bar when it was called Stanley's Pub. (RCI sent it back to MacDonald after the renovation.)

5. A lot of empty deck space; every inch seems to be covered with tables, chairs or sun loungers.

VIKING SERENADE ★★★★

Registry	**Bahamas**
Officers	**Norwegian**
Crew	**International**
Complement	**320**
GRT	**40,132**
Length (ft.)	**623**
Beam (ft.)	**89**
Draft (ft.)	**24**
Passengers-Cabins Full	**1863**
Passengers-2/Cabin	**1512**
Passenger Space Ratio	**26.54**
Stability Rating	**Fair**
Seatings	**2**
Cuisine	**Themed**
Dress Code	**Traditional**
Room Service	**Yes**
Tip	**$7.50 PPPD. 15% automatically added to bar checks**

Ship Amenities

Outdoor Pool	**1**
Indoor Pool	**0**
Jacuzzi	**1**
Fitness Center	**Yes**
Spa	**No**
Beauty Shop	**Yes**
Showroom	**Yes**
Bars/Lounges	**5**
Casino	**Yes**
Shops	**3**
Library	**Yes**
Child Program	**Yes**
Self-Service Laundry	**No**
Elevators	**5**

Cabin Statistics

Suites	**8**
Outside Doubles	**478**
Inside Doubles	**278**
Wheelchair Cabins	**4**
Singles	**0**
Single Surcharge	**150%**
Verandas	**5**
110 Volt	**Yes**

Royal Olympic Cruises

One Rockefeller Plaza, Suite 315, New York, NY 10020-2090
☎ (212) 397-6400, (800) 872-6400
www.epirotiki.com

History . . . .

Two Greek-owned cruise lines, Sun Line and Epirotiki Cruises, merged to form a new cruise line called Royal Olympic Cruises.

The line operates as two separate divisions. The upscale division is called the Blue Ships and includes three ships, the 620-passenger *Stella Solaris*, the 300-passenger *Stella Oceanis* and the 400-passenger *Odysseus*. The popular-priced line, called the White Ships, includes the 670-passenger *Triton*, the 300-passenger *Orpheus* and the 900-passenger *Olympic*. The ships sail in the Greek Islands, Turkey, Egypt and Israel.

The remaining vessels in the combined fleet, which includes the *Stella Maris*, *Jason*, *Neptune* and *Argonaut*, are made available primarily for charter service in various geographical areas. Under the agreement, each company continues to own its own vessels.

THE WHITE WORLD OF

EPIROTIKI
Make our world your world

One Rockefeller Plaza, Suite 315, New York, NY 10020-2090
☎ (212) 397-6400, (800) 872-6400
www.epirotiki.com

History . . . .

The company that is today Epirotiki started in shipping some 150 years ago, and was named for the founding Potamianos family's village of Epirus in northwestern Greece. While the line offered some specialized passenger service in pre-World War II, mostly archeological expeditions, Greek Islands cruises didn't come into prominence until after the war. In postwar Greece, war reparations vessels from Italy and later U.S.

ROYAL OLYMPIC CRUISES

warships sold as scrap but rehabilitated in Greece as passenger vessels helped the Greek companies, including Epirotiki, rebuild their fleets to provide essential services along the coast and between the islands. In 1954 the *Semiramis* set out on the first scheduled tourist cruise in the Aegean for Epirotiki.

Over the years, in addition to operating a flourishing charter business, the company has owned, sold and lost countless ships, and even scrupulous record-keepers have trouble keeping track of Epirotiki's ships except those that bring particular notice to themselves—ships such as the *Oceanos* when it sank off South Africa in August 1991; the almost-unsinkable *Pegasus*, which, after going down once as the *Sundancer* in British Columbia in 1984, was burned and scuttled in Venice harbor in 1991, then was turned into a ferry before it went down for the third and final time; and the *Pallas Athena* (the former *CarlaCosta/Flandre*), which burned at the dock in Piraeus during a fire while under reconstruction in 1994, caused, insiders say, by rehearsing performers who left sound and electrical equipment plugged in when they went home for the night.

The ships mentioned in the Royal Olympic Cruises agreement include the *Odysseus*, which has joined the Sun Line Blue Ships, and the *Triton*, *Orpheus* and *Olympic*, which make up the Epirotiki White Ships. Three other longtime Epirotiki vessels—*Jason, Neptune* and *Argonaut*—will be made available for charter rather than scheduled sailings, along with Sun Line's lovely little *Stella Maris*.

Epirotiki also had previously entered into a marketing agreement with Carnival Cruise Corp. in 1994 that was terminated a year later by mutual agreement but resulted in Epirotiki's purchase, in effect, of two former Carnival ships: the *Carnivale*, which is now the *Olympic*, and the *Mardi Gras*, now the *Apollo*.

—Owns the oldest passenger ship still sailing for a major cruise company (*Argonaut*, built in 1929).

—Made the first-ever tourist cruise in the Aegean (*Semiramis*, 1954).

Concept. . . . .

Epirotiki sails vintage Greek-flag ships with Greek crews on affordable-to-budget fares around the Greek Islands, Mediterranean and beyond. The owners describe their three basic principles as "the right ship, the right cruise, the right itinerary."

Signatures . . . .

The distinctive logo, a gold Byzantine cross on a field of blue, can be seen in ports around the Mediterranean as well as other parts of the world.

Gimmicks. . . . .

Epirotiki traditionally has marketed cruise itineraries rather than ships, mixing and matching ships in home ports depending on what was operational or what might be going out under a lucrative charter contract.

ROYAL OLYMPIC CRUISES

Who's the Competition. . . . .

With the potential end of Greek cabotage laws in sight, the exclusive advantage the Greek companies had of being able to sail roundtrip cruises from Piraeus is weakened as more and more cruise lines sail into the Aegean. While regarded as a budget line, Epirotiki's per diems on the vessels it operates under Royal Olympic Cruises vie with some of the U.S.-based mainstream lines that are cruising the Mediterranean.

Who's Aboard . . . .

A lot of first-time cruisers and package travelers to Greece from all over Europe and North America have been the backbone of Epirotiki's passenger list, but it has fewer frequent repeat passengers than Sun Line. The line also attracts Latin Americans, Asians, Australians and South Africans.

Who Should Go . . . .

The same people that have gravitated to Sun Line in the past are the most likely to go with Royal Olympic's Blue Ships, and the Epirotiki veterans and price-conscious package travelers will probably continue to patronize the White Ships.

Who Should Not Go . . . .

With two different areas of style and service, the new company covers the waterfront of potential cruisers. Generally, Greek Islands, Turkey, Egypt and Israel sailings (which is what Royal Olympic seems to be concentrating on) are port-intensive and very tour and excursion oriented, perhaps not appropriate for families with small children.

The Lifestyle . . . .

Epirotiki's cruises follow a traditional Mediterranean cruise format, with numerous ports of call in the daytimes, shore excursions, two meal seatings, fairly casual dress code suggestions, five-language announcements and variety entertainment.

Wardrobe . . . .

Casual clothing is suggested for daytime, and since it can be very hot in summer on shore excursions, lightweight clothes and sun hats are recommended, along with sturdy walking shoes for negotiating ruins.

Epirotiki suggests that men wear a jacket and tie and women a cocktail dress for the captain's welcome aboard and farewell parties. Since both the ship and the tour buses are air-conditioned, you may want to bring along a sweater to take off the chill.

Bill of Fare C

The food aboard is Greek and Continental, served in generous portions. Because of busy days in port, the deck buffets are particularly popular for breakfasts and lunches. Flaming desserts, baked Alaska and gala buffets are usually on the agenda, along with simpler treats such as hot dogs and hamburgers, Greek salads and taverna dishes.

Showtime C

Because of the number of different languages spoken by the passengers, entertainment leans more to visual variety acts including magicians, musicians and dancers rather than aural performers such as comedians and ventriloquists. You can count on an evening (or two or three) of spirited Greek folk dancing along the lines of "Dance of the Wounded Sponge Diver." Classical concerts or recitals show up from time to time, and there's always dancing in the lounge or disco.

Discounts . . . .

Cruise-only fares and all-inclusive air/land/cruise packages are offered. Singles sail without supplemental charges on the *Orpheus* except in deluxe cabins.

The Bottom Line

We have had some cavalier service on Epirotiki ships from time to time—brusque waiters or bartenders—but we've also had very friendly, caring treatment at other times. The merger with Sun Line brings an upgraded hotel management plus an expansion of marketing in North America.

OLYMPIC

★★
OLYMPIC

We've been with her through three names now, and that doesn't go back to the beginning. While she seems to do very well in the Aegean, our favorite incarnation was the brief time she spent as the FiestaMarina, a niche line aimed at the Latin American market, with some of the best food we ever had at sea, created by the chefs of Miami's trendy neo-Cuban Yuca and New York's Patria. Problem was, the Latin Americans didn't like fusion Latin food—the Brazilians said it was Mexican, the Colombians thought it was Peruvian and everybody wanted surf-and-turf and beef Wellington "like they serve on the other Carnival ships." FiestaMarina went out of business not because it wasn't good enough, but because it was too good and ahead of its time.

The *Olympic* started life in 1956 as the *Empress of Britain*, built in Fairfield's Glasgow, Scotland, yard for London's Canadian Pacific line. In 1964, she was sold to the Greek Line to become the *Queen Anna Maria* and sailed for 10 years before being laid up in Piraeus in 1975. Later that year Ted Arison bought her for his Carnival Cruise Lines, sending a young Miami architect named Joe Farcus over to Greece to supervise a makeover. "I thought all cruise ships were white and sparkling and clean," Farcus remembers. "But you should have seen that rusty old tub lying there!" As the *Carnivale*, she sailed successfully for Carnival from 1976 until she was turned into the *FiestaMarina* in 1993. There are eight passenger decks, only four of them with cabins, on the *Olympic*, with a lot of sun-and-fun upper decks and a dining room and fitness club down on the lower decks.

Between The Lines

The Brochure Says
"...one of the largest ships ever to sail the Eastern Mediterranean."

Translation
The Potamianos family, who never liked large ships, calling them "monsters of the sea," is adjusting to larger vessels.

Cabins & Costs

Fantasy Suites: C

Average Price Per Person, Double Occupancy, Per Day: $330 plus airfare.
While not exactly a fantasy, there are five suites on the *Olympic*, four of them adequately roomy and the fifth one a bit smaller. A glass partition separates the sleeping and the sitting area, and there's a dresser, hanging closets, sofa/bed, two double beds, tub/shower combination, and some units have a separate water closet.

Small Splurges: C

Average Price PPPD: $298 plus airfare.
Category TA outside double cabins have twin beds, double dressers, hanging closets and a chair, plus a bath with tub and shower. A glass medicine cabinet in the bathroom provides additional toiletries storage.

Suitable Standards: C

Average Price PPPD: $262 plus airfare.
Some of the outside doubles on the Venus Deck are large and comfortable with two lower beds and bath with shower.

Bottom Bunks: . . . . D

Average Price PPPD: $185 plus airfare.
The eight-by-12-foot insides with upper and lower berths are the cheapest cabins on the vessel; in many, the washbasins are in the bedroom.

ROYAL OLYMPIC CRUISES

The Routes

The *Olympic* sails every Friday on three-day roundtrip cruises from Piraeus to Mykonos, Patmos, Kusadasi and Rhodes on the Aegean Hellenic itinerary, and every Monday on four-day roundtrip sailings from Piraeus to Mykonos, Kusadasi, Patmos, Rhodes, Heraklion and Santorini on the Aegean Classic itinerary. The season runs from April through November.

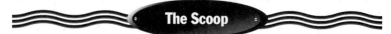

The Scoop

The *Olympic's* sleek ocean-liner figure makes her look less huge in the Eastern Mediterranean than if she were a boxy new vessel, so she doesn't necessary stand out as the largest ship in the fleet and one of the biggest in the Aegean. But doing the three- and four-day sailings does mean that's she needs more and better maintenance to keep from getting beat-up.

Insider Tips

Five Farcus Feats

1. The Nine Muses night club with its big curved bar and dance floor.
2. The Veranda, an enclosed promenade where you can sit and chat, write or read, wraps around the Hera Deck.
3. The Monte Carlo Casino was one of the hearts of the ship when it sailed for Carnival.
4. The former Salsa Plaza from FiestaMarina where the Latins danced until 4 a.m. has turned into the more sedate Horizon Lounge, but the piano bar next door still has that snazzy black-and-white tile checkerboard floor.
5. A children's pool and children's playroom on the top deck are separated by a length of promenade deck.

Five Good Reasons to Book These Ships

1. Her several stylish makeovers in this decade.
2. Her three- and four-day sailings from Piraeus, the three-day cruise calling in four ports, the four-day cruise calling in six ports. She's a new face in the Med.
3. She has a more comprehensive casino and lounges that most of the other Epirotiki ships.
4. There's more dedicated space for kids than on many Med cruisers.
5. There's an indoor swimming pool, gym, sauna, massage and fitness club.

Five Things You Won't Find On Board

1. A lifeguard working the indoor pool.
2. Any of that fantastic *FiestaMarina* Latin fusion food.
3. Your way to the fitness club without a lot of searching. Clue: Take the elevator down from the reception desk to the beauty salon, then walk down the stairs.
4. A way to watch the movie in the cinema without someone opening the door and whiting out the screen.
5. A view out of the dining room; the "windows" are photos of sunsets nicely framed and fitted around the walls.

OLYMPIC ★★

Registry	**Greece**
Officers	**Greek**
Crew	**Greek**
Complement	**550**
GRT	**31,500**
Length (ft.)	**640**
Beam (ft.)	**85**
Draft (ft.)	**29**
Passengers-Cabins Full	**1364**
Passengers-2/Cabin	**959**
Passenger Space Ratio	**32.85**
Stability Rating	**Good**
Seatings	**2**
Cuisine	**Continental/Greek**
Dress Code	**Traditional**
Room Service	**Yes**
Tip	**$6 - $8 PPPD**

Ship Amenities

Outdoor Pool	**2**
Indoor Pool	**1**
Jacuzzi	**1**
Fitness Center	**Yes**
Spa	**Yes**
Beauty Shop	**Yes**
Showroom	**Yes**
Bars/Lounges	**5**
Casino	**Yes**
Shops	**1**
Library	**Yes**
Child Program	**Yes**
Self-Service Laundry	**No**
Elevators	**2**

Cabin Statistics

Suites	**5**
Outside Doubles	**216**
Inside Doubles	**252**
Wheelchair Cabins	**0**
Singles	**13**
Single Surcharge	**150%**
Verandas	**0**
110 Volt	**Yes**

★ ★
ORPHEUS

*We stood at the rail of a ship in Piraeus one Monday morning in June 1985, and noted the names of the vessels as they sailed in—*Stella Solaris *and* Stella Oceanis *from Sun Line.* Galaxy *and* Constellation *from K-Line.* Cycladic's City of Rhodes *and* City of Mykonos. *And Epirotiki's* Jupiter, Atlas *and* Neptune, *all but* Neptune *gone now. The* Orpheus *was one of that family group.*

Chartered on a long-term basis with P & O's Swan Hellenic until the end of 1995, the *Orpheus* has been cherished and looked after for years by her devoted questers of knowledge and truth. Now, back in the fold with Epirotiki, she's part of Royal Olympic Cruises' White Ships, making Classic Aegean and Ionian Voyages every Saturday between May and October from Piraeus.

⋅ Between The Lines ⋅

The Brochure Says

"To honor the centennial anniversary of the modern Olympic Games held in Greece, Royal Olympic Cruises is pleased to present the Classical Aegean and Ionian Voyage, a seven-day exploration of the varied and beautiful lands of Greece."

Translation

It also goes to Albania.

DID YOU KNOW?

Women were not permitted to watch the original Olympic Games because all the male athletes competed naked.

Cabins & Costs

Fantasy Suites: . . . . **N/A**
N/A

Small Splurges: . . . . **C+**
Average Price Per Person, Double Occupancy, Per Day: $304 plus airfare.
The eight deluxe outside cabins boast two lower beds and a bathroom with tub and shower and some handsome wood-crafted dressers and nightstands, plus a desk, hassock, table and chair.

Suitable Standards: . . . . **C**
Average Price PPPD: $299 plus airfare.
Outside cabins with the choice of two lower beds or a double bed are the standard offerings on the *Orpheus;* there's only one of the latter.

Bottom Bunks: . . . . **D**
Average Price PPPD: $185 plus airfare.
Inside cabins with upper and lower berths are the lowest-priced accommodations on board. The bath has shower only. There are also some inside single-bed cabins available.

The Routes

The *Orpheus* makes a seven-day Classical Aegean and Ionian Voyage with some different ports of call from the rest of the White Ships—cruising the Corinth Canal, visiting Delphi; Ithaca; Saranda, Albania; Corfu; Katakolon; Zante; Rethymnon; Santorini; Mykonos; and Napflion, which is the gateway to Epidaurus and Mycenae. The ship sails every Saturday between May and October.

The Scoop

The cabins and public rooms are attractively furnished, and the ship was well taken care of during its long charter with Swan Hellenic. While the cabins are quite small, they're comfortable enough for the itinerary the ship is offering—you'll be ashore on a tour bus a lot of the time if you visit all the famous Greek sites you're offered.

Insider Tips

Five Easy Places

1. The swimming pool is surrounded by padded benches and loungers and, while not huge, is adequate to cool down a few people at a time.

2. A small taverna aft on the Venus Deck makes a casual spot to get together for a chat or a buffet breakfast, lunch or dinner.

3. The library gives a good read or a spot to admire the lovely Greek mythological murals on the walls.

4. The Apollo Pool Bar and overhead Solarium are laid-back spots to commune with nature.

ROYAL OLYMPIC CRUISES

5. The Lounge of the Muses is where after-dinner coffee is served and where you might be struck to turn out a poem or a sonata.

Five Good Reasons to Book This Ship

1. You could get an education by osmosis from the years of erudite lectures oozing from the walls.

2. There's a great sun deck and pool that could turn a scholar into a hedonist in no time flat.

3. You get to go to Albania—if only to note that you don't know why you ever wanted to go to Albania.

4. It's the only one of the White Ships that cruises the Corinth Canal.

5. You can visit the tomb of Agamemnon, the beaches at Rethymnon on Crete's northern coast and eat a fish soup called *Psarosoupa Avgholemono* in the wonderful waterfront seafood restaurants of Napflion, where the Lion of Venice still stares down from the walls.

Five Things You Won't Find On Board

1. An elevator.

2. TV sets in the cabin.

3. A fitness center.

4. A children's playroom.

5. Cabins designated wheelchair-accessible.

ORPHEUS ★★

Registry	**Greece**
Officers	**Greek**
Crew	**Greek**
Crew	**110**
GRT	**6000**
Length (ft.)	**364**
Beam (ft.)	**50**
Draft (ft.)	**15**
Passengers-Cabins Full	**316**
Passengers-2/Cabin	**308**
Passenger Space Ratio	**16.75**
Stability Rating	**Fair**
Seatings	**2**
Cuisine	**Continental/Greek**
Dress Code	**Traditional**
Room Service	**Yes**
Tip	**$6 - $8 PPPD**

Ship Amenities

Outdoor Pool	**1**
Indoor Pool	**0**
Jacuzzi	**4**
Fitness Center	**No**
Spa	**No**
Beauty Shop	**Yes**
Showroom	**Yes**
Bars/Lounges	**3**
Casino	**Yes**
Shops	**1**
Library	**Yes**
Child Program	**Yes**
Self-Service Laundry	**No**
Elevators	**0**

Cabin Statistics

Suites	**0**
Outside Doubles	**116**
Inside Doubles	**38**
Wheelchair Cabins	**0**
Singles	**0**
Single Surcharge	**150%**
Verandas	**0**
110 Volt	**Yes**

ROYAL OLYMPIC CRUISES

★★
TRITON

An English/Norwegian "Bahamarama boat" from Miami has hit the big time in the Mediterranean because of its wide teak decks and large swimming pool and standard (if narrow) cabins that don't carom back and forth in all shapes and sizes but are fitted together neatly in an orderly fashion and have beds that can be changed in a whisk from twins to queen-sized. Triton himself was the son of Poseidon and Amphitrite, a demon of the sea with a fish tail. He serves as a helpmate on a good journey, which is sort of what Triton can do for you.

The former *Sunward II* from Norwegian Cruise Line, the *Cunard Adventurer* before that (1971–1976), has settled happily into the Aegean sunshine as Epirotiki's *Triton* since the ship debuted for the Greek line in 1992. With seven passenger decks, five of them containing some cabins, the vessel has a large swimming pool, some public rooms on the two topmost decks and two-seating dining. Lighter and brighter than many of the vintage vessels plying the Med, the *Triton* has easily adaptable cabins in which most allow twin beds to be put together instantly to make a queen-sized bed instead.

Between The Lines

The Brochure Says

"Epiotiki's ships are an ideal size for cruising the Greek islands. With a maximum of 900 passengers, you won't feel lost in the crowd—and the islands you visit won't feel overcrowded."

Translation

Finally, she gets a little respect, and it's about time. Her Greek owners obviously dote on her. When she was NCL's *Sunward II*, she did the Bahamarama mini-cruise run and was the smallest ship in the fleet. Now she's one of the biggest.

Cabins & Costs

Fantasy Suites: . . . . **N/A**
N/A

Small Splurges: . . . . **C**
Average Price Per Person, Double Occupancy, Per Day: $313 plus airfare.
The largest cabins on board are the outside doubles on the Apollo Deck, about 13 by 17 feet, with twin or queen-sized beds, bathroom with tub, a small sitting area, dresser and nightstands.

Suitable Standards: . . . . **D**
Average Price PPPD: $293 plus airfare.
Standard outside doubles have two lower beds that in most cases can be combined into a queen sized bed, plus a chair, desk/dresser with stool, nightstand with drawers and bathroom with shower. These rooms are quite narrow.

Bottom Bunks: . . . . **D**
Average Price PPPD: $185 plus airfare.
The lowest-priced cabins are the inside doubles with two lower beds that can be put together for a queen-sized bed; these are almost identical to the outsides (see "Suitable Standards," above) except without a window or porthole.

The Routes

The *Triton* sails the Golden Fleece Route for the White Ships division of Royal Olympic, departing Piraeus on Friday and calling in Santorini, Heraklion, Rhodes, Patmos, Kusadasi, Istanbul, Delos and Mykonos. The season begins in March and ends in November.

The Scoop

The *Triton* is a surprisingly sleek-looking ship with an interesting itinerary for a destination-oriented traveler, perhaps someone making a first visit to the Eastern Mediterranean. Cabins are fairly small but attractively furnished, and the pool and deck areas are expansive. We'd love to hear a comment from former owners NCL about her average per diem cruise-only prices in the Med, however, compared to what they were in the Caribbean (clue: much, much cheaper in the Caribbean).

Insider Tips

Five Sensational Places

1. A great pool deck has an oval pool with tile surround and a curved teak deck filled with sun loungers.
2. The Nine Muses Nightclub has panoramic windows opening forward to the sea, the same view the navigation bridge has, only higher up.
3. A light and bright dining room makes a contrast to some of Epirotiki's below-decks windowless restaurants.

ROYAL OLYMPIC CRUISES

4. A full casino, operated by Casinos Austria, with discreetly patterned decor and small bar at one end.

5. The Nefeli Bar, a covered outdoor bar amidships on an upper deck with a big overhead awning for when you realize you're getting too much sun and want something cold to drink.

Five Good Reasons to Book This Ship

1. There's an around-the-ship jogging track, rarer than hen's teeth in the Aegean.

2. Her seven-day Golden Fleece itinerary that calls in seven ports in Greece and Turkey.

3. She's a bigger star in the Eastern Med than she was in Miami.

4. A friendly Greek staff who'd like to show you their Mediterranean.

5. To have an evening and all the next day in Istanbul to negotiate the purchase of a Turkish carpet.

Five Things You Won't Find On Board

1. A library.

2. Good sightlines in the Sirenes show lounge; but then it's pretty small, so you might not find a seat anyhow.

3. A self-service laundry.

4. Assigned seating at breakfast and lunch; only dinners have assigned tables and times.

5. A smoking section at meals; the White Ships have been designated entirely non-smoking in the dining rooms.

TRITON ★★

Registry	Greece
Officers	Greek
Crew	Greek
Complement	315
GRT	14,110
Length (ft.)	486
Beam (ft.)	70.5
Draft (ft.)	21
Passengers-Cabins Full	912
Passengers-2/Cabin	706
Passenger Space Ratio	19.83
Stability Rating	Fair
Seatings	2
Cuisine	Continental/Greek
Dress Code	Traditional
Room Service	Yes
Tip	$6 - $8 PPPD

Ship Amenities

Outdoor Pool	1
Indoor Pool	0
Jacuzzi	0
Fitness Center	Yes
Spa	No
Beauty Shop	Yes
Showroom	Yes
Bars/Lounges	4
Casino	Yes
Shops	1
Library	Yes
Child Program	Yes
Self-Service Laundry	No
Elevators	2

Cabin Statistics

Suites	30
Outside Doubles	206
Inside Doubles	117
Wheelchair Cabins	0
Singles	0
Single Surcharge	150%
Verandas	0
110 Volt	Yes

SUN LINE CRUISES

One Rockefeller Plaza, Suite 315, New York, NY 10020-2090
☎ *(212) 397-6400, (800) 872-6400*

History. . . . .

Sun Line was founded by the late Ch. (Charalambos) A. Keusseoglou in 1957, after he had been a co-founder and former executive vice president of now-defunct Home Lines. Keusseoglou had been in the shipping industry since he left the Greek Army in 1947, going first to Sweden to work with Swedish American Line, then becoming one of the founders of Home Lines later that same year, along with Swedish American Line and Greek interests. He worked with Home Lines until after the acquisition of his first vessel for Sun, a Canadian frigate he turned into the yacht-like *Stella Maris I* in 1959. This ship was followed by the *Stella Solaris I*, then in 1963 the present *Stella Maris* replaced the original and four years later the *Stella Oceanis* was added to the fleet to replace the *Stella Solaris I*. In 1973, the flagship *Stella Solaris* was put into service, bringing the fleet to its present three ships.

The Marriott Corp. acquired an interest in Sun Line in 1971, but the family purchased back those shares in 1987.

Isabella Keusseoglou from the beginning has taken the responsibility for decorating the line's ships and hiring the cruise staff and entertainers, and with her sons and daughter in key executive positions, has overseen the operation of the cruise line since her husband's death in 1984.

In August 1995, Mrs. Keusseoglou, with George Potamianos of Epirotiki Cruises, made a joint announcement of the merger of the two companies into a new cruise line to be called Royal Olympic Cruises. Two of the three Sun Line ships compose two-thirds of the upscale Blue Ships division of the new company, while the third, the little *Stella Maris*, is available for charter under the auspices of the new line. The New York marketing offices remain in the Sun Line quarters in Rockefeller Plaza, while operations are headquartered in Epirotiki's Piraeus offices.

Concept. . . . .

To create itineraries to take passengers to "the unusual and the unexpected," with destinations in Greece and Turkey, the Caribbean and

South America, and the services of a warm, loyal Greek crew, many of whom have been with the line for years.

Signatures

"Luxury Cruises in the Exotic Zone," with winter sailings up the Amazon and into the Yucatan, timed to coincide with special events from Carnival in Trinidad to the Maya Equinox at Chichen Itza.

Gimmicks

The hot homemade potato chips served in the Bar Grill room on the *Stella Solaris* keep passengers like us coming back.

Who's the Competition

Under the merger with Epirotiki, this pair of Greek lines performs very solidly in the Aegean, at least until the Greek version of the Jones Act is eroded in 1998 because of demands from European Community members who would like to see their ships be able to make roundtrip cruises out of Piraeus. Orient Lines' *Marco Polo*, the surprise entry in the Mediterranean, at about the same size and a slightly lower price range than the *Stella Solaris*, must have been competition in 1996, to judge from the noisy demonstrations against that ship in Pireaus by the Greek seamen's union, who wanted Orient's Filipino crew replaced with Greeks.

Who's Aboard

The *Stella Solaris* appeals mainly to older, more experienced cruise passengers, many of them frequent travelers with the line. Sometimes 45 percent of the passengers aboard are repeaters. Young couples and singles, particularly in the Greek Islands, like all three ships.

Who Should Go

The new line's division between Blue and White Ships broadens the market base for both Sun and Epirotiki and reaches more of the land tour travelers to the Aegean, including more young singles, couples and families.

Who Should Not Go

Any curmudgeon who won't join in the Greek dancing on Greek Night.

The Lifestyle

The Greek Islands and Turkey itinerary on Sun Line ships is the perfect answer for people who worry that "there's nothing to do" on a cruise. With its port-intensive itinerary, onboard lecturers and land guides, it's the most information-packed trip imaginable, so long as your stamina and curiosity hold up.

"I'd never book honeymooners on this cruise," one American travel agent sighed after a morning tour in Delos and an afternoon in Mykonos.

Passengers are a cosmopolitan lot, particularly in Greece, but language groups are sorted out and multilingual guides travel with each group. Social hosts accompany many of the cruises aboard the *Stella Solaris* in winter, when there are more days at sea and an older clientele aboard.

Wardrobe. . . . .

Both the Aegean and the South American cruises are casual by day, somewhat dressy by evening. The line suggests that on formal nights men wear dark suits or tuxedos and women gowns, cocktail dresses or dressy pantsuits. On informal nights, men are expected to wear suits or jacket and tie, while women are requested to don dresses, skirts or pantsuits. Casual evenings call for slacks and sportshirts for men, similar attire for women. There are usually two formal nights, one informal night and four casual nights during a seven-night cruise. Laundry and pressing services are available on board but there is no dry cleaning.

Bill of Fare. . . . . B

While the food is variable, depending on the chef aboard, the Greek dishes are always uniformly delicious, and we've found the deck buffets tasty as well.

The chief steward, if alerted the day before, can arrange a light cuisine or special-order meal. Dinners usually provide three main dish choices, fish, fowl and meat, plus light or vegetarian fare, and a passenger can always order broiled chicken or grilled steak on the spot if nothing on the menu seems appealing. All breads and desserts are made on board. The hot homemade potato chips and the thick, creamy homemade yogurt are two of our favorite treats.

An appealing deck buffet offers Greek salad, cold meats, hamburgers, moussaka, batter-dipped fried zucchini, fruit and cheese, in case you want to get an early start on an afternoon ashore.

Showtime. . . . . B

Mrs. Keusseoglou usually selects both the cruise staff and the entertainers who work on board and tends to keep certain passenger favorites over the long haul, including the charming and talented Caesar, a cocktail pianist. During our several cruises aboard, we've seen every sort of entertainment from the infamous Mr. Blackwell doing wildly popular fashion makeovers for volunteers from the audience to a dance team so exquisitely untalented they could bring back Velez and Yolanda. Magicians, ventriloquists and other variety artists are usually aboard, along with some really gifted performers such as jazz artists Steve and Bonnie Cole.

Discounts . . . .

Early booking discounts from 10 to 50 percent, depending on itinerary and departure date, are offered.

The Bottom Line

The Sun Line ships are well-suited to the Royal Olympic venture, and the marketing clout of the combination is good for both companies. We would like to think the Blue Ships reflect the careful, warm and fastidious service so typical of Sun for all these years.

★★★
ODYSSEUS

A ship anchored off Santorini is actually in the deep blue waters of the caldera itself and the island, thought by some to be the remnants of the lost continent of Atlantis, is the core of the volcano. We clambered up and down all over the town trying to get a photograph of the ship against the backlit sea, finally settling instead for stark white buildings with patches of vivid red, blue and yellow flowers. Late in the afternoon, as the wind grew fiercer and colder, we walked to the edge of the stone terrace that surrounded the cathedral to look at the other side of the island, and found ourselves backstage in the real Santorini, where a gaggle of tourist buses were parked and heavy traffic was bumper-to-bumper along the roadway that connects the small towns of the island. Our fantasies of a rugged remote island with no vehicles but donkeys and funiculars were dashed forever.

The former *Aquamarine* (only the last of many of her names), built in 1962, was virtually rebuilt when acquired by Epirotiki in 1988. When she made her debut in the spring of 1989, owner George Potamianos praised her extra-large cabins, 90 percent of them outside, and called her deck areas "for a ship of her size more ample than any ship afloat." Cabins are located on five of the seven passenger decks, awkwardly divided on the lowest of them, where neither forward nor aft sections has elevator service. The topmost deck is given over to exercise, beauty salon treatments, massage and sauna, with a large solarium aft and an observation deck forward. The primary public room deck is the Jupiter deck, with a main lounge forward, a cocktail lounge, casino, library, card room and nightclub amidships, and a pool and deck area aft.

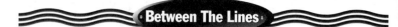

The Brochure Says

"Nearly every day brings a new island or city to explore."

Translation

These are port-intensive cruises with a number of optional shore excursions.

Cabins & Costs

Fantasy Suites: .... **B**

Average Price Per Person, Double Occupancy, Per Day: $345 plus airfare.
The top pair of suites on board are the two forward on the Apollo Deck with corner sofas, a chair, coffee table, double bed, dresser, lots of closet space, a bathroom with tub and shower and four windows in a 17-by-20-foot space.

Small Splurges: .... **C**

Average Price PPPD: $318 plus airfare.
Next best are a row of a dozen cabins measuring roughly 17-by-12, with three lower beds, nightstands with drawers, four hanging closet areas and a bathroom with shower only.

Suitable Standards: .... **C**

Average Price PPPD: $285 plus airfare.
They're getting smaller, folks. While configurations vary, outside double cabins range from 10-by-12 to 12-by-15 feet, but all are attractively furnished with two lower beds or a double bed, bath with shower and some closet hanging space.

Bottom Bunks: .... **D**

Average Price PPPD: $198 plus airfare.
The very tiniest are a handful of outside cabins with upper and lower berths scattered around on several decks; these have bath with shower.

The Routes

The *Odysseus* moves to the Baltic for a series of 12-day round-trip cruises from London calling at Copenhagen, Stockholm, Helsinki, St. Petersburg, Roenne and Hamburg during July and August. Positioning cruises of 12- and 14-day European and Mediterranean cruises flank the season. In spring and fall the ship makes three- and four-day cruises from Piraeus. In the winter of 1997–98, the ship is positioned in South America with Rio/Buenos Aires sailings, followed by Strait of Magellan itineraries between Buenos Aires and Puerto Montt and Cape Horn/Falklands cruises from Buenos Aires around the Horn.

The Scoop

Much depends on the latest renovations. The vessel is in fairly good shape from its last refurbishing. Cabins are attractively furnished although some of those on the lower decks run on the small side. Eleven of them are marketed as singles, and the line says there are some wheelchair-accessible cabins available, although we've never seen them. That may be part of the most recent refit. Certainly, under Sun Line operation the *Odysseus* comes up a notch or two.

Five Special Spots

1. The Solarium, a sheltered sun trap for serious basking on Kronos Deck aft.
2. The Trojan Horse is a cozy nightclub with bar just off the pool deck near the library.
3. The Sirenes, a large main lounge with wood parquet dance floor and tub chairs, has a charming semi-circular bar with swivel stools at one end.
4. A buffet restaurant called Ulysses Marine Club located aft of the dining room also doubles as a video and film room.
5. The top deck fitness and beauty area boasts a sauna, massage room, gymnasium, beauty salon and fitness club.

Five Good Reasons to Book This Ship

1. To see how it matches up with Sun's *Stella Solaris* in the Blue Ships fleet.
2. To set out on port-intensive three- or four-day cruises to the Greek Islands and Turkey, hitting four ports in three days or six ports in four days.
3. To snuggle into that Solarium on a breezy fall day in the Aegean.
4. To luxuriate around the pool on that lovely teak deck.
5. To splurge on a suite with lots of windows.

Five Things You Won't Find On Board

1. A private veranda.
2. A self-service laundry.
3. A single-meal seating.
4. Elevator service to all the passenger cabin decks; it stops short of the Poseidon deck.
5. A paucity of deck lounging chair space; there's plenty.

ODYSSEUS ★★★

Registry	**Greece**
Officers	**Greek**
Crew	**Greek**
GRT	**12,000**
Length (ft.)	**483**
Beam (ft.)	**61**
Draft (ft.)	**22**
Crew	**200**
Passengers-Cabins Full	**486**
Passengers-2/Cabin	**452**
Passenger Space Ratio	**22.12**
Stability Rating	**Good**
Seatings	**2**
Cuisine	**Continental/Greek**
Dress Code	**Traditional**
Room Service	**Yes**
Tip	**$6–$8 PPPD**

Ship Amenities

Outdoor Pool	**1**
Indoor Pool	**0**
Jacuzzi	**4**
Fitness Center	**Yes**
Spa	**Yes**
Beauty Shop	**Yes**
Showroom	**Yes**
Bars/Lounges	**4**
Casino	**Yes**
Shops	**1**
Library	**Yes**
Child Program	**Yes**
Self-Service Laundry	**No**
Elevators	**1**

Cabin Statistics

Suites	**14**
Outside Doubles	**168**
Inside Doubles	**38**
Wheelchair Cabins	**0**
Singles	**11**
Single Surcharge	**150%**
Verandas	**0**
110 Volt	**Yes**

★★★
STELLA OCEANIS

Our favorite thing, more than browsing through the vegetable market or sitting at one of the seafood cafes of Mikrolimano, is to stand at the rail of a passenger vessel sailing in or out of the port of Piraeus looking at all the ships and deciphering the Greek letters—ships you'd forgotten existed, ships that used to be somebody, ships that only an owner could love. One thing Piraeus has plenty of is ships.

With cabins on four of the six passenger decks, the *Stella Oceanis* has only one real public deck, the Oceanis Deck, with the dining room forward and the main lounge aft. One deck up on the Lido Deck is the popular Plaka Taverna with its wood paneling and nautical accents. The Sun Deck and pool are large enough for most of the passengers to get in some sunning and swimming between island tours.

Between The Lines

The Brochure Says

"In June, July and August, the *Stella Oceanis* will sail on 12-day alternating itineraries between Athens and Rome exploring the roots of Western Civilization."

Translation

This is a destination-oriented cruise, and you'll have plenty of time ashore with your guides to ponder the mystery of it all.

Cabins & Costs

Fantasy Suites: . . . . **C**

Average Price Per Person, Double Occupancy, Per Day: $371 plus airfare.

There are 10 accommodations designated as suites on board, two of them amidships on the Stella Deck, the remainder aft on the Lido Deck. Each has two lower beds, two chairs, a coffee table and a bathroom with tub and shower.

Small Splurges: C

Average Price PPPD: $330 plus airfare.

Two categories of deluxe cabins line the Pelagos Deck, varying a bit in size. Each has two sofa/beds with dresser, smaller table and stool, chair and two portholes, plus a tile bathroom with tub.

Suitable Standards: C

Average Price PPPD: $299 plus airfare.

Most standard outside doubles have two lower beds, small tile bath with corner shower, built-in desk and dresser, and two small individual closets with good hanging space. In some of them, one bed folds up during the daytime to make more floor space. Some have third and fourth upper berths as well.

Bottom Bunks: .... D

Average Price PPPD: $193 plus airfare.

The cheapest quarters aboard, suitable for students on a generous budget, perhaps, are quite small, with upper and lower berths and tiny baths with shower only. The two lowest passenger decks provide small, chopped-up accommodations.

The Routes

The *Stella Oceanis* makes a series of 12-day cruises between Athens and Rome calling at Istanbul, Kusadasi, Rhodes, Heraklion, Malta, Messina and Salerno during the summer. Spring and fall offer 7-day cruises to the Middle East and Greek Islands. Three- and four-day cruises are available as well.

The Scoop

The least glamorous of Sun Line's three vessels, *Stella Oceanis* nevertheless has sleeker external lines than her smaller sister *Stella Maris* and draws the youngest crowds on Greek Islands land/sea packages in summer. The ship is kept spotlessly clean, and the decking always seems to be in good shape. Still, the cheaper cabins are quite small and halls in the lower passenger decks narrow. The seven-day itinerary that visits Cairo and Jerusalem as well as Turkey and the Greek Islands is a good introduction to the area for first-time visitors.

Insider Tips

Five Favorite Places

1. The Minos Salon is decorated with murals of Greek mythology and plush furniture in autumnal shades, plus a bar with four barstools and a dance floor.

2. In the Aphrodite Restaurant, tables seat four, five or six; windows are large and let in light but the ceiling is awfully low.

3. The swimming pool is fairly large for a ship this size, and surrounded with teak decking and dark brown and blue lounge chairs. The deck buffet is served here, and just inside is a cozy bar.

4. The popular Plaka Taverna is a cozy bar that doubles as disco, decorated in nautical theme with a ship's wheel, rope knots and figurehead.

5. The Club, a tiny cardroom tucked away aft beyond the Minos Salon, makes a good hideaway when the world is too much with you.

Five Good Reasons to Book This Ship

1. To visit Cairo, Jerusalem and Ephesus plus three Greek islands, all in a week.

2. The warmth and friendliness of the Greek crew.

3. The expanse of pool and sun deck for R&R between must-see monuments.

4. To learn Greek—as well as a smattering of the other four or five languages you'll hear during public announcements.

5. To have a Greek salad for lunch every day.

Five Things You Won't Find On Board

1. A children's program.

2. 110-volt electrical current.

3. Cabins designated wheelchair-accessible.

4. A full-fledged casino, although there are slot machines.

5. A gym or fitness center.

STELLA OCEANIS ★★★

Registry	Greece
Officers	Greek
Crew	Greek
Complement	150
GRT	5500
Length (ft.)	350
Beam (ft.)	53
Draft (ft.)	17
Passengers-Cabins Full	369
Passengers-2/Cabin	300
Passenger Space Ratio	18
Stability Rating	Good
Seatings	2
Cuisine	Continental/Greek
Dress Code	Traditional
Room Service	Yes
Tip	$9 PPPD

Ship Amenities

Outdoor Pool	1
Indoor Pool	0
Jacuzzi	0
Fitness Center	Yes
Spa	No
Beauty Shop	No
Showroom	No
Bars/Lounges	3
Casino	No
Shops	1
Library	Yes
Child Program	No
Self-Service Laundry	No
Elevators	1

Cabin Statistics

Suites	10
Outside Doubles	103
Inside Doubles	46
Wheelchair Cabins	0
Singles	0
Single Surcharge	125–200%
Verandas	0
110 Volt	No

★ ★ ★

STELLA SOLARIS

It's hard to imagine anything more romantic than a balmy evening at midnight standing at the rail of the Stella Solaris *with moonlight rippling on the Aegean Sea. Even the captain had fallen in love with one of his American passengers during one of these Greek Islands cruises and later got married aboard his own ship. Yes, these week-long sailings are exhausting, exciting, exotic, fulfilling and hectic—and they're also very, very romantic.*

The largest of the three Sun Line ships is *Stella Solaris*, built in 1959 as the *Stella V*, then the *Camboge*, with eight passenger decks and a great expanse of teak decks aft. The topmost Lido deck is where you'll find the swimming pools, sunbathing loungers and Lido Bar. Down one deck from here are the suites, with a full around-the-ship promenade deck outside and a small reading and card room aft that doubles as a meetings venue. The main public lounges are on the Solaris Deck, with the dining room and galley forward, a couple of bars, the lobby and purser's desk amidships, and the main lounge and a piano bar aft. Below are cabins, plus a cinema, gym, beauty shop, disco and hospital.

The ship's 2600-square-foot Daphne Spa has a full menu of beauty and health treatments that can be booked ahead of sailing individually or in a package.

The Brochure Says

"Our Greek officers and crew are experts when it comes to welcoming you on board in the true tradition of Greek hospitality."

Translation

The new merger of Sun and Epirotiki becomes the largest Greek cruise company, Royal Olympic Cruises, who have taken the blue and white of the Greek flag as their colors and it will set you sailing with that wonderful crew.

INSIDER TIP

Better take those free Greek dancing lessons when they're offered, because on Greek night, you can count on being whirled out on the floor by an enthusiastic crew member.

DID YOU KNOW?

Celebrity passengers aboard Stella Solaris *have included Cary Grant, Rock Hudson, Jimmy and Rosalyn Carter, Eva Marie Saint and Ernest Borgnine, in whose honor the staff screened* The Poseidon Adventure.

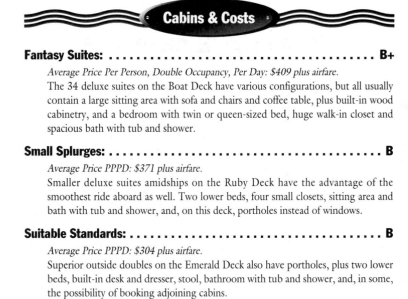

Cabins & Costs

Fantasy Suites: .... B+

Average Price Per Person, Double Occupancy, Per Day: $409 plus airfare.
The 34 deluxe suites on the Boat Deck have various configurations, but all usually contain a large sitting area with sofa and chairs and coffee table, plus built-in wood cabinetry, and a bedroom with twin or queen-sized bed, huge walk-in closet and spacious bath with tub and shower.

Small Splurges: .... B

Average Price PPPD: $371 plus airfare.
Smaller deluxe suites amidships on the Ruby Deck have the advantage of the smoothest ride aboard as well. Two lower beds, four small closets, sitting area and bath with tub and shower, and, on this deck, portholes instead of windows.

Suitable Standards: .... B

Average Price PPPD: $304 plus airfare.
Superior outside doubles on the Emerald Deck also have portholes, plus two lower beds, built-in desk and dresser, stool, bathroom with tub and shower, and, in some, the possibility of booking adjoining cabins.

Bottom Bunks: .... D

Average Price PPPD: $193 plus airfare.
The least expensive digs are the category 11 inside cabins on the Sapphire Deck, which do not have elevator access; you have to walk down from the elevator on the deck above. These cabins are small with upper and lower berths and bath with shower only.

EAVESDROPPING

Captain Michael Benas, for many years master of the Stella Solaris, *when asked about passengers fraternizing with crew, chuckled, "When we miss a passenger, we call the crew cabins."*

The Routes

The *Stella Solaris* has a variety of seven- and 14-day cruises from Piraeus along with the 21-day combination Voyage of Discovery calling at Mykonos, Istanbul, Nessebur, Odessa, Yalta, Kos, Alexandria, Port Said, Alexandria, Ashdod, Limassol, Santorini, Heraklion, Santorini, Rhodes, Patmos, Kusadasi and Dikili. In winter, the *Stella Solaris* sails the Caribbean, Amazon and Brazilian Coast, with a special Feb. 26 solar eclipse cruise.

The Scoop

With a deep 28-foot draft and steam turbine engines, the *Stella Solaris* offers a very smooth ride. Safety procedures get high marks as well, with a thorough boat drill that includes lowering the launches in front of the passengers at each boat station. One of the main assets of this ship is also one of its problems—the Greek dining room stewards who have been here forever sometimes get more involved in the logistics of "Head 'em up, move 'em out" on open seatings than is appropriate with a ship of this class. Bear in mind, too, that the *Stella Solaris* is one of those ships that changes personality by season. The longer winter voyages attract older, more affluent passengers than the seven-day summer sailings. Some of the winter passengers come back every year, stay onboard 40 or 45 days and may not get off the ship in ports they've seen before. "They don't care where the ship goes," said one longtime staffer, "they want to travel with their favorite steward."

We do, however, have to point out that we recently have received some letters of complaint about Stella Solaris, notably regarding outdated decor, the minimal gym facilities, abrupt waiter service and a rough ride in normal seas. Until we sail again (on a date after this edition goes to press) we have downgraded the vessel to a three-star rating.

Insider Tips

Five Familiar Places

1. The Grill Room Bar with its classic dark leather sofas and chairs, its horseshoe-shaped bar and clubby New York ambience, is one of our favorite spots at sea.

2. The Solaris Lounge is divided from the Piano Bar by an open sculpture wall and furnished with gold plush chairs and patterned plush banquettes, plus raised seating levels around the sides of the room facing the dance floor and stage.

3. Teatime takes place in the Piano Bar with a pianist playing pop and show tunes as waiters serve tea and cookies. A long, low bar with wide view windows behind it offers a great view of the sea.

4. The pool deck has two overlapping oval pools surrounded by a sunning platform, umbrella-covered tables and sun loungers.

5. The dining room with its wide windows lets you watch the scenery while you're cruising, or you can puzzle over the murals of legends and heroes decorating the walls.

Five Good Reasons to Book This Ship

1. Because the same Greek waiters, stewards and bartenders seem to have been here forever.

2. Because the ship never feels crowded, even when it's full.

3. For unique special event cruises such as the Maya Equinox Cruise, when passengers visit the El Castillo Pyramid in Chichen Itza for the vernal equinox, when the setting sun makes a pattern of seven triangles, one appearing at a time, along the north face of the temple, depicting the mystic descent of the "feathered serpent" that illustrates the arrival of the Maya god Kukulkan on Earth.

4. To take a seven-day crash course in Greek history and culture.

5. To socialize with some of Sun's celebrity passengers.

Five Things You Won't Find On Board

1. TV sets in most of the cabins except suites.

2. A program for children.

3. A chance to sit where you want to at open seating breakfasts and lunches, when the waiters rush you into whatever empty space is up.

4. Plenty of soundproofing between cabins; many allow eavesdropping through the walls.

5. A wheelchair-accessible cabin.

STELLA SOLARIS ★★★

Registry	**Greece**
Officers	**Greek**
Crew	**Greek**
Complement	**310**
GRT	**18,000**
Length (ft.)	**544**
Beam (ft.)	**72**
Draft (ft.)	**28.5**
Passengers-Cabins Full	**700**
Passengers-2/Cabin	**620**
Passenger Space Ratio	**29**
Stability Rating	**Fair**
Seatings	**2**
Cuisine	**Continental/Greek**
Dress Code	**Traditional**
Room Service	**Yes**
Tip	**$9 PPPD**

Ship Amenities

Outdoor Pool	**2**
Indoor Pool	**0**
Jacuzzi	**0**
Fitness Center	**Yes**
Spa	**Yes**
Beauty Shop	**Yes**
Showroom	**Yes**
Bars/Lounges	**4**
Casino	**Yes**
Shops	**2**
Library	**Yes**
Child Program	**No**
Self-Service Laundry	**No**
Elevators	**3**

Cabin Statistics

Suites	**66**
Outside Doubles	**166**
Inside Doubles	**58**
Wheelchair Cabins	**0**
Singles	**0**
Single Surcharge	**125–200%**
Verandas	**0**
110 Volt	**No**

ROYAL OLYMPIC CRUISES

ROYAL OLYMPIC CRUISES

Saga Holidays™

222 Berkeley Street, Boston, MA 02116
☎ *(617) 262-2262, (800) 952-9590*

U.K.-based Saga Holidays, with offices in the U.S., Britain and Australia, targets the mature traveler—which Saga defines at 50 years plus—looking for high quality travel at affordable prices. They say the *Saga Rose* is the only ship dedicated exclusively for passengers over 50. They sell the ship directly to passengers through phone and mail order rather than utilizing travel agents, and the package includes roundtrip airfare, transfers, gratuities, medical and baggage insurance and all port taxes. With a season of tempting northern European sailings in summer plus an around-the-world cruise in winter, the new *Saga Rose* should perform well for her previous Cunard passengers in addition to new fans.

SAGA INTERNATIONAL HOLIDAYS LTD.

★★★★
SAGA ROSE

We cherish many wonderful memories from the former Sagafjord over the years, particularly of sitting in warm Alaska sunshine while enjoying the fantastic Bavarian Brunch of sausages, roast suckling pig and sauerkraut, accompanied by aquavit and beer. When the ship was retired by Cunard a couple of years ago, we worried about what would become of her, but are delighted that a travel company whose slogan is "We give mature travelers the world" have not only purchased her and renamed her Saga Rose, but are such proud owners that they spell out "the former Sagafjord" so that all her former passengers know they can sail with her once more.

This classy vintage ship offers a comfortable but elegant atmosphere with a high passenger space ratio and some very attractive suites with verandas for fresh air fiends. Singles will be pleased to find so many cabins designated for them without the horrendous surcharges many ships make. While it takes a spirit of adventure to find the Polaris nightclub, an addition in one of her many previous renovations, the ship is generally very easy to find your way around. Most of the public rooms are on a single deck, with the dining room two decks below and the nightclub (clue: it has its own elevator) one and two decks above.

The lounge is a great place to strike up conversations with fellow passengers.

SAGA INTERNATIONAL HOLIDAYS LTD.

Between The Lines

The Brochure Says

"With our many years of experience offering cruise holidays, and the growing popularity of cruising among our customers, we felt the time was right to buy our own cruise ship."

Translation

That's a good idea, one we're very glad you had.

Cabins & Costs

Fantasy Suites: . . . .**A**

Average Price Per Person, Double Occupancy, Per Day: $717 including airfare.

The Vista Suite and the Sage Suite face forward on the Terraced Sun Deck for a captain's-eye view of the sea. The handsomely furnished quarters offer both space and privacy. Slightly less expensive are the adjacent suites with private verandas and bathrooms with tub and shower.

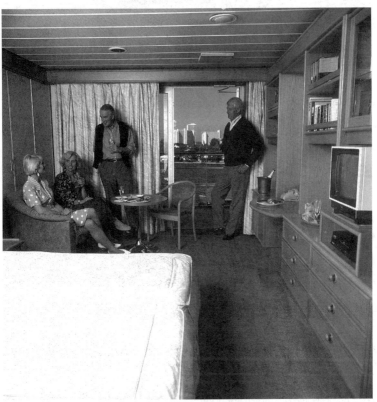

Suites and some Category A cabins offer views and spacious sitting areas.

Small Splurges: . . . . **A**
> *Average Price PPPD: $399 including airfare.*
> The Category A cabins on Terraced Officers Deck are almost as big and posh as those above, with private verandas, sitting areas and separate bedrooms with twin or king-sized bed, large closets and bathroom with tub.

Suitable Standards: . . . . **B+**
> *Average Price PPPD: $315 including airfare.*
> All the outside doubles are fairly comparable in size and furnishings, with the prices determined by deck location. The lowest category outside double is H on Main Deck; most have tub and shower, but a few have shower only. You'll find two lower beds, desk/dresser and generous storage closets. A number of outside and inside single cabins are available, and 12 are designated wheelchair-accessible.

Bottom Bunks: . . . . **B**
> *Average Price PPPD: $239 including airfare.*
> Category J inside doubles are the lowest-priced quarters aboard; most are comparable in size to the outside doubles. Number 298 is particularly nice. Two lower beds,

a desk/dresser, closets, a chair (in most) and a bath with tub or shower compose the furnishings.

The Routes

The *Saga Rose* cruises in northern Europe in the summer and sets out on a 97-night world cruise Jan. 7, 1998, from Dover. The gala sailing will take passengers to The Azores, Bermuda, South Pacific, Asian ports in the Indian Ocean, India, Egypt and the Mediterranean, returning to Dover on April 14. Passengers may opt to take only a segment of the full cruise, and American passengers can board the ship in Miami Jan. 19 for a segment or the remainder of the cruise. The latter option starts at $17,540 per person, double occupancy, for the 85-night world cruise from Miami.

The Scoop

This is a lovely ship with a clubby atmosphere. The passengers who don't already know each other from previous cruises get acquainted fairly easily, especially if they play bridge or trivia quizzes. Early bookings garner still another big discount.

Insider Tips

Five Special Spots

1. The Club Polaris nightclub, a two-deck hideaway that views the sea through a wall of glass, with a bar, a small dance floor and a bandstand. The upstairs portion of the room is even quieter, with a gallery overlooking the musicians below.

2. The North Cape Bar, an intimate spot tucked away on Veranda Deck with view windows; it can get crowded just before dinner.

3. The Garden Lounge, with a white marble dance floor, two circular levels and big windows aft, ideal for viewing the Norwegian fjords.

4. The Grand Ballroom is comfortable for shows although it doesn't offering spectacular sightlines; it's also pleasant at teatime.

5. The glamorous dining room with its crystal chandeliers and wood-framed tapestry armchairs.

Five Good Reasons to Book This Ship

1. To enjoy a classy cruise with classy fellow passengers in your age range.

2. To see northern Europe in style.

3. To be spared the ordeal of figuring out a tip; there is no tipping aboard.

4. To get your whole cruise, including airfare and port taxes, in one neat package.

5. To get a great big discount if you book early enough; call for a brochure to get the deadlines.

SAGA ROSE ★★★★

Registry	**Bahamas**
Officers	**British**
Crew	**International**
Complement	**350**
GRT	**24,474**
Length (ft.)	**620**
Beam (ft.)	**82**
Draft (ft.)	**27**
Passengers-Cabins Full	**747**
Passengers-2/Cabin	**580**
Passenger Space Ratio	**NA**
Stability Rating	**Good to Excellent**
Seatings	**1**
Cuisine	**Continental**
Dress Code	**Traditional**
Room Service	**Yes**
Tip	**No tipping**

Ship Amenities

Outdoor Pool	**1**
Indoor Pool	**1**
Jacuzzi	**1**
Fitness Center	**Yes**
Spa	**Yes**
Beauty Shop	**Yes**
Showroom	**Yes**
Bars/Lounges	**3**
Casino	**Yes**
Shops	**1**
Library	**Yes**
Child Program	**No**
Self-Service Laundry	**Yes**
Elevators	**4**

Cabin Statistics

Suites	**17**
Outside Doubles	**221**
Inside Doubles	**25**
Wheelchair Cabins	**12**
Singles	**54**
Single Surcharge	**NA**
Verandas	**26**
110 Volt	**Yes**

SAGA INTERNATIONAL HOLIDAYS LTD.

ST. LAWRENCE CRUISE LINES INC.

253 Ontario Street, Kingston, Ontario, Canada, K7L 2Z4
☎ *(613) 549-8091, (800) 267-7868*

History

The 66-passenger *Canadian Empress*, the only Canadian-flag cruise vessel, has been sailing through the Thousand Islands since 1981, when Bob Clark, a Kingston real estate developer, got the idea one afternoon while he and a neighbor were watching excursion boats carrying as many as 13,000 sightseers a day. But nobody went out overnight.

Clark set to studying river boats, since a cruise ship patterned after a traditional river boat sounded like a good idea. He went to Connecticut's Mystic Seaport Museum where he "crawled all over and measured," then sailed aboard the *Mississippi Queen* and the *New Shoreham II* (now Alaska Sightseeing/Cruise West's *Spirit of Columbia*).

He named his company Rideau St. Lawrence Cruise Ships, with the intention of cruising the mild-weather Rideau Canal between Kingston and Ottawa at the beginning and end of the St. Lawrence season. But when he set out that first year with his new vessel "the canal wasn't as we were told she was," and his four-day-old *Canadian Empress* struck an obstruction that was not on the charts and tore a 34-foot gash in the hull.

The sadder but wiser Clark later changed the name of his cruise line to St. Lawrence Cruise Lines, Inc., and cut out the Rideau Canal.

Concept

"Calm-water cruising on Canada's beautiful waterways" aboard a replica of a 1908 steamship that might have toured the St. Lawrence.

Signatures

A brass steam whistle, pressed-tin ceilings and Tiffany-style lamps and polished brass in the Grand Saloon.

Gimmicks

An after-dark campfire ashore with a hot dog and marshmallow roast is usually scheduled once during every cruise.

Who's the Competition.

The closest competition is American Canadian Caribbean Line, a U.S.-flag line that cruises in the United States, Canada and the Caribbean with small, shallow-draft vessels. ACCL makes fall foliage cruises along the St. Lawrence Seaway, the Saguenay River and Erie Canal. Their former vessel *New Shoreham II* was one of the prototypes Bob Clark sailed aboard before building the *Canadian Empress.*

Who's Aboard.....................................

People who love talking with each other, an Ontario man celebrating his 86th birthday, a couple making their 18th cruise aboard the vessel. The average age is 60 to 70, but there are some in their 50s, some in their upper 80s. They're the type of folks that would never complain, who adore the pretty young girls and boys who cheerfully wait on them and gently flirt.

Ten of the 62 passengers on our sailing were from Ontario, 10 from California, and the rest from other states and provinces.

Who Should Go ....

Anybody who wants a low-key look at life along the St. Lawrence in a down-home Canadian style.

Who Should Not Go ....

Anybody looking for glamour, glitz and gambling; families with small children.

The Lifestyle ....

The passengers are an agreeable group who enjoy sitting on the top deck watching the progress through the seven locks of the St. Lawrence Seaway, going ashore to a historic re-creation of an Upper Canada Village, engaging in a cutthroat game of Trivial Pursuit or singing along with a lively piano player after a home-cooked dinner served by pretty waitresses in Victorian garb.

EAVESDROPPING

"The only people who wouldn't like this," said one passenger, "are the people who wouldn't be happy if you gave them a million dollars."

Wardrobe...

There's nothing dressy about the *Canadian Empress.* Most of the time the women wear polyester pants or dresses and the men plaid Bermuda shorts.

Bill of Fare.................................... B+

Most meals are served on open seating, often two seatings when the ship is full, with breakfast between 7:30 and 9, lunch at 12 and 1:30 p.m., dinner at 6 and 7:30 p.m.

The traditional first-night dinner is prime rib (with some rum punch served beforehand), plus a French-Canadian dinner of pea soup and *tourtière* (meat pie) another night, roast pork loin, steak, breast of duckling and a fish fillet. These are the main courses served on different days; there is usually one set menu. Breakfast might be scrambled eggs and ham with toast, grapefruit, juice and cereal, and lunch could be hamburgers with potato and macaroni salads, raw vegetables with a dip and fruit and cheese for dessert. It's all pretty much the same menu every cruise, according to the couple who've taken 18 of them, but since there are two different cooks, they say it tastes different each time.

Showtime . . . . **N/A**

Unless you count singing along from the songbook to a tune-thumping pianist or watching the antics of a troupe of performers from Upper Canada Village, the real entertainment aboard is the sightseeing along the river.

Discounts . . . .

The highly successful *Canadian Empress* offers no discounts, but you do get five percent off the second cruise and a $25 credit for onboard purchases if you book two of them back-to-back.

⚓ The Bottom Line ⚓

The *Canadian Empress* sails from late May to the end of October, with the busiest season the fall foliage months of September and October. The ride is smooth, the crew is wholesome and friendly and your fellow passengers polite and unpretentious.

⚓⚓⚓⚓
CANADIAN EMPRESS

In the Thousand Islands, your window can drift by the autumn leaves. Most of the 1870 islands in this part of the St. Lawrence River have stands of hardwood trees, so when they put on a fall foliage show you can count on high-voltage displays in scarlet, gold, russet and orange, set off by the jade green of jack and pitch pines.

Informal and completely unpretentious, the *Canadian Empress* has no swimming pool, gambling, masquerade parties or dress-up dining. It does have a taped narration about points of interest along the river, homemade brownies and chocolate chip cookies for snacks, and a shallow five-foot draft that allows it to tie up every night at small marinas along the river. Square at the aft and high-riding in the water, she's an unlikely looking vessel when you're ashore looking at her, but when you're on board she moves smoothly and gracefully.

Between The Lines

The Brochure Says

"Sail on a replica steamship. The *Canadian Empress* is a grand ship with a warm and friendly personality. The interior is designed in charming early heritage style. Whether it is elegant furnishing, or the brass handrails complemented by ornate metal ceilings, your ship recaptures the grace of a turn-of-the-century lifestyle."

Translation

You can get away from the pressures of the 20th century by languidly moving along the river in a 19th-century atmosphere.

Cabins & Costs

Fantasy Suites: . . . . **N/A**
   N/A

Small Splurges: . . . . **C**
   Average Price Per Person, Double Occupancy, Per Day: $255
   Two of the larger cabins aboard are the premier staterooms forward on St. Lawrence Deck with double beds, folding director chairs, and small bath with shower.

Suitable Standards: . . . . **C**
   Average Price PPPD: $240
   Most of the cabins are very small, with two lower beds, one folding up into the wall during the daytime to allow space for a director's chair. While closet and drawer space is limited, the relaxed dress code and casual ambiance don't call for any fancy apparel. Basic bathrooms contain shower and toilet, with a washbasin and mirrored medicine chest in the cabin. All cabins are outside, with windows or portholes that can be opened.

Bottom Bunks: . . . . **N/A**
   N/A

The Routes

The *Canadian Empress* cruises between Kingston and Montreal on four-night excursions, between Kingston and Quebec City on six-night cruises, and between Kingston and Ottawa on five-night sailings.

The Scoop

The total experience of sailing along the St. Lawrence aboard this casual and friendly vessel is seamless, with no jarring adjustment between life on board and life on shore. The guides who take you around the sights on shore are proficient, and the experience of going back into the 1860s in Upper Canada Village is alone worth the price of the cruise. While the cabins are small—we think they may be the smallest quarters we've ever occupied on a ship—they're clean and comfortable and prettily furnished, and you can open the window for fresh air at night when the ship ties up along the shore. The only disturbance is the generator noise when we're tied up at night and the motor noise and vibration when we're running during the day.

Insider Tips

Five Down-Home Places

1. The topmost Sun Deck offers shuffleboard and a giant checkerboard behind the wheelhouse, plus yellow-and-white director's chairs for watching the scenery.

2. The Grand Saloon, a combination bar, lounge and dining room, is where indoor games are played, meals are served, the captain holds his welcome-aboard cocktail party and people sit around and talk.

3. The corner store is tucked away on the lowest passenger deck with a small stock of sundries and logo T-shirts and such.

4. A forward observation deck below the wheelhouse makes a good vantage point to watch the river ahead of you.

5. An aft observation deck below the Sun Deck makes a good vantage point to watch the river behind you.

Five Good Reasons to Book This Ship

1. To choose one of three different itineraries, each covering a pretty part of Canada.

2. To visit Upper Canada Village, included on all three itineraries, a living museum animated with costumed interpreters who show you what life used to be like along the river.

3. To watch the busy shipping along the St. Lawrence Seaway.

4. To see the rich green spring foliage or the glowing autumn leaves, or pick out one of the For Sale islands you might want to buy.

5. Because the price is right—from around $800 for a four-night cruise.

Five Things You Won't Find On Board

1. A children's program, because children under 12 are not permitted.

2. An ashtray indoors; smoking is permitted only on the outer decks.

3. A Jacuzzi.

4. A cabin designated wheelchair-accessible.

5. A nurse or doctor.

CANADIAN EMPRESS ♨♨♨♨

Registry	**Canada**
Officers	**Canadian**
Crew	**Canadian**
Complement	**14**
GRT	**467**
Length (ft.)	**108**
Beam (ft.)	**30**
Draft (ft.)	**5**
Passengers-Cabins Full	**66**
Passengers-2/Cabin	**64**
Passenger Space Ratio	**NA**
Stability Rating	**Good**
Seatings	**2**
Cuisine	**Canadian**
Dress Code	**Casual**
Room Service	**No**
Tip	**$7 - $9 PPPD**

Ship Amenities

Outdoor Pool	**0**
Indoor Pool	**0**
Jacuzzi	**1**
Fitness Center	**No**
Spa	**No**
Beauty Shop	**No**
Showroom	**No**
Bars/Lounges	**1**
Casino	**No**
Shops	**1**
Library	**No**
Child Program	**No**
Self -Service Laundry	**No**
Elevators	**0**

Cabin Statistics

Suites	**0**
Outside Doubles	**32**
Inside Doubles	**0**
Wheelchair Cabins	**0**
Singles	**0**
Single Surcharge	**175%**
Verandas	**0**
110 Volt	**Yes**

ST. LAWRENCE
CRUISE LINES, INC.

SEABOURN
CRUISE LINE

55 Francisco Street, San Francisco, CA 94133
☎ *(415) 391-8518, (800) 929-4747*

Murals depicting the classic days of cruising adorn the Seabourn Legend.

History . . . .

The buzz started in 1987 with a full-color ad in the travel trades depicting the dapper and distinguished Warren Titus, recently retired head of Royal Viking Line, clad in a tuxedo and standing on a pier at night to announce the impending arrival of a new super-luxury cruise line to be called Signet Cruises. But while the new company's first ship was still under construction, it was learned a small Texas-based company had registered the name Signet Cruises, presumably in case they might start a cruise line in the future. So the fledgling new line, owned by young Norwegian industrialist Atle Brynestad, changed its name to Seabourn and—the cliché is inevitable—the rest is history.

On a rainy mid-December morning in 1988 in San Francisco, ambassador and former child star Shirley Temple Black smashed the customary bottle of champagne against the bow of the 200-passenger *Seabourn Pride* with aplomb (to the rhythm of what some of us imagined was

"On the Good Ship Lollipop") and later requested a tour of the engine room.

The *Pride* was followed in 1989 by almost-identical sister ship *Seabourn Spirit*, both achieved great acclaim, especially in the luxury travel press. In 1991, Carnival Cruise Lines, having long touted an upscale "Tiffany product" they intended to introduce, purchased 25 percent of Seabourn, and acquired an additional 25 percent in 1996, as well as the former *Royal Viking Queen/Queen Odyssey*, now *Seabourn Legend*.

—First cruise line to implement a timeshare-at-sea program called WorldFare, in which passengers purchase 45, 60, 90 or 120 days of Seabourn cruising and use them over a period of 36 months on any cruises (1993).

DID YOU KNOW?

A seagoing timeshare concept was first discussed in 1979 when Seattle-based United States Cruises Inc. owned the SS United States, but that obviously never came to fruition.

Concept

To offer discriminating passengers all the amenities they expect aboard a full-sized cruise vessel of 10,000 tons carrying 200 in an onboard ambiance that is "casual, but elegant." Service is "warm and friendly, but impeccable. And there is absolutely no tipping."

Signatures

The blue-and-white shield logo that adorns the double funnels of all three ships.

The shore excursions, custom-designed especially for Seabourn passengers, include world-class golf options and noted special lecturers.

The "As You Like It" Air, Hotel, and Transfer programs offer the flexibility of choosing which programs work best for you. Fly Seabourn's' economy, business or first class, arrange your own air or book a private jet through Seabourn. Select a variety of pre- and post cruise hotels and lengths of stay to match your desire and budget.

EAVESDROPPING

Then-mayor of San Francisco Art Agnos, touring the newly christened ship with its godmother Shirley Temple Black and other local officials, quipped, "If the Pilgrims had come over on the Seabourn Pride *rather than the Mayflower, they never would have gotten off the ship."*

Gimmicks

Seabourn WorldFare advance purchase plan in which a passenger can buy a certain number of days aboard and use them within three years on any cruises offered by the line.

Who's the Competition

The usual suspects, of course. Silversea Cruises gives Seabourn a good run for the money-passengers with its present high-quality product.

And of course, the one and only Sea Goddess, which had a four-year head start on Seabourn, and Radisson Seven Seas' *Song of Flower.*

Who's Aboard . . . .

Veteran cruisers from Royal Viking and Sea Goddess, first-time cruisers who only want the best and can afford it, a few families traveling in three-generational groups with interconnecting suites, ranging in age from thirtysomething two-income professional couples to retired CEOs. About half the passengers on any cruise are under 50. On our several cruises with Seabourn, we've met English country squires, San Francisco restaurateurs, Hong Kong journalists, a young California-based New Zealand executive, a romance novelist, a noted jazz musician, and numerous doctors, dentists, lawyers, financiers and psychoanalysts. They're more often old money rather than nouveau riche. Passengers are always falling into small-world conversations, finding they have close mutual friends or children attending the same schools. It's a small world in that tax bracket.

Who Should Go . . . .

Anyone who books a suite at the Pierre, lunches at The Club in Pebble Beach, has a house in Vail or a condo in Deer Valley. Clubby and very posh, these ships are for couples who are rich and successful. If you want to see a cross-section of typical passengers, ask the line to send you a copy of its pretty publication for repeat passengers called Seabourn Club Herald. There, on several back pages, are color photographs of recent passengers—Stirling Moss, the legendary British motorcar racer; actress Rhonda Fleming; Teddy Roosevelt's granddaughter Sarah Gannett—along with a number of the rich and unfamous.

Who Should Not Go . . . .

Children or even restless teenagers would not find places to go and things to do on these ships. Despite the alternative casual dining in the Veranda Cafe, anyone unwilling to dress for dinner in the dining room would be out of place. And anyone who doesn't know what "out of place" means should certainly not go.

The Lifestyle . . . .

The ships are large enough to give passengers a sense of privacy when they wish but with a variety of indoor and outdoor spaces to be social or be secluded. Obviously the luxuriously comfortable cabins with seating areas, TV/VCR and full meal service entice passengers to spend more time inside. Days are casual, with many passengers lounging on deck in bathing suits reading a book, but evenings get much more formal. There are not many organized activities on board since passengers prefer to plan their own time, but they will attend outstanding lecturers.

Wardrobe . . . .

While daytimes may be spent in casual, but never sloppy, garb, people dress up in the evenings (except the "resort casual" Veranda Cafe), not because a dress code tells them they must, but because they like to, and because they are at ease in tuxedos and dressy gowns, silk or linen suits and top-label sportswear.

Bill of Fare. . . . . A+

Sophisticated contemporary cuisine prepared à la minute (when it's ordered) and served in small portions to encourage passengers to try the suggested menu rather than simply one or two dishes. We remember one chef's suggestion menu from Stefan Hamrin that we followed all the way through—an avocado fan with jumbo shrimp and scallion sauce, followed by creamy onion garlic soup with croutons, then a field salad of arugula and radishes, roast rack of spring lamb Dijonnaise, and hot macadamia nut soufflé with Tia Maria sauce. The food was light enough and the portions small enough that we were satiated but not stuffed at the end of the meal.

Mornings you can breakfast on deck under the shade of a canvas canopy or inside the jade green-and-white marble Veranda where the fresh fruits are arranged on the buffet like gemstones and the thinly sliced smoked salmon and gravlax are draped like silk with caper beading.

New dishes are regularly being added featuring regional and ethnic cuisine.

The Veranda Cafe on the **Seabourn Spirit** *is a delightful place to have breakfast on a sunny morning.*

Showtime. . . . . A

When the ships began operation, the evening's entertainment was done by the Styleliners, a quartet of singers who perform music by Sondheim, Porter, Berlin, Gershwin and other notables in a choreographed concert style. The ships still offer musical cabaret shows on the modest stage using the variety of principal artists performing during the cruise, as well as bringing in regional entertainers from the ports of call. Lecturers range from celebrity chefs to contract bridge teachers, jazz artists, astronauts and other celebrities. TV personality Robert Stack, astronauts Wally Schirra and Walter Cunningham, journalists Sander Vanocur, David Brinkley and Linda Ellerbee, composer/lyricist Richard Adler and Julliard's Gagliano String Trio were among the recent guests.

Discounts . . . .

Seabourn never allows the "D" word to creep into a discussion, but a rose by any other name can still save some money on a cruise. Repeat passengers in The Seabourn Club get "savings on the cruise tariff" of 10 percent from having made a previous cruise, plus 5 percent off the fare for friends they bring along who occupy a separate suite. Cumulative days of cruising with the company also brings "substantial fare reductions," and anyone who completes 140 days aboard the ships gets the next cruise of up to 14 days free. An "early payment program" means if you book and pay for your cruise 12 months ahead of time you save 10 percent, six months ahead of time and you save 5 percent. A "single traveler savings option" on certain cruises reduces the normal 200 percent surcharge to only 110, 125 or 150 percent. There should be something there to fit anyone opting for Seabourn.

The Bottom Line

When the *Seabourn Pride* had been running for a year and the *Seabourn Spirit* just introduced, we asked Warren Titus about the difference between operating Seabourn and operating Royal Viking. "It's much easier for us to cater to a single strata of people...They basically come form the same background and tastes...and it's so much easier to satisfy people on this ship than on a Royal Viking ship with a variety of cabins and prices."

Seabourn ships are the ultimate in patrician elegance without ever being stuffy. Your dinner table partner might turn out to have a title preceding his name, but he's unlikely to ever mention it. Everything works on these ships from the food to the service to the ambiance. You get, quite simply, a superbly satisfying cruise experience.

SEABOURN CRUISE LINE

★ ★ ★ ★ ★ ★

SEABOURN LEGEND
SEABOURN PRIDE
SEABOURN SPIRIT

Day after day, time after time, we find ourselves agreeing that there is no-where else on earth we would rather be than right here, right now, aboard the Seabourn Pride listening to Page Cavanaugh at the piano playing "Rainy Day" at cocktail time in the understated elegance of The Club.

Notes from the inaugural sailing

December 1988

Nothing makes the folks at Seabourn madder than to hear their 10,000-ton cruise ships called "small," "little," or "yacht-sized." They have, as Warren Titus pointed out on the first sailing of the *Seabourn Pride*, "all the amenities and facilities of a full-sized cruise ship but only for a few people." Everything here is scaled to the human passenger rather than cruise industry statistics, and they spent a lot of time determining what the experienced cruise passenger who books the upper end of the market would like. Suite-rooms are a spacious 277 square feet with very lavish bathrooms and sitting areas large enough to host six people comfortably at cocktail time. There are all sorts of beautiful public rooms and deck spaces, along with, at one time, a mysterious flying saucer-like device called the Star Observatory, where passengers could climb in and lie back on cushy leather seats to star-gaze through a telescope; that's not easy on a moving ship, which is why we've never saw anyone try it.

Between The Lines

The Brochure Says

"To some, Seabourn may be expensive; but it is not overpriced. In fact, the authentic Seabourn experience is an extraordinary value."

Translation

Even at $1000 a day, you can reassure yourself you're getting your money's worth.

Cabins & Costs

Fantasy Suites: . . . . **A+**

Average Price Per Person, Double Occupancy, Per Day: $1787 plus airfare, in the Mediterranean.

Owner's Suites Type E (there are two per ship) are 575 square feet with veranda, large living room with curved sofas, chairs and coffee table plus a dining table with four chairs, a marble bath with tub and twin sinks plus a second half-bath for guests, and a separate bedroom with all the amenities listed below (see Suitable Standards).

Small Splurges: . . . . **A+**

Average Price PPPD: $1634 plus airfare, in the Mediterranean.

Each of the 16 Regal C suites is 400 square feet with a small private veranda, queen-sized bed in a separate bedroom, curved sofas and chairs in the living room and lots of built-ins, plus all the amenities listed below (see Suitable Standards).

The standard suite-like cabins aboard **Seabourn Pride** *and* **Seabourn Spirit** *are large enough to have friends in for cocktails.*

Suitable Standards: . . . . **A+**

Average Price PPPD: $1021 plus airfare, in the Mediterranean.

The standard suite-rooms are 277 square feet each with a five-foot picture window placed low enough on the wall that you can lie in bed (either twins or queen-sized) and watch the sea. A tapestry-print sofa, three chairs and two round stools provide plenty of guest seating, along with a mini-refrigerator, full array of crystal and a fully stocked liquor cabinet. The coffee table can be raised to dining table height if you want to dine in, and there's a walk-in closet with lots of storage, a built-in dresser/desk with drawers and mirror, and a marble bathroom with tub, twin sinks set in a marble counter and a mirrored storage area for toiletries.

Bottom Bunks: . . . . **N/A**

There's no such thing on Seabourn ships.

EAVESDROPPING

Famous Last Words Department: A quartet of San Francisco travel agents, invited for the christening-day tour of the Seabourn Pride, walked from the gangway into the reception hall and turned up their noses at the last-minute touch-ups of artificial greenery to replace plants damaged in the stormy crossing, accepted a glass of champagne from a white-gloved waiter and flounced into the Magellan Lounge, where they sat at the back table just long enough to empty their glasses. "Hmph," one sniffed, "I don't like this room; it's too dark." "Well, this ship'll never touch the Sea Goddesses," her friend commented. "I've seen enough—ready to go?" And away they went, back down the gangway without looking at anything else.

The Routes

The *Seabourn Pride* begins the winter with Caribbean cruises from Fort Lauderdale. On Jan. 6 the ship leaves for an 18-day cruise to Valparaiso for a series of South American cruises around Cape Horn before returning for an Amazon cruise. The summer is spent in Scandinavia and the Baltic followed by fall New England/Canada sailings from New York and later Caribbean sailings from Fort Lauderdale.

The *Seabourn Spirit* spends the winter in southeast Asia with cruises from Singapore and Hong Kong to Malaysia, Bangkok and Vietnam, then positions via India to the Mediterranean and Aegean for cruises throughout the summer and early fall before returning to the South Pacific.

The *Seabourn Legend* spends the winter with cruises out of Australia and New Zealand before positioning to the Mediterranean for the summer season.

The Scoop

Yes, it's expensive, but not even the worst nitpicker could find anything to complain about with the food, service and accommodations. And there are really exotic and interesting itineraries, calling at some rarely visited ports, along with appealing mix-and-match cruises that can be combined for a sizable savings. Go for the standard suite-rooms unless you want to splurge to get a veranda. When you head for the deck, there's a steward in white shirt and tie to turn your deck chair toward the sun hourly or spritz you with mineral water. In the evening, you can slip away for cocktails in the club while the pianist plays your favorite sentimental song, or don something dazzling for dinner dancing between courses in the restaurant. Or enjoy breakfast in bed while gazing at the sea through a five-foot picture window with its own automatic window washing system.

Insider Tips

Five Unforgettable Places

1. A watersports marina that can be thrust out from the ship when it's at anchor, letting passengers swim in a giant submersible steel mesh tank with its own teak deck around it, or go windsurfing, sailing or water-skiing.

2. Forward on the top deck is the Horizon Lounge with wrap-around glass windows, cushy blue leather chairs and couches, a polished granite bar, a radar screen for passengers to play with and a computer-animated wall map of famous historic voyages as well as itinerary information.

3. The Sky Bar, a wooden bar with a circle of barstools around it plus wooden tables and lower stools fixed on the teak decking, is a popular gathering spot.

4. The Club, cool white and beige with wood, marble and woven textures, is equally handsome in the daytime with sunlight streaming in its glass dome or in the evening with the shades lowered and a pianist playing Duke Ellington compositions.

5. The Restaurant, with quiet, comfortable tables placed well apart, tapestry-patterned chairs and silky curtains; a pianist plays during dinner and there's a small dance floor for those evenings when dinner dancing is scheduled.

Five Good Reasons to Book These Ships

1. Because service is so good you don't have to lift a finger; you can let things come to you, rather than having to go fetch them.

2. Because with the "As You Like It" program you can tailor an air/land program that includes economy-class airfare or optional upgrades, premium hotel accommodations, hospitality desks at the hotels and transfers to and from the ship to fit your lifestyle.

3. Because tipping is not only not requested, but not permitted.

4. The little extras that mean a lot—bathrobes, hair dryers, combination safes, walk-in closets with four kinds of hangers, personalized stationery, a sewing kit with the needles already threaded, a 24-hour room service menu that includes everything from sandwiches to grilled steaks, complete sets of bathroom towels in two colors, peach and pewter gray, and exquisite almond-scented toiletries.

5. Instead of aspic-encased show buffets and parades of baked Alaska, you can find sevruga caviar whenever you want to order it, fresh broiled sea bass, sautéed pheasant breast with Calvados sauce, chocolate truffle cake.

Five Things You Won't Find On Board

1. A lap swimming pool; the smallish pool is adequate but wedged between the Veranda Cafe and a stairwell. The Jacuzzi is more popular than the pool.

2. A view of undersea life in the underwater viewing room on the bottom deck when the ship is moving; all you see are bubbles.

3. A delay on getting your laundry and dry cleaning back; same-day service is available.

4. A surprise when you get to the dining room; copies of the menus are delivered daily to the cabins so you can plan ahead.

5. A bar bill at the end of the cruise. Bar drinks and dinner wines are now included in the fares.

SEABOURN LEGEND	★★★★★
SEABOURN PRIDE	★★★★★
SEABOURN SPIRIT	★★★★★
Registry	**Norway**
Officers	**Norwegian**
Crew	**European**
Complement	**140**
GRT	**10,000**
Length (ft.)	**439**
Beam (ft.)	**63**
Draft (ft.)	**16.4**
Passengers-Cabins Full	**208**
Passengers-2/Cabin	**200**
Passenger Space Ratio	**50**
Stability Rating	**Good**
Seatings	**1**
Cuisine	**Contemporary**
Dress Code	**Traditional**
Room Service	**Yes**
Tip	**No tipping allowed**

Ship Amenities

Outdoor Pool	**1**
Indoor Pool	**0**
Jacuzzi	**3**
Fitness Center	**Yes**
Spa	**Yes**
Beauty Shop	**Yes**
Showroom	**Yes**
Bars/Lounges	**3**
Casino	**Yes**
Shops	**1**
Library	**Yes**
Child Program	**No**
Self-Service Laundry	**Yes**
Elevators	**3**

Cabin Statistics

Suites	**104**
Outside Doubles	**0**
Inside Doubles	**0**
Wheelchair Cabins	**4**
Singles	**0**
Single Surcharge	**110-150%**
Verandas	**6**
110 Volt	**Yes**

SEA CLOUD CRUISES

c/o Elegant Cruises & Tours, Inc.
31 Central Drive, Port Washington, NY 11050
☎ *(516) 767-9302, (800) 683-6767*

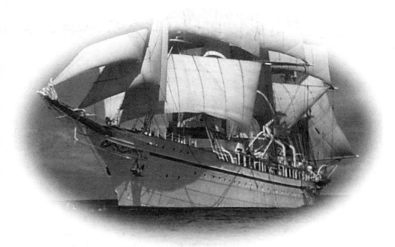

★★★★, ⚓⚓⚓⚓
SEA CLOUD

   While any vessel with white sails puffed by the wind is romantic, the sailing yacht Sea Cloud *is the most romantic of all the tall ships, not only because of her grace and beauty, but also because of her history. The yacht was built for a glamorous heiress by a fabled financier who loved her, became a nursery garden of delights for a child who would grow up to become a famous actress, and was briefly a home during the holidays for many of the world's rich and famous, as well as the rich and infamous. The legendary ship went on to become the toy of a Latin American dictator, a playpen for movie starlets, then an impounded derelict rotting away in Panama before being rescued by a group of German yachtsmen who restored her to her original glory.*

The *Sea Cloud* was built for $1 million in 1931 in the Krupp yard in Kiel, Germany, and was the largest privately owned yacht in the world when she was delivered to cereal heiress Marjorie Merriweather Post and her then-husband financier E. F. Hutton. The four-masted barque was first named *Hussar V*, since she was fifth in the series of yachts Hutton had built under that name. (See Windjammer Barefoot Cruises, the *Mandalay*, page 900 for the *Hussar IV*.) Their daughter, actress Dina Merrill, remembers in her childhood spending six months of every year sailing around the world with guests such as the Duke and Duchess of Windsor.

DID YOU KNOW?

Marjorie rented a large warehouse in New Jersey where she chalked out the deck plan on the floor and endlessly arranged and rearranged the antique furniture until it suited her, then transferred it to the ship. All the bric-a-brac and ornaments were glued to the mantels and tabletops where she meant for them to stay.

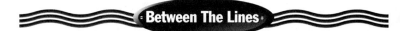

Between The Lines

The Brochure Says

"Everyone approaching *Sea Cloud* for the first time is indelibly stunned by the very sight of her, one of the last of the glorious four-masted barks (sic) lying at the pier."

Translation

You're an instant celebrity in any port when you disembark this unique and glamorous vessel, and you'll find yourself fending off street vendors in the Caribbean who think you must be very, very rich.

DID YOU KNOW?

Rafael Trujillo had come into possession of the Sea Cloud by trading a 44-passenger Viscount propjet to Marjorie for it. He then put a cannon on the side of the yacht, named it Angelina, termed it a man-of-war and rented it back from the Dominican Republic's Navy for $1 a year. His favorite illegitimate son Ramfis took it to college with him when he was enrolled in law school in Southern California. When Trujillo was assassinated in 1961, family members and loyal aides fled the country aboard the yacht with some $5 million in cash and the dictator's body in an elaborate mahogany coffin in the smoking room. After they were intercepted by a Dominican Republic gunboat, the dictator's body was permitted to go on for burial in Paris' Pere Lachaise cemetery while the yacht—and presumably the $5 million—was returned to the country to become the Patriot.

Cabins & Costs

Fantasy Suites: . . . . **A+**
Average Price Per Person, Double Occupancy, Per Day: $1191 plus airfare.

Owner's Suite #1, decorated in Louis XVI style with a marble fireplace (nonworking), marble bathroom with gold faucets, French canopy bed with damask covers, chairs and ottomans in satin brocade, flower-etched mirrors and gilded moldings, is sumptuous and spacious.

The elegant owner's suite aboard the sailing yacht **Sea Cloud** *has marble fireplaces (nonworking) and gold faucets.*

Small Splurges: .... **A+**

Average Price PPPD: $1062 plus airfare.
Suite #7 is warm and sophisticated with its softly burnished pale pine paneled walls and lower wainscoting accented with darker wood strips. The bath, a bit smaller than those in the two owner's suites, is marble with gold faucets on the tub. Best of all, there's a deep, walk-in closet with handcrafted storage cubicles.

Suitable Standards: .... **C**

Average Price PPPD: $735 plus airfare.
Now, here's the rub. There are only eight original staterooms on the ship; the remaining 24 were built in a refit when the ship was turned into a cruise vessel. They are divided into various categories; most contain two lower beds with storage drawers built in underneath, a window, a built-in dresser with four drawers, and a small bathroom with shower. There is no desk, table or chair, nor anywhere to sit except on the beds, but you do get a hair dryer, terry-cloth robes, a bowl of fruit, fresh flowers and a bottle of German champagne. In these cabins, you take turns getting up, showering and dressing, then one of you goes outside so the other can get up, shower and dress.

Bottom Bunks: .... **C-**

Average Price PPPD: $486 plus airfare.
The lowest category staterooms are furnished similarly to those, above, but are smaller.

The Routes

The *Sea Cloud* usually includes Caribbean cruises in winter and Mediterranean sailings in summer. Sailing from Antigua, the *Sea Cloud* cruises among the Windward Islands.

The Scoop

The food, prepared by German and Austrian chefs, is delicious although menus are limited in scope. Set dinner menus are posted in the mornings; if passengers spot something they don't like, they report promptly to the bartenders, who double as major-domos, and a substitute dish or entire menu will be arranged. Breakfasts are self-serve affairs set up in the dining room; lunches are elaborate buffets of hot and cold dishes with complimentary wines and beer usually eaten on the Lido deck, and dinners are formally served on linen-covered tables by candlelight, again with complimentary wines. Despite the cozy little shipshape cabins, we would go again tomorrow; it's that special.

Insider Tips

Five Glorious Places

1. The Main Deck, natural teak with brass trim, glossy wood-paneled walls and polished benches, above which you can watch young sailors, male and female, climb the rigging to set the sails in the time-honored fashion.

2. The Lounge with its elegant wood bookcases, piano and oil paintings of classic tall ships doubles as part of the dining room during candlelight dinners.

3. The dining room with its original carved wood ceilings and panels and elegant wood-and-upholstery chairs is where the captain invites each passenger to dine at his table one evening during the cruise.

4. The Lido, a big deck shaded with a tarp, is where you sit out in the breeze and enjoy the casual buffet lunches. Complimentary wines are served at lunch and dinner.

5. The Blue Lagoon, a big cushioned area aft on the middle deck where lolling sunbathers recline on a raised platform upholstered with puffy blue mattresses.

Five Off-the-Wall Places

1. Owners Suite # 1 is Marjorie's own suite, grandly done up in marble and gold.

2. Owner's Suite # 2 was E. F. Hutton's equally grand but more masculine quarters, pine-paneled with a Carrera marble fireplace.

3. Suite # 4, all its furnishings original, was where the Duke of Windsor slept when he and the Duchess cruised with Mrs. Post to Cuba. (We don't know where the Duchess slept.)

4. Suite # 7 was Dina's bedroom and nursery, with a lavish marble bathroom and walk-in closet.

5. We're not sure which cabin was occupied by Zsa Zsa Gabor in the 1950s when her friend Ramfis Trujillo had the yacht anchored off the coast of Santa Monica, but people ashore still remember waking up one morning to see a banner hanging across the Sea Cloud's side painted in foot-high bright red letters, "Zsa Zsa Slept Here."

Five Good Reasons to Book This Ship

1. Because it's there.

2. To pretend to be one of the rich and famous, if only by getting up and going out on deck early in the morning to make believe it's 1935 and this is your own private yacht.

3. To explore the Caribbean or Mediterranean on a sailing expedition.

4. To have an unimaginably wonderful experience that you'll never forget.

5. To sleep in the bed where the Duke of Windsor once slept.

Five Things You Won't Find On Board

1. A wheelchair-accessible cabin; with no elevators and extremely steep stairs, this vessel should not be booked by anyone with limited mobility.

2. A children's program; children should not be aboard this ship because there's nowhere for them to play or be looked after.

3. A casino.

4. A beauty shop.

5. A swimming pool, although sometimes when the ship is at anchor, the gangway is lowered for passengers to swim in the Caribbean or Mediterranean.

SEA CLOUD   ★★★★, ⚓⚓⚓⚓

Registry	**Malta**
Officers	**International**
Crew	**International**
Complement	**65**
GRT	**2323**
Length (ft.)	**360**
Beam (ft.)	**49**
Draft (ft.)	**16.5**
Passengers-Cabins Full	**70**
Passengers-2/Cabin	**64**
Passenger Space Ratio	**NA**
Stability Rating	**Good**
Seatings	**1**
Cuisine	**Continental**
Dress Code	**Casual**
Room Service	**No**
Tip	**$7 PPPD, 15% automatically added to bar check**

Ship Amenities

Outdoor Pool	**0**
Indoor Pool	**0**
Jacuzzi	**0**
Fitness Center	**No**
Spa	**No**
Beauty Shop	**No**
Showroom	**No**
Bars/Lounges	**2**
Casino	**No**
Shops	**1**
Library	**Yes**
Child Program	**No**
Self-Service Laundry	**No**
Elevators	**0**

Cabin Statistics

Suites	**2**
Outside Doubles	**30**
Inside Doubles	**0**
Wheelchair Cabins	**0**
Singles	**0**
Single Surcharge	**150%**
Verandas	**0**
110 Volt	**No**

S E A W I N D
C R U I S E   L I N E

4770 Biscayne Boulevard, Miami, FL 33137
☎ *(305) 573-3222, (800) 854-8787*

Teak and tile ornament the pool deck of this classic Portuguese liner.

History ∙∙

Seawind Cruise Line was founded in 1991 by a mix of Portuguese, Swedish and Greek interests to market the classic Portuguese ocean liner *Vasco de Gama* in the Caribbean on sailings out of Aruba. Until mid-1995, the ship retained the name *Vasco de Gama* while it sailed as and was marketed under the trade name *Seawind Crown*. Now it is officially *Seawind Crown*, and the double names painted on the bow are gone.

The ship was christened in Aruba on Aug. 11, 1991, by Maria Kyriakidis, wife of charterer Takis Kyriakidis, whose charter agreement was abruptly terminated Sep. 20, 1991. The then-owners, doing business as Trans World Cruises, picked up the charter themselves, and the ship resumed sailing Oct. 6, 1991, under the direction of Bo Paulson, George Potamianos and Jan Hygrell. Paulson and Hygrell represented the Swedish shipping giant Nordisk, which sold the vessel in July 1995, to a group of New York investors named Capital Holiday. They in turn sold majority control to Cruise Holdings, Ltd., who also own Dolphin

SEAWIND CRUISE LINE

Cruise Line and Premier Cruise Lines. The three lines retain separate companies at the present time but many more in the near future.

Concept

Sailing from Aruba on southern Caribbean itineraries at modest prices in a very gracious and spacious classic liner.

Signatures

The dual names on the ship's bow certainly made it stand out in a crowd, but, alas, that whimsical touch is gone now. There's an elegant wood-paneled chapel that can be used for weddings or renewal of vows. And there's always the Great American Cookout/Picnic on deck with down-home American music from barbershop quartets and such.

Gimmicks

Honeymoon and anniversary celebrations for people married within seven days of their cruise or couples celebrating an anniversary during the cruise.

Who's the Competition

Dolphin Cruise Line withdrew the *OceanBreeze* from Aruba last May, leaving little real competition year-round for Seawind except in the general Caribbean marketplace itself.

Who's Aboard

A mix of 70 percent veteran and 30 percent first-time cruisers drawn by the price and itinerary, many of them young to middle-aged couples. The median age aboard is 45–50.

The ship also attracts a sizable contingent of Europeans, Latin Americans and Asians.

Who Should Go

Veteran cruisers will love the classic ship and the excellent itineraries, while first-timers will find all the traditional cruise touches they expect presented in an un-glitzy fashion.

Who Should Not Go

Passengers who need a wheelchair-accessible cabin; there are none aboard. Families with small children, since there's no children's program or counselor. Anyone who thinks it's not a Caribbean cruise if it doesn't call in St. Thomas.

The Lifestyle

Basically, a traditional cruise pattern is followed, with exercise classes, musical and variety show entertainment, scuba and snorkel lessons. There are two formal nights during the week. Special golf packages are often available.

SEAWIND CRUISE LINE

EAVESDROPPING

Travel agent on board: "My cabin I can get to in three minutes. On a three-day cruise on those big ships, you spend the whole three days trying to find your way around. Everything is right here—you don't have to walk five blocks just to get to the lounge."

THERE IS A SPECIAL PLACE

with ocean-view suites and private verandas.

Where a yacht-like atmosphere features

all-inclusive luxuries. And a European crew

cradles you in warmth and welcome as you travel

stylishly around the world.

SILVERSEA.

"World's Best Cruise Line" *Condé Nast Traveler*
"Six Stars" *Fielding's Guide to Worldwide Cruises*

Norwegian Dream captures a rainbow.

Crystal's *Symphony* docked at Venice, Italy

Abercrombie & Kent's *Explorer* and Zodiacs

Wardrobe . . . .

Casual island resort wear is proper daytime and shoreside apparel.

There are two formal nights aboard during each week, the captain's welcome-aboard and farewell parties, which call for men to wear a tuxedo, dinner jacket or suit, or at least a jacket and tie.

Bill of Fare . . . . .B

The food is generally good, but the caterers lean toward large show buffets, flaming desserts and displays to impress first-time cruisers. There are some innovative Caribbean and Latin American dishes, as well as a couple of Greek specialties that show up from time to time to supplement the run of oxtail consomme, duckling à l'orange and cherries jubilee. There are two meal seatings at assigned tables. First dinner seating is usually 6:30 p.m., the second at 8:30.

Showtime . . . . .C+

There's a lot of entertainment with different musical productions nightly, featuring feather-clad chorus girls who, when they exit, leave the stage looking like it's molting season. Caribbean bands play poolside in the daytime, and a combo plays dance music in the Panorama Lounge. Movies run daily in the cinema and on the cabin TV sets.

Discounts . . . .

Seawind does some aggressive marketing, with advance purchase rates for anyone booking with a deposit 60 days ahead of sailing. A special Aruba land package called Free-Aruba adds on a free seven-night resort stay in Aruba at La Cabana All-Suite Beach Resort and Casino for passengers who have booked in cabin categories A through D. If you buy a cheaper cabin, in categories E through G, you'll still get three nights free at La Cabana. The airfare is included in that package too.

The Bottom Line

This is a very good buy for anyone interested in cruising on a midsized classic ship to Caribbean islands a little off the beaten track.

SEAWIND CRUISE LINE

★ ★ ★ ★
SEAWIND CROWN

It was an object lesson in how not to initiate a new cruise line—compared with, say, Crystal, which spent more than two years paving the way. The erstwhile charterer picked up the ship in a dock in Aruba at the end of a chartered Brazilian cruise (and some of the Brazilians refused to get off, so they sailed on the inaugural with us). He also flew out from Miami carrying two tons of excess baggage that consisted mostly of printed materials for the vessel. The costumes for the entertainers were impounded by Aruban officials (probably because of all the feathers), and the final blow came when the line's new president, while describing to the press all the 11th-hour travail, picked up a packet of sugar to sweeten his coffee and saw that it was marked Premier Cruise Line, a rival line that shares the same catering company.

The *Seawind Crown*, previously the *Vasco de Gama*, was built as the *Infante dom Enrique* in 1961 for the Portugal-to-Mozambique service and was laid up in Lisbon in 1976 after the African colony won its independence from Portugal and there was no further need to transport bureaucrats and their families back and forth.

In 1988, a major refurbishment supervised by George Potamianos was done in Greece to turn the ship into the *Vasco de Gama*, the name of the street in Lisbon where George lives. It would be interesting to ship buffs to make a walk-through figuring out which areas were what when it was a two-class ship. We got some clues from George. The smaller Madeira Restaurant adjoining the big dining room was the first-class dining room, the casino the first-class bar. There were even separate children's playrooms, presumably so the kids of the first-class passengers didn't have to associate with the kids of the second-class passengers. Turns out they didn't pray together either, since there was a second-class chapel where the mural behind the pool is located now. The existing chapel is, of course, the old first-class chapel. There was even, George said, a Tourist Class B, the next thing to steerage, and a lot of the cabins didn't have private baths in the old days. He also built what we believe is one of the few seagoing squash courts, but it was supplanted, alas, by an ordinary mirrored gym and fitness center.

Between The Lines

The Brochure Says

"This charming ship will remain in your memory for years to come. Because this is your comfortable home-away-from-home. It's easy to see that the Seawind Crown is beautiful. Classic. Comfortable. It's a ship that evokes feelings of a genuine quality, up-scale sailing vessel reminiscent of the world's classic liners."

Translation

Although the international crew may represent as many as 34 nationalities, there is a warmth and friendliness from them that most cruisers will enjoy.

Cabins & Costs

Fantasy Suites: .... **B**

Average Price Per Person, Double Occupancy, Per Day: $375 plus airfare but includes Aruba land stay.
The two owner's suites are spacious apartments with a large living room and separate bedroom, lots of windows facing forward, a couch that can convert to additional sleeping, coffee table, two chairs, color TV set, mini-refrigerator, built-in desk and entry hall. In the bedroom are two single beds, a long built-in table with console and nightstands, two large closets, and a huge bathroom with two wash basins, tub and shower and storage shelves.

Small Splurges: .... **B**

Average Price PPPD: $327 plus airfare but includes Aruba land stay.
Also on the topmost deck are eight suites not quite as large as the owner's but very handsomely furnished, part of the 12 suites that were created out of 24 original cabins in the 1988 refurbishment.

Suitable Standards: .... **C**

Average Price PPPD: $194 plus airfare but includes Aruba land stay.
In category H, fairly good-sized cabins with chest, dresser, three closets, optional overhead bunks, and bath with shower.

Bottom Bunks: .... **B**

Average Price PPPD: $138 plus airfare but includes Aruba land stay.
The very lowest-priced category are the 32 inside cabins with upper and lower berths, a small three-drawer chest, dresser, TV, mini-refrigerator, terry-cloth robes, hair dryers, bathroom with shower, a large mirror, altogether quite adequate unto the need.

The Routes

The *Seawind Crown* sails out of Aruba every Sunday calling at Curaçao, Barbados, St. Lucia and La Guaira (for Caracas).

The Scoop

We like the ship and the line for the money they charge, and the Free-Aruba package makes it a very good buy, the number of nights and type of hotel depending on the accommodations you booked aboard the ship. That's a creative solution to the problem of airlift into Aruba to get the passengers all in and out.

Insider Tips

Five Super Places

1. The chapel, a quiet, elegant little room on an upper deck, with an original inlaid wood mural outside, where passengers can participate in a renewal-of-wedding-vows ceremony.

2. The Panorama Lounge, used for cabaret acts and dancing in the evenings.

3. The spiffy lower-deck gym, replacing a unique squash court but probably more popular among the North American passengers.

4. The Taverna doubles as a casual breakfast and lunch buffet area but is a bit small to handle the passenger numbers. However it makes a warm and cozy hideaway between meals.

5. The pool deck has a raised platform for the musicians, a horseshoe-shaped bar, white plastic loungers, chairs and tables, plus a large, lap-sized swimming pool; there's a second, smaller one on the deck above.

Five Good Reasons to Book This Ship

1. To go back to the days of elegant transatlantic liners.

2. The price is right.

3. The itineraries let you discover a lot of the Southern Caribbean on a seven-day cruise.

4. You can get a free Aruba vacation before or after your cruise; see Discounts, above, for details.

5. Cabins are spacious and the ship never feels crowded.

Five Things You Won't Find On Board

1. That wonderful squash court that used to be there.

2. Two names painted on the bow—with the new ownership, it's now officially the *Seawind Crown*.

3. A self-service laundry.

4. Theme cruises.

5. Ushers in the cinema.

SEAWIND CROWN ★★★★

Registry	**Panama**
Officers	**International**
Crew	**International**
Complement	**320**
GRT	**24,000**
Length (ft.)	**642**
Beam (ft.)	**81**
Draft (ft.)	**27**
Passengers-Cabins Full	**824**
Passengers-2/Cabin	**720**
Passenger Space Ratio	**32.96**
Stability Rating	**Good to Excellent**
Seatings	**2**
Cuisine	**International**
Dress Code	**Traditional**
Room Service	**Yes**
Tip	**$7.50 PPPD, 15% automatically added to bar check**

Ship Amenities

Outdoor Pool	**2**
Indoor Pool	**0**
Jacuzzi	**0**
Fitness Center	**Yes**
Spa	**No**
Beauty Shop	**Yes**
Showroom	**Yes**
Bars/Lounges	**5**
Casino	**Yes**
Shops	**2**
Library	**Yes**
Child Program	**No**
Self-Service Laundry	**No**
Elevators	**4**

Cabin Statistics

Suites	**16**
Outside Doubles	**210**
Inside Doubles	**121**
Wheelchair Cabins	**2**
Singles	**4**
Single Surcharge	**150%**
Verandas	**2**
110 Volt	**No**

SILVERSEA CRUISES

110 East Broward Boulevard, Fort Lauderdale, FL 33301
☎ *(305) 522-4477, (800) 722-9055*

The pretty pink dining room of the **Silver Cloud** *serves very good cuisine cooked a la minute.*

History . . . .

Founded in 1992 by the Francesco Lefebvre family of Rome and the Vlasov Group of Monte Carlo, the former owners of now-defunct Sitmar Cruises, Silversea built its line around two 296-passenger super-luxury vessels instead of returning to big-ship cruising in the Sitmar style.

The *Silver Cloud*, which debuted April 2, 1994, and the *Silver Wind*, which debuted Jan. 29, 1995, were designed by Norwegian architects Pettar Yran and Bjorn Storbraaten, who also designed the interiors of the Seabourn and Sea Goddess ships as well as the renovated *Song of Flower* for Radisson Seven Seas Cruises.

—The Silversea name ties in with the Vlasov Group's 80-year-old British-based shipping company called the Silver Line.

—V.SHIPS, Inc., of Monte Carlo, also part of the Vlasov Group, provides many cruise lines around the world with officers and crews and other operational services.

SILVERSEA CRUISES, LTD.

Concept

The intent to provide full all-inclusive packaging in one price, including onboard beverage service, all gratuities on board, port taxes, baggage handling and selected shore excursions. Air/sea packages also factor in air travel, transfers, porterage and a choice of overnight or day deluxe five-star hotel room prior to embarkation. All-inclusive fares are available on cruise-only or air/sea packages. Free shuttles between the port and town are also offered in many ports of call.

Signatures

The Silversea Experience—a special shore excursion that is included for all passengers that explores some special aspect of local culture or hospitality, perhaps dinner in a Victorian castle, a private wine tasting in Bordeaux or a Turkish wedding party with camels and belly dancers and a lavish picnic in a pine forest.

Gimmicks

Special affiliations with prestigious companies lets Silversea produce themed sailings such as a series of Le Cordon Bleu voyages featuring chefs from the famous Paris cooking school preparing meals and demonstrating culinary techniques, along with wine tastings conducted by the head of Domaines Lafite Rothschild.

Who's the Competition

It's pretty obvious that Silversea's competition is other players in the small-ship ultra-luxury market. But with larger ships, a higher proportion of private verandas, increasingly finer food and service, and all-inclusive fares at very competitive prices, this newcomer can give Seabourn, Sea Goddess, and Radisson Seven Seas a run for the money.

Who's Aboard

Everybody from Charlton Heston (guest-starring in a film festival aboard the *Silver Cloud*) to your friendly neighborhood travel agent (if your zip code is 90210). On one recent sailing aboard the *Silver Wind*, the guest list ranged from two college-age passengers from New Jersey traveling with their parents to an Italian principessa and a number of doctors and professors; passenger home addresses included the United States, Britain, Hong Kong, Italy, Germany, The Netherlands, Mexico, Bermuda, Switzerland and Austria. Passengers are predominantly middle-aged couples, many of whom have sailed aboard some of the other super-luxury lines.

Who Should Go

Anyone who likes a lot of options, with, say, a choice of lunch in the dining room, on the canvas-shaded terrace of the Terrace Cafe, on the private veranda of your cabin or ashore in a waterfront cafe; people who stay in Relais & Chateaux hotels; people who want individual service and attention.

Who Should Not Go

Anyone whose idea of a really great meal is a Big Mac with fries; anyone whose all-time favorite vacation was a week at Disney World or a weekend in Las Vegas; anyone with small children, because there's no program or playroom for kids on these ships.

The Lifestyle . . . .

Life on board the Silversea ships will feel familiar to any veteran of the other super-deluxe vessels—luxurious, sociable, stress-free without schedules and regimentation. Two well-traveled British couples on a recent sailing around Italy never got off the ship.

Shipboard activities are low-key, ranging from nine fitness classes a day to a printed quiz, duplicate bridge, trivia, a galley tour or water volleyball. A sports marina that can be opened off the stern of the ship when it is at anchor allows passengers a chance for windsurfing, snorkeling and sailing from the ship. A larger-than-average swimming pool on board is long enough for modest laps.

Arriving guests find chilled champagne, fresh flowers and a bowl of fruit in their suites, as well as a fully stocked bar and mini-refrigerator. With a high ratio of staff to passengers (one crew member for every 1.5 passengers) and an extremely high passenger-space-ratio of 56.75, you can anticipate a leisurely, pampering cruise experience. But many veteran travelers say the detail they appreciate most about an all-inclusive cruise is the freedom from signing bar chits or figuring out tips.

Wardrobe . . . .

The Silversea ships are fairly dressy with passengers fashionably attired daytimes as well as evenings when we've been aboard (except for a couple of elderly Brits who wandered around most of the day in the terry-cloth robes from their cabins). Formal wear is requested for two evenings a week, with most men wearing either a tuxedo or dinner jacket and women in their most glamorous outfits. It's telling that the daily programs do not find it necessary to tell passengers exactly what formal dress requires. Informal dress, usually requested two or three nights out of seven, calls for men to wear a jacket and tie, while casual garb on the remaining evenings is still fairly dressy on these ships. Anyone who doesn't feel like dressing for dinner can always order dinner from the dining room menu to be served course-by-course in the cabin.

Bill of Fare . . . . .A

The cuisine is contemporary, restaurant-style cooking with a nice mix of simple and sophisticated dishes and an emphasis on fresh foods. Very early or late risers will find coffee, tea, pitchers of freshly squeezed orange and grapefruit juice, and fresh-baked croissants and other pastries in the Panorama Lounge on an upper deck between 6 and 11 a.m., followed by bouillon and crackers at 11. Full breakfast and lunch buffets and a la carte menu of hot dishes is set out daily in the Terrace Cafe, and The Restaurant serves all meals on an open seating arrangement that lets guests arrive when they wish and sit where they please. In addition, a special themed dinner may be served in the Terrace Cafe or on deck once or twice a cruise.

Showtime. . . . . **A**

The entertainment aboard usually includes a couple of variety acts, a team of magicians and a puppeteer, for instance, plus some singers and dancers, usually a quartet of Americans called the Styleliners who present music from the Gershwin/Cole Porter era as well as more contemporary show tunes and pop music, or the Matrix Dancers, a British group that perform scaled-down versions of traditional cruise production shows.

A pianist or harpist is on hand to play during teatime and dinner, a quartet plays for dancing, the casino is open when the ship is at sea and films are screened on cabin TV sets or available anytime day or night in the library for your cabin VCR.

Discounts . . . .

Besides a full air/sea, all-inclusive package price, Silversea also offers an early booking incentive of 10 percent off for passengers who book and pay a deposit four months ahead of sailing date; a combination cruise program that saves up to $3000 off the published air/sea fare for passengers booking two or more consecutive sailings; and an advanced payment bonus for 15 per cent when payment is received in full six months prior to sailing.

The Bottom Line

These all-inclusive, very luxurious ships should appeal to almost everyone who's extra-demanding about food, accommodations and service. With a sizable contingent of former Royal Viking Line personnel in the hotel operations on Silversea, you can expect the same quality that RVL always provided. The vessels themselves are well-designed, with spacious decks and public rooms, very comfortable suites, many of them with verandas, and alert and personable cabin stewardesses. A concierge is always on duty to help with any shipboard or shoreside requests. For what it costs, Silversea sailings represent a very good upscale cruise buy. (One passenger recently figured that he saved $1813 on items included in the 11-day air/sea package that he would have had to pay for on similar lines without inclusive packages.)

SILVERSEA CRUISES, LTD.

★★★★★★
SILVER CLOUD
SILVER WIND

While we thought the Silversea concept was excellent, we didn't consider it really earthshaking, at least not until the day we drove back to Monte Carlo, having spent the day touring the Silver Cloud, under construction at the shipyard in Genoa, to learn that at the same time we were aboard the ship, the Northridge earthquake, the most costly natural disaster in the history of the U.S., was taking out parts of the Los Angeles area. While we found nothing damaged when we got home, we still think of that 6.8 temblor every time we board a Silversea ship.

On check-in, passengers find a bottle of champagne in the suite, chilling in a silver ice bucket, a bud vase of fresh flowers, maybe orchids, a mini-refrigerator stocked with Evian and soft drinks, a liquor cabinet with several large bottles of different spirits, an epergne of fresh fruit, foil-wrapped chocolates on turndown, a mini-refrigerator (to keep the champagne cold if you don't want to drink it right away), and a full set of glassware in a cocktail cabinet. Everything is replenished frequently. The only extra expenses you'll have are laundry and dry cleaning, the casino, shopping and extra-premium wines and champagnes if you want to pay a surcharge. Otherwise, the wines they pour with meals are quite acceptable; there are usually two or three choices.

The layout of the sister ships makes it easy to find your way around—Vista Suites, The Restaurant, photo shop and self-service laundry on the lowest passenger deck, then The Bar, casino, boutique and entry lobby on the next deck up, along with Veranda Suites. Take one more deck up the stairs or one of the elevators to the main lobby, show lounge, card room, concierge and information desks. The Terrace Cafe, fitness center and beauty salon are one more deck up, then the pool deck and Panorama Lounge. High atop the ship is a walking/jogging track and the glass-walled observation lounge.

The Brochure Says

"At Silversea, we emphasize value—all-inclusive value—giving you far more for far less than you would expect. You will enjoy a selection of complimentary wines and champagnes from around the world, You will find that gratuities, roundtrip air transportation, port charges, transfers and porterage, as well as your pre-cruise deluxe hotel accommodations are pre-arranged and all-inclusive.... You might say we thought of everything and left you free to relax and enjoy your vacation as you please."

Translation

Who could ask for anything more?

INSIDER TIP

There are two suites for the physically challenged on the Silver Wind *(640 and 643) but none on the* Silver Cloud.

Fantasy Suites: .... A+

Average Price Per Person, Double Occupancy, Per Day: $1489 for air/sea package on Grand Suite with one bedroom, in Europe.

The term could aptly apply to virtually all the accommodations on board these ships, certainly any of those with a private veranda, but if you really wanted to book the top digs, one of the 1314-square-foot Grand Suites should do fine. A two-bedroom suite with three small private verandas, a huge living room and a second smaller sitting room, dining area with ocean view, entertainment center with CD, TV, and VCR, mini-refrigerator, two walk-in closets and two marble bathrooms with full-sized tubs.

Small Splurges: .... A+

Average Price PPPD: $1329 on air/sea package in Europe.

The Silver Suite (three to each ship) is usually the first to be booked on board these ships. At 541 square feet, it's almost twice the size of the standard suites, and has a large veranda, big living room and dining ell, a separate bedroom, walk-in closet and marble bath with tub. Also inside: Twin beds that convert to queen-sized, an entertainment center, two TV sets, VCR, refrigerator, cocktail cabinet, writing desk, wall safe, dressing table and lots of storage space.

Suitable Standards: .... A

Average Price PPPD: $869 on air/sea program in Europe.

We regard the Silversea Veranda Suite as standard, and the Vista Suite (without veranda, see below) as slumming because we love being able to sit out in the fresh sea breezes anytime day or night. The Veranda Suite has 295 square feet, including a small private veranda, with the sitting area adjacent to the veranda and furnished with sofa, three chairs, table, built-in desk/dresser, entertainment center, mini-refrigerator, cocktail cabinet, wall safe, walk-in closet, dressing table with hair dryer, twin or queen-sized bed and marble bathroom with tub.

Bottom Bunks: . . . . **A**

Average Price PPPD: $769 on air/sea program in Europe.
Despite our flip comment above, booking a Vista Suite is not exactly slumming, even if it is the lowest-price cabin category on the ships. With 240 square feet of space and all the furnishings detailed above except the private verandas (see Suitable Standards, above) it would be quite acceptable.

The Routes

The *Silver Wind* starts the year in Singapore with a 14-day cruise to Bali, followed by a series of Australian and New Zealand cruises, visits to Hong Kong, a positioning move via India to the Mediterranean for the summer. On Oct. 19 the ship moves South Africa and a return to Singapore for Asia cruising

The *Silver Cloud* starts the year in South America with seven-day cruises between Rio de Janeiro and Buenos Aires before moving to South Africa, Mombasa and up into the Mediterranean heading for Scandinavia and the Baltic for the summer. Then an Atlantic crossing to Canada and New England on the way back to the Caribbean, a circumnavigation of South America, visits to Mexico and Los Angeles enroute to Tahiti and the South Pacific fill out the season.

Looking down at the pool deck from the jogging track on the Silver Cloud.

The Scoop

After a tentative start, Silversea has really come a long way. The infusion of new staff from the Royal Viking ships and *Song of Flower* has sharpened the hotel staff, and the kitchen is turning out a more polished version of contemporary cuisine than at the beginning.

At the same time, it's a comfortable, non-intimidating cruise experience where everything is done just right without someone hovering at your elbow all the time.

While not as showy as Seabourn (you won't find silver cloches lifted in unison in the dining room here) or as sybaritic as Sea Goddess (we haven't run across serve-yourself tins of caviar among the canapes), Silversea ranks right up there on our happy vacation roster.

Insider Tips

Five Fabulous Places

1. The natural teak pool deck with its 30-by-12-foot swimming pool, long enough for modest laps, two Jacuzzis, sunny and shaded lounging areas, long wooden bar with wood barstools in one corner, loungers covered with blue/white striped cushions and tables with umbrellas.

2. The hideaway Observation Lounge high atop the topmost deck sits out on its own like a glass bubble furnished with wicker chairs, glass tables, cactus gardens and monitors showing wind speed and other operational ship's data.

3. The elegant double stairway with brass rails that is the heart of the ship; if you look up from each landing you can see the shape of a ship's keel overhead.

4. The Bar and the adjoining Parisian Lounge, Art Nouveau-style with art glass insets and Erte painted figures on each side of the stage, elaborate period lamps with wrought iron and copper trim, and glass doors etched with champagne glasses and bubbles.

5. The Terrace Cafe, more like your favorite restaurant than a ship's casual buffet cafe, with wood walls, green and yellow tapestry print chairs and lots of plants.

Five Good Reasons to Book These Ships

1. Because everything is included in one neat package (see "The Brochure Says".).

2. Because a special Silversea Experience is included on select cruises; our favorite was on the *Silver Cloud* when we were taken to a pine forest near Antalya for spectacular Turkish wedding feast—Turkish wines, two dozen cold appetizers, six or eight different kind of kebabs grilled over charcoal, a table of desserts and fresh fruits, and a costumed wedding couple who rode through the trees on decorated camels greeting guests while folk dancers and belly dancers performed.

3. For an extremely smooth ride despite the vessels' shallow drafts; in the Aegean we didn't notice any motion until we looked out and saw a 40 mph wind blowing the lounge chairs all over the deck.

4. For a toning and trimming spa routine with Steiner of London, including thalassotherepy, massage and beauty treatment rooms, saunas and steam rooms, ionotherapy, and nine exercise classes a day plus personal trainers.

5. For the super-gourmet, Cordon Bleu food and wine cruises are offered several times a year.

Five Things You Won't Find On Board

1. A snob; despite the elegance, passengers are very friendly and socialize easily.

2. A baby; the line doesn't permit infants under one and severely limits small children.

3. Enough days at sea; no matter how well-planned the itineraries, passengers never feel they have enough free time to luxuriate aboard these lovely ships.

4. A crowded shore excursion bus; the line's routine is to book enough tour buses to allow everyone to spread out and be comfortable with a maximum of 60 percent of the seats occupied and a carry-on kit of mineral water, soft drinks, etc.

5. An inside cabin, all cabins are spacious and outsides with verandas or large view windows.

SILVER CLOUD SILVER WIND	★★★★★ ★★★★★
Registry	Bahamas
Officers	Italian
Crew	International
Complement	196
GRT	16,800
Length (ft.)	514.14
Beam (ft.)	70.62
Draft (ft.)	18
Passengers-Cabins Full	315
Passengers-2/Cabin	296
Passenger Space Ratio	56.75
Stability Rating	Good to Excellent
Seatings	1
Cuisine	Contemporary
Dress Code	Traditional
Room Service	Yes
Tip	Inclusive

Ship Amenities

Outdoor Pool	1
Indoor Pool	0
Jacuzzi	2
Fitness Center	Yes
Spa	Yes
Beauty Shop	Yes
Showroom	Yes
Bars/Lounges	3
Casino	Yes
Shops	1
Library	Yes
Child Program	No
Self-Service Laundry	Yes
Elevators	4

Cabin Statistics

Suites	148
Outside Doubles	0
Inside Doubles	0
Wheelchair Cabins	2
Singles	0
Single Surcharge	150%
Verandas	110
110 Volt	Yes

SILVERSEA CRUISES, LTD.

SILVERSEA CRUISES, LTD.

Society Expeditions

2001 Western Avenue, Suite 710, Seattle, WA 98121
☎ *(206) 728-9400, (800) 548-8669*

Passengers aboard an expedition cruise in the Bering Strait on the World Discoverer *go birdwatching in a Zodiac.*

History . . . .

Seattle adventurer and entrepreneur T. C Swartz founded Society Expeditions in 1974 under the name Society for the Preservation of Archeological Monuments, dedicated to saving the giant moai statues on Easter Island, and got into the cruise business when he chartered the 138-passenger *World Discoverer* in 1979 for a five-year series of museum and university charters and independent expeditions to exotic areas of the world.

In 1984, when that charter was up, the owner of the vessel, Heiko Klein, head of a German travel company called Discovery Reederei, leased the ship to a short-lived cruise company called Heritage Cruises, which had also chartered the sailing yacht *Sea Cloud*. Heritage hired the famous decorator Carleton Varney to turn the doughty expedition vessel into a chic luxury ship that would offer exotic expeditions with music and entertainment (i.e., life after dinner).

When Heritage went out of business at the end of 1984, Klein again chartered the *World Discoverer* to Swartz. Society also acquired the *Lindblad Explorer* in 1985 when Lindblad Travel went out of business. Klein ultimately ended up buying out Swartz in 1988 to become the owner of Society Expeditions. The company ordered a new expedition ship called the *Society Adventurer*, to be built in Finland and delivered in 1991. Then Klein entered into a marketing agreement with Abercrombie & Kent to promote the two existing expedition ships and the new one coming up.

When the *Society Adventurer* was almost completed, Society Expeditions refused to accept delivery of the $68 million vehicle and started a contractual dispute with the shipyard. In January 1992, Society filed a Chapter 11 reorganization plan bankruptcy. The *Explorer* was acquired by business associate Abercrombie & Kent and the *World Discoverer* leased to Clipper Cruises, which operated the vessel through the end of April 1995. Society Expeditions came back into business in 1994.

—First line to offer a seven-continent world cruise (1982).

—First company to attempt commercial marketing of a tourist space ship cruise into outer space (1984).

DID YOU KNOW?

The erstwhile Society Adventurer languished in the shipyard another two years before making its 1993 debut as the Hanseatic, now part of Radisson Seven Seas Cruises.

Concept . . . .

To offer expedition cruises to a loyal coterie of repeat passengers, along with "the opportunity to visit small, out-of-the-way ports that are inaccessible to larger ships and the delight of traveling with like-minded individuals with whom you share common interests."

Signatures . . . .

The soaring bird logo over the blue-and-white D with the globe inside; the Zodiacs, inflatable landing craft, carried aboard and used almost daily; the inclusion in basic rates of all shore excursions, lectures and special programs; the largesse of throwing in small unadvertised "surprises" during the cruises; the strict environmentally responsible onboard program of waste management.

Gimmicks . . . .

The Ship's Log from every cruise, compiled by the captain and naturalists aboard and mailed to passengers long after they have returned home, reminding them afresh of what a good time they had. On Antarctic cruises the line sends each passenger a bright red parka, so he or she won't get lost in the ice and snow.

Who's the Competition . . . .

There was a time when Society Expeditions and Lindblad Travel virtually dominated the upscale expedition market in the U.S., but while Society was away the newcomers began to play, many of them former associates and/or employees of the two leaders. Now we have Quark Expeditions, which took up the Lindblad/Salen Lindblad banner; Zegrahm Expeditions, founded by a group of ex-Society Expeditions executives and expedition leaders; and the two new luxury expedition ships, the *Bremen* and the *Hanseatic*, originally everyone's hope for the future growth of expeditioning but both operated by companies that are more upscale-mainstream than expedition-oriented.

DID YOU KNOW?

The late Lars-Eric Lindblad of Lindblad Travel also had chartered the World Discoverer *briefly but let it go because regulars on his 80-passenger* Lindblad Explorer *thought the 138-passenger ship was "too big."*

Who's Aboard . . . .

Mostly well-traveled, well-read, upper-income couples and singles over 45—over 65 in most cases, but who's counting? On the *World Discoverer's* historic first Northwest Passage west-to-east crossing, one of the youngest of our fellow passengers was celebrating his 50th birthday. They are alert, curious, quizzical, argumentative, politically conservative but environmentally active, warm, friendly and loving.

Who Should Go . . . .

Perhaps the cost and the length of the cruises have been deterrents to younger passengers in the expedition field, but the last under-35 passenger we can recall was a stowaway on the *World Discoverer's* 32-day transit of the Northwest Passage in 1985.

DID YOU KNOW?

The young stowaway, who got aboard by wearing a Society Expeditions membership pin he had cajoled from a disembarking passenger in Nome and said he was "desperate" to be among the first to transit the Northwest Passage from west to east, was mentally noted by all the other passengers who averaged 50 years his senior but not remarked on, until crew members found him sleeping in a lifeboat (the usual hideaway for a stowaway) the first night out.

Captain Heinz Aye, a stickler for rules, put him off at the first port of call, Little Diomede Island, Alaska, in the Bering Strait three miles from Siberia. The local tribal chief promised the young man could stay for the two weeks until the next plane arrived but "would have to work for his keep." We never saw him again and have often wondered what happened after that day we sailed away and left him on Little Diomede.

Who Should Not Go . . . .

Stowaways, obviously (although Captain Aye is now master of the *Bremen*). Infants and small children, because there are no facilities for them aboard. Wheelchair passengers because there are no easily accessible cabins. Anyone looking for life after dinner.

The Lifestyle ....

Almost everyone becomes obsessed with observation and record-keeping, scribbling in journals, making photographs and sketches, even videotaping with murmured commentary into the side of the camera. We hunt the ship's library for books about the area, flock to 25-year-old documentary films and attend rambling discourses on anything having faintly to do with the subject at hand. Dress is casual in the extreme, the food is good to excellent, and life aboard becomes more comfortable and insular day by day.

Wardrobe. ....

Comfortable, sensible clothes that do not need a lot of care, practical shoes for walking and hiking, rain gear and rubber boots, spare walking shoes to replace the pair you got wet on the last Zodiac landing.

Bill of Fare. .... B+

In the Arctic and Antarctic, passengers always feel a pang of guilt when they hear about the deprivations of the early explorers, then step on the scales to find they've gained another pound or two from the excellent cuisine on board. Fresh fruits and vegetables are air-lifted, by charter plane, if necessary, into some of the most remote airports of the world to keep *World Discoverer* passengers happy and well-fed.

Showtime. .... N/A

Unless watching ancient Film Board of Canada documentaries like "Group Hunting on the Spring Ice, Part III" with a soundtrack entirely in the Netsilik Eskimo dialect is your cup of tea, you'll go to bed after dinner with a good book.

Discounts ....

Previous cruisers with Society Expeditions frequently get direct-mail brochures with early booking discounts on upcoming journeys. Call and ask to get on their mailing list, even if you're not a previous passenger; it just may work.

Explorers meet seals in the Antarctic.

The Bottom Line

Out of the 200-plus cruises we've made during the past 15 years or so, we've spent more days at sea aboard the *World Discoverer* than any other ship—something like 109 days in the Arctic, the Antarctic, Burma, India, Singapore, Indonesia, Fiji, Alaska and Siberia—more than three months altogether, under the auspices of at least three different cruise lines. Obviously we like the ship and its programs very much, but at the same time, we feel the improvements that have been made in expedition cruising with the introduction of the *Bremen* and the *Hanseatic*—private verandas, elegant dining rooms and lounges, state-of-the-art lecture halls—should not be disparaged in the reverse snobbery of the old-time expeditioners. The new ships are more environmentally correct, and they have the opportunity of attracting a larger, younger international market who might appreciate a cabin TV set that receives satellite news or a trio playing for dancing after dinner. We haven't heard the Germans or Japanese on these new ships complaining about "too much luxury."

★★★ ⚓⚓⚓⚓⚓
WORLD DISCOVERER

Along the horizon, as far as the eye could see, shimmering cliffs of ice towered, as if Dover had frozen over. It was a surrealist fantasy. The Beaufort Sea was calm and the sky was blue. Our little blue-and-white ship World Discoverer *seemed trapped between the icy cliffs on one side and the glittering sand-colored skyscrapers of an Arctic Metropolis twinkling with lights and belching flames on the other. Fire and ice in a vast, flat sea. We were five days north of Nome, looking at something no map had prepared us for, one of the Arctic's more devious tricks, a mirage called "looming." The flames and towers to our starboard side were part of the oil equipment at Prudhoe Bay. The stark icy cliffs to our port side were illusions, the flat ice cap of the Beaufort Sea reflecting against itself in the morning sunlight. How many explorers desperately searching for the Northwest Passage during the last 400 years had seen a similar wall of ice ahead and turned back?*

Her dark blue hull, which still reduces pre-1984 passengers into fits of muttering, "But it was always red!" came courtesy of Heritage Cruises' decorator Carleton Varney ("The blue looks more nautical, don't you think?"). There are three decks with passenger cabins, all of them fairly small with basic furnishings and baths with showers only, plus a lavish owner's suite on the Boat Deck and two smaller suites on A Deck. A restaurant and two lounges, one forward and one aft, plus a film/lecture hall on the topmost deck, make up the basic layout. There is a small swimming pool aft on deck and access to the forecastle forward on Boat Deck to see whales, Northern Lights and icebergs.

Between The Lines

The Brochure Says

"The *World Discoverer* is a small cruise ship accommodating only 138 passengers in a relaxed and casually elegant atmosphere. On board, a genuine camaraderie prevails among travelers. Her attentive staff presents every comfort. Each cabin has an outside view, lower beds, private bathroom and individual comfort control."

Translation

Everything is on hand to please the people "who want their adventure and their dry martini too!," as the late Antoinette DeLand, first author of the Fielding cruise guides, observed.

Cabins & Costs

Fantasy Suites: . . . . B+
Average Price Per Person, Double Occupancy, Per Day: Owner's suite $666, other suites $569 in the Antarctic plus airfare.
Although there are three suites on board, the owner's suite on Boat Deck is the largest, a big cabin with large sitting area, king-sized bed, a wall of storage closets and a spacious bath. If that's spoken for, the two 2-room suites on A Deck will do very well, each with two lower beds, dresser and nightstands in the bedroom, sofas and cabinets in the living room, and a bathroom with tub and shower.

Small Splurges: C
Average Price PPPD: $510 in the Antarctic plus airfare.
The deluxe double cabins are a bit bigger than the others and conveniently located on Odyssey Deck. They contain two lower beds, window and bathroom with shower. Closet space is barely adequate.

Suitable Standards: . . . . C-
Average Price PPPD: $431 in the Antarctic plus airfare.
The category 4 cabins on Voyager Deck are where we've spent many of those 109 days; we can still see them in our sleep. There are two lower beds, one of which folds into the wall during the daytime, and one of which makes up as a day sofa. We draw straws to see which one has to sleep in the pull-down bed. Two of them have a third

pull-down bunk, which takes up even more of the limited space. Then you have a desk/dresser with mirror, chair and three drawers, one of which locks, a space where clothes are hung back to front rather than the more standard side by side, a couple of storage shelves with wire baskets and a tiny bath with shower.

Bottom Bunks: . . . . **D**

Average Price PPPD: $333 in the Antarctic plus airfare.

Although the eight forward cabins in Category 1 on Discoverer Deck have two lower beds, they also have those washing-machine portholes with the sea splashing against the glass—when you're lucky enough not have them covered because of rough seas. Baths have shower only, of course, and the rest of the furnishings approximate those in Suitable Standards, above.

The Routes

The *World Discoverer* spends each winter in the Antarctic, as she has for the past 17 years, then sails north along the coast of South America.

The Scoop

The peripatetic *World Discoverer* offers single-seating meals (you can sit where and with whom you please but tables for two are grabbed up quickly) with fairly sophisticated cuisine, along with top-notch lecturers and wildlife experts to help passengers identify seabirds, spot and identify whales, or look for lichens. Late-night activities run more to aurora borealis gazing than disco dancing. There are no casinos or dance bands aboard— there used to be a pianist who doubled as a Zodiac driver, or was it a Zodiac driver that doubled as a pianist?—so entertainment is usually limited to lectures, films and passenger accounts of discoveries from the latest shore explorations, which on a slow day in the high Arctic sometimes deteriorated into a show-and-tell of desiccated animal droppings. It's expensive but rewarding; you should know after reading this whether it's right for you.

Insider Tips

Five Favorite Spots

1. The Crow's Nest, a tiny forward observation area higher than anything else on the ship, situated about where the crow's nest would have been on a sailing ship, with standing room only for half a dozen people at the most, a rail to get a firm grip on, and a view into the crashing, churning sea that is more exciting than any roller coaster ride in any amusement park in the country, especially when you're rounding Cape Horn.

2. The Discoverer Lounge, scene of the nightly "recaps" and once home to the long-gone brass palm trees, a nightclub touch decorator Varney borrowed from Los Angeles' Cocoanut Grove and added to the structural support posts around the room. He wrapped them in brass strips, then hung a cluster of brass "palm fronds" from the low ceiling like foliage on a tree. Unwary dancers ran the risk of getting maimed when they waltzed under them, and the captain pruned them regularly until one day they were entirely gone.

3. The Marco Polo Restaurant, once pretty in pink with chairs that used to be too big and heavy to pull up under the tables, has been trimmed down but still looks lovely, and offers open seating.

4. The lecture hall is the most popular after-lunch nap spot on the ship, especially if the documentary of the day is a couple of decades old.

5. The Lido Lounge, a big comfortable aft lounge with banquettes, tables and chairs, used all day long from buffet breakfast and lunch through needlepoint, reading, postcard-writing and chatting.

Five Good Reasons to Book These Ship

1. To go to the Antarctic and see the penguins.

2. To visit the captain and navigator on the open bridge.

3. To have the optimum opportunity for spotting marine mammals—this ship detours for whales.

4. To get a free red coat—the Arctic/Antarctic parka that is one of the perks of booking a polar cruise.

5. To check out Christmas Island or Kirabati Atoll.

Five Things You Won't Find On Board

1. A room key; passengers leave their cabins unlocked during the day, bolting them from the inside when they go to bed.

2. Room service (unless you're sick).

3. Cabins designated wheelchair-accessible; but there is an elevator aboard, albeit a small one.

4. An inside cabin.

5. Frivolous reading in the library.

WORLD DISCOVERER ★★★, ⚓⚓⚓⚓

Registry	**Liberia**
Officers	**German**
Crew	**International**
Complement	**75**
GRT	**3153**
Length (ft.)	**285**
Beam (ft.)	**50**
Draft (ft.)	**15**
Passengers-Cabins Full	**138**
Passengers-2/Cabin	**129**
Passenger Space Ratio	**24.44**
Stability Rating	**Good**
Seatings	**1**
Cuisine	**Continental**
Dress Code	**Casual**
Room Service	**No**
Tip	**$8 PPPD**

Ship Amenities

Outdoor Pool	**1**
Indoor Pool	**0**
Jacuzzi	**0**
Fitness Center	**Yes**
Spa	**No**
Beauty Shop	**Yes**
Showroom	**No**
Bars/Lounges	**2**
Casino	**No**
Shops	**1**
Library	**Yes**
Child Program	**No**
Self-Service Laundry	**No**
Elevators	**1**

Cabin Statistics

Suites	**3**
Outside Doubles	**59**
Inside Doubles	**0**
Wheelchair Cabins	**0**
Singles	**0**
Single Surcharge	**140%**
Verandas	**0**
110 Volt	**No**

SVEN-OLOF LINDBLAD'S
SPECIALEXPEDITIONS

123 South Avenue East, Third Floor, Westfield, NJ 07090
☎ *(908) 654-0048, (800) 348-2358*

Polaris *passengers explore the islands off Baja California by Zodiac.*

History . . . .

Launched in 1979 as a travel company offshoot of Lindblad Travel by
Sven-Olof Lindblad, son of the late expedition pioneer Lars-Eric Lindblad, Special Expeditions has also carved out its own very special niche
in expedition cruising. Sven bought the division in 1984 and acquired
the line's first ship, the 80-passenger *Polaris*, the former *Lindblad
Polaris*, in 1987, followed by the *Sea Lion* in 1989 and the *Sea Bird* in
1990. Sven and his wife Maria own the *Swedish Islander*, a 128-foot
ship that carries 45 passengers around the Stockholm Archipelago for a
program called "Impressions of a Swedish Summer," putting them up
overnight in small country inns. Special Expeditions also owns the *Caledonian Star.*

Concept . . . .

The logo for Special Expeditions, a giant eye in dark blue, "stands for a
different way of looking at the world, with more of an in-depth perspec-
tive," says Lindblad. Many of the places his expeditions visit are fresh
and fascinating, not always as gee-whiz name-dropper stops but visited

rather for their own unique environments, and the company's excellent expedition leaders and naturalists devote considerable time and attention to interpreting them for passengers.

Signatures . . . .

The blue eye logo on the stack of the line's flagship *Caledonian Star* and *Polaris* and the sides of the smaller *Sea Lion* and *Sea Bird.*

Zodiacs, inflatable rubber landing craft used to explore ashore or venture in close to icebergs and cliffs of nesting seabirds.

Allowing a serendipitous flexibility in the schedule when something special occurs.

Including all shore excursions and sightseeing, as well as some transfers and shore meals, in the basic fares.

A generosity of spirit in refusing to exploit on-board revenue—visits to the ship's doctor are free and the staff frequently offers free drinks or beer and wine with meals.

Gimmicks. . . . .

Publishing individual brochures for each sailing or series of similar sailings rather than an entire catalogue of cruises by the year.

Who's the Competition . . . .

The line's classic competitors in the expedition field are the *Explorer* from Abercrombie & Kent, once its Lindblad Travel stablemate, and Society Expeditions' *World Discoverer.* In Alaska and the Pacific Northwest, the *Sea Lion* and *Sea Bird* come head-to-head with Alaska Sightseeing/Cruise West's very similar small vessels, which offer fewer expeditioning extras than Lindblad.

Who's Aboard. . . . .

Mostly seniors and retirees who have the time and money for expeditioning and the thirst to learn more about the world around them.

Who Should Go . . . .

Birdwatchers of the world—these are some of the most fantastic voyages for birding we've ever been aboard; whale watchers and wildlife spotters; photographers; more young people who enjoy hiking and ecotourism.

Who Should Not Go . . . .

Families with very young children—there's no program for children and no place for them to play.

People with wheelchairs or walkers—these ships have no elevators but do have numerous steep stairs and gangways to negotiate.

The Lifestyle . . . .

The overall ambience is one of fun and discovery, due in part to the energetic young naturalists and expedition leaders. Dress is casual, and single-seating meals are served at unassigned tables. Aboard the *Caledonian Star* and *Polaris,* you'll be able to have your hair done, see a doctor or take a sauna, but don't expect a Jacuzzi, cabin TV set, casino, slot machines or after-dinner entertainment. You may, however, go ashore on an uninhabited island for a barbecue dinner or set out in a glass-bottomed boat on a balmy moonlit night to sip champagne while drifting over luminous seas sparkling with rainbow-colored fish, or go swimming or snorkeling from empty beaches in clear turquoise waters. You'll also go back to school if you wish—and everyone does—attending lectures, reading supplementary materials and watching films and slides when not actually ashore or in a Zodiac exploring.

Wardrobe . . . .

Very casual, sturdy expeditioning clothes—jeans, twills, shorts and T-shirts, swimsuits, sweaters, depending on the climate, plus sturdy shoes for deck wear and hiking ashore and rain gear in some climates. Most passengers take along one sort of dress-up outfit, not black tie and sequins but more on the order of bolo tie and knit dress.

Bill of Fare . . . . B

Food is not an obsession with Sven-Olof's passengers—most require only that it be healthful, substantial and digestible with no strange seasonings or ingredients a lifelong New Englander can't recognize. The chefs do a nice job in spite of the guests. Meals are served at a single open seating, allowing passengers to sit where and with whom they please. They do, however, as we have observed over the years, tend to stake out the same table and tablemates for most of the cruise.

Showtime . . . . N/A

Unless you count the nightly 7 p.m. "recap"—the recapitulation of what happened today and the forecast of what may or may not happen tomorrow—as entertainment, these ships have none.

The Bottom Line

Special Expeditions has moved ahead carefully and cautiously, concentrating on its strong suits rather than trying to spread itself too thin and offer too many options to its dedicated repeaters, many of whom sailed with Sven's father before him. It is a solid, predictable cruise product of very high quality and dignity, worth every penny of the sometimes substantial price.

Rather than offer optional shore excursions, Special Expeditions includes them in a seamless, free-form program that takes advantage of serendipity.

★★★   ⚓⚓⚓⚓⚓
CALEDONIAN STAR

She's not particularly handsome nor very lavish—there are no cabins with private verandas, for example, and our waiter—lovesick, homesick, the Hamlet of the dining room—never once got a single meal order correct at our table of four. But she's one of our very favorite ships in the world. Not just anybody can handle a mix of 76 very exacting British and American veteran travelers on a 24-day cruise along the coast of West Africa and leave them as happy at the end as at the beginning. We'd go again tomorrow.

Zodiacs carried aboard the Caledonian Star *ferry passengers ashore for expeditionary visits to unusual islands.*

The *Caledonian Star*, the former *North Star* from now-defunct Exploration Cruise Lines, is much better known in Great Britain than in the United States, and the company gets a tremendous amount of repeat business from there. Itineraries are exotic enough to titillate even the most-traveled members of the Century Club, and the lived-in, unpretentious vessel somehow manages to always make one feel at home. There are five passenger decks, with cabins on three of them; all cabins are outsides. The topmost deck has a sun deck and library/lecture hall, and the Veranda Deck is where the pool and main lounge are located. The dining room is one deck lower. Cabins are smallish and bathrooms are standard all over the ship with showers rather than tubs. The ship underwent a major renovation recently.

Between The Lines

The Brochure Says

"...the sense of expectation is only heightened when you are aboard an exciting ship like the *Caledonian Star*. Built for expedition travel, she accommodates 110 passengers in comfort, with special amenities such as a swimming pool. We will also make full use of her fleet of Zodiac landing craft for spontaneous landings and for exploration of the spectacular scenery."

Translation

A very apt description of the ship and its lifestyle.

EAVESDROPPING

A travel agent who specializes in expedition cruises: "You're not going to take a Seabourn person and put him on an expedition cruise. You have to be very careful and be sure you know your client."

Cabins & Costs

Fantasy Suites: . . . . **C**

Average Price Per Person, Double Occupancy, Per Day: $838 plus airfare.
There are three suites aboard, none of them to die for, but spacious enough, with separate living room, bedroom and small bath with shower. The living room sofa can convert to a bed as well.

Small Splurges: . . . . **D**

Average Price PPPD: $570 plus airfare.
The three deluxe staterooms on the lower passenger deck cannot really be recommended because of the water sloshing against the portholes in heavy seas, even though there's a sofa bed, built-in desk, and separate sitting room divided from the bedroom by a curtain.

Suitable Standards: . . . . **C+**

Average Price PPPD: $523 plus airfare.
The standards are small but comfortable enough, with windows on upper decks and portholes on lower decks. There are two lower beds, one of which converts to a sofa for daytime, plus a desk/dresser with chair, a TV/VCR, a couple of large mirrors and a mini-refrigerator. There's limited drawer space but plenty of open shelf space in the hanging closets. The bathroom has a counter and sink, marine vacuum toilet and shower, plus additional storage under the sink counter and in a mirrored medicine chest on the wall.

Bottom Bunks: . . . . D

Average Price PPPD: $477 plus airfare
The basic cabins are similar to the standards or a bit smaller (see "Suitable Standards") with two lower beds, but are located on the lowest passenger deck, with portholes instead of windows and that sloshing sea.

The Routes

The ship starts 1998 in Madagascar, cruising to Zanzibar and Dar es Salaam, then sails through the Red Sea to the Mediterranean for summer itineraries that accent history and culture. The British Isles are explored as well.

The Scoop

While not new and certainly not in the class of the glamorous *Hanseatic* and *Bremen*, the *Caledonian Star* is a handsome and comfortable expedition vessel. The food aboard is not haute cuisine, but it is well prepared and varied, with expansive breakfast and lunch buffets as well as à la carte hot dishes cooked to order. A baker prepares fresh breads, pastries and cakes daily. The Scandinavian officers keep the navigation bridge open to passengers except during severe weather or entering and leaving certain ports where local officials don't like to see passengers on the bridge. The lifestyle aboard is easygoing, and both passengers and crew are congenial. We would not recommend booking cabins on the lowest passenger deck because of the sea sloshing against the portholes like the water in an automatic washing machine.

Insider Tips

Five Favorite Places

1. The library and lecture hall has a fascinating collection of esoteric books about nature, wooden armchairs, heavy fixed tables, and self-service coffee, tea and cookies around the clock.

2. The sun deck outside the library is also where barbecues and picnics are set up at long wooden tables, along with a grill and a buffet table.

3. The swimming pool, large enough for lap swimming, unusual on a ship this small, surrounded by white plastic chairs and tables.

4. The main lounge is a handsome, comfortable room with sofas and chairs and a long banquette along one side, and a small dance floor and patio, plus (when we were aboard) plenty of live green plants.

5. A small dining room with windows, and tables for four, six and eight.

Five Good Reasons to Book This Ship

1. The itineraries, the itineraries, the itineraries.

2. The open single meal seatings that let you sit where and with whom you please, giving a good chance to get to know the lecturers as well as the other passengers.

3. The Zodiac landing craft that can take you exploring to uninhabited islands.

4. Because all the shore excursions are included in the basic fare.

5. The excellent quality of the expedition leaders and lecturers.

Five Things You Won't Find On Board

1. An elevator; you do an awful lot of walking up and down companionways on this ship.

2. A closed navigation bridge; the bridge is always open to passengers, as are the bridge wings, so long as passengers don't get in the way.

3. Room service; you don't get waited on unless you're sick.

4. Casino; the passengers are not really interested in gambling.

5. Cabins designated wheelchair-accessible; the ship is inappropriate for anyone with limited mobility.

CALEDONIAN STAR ★★★, ⚓⚓⚓⚓⚓

Registry	**Bahamas**
Officers	**Scandinavian**
Crew	**Filipino**
Complement	**63**
GRT	**3,095**
Length (ft.)	**292.5**
Beam (ft.)	**45.5**
Draft (ft.)	**21**
Passengers-Cabins Full	**134**
Passengers-2/Cabin	**110**
Passenger Space Ratio	**28.13**
Stability Rating	**Good**
Seatings	**1**
Cuisine	**Continental**
Dress Code	**Casual**
Room Service	**No**
Tip	**$7 PPPD**

Ship Amenities

Outdoor Pool	**1**
Indoor Pool	**0**
Jacuzzi	**0**
Fitness Center	**No**
Spa	**No**
Beauty Shop	**Yes**
Showroom	**Yes**
Bars/Lounges	**1**
Casino	**No**
Shops	**1**
Library	**Yes**
Child Program	**No**
Self-Service Laundry	**No**
Elevators	**0**

Cabin Statistics

Suites	**3**
Outside Doubles	**45**
Inside Doubles	**0**
Wheelchair Cabins	**0**
Singles	**14**
Single Surcharge	**150%**
Verandas	**0**
110 Volt	**Yes**

★★★ ⚓⚓⚓⚓⚓
POLARIS

Expeditioners would rather actively participate than passively observe, would be more intent at a slide lecture on seabird migration than a big-money game of jackpot bingo and are unruffled when schedules and itineraries are juggled without notice because of weather conditions or other unexpected problems. There's little ostentation—dressing for dinner may mean changing into clean clothes, and the only one-upmanship practiced at cocktail time is about rare birds spotted or offbeat destinations visited previously.

Homey, low-key and comfortable, the 82-passenger *Polaris* provides single-seating meals at unassigned tables for four or six, allowing everyone a chance to get acquainted, and wide windows in the dining room mean no one has to miss a dolphin sighting during lunch. On one *Polaris* cruise, our well-traveled fellow passengers, many near or past retirement age, included an archeologist from New Mexico, a New York architect, a Hollywood screenwriter-director, a rice farmer from California's central valley, attorneys, university professors and stockbrokers.

The Bahamian-registry ship is sturdy rather than glamorous, but the cabins are well-furnished and comfortable and the Filipino service staff and Swedish officers friendly and efficient. The captain usually allows visitors on the bridge on an informal basis.

DID YOU KNOW?

The Polaris *was the only cruise ship that passed through the Panama Canal during the U.S. military action against Panama's president Manuel Noriega in 1989. The ship was already in the canal when the firing started, and was stalled at the locks nearest Panama City for an hour or so, with some gunfire and a lot of helicopters flying overhead. The passengers were brought inside and below decks since there was shooting going on. "It was terrible for our bird list," one of the naturalists observed later.*

The Brochure Says

"...unforgettable journeys where you discover, learn and enjoy."

Translation

This is the strong suit aboard the *Polaris*, the chance to explore and discover all the wonders of the Galapagos.

Fantasy Suites: .... B

Average Price Per Person Double Occupancy Per Day: $522 plus airfare.
The owner's suite has two full-sized beds and a lot of space (but it's no bigger than the slightly cheaper #321 down the hall). Sitting areas are handsomely furnished in navy blue with sofa and matching chair piped in red, and there is a desk/dresser with its own chair, a coffee table and two windows.

Small Splurges: .... B

Average Price PPPD: $475 plus airfare.
The aforementioned #321 (see above) has much the same decor and furniture as the owner's suite and is also convenient to the public area and decks; it has two windows.

Suitable Standards: .... B

Average Price PPPD: $400 plus airfare.
The largest category of standard cabins is Category 2 with 22 examples, all but one with windows instead of portholes. (Cabin #101 one deck lower has a porthole). All cabins are outsides. Twin beds, windows, a desk/dresser with chair, lamp and telephone, and bathroom with shower are typical of this category.

Bottom Bunks: C

Average Price PPPD: $368 plus airfare.
Four outside doubles with portholes instead of windows are the lowest-priced cabins aboard, and contain the same general decor and furniture arrangement as the suitable standards, above. Your portholes will sometimes look like washing machines when seas are churning.

The *Polaris* cruises all year round in the Galapagos, making 11-day land/cruise programs between Quito and Quayaquil.

Basically it's a no-frills cruise with some largish, some smallish cabins, lectures and slide shows; inflatable rubber landing craft to take passengers ashore; and no-nonsense dinners, briskly served and sometimes eaten without a change of clothes from the last expedition of the afternoon. But the ship is a favorite of well-traveled people for its warmth and friendliness. It's expensive, but we've never been disappointed with a cruise aboard the *Polaris*.

Insider Tips

Five Good Reasons to Book This Ship

1. To get an incomparable introduction to an exotic corner of the world that is unique, Ecuador's Galapagos Islands.

2. To travel with like-minded fellow passengers who care intensely about nature and the environment.

3. To listen to some of the brightest and best naturalist/lecturers on the expedition circuit.

4. To be able to scoot around the seas in zodiacs or the ship's own glass-bottomed boat.

5. To be able to go on the "open bridge" and look at the radar and navigation charts and chat with the officers.

POLARIS ★★★, ⚓⚓⚓⚓

Registry	**Bahamas**
Officers	**Swedish**
Crew	**Filipino**
Complement	**44**
GRT	**2214**
Length (ft.)	**238**
Beam (ft.)	**43**
Draft (ft.)	**14**
Passengers-Cabins Full	**82**
Passengers-2/Cabin	**82**
Passenger Space Ratio	**27**
Stability Rating	**Good**
Seatings	**1**
Cuisine	**Continental**
Dress Code	**Casual**
Room Service	**No**
Tip	**$7 PPPD, 15% automatically added to bar check**

Ship Amenities

Outdoor Pool	**0**
Indoor Pool	**0**
Jacuzzi	**0**
Fitness Center	**No**
Spa	**No**
Beauty Shop	**Yes**
Showroom	**No**
Bars/Lounges	**1**
Casino	**No**
Shops	**3**
Library	**Yes**
Child Program	**No**
Self-Service Laundry	**Yes**
Elevators	**1**

Cabin Statistics

Suites	**1**
Outside Doubles	**40**
Inside Doubles	**0**
Wheelchair Cabins	**0**
Singles	**0**
Single Surcharge	**150%**
Verandas	**0**
110 Volt	**No**

★★ ⚓⚓⚓⚓
SEA BIRD
SEA LION

Both ships cruise the Sea of Cortez in winter, where sea lions sunning them-
selves on rocky ledges slide off into the creamy foam to swim over to our rub-
ber craft for a closer look. They show great curiosity, playfully swimming and
rolling about and deliberately splashing us, then swimming away again. One
large dominant male, who felt our presence threatened his harem, followed us
doggedly, bellowing loudly and showing his teeth in the most aggressive dis-
play he could summon. Overhead, the tropic birds darted around gossiping
shrilly with each other, and the blue-footed boobies honked hoarsely across
the guano-covered rocks. This is the noisiest island in the unspoiled group that
is North America's equivalent of the Galapagos.

This pair of sturdy little American-built expedition vessels have been re-
configured since their days with now-defunct Exploration Cruise Lines,
when they sailed as the *Majestic Explorer* and *Great Rivers Explorer*. Now
they carry only 70 passengers instead of the 92 they used to handle. Meals
are single-seating. Cabins are all outsides, but instead of windows or portholes, the four lowest-priced accommodations on the lower deck have
portlights located high up in the walls, which let in a little light but don't
allow a view. The ships carry Zodiacs, inflatable rubber landing craft, in
order to take passengers exploring ashore or in the sea. A shallow eight-foot
draft permits these small vessels to get into small ports and visit uninhabited
islands.

Between The Lines

The Brochure Says

"Your voyage is led by historians and naturalists rather than conventional tour guides, specialists who share their enthusiasm for the area with informal talks, slide presentations, and anecdotes over drinks at the end of the day. You join them for frequent trips ashore, and on forays in Zodiac landing craft to explore remote areas."

Translation

This is not a cruise, this is a learning expedition that will enrich a part of your life, or at least teach you how to recognize a frigate bird in flight.

Cabins & Costs

Fantasy Suites: .... **N/A**

There are no cabins on board in this category.

Small Splurges: .... **B**

Average Price Per Person, Double Occupancy, Per Day: $482 plus airfare.
The Category 4 aft cabins on Upper Deck, #216 and #219, are large and comfortable and only steps away from the deck when you want to run out and see the (choose one: bear, whale, porpoises, sea lions, pelicans). They have twin beds or double beds, depending on which cabin you select, a dinette seating arrangement with benches and table and large window. The bathrooms throughout the ship are quite compact with shower only.

Suitable Standards: .... **C-**

Average Price PPPD: $347 plus airfare.
Upper Deck category 2 cabins are a bit smaller than the category 4 (see Small Splurges, above) but contain twin beds and a big window.

Bottom Bunks: .... **D**

Average Price PPPD: $247 plus airfare.
The four cheapest category cabins are on the lowest passenger deck with portlights instead of windows, meaning you have a little daylight but don't get to look outside. One double bed and a single that converts to a couch in the daytime round out the furnishings, and there is a small bathroom with shower.

The Routes

Both *Sea Lion* and *Sea Bird* cruise on whale-watching cruises off of Mexico's Baja California in the winter. In spring and fall the ships cruise from Portland along the Columbia River and Hells Canyon, Idaho, "In the Wake of Lewis and Clark."

"Exploring Alaska's Coastal Wilderness" sailings depart throughout June, July and August, sailing between Juneau and Sitka on eight-day itineraries, exploring Point Adolphus and the Althorp Rocks, where humpback whales often feed; spending a full day in Glacier Bay; calling at Haines; and exploring around Admiralty Island, Le Conte Bay and Tracy Arm. During May and late August/early September, the vessels sail between Sitka and Seattle, calling in Juneau and Ketchikan and cruising British Columbia's Inside Passage, Alert Bay and Johnstone Strait, as well as visiting the San Juan Islands in Washington.

September offers departures of seven-day Islands and Wildlife of the Pacific Northwest that includes the San Juan Islands, Victoria, Princess Louisa Inlet, Johnstone Strait and Alert Bay, disembarking in Vancouver.

The Scoop

Shore excursions, visits to the ship's doctor, nonalcoholic beverages and use of snorkeling equipment are all included in the basic fare. Most of the cabins open directly onto an outer deck, which could be a nuisance in cold rainy weather like you get sometimes in Alaska. To avoid this, book one of the cheaper Category 1 or Category 2 cabins on a lower deck. While dress is casual, do bring along a change of sneakers, since you often get wet feet on Zodiac landings.

A rare spotting of a black bear provides great photo ops.

Insider Tips

Five Familiar Places

1. The dining rooms, big enough for everyone in one open seating with passengers free to sit where they please, have round and rectangular tables for five to eight.

2. In the observation lounges, the furniture is arranged in conversational groupings with swivel chairs and fixed small tables; lectures, "recaps" and social gatherings take place here.

3. The Sun Deck makes a good place for lounging and reading between wildlife spotting and bird-watching.

4. The upper deck forward is where to gather to watch the dolphins that swim with the ship in the warm waters of the Sea of Cortez.

5. Despite their modest sizes, *Sea Bird* and *Sea Lion* have full around-the-ship promenade decks for inveterate walkers who don't mind a double-digit number of laps to make a mile.

Five Good Reasons to Book These Ships

1. To learn how to identify frigate birds, tropic birds and blue-footed boobies in flight.

2. To explore the rivers, deltas, fjords and seas of the American West.

3. To ride Mexico's dramatic Copper Canyon Railway and go whale-spotting in the Sea of Cortez, all on the same unforgettable eight-day trip.

4. To take a comfortable, affordable expedition close to home in little more than a week.

5. To venture into places such as Princess Louisa Inlet looking for black bears and Point Adolphus, where the humpback whales feed.

Sea Bird *and* **Sea Lion** *take passengers for close-up looks at Alaska.*

Five Things You Won't Find On Board

1. A children's program.

2. Cabins designated wheelchair-accessible.

3. Room service.

4. Spa and beauty shop.

5. Elevators.

SEA BIRD
SEA LION

★★, ⚓⚓⚓⚓
★★, ⚓⚓⚓⚓

Registry	**Bahamas**
Officers	**Swedish**
Crew	**Filipino**
Complement	**22**
GRT	**99.7**
Length (ft.)	**152**
Beam (ft.)	**31**
Draft (ft.)	**8**
Passengers-Cabins Full	**76**
Passengers-2/Cabin	**72**
Passenger Space Ratio	**NA**
Stability Rating	**Good**
Seatings	**1**
Cuisine	**American**
Dress Code	**Casual**
Room Service	**No**
Tip	**$7 PPPD, 15% automatically added to bar check**

Ship Amenities

Outdoor Pool	**0**
Indoor Pool	**0**
Jacuzzi	**0**
Fitness Center	**No**
Spa	**No**
Beauty Shop	**No**
Showroom	**No**
Bars/Lounges	**1**
Casino	**No**
Shops	**1**
Library	**Yes**
Child Program	**No**
Self-Service Laundry	**No**
Elevators	**0**

Cabin Statistics

Suites	**0**
Outside Doubles	**36**
Inside Doubles	**0**
Wheelchair Cabins	**0**
Singles	**0**
Single Surcharge	**150%**
Verandas	**0**
110 Volt	**Yes**

⚓⚓⚓

SWEDISH ISLANDER

A common refrain among those of us who travel is that we're doing it "to get to know the people," but all too often, especially on a first visit to a country, we find ourselves herded about in groups, getting acquainted with someone from Cleveland on a shore excursion of Rome or chatting among ourselves about gasoline prices back home. But this cruise lets you get to meet the Swedes, lots of them, as you cruise from one small island to another.

Swedish Islander *passengers don colorful life vests before visiting remote islands by Zodiac.*

A charming and unusual summer cruise program is that of the *Swedish Islander*, which lets you cruise languidly with four dozen fellow passengers through an archipelago of 24,000 islands, exploring by day in inflatable Zodiac landing craft, going ashore at night to dine and sleep in Swedish country inns, some of them members of Europe's Romantik Hotels group.

Passengers get unusual views of Sweden from a Zodiac on its canals.

You'll visit glass factories, picnic on the lawn of a former royal summer palace, hike through a Swedish National Park, eat a barbecue lunch on an isolated island, search for birds and wildflowers or go fishing. Another day is spent in the delightful town of Mariefred visiting Gripsholm Castle.

The eight-day land/cruise program costs around $2580 per person, double occupancy, plus airfare, which is around $1000 roundtrip from Newark.

STAR CLIPPERS, LTD.

4101 Salzedo Avenue, Coral Gables, FL 33146
☎ (305) 442-0550, (800) 442-0551

A passenger lends a hand with the sails aboard the **Star Clipper.**

History . . . .

Swedish-born yachtsman and shipping executive Mikael Krafft introduced the first of his two classic square-rigged, four-masted clipper
ships in June 1991, in the reverse order from what he had planned.
Since the name of his company is Star Clipper, he naturally intended to
debut the *Star Clipper* first, but found himself embroiled in litigation
with St. Louis-based Clipper Cruise Line over the proprietary use of the
name "Clipper." The Missouri-based Clipper, which operates motor
vessels, not sailing ships, claimed the use of the word entailed copyright
infringement. So the *Star Flyer* debuted first (same ship, different
name) while the case was pursued, then settled by the time the *Star
Clipper* arrived in the Caribbean at the end of 1991.

—The tallest ships in the world (226 feet in mast height).

Concept . . . .

To experience the essence of sailing in its purest form, says the line, on a ship where computerized systems have not replaced human hands in the ancient ritual of raising sails.

Signatures . . . .

The 30 sails with 36,000 feet of canvas snapping taut in the wind is as distinctive an image as a cruise line could wish.

Daily sail-training classes conducted on both ships teach sailing a square rigger to every interested passenger and award diplomas of Nautical Achievement on the final night of the cruise.

Gimmicks. . . . .

The taciturn parrot named Captain Loreto was brought on board *Star Flyer* and trained to talk by owner Mikael Krafft, but the trauma of actually sailing resulted in long spells of silence in the early days. Later, either he perked up or another parrot replaced him, because he became loquacious and a popular feature of the ship.

Who's the Competition . . . .

Traditional sailing vessels such as the *Star Clipper* ships differ from the wind-cruiser vessels such as the Windstar and Club Med ships but would attract some of the same thirtysomething couples because of the romance of it all. Classic tall ships such as the Windjammers lack the luxurious cabins and public rooms the Star Clippers provide. "Wow," one Windjammer veteran said about the *Star Clipper*, "this is so luxurious compared to Windjammer," which she described as "sort of like camping out with cold showers and stuff."

Who's Aboard. . . . .

Sophisticated travelers who are successful and live well but may not have taken a cruise before; sailing enthusiasts from both Europe and America; mostly couples. It may be a person who made a safari in Africa last year who wants to cross the Atlantic on a square-rigged sailing ship this year.

The average passenger is 47, a professional, married. Half are first-time cruisers.

"A lot of our passengers," one executive says, "are people who have done a bare boat charter in the Caribbean and the wives have found out it wasn't as much fun as they thought; the husband was out fishing while the wife was in scrubbing the head."

Who Should Go . . . .

A New Jersey travel agent we sailed with aboard the *Star Clipper* said she would gear the ship toward people to whom relaxation is paramount, to couples in their mid-30s and older, to outgoing singles and to honeymooners when the ships call at romantic ports. Or to someone who doesn't cruise but takes a condo in Maui or goes skiing in Aspen for a week.

Who Should Not Go . . . .

The ships are not appropriate for people in wheelchairs or who have difficulty walking, since there are no elevators and plenty of stairs and extra-high sills. Bookings for children under 8 years old are also discouraged.

The Lifestyle . . . .

There's a wonderful sense of casual camaraderie aboard, appealing to anyone looking to unwind from a stressful job. The ports are colorful and interesting with few "must see" destinations so the obligation of shore excursions is removed. Most passengers set out on their own to stroll through the ports, perhaps lunching or dining ashore. Passengers are allowed to lend a hand with the sails if they wish, and, when seas permit, the ship anchors for swimming, sailing and windsurfing from the gangway platform. Informal classes in navigation and sail-handling are also offered. A team of sports directors supervises aerobics classes, snorkeling lessons and diving trips for passengers with certification.

Wardrobe . . . .

Dress is casual aboard, although some passengers don fashionable resortwear for dinner. Jackets are never required, but shorts and T-shirts are not considered acceptable at dinner. The term "casual elegance" crops up in the brochure a couple of times. The right footwear is particularly important, with rubber-soled deck shoes of some sort essential for getting around the ropes and gear on deck.

Bill of Fare . . . . .B

Out of necessity, food is less elaborate aboard sailing vessels because the galleys are smaller and don't allow banquet-type catering preparation. Breakfasts and lunches are often served buffet-style with a choice of several hot and several cold dishes, and dinner is served course by course but with a limited selection—two appetizers, one soup, one salad, a pasta, a choice of two main dishes and two desserts plus ice cream. A table of hot and cold hors d'oeuvres is set out on deck daily at 5:30 p.m.

Showtime C

To supplement a resident singer/pianist, local entertainment is brought on in some ports. In the Mediterranean, a pair of opera singers from Elba entertained during dinner one evening. Another night, a Corsican quartet headed up by a Dean Martin lookalike in a pin-striped suit played European pop music and American '50s rock for dancing on the deck under the stars. TV sets in the cabins play movies during the day and evening on two channels when the hotel manager remembers to load the videos. A 24-hour news crawl is updated regularly.

Discounts . . . .

From time to time, special pricing promotions on designated sailings may also include one category upgrade for early booking and special air/sea package fares. Have your travel agent inquire.

The Bottom Line

One important detail to remember is that sailing ships do not stick to itineraries as steadfastly as bigger cruise liners, since winds and sea conditions may necessitate last-minute port changes. But flexibility is part of the fun.

★ ★ ★ ★
STAR CLIPPER
STAR FLYER

Sailing represents romance to a woman, adventure to a man, we were told while standing at the rail of the Star Flyer off the Isle of Wight in 1991. The new ship had just sailed from Belgium and along with a BBC-TV crew and some British press, we sailed out from Southampton to meet her. At the last minute, we were given permission to come aboard, and climbed up the Jacob's Ladder against the steep, sheer side of the ship for what seemed a mile before being pulled over the rail onto her deck.

While passengers are not usually permitted to climb the Jacob's Ladder up the side, they can venture out on the bowsprit, which has a safety net underneath, to lie back and see the ship's sails from that vantage point, to stand on the outdoor bridge and watch the helmsman at work, or go out in an inflatable Zodiac landing craft to photograph the ship under full sail. The Star Clippers are very hands-on vessels for passengers, who lend a hand with the sails if they wish. The forward deck is where the serious work goes on; amidships and aft deck are swimming pools and lounging chairs for serious sunning.

The Brochure Says

"Perhaps nothing stirs the spirit so much as the romantic era of the great clipper ships. Today, a new name proudly carries on the tradition of the tall ships with two new sailing vessels—the first passenger sailing vessels to be classified by Lloyds since the early 1900s."

Translation

It's rare and wonderful to be able to sail aboard a square-rigger and recall the brief days of the clipper ships, the two decades between the California Gold Rush of 1849 and the opening of the Suez Canal in 1869. These classic vessels, built by Scheepswerven Langerbrugge in Ghent, Belgium, were rated A-100 by Lloyds, and passed U.S. Coast Guard inspection on the first try, a rarity in the port of Miami.

Cabins & Costs

Fantasy Suites: .... NA

Average Price Per Person, Double Occupancy, Per Day: N/A
There is a "secret" owner's suite on board—at the extreme aft end of Clipper Deck—that is sometimes put on the market or used as a special charity auction item or for the CEO on incentives and charters. With a queen-sized bed, sofas, mini-refrigerator, TV in a built-in cabinet, four bedroom portholes, a large closet, a marble bathroom with a gold faucet Jacuzzi tub and porthole, it's pretty lavish. There's even an escape hatch to the pool deck above.

Small Splurges: .... B+

Average Price PPPD: $370 plus airfare.
Category 1 cabins aft on Sun Deck near the pool have twin beds that can be put together into a queen-sized, a mini-refrigerator stocked with complimentary beverages, and a large bathroom with Jacuzzi tub. Four portholes are built up high so no one looks in while walking past. Cellular satellite direct-dial phones are in every cabin, along with TV/VCR and hair dryers.

Suitable Standards: .... B

Average Price PPPD: $320 plus airfare.
We booked a category 2 double with a king-sized bed (two lower beds pushed together with a thin fill mattress across the top) and built-in storage underneath. A built-in corner chair has a drawer underneath, and there's fairly good hanging space, one full-length about two feet wide and one half-length, a safe and three open shelves below, plus a third cupboard that is all open shelves top to bottom. The bathroom has a medicine chest, some counter space around the sink (with a faucet water control that you push on but goes off by itself just when you're ready to rinse your toothbrush), and a shower that also saves water by turning off just when you've soaped up.

Bottom Bunks: C

Average Price PPPD: $213 plus airfare.
Standard inside cabins with upper and lower berths have plenty of shelving, wall lamps and privacy curtains across doorway; this is the only cabin category aboard that doesn't have TV sets.

The Routes

Star Clipper is based in Antigua, setting out every Saturday for seven-day sailings on two alternate itineraries, one to St. Barts, Tortola, Norman Island, Virgin Gorda Sound, St. Maarten and St. Kitts, alternating with Statia; the other visiting Dominica, St. Lucia, St. Vincent, Bequia, Tobago Cays, Martinique and Iles des Saintes.

Star Flyer cruises the Mediterranean, Greek Isles and Turkey in summer and the Caribbean in winter.

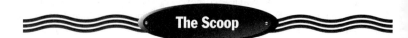

The Scoop

The Star Clippers spend more time under sail than the modern wind-cruisers, particularly in the Caribbean out of Antigua where the winds are favorable; the *Star Clipper* is under sail at sunset every day but one, and spends a full 36 hours nonstop under sail on alternate weeks in the Tobago Cays, a real treat for a sailor. While the service in the dining room may not be as polished as on the Sea Goddess, these ships are beautiful and unique, and will provide a lifetime of wonderful memories of being under sail.

Insider Tips

Five Fine Places

1. The Tropical Bar, outdoors with a white tarp covering the area, two fixed high wood tables with six built-in wood and chrome barstools at each, plus a big outdoor bar with 16 wooden stools around it.

2. The Library, cozy and comfortable, with a non-burning fireplace, a belle époque fixture from a 19th century home in Ghent, print armchairs, fixed wooden tables, cream leather sofas, oil paintings of sailing ships, CD player, and lots of hardback books and games.

3. The Piano Bar has a royal blue carpet and 12 blue leather and brass stools at the indoor marble-topped bar (which connects with the outdoor bar so one bartender can work them both). Tables, paisley-covered chairs and built-in leather banquettes make this a comfortable place to chat, and you can look through portholes into the underwater pool.

4. The dining room has royal blue carpet with a rope pattern, rose flame print chairs with wood and wicker backs but no arms, tables for six and eight and side booths set up for four but big enough for six. It's open seating, so you can sit where and with whom you wish.

5. The bowsprit, the perfect place to slip away to see the ship's sails in full glory; there's a net underneath for safety.

Five Good Reasons to Book These Ships

1. The romance of it all.

2. To learn how to sail a square-rigger.

3. To kick back and relax in a luxurious but unstuffy setting.

4. To have a once-in-a-lifetime experience at the cost of an ordinary cruise.

5. To choose between two different Caribbean itineraries out of Antigua.

Five Things You Won't Find On Board

1. A casino.

2. A beauty shop.

3. Laundry service (they can send it out for one-day service in certain ports).

4. Smoking permitted in the cabins.

5. An elevator.

STAR CLIPPER ★★★★
STAR FLYER ★★★★

Registry	**Luxembourg**
Officers	**European**
Crew	**International**
Complement	**72**
GRT	**3025**
Length (ft.)	**360**
Beam (ft.)	**50**
Draft (ft.)	**18.5**
Passengers-Cabins Full	**180**
Passengers-2/Cabin	**170**
Passenger Space Ratio	**17.79**
Stability Rating	**Good**
Seatings	**1**
Cuisine	**Continental**
Dress Code	**Casual elegance**
Room Service	**Yes**
Tip	**$8 PPPD, 12.5% automatically added to bar check**

Ship Amenities

Outdoor Pool	**2**
Indoor Pool	**0**
Jacuzzi	**1**
Fitness Center	**No**
Spa	**No**
Beauty Shop	**No**
Showroom	**No**
Bars/Lounges	**2**
Casino	**No**
Shops	**1**
Library	**Yes**
Child Program	**No**
Self-Service Laundry	**Yes**
Elevators	**0**

Cabin Statistics

Suites	**1**
Outside Doubles	**78**
Inside Doubles	**6**
Wheelchair Cabins	**0**
Singles	**0**
Single Surcharge	**150%**
Verandas	**0**
110 Volt	**Yes**

STAR CRUISE

391B Orchard Road #13-01, Ngee Ann City, Tower B, Singapore, 238874
☎ *(011) 65-733-9766, FAX: (011) 65-733-8622*

History ....

Star Cruises, which began in September 1993 and already has six ships, is headed up by a hotel, casinos and resort executive named Eddy Lee, who has been associated with Sheratons in Asia and the Pacific, the public-listed Genting Group in Malaysia, the Burswood Resort in Australia and CDL Hotels International in Hong Kong. Lee and his investors acquired and converted two passenger ferries from Sweden, the former *Athena* and *Kalypso*, into the *Star Aquarius* and the *Star Pisces*, and began cruising in December 1993. Subsequently, the new company acquired four existing cruise vessels, the *Cunard Crown Jewel*, sister ship to the *Cunard Dynasty*, *Golden Princess* from Princess Cruises and the *Aurora I* and *Aurora II*, two small luxury vessels formerly owned by a German bank and leased to New York-based Classical Cruises.

Two more ships under construction at Meyer Werft in Germany, *SuperStar Leo* and *SuperStar Virgo*, will join the fleet in late 1998, bringing the line's total to eight ships carrying a total of 12,000 passengers.

Officers for the new cruise line are English-speaking Scandinavians. Four of the ships are based in Singapore, one in Okinawa and one in Hong Kong. The fleet, one of the world's youngest, has an average age of four years.

Concept ....

This vibrant Malaysian-owned, Singapore-based cruise line, after studying the Carnival and Royal Caribbean operations in the Caribbean, created a three-label cruise line tailored to very specific markets. *"Star"* ships make short, high-density, mass-market, Asian-oriented sailings from Singapore and Hong Kong; *"MegaStar"* ships offer deluxe charters particularly targeting the upscale Asian market; and *"SuperStar"* ships are marketed internationally with particular emphasis on Australia, New Zealand and the United Kingdom. Another stated intention of the cruise line is to create a year-round rather than seasonal cruise industry in Singapore to utilize the new Singapore Cruise Centre.

Signatures ....

The Star Cruises logo is a broad funnel with a dark blue base and red-and-white striped top ornamented with an eight-point gold star.

Who's Aboard. . . . .

Hong Kong and Singapore residents make up the greater portion of travelers on the "Star" vessels, while the other ships draw from other urban areas in Asia, such as Okinawa, as well as Europe.

Who Should Go . . . .

Besides first-time cruisers from the region, anyone visiting in Singapore, Malaysia or Hong Kong who wants a short, luxurious break from business. Families with children will find teen video arcades and child care available. Meetings and incentive groups will find a variety of meeting rooms and business services offered. The five-day *SuperStar Gemini* cruises from Singapore to Malaysia and Thailand give a good cross-section view of the area for a cruiser with limited time. British travelers usually buy a two-week package that includes land programs as well, while Australians buy a one-week package that is basically transportation, transfers and the cruise.

Who Should Not Go . . . .

Traditional cruisers will find the ambiance aboard the Star label ships more similar to a Scandinavian ferry than a cruise ship, while the deluxe MegaStar vessels are marketed almost entirely to charters, particularly Korean honeymooners and incentive groups. Most sailings are between two and five nights.

The Lifestyle . . . .

Star Cruises has created a uniquely Asian-style leisure product patterned loosely on traditional western cruises. The differences include a much wider range of food options for far longer hours; private karaoke and mah-jongg booths; a membership club that provides special lounges at the port as well as on board some of the ships; and 24-hour child care. There are more surcharge options, particularly for meals, than on traditional cruise ships. On the other hand, the SuperStar and MegaStar ships are tailored for the international cruise market.

Wardrobe. . . . .

Given the tropical climate and the general lifestyle of the area residents, any idea of dress code is out the window. On the Star ships, passengers come aboard in whatever they wear at home and continue to follow what the line terms "smart casual" dress style throughout the cruise. The Australians and British on the *SuperStar Gemini* are usually in sport shirts for the men, cotton frocks for the ladies. But some of the honeymooners and incentive groups on the *MegaStar* ships do dress up.

Bill of Fare. . . . . .A to B+

The Star label ships provide passengers with vouchers for three meals a day, which may be taken at any hour in the buffet restaurant, or which serve as a base price for dining in the optional restaurants—Chinese, Japanese, Italian, seafood—with a surcharge added, depending on which dishes are ordered. On the *Star Aquarius* we noted a live fish tank, surely the only one at sea, in the surcharge seafood restaurant. The *SuperStar Gemini* sets out a copious eastern and western buffet that stretches for miles—from cream of tomato soup to sushi, roast beef to fried rice—plus offering at no extra charge a choice of western or Chinese meals in the dining room. The little MegaStar ships offer "the ultimate gastronomical adventure" for passengers willing to spring for caviar, Peking duck, fresh lobster and rack of lamb.

Cuisine Report Card: Asian dishes A, western dishes B+

Showtime . . . . .C+

The *Star Aquarius* and *Star Pisces* include a karaoke nightclub, adult disco, children's disco, cinema, a mah-jongg and card room, a 400-seat cabaret and show room, and an activity center where you can rent library books, videotapes, karaoke discs, cards and games. In Asia, the mah-jongg and card room, along with the karaoke facility, is customarily rented to users on a reservation basis rather than being a free, public area. The Admiral Club, a private membership club, offers extra perks such as a private lounge aboard and in the cruise center.

On the *SuperStar Gemini*, a large show lounge, a cabaret lounge, karaoke lounge, disco and a number of indoor and outdoor bars are sited where their equivalents were on the former *Crown Jewel*. The Admiral Club is located where the casino used to be, and the casino is in the Star Club.

On the former Auroras, the very small vessels, there's a main lounge, a karaoke room, an auditorium (for groups and meetings when the ships are chartered) and another Admiral Club houses the casino.

Discounts . . . .

Fifty percent discounts are offered for the third and fourth passengers sharing a quad cabin on the Star and SuperStar ships.

The Bottom Line

While there have been ocean-going cruise lines based in Asia for some time—primarily in Japan—this is the first major, English-speaking, mainstream cruise company aiming primarily at the Asian market with its first vessels, but also eyeing the international cruise market with the last three ships. The construction design and quality of all the ships is excellent; they have been altered only enough to add items westerners would consider optional but easterners think essential, niceties such as private mah-jongg and karaoke rooms and larger casinos.

★ ★ ★ ★

MegaStar Aries
MegaStar Taurus

When we boarded the pretty little Aurora II *in Topolobampo, Mexico, it was love at first sight, not only for us but for a frequent-cruiser couple traveling with us. She had lovely sleek yachtlike lines, a dark blue hull, big windows, elegant cabins with big tile bathrooms, broad expanses of teak deck.*

This pair of elegant little ships were actually ordered in the late 1980s by a now-defunct German company called Windsor Cruises (reflecting the German fascination with the British royal family), and the two ships were going to be Sea Goddess clones named the *Lady Diana* and the *Lady Sarah*. Given the way that whole affair turned out, it's probably just as well they weren't delivered under those names. A German bank ended up as the reluctant owner of the pair and chartered them out to Classical Cruises, a division of New York's Travel Dynamics, which books university and museum groups on educational cruises aboard a variety of small ships. We first met them on a Sea of Cortez nature cruise in the spring of 1994 and were enchanted. For the record, the *Aurora I* is now the *MegaStar Taurus*, the *Aurora II* the *MegaStar Aries*.

The Brochure Says

"It's not true we're exclusive. We're very, very exclusive. Few hear of it. Even fewer experience the luxurious high life on a Star Cruises MegaStar vessel. Because each cruise is limited to a select number of guests who barely outnumber the impeccably discreet staff."

Translation

Wow, a textbook case in subliminal selling, aiming at everyone from someone who wants to be au courant ("Few hear of it") to a business executive out for a fling with his secretary ("impeccably discreet staff"). But actually, more and more of the Asian market are hearing of it, because most sailings are sold-out charters.

Cabins & Costs

Fantasy Suites: . . . . **A**

Average Price Per Person, Double Occupancy, Per Day: Available by request only.
The Commodore Suite is a large two-room suite with a king-sized bed, a marble bathroom with tub off the bedroom, a living room with chairs and sofa and a second bathroom with shower instead of tub off the living room.

Small Splurges: . . . . **A**

Average Price PPPD: $265, cruise only.
The 34 Admiral Suites (we would call them deluxe cabins) have twin beds that can be cranked up or down by remote control, TV/VCR, desk, mini-refrigerator, large corner table, reading lamps, two chairs, two chests, two large closets, and a tile bathroom with tub/shower, marble counter and good storage.

Suitable Standards: . . . . **A**

Average Price PPPD: $250, cruise only.
"Deluxe cabins"—there are only two of them, would be the cheapest cabins aboard—and they are very similar to the Small Splurges, above, except the bathrooms have shower only.

Bottom Bunks: . . . . **N/A**

N/A

The Routes

The *MegaStar Taurus* is based in Singapore, and makes two-night luxury cruises from Singapore to Port Kelang, Malaysia, leaving Singapore every Monday, Wednesday and Friday at 9 p.m.

The *MegaStar Aries* sails from Singapore on Mondays, Wednesdays and Fridays to Port Kelang and returns on Tuesdays, Thursdays and Saturdays. A free city tour is included.

Both vessels are frequently under charter and not available for individual bookings.

The Scoop

Obviously aimed at a short cruise getaway market, these pretty little ships should be able to charge whatever the traffic will bear, so the prices seem relatively modest for the quality of accommodations being offered. There's no tipping aboard, and there are some theme cruises built around holiday celebrations such as Christmas (a major big deal in Singapore) and Chinese festivals such as New Year and Autumn Moon. Most often, however, the vessels go out under charter. They are particularly popular with groups of Korean honeymooners.

STAR CRUISES

Insider Tips

Five Special Spots

1. The expanded aft deck Admiral's Club contains blackjack, roulette, slots and baccarat.

2. Oscar's Unisex Salon beauty shop is actually operated by Steiners.

3. The Aquarius Lounge, a warm living room with wood-paneled walls and comfortable sofas and chairs in bright silk tapestry.

4. The Pisces Dining Room, also wood-paneled, serves all the guests at one seating.

5. The Aurora Auditorium is comfortable enough to nap in, with padded blue theater seats in rows, and a full video and slide presentation facility.

Five Good Reasons to Book These Ships

1. They're small, elegant and exclusive.

2. Cabins are extremely comfortable and the bathrooms are some of the largest at sea.

3. To become a member of the Admiral's Club for those special perks.

4. To sail into smaller ports than the big ships can.

5. To have all the Beluga caviar and Peking duck you ever wanted—so long as you order it in advance.

Five Things You Won't Find On Board

1. Tables for two.

2. Elevators; you'll have to walk.

3. A children's program; this is not really a family cruise.

4. Tipping; there's no tipping necessary.

5. A private veranda; if they'd been as routine in 1991 as they are now, you can bet these ships would have had them.

MEGASTAR ARIES ★★★★
MEGASTAR TAURUS ★★★★

Registry	**Panama**
Officers	**International**
Crew	**International**
Complement	**80**
GRT	**3264**
Length (ft.)	**267**
Beam (ft.)	**45.5**
Draft (ft.)	**11**
Passengers-Cabins Full	**72**
Passengers-2/Cabin	**72**
Passenger Space Ratio	**45.33**
Stability Rating	**Good**
Seatings	**1**
Cuisine	**Continental and Asian**
Dress Code	**Smart Casual**
Room Service	**Yes**
Tip	**No Tipping**

Ship Amenities

Outdoor Pool	**1**
Indoor Pool	**0**
Jacuzzi	**1**
Fitness Center	**Yes**
Spa	**No**
Beauty Shop	**Yes**
Showroom	**No**
Bars/Lounges	**1**
Casino	**Yes**
Shops	**1**
Library	**Yes**
Child Program	**No**
Self-Service Laundry	**No**
Elevators	**0**

Cabin Statistics

Suites	**1**
Outside Doubles	**35**
Inside Doubles	**0**
Wheelchair Cabins	**0**
Singles	**0**
Single Surcharge	**150%**
Verandas	**0**
110 Volt	**No**

STAR CRUISES

★ ★ ★

STAR AQUARIUS
STAR PISCES

This good-looking pair of ferrylike vessels are a major introduction to cruising for the Asian market, offering short, snappy getaways tabbed "resort vacations" for one of the world's biggest yuppie markets. Since many of Singapore's ethnic Chinese have friends and relatives on the island of Penang in Malaysia and like to vacation there, it was a logical destination choice when the first ship, *Star Aquarius*, was introduced in December 1993. The savvy marketing arm of Star Cruises made a big selling pitch to young singles, couples and families to get rid of "the popular misconception of cruise holidays as being only suitable for the middle-aged or retirees."

Frankly, we've never seen a middle-aged, white-collar worker in Singapore in the dozen or so times we've been there. Everyone we meet is 35 or under. We've never been able to figure out what they do with citizens over 40, but we suspect they're put out to pasture in those endless blocks of high-rise apartment complexes in the suburbs.

• Between The Lines •

The Brochure Says

"An all-inclusive package in a fabulous cruise resort."

"Bring your staff for a seminar or convention they'll never forget."

"Every night is party night on *Star Aquarius*."

"Fettucini yesterday, sashimi last night. How about shark's fin soup for now?"

"A nonstop party for the whole family."

Translation

The public rooms run the gamut from optional specialty restaurants and fast-food counters to private karaoke and mah-jongg parlors. Activities for kids and teens, conference meeting room facilities, a computer center, duty-free shopping, cabaret and showroom and separate discos for kids and adults, even a Singapore-style satay stand selling skewers of meat or chicken with peanut sauce—what's not to like?

Cabins & Costs

Cabins on the two ships are shipshape Scandinavian ferry-style accommodations in the lower categories. There's a standard family quad with four beds two desk/dressers with chair, TV, phone and small bathroom with shower; a standard twin with twin or double bed, two chairs and a small table, desk/dresser and bathroom with shower. Per diem prices range from $117 to $463 per person, double occupancy.

The Routes

The *Star Pisces* sails from Hong Kong on a Tuesday cruise to nowhere, and a three-night to the beach resort of Haikou and Xiamen in China.

The *Star Aquarius* makes a two-night cruise to nowhere from Singapore every Friday night, plus a two-night sailing to Penang and a three-night sailing to Port Kelang, gateway to Kuala Lumpur and the Langakawi Island in Malaysia.

The Scoop

Embarkation is like a replay of the early 1980s in Los Angeles or Miami, when the three-night cruises loaded with first-timers starry-eyed with excitement set out for the Bahamas or Ensenada. Star Cruises is making cruising a high demand holiday for mass market travelers in Singapore and Hong Kong. This could be the start of something big.

STAR CRUISES

STAR AQUARIUS ★★★
STAR PISCES ★★★

Registry	**Panama**
Officers	**International**
Crew	**International**
Complement	**750**
GRT	**40,000**
Length (ft.)	**574**
Beam (ft.)	**94**
Draft (ft.)	**11**
Passengers-Cabins Full	**1900 /2196**
Passengers-2/Cabin	**1378**
Passenger Space Ratio	**29.02**
Stability Rating	**Good**
Seatings	**1**
Cuisine	**Asian/International**
Dress Code	**Smart Casual**
Room Service	**No**
Tip	**No Tipping**

Ship Amenities

Outdoor Pool	**1**
Indoor Pool	**1**
Jacuzzi	**4**
Fitness Center	**Yes**
Spa	**Yes**
Beauty Shop	**Yes**
Showroom	**Yes**
Bars/Lounges	**4/2**
Casino	**Yes**
Shops	**2**
Library	**Yes**
Child Program	**Yes**
Self-Service Laundry	**No**
Elevators	**5**

Cabin Statistics

Suites	**82**
Outside Doubles	**182/209**
Inside Doubles	**415/445**
Wheelchair Cabins	**0**
Singles	**0**
Single Surcharge	**150%**
Verandas	**0**
110 Volt	**No**

★ ★ ★

SuperStar Capricorn

We'll always think of this ship as the Royal Viking Sky, an elegant seagoing lady, and remember sailing her to the Norwegian fjords and North Cape, watching the Norwegian crew grow warm, fulsome and joyous as they got closer and closer to home. Another summer we saw her in Stockholm in her startlingly garish livery as the Birka Queen, looking over-rouged and altogether inappropriate. ("The Finns were cooking sausages in the sauna!" sniffed one beauty salon attendant who had stayed aboard). The ship came back to Miami in 1991–92 for a humiliating season as NCL's Sunward, making three- and four-day cruises to the Bahamas, then reverted to her new Finnish owners, Birka Line. They leased her in 1993 to Princess to make Alaska sailings as the Golden Princess, which called for a major renovation, and when we visited her in Ketchikan, she looked like her old self again. Now she's sailing for Asia-based Star Cruises as the SuperStar Capricorn, cruising from Okinawa on three-, four- and seven-night cruises.

Through her various name changes, the ship has been renovated several times. Currently the vessel's density has been increased to accommodate as many as 1375 passengers and 600 crew members. The cuisine in the Ocean Palace Restaurant swings a wide pendulum from Asian to Japanese to western dishes, including Italian and French cuisines, Japanese "home-style" dishes and Szechuan specialties.

Fitness activities include a golf driving range, basketball court, paddle tennis court, ping-pong table, a gymnasium and a whirlpool spa for relaxation. A disco, karaoke lounge, library, conference room and a beauty salon are also on board.

Families will find a child-care center that offers activities and baby-sitting so parents are free to pursue their own activities. Teenagers will find the Light House Video Arcade makes money disappear rapidly. Headline entertainers from the U.S., Australia, Hong Kong, Japan and Taiwan appear nightly in The Galaxy of the Stars showroom.

Ocean Palace dining room features international cuisine.

Since passengers come from numerous countries, languages used on board include English, Mandarin and Japanese, and currencies used on board include Singapore dollars, U.S. dollars, Japanese Yen and Taiwan NT. Credit cards may also be used.

The ship carries a five-category cabin range from penthouse suites and junior suites to deluxe doubles, outside doubles and inside doubles. Each cabin has a private bathroom with shower and/or tub, TV for in-cabin movies, telephone and personal save.

The *SuperStar Capricorn* makes three-night roundtrip sailings from Naha, Okinawa to Keelung, which accesses Taipei, Taiwan, and Ishigaki in the lovely Ryuku islands of Japan. Four-night sailings add the port of Zanami. Seven-night sailings cruise from Naha to Keelung, Hong Kong and Xiamen.

SuperStar Capricorn *features two outdoor pools with inviting deck areas.*

SUPERSTAR CAPRICORN ★★★

Registry	**Panama**
Officers	**Scandinavian**
Crew	**International**
Complement	**600**
GRT	**28,000**
Length (ft.)	**674**
Beam (ft.)	**83**
Draft (ft.)	**24**
Passengers-Cabins Full	**1375**
Passengers-2/Cabin	**860**
Passenger Space Ratio	**34.82**
Stability Rating	**Good to Excellent**
Seatings	**Open**
Cuisine	**Asian/International**
Dress Code	**Smart Casual**
Room Service	**No**
Tip	**No tipping**

Ship Amenities

Outdoor Pool	**2**
Indoor Pool	**0**
Jacuzzi	**1**
Fitness Center	**Yes**
Spa	**No**
Beauty Shop	**Yes**
Showroom	**Yes**
Bars/Lounges	**3**
Casino	**Yes**
Shops	**1**
Library	**Yes**
Child Program	**Yes**
Self-Service Laundry	**No**
Elevators	**5**

Cabin Statistics

Suites	**20**
Outside Doubles	**346**
Inside Doubles	**64**
Wheelchair Cabins	**1**
Singles	**0**
Single Surcharge	**150%**
Verandas	**9**
110 Volt	**Yes**

STAR CRUISES

★ ★ ★ ★
SUPERSTAR GEMINI

The Star Cruises team, some recruited from existing cruise lines, some hired and trained in Singapore, really pitch in and work hard to meet and greet their passengers. From Charley Penguin (the mascot) to pretty female staffers at the gangway dressed in exotic regional costume, everyone seems to be right where they're supposed to be doing what they're expected to do with a bright, wide smile—and there's no tipping.

The former *Crown Jewel*, which made a splashy debut during the Barcelona Olympics in 1992, is a jewel box of a ship, big enough to give a sense of stability and comfort, but intimate in its public rooms and lounges so guests can meet each other and socialize easily. Cabins are dispersed among five of its seven passenger decks, with a topmost deck housing a fitness center, video arcade, teen and youth center, beauty salon, pool, pool bar and mah-jongg and card room where the former teen area was located. The other major public rooms deck is Deck 5, anchored by a show and cabaret lounge forward and the Gemini Bar amidships.

Between The Lines

The Brochure Says

"In Singapore, home port of the *SuperStar Gemini*, you can breakfast with hundreds of colorful exotic birds on the celebrated terrace of the Jurong Bird Park, with the world's largest walk-in aviary. You can share morning tea with Ah Meng, the friendly orangutan at the famed Singapore Zoological Gardens. And in the evening when you sail through the glittering city of lights that is the world's busiest port, you may even find yourself seated with the Captain. He may not be as exotic. But we guarantee he has better manners."

Translation

(Also from the brochure) "Breakfast with the birds. Tea with the Orangutans. Dinner with the Captain. He's a Scandinavian, and he speaks English."

Cabins & Costs

Fantasy Suites: .... **A**

Average Price Per Person, Double Occupancy, Per Day: $371, cruise-only.
Executive suites, some with private verandas, some with bay windows and some
with forward-facing picture windows, have twin beds that can convert to doubles,
separate sitting areas, mini-refrigerators and extra large closets with cabin safes;
bathrooms have tub and shower in most. The space is around 350 square feet altogether.

Small Splurges: .... **A**

Average Price PPPD: $242, cruise-only.
Junior suites have sitting areas with sofa and coffee table, twin beds that can convert
to queen-sized, and desk/dresser with chair, cabin safe and bath with shower.

Suitable Standards: .... **B**

Average Price PPPD: $199, cruise-only.
While they're called Admiral Suites, they're really standards measuring around 146
square feet, with twin or queen-sized bed, chair, coffee table, desk/dresser with
chair, cabin safe, telephone, and bath with shower.

Bottom Bunks: .... **B**

Average Price PPPD: $170, cruise only.
The cheapest quarters are the inside cabins, measuring around 132 square feet each,
with two lower beds that can be combined, remote-control color TV, combination
safe, mirrored built-in dresser/desk, telephone and bath with shower, cabin safe and
telephone.

The Routes

The *SuperStar Gemini* sails Sunday nights from Singapore, calling Mondays at Port
Kelang, Malaysia; Tuesdays at Langkawi island, Malaysia; Wednesdays at Phuket, Thailand; and spends a day at sea on Thursdays before sailing back into Singapore on Friday
afternoon. On weekends, she makes a two-night cruise to Malacca, Malaysia, for half the
year and Tioman Island, Malaysia for the other half.

The Scoop

If you were a resident of this tiny but prosperous little country, say, a young, single Sin-
gaporean making a good living working in a bank or office, perhaps still living at home
with your parents, and you loved western-style amusements, wouldn't you take a short
cruise on one of these ships?

Insider Tips

Five Special Spots

1. The Star Club casino offers dai sai (Chinese roulette), blackjack, roulette and mini-baccarat.

2. The Galaxy of the Stars main lounge has four graduated levels, swivel club chairs and cocktail tables, and handsome draperies. Sightlines are spotty.

3. The pool deck area with natural teak and green Astroturf underfoot, padded sun loungers and a pool flanked with Jacuzzis in a three-step teak platform.

4. The Universe Fitness Center is surprisingly elaborate for a ship this size, with exercise equipment and beauty services, plus the Star Track for jogging.

5. The children's playroom with a slide into colored balls, a special nap area and 24-hour baby-sitting.

Five Good Reasons to Book This Ship

1. To have tea with the orangutan at the Singapore Zoo.

2. To visit the James Bond Islands of Phi Phi from the film *Man With the Golden Gun*, and "be shaken, not stirred."

3. To be able to choose between an eastern and a western menu.

4. To relax on the Palm Beach-style pool deck in a trim blue-and-white cushioned lounger.

5. To take a two-country cruise in six days, visiting Malaysia and Thailand from Singapore.

Five Things You Won't Find On Board

1. Durian fruit; it is forbidden on board due to its strong aroma.

2. A limited version of mealtimes; since many Singaporeans snack frequently from the street carts in their spotless city, they expect to be able to eat anytime. *SuperStar Gemini* tries to have something around to munch on all the time.

3. Anyone chewing gum; it's forbidden in the country of Singapore.

4. A self-service laundry.

5. A gratuity envelope. There is no tipping.

SUPERSTAR GEMINI ★★★★

Registry	**Panama**
Officers	**International**
Crew	**International**
GRT	**19,089**
Length (ft.)	**532**
Beam (ft.)	**73**
Draft (ft.)	**17.5**
Crew	**470**
Passengers-Cabins Full	**900**
Passengers-2/Cabin	**800**
Passenger Space Ratio	**23.86**
Stability Rating	**Fair to good**
Seatings	**2**
Cuisine	**Continental and Asian**
Dress Code	**Smart Casual**
Room Service	**Yes**
Tip	**No Tipping**

Ship Amenities

Outdoor Pool	**1**
Indoor Pool	**0**
Jacuzzi	**3**
Fitness Center	**Yes**
Spa	**Yes**
Beauty Shop	**Yes**
Showroom	**Yes**
Bars/Lounges	**3**
Casino	**Yes**
Shops	**1**
Library	**Yes**
Child Program	**Yes**
Self-Service Laundry	**No**
Elevators	**5**

Cabin Statistics

Suites	**196**
Outside Doubles	**68**
Inside Doubles	**123**
Wheelchair Cabins	**4**
Singles	**0**
Single Surcharge	**150%**
Verandas	**12**
110 Volt	**No**

STAR CRUISES

77 New Oxford Street, London WC1A 1PP
☎ (01144) 171-800-2200 (in U.K.), in U.S. ☎ (888) MINERVA, (800) PRINCESS
www.swan-hellenic.co.uk

History . . . .

Swan Hellenic's European tours have been offered since the 1920s; the company began Greek ship-based tours in 1952 when the war-torn country had little tourism infrastructure. Everyone from the former Archbishop of Canterbury to the Deputy Keeper at the British Museum takes a turn at talking about archeology, history, mythology, geology, military history, astronomy, marine biology, art, music, drama and medical history.

With its new ship and new attitude, Swan Hellenic, a P & O company, is enjoying more young cruise passengers and more North American clientele. For this reason, bookings are available in the U.S. through Los Angeles' Princess Cruises, the latter also a P & O company.

⚓⚓⚓⚓⚓

MINERVA

Swan Hellenic's *Minerva* is just the size ship the company seems to prefer for its cultural and intellectual European programs. While the clientele is primarily British, a lot of Americans also enjoy these cruises because of their unusual itineraries and in-depth lecture programs.

An open-seating policy in the dining room gives passengers a chance to get acquainted with a wider range of people, including the lecturers, than with the customary assigned seating. Passengers may arrive within a time frame and sit where they like. There is a no-tipping policy as well. Dress aboard is casual during the daytime, and gets a bit dressier (say, a floral frock or pantsuit) for evenings. There is one gala night where dressing up is expected. There's a fitness center, pool, beauty shop, library and self-service laundry, but no casino.

Cabins & Costs

Twelve of the accommodations aboard are suites, with 128 outside double cabins and 52 inside double cabins. Single rates are offered on all cabins. Four of them are wheelchair-accessible, and the vessel has two elevators.

Anyone under 26 accompanying a full-fare adult gets a 50 percent discount on the regular adult fare. Group discounts are also available on request.

The Routes

Swan Hellenic's usual cruising patterns include the Eastern and Western Mediterranean, the Aegean, Black Sea, Red Sea, North African coast and Iberian peninsula, as well as British Isles, Scandinavia and Baltic cruises. All-inclusive rates cover air from London, tips and shore excursions.

MINERVA ⚓⚓⚓⚓

Registry	**Bermuda**
Officers	**British**
Crew	**International**
Crew	**160**
GRT	**12,000**
Length (ft.)	**416**
Beam (ft.)	**65**
Draft (ft.)	**19.5**
Passengers-Cabins Full	**400**
Passengers-2/Cabin	**384**
Passenger Space Ratio	**31.25**
Stability Rating	**Good**
Seatings	**1**
Cuisine	**International**
Dress Code	**Casual**
Room Service	**No**
Tip	**No Tipping**

Ship Amenities

Outdoor Pool	**1**
Indoor Pool	**0**
Jacuzzi	**0**
Fitness Center	**Yes**
Spa	**No**
Beauty Shop	**Yes**
Showroom	**Yes**
Bars/Lounges	**2**
Casino	**No**
Shops	**2**
Library	**Yes**
Child Program	**No**
Self-Service Laundry	**Yes**
Elevators	**2**

Cabin Statistics

Suites	**12**
Outside Doubles	**128**
Inside Doubles	**52**
Wheelchair Cabins	**4**
Singles	**0**
Single Surcharge	**150%**
Verandas	**12**
110 Volt	**No**

TALL SHIP ADVENTURES

1389 South Havana Street, Aurora, CO 80012
☎ *(303) 755-7983, (800) 662-0090*
www.tallshipadventures.com

History . . . .

The three-masted schooner *Sir Francis Drake* was constructed in Germany in 1917 as the *Landkirchen* and carried copper from Chile around Cape Horn to Europe. Then, with an engine added in the 1920s, it spent 40 years carrying cargo in the Baltic and North Seas. In 1988 Eckart Straub and Captain Bryan Petley purchased the vessel and renamed it after the dashing English buccaneer. Captain Petley, a New Zealander, has been sailing since he was 13, and brings a cheerful, off-beat attitude of fun that rubs off on all the passengers.

—One of fewer than 100 tall ships remaining that was built to transport cargo solely under sail.

Concept . . . .

"We advertise ourselves as a middle-of-the-road soft adventure," says Captain Petley, "not as luxurious as the Star Clippers or *Sea Cloud* but a bit less basic than the Maine Windjammers or the Windjammer Barefoot Cruises." What he means is that the cabins are carpeted, air-conditioned and have private bathrooms, but you can still show up to dinner barefoot and in shorts.

Signatures . . . .

The B.L.T. party, every Tuesday night, when passengers are required to wear (1) Buccaneer dress, (2) Lingerie or (3) Toga.

Gimmicks . . . .

Pirate's Punch is free.

Who's the Competition. . . . .

Probably the Windjammer ships come the closest in style and authenticity, but the cabins don't all have private facilities on those vessels.

Who's Aboard . . . .

Young to middle-aged couples and singles, with a median age in the mid-40s, but they can be as young as 20 or as old as 80, plus an occasional family with children over 8. Captain Petley discourages children any younger than 8.

Who Should Go . . . .

People who want to relax. One veteran of many Tall Ship Adventures says, "The first day you're a little uptight, the second day you begin to unwind and by the seventh day, you don't have a clue what's happening in the world and you don't care."

Who Should Not Go . . . .

Fussbudgets and nitpickers; clothes horses; shoppers (there are very few shopping stops on the itinerary); people who hate sun, sand and sea.

The Lifestyle . . . .

The usual drill in the U.S. and British Virgin Islands is to sail in the mornings, anchor at midday and have lunch on the beach, spending the afternoon snorkeling, swimming, windsurfing, sailing or water-skiing. Dinner is served on board, and afterwards the captain and whoever wishes to join him usually go ashore "to where the bands are" and party. For a 10-minute video preview of the ship, send a refundable $15 deposit to Tall Ship Adventures (address above).

Wardrobe. . . . .

Anything goes. Bare feet and shorts are acceptable dinner attire except perhaps on the Sunday night captain's dinner. "That's when I dress in my uniform," Captain Petley says.

Bill of Fare. C

In the tiny galley below decks, the chef prepares a mix of popular standards including hamburger and barbecued ribs with elegant lobster sandwiches on homemade bread or Caribbean-accented specialties such as chicken-and-shrimp stir-fry and West Indian baked chicken. Lunch is often served on the beach, and deck barbecues are popular.

Showtime. . . . . .N/A

Going ashore after dinner to small island nightclubs with the unflappable Captain Petley.

Discounts . . . .

Early booking bonuses up to 20 percent are available on certain cruises; call the company for details. A group of 10 to 19 passengers gets a 5 percent group discount, while a group of 20 or more gets a 10 percent discount.

The Bottom Line

This is Captain Petley's ship, run in his own inimitable fashion. He formerly sailed as a captain with Windjammer and describes one primary difference between his ship and theirs: "They sail at night every night and stop during the day. We sail during part of the day and anchor at night."

⚓⚓⚓⚓
SIR FRANCIS DRAKE

The first time we saw the Sir Francis Drake *was in the Boston Harbor during the Tall Ships celebration in 1992, and even there amid so many vessels its three masts stood out above the crowd.*

You won't get lost aboard the ship if you can just remember which companionways go where. There are only 14 cabins, a dining room, a lounge and the open deck, but a recent refitting has spruced it up, and if you had 33 like-minded friends could probably arrange your own charter. The last going price we heard was $4000 a day, which would work out to about $118 apiece a day if you had the full 34 people.

Between The Lines

The Brochure Says

"Visit palm-fringed beaches kissed by gin-clear waters and discover enchanting coral reefs. Dance the night away to the Caribbean beat at romantic island hideaways."

Translation

There's the answer to the question, What's there to do?

EAVESDROPPING

"The people we get don't ever want to go back on a floating hotel or a wimp cruise again," says Captain Bryan Petley.

Cabins & Costs

Fantasy Suites: . . . . **C-**
Average Price Per Person, Double Occupancy, Per Day: $199 plus airfare.

TALL SHIP ADVENTURES

There is one luxury suite on board, contoured into the aft corners of the vessel, not huge but it certainly seems spacious beside the others. Anyhow, the bed is big enough for two, it's carpeted, air-conditioned and has a wall-mounted chest for a modicum of storage.

Small Splurges: .... C-
Average Price PPPD: $170 plus airfare.
Small is the operative word here. You can book the next category down, a double bed with upper twin (there are six of these), carpeting, air conditioning and private toilet and shower.

Suitable Standards: .... C-
Average Price PPPD: $170 plus airfare.
Side-by-side twin beds mean only one of you gets up and gets dressed at a time; there are four of these, with very compact bathrooms.

Bottom Bunks: .... D
Average Price PPPD: $142 plus airfare.
And you thought the small splurges were small! Three of these with upper and lower bunks are pretty basic; one is aft, opposite the suite, and the other two forward, but you can't get from the aft one to the forward ones without going up, across the next deck and back down.

The Routes

While the captain changes itineraries frequently, he stays in the Caribbean, usually around the British Virgin Islands. Most recently the ship sails from Tortola on the first, third and fifth Saturday of each month to most of the little islands in the BVI, and on the second and fourth Saturdays to the rest of them. In summer, the ship sails in the Grenadines between St. Vincent and Grenada.

The Scoop

The *Sir Francis Drake* is a handsome old ship, especially after its recent refurbishment, but housekeeping is not always pristine and the casual lifestyle may verge on the raffish occasionally. Still, the prices are very low, the beach activities super and the food isn't bad either. If you're not fussy and want a relaxed and relaxing barefoot cruise, you should try it.

Insider Tips

Five Shipshape Spaces

1. The lounge, which doubles as bar, video room, gift shop, TV room, library and gathering spot.

2. The deck, clean, natural teak bleached to a weathered gray, is ringed with chairs, lounges and small tables.

3. The dining room, elegantly wood-paneled and prettily redecorated in beige with wood armchairs.

4. The bowsprit has a safety net underneath that can support a foolhardy passenger or two.

5. The deck bar, sometimes the setting for an onboard wedding.

Five Good Reasons to Book This Ship

1. To join Captain Petley at the Tuesday night B.L.T. (buccaneer, lingerie or toga) party; he himself may appear in filmy lingerie with his captain's bars pinned to one spaghetti strap.

2. It's a good blend of land and sea vacations for a watersports-and-party crowd.

3. Because all you need to pack are shorts, T-shirts and tennis shoes.

4. Because you can cruise through the unspoiled British Virgin Islands or Grenadines.

5. Because you can take a seven-day cruise for as little as $796 if you get in on an early booking discount.

Five Things You Won't Find On Board

1. Room service.

2. A concierge.

3. Anybody with a stuffy attitude.

4. Anyone wearing pantyhose and high heels—except maybe on B.L.T. Night.

5. An elevator.

SIR FRANCIS DRAKE   ♨♨♨

Registry	**Honduras**
Officers	**International**
Crew	**International**
Complement	**14**
GRT	**450**
Length (ft.)	**165**
Beam (ft.)	**23**
Draft (ft.)	**9**
Passengers-Cabins Full	**34**
Passengers-2/Cabin	**28**
Passenger Space Ratio	**NA**
Stability Rating	**Fair**
Seatings	**1**
Cuisine	**Caribbean**
Dress Code	**Casual**
Room Service	**No**
Tip	**$10 PPPD**

Ship Amenities

Outdoor Pool	**0**
Indoor Pool	**0**
Jacuzzi	**0**
Fitness Center	**No**
Spa	**No**
Beauty Shop	**No**
Showroom	**No**
Bars/Lounges	**2**
Casino	**No**
Shops	**1**
Library	**Yes**
Child Program	**No**
Self-Service Laundry	**No**
Elevators	**0**

Cabin Statistics

Suites	**1**
Outside Doubles	**13**
Inside Doubles	**0**
Wheelchair Cabins	**0**
Singles	**0**
Single Surcharge	**NA**
Verandas	**0**
110 Volt	**No**

WINDJAMMER BAREFOOT CRUISES, LTD.

1759 Bay Road, Miami Beach, FL 33139
☎ *(305) 672-6453, (800) 327-2601*
www.windjammer.com

History . . . .

In 1947, Captain Mike Burke, just out of the U.S. Navy after serving four years in submarines, says he headed first for Miami, then after a few drinks, on to the Bahamas with $600 back pay in his pocket. He woke up the next morning on the deck of a 19-foot sloop with no money and a splitting headache. He had bought a boat. He named it the *Hangover.*

Soon Burke found himself taking paying friends and guests on cruises to the Bahamas, and after a year or so of that, combined his entrepreneurial skills with his love of tall ships and founded Windjammer Barefoot Cruises. His first boat was a 150-foot schooner named *Janeen* that had been run aground. Burke fixed her up and renamed her *Polynesia I.* By 1958, his fleet numbered four, *Polynesia I, Polynesia II, Brigantine Yankee* and his prize, the *Yankee Clipper*, originally built for German industrialist Alfred Krupp and confiscated as a prize of war by the United States in 1945.

Burke says his secret is to buy the ships in bad shape and then fix them up. In that way he acquired his present fleet of six tall ships (the newest, the former *France II*, is to be named *Lagacy* and was expected to debut in late 1997) and one motor vessel, *Amazing Grace*, his supply ship. His six children have joined him in his company.

—The largest single fleet of tall ships in the world (six). Burke says the Norwegian government comes in second with three tall ships.

DID YOU KNOW?

The Polynesia I *was confiscated by Fidel Castro in 1971 when a storm blew her off course into Cuban waters and government officials seized her. Burke had to bail his crew out of jail in Cuba; fortunately, there were no passengers aboard. But Castro kept the vessel as his own private yacht.*

Concept . . . .

To provide "memorable, affordable vacations for would-be "ol' salts of all ages" where informality rules. Passengers set their own pace, doing as much or as little as they like, from helping hoist a sail to lolling in the sun doing nothing.

Signatures . . . .

The logo tall ship and the word "barefoot" in the company name describe the product clearly to would-be passengers. Four or five designated singles cruises are among each year's big sellers, in which an entire sailing is devoted only to singles, sometimes within a certain age bracket, and always promising an equal mix of men and women. The line claims five marriages so far from couples that have met on singles sailings. Their longtime sailaway anthem is "Amazing Grace."

Gimmicks . . . .

"Drinker's Doubloons" are tokens you buy from the bartender on board to pay for drinks without having to carry cash around.

"Story hour" is the daily morning briefing (8:45 a.m.) from the captain, telling you what is likely to happen during that day.

Who's the Competition . . . .

The only really comparable product is Tall Ship Adventures' *Sir Francis Drake* (see above), but with only one ship, it doesn't put a dent in Windjammer's business. None of the more upscale sailing ship cruise lines—Star Clipper, Windstar or Club Med Cruises—come close to the bargain prices and informality on board the Windjammers.

Who's Aboard . . . .

The company says, "Singles, nearlyweds, newlyweds, retirees and families alike," which pretty much covers the waterfront.

Who Should Go . . . .

People who love sailing and the sea and want to meet like-minded folks.

Who Should Not Go . . . .

Tradition-mined cruisers; Sea Goddess veterans; anyone susceptible to mal-de-mer; infants and toddlers.

NO-NOs

Open bottles of personal liquor in the cabins are not permitted; smoking is forbidden anywhere except on the open decks; and flip-flops are not advised for deck and island wear.

The Lifestyle . . . .

"Barefoot" is the operative word here; you'll never need dress-up clothes or even shoes, if you don't feel like wearing them. Free Bloody Marys before breakfast, Rum Swizzles at sunset, free wine with dinner (which is served in two seatings), and always time for a party. Passengers may help the crew with the sails or take a turn at the helm, and swimming, diving and snorkeling are favorite pastimes. Cabins range from dorm-like rooms to doubles to suites, most but not all with private bathroom facilities.

Wardrobe . . . .

As little as possible, because the cruises are very casual with no dressing up even considered, let alone required, and because there's very little storage space in the cabins. Take plenty of bathing suits, shorts and T-shirts, perhaps a long-sleeved shirt and long pants or skirt to cover up from the sun.

Bill of Fare . . . . .C+

The food is hearty, simple and family-style. Breakfasts feature freshly baked breads and pastries, preceded, if you wish, by a complimentary Bloody Mary. Lunch may be a picnic on the beach or a buffet on deck. At cocktail time, hors d'oeuvres are served with rum or soft drinks, and dinner includes wine, beer or soft drinks of your choice. A late-night snack provides "midnight munchies." Many of the dishes have a Caribbean accent.

Showtime . . . . N/A

Drinking Rum Swizzles and nibbling hot hors d'oeuvres on deck is the evening's pre-dinner entertainment. What you do later is up to you.

Discounts . . . .

Windjammer Club members ($25 initiation fee) get to take along a friend on a fall cruise for half-price on the "bosom buddy" program on some sailings.

The Bottom Line

Windjammer delivers exactly what it promises its passengers, which explains its high repeat factor, with one loyal who's passed his 160th sailing. Like Carnival, you know pretty much what you're getting so you can figure ahead of time whether it's what you want. The prices are right and the supply of food and grog plentiful; what's not to like?

Unrated
AMAZING GRACE

The supply ship *Amazing Grace*, built in 1955 in Scotland as the *Pharos* and acquired by Windjammer in 1988, is a former British Navy motor vessel that sails on 13-day voyages between Freeport, Bahamas and Trinidad. She rendezvous with Windjammer's tall ships and delivers their monthly supplies, just as she once delivered supplies to lighthouse keepers along the rugged North Sea coast in Scotland on weekdays and entertained royalty at tea on weekends.

A period dignity has earned her the nickname "Orient Express of the Caribbean," and both a smoking room and a piano room with fireplace have been preserved in their original style. A spacious deck gives passengers room to move around or relax with a book.

Cabins & Costs

Cabins are somewhat larger than on the tall ships, a few with twin or double beds. Some have private toilet facilities and some offer a wash basin in the room and toilet down the hall. The **Fantasy Suite** equivalent is Burke's Berth, which has a sitting room, sleeper sofa, TV/VCR and CD stereo with tape player and honor bar, a separate bedroom with double bed and a marble and teak bath with its own Jacuzzi.

Suitable Standards with private toilet and shower facilities include cabins 1BB, 1BI and the Officer's Deck cabins. All have upper and lower berths.

Bottom Bunks would include 1TP, 2TP and 2BP; the first two have twin beds and wash basin, porthole and desk or vanity, the latter upper and lower berths with porthole and wash basin.

Prices for the 13-day cruise range from $950 to $2800 per person, double occupancy, the latter, of course, for Burke's Berth. Add $100 a person for sailings between the first of November and the end of May. Calls are made at any of nearly three dozen islands between Freeport, to the north not far off Florida, and Trinidad.

AMAZING GRACE — Unrated

Registry	**Honduras**
Officers	**British/West Indian**
Crew	**West Indian**
Complement	**40**
GRT	**1526**
Length (ft.)	**254**
Beam (ft.)	**38**
Draft (ft.)	**17**
Passengers-Cabins Full	**94**
Passengers-2/Cabin	**94**
Passenger Space Ratio	**NA**
Stability Rating	**Fair**
Seatings	**2**
Cuisine	**Caribbean/Continental**
Dress Code	**Casual**
Room Service	**No**
Tip	**$7.50 PPPD**

Ship Amenities

Outdoor Pool	**0**
Indoor Pool	**0**
Jacuzzi	**1**
Fitness Center	**No**
Spa	**No**
Beauty Shop	**No**
Showroom	**No**
Bars/Lounges	**1**
Casino	**No**
Shops	**1**
Library	**Yes**
Child Program	**No**
Self-Service Laundry	**Yes**
Elevators	**0**

Cabin Statistics

Suites	**10**
Outside Doubles	**36**
Inside Doubles	**1**
Wheelchair Cabins	**0**
Singles	**0**
Single Surcharge	**140-200%**
Verandas	**0**
110 Volt	**Yes**

⚓⚓⚓⚓

FANTOME
FLYING CLOUD
LEGACY
MANDALAY
POLYNESIA
YANKEE CLIPPER

"Romantic" is the word most commonly used to describe sailing ships, perhaps because these age-old craft take us back to what we imagine as a more stress-free time. Shirley says white canvas sails puffed by the breeze are the perfect accessory to romance, far better than a ruffled parasol or a bearskin rug, because they seem to make most men act like Mel Gibson.

This fleet of tall ships—the four-masted stay-sail schooner *Fantome*, built in 1927 for the Duke of Westminster; the *Flying Cloud*, a former French naval cadet training ship decorated by General Charles de Gaulle for sinking two Japanese submarines when she was carrying nitrates from Tahiti; the *Mandalay*, the former luxury yacht of financier E. F. Hutton, originally the *Hussar IV* and predecessor to the famous *Sea Cloud*; the *Polynesia*, a former Grand Banks fishing schooner acquired by Windjammer in 1975, previously the *Argus*, subject of a National Geographic feature and an Allen Villers book; and the two-masted sailing ship *Yankee Clipper*, probably the only armor-plated yacht in the world, built in 1927 for German industrialist Alfred Krupp as the *Cressida*. The *Legacy*, newest member of the fleet, is a 294-foot four-masted topsail schooner built in 1959 in France as the *France II*.

She was formerly a meteorological research vessel operated by the government. After her extensive rebuilding, it is expected she'll be able to sail into U.S. ports.

DID YOU KNOW?

The Fantome *was purchased by Aristotle Onassis from the Guinness Brewing family to present as a wedding gift to Princess Grace and Prince Rainier. When he wasn't invited to the wedding, he didn't send the gift. Captain Mike picked her up in 1969 as the flagship of his fleet.*

DID YOU KNOW?

The Yankee Clipper, *originally a yacht named* Cressida *built for German munitions king Alfred Krupp, hosted Adolf Hitler during World War II, was acquired by the Vanderbilt family after the war and raced regularly off Newport Beach, California, as the* Pioneer, *once clocked at 22 knots under sail. She's still considered one of the fastest tall ships sailing.*

Between The Lines

The Brochure Says

"Informality rules! T-shirts and shorts are all you'll need to pack, so trash the tuxedos and ballgowns. Stow your gear in your air-conditioned cabin. From dorms to Honeymoon Suites, all feature modern amenities. Who said anything about roughing it?"

Translation

This is the ultimate in casual cruising, and Windjammer's multiple repeaters like it like that. Some of the cabins are pretty basic, however, and while everything is more or less air-conditioned, the modern amenities aboard may or may not include a private toilet facility.

Cabins & Costs

Fantasy Suites: . . . . **B**
Average Price Per Person, Double Occupancy, Per Day: $187 plus airfare.
The best digs (apart from Burke's Berth on the *MV Amazing Grace*, above) would be the Honeymoon Suite aboard *Flying Cloud*, which is below Main Deck with its own private entrance, windows, a queen-sized bed, mini-refrigerator, private toilet and shower, TV/VCR, CD and wet bar.

Small Splurges: . . . . **C**
Average Price PPPD: $170 plus airfare.
The Admiral's Suite on the *Fantome* with a queen-sized bed, private bathroom with toilet and shower and a mini-refrigerator, relatively lavish comfort for Windjammer.

Suitable Standards: . . . . **C-**
Average Price PPPD: $154 plus airfare.
Par for the course double cabins on the Windjammers are compact but livable, as in the *Yankee Clipper's* Main Deck cabins with upper and lower berths, mini-refrigerator, picture window, private toilet and shower.

Bottom Bunks: . . . . **D**

Average Price PPPD: $107 plus airfare.

There's a wide range to choose from on the fairly basic Windjammers. Typical would be the Bachelor/ette dorm rooms on the *Polynesia* or *Flying Cloud*, which sleep six in bunks with a private shower and toilet for the dorm. It's sold to all-male, all-female or a family of five or six.

The Routes

There's never a hard and fast schedule on the Windjammers; that's part of their charm. The captain chooses where to go based on a certain group of islands, and every time there's a fifth Monday in the month, it's a Captain's Choice cruise hitting all his top favorites.

The *Fantome*, based in Belize, checks out the Bay Islands of Honduras and their fabled dive spots, as well as unspoiled little Placencia and its snorkeling.

The *Flying Cloud* covers the British Virgin Islands from its home in Tortola, choosing among Jost van Dyke, Beef Island, Virgin Gorda, Peter Island and Norman Island.

The *Mandalay*, home-ported in Grenada and Antigua, visits the Windwards and the Grenadines, selecting from Nevis, Montserrat, Iles des Saintes, Dominica, Martinique, St. Lucia, St. Vincent, Bequia, Canouan, Mayreau, Palm and Carriacou.

From Sint Maarten, the *Polynesia* sails out to see Anguilla, St. Barts, Saba, St. Eustatius, St. Kitts, Nevis and Montserrat.

The *Yankee Clipper* is based in Grenada and sails to several of the following islands: St. Vincent, Bequia, Canouan, Mayreau, Union, Palm and Carriacou.

The Scoop

Prices are very modest on the Windjammers, so much so that if it's a special occasion like a honeymoon, you should spring for the best you can afford. If you're footloose and fancy free, book anything and spend your spare time on the deck. Don't worry about sailing experience; you don't need it. Just go with the flow. If you're concerned about getting seasick, take a dramamine or other approved medication in the prescribed amount of time before boarding rather than waiting until you feel queasy. But bear in mind that seasickness is much rarer than people think—neither of us has ever experienced it in more than 200 cruises in some of the roughest seas in the world. (See Seasickness, page 113, for more about the malady and the treatment.)

Insider Tips

Five Fun Places

1. The *Mandalay* interior, extensively renovated in the style of its period (the 1920s) has always been considered one of the most luxurious private yachts in the world. Reminiscent of the *Sea Cloud* in her original rosewood-paneled cabins and marble bathrooms, and of the modern-day ultra-luxury vessels with a pair of suites with private verandas.

2. The *Fantome's* dining room is a trim and shipshape wood-paneled area with comfortable booths and resin-coated tables.

3. The deck on any Windjammer, where you sun, hang out, chat or read, meet your fellow passengers or learn about sails and charts from the captain during a sailing lesson.

4. The beach, a frequent part of any Windjammer cruise, where you may have a barbecue or buffet lunch, a swim or rum and nibbles at sunset.

5. The deck bar, where you check in with your $10 paper doubloon and have the bartender nick it with a hole punch every time you buy a drink.

Five Good Reasons to Book These Ships

1. To take advantage of the modest prices that include a lot of things other lines charge extra for such as sunset cocktails and wine with dinner.

2. To take a singles cruise and meet the mate of your dreams.

3. To learn how to handle the sails on a tall ship.

4. To see (and be seen in) the Caribbean aboard a classic ship, which automatically makes you a celebrity.

5. To kick back and relax and take off your shoes.

Five Things You Won't Find On Board

1. Elevators.

2. Jacuzzis.

3. Fitness centers.

4. Swimming pools; they claim theirs is the Caribbean sea.

5. Casinos.

FANTOME   ⚓⚓⚓

Registry	**Honduras**
Officers	**British/West Indian**
Crew	**West Indian**
Complement	**45**
GRT	**676**
Length (ft.)	**282**
Beam (ft.)	**40**
Draft (ft.)	**17**
Passengers-Cabins Full	**128**
Passengers-2/Cabin	**128**
Passenger Space Ratio	**NA**
Stability Rating	**Fair**
Seatings	**2**
Cuisine	**Caribbean/Continental**
Dress Code	**Casual**
Room Service	**No**
Tip	**$7.50 PPPD**

Ship Amenities

Outdoor Pool	**0**
Indoor Pool	**0**
Jacuzzi	**0**
Fitness Center	**No**
Spa	**No**
Beauty Shop	**No**
Showroom	**No**
Bars/Lounges	**2**
Casino	**No**
Shops	**1**
Library	**Yes**
Child Program	**No**
Self-Service Laundry	**No**
Elevators	**0**

Cabin Statistics

Suites	**24**
Outside Doubles	**20**
Inside Doubles	**22**
Wheelchair Cabins	**0**
Singles	**0**
Single Surcharge	**175-200%**
Verandas	**0**
110 Volt	**Yes**

FLYING CLOUD   ⚓⚓⚓

Registry	**Honduras**
Officers	**British/Australian**
Crew	**West Indian**
Complement	**28**
GRT	**400**
Length (ft.)	**208**
Beam (ft.)	**32**
Draft (ft.)	**16**
Passengers-Cabins Full	**74**
Passengers-2/Cabin	**66**
Passenger Space Ratio	**NA**
Stability Rating	**Fair**
Seatings	**2**
Cuisine	**Caribbean/Continental**
Dress Code	**Casual**
Room Service	**No**
Tip	**$7.50 PPPD**

Ship Amenities

Outdoor Pool	**0**
Indoor Pool	**0**
Jacuzzi	**0**
Fitness Center	**No**
Spa	**No**
Beauty Shop	**No**
Showroom	**No**
Bars/Lounges	**1**
Casino	**No**
Shops	**1**
Library	**Yes**
Child Program	**No**
Self-Service Laundry	**No**
Elevators	**0**

Cabin Statistics

Suites	**7**
Outside Doubles	**12**
Inside Doubles	**15**
Wheelchair Cabins	**0**
Singles	**0**
Single Surcharge	**175-200%**
Verandas	**0**
110 Volt	**Yes**

MANDALAY ⚓⚓⚓

Registry	**Honduras**
Officers	**Irish/US**
Crew	**West Indian**
Complement	**28**
GRT	**420**
Length (ft.)	**236**
Beam (ft.)	**33**
Draft (ft.)	**15**
Passengers-Cabins Full	**72**
Passengers-2/Cabin	**72**
Passenger Space Ratio	**NA**
Stability Rating	**Fair**
Seatings	**2**
Cuisine	**Caribbean/Continental**
Dress Code	**Casual**
Room Service	**No**
Tip	**$7.50 PPPD**

Ship Amenities

Outdoor Pool	**0**
Indoor Pool	**0**
Jacuzzi	**0**
Fitness Center	**No**
Spa	**No**
Beauty Shop	**No**
Showroom	**No**
Bars/Lounges	**1**
Casino	**No**
Shops	**1**
Library	**Yes**
Child Program	**No**
Self-Service Laundry	**No**
Elevators	**0**

Cabin Statistics

Suites	**9**
Outside Doubles	**12**
Inside Doubles	**0**
Wheelchair Cabins	**0**
Singles	**0**
Single Surcharge	**175-200%**
Verandas	**0**
110 Volt	**Yes**

POLYNESIA	⚓⚓⚓
Registry	**Honduras**
Officers	**South African/US**
Crew	**West Indian**
Complement	**45**
GRT	**430**
Length (ft.)	**248**
Beam (ft.)	**36**
Draft (ft.)	**18**
Passengers-Cabins Full	**126**
Passengers-2/Cabin	**114**
Passenger Space Ratio	**NA**
Stability Rating	**Fair**
Seatings	**2**
Cuisine	**Caribbean/Continental**
Dress Code	**Casual**
Room Service	**No**
Tip	**$7.50 PPPD**

Ship Amenities

Outdoor Pool	**0**
Indoor Pool	**0**
Jacuzzi	**0**
Fitness Center	**No**
Spa	**No**
Beauty Shop	**No**
Showroom	**No**
Bars/Lounges	**1**
Casino	**No**
Shops	**1**
Library	**Yes**
Child Program	**No**
Self-Service Laundry	**No**
Elevators	**0**

Cabin Statistics

Suites	**14**
Outside Doubles	**3**
Inside Doubles	**40**
Wheelchair Cabins	**0**
Singles	**0**
Single Surcharge	**175-200%**
Verandas	**0**
110 Volt	**Yes**

YANKEE CLIPPER   ⚓⚓⚓⚓

Registry	**Honduras**
Officers	**British/Australian**
Crew	**West Indian**
Complement	**29**
GRT	**327**
Length (ft.)	**197**
Beam (ft.)	**30**
Draft (ft.)	**17**
Passengers-Cabins Full	**64**
Passengers-2/Cabin	**64**
Passenger Space Ratio	**NA**
Stability Rating	**Fair**
Seatings	**2**
Cuisine	**Caribbean/Continental**
Dress Code	**Casual**
Room Service	**No**
Tip	**$7.50 PPPD**

Ship Amenities

Outdoor Pool	**0**
Indoor Pool	**0**
Jacuzzi	**0**
Fitness Center	**No**
Spa	**No**
Beauty Shop	**No**
Showroom	**No**
Bars/Lounges	**1**
Casino	**No**
Shops	**1**
Library	**Yes**
Child Program	**No**
Self-Service Laundry	**No**
Elevators	**0**

Cabin Statistics

Suites	**12**
Outside Doubles	**5**
Inside Doubles	**15**
Wheelchair Cabins	**0**
Singles	**0**
Single Surcharge	**175-200%**
Verandas	**0**
110 Volt	**Yes**

WINDSTAR® CRUISES
A HOLLAND AMERICA LINE COMPANY

300 Elliott Avenue West, Seattle, WA 98119
☎ *(206) 298-3057, (800) 258-7245*
www.windstarcruises.com

History . . . .

In Helsinki, Finland, in the early 1980s, ship designer Kai Levandar and his Finnish workshop group came up with a number of revolutionary cruise vessel concepts, including several that looked like major high-rise urban hotel towers floating on a ship-like hull, somewhat similar to the long-in-progress Phoenix World City project. But following a suggestion from an imaginative entrepreneur named Karl G. Andren, owner of Circle Line sightseeing boats, they created a design in 1983 called Windcruiser, a motor-sailing vessel with computer-trimmed sails.

In 1984, Andren contacted a French-born, Miami-based cruise line veteran named Jean-Claude Potier to make a feasibility study and find a yard to build it. Potier, who subsequently became the line's president, announced the project, Windstar Sail Cruises, in December 1984, and hired a French shipyard (Societe Nouvelle des Ateliers et Chantiers du Havre) to build it and French architect-designer Marc Held to create an interior design. The French government assisted in the financing.

Jean-Claude Potier saw romance in the design. "A sailing ship, unregimented, not organized, fun, an experience in feeling, not glittery, beautiful." He coined the term "casual elegance" to describe the onboard dress code for the vessels.

The 148-passenger *Wind Star* was the first of the trio, debuting in 1986 to immediate acclaim. The *Wind Song*, to be based year-round in Tahiti for a decade, followed in 1987, and the *Wind Spirit* in 1988. Andren sold the company to Holland America Line in August 1988, and Carnival Cruise Lines subsequently acquired Holland America in January 1989, and with it Windstar. Potier departed not long afterward, and the company subsequently changed its name to Windstar Cruises, eliminating the word "Sail." The ships do a substantial number of charter and incentive sailings.

In 1990, a new division of Club Mediterranee called Club Med Cruises introduced the first of two similar but larger motor/sail vessels, *Club Med 1*. (See Club Med Cruises, page 305.) This ship, but not its sister *Club Med 2*, was acquired by Windstar in 1997 to become the *Wind Surf*, scheduled to enter Windstar service in May 1998.

—First cruise passenger vessels with computer-operated sails.

> ## DID YOU KNOW?
>
> *How does it work? Sails on these sophisticated 440-foot, four-masted ships are set and trimmed by computers that monitor wind velocity and direction and control heeling to less than six degrees. This, in combination with the usual cruise-ship stabilizers and bow thrusters, gives the comfort of a cruise vessel with the romance and grace of a sailing ship. If you want to see it work, the captain welcomes passengers to the navigation bridge anytime.*

Concept

A relaxed, nonregimented, nondressy version of a cruise with an emphasis on watersports, tropical and Mediterranean ports and an upscale onboard lifestyle.

Signatures

The four-masted sailing vessels maintain an open bridge with passengers permitted to come inside and watch the computers trim the sails.

Gimmicks

In some seasons on certain itineraries, two of the ships may meet to sail side-by-side, so each vessel's passengers can photograph or videotape the other.

Who's the Competition

Windstar has found itself a fairly solid niche with a lot of repeat passengers in the younger, nontraditional cruise area. Club Med Cruises competes in the Med and the Caribbean, but attracts a slightly different crowd and more Europeans. Star Clippers, although more traditional sailing vessels, also compete somewhat with Windstar, but Windjammer Barefoot Cruises is not a strong competitor.

Who's Aboard

Mostly urban thirtysomething-and-up couples in high-pressure jobs out to relax. A few sailing enthusiasts (but purists turn their noses up at computer-trimmed sails), a lot of destination-oriented passengers (particularly on the Tahiti itinerary). One executive described the average Windstar passenger as 45, affluent, well-traveled, pays a lot of attention to travel plans and is interested in the sports activities available. He may or may not have taken a cruise before.

Who Should Go

Anyone who wants to have an upscale but casual resort sort of holiday. The ships are beautiful and the cabins and bathrooms efficient and well-designed. All are identical, so there's no problem deciding what cabin category you'll book.

Who Should Not Go

Sometimes there are families with children on board, but this doesn't work as well with kids under 12 because there's nowhere for them to call their own and they end up belly-flopping in the swimming pool and being general nuisances. The line discourages toddlers and young children specifically. Also, because there's no elevator, anyone with mobility impairment should not book because getting from cabin to breakfast cafe can mean climbing as much as four flights of stairs.

The Lifestyle . . . .

There is no regimentation. No mileage pool or deck games, no ship's photographer treading on the punch line of your best joke to ask everyone to sit closer together, no table assignments or specified meal seatings, no waiter choruses of "Happy Birthday" in the dining room, no tipping required, and no dress code beyond the genially vague "casual elegance."

These are ships for those who eschew a standard cruise, for couples who want to be alone together on a remote island beach instead of a bus tour of St. Thomas, for erstwhile or would-be skippers who like to stand on the bridge with the captain instead of lying in the sun, and for anyone who would rather snorkel and go windsurfing than play bingo or line up to photograph the midnight buffet.

Wardrobe . . . .

"Casual elegance," the ambiguous dress code term suggested by Jean-Claude Potier, has been variously interpreted over the years, but generally means elegant resort wear with jacket and tie optional. You see a lot of open-necked silk shirts and linen pants on both men and women. Daytime wear is very casual, usually a lot of shorts and swimsuits, and going ashore garb, except in the fashionable Mediterranean resorts, is equally basic.

Bill of Fare . . . . A

With Los Angeles' super-chef Joachim Splichal, owner of Patina, creating his signature cuisine on board all the ships, you can count on delicious fare. Splichal is not the type to wander away after stamping his name on a menu; the name of the cuisine concept is "180 Degrees from Ordinary." Consider marinated salmon with horseradish, potatoes and creme frâiche; chilled gazpacho with cilantro creme; roast young chicken with creamy polenta, artichoke, truffle oil and crispy Parmesan chips; chocolate croissant pudding with Wild Turkey bourbon sauce. Some of the best food at sea is served aboard these ships.

The seating at meals is open, meaning you arrive when you wish and sit where and with whom you please. Besides the dining room, there is a casual buffet cafe atop the ship where breakfast and lunch is served; it sometimes doubles as a cabaret or disco late at night.

Showtime . . . . N/A

Entertainment is too organized a concept for the Windstar ships, but there is usually a trio playing for dancing and a small casino, as well as a large library of videotapes, some of them X-rated.

Discounts . . . .

The Advanced Sailings Advantage Program allows discounts up to 50 percent for early bookings on a first-come first-save basis; a limited number of cabins is available. From time to time, two-for-one sailings are also announced. The best idea is to get on the Windstar mailing list, either by requesting it from the 800 number above or by being a repeat passenger. Then you'll get all the information as soon as the deals come up.

The Bottom Line

Since the emphasis is on low-key camaraderie and offbeat, noncommercial ports of call in Costa Rica and the Caribbean, people looking for nightlife, disco and casino action and born-to-shop types should opt only for the Mediterranean itineraries. While the sails initially attract the passengers, it is the pleasurable experience—friendly, relaxed and low-key—along with the very nice staff and crew, that keeps everybody on board happy. Windstar is a real winner.

★★★★★
WIND SONG
WIND SPIRIT
WIND STAR

They are most uncommon cruise ships, their long, trim hulls cutting through the indigo sea like a knife through silk, their sails catching the breeze and rising like romantic whispers from four tall white masts. The ports of these dream ships are fantasies themselves, fragments of the world's surreal estate— the wave-worn black sand beaches of Tahiti where Paul Gauguin spilled out his life painting women as lush as overripe mangoes...the fortress fastness of Elba, where Napoleon would sit for hours on a cold marble bench in a prim little garden staring across the sea toward France...the elemental water-smoothed stones of The Baths rising from the sapphire-and-turquoise Caribbean Sea at Virgin Gorda.

Sleek and sexy, these high-tech 148-passenger ships are fitted out like yachts, with dark wood and brass, rich colors and glove leather. The futuristic gray modular bathrooms, a marvel of design by France's Marc Held, make you want to say, "Beam me up, Scotty!" when you step into the shower. Casual elegance is the keynote for the lifestyle on board. A cover-up over your bathing suit will allow you to lunch in the handsome glass-walled Veranda Cafe, and after a busy day ashore or a bare-feet-and-bikini day in the sun, you can slip into sandals and something loose, soft and silky for evening.

DID YOU KNOW?

On the 1986 maiden voyage of the Wind Star, in Mustique, William F. Buckley came over from his yacht and requested permission to board, and David Bowie wangled an invitation to lunch. In St. Lucia, Princess Margaret admired the ship, and Colin Tennant, Lord Glenconnor, was so enchanted he invited the ship and its passengers to spend the afternoon at his private beach (later to become the posh resort Jalousie) with his pet elephant Bupa, along with steel drummers, fire eaters, limbo dancers and acrobats.

Between The Lines

The Brochure Says

"Like great white wings, Windstar's sails unfurl. And as they billow and fill with the power of the wind, you fly."

Translation

If you've booked this vessel for a vacation and didn't know about the sails—let's face it, they no longer mention them in the company name—you may not notice they're there until a shadow suddenly falls across your body when you're sunbathing, and you look up with faint annoyance.

Cabins & Costs

Fantasy Suites: .... N/A

All the cabins aboard are fantastic but not in the sense Fantasy Suites implies.

Small Splurges: .... A

Average Price Per Person, Double Occupancy, Per Day: $620 plus airfare.
There is an Owner's Suite, cabin # 107, that is somewhat larger than the standard cabins and sold at a 30 percent higher price than the standard cabins.

Suitable Standards: .... A

Average Price PPPD: $485 plus airfare.
All the cabins on board, with the single exception of the Owner's Suite (see above) are identical, clean-lined and efficient rooms that have twins or queen-sized bed, color TV with VCR, mini-refrigerator and bar, makeup table, safe, desk, bookshelves and drawers. Bathrooms have space-age showers, hair dryers, plenty of counter space and thick terry-cloth robes. Some have a pull-down third berth and some an adjoining private door to make a two-room suite.

Bottom Bunks: .... N/A

This category does not apply; all cabins have two lower beds.

Twilight on the **Wind Song** *in tropical seas.*

The Routes

The *Wind Song* repositions to its new home port of Puerto Caldera, Dec. 13, 1997. The ship spends the winter making seven-day sailings to Isla de Cano, Bahia Drake, Quepos, Playa Flamingo and Isla Coiba, all but the last in Costa Rica. Isla Coiba is in Panama.

In May, the ship begins its summer season in the Western Mediterranean, sailing Sundays from Rome and visiting Livorno, Ajaccio, Amalfi, Capri and Ischia.

The *Wind Star* alternates north and southbound Caribbean cruises out of Barbados in winter, visiting Nevis, St. Martin, St. Barts, Iles des Saintes and Bequia on the northbound itinerary, and Martinique, Grenada, Tobago, Tobago Cays and St. Lucia on the southbound. In summer, *Wind Star* cruises the Greek Isles between Athens and Istanbul.

The *Wind Spirit* cruises the Virgin Islands in winter from St. Thomas, visiting St. Barts, Virgin Gorda, St. John, Tortola and Jost Van Dyke. In summer *Wind Spirit* sails the Greek Islands and Turkey.

The Scoop

These unique vessels, which capture the imagination of all who see them, the admiration of all who sail on them, have changed the face of small-ship cruising, offering an alluring alternative to sophisticated travelers looking for a fresh and more personal vacation experience. They have our highest recommendation.

Insider Tips

Five Fun Places

1. The lounge is filled with natural light flooding in from a large skylight in daytime, and furnished with a lot of comfortable chairs and sofas in convivial groupings.

2. The glass-walled Veranda is a casual breakfast and lunch cafe that sometimes doubles as a disco when somebody can figure out where to turn on the fog machine and turn out the lights.

3. The Restaurant is a charming room with wood paneling and windows that let in the view. While there are plenty of tables for two, the ambiance onboard is such that passengers tend to clump together in larger groups.

4. The outdoor Piano Bar is conveniently close enough to the outdoor bar that joining in on a familiar song is irresistible.

5. The instruction wheel is on the top deck, a fixed ship's wheel that offers some sailing lessons to passengers, and makes a dandy place to be photographed.

Five Good Reasons to Book These Ships

1. Romance, romance, romance.

2. To eat the delectable cuisine of Joachim Splichal without having to pay the Patina price.

3. To go to the remote islands of French Polynesia and see it almost like Gauguin did.

4. To use the watersports deck in the balmy Caribbean, the sunny Mediterranean or Costa Rica to swim off the ship.

5. To enjoy an unusually smooth ride, even in notoriously temperamental waters.

Five Things You Won't Find On Board

1. A cruise director leading the fun and games.

2. A children's program.

3. An inside cabin; all accommodations have a view.

4. Anyone nudging you for a tip; tipping is at the passenger's discretion.

5. An elevator.

WIND SONG   ★★★★★
WIND SPIRIT   ★★★★★
WIND STAR   ★★★★★

Registry	**Bahamas**
Officers	**European**
Crew	**International**
Complement	**88**
GRT	**5350**
Length (ft.)	**440**
Beam (ft.)	**64**
Draft (ft.)	**13**
Passengers-Cabins Full	**159**
Passengers-2/Cabin	**148**
Passenger Space Ratio	**36.14**
Stability Rating	**Good**
Seatings	**1**
Cuisine	**Contemporary**
Dress Code	**Casual elegance**
Room Service	**Yes**
Tip	**Not required**

Ship Amenities

Outdoor Pool	**1**
Indoor Pool	**0**
Jacuzzi	**1**
Fitness Center	**No**
Spa	**No**
Beauty Shop	**Yes**
Showroom	**No**
Bars/Lounges	**3**
Casino	**Yes**
Shops	**2**
Library	**Yes**
Child Program	**No**
Self-Service Laundry	**No**
Elevators	**0**

Cabin Statistics

Suites	**1**
Outside Doubles	**74**
Inside Doubles	**0**
Wheelchair Cabins	**0**
Singles	**0**
Single Surcharge	**150%**
Verandas	**0**
110 Volt	**Yes**

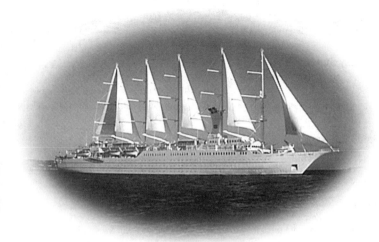

★ ★ ★ ★ ★
WIND SURF

Her first captain, Alain Lambert, loves the Club Med 1. *"She's like a fish, just like a fish when she's running. She's lovely. She puts her nose in the water, she likes the water." Her maximum list is two percent but he can control it from one degree to five degrees. "If I have sportive passengers, I can put it five degrees." The combination of sails and engine saves seven tons of bunker fuel a day. Twenty tons are consumed in the average day. The ship makes 14 knots under motor and sail with favorable winds, and he can raise or lower the sails in one-and-a-half minutes. "She's very stable."*

Launched as the *Club Med 1* in 1990, the ship was sold in mid-1997 to Windstar to debut as the *Wind Surf* in May 1998. The name was the one originally planned for a fourth Windstar ship that was never built. Changes made to the vessel for Windstar service include the addition of 30 deluxe suites and a full spa program called The Wind Spa. Passenger density will be reduced; the *Wind Surf* will carry 312 passengers two to a cabin instead of the 376 carried by *Club Med 1*.

Between The Lines

The Brochure Says
"Come, let's sail away to the secret isles, the intimate ports, to the ultimate destination called Windstar that lies 180 degrees from ordinary."

Translation
As the *Club Med 1* this ship was always 180 degrees from ordinary.

Cabins & Costs

Fantasy Suites: .... A

Average Price Per Person Double Occupancy Per Day: NA
Thirty new suites, each approximately 400 square feet with ocean view dining/living area, twin beds convertible to king-sized and two bathrooms are being added to the ship.

Small Splurges: .... A

Average Price PPPD: NA.
Suites (two measuring 321 square feet each containing the same basic furnishings as standards (see "Suitable Standards," below) are also available.

Suitable Standards: .... A

Average Price PPPD: NA
All the cabins are outsides with portholes rather than windows and measuring 188 square feet, with white walls, mahogany trim, twin beds that can be made into a queen-sized bed and space module bathrooms that are trim and sleek with excellent pulsating shower heads. Some 23 cabins have a third upper berth. Furnishings include a long dresser/desk with six drawers, a mirror wall, wide counter, built-in TV set fitted into a wooden base (most of the programming is in French) and a hotel-type folding suitcase rack. Niceties include attractive art, reading lights over the beds, hair dryers, terry-cloth robes, fresh fruit in each cabin and toiletries. A stocked mini-refrigerator and mini-bar carry price lists for the contents. Except for continental breakfasts, room service carries a charge.

Bottom Bunks: .... NA

There are no accommodations that fit this category.

The Routes

Wind Surf summers in the Mediterranean, calling at chic ports such as St. Tropez, Cannes, Monte Carlo and Portofino and out of the mainstream with the likes of Portovenerre and Portoferraio. In winter the ship is based in Barbados for Caribbean cruises.

The Scoop

Finally this lovely ship is getting the high quality staff and passengers she deserves. With some of the former Club Med cabins converted to spacious luxury suites. all the Windstar regulars should be overjoyed. Happy sailing!

WIND SURF ★★★★★

Registry	**Bahamas**
Officers	**European**
Crew	**International**
Complement	**178**
GRT	**14,745**
Length (ft.)	**617**
Beam (ft.)	**66**
Draft (ft.)	**16**
Passengers-Cabins Full	**335**
Passengers-2/Cabin	**312**
Passenger Space Ratio	**47**
Stability Rating	**Good to Excellent**
Seatings	**1**
Cuisine	**Contemporary**
Dress Code	**Casual elegance**
Room Service	**Yes**
Tip	**Not required**

Ship Amenities

Outdoor Pool	**2**
Indoor Pool	**0**
Jacuzzi	**1**
Fitness Center	**Yes**
Spa	**Yes**
Beauty Shop	**Yes**
Showroom	**No**
Bars/Lounges	**5**
Casino	**Yes**
Shops	**1**
Library	**Yes**
Child Program	**No**
Self-Service Laundry	**No**
Elevators	**2**

Cabin Statistics

Suites	**32**
Outside Doubles	**124**
Inside Doubles	**0**
Wheelchair Cabins	**0**
Singles	**0**
Single Surcharge	**150%**
Verandas	**0**
110 Volt	**Yes**

WINDSTAR CRUISES

WORLD EXPLORER CRUISES

555 Montgomery Street, San Francisco, CA 94111-2544
☎ *(415) 393-1565, (800) 854-3835*
www.wecruise.com

History

San Francisco-based World Explorer Cruises was a division of the widespread C.Y. Tung family shipping interests, marketing the *Universe* for summer Alaska sailings when the vessel was not in use as a floating university.

The Seawise University concept had been a passion in this family since the late Mr. Tung acquired the *Queen Elizabeth 1* for the purpose of creating a university that would sail around the world. Unfortunately, that poor ship never got out of Hong Kong harbor, where she burned and sank during the refitting in 1972.

Concept

Education, eco-tourism and a close-up, first-hand look at Alaska are the main aims of the summer sailings. The slogan, "a 14-day adventure for the heart, mind & soul" seems to be the company's concept. The new *Universe Explorer* has also added winter Latin America and Caribbean sailings on Dec. 28, 1997, and Jan. 6 and 21, 1998.

Signatures

Classical music instead of production shows, a full audience listening to lecturers instead of playing blackjack, hands-on crafts lessons.

Gimmicks

Fitness class hearts—12 laps around the deck net you one heart, and 20 hearts gets you a T-shirt that says Sound Mind, Sound Body, Universe.

Who's the Competition.

Nobody really offers a cruise like this one—14 days hitting more ports in Alaska than any other ship, and promoting the educational and cultural level of the cruise.

Who's Aboard

The entire membership of Elderhostel, families with children, staffers from the University of Pittsburgh (who accredit the Semester at Sea program), grandparents bringing their grandchildren on a cruise, one family with several children including an infant. Many, many repeaters. According to one longtime staffer, "Our passengers are those that have never taken a traditional cruise and didn't want the glitz."

Who Should Go . . . .

People interested in getting a close-up look at Alaska and a lot of lectures; people who don't want to dress up.

Who Should Not Go . . . .

Anyone fussy about food and service; anyone who usually books a suite on a cruise ship; anyone who likes to dress up.

The Lifestyle . . . .

While the educational and eco-tourism aspects of the voyage are emphasized almost constantly, they still get passengers stirred up with typical cruise ship frivolities including bingo, singalongs, horse racing, mileage pools, a masquerade parade, passenger talent shows, bridge competitions and dancing gentlemen hosts. This is not exactly Mensa on vacation.

INSIDER TIP

Unlike expedition ships, the Universe Explorer *does not include shore excursions in its fare; passengers pay from $12 for a botanical walk in Wrangell to $275 for a flightseeing excursion to Mt. McKinley.*

Bill of Fare. C

Breakfast usually offers a blackboard special of the day, with one fresh fruit, one egg dish, and side dishes that include oatmeal, blueberry pancakes and such.

A typical lunch starts with three appetizer choices—perhaps fresh asparagus, fruit or a cheese plate, a smoked chicken risotto soup, a salad bar, and a choice of pan-fried fillet sole of lemon butter and almonds; Seafood Louie salad; beef Stroganoff over noodles; or the "light" selection of the day. There is also a continental self-service breakfast served on the enclosed promenade deck.

Dinners also feature several appetizers, one soup, the salad bar and a choice of several main dishes, perhaps salmon, barbecued chicken and steak, along with a vegetarian main dish.

Showtime. C

The staff musicians are Peggy Wied and the Voyagers, who bill themselves as "seniors playing for seniors." Classical concerts are interspersed with folk singers and a belting country, blues and pop singer who also leads singalongs.

The Bottom Line

This is the favorite Alaska cruise for a great many people, but we were amused to find the passengers being so self-congratulatory—"Aren't we clever not to be on some tacky cruise ship that doesn't really show you Alaska?"—every time a more handsome ship passed us along the Inside Passage. We restrained ourselves from pointing out that they're taking the same optional, land-operated shore excursions in Alaska that, say, Princess and Holland America passengers do.

★★ ⚓⚓⚓
UNIVERSE EXPLORER

The weary, sagging old *Universe*—still sentimentally recalled by both Semester-at-Sea students and Alaska cruisers—has been sent to the breakers in India and replaced with Commodore's *Enchanted Seas*, which carries a new name, *Universe Explorer*, the twelfth name-change this ship has had in its 39-year-history. During the years, a second swimming pool was added on deck and the casino and boat deck stern extended so the latter could house a disco. For World Explorer sailings, the casino has been turned into the library, complete with all the former *Universe's* 12,000 volumes, and a computer room has been added.

The Brochure Says

"On a World Explorer cruise, you'll have the chance to participate rather than just spectate. Not only do we give you more time on shore to really discover the land, we offer you an extensive program of educational lectures and slide shows...We pride ourselves on being the uncommon route to Alaska. And we invite you to enrich your mind, as well as your senses, at our unusually low fares."

Translation

To the unusually low fares, add the cost of excursions.

Cabins & Costs

Fantasy Suites: .... **N/A**
N/A

Small Splurges: .... **C**

Average Price Per Person, Double Occupancy, Per Day: $285 plus airfare.
Four cabins of different shapes and sizes are designated suites, and are larger than most but not all the other cabins. Two of them, #618 and #628, also have bathtubs. Furnishings are trim and attractive if hardly glamorous, but a striking improvement over the old *Universe.*

Suitable Standards: .... **C**

Average Price PPPD: $249 plus airfare.
A large percentage of the cabins on board are standard or deluxe outside doubles, many with twin beds that can be converted to queen-sized. A desk/dresser, TV set, chair or small sofa/bed for a third cabin occupant are the usual furnishings. some accommodate a third and fourth occupant at a flat rate of $995 for the cruise.

Bottom Bunks: .... **C**

Average Price PPPD: $164 plus airfare.
The cheapest beds aboard are in the category 9 insides with upper and lower berths, but there are only nine of these.

The Routes

The *Universe Explorer* sails roundtrip from Vancouver on 14-day itineraries from mid-May to late August, calling in Ketchikan, Juneau, Skagway (with optional shore excursions to Haines), Valdez, Seaward (for Anchorage), Sitka, Wrangell and Victoria, and cruising B.C.'s Inland passage, Glacier Bay, Yakutat Bay and Hubbard Glacier. In winter the ship offers Caribbean and Latin American sailings. The Institute for Shipboard Education celebrated its 20th birthday recently. The Institute, in partnership with the University of Pittsburgh, takes student passengers on 100-day educational voyages around the world, one in the fall, the other in spring. A record 764 people of all ages signed up for the spring 1997 program.

The Scoop

For the money and the numbers of ports, this is one of Alaska's best buys for travelers who are destination-oriented. An added attraction is the new ship. Although built 40 years ago, the *Universe Explorer* is a tremendous improvement over the line's dowdy *Universe,* offering more indoor and outdoor areas for passengers to explore, along with much larger, nicer cabins and baths.

UNIVERSE EXPLORER	★★, ⚓⚓⚓
Registry	**Panama**
Officers	**European/American**
Crew	**International**
Complement	**330**
GRT	**23,500**
Length (ft.)	**617**
Beam (ft.)	**84**
Draft (ft.)	**28**
Passengers-Cabins Full	**739**
Passengers-2/Cabin	**726**
Passenger Space Ratio	**32.36**
Stability Rating	**Good**
Seatings	**2**
Cuisine	**International**
Dress Code	**Casual**
Room Service	**No**
Tip	**$8.50 PPPD, 15% automatically added to bar check**

Ship Amenities

Outdoor Pool	**1**
Indoor Pool	**0**
Jacuzzi	**1**
Fitness Center	**Yes**
Spa	**No**
Beauty Shop	**Yes**
Showroom	**Yes**
Bars/Lounges	**3**
Casino	**No**
Shops	**3**
Library	**Yes**
Child Program	**Playroom**
Self-Service Laundry	**No**
Elevators	**3**

Cabin Statistics

Suites	**4**
Outside Doubles	**286**
Inside Doubles	**74**
Wheelchair Cabins	**2**
Singles	**2**
Single Surcharge	**130%**
Verandas	**0**
110 Volt	**Yes**

WORLD EXPLORER CRUISES

OTHER CRUISE COMPANIES

The following are cruise marketing companies that represent various lines
or charter various vessels seasonally over a period of years.

Golden Sun Cruises

c/o Dolphin Hellas
71 Atki Miaouli, Piraeus 185-37, Greece
☎ *[30] (1) 452-1260, in North America (800) 473-3239 (Aegean TravelVisions)*

After watching the successful merger of Sun Line and Epirotiki into Royal
Olympic Cruises, other Greek lines are considering the same thing. One of
the newest is a planned merger between Dolphin Hellas Shipping and Attika
Shipping, to be based in Piraeus. Each line is putting one ship in, Attika the
Arcadia (not to be confused with P & O's new *Arcadia*, the former *Star
Princess*) and Dolphin Hellas the *Aegean Dolphin* as soon as it is released
from its current charter to Renaissance Cruises as the *Aegean I*. The pair is
said to be looking for other Greek operators to join them for a series of
three-, four- and seven-day sailings in the Aegean beginning in the spring of
1998.

Jadrolinjia Cruises

c/o Malta National Tourist Office
Empire State Building, 350 Fifth Avenue, Suite 4412, New York, NY 10118
☎ *(212) 695-8229*

This Croatian cruise line, marketed by two German companies, is also
being touted by the New York office of the Malta tourism people for the
300-passenger *Dalmacija*, one of the former Yugoslavian vessels that got
sidetracked during the long war. Built in 1965, the ship has five passenger
decks, a single-seating restaurant, two bars, a lounge, an indoor swimming
pool and a German/Croatian crew.

It has a fairly good-sized sun deck and basic cabins with tiny bathrooms,
but modest per diem prices, from $76 for an inside quad to around $190 for
an outside cabin with two lower beds and a sitting area.

Jadrolinjia also runs the *Adriana*, the former *Aquarius*, which cruises the Adriatic and is marketed in North America by OdessAmerica (see above).

13 Hazelton Avenue, Toronto, Ontario, Canada M5R 2E1
☎ *(416) 964-9069, (800) 263-9147*

This fast-growing Canadian expedition company, founded in 1992, claims it cruises "to the ends of the earth" with its active, moderately priced cruises to the Arctic in summer and the Antarctic in winter (austral summer in the Southern Hemisphere).

It uses six chartered Russian and Estonian ice-rated research vessels manned by Russian and Estonian crews with a North American and European cruise staff. Ships currently in the fleet include the 120-passenger *Marine Discovery* (the *Alla Tarasova*), the 38-passenger *Marine Challenger* (the *Livonia*), the 44-passenger *Marine Spirit* (the *Professor Shuleykin*), the 44-passenger *Marine Intrepid* (the *Professor Multanovsky*), the 80-passenger *Marine Adventurer* (the *Akademik Ioffe*), and the 80-passenger *Marine Voyager* (the *Akademik Sergey*).

Cabins aboard are generally small, with portholes or windows, and some in the bottom categories have shared bathroom facilities. One, two or three suites with sitting area, two lower beds and private bath facilities with shower are available on all the vessels except the *Marine Discoverer*. Furnishings are basic, with bunks, a table and a chair. Food is served family-style and consists of "basic comfort food," as one recent passenger described it. Dinners usually offer a soup, salad, hearty casseroles or pasta dish and fruit for dessert, while lunches may be soup and cheese sandwiches or fried chicken and french fries.

Passengers are most often veteran expeditioners or independent adventurers of various ages from the late 30s to the 70s. Excursions ashore are made by Zodiac, inflatable rubber landing craft. Lecturers who specialize in the flora, fauna or geology of an area are aboard, and a comprehensive handbook is provided about each region.

Marine Expeditions emphasizes controlled tourism and adheres to all international environmental regulations, frequently participating in programs with international scientific groups.

In the summer, Marine Expeditions cruises part of the Northwest Passage from Sondre Stromfjord, Greenland, to Nanisivik/Arctic Bay, Canada, on a nine-day itinerary; sails from Sondre Stromfjord to Churchill, Canada, on a 12-day program; sails from Vladivostok, Russia, to Nome through Kamchatka Peninsula and the Kuril Islands on a 13-day cruise that includes roundtrip airfare from Anchorage beginning at $4795 per person, double occupancy; sails the Aleutians on a 17-day program from Prince Rupert to Nome, with calls in Kodiak, the Semedi and Shumagin Islands, Unimak Island, the Fox Islands, Dutch Harbor and Unalaska, the Pribilofs, St. Matthew and St. Lawrence in the Bering Sea, the Chukotskiy Peninsula, Yttygran Island and Providenya in the Russian Far East, with a connecting flight to Nome; fares start at $4795 per person, double occupancy.

The company is also offering new Greenland cruises aboard the 92-passenger *Disko*, a 2162-ton Danish-built ice-class ship with private baths in all cabins. While most of the sailings are seven-day itineraries, there are some shorter two-day cruises starting from $795 per person, double occupancy, including roundtrip airfare from New York.

QUARK
EXPEDITIONS

980 Post Road, Darien, CT 06820
☎ *(203) 656-0499, (800) 356-5699*
www.quark-expeditions.com

Quark Expeditions was founded in 1990 by veteran expeditioners of countless Arctic and Antarctic programs who were able, thanks to the thaw in U.S./Russian relations, to charter former Soviet atomic fleet icebreakers to cruise not through balmy oceans but rather pack ice as thick as 16 feet. Many of the nuclear-powered vessels were built in Finland's Wartsila shipyard in the early 1980s, during the period when we were there observing construction of more traditional cruise ships such as the *Royal Princess* and Carnival's *Fantasy*.

The fleet employed by Quark includes the *Kapitan Khlebnikov*, the *Akademik Golitsyn*, the *Professor Molchanov*, the *Sovetski Soyuz* and the *Kapitan Dranitsyn*. The company also offers occasional expedition sailings aboard the *Bremen* (see Hapag-Lloyd, above) and the *Clipper Adventurer* (see Clipper, above).

The once-in-a-lifetime itineraries in the summer of 1998 include a visit to the North Pole roundtrip from Murmansk July 4–18; a transit of the Northwest Passage between Providenya, Siberia, and Resolute, Northwest Territories, July 28 to Aug.13; a Northeast Passage voyage between Providenya and Longyearbyen, Spitsbergen, Aug. 13 to Sept.1; a circumnavigation of the High Arctic roundtrip from Longyearbyen July 2 through Sept. 1; a Greenland voyage between Longyearbyen and Sondre Stromfjord July 2 through July 16; an exploration of Greenland and Canada's High Arctic July 16–28; a circumnavigation of Baffin Island Aug. 4 through 17; a Spitsbergen and

Norway cruise July 15 through July 27 between Longyearbyen and Bergen; and a British Isles sailing aboard the *Clipper Adventurer* June 6–18.

Quark's Russian icebreakers sail both polar regions.

In winter, Antarctica is the big destination, with numerous departures, one to the Ross Sea that is already sold out and waitlisted; others to the Antarctic Peninsula and South Shetland Islands. Visits to the Falkland Islands, an early spring South Atlantic sailing between Ushuaia, Argentina, and Vlissingen, The Netherlands, March 18 through May 12; and a special Shackleton Commemorative Crossing of South Georgia (no relation to Sherman's march through Georgia) roundtrip from Ushuaia Feb. 25 through March 17. The Upper Amazon is scheduled for Oct. 21–28, 1998, roundtrip from Manaus aboard the *Clipper Adventurer.*

The "because-it's-there" adventurers generally need big bankrolls for the longer name-dropping sailings, but prices for the Antarctic are relatively modest, beginning as low as $2950 per person, double occupancy.

1414 Dexter Avenue N # 327, Seattle, WA 98109
☎ (206) 285-4000, (800) 628-8747

This small Seattle-based expedition company, made up of experienced expedition veterans from pioneer outfits such as Lindblad Travel and Society Expeditions, has grown by leaps and bounds since its debut in 1991. Over the years, Zegrahm has offered some of the most exotic and far-out cruises you could take around the world.

On Aug. 3, 1997, it made the first-ever passenger-ship circumnavigation of Baffin Island aboard the icebreaker *Kapitan Khlebnikov*, 17 days of cruising, sometimes through pack ice, in search of the rare, one-horned narwhal, walrus, beluga whales and polar bears. Company founder Werner Zehnder said it had been a dream of his to make this journey since 1985, when he, along with the authors, was aboard the first west-to-east transit of the Northwest Passage with the late Captain Tom Pullen, an icemaster who knew intimately all the waterways of the Canadian Arctic. This journey was a culmination of years of planning and dreaming.

Aboard the same vessel, Zeghram offers a Canadian Arctic and Greenland itinerary, and, in 1998, a cruise through the Aleutians and the Pribilofs to the beautiful Kamchatka Peninsula in the Russian Far East aboard the *World Discoverer* (see Society Expeditions, page 833).

566 Seventh Avenue, New York, NY 10018
☎ (212) 221-0006, (800) 447-5667

Zeus, a New York-based, 47-year-old company that specializes in Eastern Mediterranean tours and cruises, is operating an extensive range of mainstream Aegean cruises as well as sailings aboard its sailing ships and private yachts (See "Alternative Cruises," below.)

Zeus also markets the sleek 50-passenger *Lady Caterina*, a new, 25-cabin, 70-foot mega-yacht, one of those long white jobbies with the dark windows that remind us of Darth Vader in *Star Wars*. She makes seven-day Mediterranean and Aegean cruises.

Another new ship for the company is the two-masted sailing ship *Galileo Sun*, carrying 36 in outside air-conditioned cabins with private bath.

The 50-passenger *Pan Orama*, a trim, three-masted sailing cruiser commissioned in 1993, is another Zeus product. All 25 cabins are outsides with private bathrooms, telephones and radios and a choice of twin or double beds. The yacht-like vessel has a topmost deck with sun loungers and deck bar and a second deck with an elegant, single-seating restaurant furnished in banquettes and tables for two or four and its own sociable bar. The top-category cabins are also on this deck, Trim and prettily furnished, the *Pan Orama* cruises the French and Italian Rivieras and the Aegean Islands in summer on seven-day itineraries. The ship carries a full range of watersports equipment.

The Evolution of Adventure Cruising

Introducing the 122-Passenger M/S *Clipper Adventurer*

In April 1998, the *Clipper Adventurer* will set a new standard in adventure travel as she begins her inaugural season. Built in 1975 as the *Alla Tarasova*, this classic ship, completely converted in 1997 by Scandinavian craftsmen, is reminiscent of the great ocean liners – when ships preferred varnished woods and polished brass to plastic and vinyl.

Cousteau's *Calypso*

With 61 all-new outside staterooms and superb American and Continental cuisine served in the window-lined dining room, passengers will enjoy the comfort and service that have made Clipper Cruise Line one of *Condé Nast Traveler*'s Top Ten Cruise Lines in the world.

Darwin's *H.M.S. Beagle*

Exploring the natural history and cultural diversity of our planet will be fun and educational. The *Clipper Adventurer*'s ice-hardened hull allows her to easily navigate in the most rugged environments, and her fleet of Zodiac landing craft permits landings anywhere nature or curiosity dictate.

If there's a little bit of Christopher Columbus, Charles Darwin or Jacques Cousteau in you that wants to get out and explore the world, see your travel agent or call Clipper toll free at **1-800-325-0010**.

❖ *CLIPPER*

The Beauty of Small-Ship Adventure Travel

Columbus's *Nina*

In 1998, the *Clipper Adventurer* will visit Portugal • Madeira • Canary Islands • Morocco Gibraltar • Spain • France • Belgium • Holland • Germany • Denmark • Poland • Lithuania Latvia • Estonia • Russia • Finland • Sweden • England • Ireland • Scotland • Orkney Islands Shetland Islands • Norway • Spitsbergen • Faroe Islands • Westmann Islands • Iceland • Greenland Baffin Island • Hudson Bay • Labrador • Newfoundland • Nova Scotia • U.S. East Coast • Caribbean Orinoco River • Brazil • Amazon River • Uruguay • Argentina • Falkland Islands and Antarctica.

INDEX

Order Your Guide to Travel and Adventure

Title	Price	Title	Price
Fielding's Alaska Cruises and the Inside Passage	$18.95	Fielding's Indiana Jones Adventure and Survival Guide™	$15.95
Fielding's America West	$19.95	Fielding's Italy	$18.95
Fielding's Asia's Top Dive Sites	$19.95	Fielding's Kenya	$19.95
Fielding's Australia	$18.95	Fielding's Las Vegas Agenda	$16.95
Fielding's Bahamas	$16.95	Fielding's London Agenda	$14.95
Fielding's Baja California	$18.95	Fielding's Los Angeles	$16.95
Fielding's Bermuda	$16.95	Fielding's Mexico	$18.95
Fielding's Best and Worst	$19.95	Fielding's New Orleans Agenda	$16.95
Fielding's Birding Indonesia	$19.95	Fielding's New York Agenda	$16.95
Fielding's Borneo	$18.95	Fielding's New Zealand	$17.95
Fielding's Budget Europe	$18.95	Fielding's Paradors, Pousadas and Charming Villages of Spain and Portugal	$18.95
Fielding's Caribbean	$19.95	Fielding's Paris Agenda	$14.95
Fielding's Caribbean Cruises	$18.95	Fielding's Portugal	$16.95
Fielding's Caribbean on a Budget	$18.95	Fielding's Rome Agenda	$16.95
Fielding's Diving Australia	$19.95	Fielding's San Diego Agenda	$14.95
Fielding's Diving Indonesia	$19.95	Fielding's Southeast Asia	$18.95
Fielding's Eastern Caribbean	$17.95	Fielding's Southern California Theme Parks	$18.95
Fielding's England including Ireland, Scotland and Wales	$18.95	Fielding's Southern Vietnam on Two Wheels	$15.95
Fielding's Europe	$19.95	Fielding's Spain	$18.95
Fielding's Europe 50th Anniversary	$24.95	Fielding's Surfing Australia	$19.95
Fielding's European Cruises	$18.95	Fielding's Surfing Indonesia	$19.95
Fielding's Far East	$18.95	Fielding's Sydney Agenda	$16.95
Fielding's France	$18.95	Fielding's Thailand, Cambodia, Laos and Myanmar	$18.95
Fielding's France: Loire Valley, Burgundy and the Best of French Culture	$16.95	Fielding's Travel Tool™	$15.95
Fielding's France: Normandy & Brittany	$16.95	Fielding's Vietnam including Cambodia and Laos	$19.95
Fielding's France: Provence and the Mediterranean	$16.95	Fielding's Walt Disney World and Orlando Area Theme Parks	$18.95
Fielding's Freewheelin' USA	$18.95	Fielding's Western Caribbean	$18.95
Fielding's Hawaii	$18.95	Fielding's The World's Most Dangerous Places™	$21.95
Fielding's Hot Spots: Travel in Harm's Way	$15.95	Fielding's Worldwide Cruises	$21.95

International Conversions

TEMPERATURE

To convert °F to °C, subtract 32 and divide by 1.8.

To convert °C to °F, multiply by 1.8 and add 32.

Fahrenheit   **Centigrade**

Fahrenheit		Centigrade	
230°	—	—	110°
220°	—		
210°	—	—	100° Water Boils
200°	—		
190°	—	—	90°
180°	—	—	80°
170°	—		
160°	—	—	70°
150°	—		
140°	—	—	60°
130°	—		
120°	—	—	50°
110°	—		
100°	—	—	40°
90°	—	—	30°
80°	—		
70°	—	—	20°
60°	—		
50°	—	—	10°
40°	—		
30°	—	—	0° Water Freezes
20°	—	—	-10°
10°	—		
0°	—	—	-20°
-10°	—		
-20°	—	—	-30°
-30°	—		
-40°	—	—	-40°

WEIGHTS & MEASURES

LENGTH		
1 km	=	0.62 miles
1 mile	=	1.609 km
1 meter	=	1.0936 yards
1 meter	=	3.28 feet
1 yard	=	0.9144 meters
1 yard	=	3 feet
1 foot	=	30.48 centimeters
1 centimeter	=	0.39 inch
1 inch	=	2.54 centimeters

AREA		
1 square km	=	0.3861 square miles
1 square mile	=	2.590 square km
1 hectare	=	2.47 acres
1 acre	=	0.405 hectare

VOLUME		
1 cubic meter	=	1.307 cubic yards
1 cubic yard	=	0.765 cubic meter
1 cubic yard	=	27 cubic feet
1 cubic foot	=	0.028 cubic meter
1 cubic centimeter	=	0.061 cubic inch
1 cubic inch	=	16.387 cubic centimeters

CAPACITY		
1 gallon	=	3.785 liters
1 quart	=	0.94635 liters
1 liter	=	1.057 quarts
1 pint	=	473 milliliters
1 fluid ounce	=	29.573 milliliters

MASS and WEIGHT		
1 metric ton	=	1.102 short tons
1 metric ton	=	1000 kilograms
1 short ton	=	.90718 metric ton
1 long ton	=	1.016 metric tons
1 long ton	=	2240 pounds
1 pound	=	0.4536 kilograms
1 kilogram	=	2.2046 pounds
1 ounce	=	28.35 grams
1 gram	=	0.035 ounce
1 milligram	=	0.015 grain